THE WIND IS MY NEMESIS
I SHALL WANT
IT LEADETH ME INTO ERROR
YEA, THOUGH I SHOOT
UPON THE RANGES OF HELL
I WILL FEAR NO EVIL
FOR MY EQUIPMENT IS
RIGHTEOUS

CENTREFIRE RIFLE ACCURACY

Creating and Maintaining It

W Hambly-Clark Jnr...

CENTREFIRE RIFLE ACCURACY — Creating and Maintaining It.

SUBJECTS: RIFLES.
RIFLES — MAINTENANCE AND REPAIR. FIREARMS.
FIREARMS — MAINTENANCE AND REPAIR. DEWEY NUMBER: 683.422

Published in the United States of America by:
REDD INK PRESS,
123 NEZ PERCE RD,
DARLINGTON,
SC 29532, U.S.A.

ISBN 978-0-9905687-3-5

Cover : The Author, on the 1210 yard (1100 meters) mound, competing in the 2012 Queensland Long Range Championships, held at Raglan, Queensland, where he had the winning score by 22 points.

Photo by Lyn Hambly-Clark.

Back Cover: The Author chambering a barrel for his Panda action.

FOR

MY BEST MATE

MY HUNTING PARTNER FOR OVER 40 YEARS

MY NUMBER ONE OFFSIDER

MY MOST DEDICATED SUPPORTER

MY LOVELY WIFE OF 47 YEARS

THE LIGHT OF MY LIFE

LYN.

CONTENTS

DISCLAIMER

This book is entirely a work of fiction. Any resemblance of any procedures, methods or theories, described within, to procedures, methods or theories, in the real world are entirely coincidental.

The Author does not recommend that you read this book for fear that you may get eye strain, or RSI from turning the pages. If you do read this book it is entirely at your own discretion and risk. The author believes that if you take any notice of any of the material presented herein, you are madder than he is, and should seek medical help.

Expressly disclaimed, or any, associated, liable, in any event, for any direct, indirect, punitive, special, incidental, consequential, injury, revenues, monetary, profits, loss, anyway, denunciation, misuse, lugubrious, express, imply, responsibilities, liability, lack, not limited to, expressed, independently verified, technical, warranty, infringe, merchantability, representation, infringement, copyright, are all words that usually appear on pages like this. Fit them in wherever you wish.

In short the author is not recommending that you do anything at all. You are an autonomous person. If you choose to do something really stupid and stuff yourself up, you did it of your own volition, so don't go looking to blame someone else for your stupidity. Accept the responsibility of your actions and live with the consequences. I certainly do.

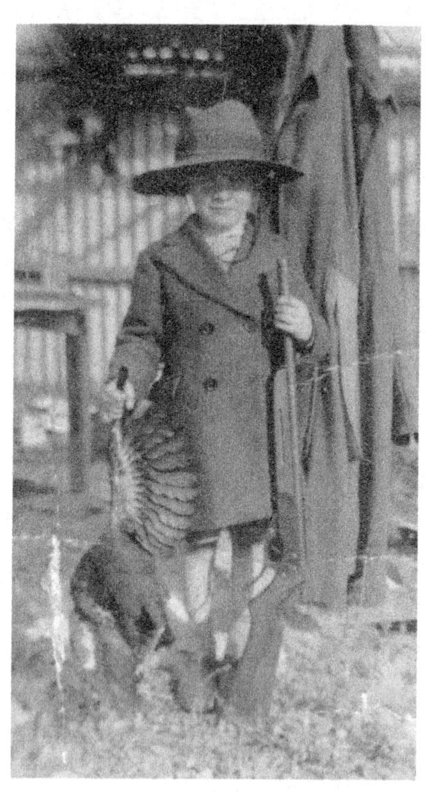

The Author.

Photo taken around 1948.

Catch 'em young and teach 'em tricks!

PREFACE

My intention in producing this book is not so much to show you, step by step, how I create and maintain an accurate rifle, but to prompt you to think about the process, probably more than you ever have, and draw your own conclusions as to how the job should be accomplished.

You can't be expected to draw any valid conclusions unless you have all of the information at hand, so with that in mind, I have not only detailed my procedures, step by step, but have also tried to explain, as much as possible, why I do what I do. It is the 'why' that is important, for unless you understand the theory behind what you are doing, you are merely doing the job by rote. Monkey see, Monkey do. Doing this job that way will stunt your development and grind it to a halt.

I am assuming that you, the reader, have at least a basic knowledge of the tools a Gunsmith uses; at least enough to understand the terminology I will be using. If not, I'm afraid you are on your own, though that knowledge is readily available elsewhere.

The buck with any problems with this book stops with me, so, right up, I should make my apologies. I apologize for the wording; I'm no writer, and I apologize for the quality of the photographs; I'm no photographer. With regards to the photographs, some of them will be mockups to show you something that I am finding hard to explain. All through the years I was doing this work I didn't take a lot of photographs due to financial and time constraints, except when I wrote articles for shooting publications in the 1970s. If the mockups get the required information across they will have done their job.

In between chapters I will include a photo gallery of rifles I have built over the years, starting from the earliest to the latest. I hope you enjoy them. I'll also include photos of rifles, in the field, that were significant in my career.

Finally, I'd exhort you not to dismiss anything you are shown unless you are positive that you understand the theory behind it thoroughly. Only by doing that can you move forward. It's pretty well guaranteed, that when this is done and dusted, I am going to discover omissions; things I wish I'd told you, things I will think I could have explained better, so I guess I'd better apologize for that too. I am trying my best though.

W (Bill) Hambly-Clark Jnr...
2013

ACKNOWLEDGEMENTS

Lyn, who else but Lyn. She has a knack of taking my hare brained projects and working on them until I complete them. Thanks, luv, for all the typing, compiling, suggestions, and especially the editing. In the end, she could recite this book off by heart. I did mention something about another book, but when I saw her eyes glaze over and a nervous tic start in one, I thought I'd better drop the idea!

Twice, she has saved my miserable life, and for that she has my eternal gratitude and love.

INTRODUCTION

In mid 2012 I had no intention of writing this book, but around that time a couple of things happened that changed my mind.

I have been involved with firearms for as long I can remember. My Father was a somewhat flamboyant character who owned a Gun Shop in Adelaide, South Australia. Until 7TH grade primary school we lived above the Gun Shop at 262 Rundle Street, so my early years were spent around the feet of shooters and hunters that frequented the shop, and my playground was the East End Market. When my sister and I walked to Flinders Street Primary School, every day, we passed the Sporting Arms Factory, located at the east end of Pirie Street, and often called in on the way to school to deliver parts, or later a rifle, and on the way home to pick up parcels to take back to the shop.

In the early days my Father did some hunting, and even at a very early age I was taken along too. I had my own air rifle, a lever cocking .177 muzzle loader, and I terrorized everything that crossed my path with it. Dad soldered a piece of tube onto the barrel with a couple of wires in it for a reticule, so very early on I knew how to use a telescopic sight.

In 1954 Dad and his brother, Ray, went up to the Northern Territory to hunt Buffalo and Crocodile, and I was included in the trip, which was made by vehicle through the centre of Australia. For the trip he had the Sporting Arms factory make me a shortened .22 Sportamatic rifle with a stock proportioned to suit my small stature, and mounted with a 2¾ power Pecar telescopic sight. By the end of that trip I had accounted for numerous crows, hawks, foxes, kangaroos (really big ones) and 11 Buffalo, all taken just after my 11TH birthday. I had a lot of adventures to boot. My first Buffalo was taken with a 30M1 carbine, which everyone deemed was not enough gun, so the remainder were taken with a P14 .303, using MK6 military ammunition. That rifle was longer than I was tall, and booted the blazes out of me.

When I was 14 Dad sent me over to Kangaroo Island to stay with a friend of his, who had the run of the Flinders Chase Sanctuary, culling feral animals. Goats were the main quarry and I accounted for many of them, but it was there I shot my first pigs, all on my own. I remember it like it was yesterday. I had been told where I might find some, so I rose in the early hours of the morning while it was still dark and walked five miles with my Sportco .22 Hornet, mounted with a 4 power Nikko telescopic sight, over my shoulder to reach the spot just on daylight. I didn't go far before I spotted three pigs rooting up the ground in a wet and soggy field. I stalked up to within about 80 yards of my quarry, assumed a sitting position and shot the closest pig to me between the eye and the ear. It dropped as if poleaxed. The two remaining pigs looked up, but by this time I had reloaded, and shot the second pig exactly as I had the first. Now the third pig was off and running. I can still see him in my telescopic sight splashing through the water making his escape. My shot took him in the neck and poleaxed him as well. Three pigs in as many seconds, all off my own bat at 14 years old.

When I went to High school I met a lad who was as interested in firearms and hunting as I was, and we became mates. We spent many weekends riding our push bikes to remote locations hunting for rabbits and foxes. When we turned sixteen, and received our driving licenses, we swapped our push bikes for clapped out old motorcycles, and ranged further after kangaroos, wombats and foxes.

By this time I had used an impressive variety of firearms from a .22 black powder Martini Hornet through to a .577 Snider, and for a young city bloke, I had done a lot of hunting.

When I was seventeen I joined the army for 3 years, but ended up serving 4 years after I went for a sojourn over the side of the mountain, on my Manx Norton 350cc motorcycle, during practice for the Easter races at Mount Panorama, near Bathurst, N.S.W. This resulted in a nine month hospital stay of which seven months were spent in traction, and ultimately my medical discharge from the army. They had found I was only entitled to be paid for 6 months, and they had paid me for 9 months. By the time that was all squared up I lobbed back in Adelaide with a caliper strapped to my right leg, and stony broke. Fortunately Dad took me on, so I went to work in his gun shop, caliper and all.

For a young bloke interested in guns and hunting this was a good place to be. So many interesting firearms to pore over, and so many interesting people passing through the shop. By this time I had graduated to a Krico Model 600 sporting rifle in .222 Remington calibre, mounted with a 6 power Weaver K6 telescopic sight in EAW rings, and had set about learning the ins and outs of .222 ballistics.

I met my mate, and later my best man, Ron Pridham in the gun shop.

Ron had a farming property near Naracoorte, in the South East of South Australia, with an abundance of rabbits and foxes, and it was there my interest in long range precision shooting was born.

In 1964 two things happened that had a profound effect on my future. First up I met my best mate, who was later to become my wife and lifelong partner, and second I became aware of bench-rest shooting, and the quest for ultimate accuracy. A group of shooters had formed a club and were shooting on a range at McHargs Creek in the Adelaide hills.

Up until that time the thought of loading ammunition to extract the best accuracy possible had not really occurred to me. Sounds crazy today, but back then that was a revelation. You either shot factory ammunition, or if you reloaded, just picked a load from the load sheet that came with your can of powder (usually ex military 4740 or 4831) and went hunting with it.

I embraced the new discipline, eager to learn what made a rifle tick, and how to squeeze the best accuracy from it. I attended the 1967 National Bench-rest Championships, and took 2ND place in the Sporter class with my Krico .222, amid a sea of Sakos, first place in the Varmint class with my Fathers 40x Remington in 6mm Remington, and 3RD place in the Open class using the same 40x. I also shot the smallest grand aggregate for the match in pretty ordinary conditions. I won the State Championships in 1967 also, and again in 1968, after which I decided I'd had enough of punching holes in paper and, really, preferred to go hunting.

At this time I was a keen crow shooter, and needed accurate rifles to reach out and swat those varmints, so I never faltered in my quest for the ultimate accurate long range rifle. Most weekends were spent cruising remote country roads within 100 miles of Adelaide pranging almost every crow I saw, and all holiday weekends away hunting goats or foxes.

I met my good mate Tony Greenfield in 1965. Tony and I were kindred spirits, with an intent interest in accurate long range rifles. His property, Purple Downs, was the ideal place to field test the examples I created, and they were many and varied.

I started rebarreling my own rifles in late 1967. Hector Bridgeman, who owned Sprinter Arms, based at Hahndorf in the Adelaide Hills, showed me how he did it, and I took it from there. My father had an old lathe on the first floor above the Gun shop, and that is where I cut my teeth, spending more time than I care to remember, after hours, teaching myself to operate it.

I was already bedding my rifles (in Plastibond) before I started to rebarrel them, and it wasn't long before I started restocking them, using Fajen semi inletted wood blanks imported from the USA. As things progressed my focus became centred on hunting rifles, and what it takes to make something that feels like it is an extension of your arm, so much so that you hardly have to think about it when you use it. It soon became apparent that the shape I was looking for could not be found using semi-inletted blanks. In 1978 I made my stock making pantograph which started me on the road to designing my perfect hunting rifle, that culminated in the rifles I was building in the late 1980s.

Financially we were always struggling, and the situation came to a head when work suddenly dried up in 1990, and I was forced to find other employment. To us, having a regular wage each week was like winning the lottery, so I kept the job until 1998, when my Mount Panorama indiscretion finally caught up with me in a big way, and forced my retirement on disability.

Now, at over 70 years of age I am still an active shooter, and still do my own rifle work. I shoot 100 yard bench-rest for score, 200 yard bench-rest for group, and F Open Class at our local rifle club. I also travel to some Open F Class Prize matches whenever I can. Health problems have prevented me from hunting the last few years — maybe next year!

When I started to gain some knowledge, doing this job, I began to think I was pretty smart. The more knowledge I gained, the more I began to realize I was not as smart as I thought I was. By the time I finished with the job I didn't think I was very smart at all. That was a large part of the reason why I had no intention of ever writing this book.

Then in mid 2012 I ran into two guys, while competing at a couple of F Class prize shoots, that prompted me to change my mind. I realized that those two guys would benefit greatly from the knowledge I possessed, and, in reality, it would be criminal of me to not write it down, and make it readily available to anyone who was interested. Thus began my odyssey, and this book is the result

Being entirely self taught, with no formal training, whatsoever, in either metalwork or woodwork, I would have loved to have had the information that is in this book at my disposal when I started out. I hope you get something out of it. If so my mission is accomplished.

W (Bill) Hambly-Clark Jnr... 2013

Tony with a big roo taken for dog meat, on Purple Downs Station, with my .14 Walker Hornet. This photo would have been taken in 1971

ALAN ANTHONY GREENFIELD

6-2-1941 — 7-2-2008

This book would not be complete if I did not mention my good mate Tony Greenfield.

I met Tony in my Fathers Rundle Street Gun shop in 1965 and we became mates.

We both shared a passion for accurate long range sporting rifles, so we had a lot in common.

Tony owned Purple Downs Station, a 300 square mile grazing property near Woomera in South Australia, consisting of mostly sand hills and salt bush country. It was literally the home of foxes and rabbits. Between us we were the perfect match. I made the experimental rifles, and Tony had the place to test them on. He used to love playing with the concoctions I dreamed up.

Every holiday weekend I would haul my young family up the Port Wakefield road, heading to Greenie's place, with some new cartridge and rifle to try out. Tony drove the Toyota, Lyn drove the spotlight, I drove the rifle, and my young bloke slept in the passengers foot well of the vehicle, while we hared around Purple Downs all hours of the night after Brer Fox.

When I went out on my own, in 1978, my Father refused to sell me the Orn lathe I was using up until then; I suppose to punish me for leaving his employ, even though he had no use for it. Twenty years later he gave it to me — go figure! I didn't have enough money for a new lathe. Somehow Greenie learned of my predicament, and out of the blue loaned me $5000.00 with no strings attached, no interest, pay it back whenever you can. It took me twenty years to pay him back, and he never mentioned the loan in all that time. He had faith in my ability. He was a very good mate.

Sadly, my mate passed away from Oesophageal Cancer in 2008. Wherever he is, I can imagine him roaring over sand hills, or through salt bush, with a big grin on his face making impossible shots on long range foxes, rabbits, and crows.

Save a few for me mate. I'll be there soon enough. Bomb me a hole!

CENTREFIRE RIFLE ACCURACY

Creating and Maintaining It

W Hambly-Clark Jnr...

CHAPTER ONE

THE ACTION

The centrefire rifle action is the foundation upon which all of the associated systems rely for their correct operation. If the action is bad, then nothing else will work properly, and the rifle will never be a really accurate one. The Holy Grail in a quality action is alignment, as perfect as it is possible to achieve.

The bolt hole is the principal component to which everything else must be aligned, yet, in commercial actions, nothing is ever aligned to the bolt hole. In fact, some are so badly misaligned, you wonder how they work at all. A good action should have the following attributes.

1. Receiver bolt hole straight, round, and parallel.
2. Receiver thread centre-line exactly the same as bolt hole centre-line.
3. Receiver threads parallel and square to bolt hole centre-line.
4. Receiver front square to bolt hole centre-line.
5. Recoil lug square to bolt hole centre-line.
6. Receiver externals parallel to bolt hole centre-line.
7. Recoil lugs, in receiver, square to bolt hole centre-line.
8. Bolt, a close fit to receiver bolt hole.
9. Recoil lugs, on bolt, square to bolt centre-line.
10. Bolt face square to bolt centre-line.

Those are the main attributes an action needs to be really accurate. They are what you need if you are ever to own that elusive Hummer rifle.

Right off the bat I'm going to go ahead and recommend, that if you are building a rifle from scratch, go and buy yourself a custom action. You will not regret it. Just have a look at the equipment lists of the winning rifles in recent matches, and base your choice of brand on that information. A good custom action *should* have all of the attributes you need.

My preference would be an action with a flat bottom and octagon shaped top. Receivers of this shape have a large bedding area, especially at the rear tang. They are very resistant to bending, and provide a very stable bedding platform. If you ever get to bed both flat/octagon, and round action types, you will understand what I am talking about here.

Two locking lugs or three? My background has been hunting, and I have always preferred a two lugged action for its opening and closing strength. A good two lugged action will get a cartridge in, and a case out of the chamber easily, that you would have to hammer in and out of a three lugged action. If you are a hunter, that would be my recommendation. After having been let down by various actions in the field, when I was most depending on them to work, I only use Mauser M'98 actions, on my personal hunting rifles, for their controlled feed, classic lines and ultra dependability. They always work.

Target competition, however, is a cat of another colour. You don't have to cram another cartridge into the chamber, while running flat out through the bush after some animal. Nor is your target rifle banging around in a 4WD, or on the back of a motor bike, in hot dusty conditions for weeks at a time.

In short, target rifles lead a much more pampered life than do hunting rifles, and as a result, features that would be considered to be not acceptable in a hunting rifle may well be beneficial in a target rifle. For instance, I would never consider a 3 lugged action for a hunting rifle, but it may very well be the best design to use in a target rifle. The tripod design of a 3 lugged action is a very stable platform through which to transfer recoil forces to the rest of the system. Used with quality well cared for ammunition, that is properly full length sized, (more on that later) such actions will function perfectly ok in that situation.

In the final analysis you make your choice, pay your money, and live with what you receive. Be it two lugs, 3 lugs, 4 lugs, or even one lug, matches have been won with all of them — though not lately with one lugged actions.

While the recommendation is to go with a good custom action, that recommendation is largely given with a view to resale value in addition to inherent accuracy. It's a valid point. Any reworked factory action is suspect, unless you did the work yourself, and know beyond any doubt that it was a good job. You may have difficulty convincing a prospective buyer of that fact, and the usual result of that is a marked down selling price.

Be that as it may, there is no reason that a factory action, with the right attributes, should not be aligned, and once properly aligned, there is no reason to prevent it performing every bit as good as a custom made action. Surprisingly, it takes very little machining time to do the job, but a bunch of set up time. That's the way it is with a lot of rifle smithing, 30 minutes to set up, and 30 seconds to machine.

There is a saying that goes, "You can't make a silk purse out of a sows ear," and that is certainly true. You should consider carefully whether the action you have is worth expending the effort required to do this job. Ultimately that choice is yours, but I would suggest not bothering with anything that does not have a good straight bolt hole. I have seen receivers where two close fitting mandrels, inserted in each end of the part, met somewhere down in the magazine well. Those same receivers also had receiver threads similarly misaligned. I would not proceed with a receiver like that. You can't polish a turd!

In Real Estate the word is position, position, and position. In centrefire rifle accuracy it is alignment, alignment, and alignment. The theory behind the job is to make every relevant surface either parallel to, on the axis of, or square to the bolt hole. In order to accomplish that it is necessary that we find a way to hold, and rotate, the receiver bolt hole, and bolt body, perfectly in line with the centre-line of the spindle of the lathe. Only in that way can we be sure that the machining work we will do will be accurate. *We can accept nothing short of absolute accuracy here.* Anything less, and we might as well leave the action as it is.

As I said earlier there is, in fact, very little machining work required. Most of your time will be spent in setup. Actually, you should aim to do the absolute minimum amount of machining required to true the surfaces we will be working on. To accomplish that you will be taking cuts of .001" or less, and as soon as the witness marks on the surface indicate true, you stop. Don't take an extra cut to be sure. True is true, and all we want is to machine off the absolute minimum amount necessary to make it so.

You'll be seeing photos of two actions as we go along. One is a Remington 40x I've had for 40 years doing duty as a varmint rifle through several barrels, and lately as an F Class practice rifle in .22PPC shooting the 80 grain match projectile. I decided I should look to squeeze some more accuracy from it awhile ago, and took some photos while I did the job. The Remington 700 series of actions (and 40x, which is simply a single shot Remington 700) are ideal for this modification, having many attributes of a good target action. They would be my #1 choice for the foundation of a super accurate varmint rifle.

The other action is a Shilen DGA I obtained when Ed first started making them. I've had it for 40 odd years also. It's number 037, so it's an early one, and has done duty originally as a .25/222 magnum, and lately, after I opened up the bolt face and fitted a Tikka extractor, as a .22PPC/80GN through several barrels. A while ago I decided to turn it into a .30BR and, not wanting to leave any stone unturned, aligned it and took a few photos along the way. We all deserve to own at least one Hummer rifle in our lifetime and I do believe this rifle is mine. It really does hammer them in one little hole with very little effort. Anyway, lets get on with it.

Check your receiver and bolt over carefully for defects. If you want to smooth the bolt hole, raceways, or anything else, now is the time to do it. Get all of that work out of the way, and wash the parts taking particular care to remove any glue/locking material the manufacturer may have put in the receiver threads when they fitted the original barrel. When you look at the locking lug recess in the receiver you will probably find them poorly machined, and often you can see that only one locking lug on the bolt is bearing. Likewise the barrel breeching surface is pretty ordinary, along with the threads in the receiver. Not to worry, we will be making them all bright and shiny, but most importantly, accurate.

1. We need to make a mandrel that is custom fitted to the receiver. The most convenient material to make this from would be a piece of old stainless steel barrel. If you don't have that you will have to obtain a piece of bright mild steel rod, or something similar, at least .050" larger in diameter than your bolt body.

1.1. The mandrel should be long enough to reach from the rear of the rear bridge, on the receiver, to about 4" past the front of the receiver, plus 2" to hold it in a 4 jaw chuck.

1.2. The diameter of the bolt hole at the front and rear bridges of the receiver are seldom (read: never) the same. The mandrel must be a tight fit in both of these holes. My preference is to determine their diameter with oversize pin gauges, for want of a better description. I am not satisfied to rely on a measurement, preferring to determine the fit physically. You will be expending a deal of effort in making this mandrel, so best get it dead right the first time.

1.3. To prevent interference by the bolt hole, the mandrel needs to be relieved between the front and rear bridges; .005" to .010" is fine.

1.4. The mandrel should protrude past the front of the receiver at least 4".

1.5. Turn your piece of steel between centres to a size about .050" larger than your bolt diameter. Chapter 2, 'Barrel Setup,' explains how to correctly centre a barrel (page 51). Secure it in the 4 jaw chuck by at least 1½" and true it with a dial indicator to +/- 0. Support the end with the tailstock for the roughing out work. Turn the length of the mandrel to within .020" of the diameter of the larger of the bridge diameters. Mark the width and position of both bridges with a texta, and relieve the mandrel between them to between .005" to .010" under bolt hole diameter. Photo 1-1 shows me turning the mandrel.

PHOTO 1-1.
Pre-turning the stainless steel mandrel.

Do the same to that length of mandrel that protrudes past the front bridge. Remove the centre from the rear of the mandrel, and using a very sharp high speed steel cutting tool, and taking shallow cuts of no more than .005", turn the two bridge sections to size. Be very careful. If you overdo it you will need to start over. The fit we are looking for is tight, but not so tight that you need to hammer it in and out of the receiver. If you took the trouble to check the fit physically with large pin gauges you should not make a mistake. You will need to remove it from the receiver, later on, without upsetting the accuracy of the receivers alignment in the lathe, so the fit needs to be one that allows you to rotate it back and forward, although with resistance, in order to remove it. When you have achieved that fit, turn the end of the mandrel true in front of the front bridge. Take small cuts at a slow feed to avoid chatter. When finished, you will have a dead straight mandrel that fits your receiver perfectly.

1.6. If you cannot turn the mandrel without chatter, turn a true section as far from the lathe chuck as you can, and mount a steady rest, bearing on that section, as I have described on page 16. Turn another true section, move the steady rest onto it, and you should be able to turn the rear of the mandrel ok.

1.7. Cut the oversized back piece off, face it, break the edge with a file and we are finished.

1.8. These mandrels are a custom fit to each action that you are accurising. You will be lucky indeed if you find another receiver that it fits properly, but stranger things happen at sea. Photo 1-2 shows the mandrel I used to true my Shilen receiver.

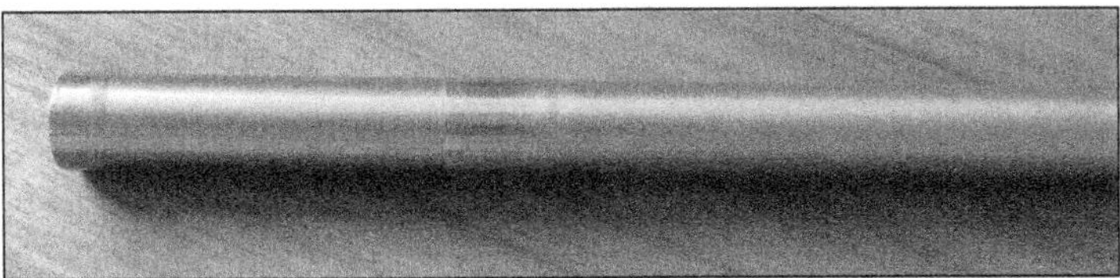

PHOTO 1-2.

An action truing mandrel. Note the relief between the two diameters that will engage the front and rear bridges of the receiver. There is also relief in front of the diameter that will engage the front bridge.

2. Now we need a cathead that will accept the receiver. If you don't have one it is easily made. Photo 1-3 shows mine. The receiver will be held between the rear of the front bridge and the front of the receiver. My cathead is 1.800" long and the bolts are 5/16" Whitworth cap screws. You can use a cap screw with a finer thread if you wish, though I can say the coarse Whitworth thread has not been a problem for me; your choice. My cathead is 2.250" in diameter, the hole is 1.500" in diameter, and the screw spacing is 1.000". It has been milled out to accept an octagon action.

3. Secure the receiver in the cathead, and place the mandrel in the bolt hole of the receiver. Secure the cathead in the 4 jaw chuck and true it to +/- 0 with a dial indicator.

3.1. When you have trued the cathead in the 4 jaw chuck, the jaws will be tight. All subsequent adjustments will be made with the cap screws on the cathead.

3.2. The front of the receiver must protrude past the end of the cathead by .020" minimum. We will be taking a facing cut here later.

3.3. You may want to place some brass shims under the screws of the cathead to protect the surface of the receiver. In reality, the ends of the screws should be rounded, and polished bright, but I mention it none the less.

PHOTO 1-3.

The Cathead I use for receiver and bolt truing.

4. We need to place two dial indicators with their probes located on the mandrel. Photos 1-4 and 1-5 show this better than I can explain it. Now the fun part begins!

5. In a nutshell, we rotate the lathe chuck by hand, and by adjusting the screws on the cathead, bring the runout of the mandrel into a $^{+}/-$ 0 condition on both of the dial indicators. Be advised, this is a formidable task.

PHOTO 1-4.
The setup I used to align the bolt hole of my 40X Remington receiver with the centre-line of the spindle on my Colchester lathe.

PHOTO 1-5.
The same setup, this time to align my Shilen DGA receiver bolt hole with the centre-line of the spindle on my Orn lathe. I had to use the Orn for this job as the DGA would not fit through the hollow mandrel of the Colchester.

5.1. The best advice I can give you is to mark the lathe chuck with a texta (Permanent Marker), top, bottom, right or whatever. Work out a system so you know where you are at any time.

5.2. Start by getting both dial indicators reading the same at one position of the lathe chuck, the top position for instance.

5.3. When you adjust one screw it will affect the adjustment of the other screw. At times you will feel like you are chasing your own tail, but as you progress you will get a feel for how one adjustment affects the other, and things will start to come together. Before you make an adjustment, work out in your mind how it is going to affect the other dial indicator, then watch both dial indicators as you adjust.

5.4. I have found it beneficial to draw an arrow on the dial of both indicators, in texta, with the word 'in' next to it. This indicates to me when the probe is moving in, and so is the mandrel moving in, towards the indicator. In other words, you have to know where you are at all times, otherwise you will be making wrong adjustments, and believe me, that's just downright throw yourself off a cliff frustrating, especially when you're almost there.

5.5. Getting both dial indicators reading $^{+}$/- 0 on the mandrel will take me more than an hour, and I am pretty quick with a dial indicator. I will probably do it in 3 or 4 sessions to ease the pain I suffer doing this job. Work it out for yourself, but when you have it right give yourself a good pat on the back; you deserve it! It's a really frustrating job.

6. We now have our receiver held in the lathe chuck with the centre-line of the bolt hole exactly on the centre-line of the lathe spindle. Any machining we now do, on the receiver, will be exactly parallel to, or square to, the bolt hole centre-line. Very carefully remove the mandrel from the bolt hole, oil it and put it away. Your chances of using it again are pretty remote, but you never know your luck in a big city.

7. Our first job will be to true the receiver threads. Generally these threads are quite eccentric to the bolt hole, and you will have to enlarge their diameter by up to .010", in order to clean them up, and make them true. Because of this, our first job will be to open up the minor diameter of the threaded hole by .010".

7.1. Centrefire rifle receivers are made from 4140, or similar, chrome moly steel, or 17–4PH, or similar, stainless steel heat treated to around 40RC. The important feature of these steels is their impact resistance. They are ideal to resist the hammering locking lugs receive during the stresses of firing the rifle. These steels, while resisting an impact machining process such as milling, are easily machined with a lathe turning process using hi-speed steel tools. I have found no reason to employ tungsten carbide tooling for this job.

7.2. Select a sharp boring bar that will reach into the locking lugs of the receiver. Stone a small radius on the tip of the tool. A radius of about .015" is ok. We don't want to leave a sharp corner at the end of the cut, as sharp corners are spots where cracks can start.

7.3. Mount the boring bar in your tool post, and run it into the receiver until it stops against the locking lugs. Lock the travel stop down, move the boring bar back about .010" with the cross-slide adjustment, and wind it back out of the receiver.

7.4. Start the lathe, running at around 570RPM. You will be standing on tippy toes trying to see the tip of the tool inside the receiver. Move the tool longitudinally back and forth, with the carriage handle, while you slowly bring the tool tip into contact with the top of the threads, using the cross-slide feed. You will hear, and feel, the tool touch the top of the threads. With the carriage feed, wind it out of the receiver and zero the dial on the cross-slide wheel.

7.5. Wind the cross-slide feed in .020" to .030", so that the tool is clear of the threads, and with the lathe still running move the carriage forward to its stop and lock it in position. Using the feed on your compound rest, advance the boring bar until the cutting tip just touches a locking lug. When it does, zero the dial on the compound rest feed wheel.

7.5.1. Again you will be on tippy toes to look past the boring bar into the receiver to see when the tool touches a locking lug.

7.5.2. It's very rare that the tool will touch the two lugs simultaneously. We are not cutting yet, just setting our controls to a zero starting point. You should have advanced the tool to a scratch, on a locking lug, not a cut.

7.6. Lubricate the threads in the receiver with cutting oil (I use Rocol Ultracut Metalworking Fluid). Back the compound rest up .005", so the tool doesn't quite reach the locking lugs, and take a .005" cut along the top of the receiver threads up to the carriage stop, using a slow feed.

7.6.1. The cut will be an intermittent one until it reaches the end of the threads.

7.6.2. Move the carriage feed in .010" so as not to rub the tool when you remove it from the receiver, and wind it out of the receiver. Have a look at the cut you have made just in front of the recoil lugs. You may find that you have only cut around 2/3RDS of the diameter. That's ok. It's an indication of the eccentricity of the threading job in the receiver.

7.6.3. Relube, take another .005" cut and re-inspect. Most receivers clean up with .010" in total enlargement. You can easily see what you have done, as the inside of the receiver is blued, and your cuts will be bright and shiny. If you see bright and shiny for the full 360° over the full length of your cut, then that job is done. Re zero the cross-slide dial to the new setting, which is, of course, back .010" from zero.

7.6.4. If the receiver does not clean up in .010", then I will take another cut at .002" — I don't think I have ever had one that needed more than .014" to clean up. Take the smallest amount necessary to true the surface and no more.

7.7. Lubricate the locking lugs, and wind the cross-feed wheel in, so that the tool is just past their inside face. Run the carriage into the stop and lock it in position. Move the compound rest slide .001" past zero, and take a .001" cut, with a slow feed, across the locking lugs out to the zero on your cross-slide handle. Back the tool off a couple of thou so it doesn't rub and inspect the cut.

7.7.1. You will see the cut easily. A small torch may assist. Rotate the chuck by hand so you can view both lugs. You may have machined only one lug, or maybe only part of one lug. Again, we want to remove only the bare minimum of material in order to bring the two surfaces into alignment. Take .001" cuts until you can see you have machined both locking lugs, over their entire surface, and stop. Remove the boring bar and put it away. We are finished with it for the time being.

7.7.2. Don't take extra cuts here. As soon as the locking lugs are aligned *STOP!* We are removing the absolute minimum amount of material to true the surface, and no more. True is true. It won't get any truer if you take an extra (unnecessary) cut.

8. The minor diameter of our receiver threads is now parallel to the centre-line of our bolt hole. Both locking lugs are square to it and on the same plane. We now need to chase the receiver threads to make them parallel to the centre-line of the bolt hole also. The tool I use to do this is shown in Photo 1-6, along with a couple of washers I use to set the end of the cut. The tool is home made, and uses a high speed tool steel insert I sharpen on a tool and cutter grinder. It has served me for 30 odd years. You may find buying a TC insert tool more convenient, and if you do that make sure you obtain thread cutting inserts that are capable of taking very fine cuts. They need to be very sharp. Unfortunately I am of no use giving advice in this area because I have never used TC for this job; sorry.

PHOTO 1-6.

The tools I use when truing the threads in a receiver. My Remington 40X has just been removed from the lathe, the job having been completed. On the left is the 1.072" diameter thread gauge I use so I know when to stop enlarging the thread. In the middle is my thread chasing tool. The slot on the end holds the insert, when I sharpen it, in a tool and cutter grinder. The two washers are simply spacers that allow me to set the end of the cut at the end of the receivers thread. On the right is the alignment mandrel.

8.1. You will need to determine the depth/length of the cut you will be making. There may be no need to cut the full length of the existing thread. It has been made with an intermediate tap so the last bit of its length will be tapered. You only need to chase the thread about 1½ turns past the length of your barrel thread. I have that already worked out, so I simply put my two washers in the receiver, against the locking lugs, then run my tool holder in until it stops against the washers, and that's the length of my cut. If you have the old barrel, that came from the action, you can work out how deep to chase the threads easily enough. Don't forget to take into account recoil lug thickness on Remington style actions, or any other little traps waiting for unwary players.

8.2. Unlike cutting external threads, when cutting internal threads, to what is essentially a blind end, we need some way to know when to end the cut. Once you get a little bit of depth in the cut you will probably break the tip off the tool if you cut past that point. Photo 1-7 shows the setup I use to determine when to disengage the tool.

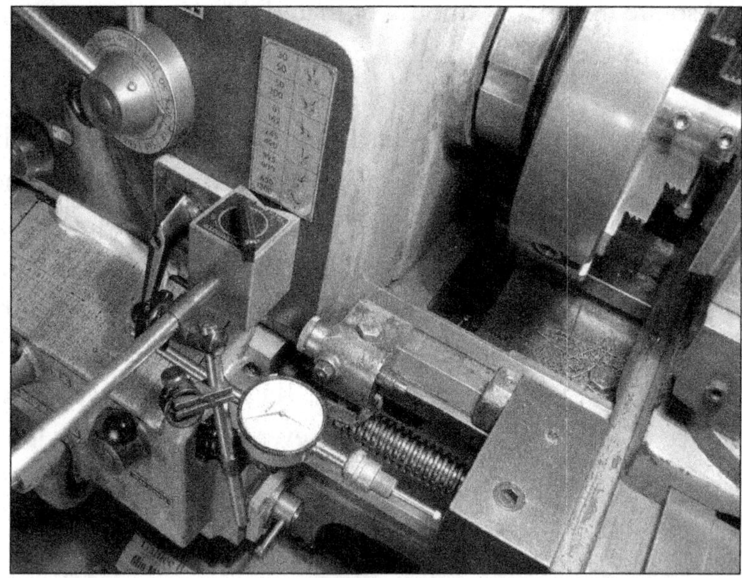

PHOTO 1-7.

The setup I use to indicate when to stop at the end of the thread.

8.2.1. The dial indicator has 2" of travel, which is more than needed. One inch would be enough. You could get by with a ½", but 1" would be better. I don't think I could get psyched up enough to disengage on time with only half an inch of warning. The indicator is magnetically clamped onto the headstock, and the probe bears against a flat surface on the carriage of the lathe. First we run the carriage forward to where we want our cut to finish. In my case I simply run the thread chasing tool up against the two washers I have placed against the locking lugs. Adjust the dial indicator out until it indicates zero on the one inch of travel mark. Now, when I back the carriage out of the cut the dial indicator probe comes out, with the dial pointer rotating backwards. When I make my cut, I can watch the dial on the indicator, and see the pointer moving, one rotation for every 1/10" of travel, and count the tenths as the carriage moves forward. 5, 6, 7, 8, 9,10 *STOP!* But I'm getting ahead of myself. Now you have an idea of what gives here, let's go back and get into sequence.

8.3. Mount your thread chasing tool on your tool post, taking care to have enough protrusion, to make the depth of cut you have worked out. Set the compound rest to 60°, and square the threading tool to the lathe spindle centre-line.

8.3.1. Remember, we are chasing existing threads here, not making new threads, so we want the tool to cut on both sides. If we were making a new thread we would set the compound rest at 59°. If you don't know why don't worry about it, as I'll explain in the chapter on barrel fitting. Just go with 60° now.

8.3.2. Also, make sure your cutter height is on the centre-line of the lathe spindle. Be careful from now on, as it's easy to catch the tip of your cutter on the receiver, or in the threads, and break the tip off. Yes — I've done that!

9. Set the gearbox of your lathe to the pitch of your receiver threads. In my case that is 16TPI for the Remington and 18TPI for the Shilen. Now we need to pick up the thread; that is synchronize the position of our chasing tool to the position of the thread with the lead screw engaged.

9.1. Your lead screw will have a degree of slack when engaged. In other words, with the lead screw engaged, it will be possible to move the carriage back and forth. When picking up the thread, be sure that all of the slack is taken up, by having the carriage as far as it can be to the rear. The lead screw will be driving the carriage forward, thus all slack is removed from the back of the thread. Pick up the thread with the drive in the same condition.

9.2. Make sure you can run the chasing tool into the front of the receiver without scraping its tip over the threads, and breaking it off, then set the lathe going at 30RPM. Engage the lead screw and the tool will move into the receiver front. Stop the lathe so that the tip of the tool is about 1½ threads inside the recess, and switch it off. Now, by using both the cross-slide feed, and compound rest feed, adjust the chasing tool so that it fits into, and bottoms out, in the receiver threads with the handle of the cross-slide wheel at 12:00, and the lead screw still engaged.

9.3. It's hard to see properly in there, so this is done by feel as well as by the little you can see. Start by adjusting both slides until you think the point of the tool is centred over the bottom of the V of the threads, then wind it in against the thread with the cross-slide wheel. Don't be too ham fisted. You will feel the tool touch the receiver thread. You will see one side of the V and the fit of the tool against it. If there is a gap, wind the cross-slide in a bit, and advance the compound rest in a bit, then bring the cross-slide back again and check. If there is a tiny gap, you have to be close, so go halfway and check again. You get the picture? Get it as close as you can, and then zero the dials on both the cross-slide and compound rest handles. All the time you are doing this be sure that you have back pressure on the carriage wheel; enough to simulate the pressure when the lead screw is driving the carriage forward.

10. Now that our chasing tool is in the position it needs to be to follow the receiver threads, when being driven by the lead screw, we can set our dial indicator up to indicate the end of the cut. I discussed that in step 8, so refresh your memory, and then set the carriage to that point where the cut will end.

Mount the dial indicator and adjust it to zero at the point of travel you have selected. In my case this is 1" of travel. Wind the carriage back so that the chasing tool is clear of the receiver, lubricate the receiver threads with cutting oil (Rocol Ultracut in my case) and we are ready to start chasing the thread.

11. Before we do that, let's discuss what is going to happen here. For starters we need to sneak up on this cut. If we set our cross-slide wheel to zero and make a cut, no matter how well we think we picked up the thread, there's a good chance we will take a good slice out of one side of the thread, while not touching the other side. Then, at the end of the cut, we will run into a veritable brick wall and break the tip off the tool. Also we need to be practiced at disengaging the tool at the end of the cut. *Very practiced!*

11.1. The reason we wanted the handle of the cross-slide wheel in the 12:00 position in step 9.2 is so that we can snap it down, clockwise, to the 6:00 position very quickly, thus disengaging the cutting tool completely from the thread at the end of the cut. At the same time we snap the cross-slide wheel down we have to quickly disengage the lead screw nut. Both actions are done simultaneously when the dial indicator point reaches the zero mark you have selected. You will notice that, when cutting a 16TPI thread at 30RPM, the dial indicator needle moves pretty quickly, so you need to perform those simultaneous actions very smartly. If you haven't done this sort of thing before, I'd recommend that you practice it until you're good at it with the cutting tool disengaged. Otherwise, if you make a mistake, you will damage the chasing tool. Ok, we've got that down pat, let's do it!

11.2. Oh yes, I'd better mention, you will be nearly standing on your head trying to see the progress of your work inside the receiver, unless you have a swish little camera mounted on the tool so you can watch the whole thing on a TV screen. Just kidding! Do the best you can, though it is difficult to see past your tool post, tool holder and light source. You will only be able to see the first 2 or 3 threads, and the rest will be blind. That's ok, as by then our attention should be fully focused on psyching ourselves up for the stop; 6, 7, 8, 9,10 *STOP!*

12. To avoid smacking the tool into a ledge formed by the tap that made the thread initially, I make my first pass with the cross-slide dial set at zero +.050" in. That's no cut at all on the main part of the thread, but what I am looking for is to pick up the tapered rear. If there is no evidence I have touched the thread at the rear (you will see a chip on the tool tip) then I will take .005" cuts. It doesn't take long to make 10 passes; a lot less than resharpening a chipped cutting tool. Also, making these passes gets me in the zone for stopping efficiently. When the tool starts to cut at the back of the thread, don't forget to add some cutting oil there before the next cut.

12.1. As the cross-slide dial approaches the zero mark, start to pay close attention to the tool as it enters the thread. Perfection would be to see it begin to skim the rear of the thread V, and miss the front of the V (that's the face you can see looking inside) by a tiny bit. Then, all you need to do is set the cross-slide to it's last position for the next cut and advance the compound rest, a thousandth or so at a time, until the front of the tool skims the front of the V. Then we are centred in the V and can make all further cuts with feed from the cross-slide only.

12.2. If the chasing tool starts to cut on the front face first (you'll see that within the first revolution of the tool entering the thread) stop the cut and back the compound rest out a couple of thousandths, and then advance the tool with the cross-slide a thousandth at a time, until the tool starts to skim again. If its still on the front of the V, repeat until you have the tool in the bottom of the V, and scraping both sides.

13. Once I have the tool properly set, I take .002" cuts (there's only five of them to take) enlarging the major diameter of the thread .010". After the last cut take several more passes at the last setting (i.e. don't advance the tool). The tool will skim a little from the V up to the last pass. Of course, we are lubricating the thread before every cut aren't we?

13.1. Now blow the recut thread clean with compressed air and have a look see at the result. Use a small piece of mirror to look at the rear of the thread. What we want to see here is bright shiny surfaces front and back of the thread for its full length. I have a test piece I made from a piece of barrel, 1.072" diameter x 16TPI, that I use to be sure all of my threads are the same size. You can see it in Photo 1-6. (page 9)

13.2. I have seen receivers with a recess on one side of the threads, probably caused during heat treatment; a patch, sort of like a 5 cent coin not touched by the tool. Sometimes the cutting tool misses one side or the other of a thread or 3. If this happens I will take another .002" pass, and check again, up to a maximum of .015" total enlargement. I have never had a receiver not clean up by .015". Of course, as soon as the threads have cleaned up take a few passes at the last setting then stop. Our thread chasing job is complete. Put the chasing tool and indicator away, and straighten the compound rest.

14. Now take a sharp facing tool, and face the front of the receiver the minimum amount necessary to make it true; probably .002" or less. Then chamfer the end of the thread 60°, to prevent a burr appearing when the barrel is screwed in, and our work on the receiver is done for now. Remove the cathead from the lathe and the receiver from the cathead. Now we turn our attention to the bolt.

15. Before we start on the bolt we need a plug that will screw into its rear. Make it a bit over bolt diameter and long enough to fit through the cathead. Photo 1-8 shows the ones I use. (page 14)

15.1. At this point I'd like to say your bolt is a precision piece of engineering. That's what I would like to say, but sadly that is rarely the case. Attachment of bolt handles and bolt heads by heat intensive processes doesn't help. They are rarely truly round, especially if they have been used. They rarely have true surfaces, and often have hard spots in the steel around where the heat processes have been applied. The upshot of all this is, when it comes to bolts, you will have to compromise in your setup. We will still do the best we can, and it will be good enough.

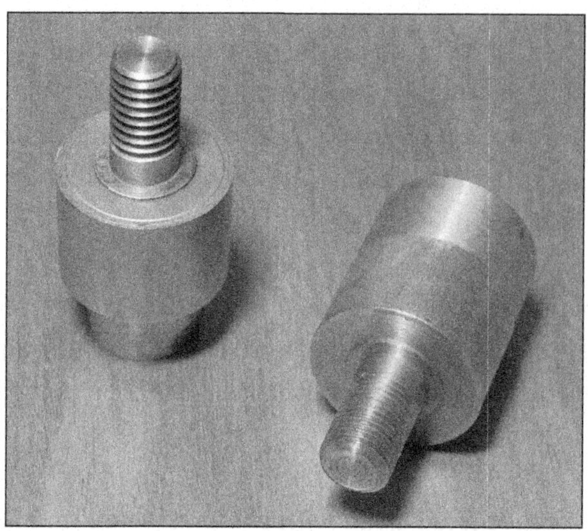

PHOTO 1-8.

The bolt plugs I used to align my Remington 40X (on the left) and my Shilen DGA (on the right). Note the ledge left at the root of the minor diameter, so that the plug tightens only on the rear of the bolt body diameter, and not against the handle.

16. To start with we need a square surface, at the rear of the bolt, to tighten our plug against. You'd think the rear of the bolt would be square, but it never is.

16.1. Secure the bolt in the 4 jaw chuck, with enough of the bolt handle end protruding, so you can get a dial indicator onto the body just ahead of the bolt handle to true it +/- 0. Here you may have to use a TC tool to face the rear of the bolt square. I always try a hi-speed steel tool first, and quickly find out if it is not up to the job, then switch to TC if necessary. The problem is there are often hard spots in the steel caused when attaching the bolt handle, and it will take a TC tool to cut them. Remove only the bare minimum of material needed to square the surface. Also, make sure the diameter of your squared surface will accommodate the diameter of the breeching surface on your plug. Photo 1-9 refers.

PHOTO 1-9.

Squaring the rear of the bolt body. This bolt had hard spots in it, and needed a tungsten carbide tool to make the cut.

16.2. Screw the plug into the rear of the bolt nice and tight, and turn its length until it is running true with the bolt body. Remove the bolt from the lathe.

Before we start on the bolt there is something we should consider. If a Remington action has a fault (apart from the obvious) it has to be the diameter of its firing pin coupled with the diameter of the firing pin hole. Simply put, they are both too large.

On this action the diameter of the tip of the firing pin is .0750" and the diameter of the hole it fits through is .0776", leaving a gap between the two of .0026". This action will see service on my practice rifle, barreled to .22PPC using the 80^{GN} projectile, and I know from experience that a firing pin and hole of those dimensions will not be able to withstand the extended pressure peak generated in the .22PPC.

If I try to use it unaltered I will be suffering disked primers, and a face full of gas every time I fire the rifle. Something needs to be done, and now is the time to do it, before we begin to align the bolt.

To cure the problem we have to reduce the frontal area the firing pin presents to the primer, and at the same time reduce the gap between the firing pin and its hole. We do that by bushing the firing pin hole, thus reducing the hole diameter, and machining the firing pin tip to a smaller diameter and a closer fit to the bushed hole.

We have already made the plug we will use to align the bolt, and we will make use of that here too. Let's do it.

A. Hold the plug in the 4 jaw chuck, mount a dial indicator with its probe just behind the locking lugs of the bolt, and adjust the 4 jaw chuck until the dial indicator reads $^{+}/-$ 0. Photo 1-10 shows this happening.

PHOTO 1-10.

Truing the bolt just behind the recoil lugs where the steady rest fingers will bear.

B. Mount a 3 jaw steady rest onto the lathe bed, positioned behind the locking lugs of the bolt.

C. Bring the steady rest forward so that the fingers will bear behind the locking lugs of the bolt, and lock it down.

D. Now, mount a dial indicator on the carriage, with the probe bearing on the nose of the bolt, opposite one of the bottom supports. Wind the support in very carefully, until the dial indicator needle registers .0001" of movement, and lock that support down. Reposition the dial indicator so that its probe bears opposite the other bottom support. Wind the support in very carefully until the dial indicator registers .0001" of movement, and lock that support down. Now move the dial indicator, so that the probe bears under the bolt nose, opposite the top support. This time move the support down until the needle on the dial indicator registers .0002" of movement, and then lock it down. We are now ready to machine the bolt. Photo 1-11 demonstrates this.

PHOTO 1-11.

The first steady rest finger has been brought into contact with the bolt body, and the dial indicator is in position for adjusting the second finger.

E. Fit a #19 drill in a drill chuck in the tail stock, and drill the firing pin hole out to a depth of .180". Photo 1-12 shows the drilled hole.

F. With a small boring bar, bore the drilled hole to a diameter of .200" x .187" deep, finished square at the bottom. Photo 1-13 shows the hole being bored to size.

PHOTO 1-12.

The firing pin hole has been drilled out to depth.

PHOTO 1-13.
Boring the hole to diameter and depth for the bush.

G. I use a small gauge I made to size the hole precisely. It can be seen in Photo 1-14. The small end is .199" diameter and the large end is .200" diameter. When the small end fits I know I have close to .001" to go, to make the hole exactly right.

PHOTO 1-14.
Some tools mentioned in the text. At the top is the tool I will use to face the bolt face of the Remington 40X bolt. Under it is the small boring bar I used to bore out the firing pin hole to accept the bush. Under that is the firing pin bush itself, back up. To the left is the gauge I use to size the hole.

H. Undo the steady rest, and remove the bolt from the lathe. Remove the plug from the bolt, and put both of them aside. Remove the steady rest from the lathe, but don't put it away just yet.

I. I make the firing pin bush from a ¼" Unbrako Allen head cap screw. You can get a few bushes from a 2" screw, and the steel it is made from is plenty tough enough for the job, and machines ok.

I.1. Set the screw up in your 4 jaw chuck, and true it with the dial indicator.

I.1.1. If it's too small to fit in your 4 jaw chuck, make a split sleeve like the one in Photo 1-15, and hold it in that. Easy!

I.2. Face it off and turn the outside diameter to .201" x .250" long. Don't polish it with abrasive cloth. Make a fine off tool finish exactly to size and that will be fine.

Photo 1-15.

The firing pin bush is held in a split sleeve for machining.

I.3. Spot the centre with the tip of your facing tool or your turning tool, whichever you like. Just be sure they are exactly on centre so they do not leave a nib at the centre of the spot. The bush has been spot centred in Photo 1-15.

I.4. Drill the bush with a #1 centre drill. You should drill to a depth that leaves only .050" of flat surface left at the edge of the bush. This tapered hole is a leade in for the tip of the firing pin. Photo 1-16 shows the bush centre drilled.

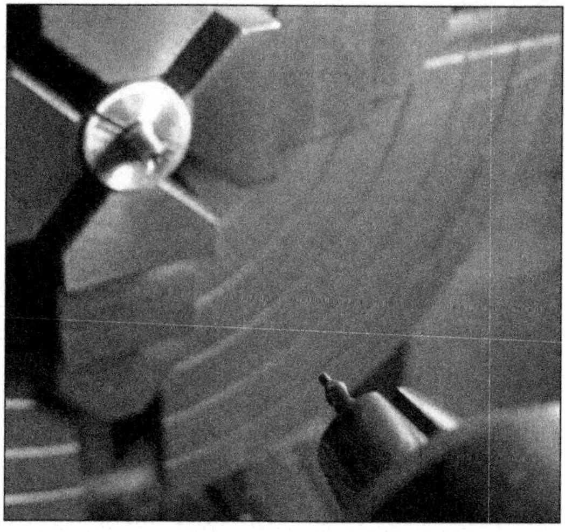

Photo 1-16.

The bush has been centre drilled.

I.5. Replace the #1 centre drill with a 1.5mm twist drill, and drill to a depth of .250" from the back of the bush. Be careful, these drills are relatively fragile. I take .015" deep passes, advancing the feed slowly, and lubricating with Rocol Ultracut.

I.6. Open the hole with a #52 number drill. Don't forget to lubricate with Rocol and be careful. The drill is still fragile. The hole diameter should be .0635". Photo 1-17 shows the hole about to be opened up.

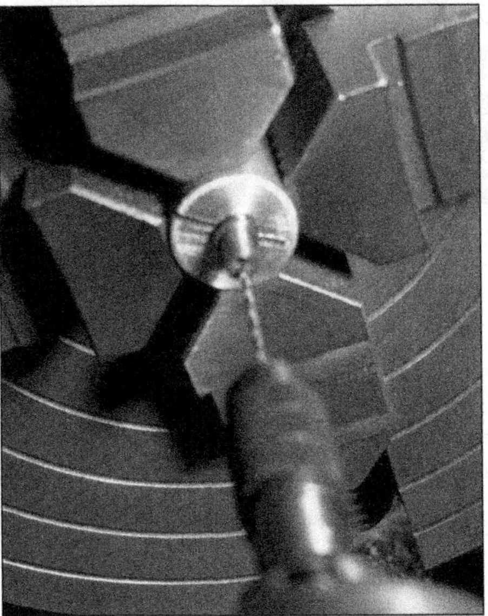

PHOTO 1-17.
Opening up the bush hole. The small drill is held in a pin vice.

I.7. Make a good 45° chamfer on the back of the bush at least .010" to .015" deep to provide a leade in when we install it in the bolt, and a clearance so that it will go right to the bottom of the hole when we install it.

I.8. Part the bush off at a length of .215", degrease it and place it in your refrigerator freezer for a couple of hours. Photo 1-18 (page 20) shows the bush being parted off.

I.9. Pour yourself a Rum and Pepsi Max (or substitute your personal favorite poison). You deserve it!

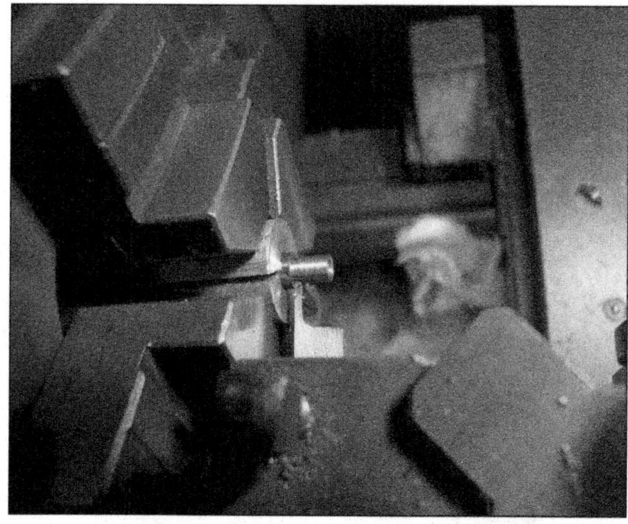

PHOTO 1-18.
Parting off the newly made firing pin bush.

J. While you're having that drink, consider how you are going to press the sleeve into the hole we made in the bolt. We have put it in the freezer to reduce its diameter, a little bit, by reducing its temperature. We will be heating the bolt nose up, thereby increasing the diameter of its hole. When we press the parts together, and they return to room temperature, we will have effected a permanent shrink fit.

J.1. I have a fairly powerful arbor press I use to do this, and it does double duty when I'm home as a reloading press. You can see it in Photo 1-19 having just pressed the sleeve into my bolt.

J.2. If you don't have a suitable arbor press (and one of the light reloading ones is not suitable) you could probably get it started in a drill press and then tap it right home with a brass drift. Just make sure it bottoms right out when it is inserted. We don't want it moving back when the rifle is fired.

K. Heat the end of the bolt up so that it is just uncomfortable to touch. Don't go stupid here — we don't want to be drawing the temper of the bolt head. Just good and warm is all that is needed.

L. Have everything at hand so you can do this quickly. Retrieve the bush from the freezer and, as quick as you can, press/tap it into the hole in the bolt. Even though I press it in with a strong arbor press I still move it to my vice and give it a couple of taps with a brass drift to ensure it is fully bottomed. That's it for the bolt. We will finish the bush when we do the alignment job shortly.

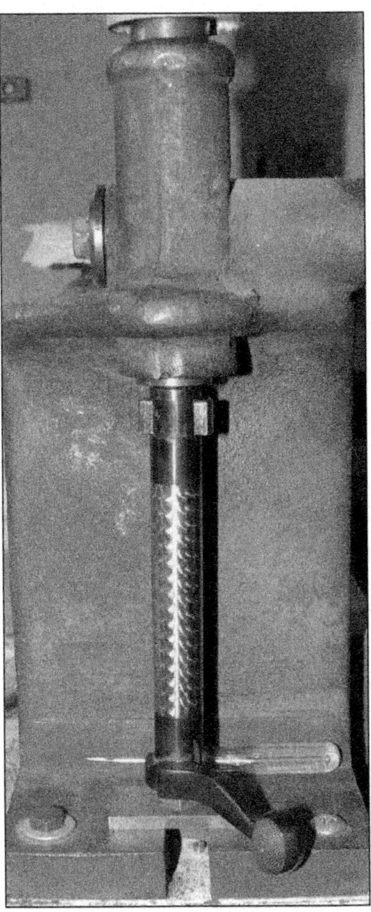

PHOTO 1-19.
The bush has been pressed into the bolt.

M. Time to turn our attention to the firing pin. Firing pins need to be tough, rather than hard, so that they can withstand thousands of impacts without cracking or breaking. As such, it is unusual not to be able to turn them easily. All we have to do here is reduce the tip of the firing pin from a diameter of .0750" to .0625", a reduction of only .0125", while maintaining the shape of the tip. It will turn easily.

M.1. To maintain the shape of the firing pin tip requires a shaped turning tool to be made, just for this job. The one I use can be seen in Photo 1-20.

PHOTO 1-20.
The shaped firing pin turning tool.

N. Set up the firing pin, in the 4 jaw chuck, held immediately behind the collar. True the tip of the firing pin.

N.1. I don't bother with carriage stops or automatic feed for this job, but do it by hand. Simply bring the tool into contact with the tip and take a .005" cut, just skimming the contour at the end of the tip.

N.2. Measure the diameter you have made and press on. I will reduce the diameter to .0640", then take at least 3 passes with the tool set in the same position to ensure parallelism, and measure the tip between passes.

N.3. When it is at its correct size (.0625"), give the tip a light rub with a fine file to remove the sharp corner. I mean '*remove the sharp corner*'; don't go reshaping the tip. Finally, give it a polish with a bit of worn 320 grit abrasive cloth.

O. Remove it from the lathe and test fit it into the bolt. It should slide in like a finger in a .... well, you know what I mean!

P. Reassemble the firing pin assembly and we'll move on with aligning the bolt. Replace the bolt plug, and tighten it up.

17. As with the receiver we need to set up the bolt so that its centre-line is exactly on the centre-line of the spindle of the lathe. The only way we can do that is with our cathead, so mount the bolt in that. Secure the cathead in the 4 jaw chuck and true it with a dial indicator. Mount two dial indicators, one to bear at the rear of the bolt body, and the other at the front of the bolt body. Photo 1-21 shows this far easier than I can explain. Now all we have to do is rotate the lathe chuck, and adjust the cathead bolts, to bring both of the dial indicators reading $^{+}$/- 0 run out. When we have achieved that, the bolt will be turning with its centre-line true to the lathe spindle centre-line.

PHOTO 1-21.

Truing the bolt body to the centre-line of the lathe spindle.

17.1. If you had trouble truing the receiver the bolt is going to give you fits. Sorry, but it's a real mongrel! The problem is out of roundness, so we need to compromise a tad with our setup. We do this by truing the body at each quarter of its circumference. The best points to do this from are level with the adjustment screws on the cathead. Mark the bolt body, front and back, with a texta at these points, along with 'up' and 'down', or whatever info you need to keep track of what you are doing. It also helps to still have the dial indicators marked as before. You can see the texta marks on my Shilen bolt in the above Photo (1-21).

17.2. As before, I find it best to get the dial indicators indicating equally, and then true the bolt from there. Think about each adjustment before you make it and keep track of where you are at all times. If it gets too much, walk away for a few hours (before you throw it in tall grass) and come back to it with a fresh approach. I certainly do.

17.3. When you finally achieve a reading of $^{+}/-$ 0, on both indicators, at all eight quadrants of the bolt body, you have it running with its centre-line as perfectly in line with the axis of the lathe spindle as possible. All cuts we make on the bolt will be either parallel to the centre-line or square to it, which is exactly how we want it to be. But first we need to support the end of the bolt to withstand the pressure applied when being machined.

18. Mount the steady rest on the lathe bed and slide it behind the locking lugs of the bolt. Be very careful not to bump it into the bolt and compromise all of the good work you have just done.

18.1. I like to do all of the work on the front of the bolt in one setting, so I position the steady rest along the bolt body so that I have enough room, behind the locking lugs, to squeeze a tool in, and then I lock the steady rest down.

18.2. Now, mount a long probe dial indicator on the carriage with the probe bearing on the nose of the bolt opposite one of the bottom supports. Wind the support in very carefully until the dial indicator needle registers .0001" of movement and lock the support down. We've done this before, haven't we? If you don't remember, go back and refresh at step D (page 16), when we set up our bolt to install the firing pin bush. No need to repeat it all here. We are now ready to machine the bolt. See Photo 1-11 (page 16) if you're not sure.

19. First step is the bolt face. On many bolt faces this is a simple boring job; that is a simple boring bar will suffice to make a shallow surfacing cut across the bolt face to true it. My Shilen is such a bolt face. Again, take the absolute minimum necessary to make the bolt face true to the axis of the centre-line of the bolt. .001" should do it. I have rarely had to take .002" of material away.

19.1. Remingtons require a specially ground tool which can be seen in Photo 1-22. The bit is ground by hand on a bench grinder, and the slot is made with an abrasive wheel on a Dremel tool. The slot is necessary to clear the extractor on the Remington bolt, which is non removable, unless you want to buy a new extractor and fit it. That's not necessary as this cutter will dodge it very nicely. Just be very careful setting it up. Bring the tip to within .001" of the bolt face, lock the carriage and zero the compound rest feed dial. Now rotate the lathe chuck (lathe in neutral) by hand, and using the cross-slide feed, wind the tool towards the outside of the bolt face. Watch carefully and you will see the instant the tool touches the outside edge of the bolt face by the witness mark it leaves. Zero the cross-slide feed dial, and take a .001" cut back to the zero mark with slow hand feed, and the bolt face lubricated with cutting oil. The job should be done. If not, take a .0005" cut and recheck. Don't be taking extra cuts trying to make a fine finish. If your tool is sharp the finish will be good. We must remove only the minimum needed to true the surface. Give it a light polish with some worn 320 grit cloth held on the blade of a screwdriver, and it will be bright and shiny. If we bushed the firing pin hole, that cut will have finished that job at the same time.

PHOTO 1-22.

Lathe tools for facing the bolt face on a Remington Model 700.

19.2. Next we turn our attention to the locking lugs. Again this is a simple facing operation and, as with the end of the cut made in the receiver, we do not want to leave a square/sharp corner at the root of the lugs, so the tool we use to make the cut must have a small radius at its tip. Photo

1-23 shows mine. I left clearance for this tool between the steady rest and locking lugs. As I am using a universal tool, that cuts on the left side, I mount it in the tool post upside down and run the lathe in reverse to make the cut. If you want to make a special right hand cutting tool, just to do this, feel free to do so. Makes no matter! Find your depth against the bolt body and zero the cross-slide feed dial, then bring the tool back to touch a locking lug. I start at the inside (zero) and face the lugs out. Take a .001" cut and see what you have done. You may have only cut one lug, and if so take another cut, .0005" this time and continue until both lugs clean up. Rarely do you have to cut past .002".

19.3. Move back to the front of the bolt. Here I use the same tool I used on the locking lugs, except now I can use it with its normal left hand cut.

19.3.1. Face the front of the bolt nose. With a Remington 700 be especially careful to face the absolute minimum, as this section is thin.

PHOTO 1-23.

Facing the back of the locking lugs. The lathe runs in reverse. Note the radius on the leading edge of the tool, necessary to avoid a sharp corner at the root of the lugs.

19.3.2. True the bolt nose itself. Again, minimum, blah, blah, blah.

19.3.3. Face the front of the locking lugs until they are both true.

19.3.4. Break the sharp edge at the end of the bolt nose with a fine file.

19.3.5. Give the surfaces a lick with a worn piece of 320 grit abrasive cloth to make them bright and shiny.

20. On some actions the fit between the bolt and the bolt hole leaves a bit to be desired. My Shilen was good having only a .001" gap but the Remington didn't measure up, having a .010" gap. With a

gap like that, when the bolt is in the cocked position, the rear of the bolt will be forced into the up position against the top of the rear receiver bridge, which will, in turn, unload the top (left) recoil lug. That is to be avoided. We don't want the bolt to be rattling around before or during ignition. The fix is to sleeve the rear of the bolt where it resides inside the rear bridge of the receiver, thus taking up any looseness that exists. There is no need to be concerned with the fit of the front of the bolt, on a Remington, because we have trued the bolt nose, and subsequently can support the front of the bolt in its recess in the back of the barrel. The preparation work to do this job should really be done before the bolt itself has been set up in the lathe for truing, unless you have a second lathe you can use.

20.1. Place the bolt in the receiver in the locked position, and mark the body with a texta on the underside at the front of the trigger cut out and the back of the magazine well. This is where our sleeve will be.

20.2. Now make a sleeve out of a piece of old barrel steel. This is a simple facing, turning, boring and parting job. Turn the OD to .750" diameter, bore the hole to .680" diameter and part the piece off .400" long. Don't worry about making a super finish anywhere. Give it a good 45° chamfer at each end with a file.

20.2.1. Cut the sleeve in half along its length. I use a thin cut off saw in my milling machine. Long ago I used to cut them in half with a thin abrasive disc in a Dremel tool. See Photo 1-24.

PHOTO 1-24.
Cutting the sleeve in half.

20.2.2. Now take each half in the jaws of a pair of vice grips and squeeze the edges in slightly. Use vice grips here, as they are adjustable, so you can adjust to the exact amount of squeeze you want, which isn't much. If you use pliers you are in danger of overdoing the squeeze big time.

21. Our bolt is already set up perfectly in the lathe, so we will want to do this job while it is still in that position, but we need to get our carriage behind the steady rest. We can't do that, as there is not enough room to fit it in. We need another method with which to support the end of the bolt.

21.1. I do this with an adjustable cap that fits over the nose of the bolt, and is supported by a live centre in the tailstock of the lathe. It can be seen in Photos 1-25a and 1-25b.

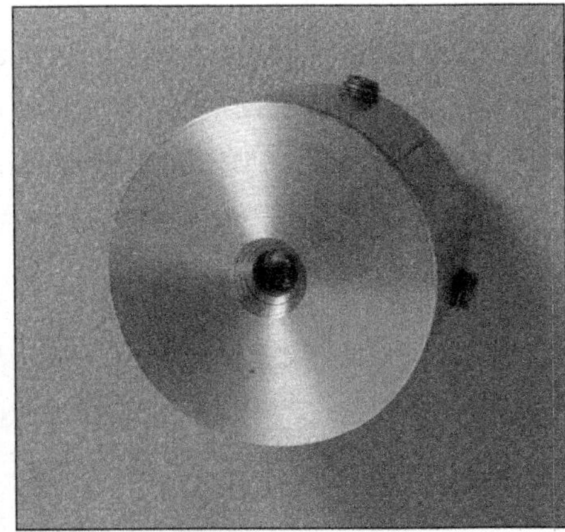

PHOTOS 1-25A AND 1-25B.

The adjustable nose cap I use to support the end of the bolt for further machining.

Photo 1-26 shows the cap installed on the nose of the bolt, and supported by the live centre in the tailstock.

PHOTO 1-26.

The bolt nose cap in place supporting the end of the bolt for further machining.

21.2. The cap is 1.125" long x 1.375" in diameter. It is bored out 1.100" in diameter x .600" deep to accept the end of the bolt. The other end is centre drilled to enable it to be supported by the tail stock centre, and the four adjustment screw holes are drilled and tapped .200" from the open end. The screws themselves are 5mm grub screws, 10mm long.

21.3. Install the cap on the end of the bolt, and true it with the dial indicator before you remove the steady rest from the lathe.

21.4. Remove the steady rest, wind the carriage back to the lathe chuck, and bring the live centre, in the tail stock, into the centre in the nose cap. Make sure you have enough room to maneuver with the carriage at the end of the bolt before locking the tail stock.

21.5. Clamp a dial indicator onto the carriage, and adjust any run-out just behind the bolt lugs to $^{+}$/- 0 using the adjusting screws on the bolt nose cap. There is no need to worry about the back of the bolt as that is already true. See Photo 1-27.

PHOTO 1-27.
Adjusting the bolt nose to zero run-out.

22. Now we need to cut a groove in the bolt, between the marks we put there previously, to accept the sleeve we made. In my case that would be .402" wide (sleeve width +.002") x .670" in diameter. By making the diameter .010" smaller we will allow the ends of the sleeve to be closer together when we attach it.

22.1. I find a parting tool is the most convenient tool to make this cut with. I prefer to have a carriage stop at each end of the carriage, and then adjust the final width of the groove with the compound rest. There is no need to make a fine finish here either; straight off the tool is ok. I set my stops to width, and plunge cut to rough out the groove. The parting tool will cut on the edges so, for my final cut, I start at one end, go in to depth, wind back to the other end, and bring the tool straight out. It's a simple job. Check the fit of the sleeve before removing the tool. Photo 1-28 refers.

PHOTO 1-28.
Turning the recess in the bolt body.

23. Now we will glue the sleeve onto the bolt. 24 hour Araldite is fine for this job. You will note that the sleeve is nearly a snap fit to the groove. That's why we squeezed the edges in a little, so that it would fit the groove more closely. Also you will note it will be prone to pop off on its own. Be aware of this!

23.1. Degrease the sleeve and the groove, carefully, with alcohol. Mix up some 24 hour Araldite, and while it is combining, warm up the bolt and sleeve a bit with a hair dryer.

23.2. Coat the groove and the inside of the sleeve halves with glue; rub it well in, and fit the sleeve halves into the groove. Hold them in with a pair of vice grips. Mild pressure on the vice grips will be sufficient.

Clean off excess glue with cotton buds dampened with alcohol.

23.3. A bit of heat will assist the Araldite to harden properly. I place my lathe light over the sleeve, so that it gets the heat from the light, for a couple of hours minimum. The problem with gluing metal is it is a conductor, and conducts the heat the Araldite creates itself, and needs in order to cure properly, away into the atmosphere. You will achieve a better cure if you supply a heat source, to compensate for the loss through conductivity. Go and do something else for a day while the Araldite goes good and hard. See Photo 1-29.

PHOTO 1-29.

The sleeve is held tightly to the bolt body with vice grips while the Araldite hardens. A small pair of vice grips are the best tool with which to hold the sleeve to the bolt with tension. The chamfer mentioned in step 20-2 can be seen here too. (page 26)

24. We already know the diameter of our rear bridge hole from when we made the mandrel to true the receiver, so all we need to do now is turn the outside diameter of the sleeve to .001" under that diameter. You can make a nice fine polished finish here. The bolt is done, so remove it from the lathe and put everything away. Photo 1-30 (page 30) shows the sleeve turned to diameter.

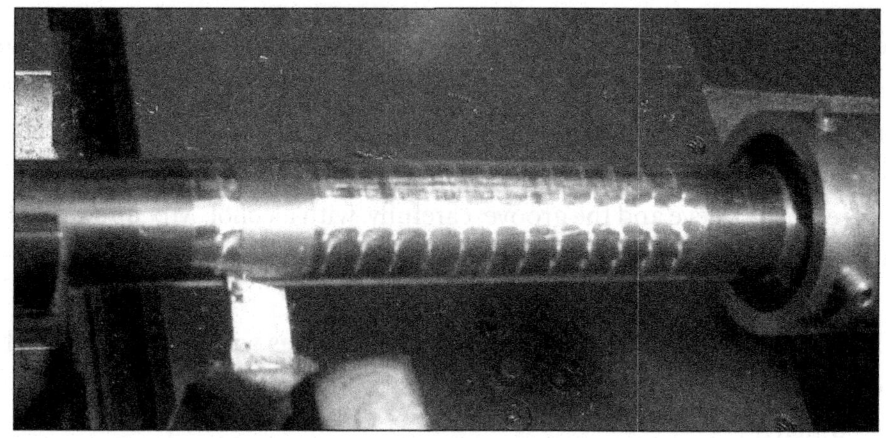

PHOTO 1-30.
Taking the final cut on the bolt sleeve.

25. All that remains is to lap the locking lugs, which really is a formality, as the machined surfaces are as true as it is humanly possible to make them. Nevertheless, twenty strokes with 400 grit non imbedding lapping compound will prove the accuracy of your job, with lug contact 100%. Clean the whole works and jerks up and we are done.

PHOTO 1-31.
My finished Shilen DGA action and the tools I used to align it.

Our action, trued like this, is every bit as good as a custom action, and may be even better, as you know beyond doubt that the action is dead straight. It will be a fine foundation on which to build a super accurate varmint rifle, and at well below the cost of a custom action.

PHOTO GALLERY

This page begins the photo galleries I am including, between each Chapter of the book, depicting significant rifles I built during my career.

I began rebarreling my own rifles in late 1967. I had been fiberglass bedding them since around 1965, and it was a natural progression to begin restocking those rifles, using semi inletted blanks, mainly from Fajen in the USA, sometime in 1968. I had no formal metalwork or woodworking training, so was in effect bumbling around in the dark and feeling my way. What I did have was a determination to do the best job I could, and see it through until it was right, coupled with a desire to learn as much as I could from whatever source that was available to me.

De Rigour at the time was Thumbhole stocks, rollover cheek pieces, recurved grips, basket weave checkering etc. Naturally my early efforts reflected these styles. You won't find any photographs of those rifles here; they are sort of like something I don't like to admit I ever did. I am not alone in this. I have been fortunate, in my time, to meet some really talented people, and none of them liked to be confronted with their early work, even though it may have been very good. Real talent forces progression, and each piece is a stepping stone towards the makers conception of perfection. Thus, when one is confronted by an example that is mid stream you sort of go — "UGH! — That's not what I'm doing now," even though the example may be fantastic. I guess beauty is in the eye of the beholder.

Most of those early rifles featured barrels of #4 contour for hunting versions and #5 or Shilen's #5A for varmint versions. They were heavy rifles, especially the thumbhole stocked examples. For instance, my little .17 Ackley Hornet was fitted with a #3 profile Douglas barrel blank in 1968. When I restocked it, with a Fajen thumbhole design Claro walnut stock, in 1969, it weighed in at 13.5 pounds, mounted with a Kahles 8x scope in a Hillver bridge mount. That's heavy!

These designs worked ok for spotlighting from a vehicle, but they had definite short comings when it came to hunting, and in particular shooting at running game. In the mid 1960s I mostly hunted goats and pigs, but also gave crows and rabbits a hard time with my Krico .222, and later my Remington 700 in 22-250, both with light barrels. In the late 1960s my focus shifted to long range spotlighting of foxes which prompted a change in rifle design to heavy barreled rifles.

By the beginning of 1970 I was doing a lot of hunting and my varmint rifles were doing double duty. Small game such as foxes, dingos, crows and rabbits were taken either by spotlighting, or in daylight from a vehicle at long range. Medium game, such as pigs and goats, were hunted on foot, and mostly taken running. It soon became apparent to me that a heavy barreled rifle does not make an ideal hunting rifle.

The real wake up call came to me in early 1974. We were culling goats in the Flinders Ranges, on a sanctuary, using mostly semi automatic 308 Winchester and .223 Remington rifles. I wanted a very light rifle to carry with me on a motorcycle that I used for scouting trips, to locate mobs of goats, which were then hunted in the rugged hills on foot.

I had been importing fiberglass stocks made by Chet Brown and Lee Six in the U.S.A for awhile, and had Chet make me a blank with no filling in it other than urethane, which made it very light. At that time all of Brown Precisions stocks were knock offs of their respective factory designs, so my blank was a copy of Remington's short Model 700 ADL design.

I obtained a Remington 700 barreled action in .308 Winchester (the calibre of the SIG AMT rifle I was using), pulled the barrel, turned it down to a super light profile and cut it off to 20" long. I finished the stock in a 2 pack urethane paint and glued the barreled action into it, making a rifle that weighed 6 pounds, complete with a 2-7x Redfield Widefield scope in Weaver mounts, a full magazine and sling.

At the time the general wisdom, as espoused in the hunting/shooting magazines of the era by the gurus, who were supposed to know, was that light barreled hunting rifles were useless, because you couldn't hold them steady and they were not accurate.

When I completed the rifle I went to sight it in on my Fathers 40 acre property at Brown Hill Creek, and did the preliminary sight in at 25 yards from a sitting position, facing slightly downhill. I discovered two very important things that changed my thinking about the design of sporting rifles, and the path I would ultimately follow in their creation.

First up, as I sighted on the target in preparation for the first shot, I was shocked at how steady I could hold it. By this time I was a very experienced hunter, and had taken many thousands of head of medium game shooting from field positions, prone, sitting and standing without a rest. I knew well the difficulties of shooting from these positions, and why they were difficult. The enemy you have to overcome to be successful, when shooting at running game, is inertia.

Simply put, the faster you have to swing a rifle, to get on to target, the harder that swing is to stop or slow. The more weight you have in the rifle, especially that weight from the receiver forward, the harder it will be to stop or slow the swing.

I knew well how this worked as I had experienced it over and over again; a thousand times over. Animal breaks from cover hitting 35mph in about 3 strides. You swing to lead it, but can't slow the momentum of your swing quickly enough. By the time you do slow it you've over compensated and are behind the lead, so you have to speed it up, and so on, and so on, wasting precious time, often allowing the animal to escape unscratched. Been there, done that!

This new rifle, however, had virtually no inertia problems, and was dead easy to hold rock solid on the target. I was somewhat surprised.

The second important thing, I noticed, was I let go of the grip when I mounted the rifle. I don't know why this became apparent at this time because I'd used this stock design extensively before this moment. I remember thinking to myself, "What the hell happened there?" I mounted the rifle a few times, and observed that, when I brought it to my shoulder, my right hand circled the grip completely (and properly), but when I took aim I let go of the grip and moved my hand to the rear, so that I could reach the trigger with the ball on the end of my trigger finger. When I gripped the stock, as it should be held, the grip was way too short, and to be comfortable I would have had to pull the trigger with the second joint of my finger, not with the ball of the first. Interesting huh!

It would seem the short grip was a result of the Remington 700S heritage. Its Father was the Remington 722, and its Grandfather was the M17 30/06 Military rifle Remington made, in their tens of thousands, during the second world war. If you look, you will see similarities between the old M17 and the Remington 700. In the military they were taught to pull the heavy weight two stage triggers with the second joint of their finger, to gain more leverage, and the grip on those stocks was short so they could reach it. With the relatively light single stage triggers we use these days we don't need to do that, and find we have more control using the ball at the end of our trigger finger. However, to do that, we have to let go of the grip.

From that day on the design of my sporting rifles would reflect a philosophy of combining correct grip length, minimum frontal inertia, and slim feminine lines. When a rifle was finished I would examine it critically, and make whatever small adjustments I felt were needed in the next one. When you peruse the photographs from the front of the book to the back you will see the subtle differences in design.

Mostly I built rifles on M'98 Military Mauser actions made in the 1950s by FN, as I believed they were a good action, being through hardened. I never used the 1909 Argentine action everyone else seemed to like, as every example I saw had set back locking lugs from use with the low pressure 7x57 Mauser Military ammunition of the time. I did not believe them suitable for high pressure cartridges.

I know my design philosophy was right from personal experience. My own hunting rifles are of my last design, and I do not have to think when I use them. When I mount them they are pointing right at the target. They are like an extension of my arm. I have taken so many terrific shots with them wondering afterwards, "How did I do that?" It's like magic. As natural as breathing.

Phil Vinnicombe engraved these rifles for me. Apart from being a nice unassuming bloke, Phil was a master craftsman.

I hope you enjoy looking at them.

W (Bill) Hambly-Clark Jnr...
2013

A REMINGTON MODEL 700 IN .17 REMINGTON

BUILT IN THE MID 1970S

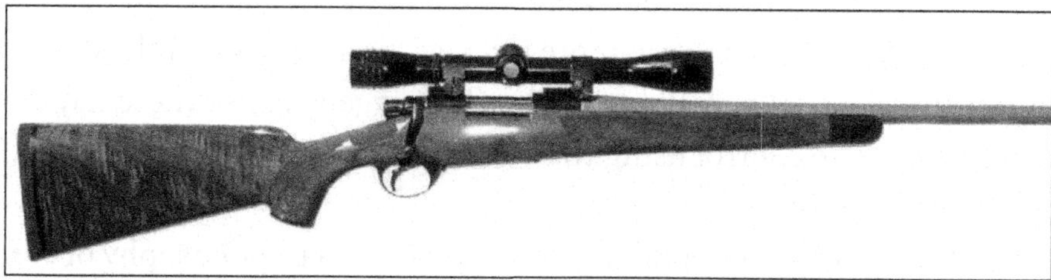

PHOTO C1-1.

This rifle is representative of my last work using Fajen's semi-inletted stock blanks.

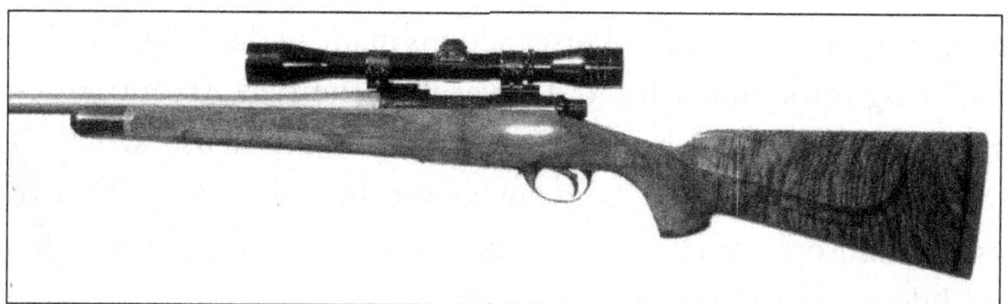

PHOTO C1-2.

The barrel was a #3 profile Shilen in stainless steel. The forend tip was rosewood.

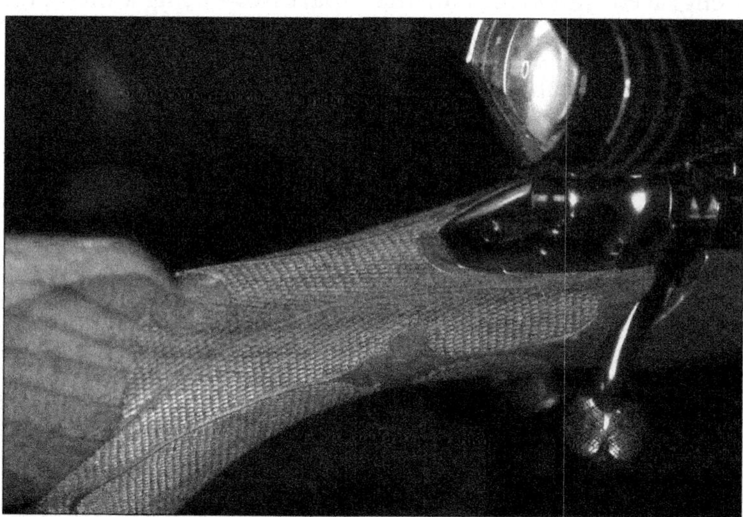

PHOTO C1-3.

Of note is the unmodified rear tang that I have taken much trouble to make flush with the line of the grip. Later I would modify this area considerably.

PHOTO C1-4.
The stock was a fancy grade of Claro Walnut.

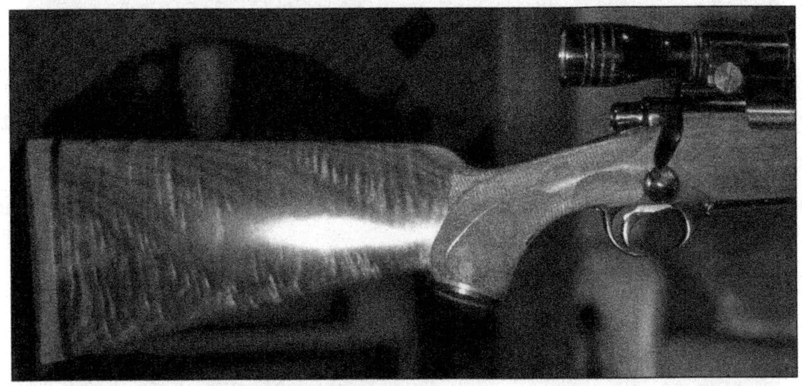

PHOTO C1-5.
Claro Walnut in the fancy grades had striking figure, but was a relatively soft stock wood.

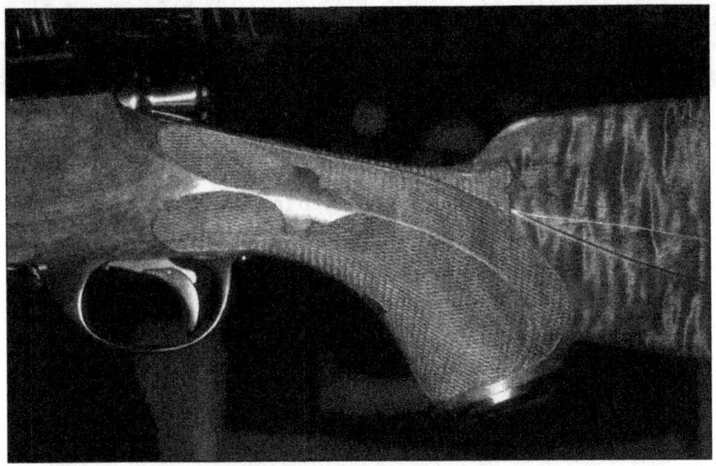

PHOTO C1-6.
This is probably one of the first Fleur-de-Lis checkering patterns of this design I did. It would become a trademark of mine with slight variations.

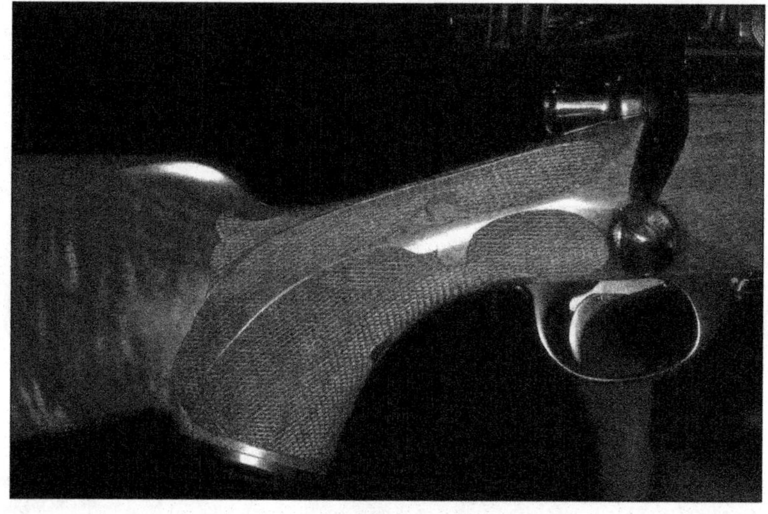

PHOTO C1-7.

The bolt handle is one of Len Brownells welded onto the stub of the original Remington handle. The bolt knob checkering was in four circular panels. The trigger guard I made from solid steel in Remington ADL style and grafted it onto the BDL frame.

PHOTO C1-8.

I made the skeleton grip cap from solid steel.

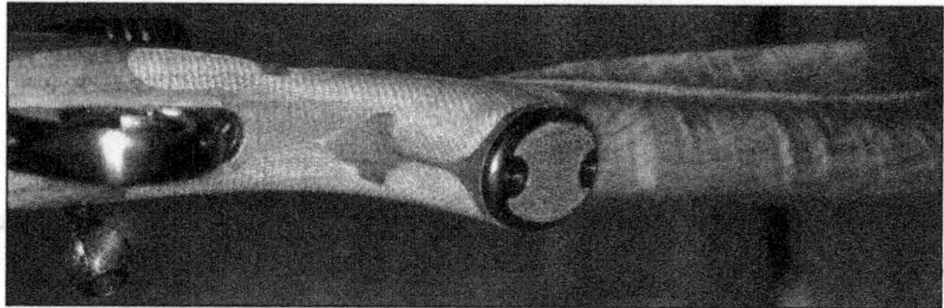

PHOTO C1-9.

This is probably the first stock where I continued the checkering pattern under the grip without a break. The thicker grip is typical of its vintage.

This is a sober reminder to be very careful around high power, high velocity rifles, or any rifle for that matter. I snapped these Photos at the instant my mate, Tom Buvac, hit these rabbits with his .22-250 Improved. These hot calibres do the same damage to us, so always be careful. Very, very careful!

A BFA ACTIONED RIFLE IN .17 MACH 1V

BUILT IN THE LATE 1970S

PHOTO C1-10.

The left hand stock on this rifle is pre pantograph. It was cut from the blank, with a hand saw, and shaped completely by hand.

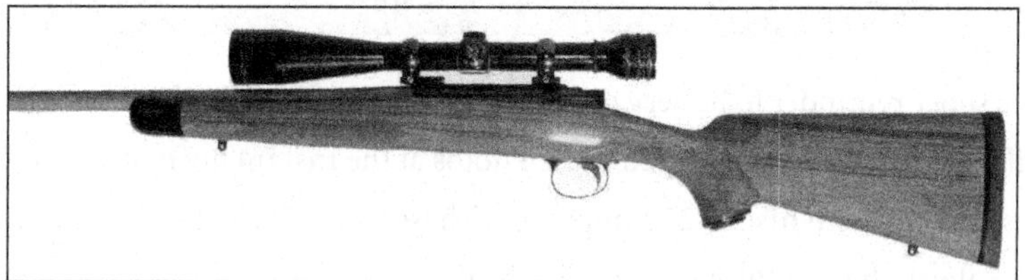

PHOTO C1-11.

The stick was a standard grade of New Zealand walnut. I rarely obtained any satisfactory blanks from there. Many I could not use at all, they were so bad. They made expensive firewood at a time when we were counting every cent.

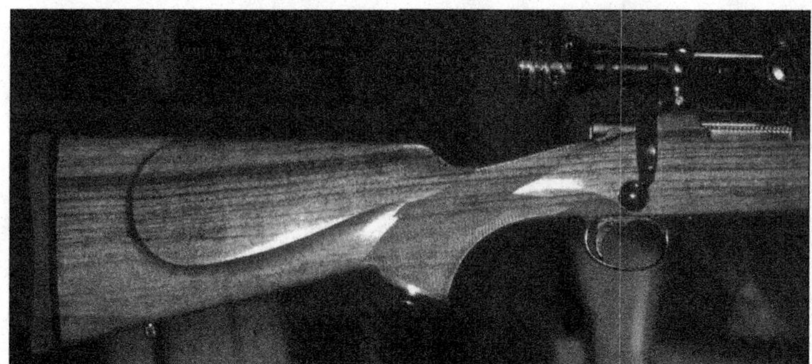

PHOTO C1-12.

The cheek piece has no shadow line. The telescopic sight rings are Conetrol. The trigger is a Canjar 700–2/S2 tuned to a 1¼ pound pull.

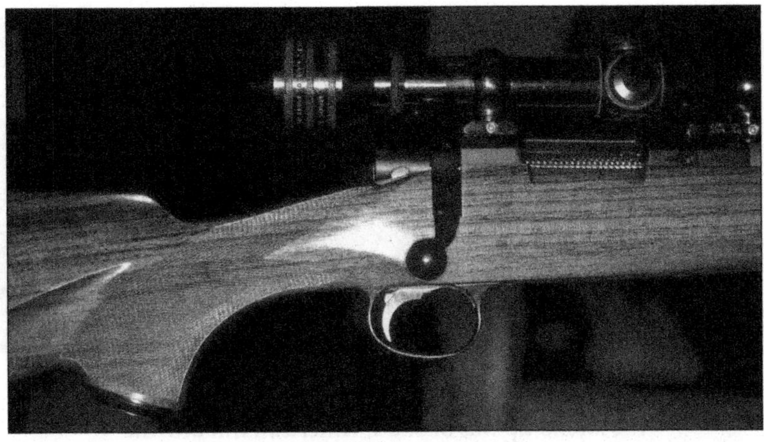

PHOTO C1-13.

I designed this action and made them from investment castings. Unfortunately I was lucky to get one good casting from five, and every time I received a new batch they had new problems, so in the end I had to abandon the project.

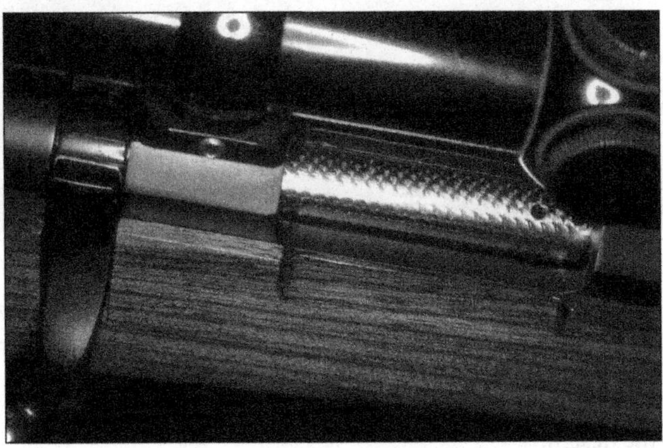

PHOTO C1-14.

The action was of octagon shape on top, with a flat bottom, and integral recoil lug. There was a large rear tang bedding area, and a long barrel thread. It was a very stiff and strong action designed for the .222 case head sized cartridges. Any Remington Model 700 trigger could be fitted.

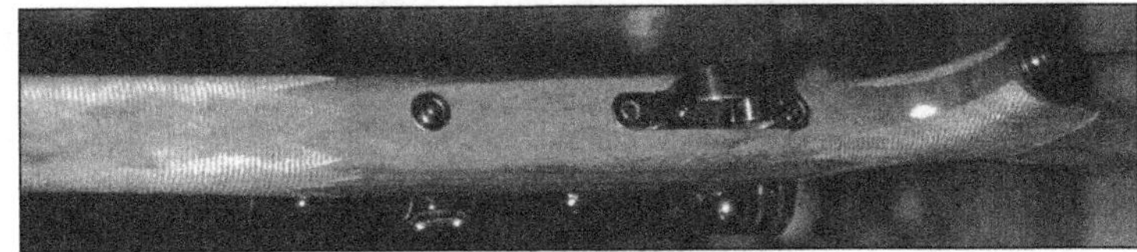

PHOTO C1-15.

I used Remington 700ADL trigger guards. The grip cap was from Len Brownell.

photo C1-16.
The forend tip was of South American Imburi. The swivel base was a standard Uncle Mikes part.

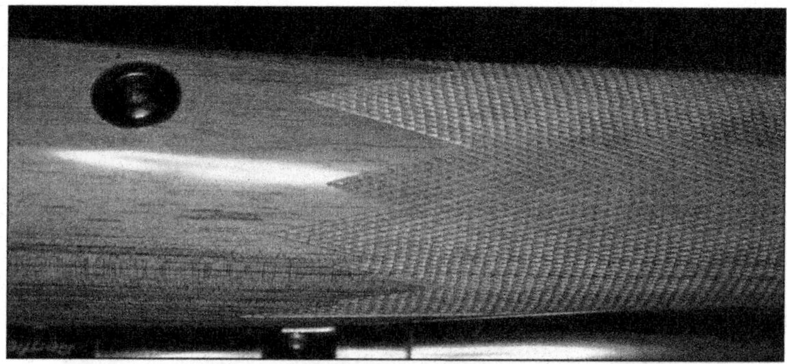

photo C1-17.
The Checkering pattern was of classic point design. The action initially was of Remington ADL configuration, and I used the standard Remington front screw escutcheon. The project came to a halt before I could start making a dropped floor plate magazine design.

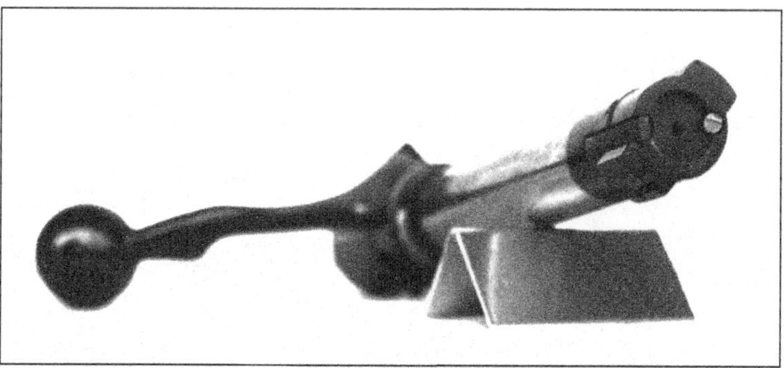

photo C1-18.
A BFA Bolt. The body and handle were machined investment castings.

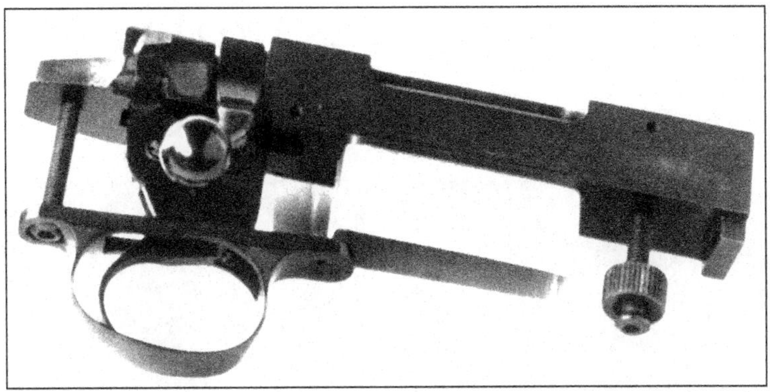

PHOTO C1-19.

At the time I made this action there was a shortage of Sako L461s in Australia. Also the L461 had its feed rails redesigned so that it would no longer feed short cartridges like the .17 Mach IV reliably. I designed the action with feed rails specifically for the .17 Mach IV, and altered them to suit longer cartridges, like the .223 Remington and .17 Remington, as needed. Using the Remington Model 700 trigger also allowed the use of 2^{oz} triggers such as the Canjar 700–LP, or Remington 2^{oz} conversions.

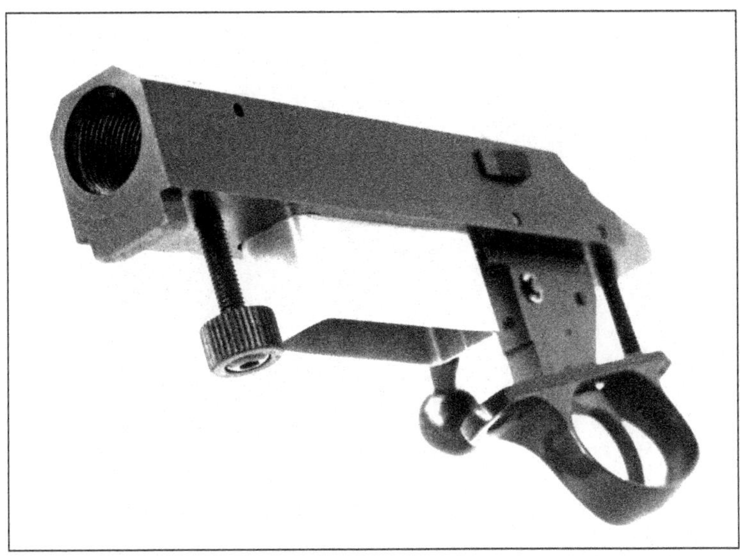

PHOTO C1-20.

The flat bottom design, along with the large rear tang area, made a very stable bedding platform. It was very disappointing to have to abandon the project because of the terrible quality of the investment castings I was receiving. Every batch we received had a problem we had to pay to fix, and every new batch had a new problem. I ended up machining the castings all over, so might as well have made the action from scratch at the beginning. Unfortunately we had sunk all of our meagre finances into the castings. In the end we simply ran out of money, and had to say, "enough is enough!"

SIGNIFICANT RIFLES AND EVENTS

PART 1: THE 1960S AND BEFORE

PHOTO C1-21. **PHOTO C1-22.**

PHOTO C1-21: I was exposed to the outdoors and hunting at a very early age. The rifle is one of my fathers BRNOs, probably in 6.5x57. The Fallow Doe was probably taken for meat at Buckland Park in South Australia. Photo circa 1945.

PHOTO C1-22: Dad said, "When you can cock this airgun you can have it." I figured out how to do it pretty quick, and won my first gun. Photo taken around 1947.

PHOTO C1-23.

This slug gun was significant because I learned to shoot with it at a very early age. This photo is probably my first shot after figuring out how to cock it. Dad cut the butt off to make it shorter for me. If you look back to the photo in my Preface (Page ii) you will see that it is significantly shorter. Later he soldered a tube to the barrel with cross-wires in it. Photo circa 1947.

PHOTO C1-24.

This big red kangaroo was taken with a specially made small stocked Sportamatic .22 on a trip through the centre to Darwin in 1954. The rifle was mounted with a Pecar 2¾ power telescopic sight. I still have the tanned skin from this roo.

PHOTO C1-25.

The rifle in this PHOTO is a P14 .303, and I have just turned 11 years of age. I killed one buffalo with a .30M1 carbine using military ball ammunition, and it wasn't enough gun by a good margin. I killed 10 more buffalo using the P14, and military Mark 6 215 grain hard ball round nose ammunition, which was the preferred ammunition for that job. We were shooting buffalo for skins on Mount Bundy station in the Northern Territory. In those days the N.T. was the wild west. PHOTO circa 1954.

PHOTO C1-26.

This is a significant rifle as it marked my graduation from .303s and .30M1 Carbines etc, to a rifle you could actually hit something with at long range. It was a sporter weight Krico model 600 in .222 Remington, mounted with a Weaver K6 in EAW rings. I learned to become very deadly with it out to 300 yards. This Billy fell to it in late 1964.

PHOTOS C1-27, C1-28, C1-29.

In 1967 I competed in the National Bench-rest Championships held at Belmont in Brisbane, Queensland. I took first place in the Heavy Varmint Class, second place in the Light Sporter class, and third place in the Open class. I also had the lowest grand aggregate for the competition. I am shown here with my trophies, Sporter on the left, Varmint in the middle, and Open on the right, with the rifles I used.

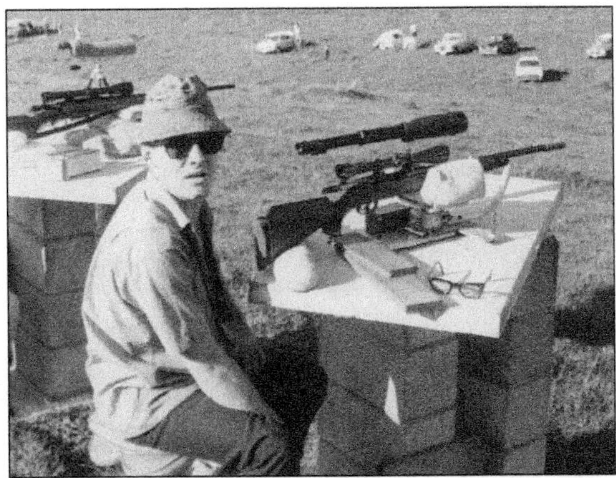

PHOTO C1-30.

200 yard bench-rest competition at McHargs Creek range, October 1967. The rifle is my heavy barreled Krico model 600 in .222 Remington. I had taken 2ND place in the National Bench-rest Championships, Sporter Class, 4 months earlier with it.

PHOTO C1-31.

I started to work with .17 calibre in early 1968 after hearing about their exceptional performance from a friend in the USA. There were no commercially made projectiles available, so I obtained bullet making dies, and jackets, and made them myself. The first rifle was a .17/222 Improved Magnum. I fitted the Shilen barrel to my Krico Model 600 bench-rest rifle. That's it in PHOTO C1-31. I made 25 grain Projectiles, and that case pushed them to just over 4150 feet per second. Recoil was negligible, and accuracy was ½", and under, at 100 yards. I tested it extensively and was very surprised with the results I obtained. In PHOTO C1-32 I am testing its trajectory to 500 yards at the shearing quarters on Purple Downs. I tried it on all manner of game before going public with it, in an article entitled 'Sweet 17' in Sporting Shooter Magazine, March 1970. That article certainly stirred up a deal of controversy. .17 calibre was here to stay, however, and for quite a few years the bulk of my bread and butter work consisted of making, or rebarreling, rifles in .17 calibre.

PHOTO C1-32.

PHOTO C1-33.

Part of a nights fox tally on Purple Downs Station, some time in late 1969. This particular .17/222 Improved Magnum was built on a Remington Model 700 Action.

PHOTO C1-34.

PHOTO C1-35.

I rebarreled a good 1963 BRNO ZKW465 rifle in September 1969, and made my first .17 Ackley Hornet. Its first outing was on rabbits and foxes at Ron Pridham's place in the south east of S.A. It was a bit of a surprise. I knew the .17 Magnum was good, but I didn't expect the Hornet to be so close to it. Crows are never safe around me and PHOTO C1-34 (Page 46) shows one that sat for a tad too long to stay healthy. Lyn has taken a fox with it in PHOTO C1-35.

PHOTO C1-36.

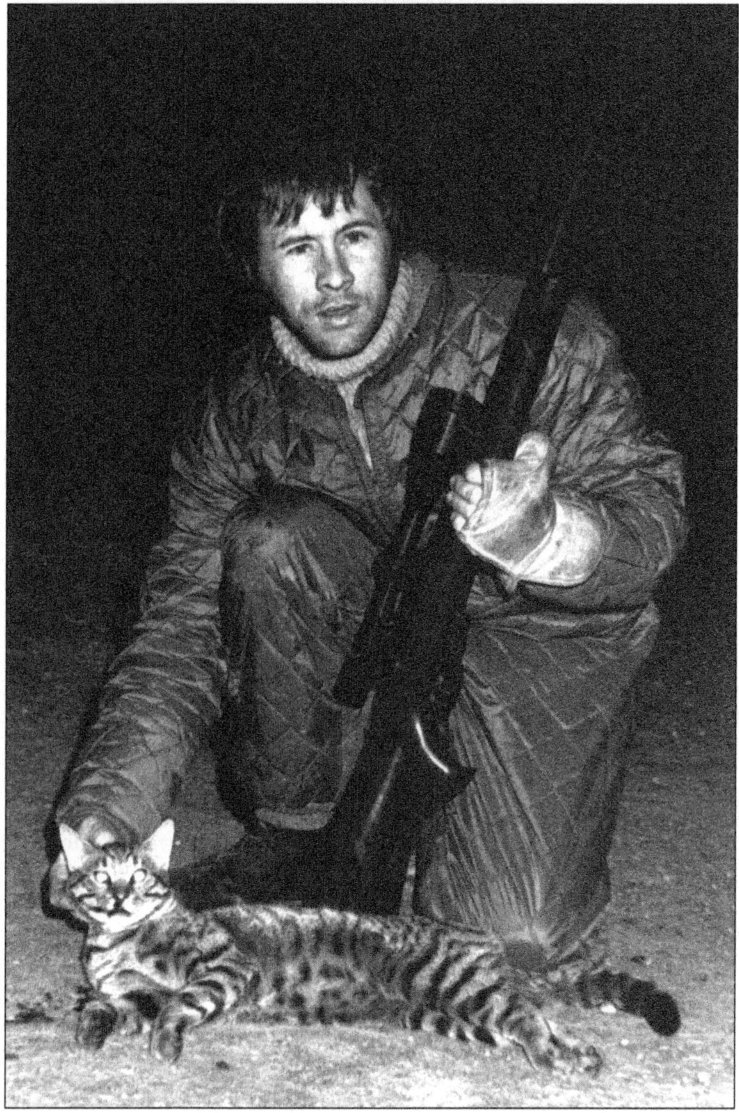

PHOTO C1-37.

I restocked the .17 Hornet in mid 1970 with a thumb hole design in Claro Walnut. It seemed to be very comfortable to use, but was very heavy. Later I would work out that a thumb holes comfort is a deception. A good classic design is much better.

PHOTO C1-36 shows the newly stocked rifle with my arch enemy, and PHOTO C1-37 shows it with a feral cat. Cats were a real problem on Purple Downs as it was close to the Woomera township, and a lot of cats were dumped in the bush when expatriate Americans returned home. Greenie's rule #1 was, 'shoot the cat before you shoot the fox!' Any cat in front of this rifle was in mortal danger.

This .17 Ackley Hornet rifle was absolutely deadly out to 250 yards. It shot the 25 grain projectile out at 3650FPS, and in my testing matched a 22-250 Remington for trajectory to just past 200 yards. Recoil was nearly non existent, so much so that you could easily see the bullets impact in the scope. It was a formidable combination, and was one of my favorite rifles.

PHOTO C1-38.

While all of that .17 calibre stuff was going on, I was still very active with .22 calibre rifles. In 1967 I moved from .222 Remington to .22–250 Remington, and then onto the improved versions of that case. I favored the 28° version over the 40° because it fire formed with accuracy, velocity and no hassles. Essentially, it was a .220 Swift with a much better case shape. In PHOTO C1-38 I rolled the 4 pigs, all with head shots, at 240 yards in the same group. I did this often with up to 6 pigs, the trick being to shoot the closest pig to you, and work backwards, so the others didn't hear the sonic crack because the projectile did not pass a living pig. I was far enough away that the sound of the rifle never bothered them.

In PHOTO C1-39 you can see the tools I used for my weekend forays after crows. This PHOTO is circa 1968, and the Mini Cooper S is only a couple of months old. The rifle is a Remington Model 700 Varmint Special in .22–250 Remington Improved 28°. The scope is a Lyman Super Targetspot with a 16X eyepiece fitted.

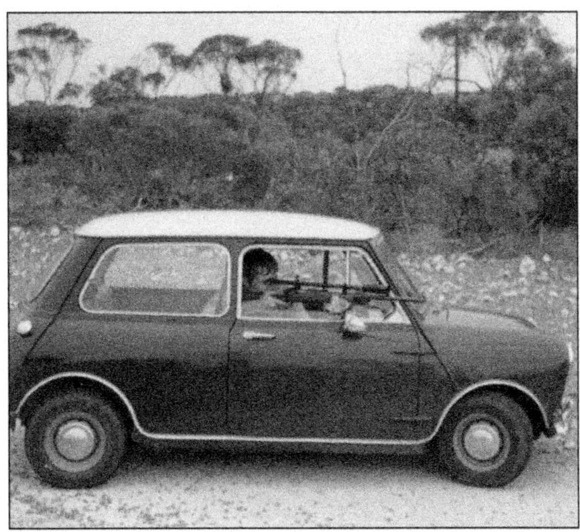

PHOTO C1-39.

CHAPTER TWO

BARREL SETUP

Of the many procedures we undertake to fit a blank to an action, barrel setup is arguably the most important. Initial setup will determine the final accuracy of the overall job. It is the foundation upon which all other steps are taken. Simply put, it is highly unlikely you will make an accurate finished job if you have started with an inaccurate initial setup.

There are several ways to set a barrel blank up in a lathe with the aim to fit and chamber it to an action. I am confident that all of the methods I will detail here are in use as I write this. I am not describing these methods because I endorse them, but rather to supply you with information that I hope will make you think about what you are trying to achieve with the job, and conclude whether you think it is the best way to achieve your goals. Be assured that match winning rifles have been produced using all of these setup methods. The question one needs to ask is, "How often could I reasonably expect this method to produce an accurate result, given my knowledge of the theory behind its execution?" The answer to that I will leave up to you. In the next chapter I will describe and show what I do, and detail the reasons I do what I do. You make up your own mind.

SETUP METHOD 1

Setup method 1 is probably the simplest way to set up a barrel for fitting to an action. It is the method I was shown when I started to fit barrels in the 1960s, and is still in use by many gunsmiths today. This is how to do it.

1. Install a centre in the tail stock of the lathe, and a 3 or 4 jaw chuck on the headstock. A 3 Jaw chuck would be mostly used.

2. Hold about 1" of the muzzle of the blank in the 3 or 4 jaw chuck, and bring the tailstock centre into the centre at the breech end of the barrel blank. Install a steady rest on the parallel section at the end of the blank.

3. If you are using a 3 jaw chuck the barrel is already set up. If you are using a 4 jaw chuck you will need to indicate the outside of the barrel, close to the chuck, so that it runs true.

That is probably the simplest method we could use to set a barrel up in a lathe for fitting to an action. As I said, it is the way I was shown when I wanted to fit my own barrels in the 1960s, but is not a method that I ever used. I know that it is in use even today, despite it being fundamentally flawed. Photo 2-1 is evidence of that.

PHOTO 2-1.
By the factory stamping, at the rear of this fitted barrel, one can assume that the original centre was used when it was set up for chambering. This barrel was fitted within the last five years (I don't know by whom).

Why is it flawed? Well...

1. The section of muzzle that is held in the chuck has no relationship with the bore of the blank. It can be .010" or more eccentric.

2. The centres in both ends of the blank have been subjected to a great deal of sideways pressure during the profiling phase of manufacture, and are (in manufacturing terminology) freshed out. In other words, any accurate relationship they might originally have had with the bore of the blank has been lost.

So, any chance of making an accurate setup is compromised before we start. If you must fit a barrel using the 'Between Centres' setup method this is the proper way to do it.

It follows that we need to make new accurate centres and we do that like this:–

1. Install a 3 jaw steady rest on the bed of the lathe. Secure the muzzle end of the barrel blank in the 3 jaw chuck, and insert a live centre into the existing centre at the other end.

2. With the lathe running at slow speed, bring the steady rest jaws into contact on the outside diameter of the barrel tenon. Secure them, slide the tailstock out of the way, and face back the end of the blank to remove the old centre.

2.1. Make sure you remove the old centre completely; we do not want the new centre, we will be making, to begin following a vestige of the old centre we left behind.

2.2. Before you stop the machine, break the sharp outside edge with a file, and break the sharp inside edge with a 320 grit round stone ground to a 60° angle. Dip the end in lubricating oil first.

2.2.1. Dress the stone by holding it in the chuck of an electric drill, and with the drill rotating, hold the stone against the rotating wheel of a bench grinder.

2.3. With a 10x jewelers loupe, check that you have broken the edge enough. Just remove the burrs so that there is a smooth exit from the bore.

2.4. Reverse the blank in the lathe, and repeat the process, to remove the old centre from the muzzle end. Remove the steady rest and barrel.

3. Install a centre in the tail stock, and one in the head stock, or in the lathe chuck.

3.1. The tailstock centre can be either live or dead; your choice. A live centre is quite accurate enough, and far more convenient.

3.2. To install a centre in the headstock requires removal of the chuck, so I prefer to make a centre that is held in the chuck. This is simply a length of ¾" diameter mild steel that has already been taper turned to a 60° angle (for previous jobs). In use I set it up true in the 4 jaw chuck, set the compound rest to 60° and skim the surface to make a very accurate centre in only a few minutes.

4. Place a driving dog on the muzzle end of the blank and install the blank between the centres. Now you can position the driving dog properly, so that it engages one of the chuck jaws with a little clearance to the chuck face. Photo 2-2 (Page 62) shows the dog installed on a blank. Note there is a bit of rubber tubing on the drive spigot which acts as a shock absorber. The dog only needs to be tightened snug, so don't over do it.

PHOTO 2-2.

This centre has been trued in the 4 jaw chuck, and then taper turned, with the compound rest set at a 60° angle, to make a very accurate centre. Doing this also allows me to dodge removing the heavy 4 jaw chuck from the machine. It actually takes less time to make the centre like this than it does to remove and replace the chuck.

5. Remove the blank from the centres with the dog installed, remove the tailstock centre and replace it with a 3 jaw drill chuck.

6. Place an appropriate centre reamer in the 3 jaw tailstock chuck with a correctly sized pilot installed.

6.1. These reamers are piloted, and are available from reamer manufactures in .17, #1, #2, and #3 sizes to cover the spectrum of calibers we normally use. They accept the same pilots we use on our chambering reamers, with the exception of .17 caliber which has a solid pilot. Photo 2-3 shows what they look like.

6.2. Run a patch or two through the barrel, to clean it, and select a reamer pilot that is a close fit in the bore of the barrel. Close means no smaller than .0002" under bore size. To do this you need a selection of pilots in .0001" increments. Find the right size by simple trial and error. Go up in size until you find the one that doesn't fit, then use the next size down.

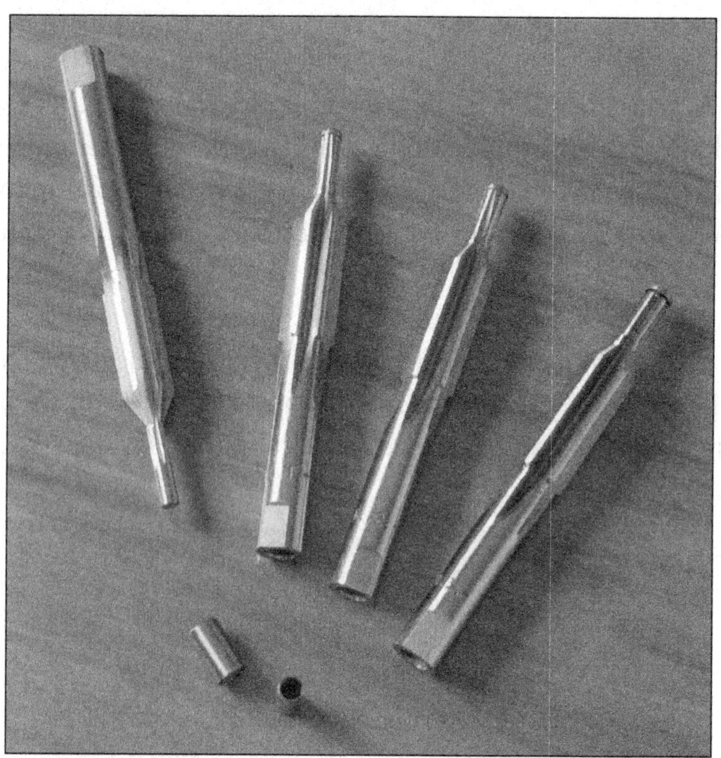

PHOTO 2-3.
Centre reamers, from the left: .17CAL, #1, #2, #3 and pilots.

6.3. If you are stuck for a particular size of pilot, don't be afraid to make your own. It doesn't need to be hardened to do a perfectly adequate job on half a dozen jobs, or maybe more. I prefer to make them from oil hardening drill rod, and the only caveat is they must be made in the one setup. Drill and bore the hole to size, to accept the reamer nose, and then turn the O.D. to size without removing the part from the chuck, and part it off to length. Chamfer the ends to finish. Any lathe operator worth his salt should be able to turn stock to exact dimensions +/- 0. If you can't do that, better practice until you can. The pilot will always be running in good quality oil so wear will be negligible.

7. Now you need to be a little bit nimble. Have your reamer oil close at hand and set your lathe speed to slow, 30RPM is fine. Put a little bit of reamer oil in the bore of the blank, place the muzzle end of the blank onto the headstock centre, and bring the tail-stock forward. At the same time hold the blank back against the head-stock centre.

7.1. Watch out here. The blank (especially target profiles that are heavy) will want to slide off the taper of the headstock centre. If you let it get away from you, when the reamer pilot has entered the bore, there is a good chance it will break the pilot off the reamer. Be sure to keep good backward pressure on the barrel at all times.

8. Apply some reamer oil to the cutting edges of the reamer, and while holding back on the blank turn the lathe on. As the blank turns, let your hand slip a bit, but maintain backward pressure on the blank and keep it solidly against the headstock centre.

9. With the lathe running bring the reamer into the bore with the tailstock hand wheel. Continue to advance the reamer, until you have made a good centre in the end of the blank, while continuing to hold back against the headstock centre. Let the lathe run on after the cut has finished at least one and a half revolutions.

9.1. This won't take long. Probably only 3 or 4 revolutions of the barrel, and you will have advanced the tailstock maybe .050" to .075", after the reamer begins to cut, to make the centre. Photo 2-4 shows me making a centre.

9.2. If you are not sure about this, place a dogged barrel blank between centres in the lathe, set the machine running and put your hand in place with a bit of backward pressure to get the feel of it. You will see there is nothing to be worried about.

PHOTO 2-4.

Cutting a centre in the end of a barrel blank.

9.3. Photo 2-5 shows a perfectly adequate centre. You don't need to go very deep. A width of .050" on the flat surface is quite adequate.

PHOTO 2-5.
An adequate centre.

10. Switch off the lathe and back out the tailstock. Reverse the blank and fit the dog to the breech end. Clean the centre you have made, and repeat the procedure to cut a centre at the muzzle end of the barrel.

The whole procedure takes a lot longer to describe than it does to execute. In practice the job will be done in a few minutes.

11. Remove the centre reamer and chuck from the tailstock, clean them up, put them away and install a live centre. The driving dog is already in the correct place on the breech end of the blank so leave it there. Run a patch through the barrel and be sure the centres you have created are clean. Blow them out with compressed air to be sure.

12. Place the blank between centres in the lathe and turn a parallel section at the muzzle end of the blank about 1" long. Turn only enough off the diameter to make the 1" parallel section. Don't overdo it. Remove the blank from the lathe.

13. Remove your centre from the headstock. If you were using a 3 jaw chuck replace it with a 4 jaw version. Remove the dog from the breech end of the barrel.

14. Place the barrel back in the lathe, but this time hold the trued muzzle end in the 4 jaw chuck, and the breech end in the live centre in the tailstock. Have enough of the parallel turned section, on the muzzle end, protruding so that you can get a .0001" dial indicator onto it.

15. Indicate the run out on that turned section, and adjust until it runs true to +/- 0.

That's it. The barrel blank is set up ready to go to work. In practice the breech end will be turned parallel for its full length, a tenon created which will then be threaded. Then a steady rest will be installed onto the parallel section of the breech so that the necessary operations can be completed at that end. Then the blank is reversed and set up for crowning in the same way.

This setup is useful if you are using a lathe that will not accept the barrel blank through the hollow mandrel of the headstock. Maybe the hollow mandrel is too small in diameter, or maybe the blank is too short to fit right through. However, the accuracy of this setup is highly questionable for reasons I will discuss later.

SETUP METHOD 2

Setup method 2 requires that you be able to fit the barrel blank comfortably through the hollow mandrel in the headstock of the lathe. You must have enough barrel protruding from the 4 jaw chuck to machine the necessary threads etc, and at least ¼" protruding from the 4 jaw spider you need, at the other end of the hollow mandrel, in order to support the muzzle end of the blank. Lathes don't come with a spider at the end of the hollow mandrel, so if you don't have one you must make one. Photo 2-6 shows the one I made for my Colchester lathe over 35 years ago. When you make it, maintain the internal diameter of the hollow mandrel if at all possible. They are never big enough. The 'jaws' are simply long ¼"UNF cap screws with the Allen heads cut off and screw driver slots cut in the end. Don't over tap the holes, as we want minimum clearance here. This is an indispensable bit of kit on a gunsmiths lathe, so make it permanent by shrinking it onto the mandrel. Also index it with your 4 jaw chuck so the jaws are all in line. That is both headstock and spider jaws push the same way.

1. Prepare the barrel blank by cutting off the centres, front and back, that were used in the factory to profile it, and face both ends to remove the saw marks and square them.

1.1. Barrel blanks that have been lapped are always oversize (lapped out) in the bore at each end of the blank, so in practice it is advisable to cut off at least one inch, from both ends of the barrel, to remove the tapered section. We will discuss that more in the next chapter.

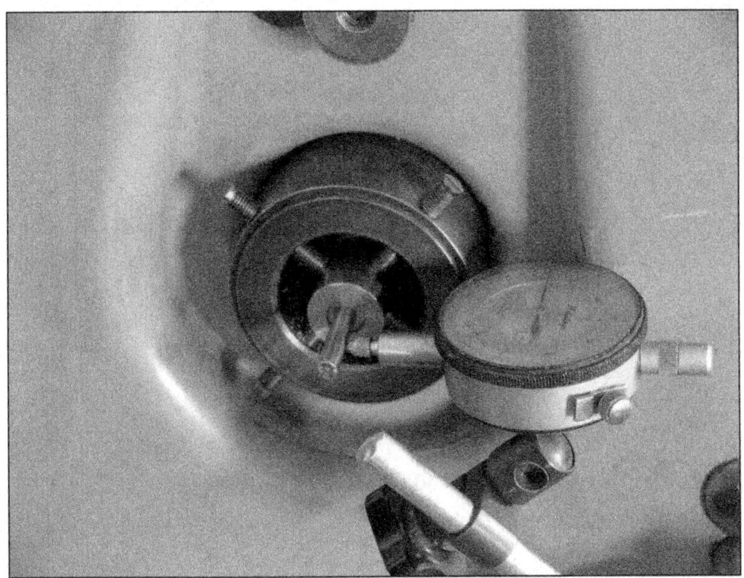

PHOTO 2-6.
The spider I have used on my Colchester lathe for over 35 years.

1.2. This time you can face the ends of the blank with it held in the 4 jaw chuck and spider — much easier.

2. As you face each end (before you stop the machine) break the sharp outside edge with a file, and break the sharp inside edge with a 320 grit round stone ground to an angle of 60°. Dip the end of the stone in cutting oil.

2.1. Dress the stone by holding it in the chuck of an electric drill, and with the drill rotating, hold the stone against the rotating wheel of a bench grinder.

2.2. With a 10x jewelers loupe, check that you have broken the edge enough. Just remove the burrs so that there is a smooth exit from the bore.

3. Remove the blank from the lathe and run a couple of patches through the bore to clean it.

4. We are going to need a couple of pin gauges now, so best we make them before we go any further. If you adopt this method of barrel fitting you will accumulate a large selection of these gauges. I used it myself for many years and I must have hundreds!

4.1. Bright mild steel is fine to make these gauges from. .17 to .22 caliber gauges can be turned from ¼" diameter stock, 6mm to 7mm from 5/16" stock, and larger calibers from 3/8" or ½" stock.

4.2. Chuck the stock in the lathe with about 2" protruding, and using a very sharp high speed steel tool turn it to the diameter you believe the bore of the blank to be. Your final cuts should be only in increments of .001" with the slowest feed on your machine. About .002" from final diameter take a couple of extra passes without advancing the cross-slide. You should have a very fine finish on the gauge which can be polished to a high mirror finish by the application of a bit of worn 320 grit polishing cloth.

4.3. The gauge will have sprung away from the turning tool, a little bit, creating a slight taper to the order of .001" over its length, which is a good thing.

4.4. Face off both ends, chamfer them with a file, make a mark at the big end, so you can easily identify it, and try it for fit in the barrel.

4.5. Ideally the gauge should go into the bore about half to three quarters of the way, and you should feel it tighten up, as it goes in, until you can't get it in any further without using a lot of force. *Don't do that*; finger pressure is all that is required. You will probably need to remove it with pliers gripped right at the end. Be gentle; a bit of backward pressure, rotating it back and forth slightly, will do the trick. Keep them oiled or they will rust, unless you can find a source of stainless steel drill rod to make them from.

4.6. Bores are not parallel. When they are lapped the aim is to choke them slightly towards the muzzle. If your gauge fits the breech end of the blank properly it will probably (almost certainly) be too large in diameter to fit in at the muzzle. You need two gauges. Take the time to make gauges sized correctly as their proper fit is important.

5. Replace the barrel blank in the lathe, breech end held in the 4 jaw chuck, and muzzle end held in the spider at the end of the hollow mandrel.

5.1. The breech end will need to protrude enough so that you can carry out the necessary machine work required to screw and chamber it for the receiver. These dimensions are worked out from the action and I will discuss them in detail in the next chapter.

5.2. We don't want the blank to be held very tightly at this stage. The chuck jaws and the spider should be just touching, not loose, but not tight.

6. Install your pin gauges in the breech and muzzle ends of the blank, and set up a .0001" dial indicator close to the gauges, but not on them just yet.

6.1. It is an advantage to have two dial indicators for this job. At the chuck end a magnetic base unit works best. At the muzzle end you will probably need a permanent mount. Photo 2-7 shows the setup I have had on my Colchester machine for over 35 years.

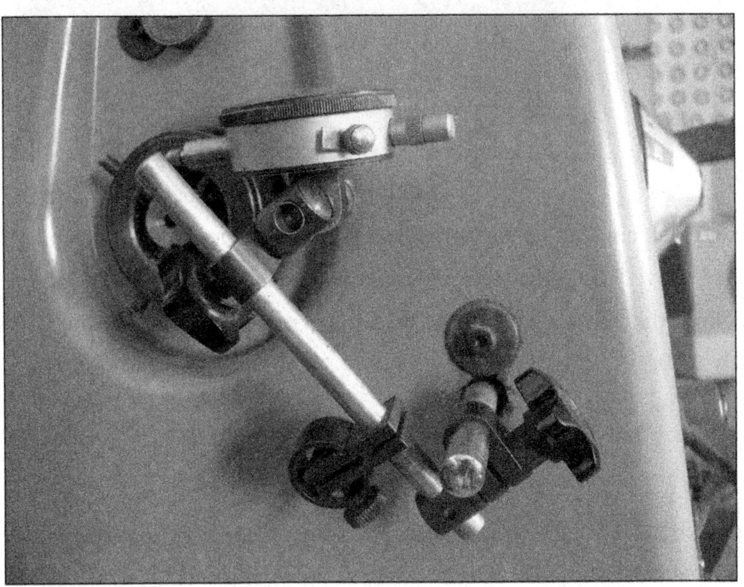

PHOTO 2-7.

This dial indicator mount is a permanent fixture on the lathe.

7. With the lathe out of gear (so you can easily rotate the spindle) adjust the chuck and spider jaws until the dial indicator probes can be engaged, without exceeding the dial indicators maximum travel. Then engage them, and adjust until the dial indicators indicate +/- 0 run out at each end.

7.1. Dial indicators that indicate .0001" with an overall travel of ½" are very good for this job.

7.2. Keep holding the blank softly in the jaws until you are indicating on the pins to within about .005" concentric, then start applying a bit of pressure as you bring the readings to +/- 0.

7.3. The tightness you end up with, when the pins indicate +/- 0 front and back, is very subjective. Experience is a great teacher, especially if you have a barrel rotate in the chuck while you are threading it. That's definitely a wake up call, and a hard lesson. Probably 'firm' is the best word to describe the tension you should aim for. Not extra tight.

8. Remove the indicators and pin gauges, and your barrel blank is set up ready to work on.

This setup method 2 is probably the method in most use today. Indeed, with many of the barrels I fitted in my early career, I used this setup method. However, like setup 1, its accuracy is highly questionable. As setup methods go, I think it is better than 1, but still flawed. Again, I will discuss this later.

PHOTO 2-8.

This barrel is being set up for threading and chambering using setup method 2 described above. I used that setup method for many years, myself, believing that I was making the best job possible at the time. *I was wrong!* This photo dates from the early 1970s.

SETUP METHOD 3

Setup method 3 is very similar to setup method 2, except it goes one step further in order to try and achieve a higher degree of accuracy. In order to use it we will need an additional tool in the form of a dial indicator with a very long probe. Photo 2-9 shows the one I use. It is a Swiss made Interapid .0005" model 312B-15 tool, with a probe 2¾" long, and is perfectly adequate for the job.

PHOTO 2-9.

An Interapid long probe dial indicator. Note the texta marks indicating chamber length from the last job I used it on.

Method 3 goes like this:–

1. Set up the barrel blank in the 4 jaw chuck and spider, exactly as you did using setup method 2, except that when you arrive at the point where the two indicators read +/- 0, do not have the chuck or the spider at final tightened tension. The blank should be only lightly held.

2. Remove your pin gauge from the rear of the barrel. Leave the gauge in the muzzle end.

3. Now, we need to find out where the throat of the chamber will be when the job is finished, and mark the probe of the indicator at the appropriate place.

3.1. This is simply determined by using a cartridge case. Lay the cartridge case along the side of the probe of the dial indicator, with the probe ball just past the shell neck. Mark the back of the indicators probe with a texta, at the appropriate place, where the end of the barrel will be.

3.2. Don't forget that on some actions the case will protrude around .120" from the back of the barrel, while with others (e.g. Remington 700) it will be nearly flush with the end of the barrel. Take this into account.

4. Mount the dial indicator on the saddle of your lathe and run it up into the bore of the blank until the Texta mark on the probe is level with the back of the barrel. Photo 2-10 refers.

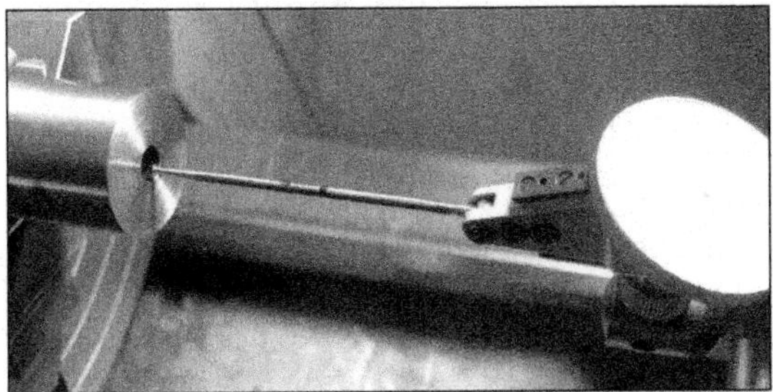

PHOTO 2-10.

A long probe Interapid dial indicator in position to enter the bore and align it as per setup 3. Note the texta marks indicating where to place the probe.

4.1. It takes a bit of fiddling to get the probe in the bore properly. You need a little bit of down angle in order to get the ball to engage the surface of the bore, but not enough that the probe is bumped at the rear by the rifling. Too little angle and you will engage the shaft behind the ball instead of on the ball. Get it right and get it straight.

5. Now it is simply a matter of making final corrections to bring both dial indicators into a reading of +/- 0 while arriving at the correct 'firm' tension on the barrel as before.

5.1. The ball on the end of the dial indicator will be bumping over the rifling in the barrel, and the indicator needle will be swinging back and forth on the dial. The idea is to read the eccentricity at the bottom of the grooves in the rifling, as that is where the projectile will ride, on its way through.

5.2. The easiest barrels to set up like this are those with 4 rifling lands and 4 grooves, especially if the grooves line up with the adjusters on your 4 jaw chuck. Six groove barrels can be a bit of a trial, and a barrel with more than 6 grooves may not let the dial indicator probe ball right into the groove of the rifling. Check to make sure, and if not, your only option is to indicate on the top of the lands.

6. Once you have achieved +/- 0 run-out on both indicators, along with the correct tension on the chuck jaws, setup is complete and the barrel is ready to receive its further machining. Some may also indicate inside the bore at the muzzle instead of on a pin gauge; your choice. I doubt the setup will suffer which ever way you do it.

I would hazard a guess that most of the barrels for bench-rest competition are fitted using this method 3. However, like the two previous methods it is still fundamentally flawed. Of the three it is probably the best one to use, if you were insisting on using one of these methods.

As stated previously all of the three setup methods described have been used to make match winning rifles, but it does not follow that the three setup methods described always make match winning rifles, and therein lies a problem.

We need to stop here, put on our thinking caps for a while and ask some very pertinent questions. The question I most often ask myself is, "What am I trying achieve here?" This is usually followed by another question, "Is what I am doing going to produce the result I am trying to achieve?" Believe me — you need to think about and understand, at the most basic level, every single thing you are doing. Monkey see, Monkey do produces only mediocre results. I am hoping here to encourage you to think carefully about everything you do, and if that comes about I will consider I have achieved something.

So, what are we trying to achieve when we fit a barrel to an action? Think about it and write it down, and we will see if your answer is the same as mine. Go on, do it! Don't turn the page until you have written it down. Think about it carefully before committing yourself.

I hope you have followed through with that exercise. If you did that, it makes me very happy because, as stated previously, my goal is to get people thinking about what they are doing.

My answer to the question is this:-

> *'My aim, when I fit a barrel to an action, is to do the job without detracting, not even .0001% from the inherent accuracy that the barrel blank is capable of.'*

The barrel blanks 'inherent accuracy' is not a tangible thing we can measure, but rather imaginary. What accuracy would that barrel blank be capable of if we could fire a group in a vacuum with no external forces acting on it? No action fitted, no chamber, no stock, nothing but the barrel suspended magically in mid nothing spitting perfect bullets out into a group. What would its potential be? No one will ever know, but whatever it might be, when I install it on an action I do not want to have done any harm to that potential at all. Nil, zero, nada, zip.

At this point we need to know a little about barrel blanks. It is important to understand that barrel blanks are not straight. They are pretty straight, fairly straight, and almost straight; whatever terminology you might want to use, but they are not straight, straight. Nor are they curved in any sort of even manner.

The bar the barrel is made from is rotated at high speed, and a single point drill is run through it, with chips being flushed out by oil at very high pressure, to initially make a hole through it. The drill stays pretty much in the middle of the bar when passing through, but during that passage it wanders around randomly, probably depending on purity and hardness variations found in the metal it is passing through.

The result is a randomly wandering hole through the bar, with no rhyme or reason for where it will be actually located at any point along the bars length. Subsequent reaming, rifling and lapping operations do little, if anything, to correct where the drill originally wandered. It is simply a fact that it occurs and we need to deal with it.

This is important knowledge. You need to understand it, think about it, and having done that answer me this before we go any further. I said that the accuracy of the setups 1, 2, and 3, described previously, was highly questionable and fundamentally flawed. Why do you think I am of that opinion? Think about it and write down your answer.

When we fit and chamber a barrel to an action our overall aim is to produce a rifle that is colloquially called a "Hummer." A Hummer is not only a very accurate rifle, but also one that maintains its accuracy over a wide range of conditions and powder loads. It also shoots through windy conditions that would normally cause considerable windage movement. Owning a rifle like this is a real treat, and owning one is the Holy Grail of all short range bench-rest shooters.

Conventional wisdom says that producing a hummer is solely dependent on the quality of the barrel blank you begin with. In other words, if you don't start with a hummer blank you can't make a hummer rifle. Personally, I don't entirely agree. Certainly, the quality of the barrel blank is of major importance. However, given the quality of barrels available from the better manufacturers on offer today, I think that how the barrel is fitted has more of a bearing on how well the finished product will perform, than most people think. Certainly, a potential hummer can be turned into an also ran by less than adequate fitting. I don't think anyone would disagree with that.

So what is the theory behind what we are talking about here? Simply put it has to do with alignment. Our ultimate aim is to have the projectile exit the muzzle of the barrel spinning perfectly around its centre-line, without even the tiniest amount of yaw. We want it to be gyroscopically dead, like a spinning top that has gone to sleep. Additionally, we would like every projectile to exit the barrel at the same point in the barrels oscillations, preferably when it is at the limit of its upward or downward movement. Projectiles launched like this will present a smaller profile to the wind, both side wind, and to the air they are pushing through. They will be deviated less by external forces, compared to projectiles that exit the bore yawing even the tiniest amount.

Given all of the above, what is the answer to the question I posed above? There are several reasons, not all of which apply to every method, but one that applies to them all is — *they all rely for their accuracy on the barrel blank being straight*, and if there is one thing barrel blanks are, it's *not* straight. Methods one and two are set up at each end of the blank with no regard, whatsoever, to what is happening further inside the bore. Method 3, at least, indicates the bore at the throat, but fails to take into account in what direction that section of bore is heading. If a projectile is started gyroscopically straight in the bore of a barrel set up using any of these methods, it would be pure coincidence. There are other problems.

Method 1 relies on a high degree of accuracy in the lathe, from the headstock to some 3 feet down the bed; accuracy that is pretty well guaranteed not to be there. If this method is all that is available to you then you are in a bind for, be assured, the sort of precision needed to give you a good chance to produce a hummer is not available here, except by happenstance.

Methods 2 and 3 have another major problem. To help you understand it we will do a little experiment. Take one of your rifles, the heavier the barrel the better, and place it in the padded jaws of a bench vice held by the barrel about half way between the forend and muzzle. Now stick a boresighter, either in the bore or on the muzzle, if it's magnetic, and without touching the rifle in any way, note where the cross-wire, or dot, of the Telescopic Sight is on the grid of the boresighter. Now, apply a bit of sideways pressure to the butt of the rifle and note what happens to the cross-wire. *It moved across the grid of the bore sighter didn't it?* Go on, move it around. Left, right, up, down. Every time you put a bit of pressure on the butt in any direction the reticule moves on the boresighter grid. My F class rifle has a Heavy Varmint Krieger barrel fitted, 27" long. With a Leupold boresighter stuck on the muzzle, it takes very little pressure on the butt, in any direction, to move the reticule half of a square on the grid from its resting position. You know what is happening here, don't you? *You are bending the barrel.* I am doing that in Photo 2-11. The relationship between the telescopic sight, action, barrel and bore sighter is fixed and permanent. The only way to change that relationship is to either move the telescopic sight adjustments, or deflect (bend) something out of alignment. In this case it is the barrel that is being deflected (bent).

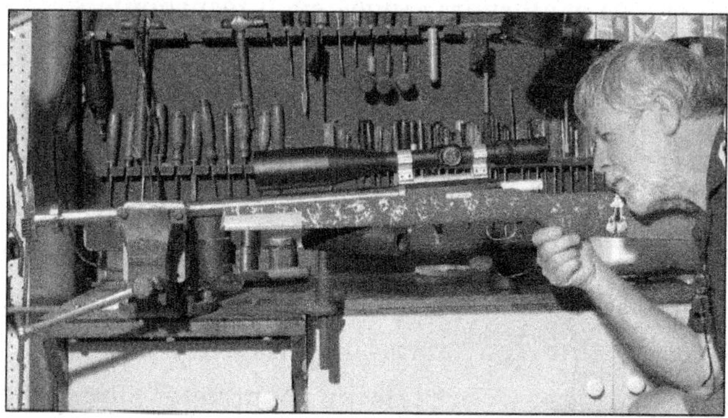

Photo 2-11.

I have a Leupold bore sighter stuck on the end of the barrel. When applying very little pressure to the stock in any direction I can see the telescopic sight reticule move around on the grid of the bore sighter. Hmmm... I wonder why that is?

Now consider this. Your lathe is designed (among other things) to turn a piece of steel, protruding from the chuck up to 12", to precision dimensions and parallelism. If there were any play in the bearings this would be impossible to do. The headstock bearings are pre-loaded to allow this.

Get the picture? When you tighten the chuck jaws on the parallel section of barrel at the breech end, that's the end of the setup process. *All of the adjustment you make at the muzzle end with the spider is futile. All you are doing is bending the barrel, with no effect whatever on the overall line up of the bore.* That lineup is solely determined by how straight the bore is to the outside of the parallel section, at the breech end of the blank you have clamped, and it will nearly never be straight.

When I worked all of that out for myself it was a bit of a shock. For many years I used method 2 and later method 3, thinking I was doing the best I could, and produced some fine shooting rifles. You may well ask, "How can that be. If the setups are flawed how can they produce accurate rifles?" Well, the answer to that lies in odds. How good the odds are, for instance, of producing a hummer rifle using these methods can pretty well be gauged by the experience of experts in the short range bench-rest game. Those competitors who are at the top of their game, and who have been competing for 15 or more years.

The general consensus seems to be that these experts only obtain one, and on rare occasions, two hummer barrels in their shooting career. Considering that many, if not most of these top shooters, choose their match barrels from between 10 to 20 (or more) blanks each year, it follows that the odds of getting a hummer rifle are very slim indeed.

So occasionally, despite the setup method being flawed, one out of spec cancels out another out of spec, and so on, and lo and behold, by pure happenstance, the setup is perfect and a hummer is born. By the law of averages there will also be a number of almost perfect setups, and even more pretty good setups, so results will vary. We won't mention the really bad setups. The blame for them will probably be put on the barrel for their inaccuracy, rather than the setup.

The question is, what are we going to do with this information? Are we going to use it, or go on blithely doing what we have always done? I don't know about you, but I want every job I do to be a hummer, and while that may not be achievable (except in theory), I don't want anything I am doing to prevent that from happening.

Armed with that information, I gave it a lot of thought, experimented, and worked on it until I arrived at a solution that I believe is the best way to do the job. The method I use is current as I write this, and I haven't been able to think of any way to improve it. Not that I am not working on it.

Now, put on your thinking cap and see if you can come up with a solution. Don't worry about the mechanics, they will come later. I am talking about the theory. What do we need to do to correct the deficiencies in the setups I have described above? I'll give you the answer and describe the mechanics of how and why I do what I do in the next chapter.

I know I'm a pain in the ass with this thinking thing, but it is so important that you know and understand what it is you need to do. The mechanics of the solution follow, after you have the theory, as a natural step. As I said before, Monkey see Monkey do won't cut it. It will only produce Monkey results.

AN M'98 MAUSER IN .270 WINCHESTER

BUILT AROUND 1979

PHOTO C2-1.

The stick was a piece of New Zealand English walnut of standard grade. Do they grow anything else? The forend tip was South American Imburi.

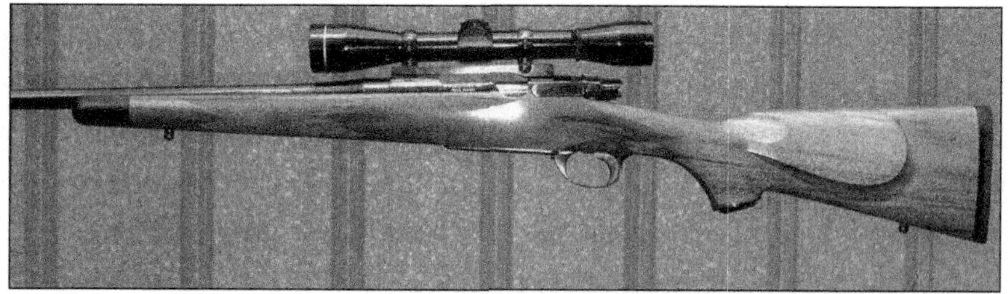

PHOTO C2-2.

This stock may have been the first example from my pantograph.

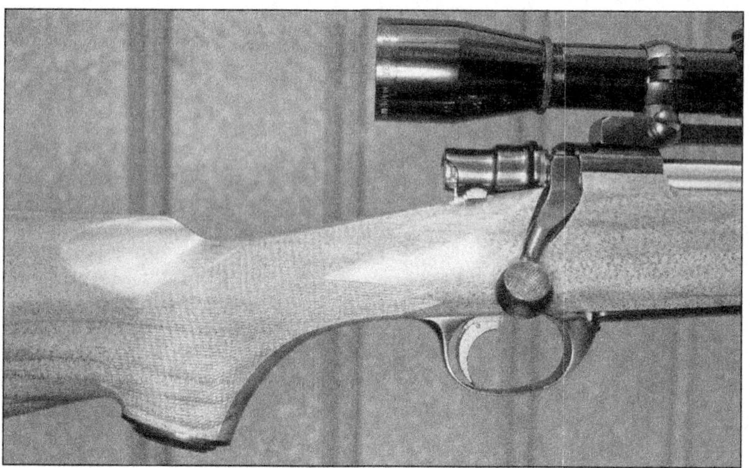

PHOTO C2-3.

I made the trigger guard assembly in shop. Of note are the Len Brownell bolt handle, the FN bolt shroud, and the Redfield bridge mount. This is probably the last time I would use parts like these. Becoming more sophisticated I guess!

The trigger was a Canjar MS2/2, tuned.

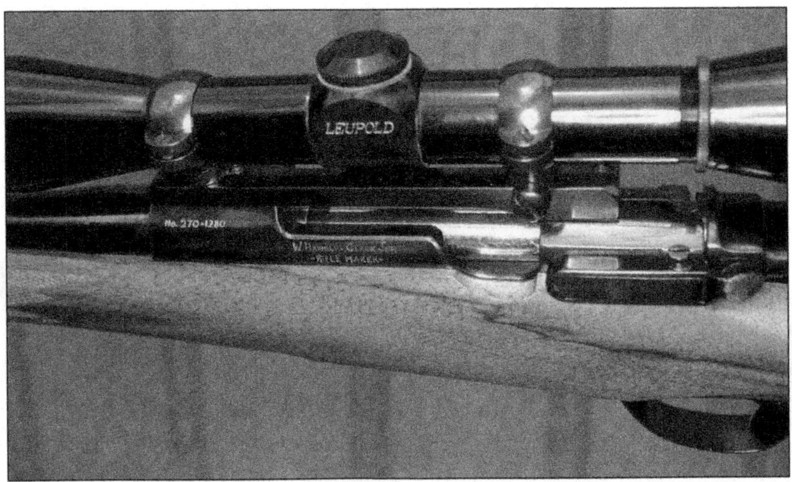

Photo C2-4.

The receiver was profile ground and the name engraving done with a Dremel Tool.

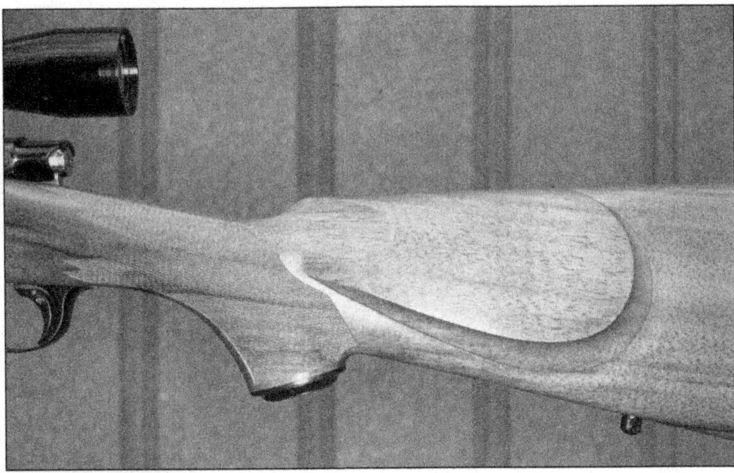

Photo C2-5.

Left side butt profile. I am using a shadow line around the cheek piece now. The checkering pattern was a classic point pattern at 22 LPI.

Photo C2-6.

The grip cap was one of Len Brownells.

A SAKO L61R IN .270 WINCHESTER

BUILT IN THE LATE 1970S

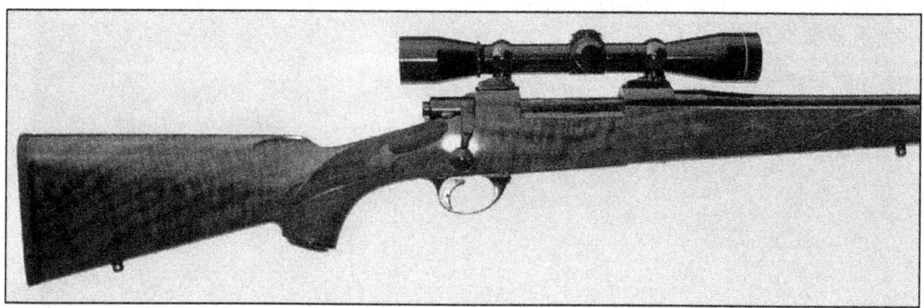

PHOTO C2-7.

The stick was a nicely figured piece of California Claro walnut.

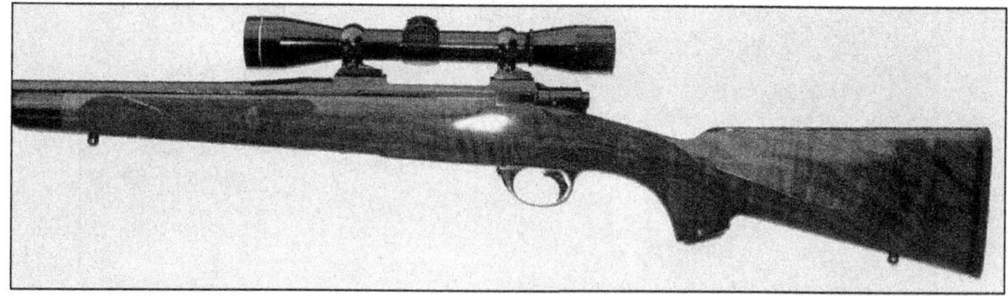

PHOTO C2-8.

The barrel was a Shilen, #3 profile Chrome Moly, 22" long. The scope rings are Conetrol Custum, on bases that I have profile milled for that extra custom touch.

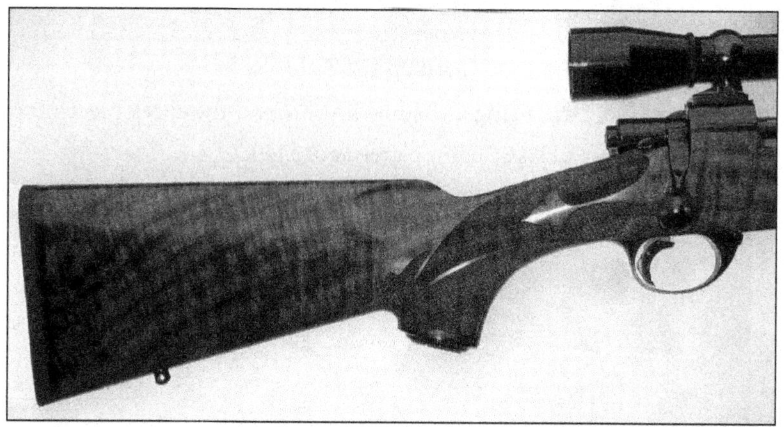

PHOTO C2-9.

California Claro Walnut was a softer stock wood than English Walnut, but it did have striking figure in the exhibition grades, and at much lower cost than English. I designed the checkering pattern, which is a one off as I don't think I ever repeated it exactly the same as this example.

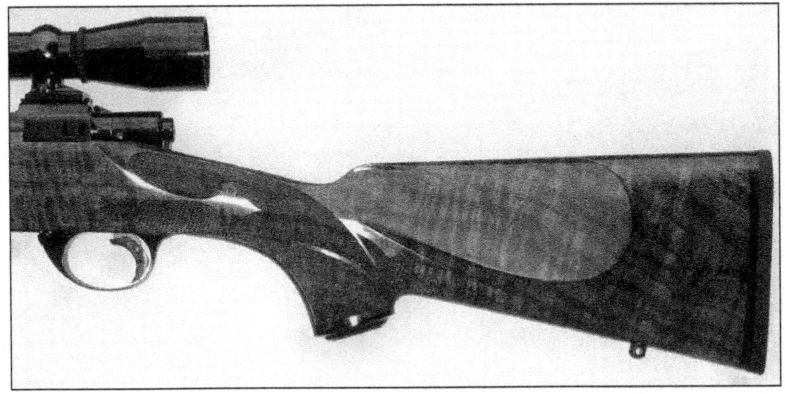

PHOTO C2-10.

The trigger is a Canjar 61–1/2 that has been tuned.
There is a shadow line around the cheek piece.

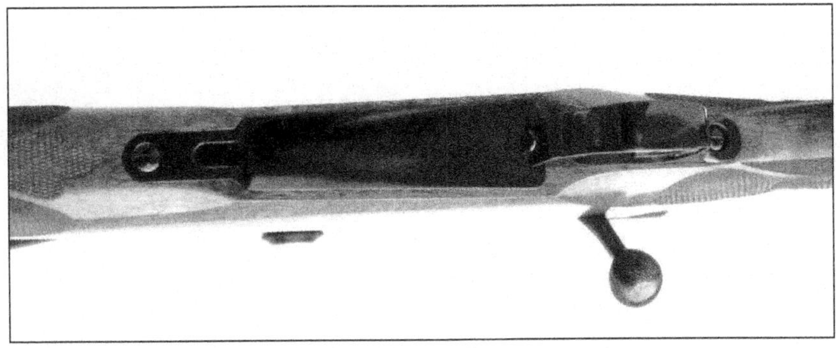

PHOTO C2-11.

The Sako floor plate was converted to a straddle design.

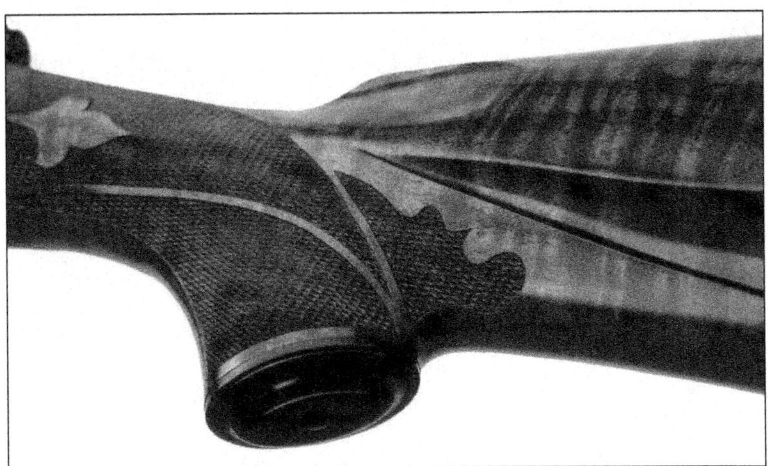

PHOTO C2-12.

Checkering was 24 lines per inch.

PHOTO C2-13.
The grip cap was from one of Len Brownell's investment castings. They were a real bear to polish ready to blue.

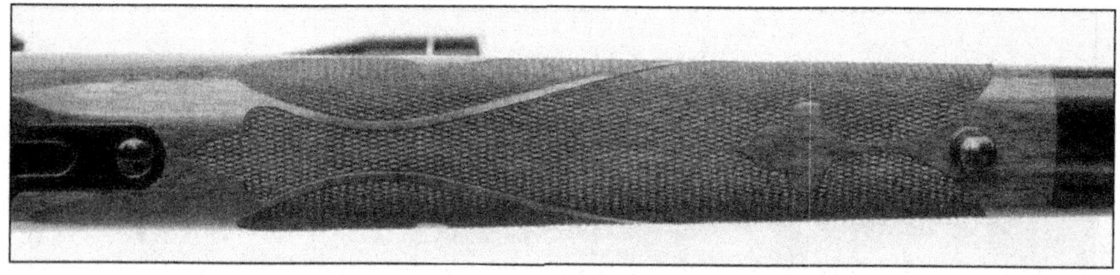

PHOTO C2-14.
The forend tip was African Ebony. Sling swivel studs were Uncle Mikes.

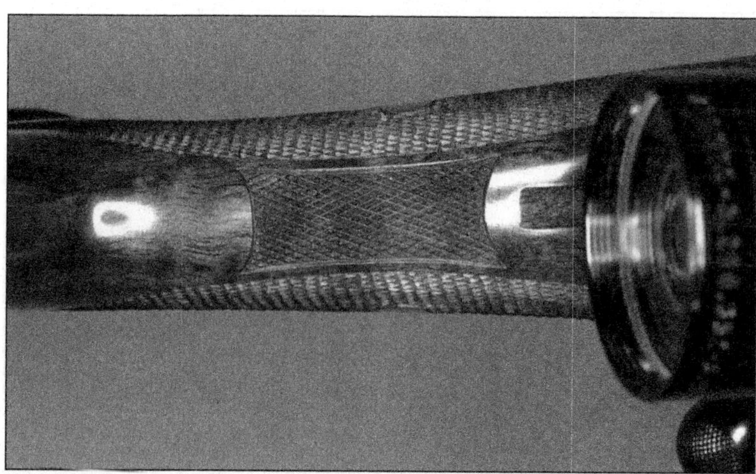

PHOTO C2-15.
The panel of checkering on the top of the grip is separate from the side grip panels. As I progressed I would modify this Fler-de-Lis checkering pattern until it ended up going right around the grip, through all of the ribbons, without a break. I am not aware of anyone else in Australia who has done that.

PHOTO C2-16.

Classic bolt handle with 3 panels of checkering. The safety catch was modified for a lower profile to the stock. The trigger guard was cut from the solid and welded to Sako's frame.

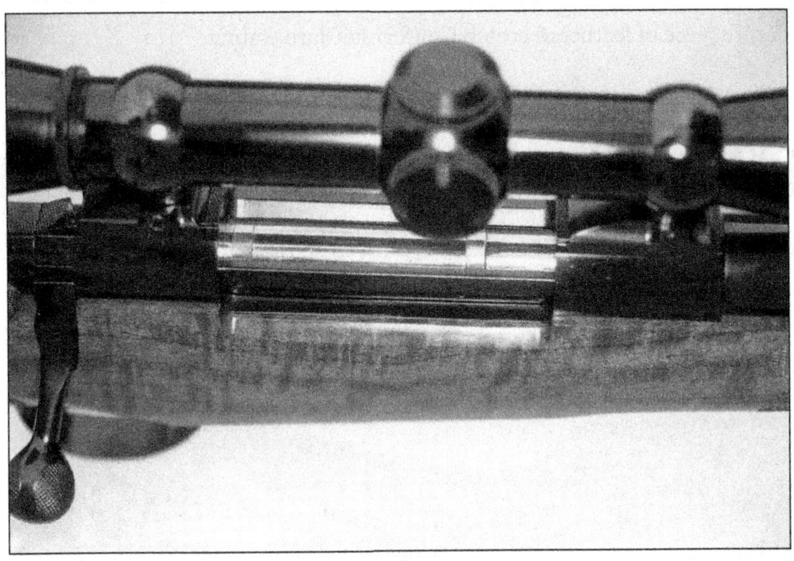

PHOTO C2-17.

The scalloped treatment of the scope mount bases was a custom touch that would stay with me, and end up a feature on all of the scope bases I made later on.

Up until 1982 I worked out of a single car shed in the backyard of my house. It was pretty hot in the summer after 11AM, so I would go and do my checkering in the bedroom, where we had a small in wall air conditioner. I'm lucky I had a tolerant wife. In the evening, when the shed cooled down, I'd continue on with metal work and stock work. This was necessary, as working on stocks and dripping sweat all over them just didn't work.

A SAKO L61R IN .25/06 REMINGTON

BUILT IN THE LATE 1980s

PHOTO C2-18.

These are the only photos I have of this rifle, and I have included them here so you can compare the shape of this 1980s rifle to that of the 1970s rifle in the previous pages. You will note that the stock is much slimmer and more streamlined. The stick was a nice piece of feathered crotch California Claro walnut.

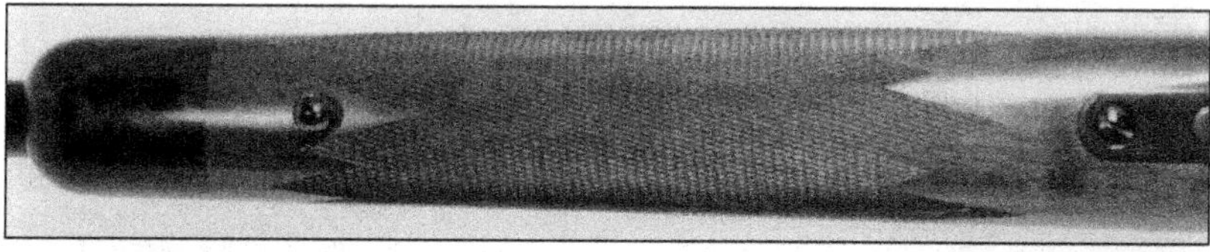

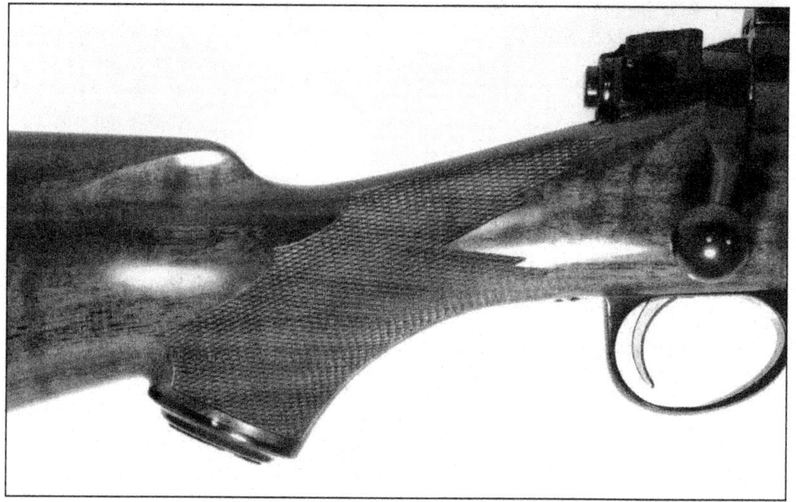

PHOTO C2-19 AND PHOTO C2-20.

Note the M'70 style side swing safety on the bolt shroud. Nearly all of the rifles I built in the 80s and 90s featured safeties like this. Checkering was 22 lines per inch.

In the mid 1970s Lyn and I culled many thousands of feral goats from a sanctuary in the Flinders Ranges. All of this work was carried out on foot in very rugged country. In the photo above I have used a H&K .223 Remington Semi Automatic. In the bottom photo I am with my favorite rifle for that job, an SIG AMT Semi Auto .308W, which was a shooting machine. It was a roller locked design that had nearly no recoil, and for a semi-auto was quite accurate, grouping just under 1MOA. I used a 6X Kahles scope on the .223, and an 8X Kahles on the 308. We used 60^{GN} projectiles in the 223. I made my own 150^{GN} Hollow Point projectiles for the 308, which were very effective in making clean kills on these soft skinned critters. At the time, we quickly found that the commercially available projectiles were too hard to expand properly in the 150+ grain weights, and 130^{GN} was too light. My projectiles were ideal.

SIGNIFICANT RIFLES AND EVENTS

PART 2: THE 1970s

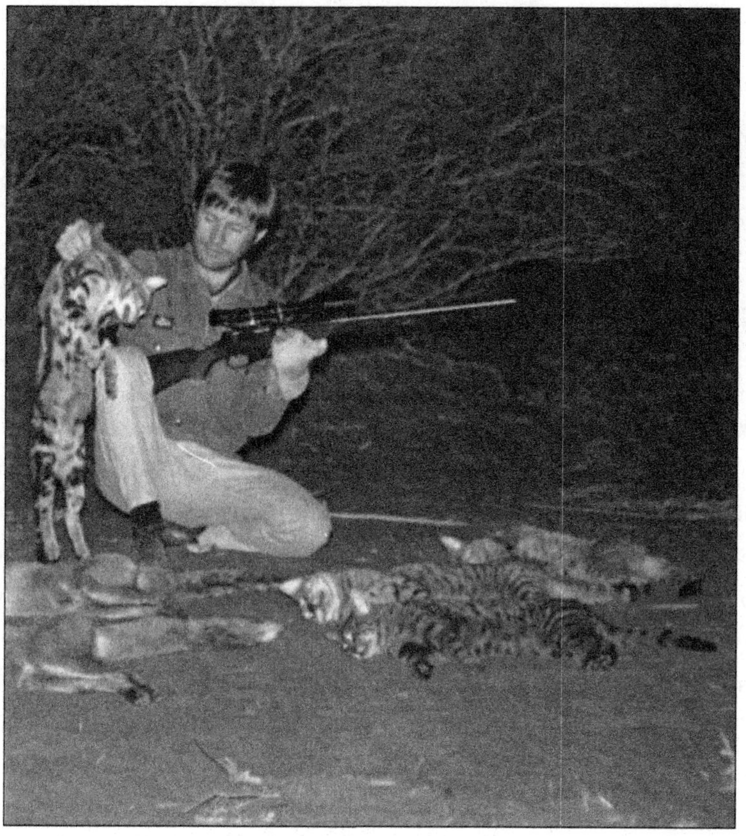

PHOTO C2-21.

As if .17 calibre was not small enough I started playing with a .14 Walker Hornet some time in early 1970. I obtained a chambered barrel, bronze brushes and 17 grain projectiles from the USA. There was no point in getting a chambering reamer for it, as I didn't expect the project would be commercially viable. I threaded the blank and fitted it to a good early ZKW465 BRNO action. Velocity with the 17^{GN} projectile was over 3750 feet per second, and the projectile was very fragile, printing comet tails on the chronograph screens. The rifle didn't begin to really work until I obtained a batch of 11 grain projectiles. The 11^{GN} projectile could be pushed as high as 4437FPS, and I used it in the field running at 4200FPS. For such a tiny projectile the .14 calibres performance was amazing. Sighted 1" high at 100 yards it printed ½" high at 150 yards, ¾" low at 200 yards, and 5¾" low at 250 yards. Though it ran out of steam after 200 yards it was amazing that the little gramophone needle like 11^{GN} projectile could produce such impressive drop figures out to 200 yards. As you can see in Photo C2-21 it was good cat and fox medicine. I could never find a bullet entry wound without peeling the skin off the critter, as it was never more than a pin prick in the skin. Cleaning the barrel was a chore though — like .17CAL times four.

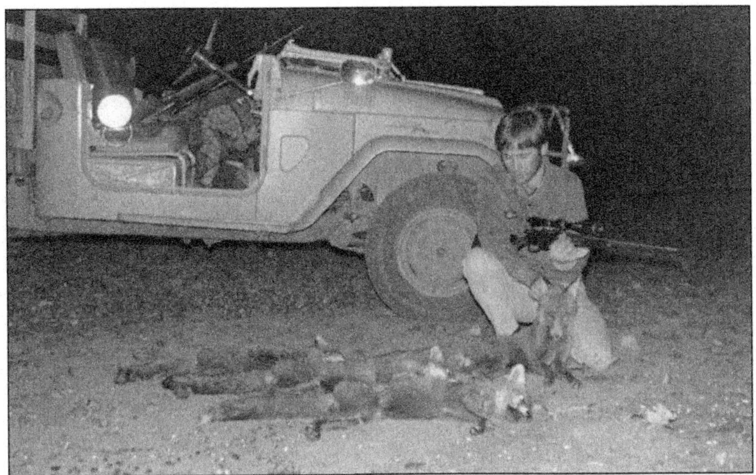

PHOTO C2-22.

Here is the .14 Walker hornet with a bunch of foxes taken in the one spot. In the Toyota can be seen a backup rifle, probably the .22–284 Winchester I was working with at the time. We always had a backup quickly available when using the .14 in case it failed to kill quickly, especially on larger critters.

PHOTO C2-23.

We did a lot of experimenting with .22 calibres in parallel with the work I was doing with .17 and .14 calibres. Here I am with part of a nights fox tally, taken with a .22–284 Winchester. I also tried .22–308 Winchester and a shortened .22–308 Winchester I named the .22 Cheetah. I shortened it to match the available powder to the capacity of the case, looking to get $100^{\%}$ powder capacity. I used 12" pitch barrels that spun the 60^{GN} hollow point projectiles fast enough to make them explosive. All of these cases spat the 60^{GN} projectile out at over 4000FPS, which was very fast and flat shooting.

PHOTO C2-24.

The .14 Walker Hornet worked so well I decided to follow it up with a .14–221 Fireball, and made it on a Sako L461 action stocked in a thumbhole design. I used both 11^{GN} projectiles at 4400FPS and 15^{GN} projectiles at 3800FPS in it. In the photo above Lyn poses with a crow she shot, that got too smart for its own good around the chook pen, on Purple Downs, and in the photo below I can be seen with a small boar I took on the Thomson Channel country in 1972. Later I replaced the claro walnut stock with a laminated thumbhole version. Playing with these small calibres was an interesting diversion, but I had no thought of going commercial with them.

PHOTO C2-25.

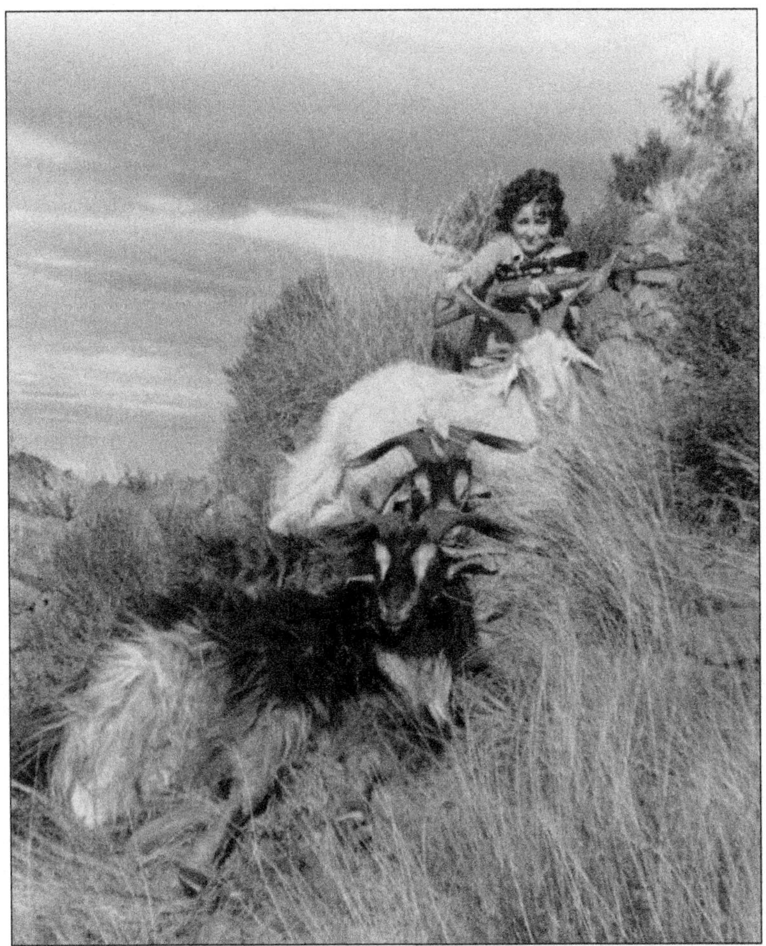

PHOTO C2-26.

The sub calibre and .22 calibres were impressive enough in the field, but with the extensive use I was putting them to they exhibited a trait that would probably go unnoticed to someone who only used them casually. The problem that reared its ugly head was mystery misses with shots where I was dead certain everything was perfect, and I should have connected. Eventually I worked out the misses were caused by something, probably a blade of grass or a small stick, in the path of the projectile that couldn't be seen when the shot was taken. This prompted much thought and research until I decided that the best shootable combination would be a 25/06 Ackley Improved cartridge shooting the 87^{GN} projectile out at 3650FPS. I built it on a Remington Model 700ADL long action fitted with a Shilen #5A x 27" long barrel, and stocked with a laminated thumbhole design. Lyn can be seen with it in the above photo with 3 big billies she pranged, one after the other, at around 220 yards shooting up hill in the Flinders Ranges, South Australia.

The mystery misses disappeared when I started using this rifle, and it was absolutely deadly on foxes well past 300 yards. On crows I needed to be very careful to hold the rifle so that it would recoil straight back into my shoulder, and if I did my part it would reach out past 250 yards and smack those varmints like the Hammer of Thor. I used Remington .270 Winchester brass in it as that was a very strong case. With its weak Norma brass the .257 Weatherby Magnum could not match the .25/06 Imp.

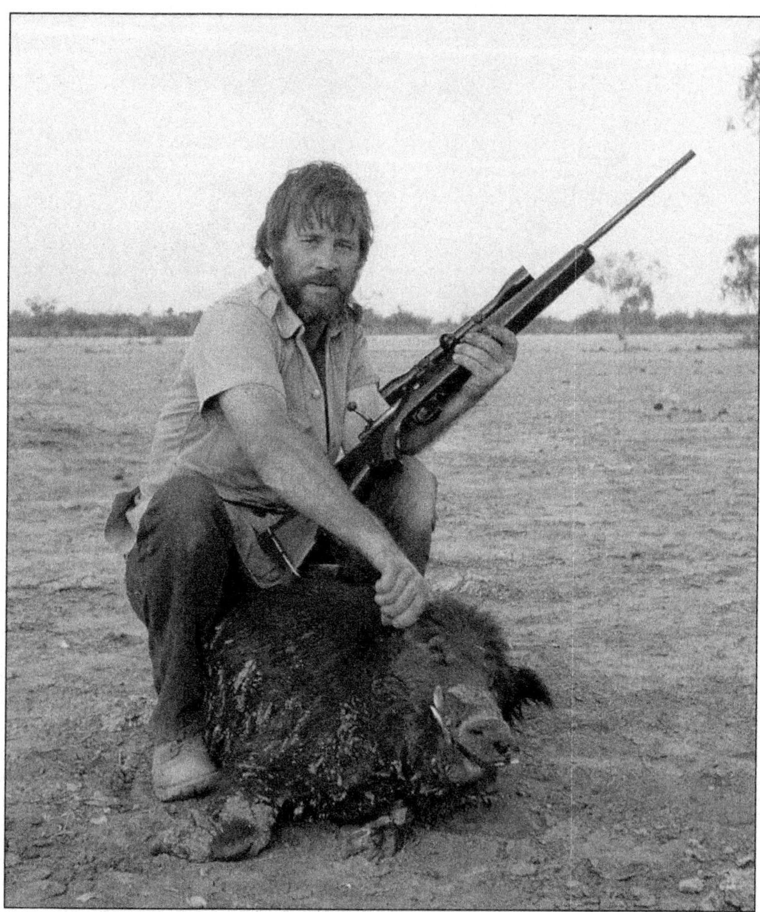

PHOTO C2-27.

This is the rifle that changed my thinking radically as to what the design of a hunting rifle should be. I used it extensively for medium game over a 6 year period. Up until I made this rifle I had not considered that such a light weight rifle could be so effective in the field. The design of my sporting rifles would reflect the lessons I learned from the first shot I fired out of it. It was a fibreglass shell stocked Remington Model 700 in .308 Winchester Calibre, and weighed in at 6LBS fully kitted out ready to shoot. Its secret was not in the super light weight, but in its 'front light' balance.

PHOTOS C2-28 AND C2-29.

Tony Greenfield sighting the .14/221 on the left. Goats in the Flinders Ranges on the right.

PHOTO C2-30.

This is the first prototype of the BFA action I made in the late 1970s. Lyn is with a goat she took with it on its first outing. The calibre was .223 Remington, for which I had Winchester Proof ammunition. Once we were satisfied that everything worked we went in to production. Pity it didn't last.

PHOTO C2-31.

The 25/06 Ackley Improved was without peer as a long range fox rifle and did double duty as a long range medium game rifle. For medium game I switched to 100^{GN} projectiles at 3400FPS, which was also a deadly combination. Were I to be restricted to one rifle only, I think the 25/06 Improved would definitely be on the short, short list.

CHAPTER THREE

FIT THE BARREL

A mate directed me to an internet forum a while ago where there was a guy, I'd imagine, trying to impress everybody with his skill and knowledge. He made the statement that, in his workshop, fitting barrels was the least precision job he does. I think what he was trying to do was put the guys on the forum, that fit barrels, down by inferring that it's a simple job that any moron can do. I remember thinking to myself, "Hmm, I must be among the morons, because I don't think it's that simple at all."

Of course it can be a simple job, depending on how you go about it. I guess if all you wanted was to fit a barrel that would accept a cartridge and go 'bang', you could achieve that with a file, a couple of twist drills and some emery paper. They do it like that somewhere in Pakistan, but here we are looking for something with a little more precision.

As we have seen in the previous chapter, the job can be accomplished with varying degrees of accuracy depending on how you set the barrel up. I posed a question at the end of the last chapter that said in essence, "Theoretically, what do we need to do to correct the deficiencies of the setups I described in this chapter?" My answer to that question is, "I need to make it so that the projectile starts dead straight into the bore." That is, as perfectly aligned as possible with the centre-line of *that section of bore it is entering.* It should be obvious, that with the speed these projectiles are rotating, any deviation from dead straight will have a detrimental effect on both accuracy, and wind drift, due to wobble when the projectile leaves the muzzle. It's also perfectly possible that the projectile, spinning eccentrically about its axis, can be detrimental to a barrels harmonics on its way to the muzzle. Many factors effect accuracy, not all of which are fully understood, and much of our thinking is more theory based on small samples of data, rather than hard proven fact beyond doubt. Be that as it may, it seems logical to me that it would be very advantageous if we could start every projectile on its way down the bore perfectly straight, in line with the centre of the bore axis immediately in front of the chamber. *It certainly won't do any harm.*

Having worked out the theory, all we need to do is work out the mechanics required to make it happen. The nuts and bolts as it were. I will now describe how I go about fitting a rifle barrel to an action and, more importantly, why I do it the way I do. I'm going to start from scratch; that is as if I have never fitted this caliber ever before, and I am using a brand new chambering reamer just arrived in the post. We are going to need a few tools to do this job so I will describe them as I go along. I hope you can follow it all.

As this is a fresh start for me, I am going to want to make three little tools that will be very useful later on. Also, as this is a new reamer, these tools will give me information, about the dimensions of the tool, that will assist me in working out some things that I will need to take into consideration. These tools are made from a piece of old stainless steel barrel.

They are:

1. A case head-space gauge.
2. An overall cartridge length gauge.
3. A case length gauge.

I use reamers made by Hugh Henriksen in the U.S.A. Hugh makes a terrific tool, with very accurate dimensions, that cuts superbly, and with one feature that is, in my opinion, extremely important. That is a correctly dimensioned throat and leade. Photo 3-1 shows exactly how the leade and throat should be on a finish reamer, and Hugh gets it right every time. The throat in the chamber is a parallel section, immediately in front of the neck, and is needed to allow us to seat the bullet at least some way out from the end of the cartridge case. The leade (pronounced leed) is the tapered section at the end of the throat that eases the projectiles passage into the bore proper. On my finish reamers I want the throat diameter to be no more than .0005" over nominal caliber diameter. For a 7mm reamer, whose nominal calibre diameter is .2840", I want the throat to be cut at no larger than .2845". I prefer to have my reamers short throated so that I can have some flexibility with throat length. That way I have the option to cut a chamber suitable for light (short) projectiles, or by lengthening the throat with a throating reamer, that is made to cut the throat and leade only, I can make the chamber suitable for heavy (long) projectiles. As an example, my 7mm Remington Saum reamer cuts a throat .100" in length that I extend to .220" with a throating reamer to accept 180 grain Berger Hybrid projectiles.

The leade on a reamer typically has an angle of 1.5° for small calibers up to 6mm, and 3° from .25 caliber up. With the advent of the sharp VLD projectiles we are using today, for target competition, I prefer to use a 1.5° leade on any barrel job that will be put to that use. So my 7mm Saum reamer, for instance, cuts a 1.5° x .100" deep throated leade which I deepen to a 1.5° x 220" deep throat and leade with the throating reamer.

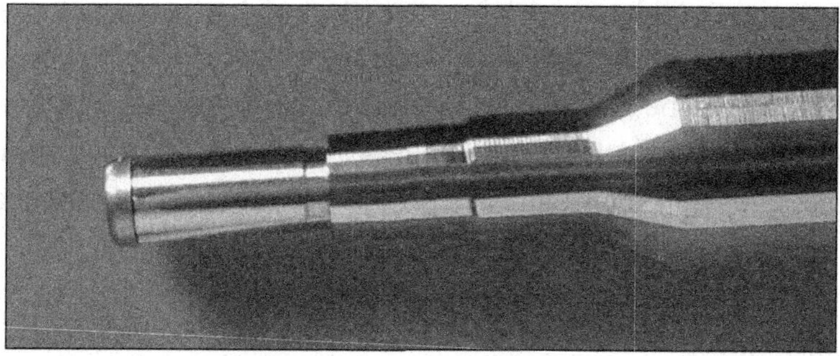

PHOTO 3-1.

The throat and leade of a Henriksen reamer. The transition from the parallel throat section to the tapered leade section can be seen .100" in front of the neck. This reamer cuts through steel like a knife through soft butter.

The dimensions I hassle Hugh with when I order a reamer are:–

1. Throat length, diameter, and leade angle.
2. Neck diameter.
3. Base diameter .200" ahead of the bolt face.

There are specifications published by the Sporting Arms and Ammunition Manufacturers Institute Inc (SAAMI) for the dimensions of a maximum cartridge, and a minimum chamber. The idea is that if ammunition manufacturers do not exceed the dimensions of a maximum cartridge, and rifle manufacturers do not exceed the dimensions of a minimum chamber, the two will always fit together. In practice that works pretty well, but in execution it leaves a bit to be desired for the kind of precision work we are about here. Were I to order a 7mm R Saum reamer from Hugh, without specifying any special dimensions, he would supply me a high quality tool that cut through barrel steel like butter, and produced a nearly mirror off tool finish to SAAMI minimum chamber specifications. A tool like that would be fine if I were using it for mass production, but the use I am intending it for is, shall we say, more precise, so I want to specify those three dimensions on my reamer.

You can access the SAAMI specifications for most cartridges and chambers on their website (www.saami.org) and therein you should note that those dimensions allow for a manufacturing tolerance. In the case of the chamber – 0" and +.002", and in the case of the cartridge the tolerance is + 0" – .008". These tolerances are significant. For instance on the 7 R Saum, in the case of the throat diameter, it is specified at .2846", however the diameter at maximum SAAMI specification could be anything up to .2866", which is significantly large. Some reamer makers specify a tolerance of – 0" +.001", which can still make a throat diameter of .2856". That is too large for my liking.

Similarly, we have a problem at the base of the chamber. The dimension here is taken .200" in front of the bolt face, as that is about where the solid head of the case thins sufficiently enough to be upset, or deformed, by chamber pressure. The SAAMI spec here is .5510" diameter. The SAAMI spec for a maximum cartridge case could measure .5420", which would result in a large unsightly, accuracy compromising bulge at the rear of a case dimensioned like that. You need to take into account the dimensions of the cases you will be using when you order a reamer to avoid this.

Figure 3-1 shows the print Hugh provided when he supplied my reamer. For me Hugh's reamer is just perfect. He supplied exactly the dimensions I specified, which I view as no mean feat. Cases fired in the chamber cut with this reamer expand .0014" in diameter at the head. The throat and leade are exactly dimensioned and perfectly formed, and the neck diameter allows me to neck turn cases to just clean them up with a .0035" clearance.

Regardless of where the reamer was made, we need to check the dimensions it will actually cut in the real world, and making these three small tools will give us advance information on what to expect. Beg, borrow, or steal a piece of barrel, in the caliber you will be chambering, at least 6" long or more. We need to face off both ends and make 60 degree centres in them, then turn the length parallel. The diameter we turn it to is not important, as long as it is larger than the diameter of the shoulder and body junction of the case. The procedure to prepare the basic piece was described in the chapter on barrel setup — setup 1 (Page 52).

With the steel thus prepared proceed as follows:–

1. Chuck the steel in a 4 jaw chuck with about 1" protruding and insert a correctly fitted pin gauge in the bore.

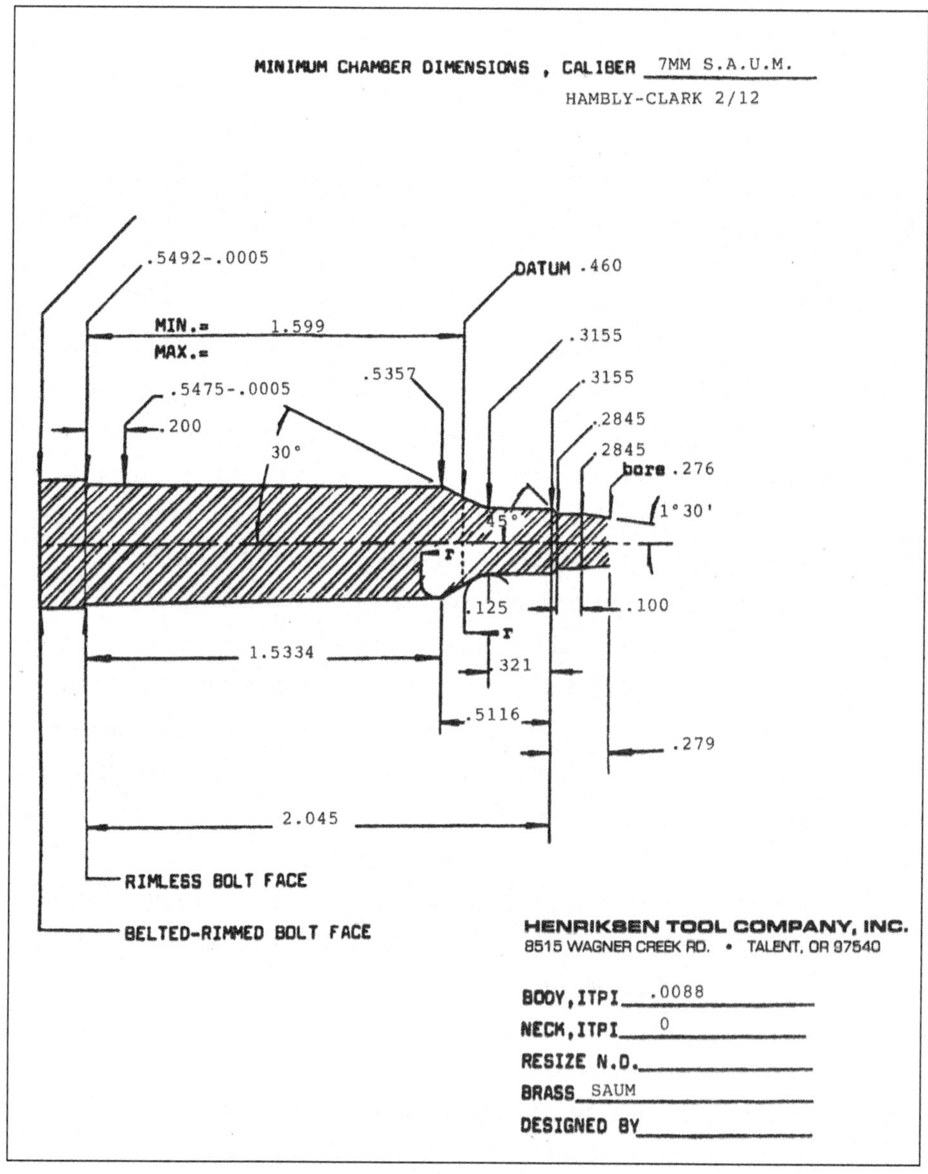

FIGURE 3-1.
Henriksen 7MM R SAUM finish reamer print.

2. Use a .0001" dial indicator and true the pin gauge to +/- 0. Photo 3-2 shows this happening.

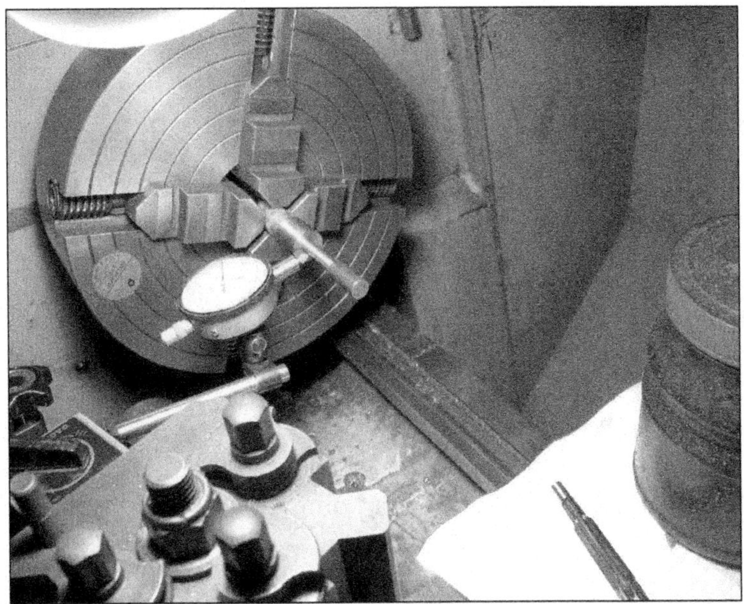

PHOTO 3-2.
Indicating a barrel stub that will be used in making our measuring tools.

3. Place a dead centre in the tail-stock of the lathe, and set it up for reaming a chamber.

 3.1. I will discuss reaming and tail-stock accuracy in detail later. If you want to get started with that, skip to the relevant section before you begin, where ever it is! (Page 113)

4. With the lathe running at slow speed (around 30RPM) run the reamer into the, lets call it a barrel, until the depth is about .025" past the junction of the shoulder and body on the reamer.

5. Remove the piece of barrel from the lathe and cut it off about ¼" in front of the point where the chamber neck ends.

6. Face off the cut end, and break the outside edge with a file, and the inside edge with a stone.

7. Now with a bandsaw (or a hacksaw, the hard way) make a cut from the outside to the centre-line, of the piece, along its length.

8. Make a second cut, likewise, at 90° to the first cut so that you expose about 1/10" of the bore.

9. Place the piece in a milling machine, and clean up the sawn surfaces to remove the saw marks, and make them look nice.

 9.1. If you don't have a mill you will need to clean up the rough surfaces with a file, the hard way.

10. De-burr the piece inside and outside and clean it up.

This is a handy case length gauge (more on that later). It also allows you to get a preliminary measurement of actual neck diameter, and see what the throat and leade will be on your finished chamber. I think it is an essential tool. Photo 3.3 (Page 87) shows a couple of mine.

Let's move on to tool #2.

1. Face off the barrel piece and set it up in the 4 jaw chuck as before.

2. Ream it again, but this time run the reamer in to only the junction of the shoulder and body, no more.

3. Remove the barrel piece, and cut it off at a point about .100" ahead of where the neck of the chamber ends.

4. Face the cut end off. Be careful not to face it past the end of the chamber.

5. Break the sharp outside edge with a file, and the sharp inside edge with a stone. Clean it up.

This is a full length case sizing gauge. It will be indispensable when it is time to set up the full length sizing die. More on that is discussed in the appropriate chapter.

We need one more tool.

1. Again, prepare the remaining piece of barrel, and set it up in the 4 jaw chuck.

2. Now, if you are going to finish the throat and leade of the chamber entirely with your finish reamer, then that is the tool you should use here. If, however, you are going to finish the throat and leade of the chamber with a separate throating reamer, then that is the tool you should be using.

3. Run the reamer of your choice into the barrel piece. In the case of a chambering reamer, stop just as you come to the bottom of the 45° chamfer at the end of the neck of the reamer. In the case of a throating reamer you can stop when the throat has been cut in about .100".

4. Remove the barrel piece from the chuck, and patch it out to clean and dry it.

5. Find out where the tip of the projectile you will be using ends up in the piece, and cut it off about .100" ahead of this point.

    5.1. Use a dial caliper. Measure the length of the projectile and write that down. Place that projectile, nose first in the throat you have cut until it stops, and measure the amount the base of the projectile protrudes from the back of the barrel. Write that down. Subtract the second measurement from the first and that is how far up the barrel you need to cut it off +.100".

6. Face off the cut end, and de-burr it as before.

This is a very exact overall length gauge that will be used, in conjunction with a dial caliper, to measure overall cartridge length. Again, it is an essential tool. Photo 3-3 shows a couple of mine.

PHOTO 3-3.
The three tools we have just made. On the left for .30BR, and on the right for .22PPC.

We will start with the first tool we made, the case length gauge.

The SAAMI spec for the chamber length on the Remington 7MM SAUM is 2.045" - 0 + 015".

In order to clean up all the necks of the 200 cases I had for my 7 SAUM I had to trim them to 2.030" in length. Hugh made the reamer to the exact minimum SAAMI spec of 2.045" which is ideal. However, if I had a batch of short cases I would have made an adjustment to the head-space specs of the chamber, in order to get the case neck closer to the end of the chamber. The clearance you want here is .010". I have .015" which is not a tragedy. In practice, I simply let the cases grow .005" and keep them trimmed to 2.035" in length.

However, for instance, when I did my 6x47 Lapua I needed a correction, and the same with my .22PPC. The 6x47 Lapua cases shortend when they were sized from 6.5x47 Lapua, and the .22PPC cases shortened when they were fireformed from .220 Russian brass. The gauge we made is for checking this out, then measuring the correction we will have to make. The correction is simply made by pushing the case further into a full length die, until the end of the shortest case you have is within .010" from the end of your test tool neck.

If you can't get it far enough into the die you will need to grind a bit from the end. You can get all sophisticated, with this, with a tool and cutter grinder, but it is easily accomplished with a bench grinder, and a battery drill.

1. Wind the decapping rod back until it is inside the die and lock it down.

2. Chuck the decapping rod in the battery drill.

3. Measure the overall length of the die. From the gauge you know how much you need to remove from the bottom.

4. Use the fine end of the grinder. Hold the threaded body of the die in your hand and start the electric drill.

5. With the grinder and drill running bring the die end into contact with the stone — sparks will fly.

6. Don't over heat the die, and check the overall length often.

7. When you have ground the die to length, polish the end and chamfer (leade in), and wash it in solvent.

8. Test it with a case. Photo 3-4 shows the method.

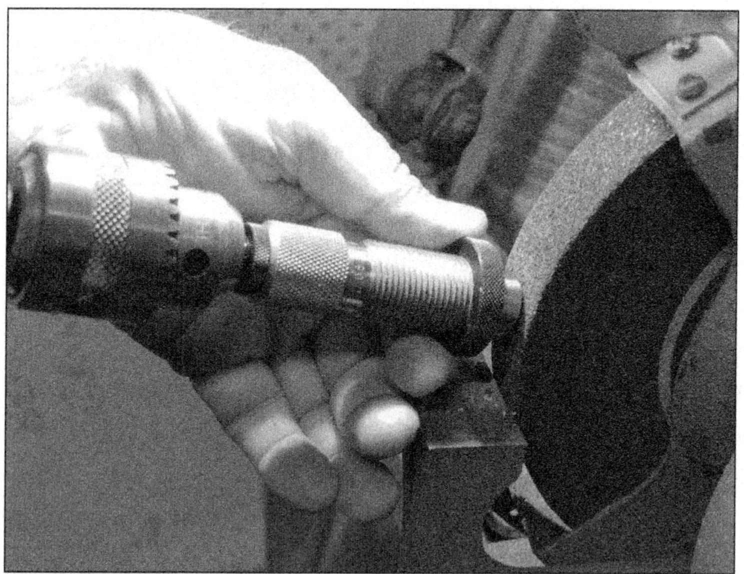

PHOTO 3-4.
Shortening a commercial FLD. Only around .010" will be removed, so tread lightly. With the grinder running, start the drill in slow, and bring the end of the die into contact with the wheel. The lock ring will wind back, so deal with that. The job will only take a few seconds.

What we are doing here is shortening up the head-space of the chamber in order to get the end of the neck of the case in its proper place, .010" from the end of the chamber. There is no problem with this as the head-space has been shortened. However, should those cases be later fired in a rifle, chambered with a SAAMI specification head-space gauge, they could have excessive head-space, *so that should be avoided.* The choice is yours of course. I am merely presenting the information.

For my own rifles I don't head-space with a SAAMI gauge. I head-space with a new cartridge case that has been full length sized. If I use a gauge I am being subjected to tolerances that I would prefer to avoid. I will head-space the chamber so that I can feel the bolt close on a new full length sized case. That way the case is fully supported by the shoulder on its first firing. This is why I have been discussing the above a bit out of sequence. I need to determine the head-space dimensions I will be using before I start the job, and the case length gauge I made allows me to do that.

I would never fit a barrel with those head-space dimensions for anyone else, a customer or even a friend. If they go and do something stupid and blow themselves up, you know who will be blamed. When doing this job, for anyone else, adhere rigidly to SAAMI minimum specifications. No matter how well you think you know the guy, or no matter how much he assures you it will be ok, if the crunch comes you will be hung out to dry, even if the problem is not of your making. Stay safe!

Let's fit a barrel to an action:–

1. I prepare the blank by removing the front and rear centres. I cut only about ½" from the end of the muzzle, face it off and break the sharp edges with a file and stone as previously described. I then only face off the rear of the barrel enough to remove the centre, and break the sharp edges.

PHOTO 3-5.

Breaking the sharp edge at the back of the bore with a 3/8" round 320 grit stone.

1.1. I am not concerned about the lapped out end of the blank at the rear — it is of no consequence, and I am looking to maintain as much length in the barrel as possible on a long range match rifle.

1.2. At the muzzle end select a reamer pilot that will just fit inside the bore and fit it to your range rod (more about range rods later). Put a drop of lubricant in the mouth of the bore and one on the pilot, and see how far you can insert the pilot in the bore; probably not very far. Select the next size pilot down (-.0001") and try again until you find the exact size pilot that goes into the bore at least 2". Now go up one size (+.0001").

Push the pilot into the bore until it stops and mark the rod with a texta at the muzzle. The distance from the mark to the end of the pilot denotes the point where the bore begins to taper out towards the muzzle. That taper was caused during the lapping operation. You want the bore to be parallel where the projectile exits. Any belling of the bore at the muzzle will be detrimental to accuracy. Cut the barrel off ½" behind the point you found to be sure you have a good section of barrel at the crown. Face it off and break the outside and inside edges with a stone and file.

1.3. That is the only preparation needed. Remove the blank from the lathe and run a couple of patches through it to clean out any shavings and stoning residues that have found their way into the bore.

2. With a texta, mark the position on the outside of the blank where the end of the chamber will be when the blank is chambered.

2.1. Don't forget to take into account any protrusion of the case from the rear of the barrel when it has been chambered.

Now I must digress for a bit. We have already discussed the short comings of the various setup methods, so now we need to address those short comings. Our aim is to start the projectile dead straight into the bore. To achieve that aim it follows that we need to be able to determine in what direction the section of barrel, just in front of the end of the chamber, is heading. Where was the drill wandering when it passed through that section of the bar?

If we can know the angle the bore is heading, from the end of the chamber for about 1½" to 2", and we could align the centre-line of our chamber with the centre-line of that section of barrel, it follows that we have the very best chance possible to start our projectile dead straight into that section of barrel.

Once started dead straight, common sense dictates that it should follow the bore, remain straight on its trip through the barrel, and exit from the muzzle gyroscopically stable.

Being able to find the angle the bore is heading in is not enough though. *We also need to be able to adjust the barrel blank in the lathe so that the centre-line of that 1½" to 2" section of barrel rotates perfectly in line with the centre-line of the spindle of the lathe.* If you can follow all of that it should be pretty apparent that simply holding the blank in the chuck and spider, and indicating at each end, falls far short of what we want to do. Just indicating at the front of the chamber does too!

To make all of that happen we need some accessories. First we will address positioning the barrel in the lathe, and then we will address finding the direction our little section of barrel is heading in.

To address our first problem we need 4 pieces of half round steel 3/8" in diameter and about 1¼" long. I made mine by simply cutting a length of 3/8" diameter silver steel (oil hardening drill rod) down the middle with a saw for 2½" then cutting it for length. Leave the saw ends rough, as they will grip the blank better, and will do no harm. See Photo 3.7 (Page 91).

Also, we need to modify the jaws of our lathe chuck slightly. The jaws on the Colchester lathe I use for chambering already had several grooves ground on their inside surface. All I needed to do was break the sharp inside edge of the 4 grooves closest to the tailstock, with a 3/8" diameter stone, to allow the 3/8" diameter section of my parts to rotate freely, rather than bind on the sharp edges of the cutouts. Figure 3-2 (Page 92) shows what I am talking about here. If your chuck does not have the cutouts like mine (my Swedish Orn lathe lacks them) you will need to have them ground into the jaws. A 3/8" diameter section ground .050" deep would be fine. All it needs to do is locate the ½ round pieces, and allow them to rotate.

Now we can start to set up our barrel blank.

3. Go back and read setup 2 in the previous chapter — saves me repeating it. Set up the barrel blank exactly like that, with the following exceptions:-

3.1. Place the texta mark we made in step 2 under whatever recess we have in the chuck jaws to accept our ½ round pieces of drill rod. Photo 3-6 (Page 91) shows what I am talking about.

3.2. Don't have the chuck or the spider tightened up when you get the dial indicators reading +/- 0. The barrel should be held only lightly.

4. Now back out each chuck jaw enough so that you can slip in each of the 4 pieces of drill rod in turn. Wriggle them around to be sure they are seated properly in the cutout on each chuck jaw, and remember we only want the jaws tightened lightly. Photo 3-6 (Page 91) shows the barrel blank being pre-indicated. Photo 3-7 (Page 91) shows a gimbal piece in position under the groove of one of the four jaw chuck jaws.

PHOTO 3-6.

Pre-indicating the barrel blank. Note the texta mark indicating where the end of the chamber will be located, just behind where the gimbal pieces will grip the blank.

PHOTO 3-7.

A gimbal piece in place under the groove of a four jaw chuck jaw. The sharp edge of the groove has been broken, with a 3/8" round stone, to allow the gimbal piece to rotate when the blank is moved into position. Only in this way can the bore of the barrel blank be adjusted

Let's stop a moment to think about what is happening here. In effect, what we have done is to create a gimbal that allows the barrel to be moved into position, at pretty well any angle within the hollow mandrel, without being bent or stressed. Test it out if you like. Wind out the spider screws and move the muzzle around. It moves easily, and more importantly, when you move the muzzle you also move the back of the blank, and when you move it into a position it stays there. *Now, those small corrections you will make, with the spider at the muzzle, will actually be reflected by movement at the rear of the blank.* This is crucial if we are going to set up the blank properly. Figure 3-2 demonstrates the action of the gimbal. Notice, that in the left drawing, the outside of the barrel blank is parallel to the jaws of the lathe chuck, but the bore, represented by the dotted line, is not. This is what happens when the barrel is held directly in the jaws of the chuck. However, in the right hand drawing the barrel is free to move independently from the chuck jaws. In this way we can align the bore of the barrel without regard to the outside of the barrel blank, or the chuck jaws.

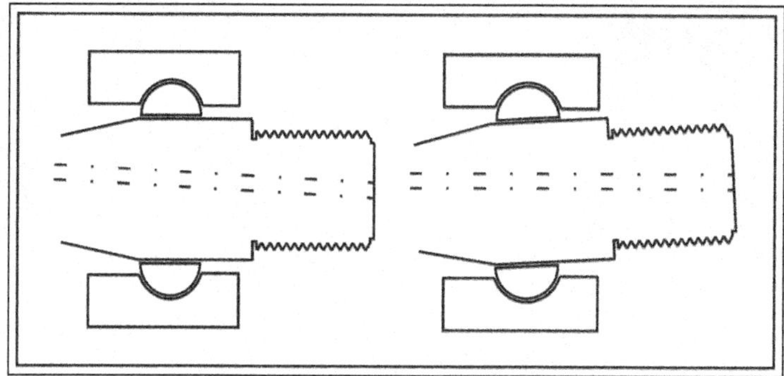

Figure 3-2.

In the left drawing the outside of the barrel blank is being held parallel with the lathe spindle centre-line. In the right drawing the gimbal has allowed the barrel blank to be positioned, in the lathe chuck, at an angle that would be impossible if it were held directly in the jaws of the chuck.

Now that we can place the barrel blank pretty well anywhere we please inside the hollow mandrel of the lathe, we need to have a method of determining in what direction the short section of bore we are interested in is heading. To do this we need a simple tool to do a complicated job.

The tool is called a range rod, and it can be easily made from a piece of drill rod about 12" long, turned at one end to accept a reamer pilot, and drilled and tapped to accept a screw to retain the pilot. Photo 3-8 shows the four rods I routinely use. Sizes of .204" (#6) diameter for #1 pilots, .234" (Letter A) diameter for #2 pilots and .302" (Letter N) diameter for #3 pilots work fine. For .22 caliber barrels I use a separate rod .195" diameter that has been relieved to .165" diameter for 4¼" behind the pilot. This ensures I have clearance to the bore, as a .218" diameter pilot is not very much larger than the #6 rod diameter. The rod does not need to be hardened, so it is not a big ask to turn the end to fit a reamer pilot very closely. Just be sure to true the rod in the chuck to +/- 0 before turning it to size. Drill and tap the end at the same time. If you have a 4–40 UNC tap you can use the retaining screw from one of your reamers. With the rod in hand it is time to proceed.

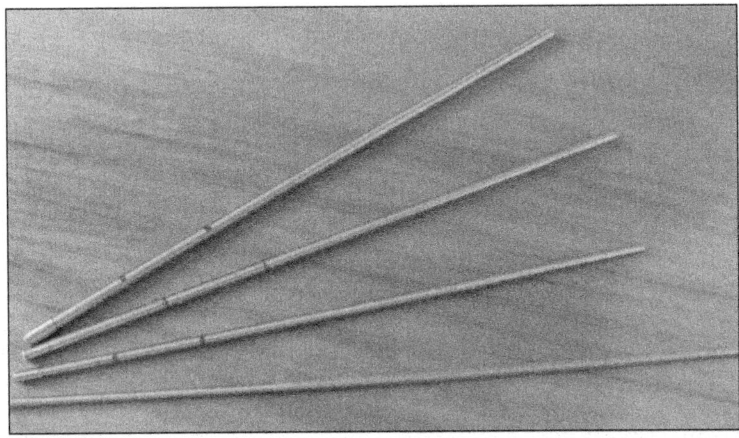

PHOTO 3-8.

Four range rods I routinely use that will allow me to set up barrel blanks from .22 caliber right through .458 caliber. Note the texta marks from previous jobs.

5. The range rod is handy for this step. Remove the pin gauge from the rear of the blank and find a close fitting reamer pilot that will go into the bore of the blank at least 3" to 4" past the mark you have made on the blank previously with a texta.

5.1. Remember that the rear of the barrel will be lapped oversize, so you will need to start with a size a few tenths of a thousandth under what will fit in the end of the blank.

5.2. Leave the pin gauge in the muzzle for the time being — we will use it later, however back the dial indicator well away from it.

5.3. Put a couple of drops of oil on the pilot and in the bore. We don't want to jam it in there if we can help it. With such small clearances that's easy to do.

5.4. By close fitting I mean .0001" under bore size. In practice you simply keep trying +.0001" pilots until you find one that won't go all the way into the bore, and then pick the previous size that would.

5.5. Feed the pilot in as carefully, and as straight as you can using the range rod. You can get trapped into thinking a pilot won't fit when it is actually not entering the bore straight. Be aware; the fit is very close.

6. With a correctly fitted pilot on the range rod, lay the rod along side the barrel blank, so that the mid point of the pilot is in line with our texta mark, and make a texta mark on the shaft of the rod level with the rear of the blank.

7. Now measure back from that mark 2" and make another texta mark on the shaft of the rod.

8. Install a drill chuck in the tailstock of the lathe and secure the range rod in the chuck.

9. Put a drop of oil at the mouth of the bore, and a drop on the reamer pilot. Bring the pilot up close to the end of the barrel blank, and lock the tailstock onto the lathe bed, Photo 3-9 shows this.

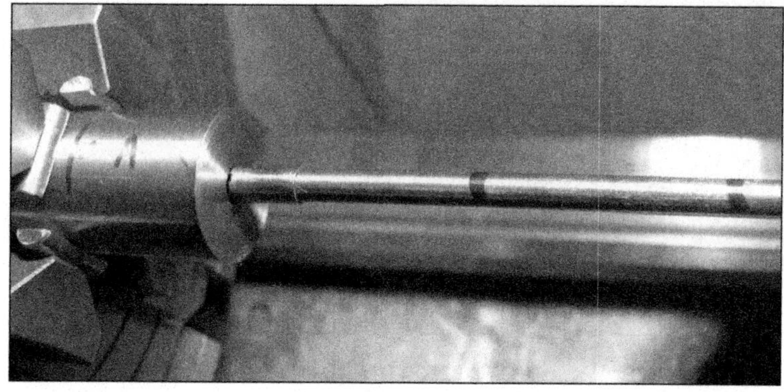

PHOTO 3-9.

The range rod is about to enter the bore of the barrel blank. Note the Gimbal pieces in place under the chuck jaws. The slight misalignment is of no consequence.

10. Using the tailstock feed, advance the rod until the reamer pilot just enters the bore of the blank. Then, rotating the lathe chuck by hand, feed the range rod into the bore until the first texta mark on the shaft is level with the back of the blank.

10.1. The range rod will very likely not be lined up with the bore so that it can go straight in. You will need to spring it a little to one side or the other, maybe up or down, to get it to enter. This is ok.

10.2. If there is a major misalignment, like ½ a hole or more, try rotating the rod in the chuck until it lines up, at least no more than .020" out.

10.3. If rotating the rod doesn't work, either get a straighter rod, or try shimming the drill chuck jaws to line it up.

11. Now mount a dial indicator so that its probe is resting on top of the shaft of the range rod at the back of the barrel blank. Photo 3-10 shows the dial indicator in position.

PHOTO 3-10.

Dial indicator in position to begin trueing the bore of the barrel blank at the end of the chamber.

11.1. I prefer to use a sensitive dial indicator, with a probe, as seen in the picture. You make up your own mind.

Let's discuss what we are doing here. Remember that we set up the barrel blank to a tolerance of +/- 0 using pin gauges in each end of the barrel, so if that setup method (2) was valid the bore would indicate true, right? We will see.

When we rotate the barrel blank any eccentricity in the bore will displace the range rod, and we will be able to measure the amount of deflection, with the dial indicator, reading off the top of the range rod at the back of the barrel blank. Even though we set up the blank as per Method 2, Chapter 2, you will see that the eccentricity we will measure at that point where the chamber ends is considerable. I have never fitted a barrel where the run out was zero, at this point, straight away.

You will remember we were careful to mount the blank in the chuck at that precise point where the chamber is to end. This is important to make our setting up a little easier, as it is at that position the blank will be pivoting when we make adjustments at the muzzle end. So once that point is running true, adjustments at the muzzle will not be reflected with extreme changes at the end, where our gimbal is holding it.

Let's move on.

12. Rotate the chuck, and adjust it to bring the dial indicator into a reading of +/- 0.

12.1. You will only need to move the chuck jaws a little at a time, but be careful not to drop one of your 3/8" gimbal pieces out of the chuck when you loosen one of the jaws.

12.2. Remember we are not using much pressure on the chuck jaws yet. The blank should still be held gently.

13. Rotate the chuck and wind the tailstock in until the second texta mark, on the range rod, is level with the end of the barrel. Continue to rotate the chuck and bring the dial indicator into a reading of +/- 0, this time by adjusting the spider jaws at the muzzle end of the blank.

14. Keep repeating this procedure, winding the range rod in and out to the marks, and adjusting the chuck and spider, until the dial indicator reads +/- 0 at both marks on the range rod.

14.1. When you have both points reading within .0002", start increasing tension on the screws so that you arrive at final firm tension, both on the chuck and spider, when the indicator reads +/- 0 at both points.

14.2. If you find the dial indicator needle is jumping around you may have too tight a pilot fitted. Try the next size down. The indicator needle should move smoothly.

What exactly have we achieved here? Well, we have mounted our barrel blank in the lathe with the short section of barrel, immediately in front of the chamber, rotating with its centre-line exactly true with the centre- line of the axis of the lathe spindle. *This is very important.* Now, if we can line the centre-line of our chamber up perfectly, with the centre-line of the axis of the lathe spindle, *we will have achieved our aim of starting the projectile, as perfectly as possible, straight into the bore.* Further, all other operations we need to do, on the rear of the barrel, will be carried out in alignment with the centre-line of that short section of barrel

15. Remove the range rod, and as a final check test your setup with your long probe dial indicator, as described in setup 3 in the previous chapter.

15.1. The dial indicator will bump up and down over the grooves and lands of the barrel blank, so you need to note the measurements and be aware of where the ball is — on a land or in a groove.

15.2. The probe won't get all the way into where it should be on long chambers, so just do the best you can.

15.3. I, personally, have never needed to change the setup I made with the range rod, however I still make this final check. If you find a discrepancy, your initial setup probably wasn't quite right. I would reinstall the range rod and check it again. Photo 3-11 shows the long probe dial indicator about to enter the bore.

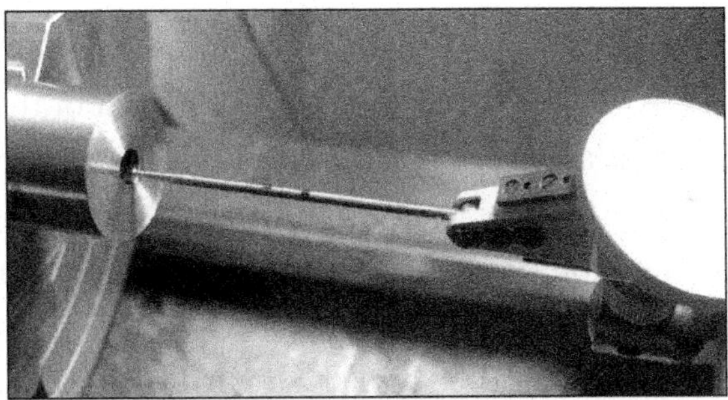

PHOTO 3-11.

I am about to double check the barrel setup at the chamber end with a long probe dial indicator.

16. Re engage the dial indicator at the muzzle onto the pin gauge we left in there, and measure the amount of run out. It will be considerable, anything up to and including .025". Don't be alarmed — it isn't important. *What we have just done at the other end is important.*

17. Rotate the barrel with the dial indicator engaged, and find the point on the muzzle where the pin gauge indicates at its highest point (closest to the indicator).

On my lathe the dial indicator probe is at the 9:00 o'clock position, so I rotate the barrel until the indicator shows that it is closest to me. Now move to the breech end of the blank and make a visible mark, with a texta, at the same 9:00 o'clock position, and write the word 'up' next to it. Photo 3-12 shows this. We will be referring to it later.

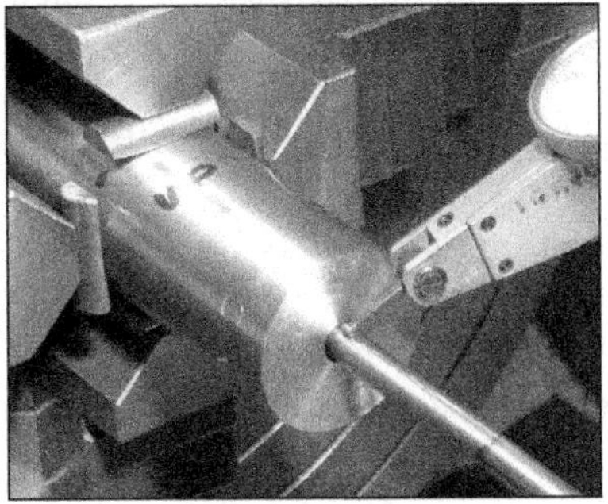

PHOTO 3-12.

Note the line, and the word 'UP' in texta, indicating the position of the mass of the blank.

For the next steps I will use my Panda action as an example, because it is a simple one. We need to take some measurements from the action before we can proceed. If you have already removed a barrel from the action you will be able to easily see, and measure, the dimensions. You will also see the shape the barrel tenon needs to be to fit it to the action. In the Appendix of this book I will put drawings for the tenons of many of the actions I have fitted barrels to over the years. These drawings are primitive, to say the least, but they served me well for over 40 years, and are the results of my own observations. I still use them today. No doubt there are better more complicated drawings available, but some times simpler *is* better. *Do not take any of those measurements verbatim.* Always double check every measurement you have to deal with, or one day you will be bitten.

Oh, yes. On page 95 I said, "We will see." When the barrel you see in Photo 3-14 (Page 99) was set up, I re-inserted the pin gauge at the rear, and re-measured the run out. The muzzle end ran out .012", and the breech end ran out .0005". Had I set up that barrel using any of the methods in the previous chapter, that critical short section of bore just in front of the chamber would have been nowhere near the centre-line of my lathe spindle, and the alignment of my chamber would have been severely compromised.

To digress a little bit (*again*) we should discuss lathe cutting tools. It seems to me that it is de rigueur to use Tungsten Carbide tooling. Virtually everyone I run into uses TC Tooling, especially gunsmiths. I don't. All of the tooling I use is home formed and sharpened hi-speed steel. I do not resort to using TC unless I run into a piece of stock that is within a few points of, or harder than the hardness of high speed steel. Of course, then I have no choice. The reason I use hi-speed steel is simply that when I started doing gun work, over 45 years ago, the, TC tools I tried would not make the extremely fine cuts I wanted. Their design at that time was for high speed and heavy cuts. *I don't make any high speed or heavy cuts.*

High speed steel tool stock typically runs over 60 on the Rockwell C scale, and most of the material we work on will test much lower than that. Barrel steel for instance will run at only around 26RC, and actions at around 40RC. High speed steel will cut anything below 50RC easily.

It didn't take me long to find out that a sharp high speed steel lathe bit was easily capable of shaving cuts as small as .0001" from the rifle steels I was encountering. It is durable enough to easily last through an entire job or two, and takes only a few minutes to sharpen. I have never found the need to bother trying anything else.

Now, I could be well behind the times with this, as TC tooling may well have improved over the years, so I will only say this. Making small diameter pin gauges is probably as good a test as there is if you are using TC tooling. Unless a TC lathe turning bit is very sharp it will push a .218" diameter pin gauge away rather than cut it. So if you are unable to take a .0001" cut from the diameter of a .218" diameter pin gauge you should seriously consider switching to high speed steel. Your choice; back to business.

18. I need two measurements from my Panda action. First up I strip everything off it so I am left with only the receiver and bolt body. Using a depth micrometer I measure from the front of the action to the face of the bolt installed in the receiver, and I write that measurement down (measurement A).

18.1. Be sure you are not interfering with the bolt being firmly back against the locking lugs of the receiver when you make this measurement.

19. Now measure from the front of the action to the front of the bolt nose, and write that measurement down (measurement B). I deduct .010" from measurement B, and that will be measurement C.

20. Now we know the length we need to make our barrel tenon (measurement C), and we also know how far the cartridge case will be protruding from the rear of the barrel when it is chambered; measurement A minus measurement C = measurement D.

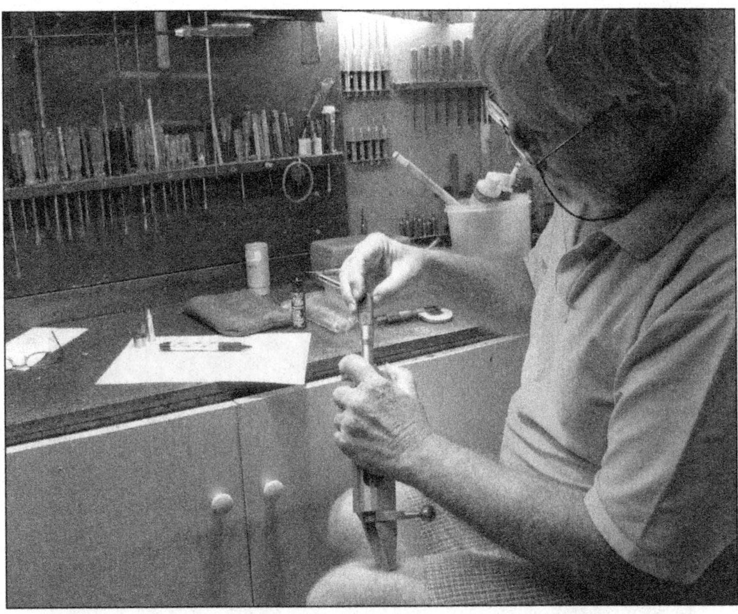

PHOTO 3-13.

Measuring the action, with a depth micrometer, to determine the length of the barrel tenon, and the amount the cartridge must protrude from the rear of the chamber, to make the correct head-space dimensions.

21. Back to the lathe; Set up a turning tool that will turn to a sharp corner (Photo 3-14 shows mine), and advance it along the lathe bed until it touches the back of the barrel. Using the cross-slide, wind it out from the blank, and zero the carriage travel measuring dial. Now wind the carriage towards the headstock a distance equal to measurement C plus .010". Set the carriage automatic stop at that point and tighten it up.

PHOTO 3-14.

I have run the cutting tool up to the back of the barrel with the longitudinal travel, and withdrawn it with the cross-slide, as witnessed by the scratch on the face, in preparation for delineating my tenon length +.010".

22. Now, turn the outside diameter down to the diameter we want our thread outside dimension to be. In my case that is 1.062" diameter. Photos 3-15 and 3-16 show that happening.

PHOTO 3-15.
Turning the barrel tenon to diameter and length + .010".

22.1. Use good cutting oil, applied by brush, prior to every cut.

22.2. I cut a depth of .020" with a chuck RPM of 570, and slow carriage feed, as I do not want to burn my cutting tool up, overheat the job, or am I in any particular hurry. Also, by being gentle, I will be putting as little stress on my setup as possible.

22.3. I make my last cut no deeper than .005", with the slowest carriage speed on my machine, to make a fine finish.

22.4. At the end of the last cut, when the carriage stop clicks off, I lock the carriage and advance the cross-feed about .010". Then I advance the cross-slide about .005", and back the carriage cross-feed out very slowly. This just clears the sharp corner at the end of the cut. There is probably no sane reason to do it, but I've been doing it forever. Go figure! Didn't I warn you earlier about doing things by rote? Oh well…

PHOTO 3-16.

The barrel tenon has been turned to diameter for my Shilen DGA, the one we aligned in Chapter 1. Note the shape of the cutting tool I used. The relief, at the end of the shank, is also needed on Remingtons to clear the end of the thread.

23. When the shank is at diameter, change to a facing tool. Bring the tool to touch the end of the blank, lock the carriage and, using the cross-slide feed, face the end of the barrel to length. Take a shallow cut across the face of the rear of the blank, only about .002" deep. Measure the distance from the back of the blank, to the shoulder formed, when you turned the shank down. You want to end up with measurement C.

PHOTO 3-17.

The barrel blank for my Shilen DGA .30BR faced to length.

Your measurement should be larger than measurement C, and the difference between them is the amount you will have to remove to bring it to correct size. Take the final .002" deep cut at a slow automatic cross feed, moving to the centre, and you will make a fine finish. In Photo 3-17 that job has just been completed.

24. Swing the facing tool around on the cross-slide so that its cutting face makes a 30 degree angle to the rear of the barrel, and break the sharp edge at the rear enough, to provide a good lead in, for the threading tool we are going to use next

25. While the barrel is still rotating give the shank a lick with a bit of worn 320 grit cloth abrasive and it will shine like a mirror. That will assist us to see the end of our cut when we do the threading operation.

26. Replace the facing tool with a 60° threading tool, and set the compound slide of the lathe to an angle of 59°. Using a thread angle gauge, set the threading tool square to the centre-line of the barrel, and lock it down. See Photo 3-18.

26.1. I use high speed steel threading tools that I sharpen, using a tool and cutter grinder, to make the correct angle easily and precisely. You can sharpen them by hand on a bench grinder with a bit a practice. I did it that way for many years before I obtained the T&C grinder.

PHOTO 3-18.

Setting the threading tool square to the centre-line of the lathe spindle. I do this by placing a tissue on the bed of the lathe, and locating my light so that I can see what I am doing in shadow relief.

26.2. If you have a tungsten carbide threading tool that will take a cut of only .0001" positively, then by all means use it. If not, use high speed steel.

27. With the compound rest slide in its normal operating position, bring the point of the threading tool to within about .005" of the barrel shank outside diameter, using the cross-slide. Now adjust the compound rest slide, and cross-slide, until the cross-slide handle is at a position of about 11.00 o'clock. This will allow you to easily, and quickly, back the threading tool out, by bearing straight down on the handle. Zero the cross-slide dial.

27.1. You need to be able to move the handle down very quickly, so if you are unsure, practice it until it is second nature.

28. Set the lathe at its slowest speed, mine is 30rpm, and set the gearbox to cut the number of threads per inch needed for your receiver. For my Panda that is 18tpi.

28.1. You need to know your lathe, and its individual threading characteristics. We are going to make multiple threading passes to cut the thread to depth, so it figures that we want to follow the same groove every time we make a pass. My machine is equipped with a threading dial with numbers at 1, 3, 6, and 9 o'clock and marks at 1.30, 4.30, 7.30 and 10.30 (Photo 3-19). In order to cut a thread we need to drop the lead screw dog into engagement, at a pre determined point on the dial, every time we make a cut. For instance, if I am cutting a thread pitch of 16 threads per inch, I can drop the dog in at any point on the dial; that is any o'clock, any mark, and anywhere in between. Very convenient! Why can't all receiver threads be 16tpi? For the 18tpi thread we will be cutting for my Panda, I can only drop the dog in at a number for every cut, or at a mark for every cut, not both. If I am cutting a metric thread, I have to keep the dog engaged, and shut off the motor at the end of the cut, quickly backing the tool out, then reverse the motor back to the beginning to make the next cut. So, sort out what your machine requires before proceeding any further.

PHOTO 3-19.

My thread chasing dial at the point where I will drop in the lead screw dog. Also can be seen the carriage longitudinal measuring dial.

29. Set the lathe running at 30rpm, and bring the threading tool close to the barrel shank, using only the cross-slide, to the zero we set in Step 27. Move it back behind the barrel tenon using the carriage feed, and put some cutting oil on the barrel shank with a brush. For my Panda, I will now wait until the indicator reaches a number on the dial, and then engage the lead screw dog. The threading tool will now be moving towards the head stock.

29.1. The cutting oil I use is Rocol Ultracut Metal Working Fluid. It is fantastic threading oil for use on both lathe threading and tap and die threading. I apply it with a small bristle brush before every threading pass, brushing off any chips first, and then applying the fluid.

30. Using the compound rest slide, advance the threading tool until it is just beginning to mark the barrel shank, and zero the dial on the compound slide.

30.1. By the time you zero the compound rest dial the threading tool will have marked the barrel shank for probably ¾ of its length. That's fine.

30.2. If you can't get the slide dial zeroed in time, back it out, disengage the dog, and come at it again. A little practice will have you doing this easily.

31. When you have the compound rest dial zeroed, back the tool out using the cross-slide handle. Wind it back to the rear of the barrel shank with the carriage feed, brush the chips away and shut off the machine.

32. Using a thread gauge — in my Pandas case an 18TPI one, check that you are cutting the correctly pitched thread.

32.1. *Do this!* I once cut a thread for a Remington model 700 without double checking, and when it was to depth wondered why it wouldn't fit, only to discover I had the gearbox set on 2 instead of 1. So, I cut an 18TPI thread instead of 16TPI. How I managed to cut the whole 18TPI thread without missing the index point (see 28.1, page 103) beats me, but I did. I double check it every time now. I wonder why!

33. To make the thread we will make multiple passes, each one a little deeper than the last. Wind the cross-slide wheel back to 0 on its dial, and advance the compound rest wheel .010" on the dial. Start the lathe running at 30RPM, apply cutting oil to the shank, and when the thread indicator dial (again for my Panda) points at any number, drop in the lead screw dog. The threading tool will follow the marks it made previously (if it doesn't back it out toot smart and find out why), and begin cutting the thread. Watch it closely. I use 4x magnifying glasses so I can see it better. When the tool is within about 1/10" of the shoulder of the tenon, snap the cross-slide handle down (and thereby the tool out) at the same time disengaging the lead screw dog. A bit of coordination required here. Practice it until it is second nature to you.

33.1. We have now delineated the end of our thread. We have to back out the cross-slide, and disengage the lead screw dog, at or just before that point every time we make a cut. You need to concentrate, because if you over cut you will break off the tip of the tool or worse, spin the barrel blank in the chuck, both requiring much extra work to fix. If that happens you won't be alone. Both disasters have happened to me more than once.

33.2. A .010" cut is ok for the first pass, but for subsequent cuts it will be too aggressive, for my liking, if we maintain that depth of cut. I don't want to over stress my setup, or my threading tool, so I monitor the cut and how the machine is reacting to it, and adjust the depth as needed. Generally it goes something like this. Pass 1: .010", pass 2: .010", pass 3: .005", pass 4: .005", pass 5: .0025" for several passes, then reduce to .001" until the receiver starts onto the thread. At that point I will be making only .0005" passes. All of these cuts, up to this point, are made by advancing the compound rest only. For each cut the cross-slide is returned to zero, following its quick disengagement at the end of the cut.

PHOTO 3-20.

Cutting the thread on the barrel tenon. I am about half way to depth here, taking a .0015" cut. With this 18TPI thread it is expedient to stop the lathe at the end of each cut, as by doing this the indexing for the next cut is correct, with the threading tool ready to start the next cut. If the thread pitch was 16TPI, I would leave the lathe running because there is no need to drop the dog in at a specific place.

33.3. Because we set the compound rest at 590, and we are cutting a 60° thread, you will notice that, as the cut deepens, the tool is only cutting on the leading edge (the one closest to the chuck). This is done to ease the load on the cutting tool, and on the setup.

33.4. You will also notice, that as we deepen the cut, the tool moves forward. This is the reason we did not run our first cut right up to the shoulder of the tenon. We need a bit of clearance to allow for this forward movement.

34. The thread fit I aim for, is to be able to screw the receiver all of the way against the shoulder *easily,* back it out about .005", and have no movement when I try to move the receiver up and down at the rear tang. To achieve that fit requires a deal of patience, and a little bit of cunning, as it will need a good number of threading passes, and some second guessing at what is happening with the thread inside the receiver. I have it pretty well worked out, on my machine, at what depth I will start to check whether the receiver will start to screw onto the tenon thread. Mostly knowledge gained from experience.

35. When I reach that predetermined depth, .030" in the case of my Panda, I stop the threading tool at the end of the cut and try the receiver on the thread. Clean the chips off first of course. From now on I will be trying the fit of the receiver on the thread after every pass. This can be pretty tedious but, unless you don't care whether or not you end up with a good rattling fit, it is very necessary. By now I am taking cuts .001" deep on the compound rest slide.

36. Finally after a .001" pass the receiver will accept the tenon thread, probably by only a 1/16TH to an 1/8TH of a turn. Now it is time to pick up that 1° clearance on the thread that we made when we set the compound rest to 59° instead of 60°. On the next pass leave the compound rest slide where it is, and increase the depth of your cut by .001" using only the cross-slide adjustment. You will probably only need to make 2 or 3 passes, adjusting the cross-slide only, (and trying the receiver fit after every pass) to fully engage the cutting tool, on both of its faces, thus making your thread a true 60°. By this time the receiver is probably engaging the thread by one to two turns before tightening up.

37. Now I juggle both the compound rest slide and cross-slide depth in order to keep the pressure of the cut at the minimum. What I am about is making my main cut on the front face of the tool, while just making a skimming cut on the back face of the tool. I base the amount I advance both adjustments depending on how the cut looks. Probably .0005" on the cross-slide and .00025" for the compound rest slide. If I see the cutting tool is not skimming enough on its rear face I will advance the cross-slide a little extra on the next cut to catch it up.

38. With every pass the receiver is screwing further onto the thread. By now I will be winding the carriage well behind the barrel tenon in order to get a clear go at the end of the barrel. You must be sure the threads are very clean, at this point, before trying the receiver for fit, and be very careful screwing it on. The last thing we want is for the threads to seize up, which can easily happen if you get too aggressive, especially with stainless steel receivers fitted to stainless steel barrels. Remember the fit I said I wanted. Screw on easily — not tight. At the first indication of tightness back the receiver out and take another cut.

39. Finally the receiver will be screwing on easily to within a couple of turns of the breeching face, at the end of the barrel tenon, before tightening up on the thread. At this point I advance only the cross-slide .0001" to .0002" at a time until the receiver screws easily all the way up to the breeching face. The threading tool will be cutting on both of its faces making a true 60° thread, and I will have done all I can possibly do to make a perfect threading job. The thread thus cut will be smooth, bright and shiny, as in Photo 3-21.

40. As I said, my Panda is an example of a simple fitting job. No extra work is required before we turn our attention to chambering. No thread relief is needed, as that is in the receiver threads, and no extra work at the rear of the blank, as the bolt nose is flat. Also my Panda is blessed with a parallel threading job in the receiver, which makes life easy. Not all receivers are blessed like this. I'd better pause here and discuss this in more detail.

Many receivers you encounter will not have parallel threads, but will have threads tapered to a degree, some more than others. This isn't done by design. Probably it comes about during heat treatment, or even from a slightly tapered thread cutting tool. Whatever the cause, it is our lot to have to deal with it. You may be able to get an idea of what to expect if the receiver already has a custom barrel fitted, though probably not. I don't think I have ever seen a barrel threading job that wasn't a good rattling fit.

PHOTO 3-21.

The finished thread. You can see the scratch where my first thread end delineating pass was made, and the amount the threading tool has moved forward, because our depth of cut was made from the compound rest to ease the load on the cutting tool and the setup. Note that each pass has stayed well away from the end of the thread.

Unless you have fitted a barrel to the receiver before, and know its characteristics, my advice is to proceed very carefully. If you proceed to blithely deepen a thread, without any consideration for a possible taper in the receiver thread, you will end up with a thread that engages only at the back, and is very loose from there forward. When you back such a job away from the breeching face, a bit, the rear tang will probably wiggle up and down 1/8" or more. Not much precision there. Figure 3-3 demonstrates what I am on about here.

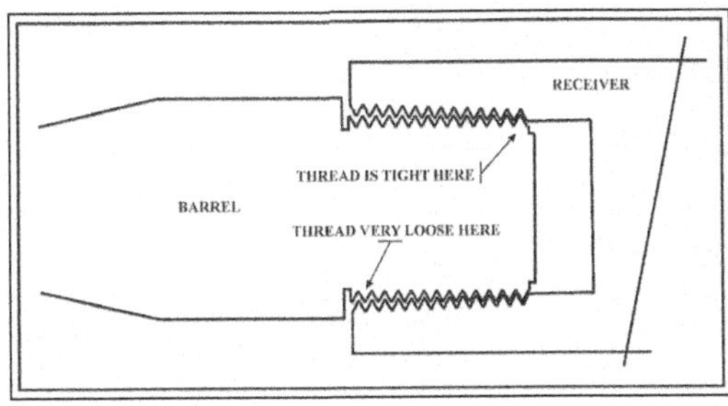

FIGURE 3-3.

If you do not allow for a tapered receiver thread your barrel thread will make contact only at the end of the receiver thread, and miss the threads from there forward, as in this drawing.

What I do, is begin to test for receiver taper when the receiver will screw onto the thread a little less than ¼ of the way. I do this by taking my next pass only ¼ of the way along the thread, and then backing the tool out with the cross-slide slowly, while the barrel is still turning. If the receiver will still screw on the thread the same amount, there's a good chance there is no, or very little taper in the thread. If, however, the receiver makes an extra turn, or partial turn, on the thread, then you are certainly dealing with a tapered thread. If the receiver didn't go on any further, I would take my next pass at the same depth setting as the previous one. In other words finish the previous cut, and see how the receiver fits. Try and suss it out by backing it off ½ a turn from its stop point, and wriggle it about and see if there is any slack there. If there is none proceed, but if there is best stop and think about it. If the receiver went on an extra turn I would take another cut a little deeper, but this time only cut 1/8TH of the way along the thread before backing the tool out, and trying the receiver again. This can be really tedious, and obtaining a good fit comes down to experience and feel. In the end it is possible to make a really good fitting threading job, on taper threaded receivers, by proceeding carefully a bit at a time. You will pretty well have to contend with this when fitting barrels to every unmodified factory action you encounter, so be prepared to deal with it. Even custom target actions may have a little bit of taper in the receiver threads. Be mindful that it will take very little taper, maybe only .0001" to bind the threads on a precision job, so look for it in every job you do. It does feel good, though, when you make that perfect threading job.

41. You may remember we went to some trouble in step #17 to find the high point at the muzzle, and mark its position at the breech end with the word 'up', and a line in texta. Now we will make use of that. With the receiver screwed all the way on to the thread, and butted against the breeching face of the barrel, I now take note of the position of the top of the receiver in relation to the texta mark we made previously, denoting the top of the run out at the muzzle. If the two do not coincide (and they probably won't) I face back the breeching face until I can screw the receiver on, and the centre of the top, or the bottom of the receiver, comes to a stop about a lines width before the line we marked on the barrel blank. It will tighten up to the line when it is fully breached. Don't forget to face off the rear end of the barrel a corresponding amount to maintain bolt clearance. See Photo 3-22.

Photo 3-22.

I had to set the barrel tenon back .013" to index the receiver like this. When the barrel is finally tightened the index point will be exactly where I want it.

41.1. I will be the first to admit that I have absolutely no basis in fact to warrant indexing the receiver like this. Rim fire bench-rest shooters are of the opinion that a barrel indexed to print its groups at the 12 o'clock position shoots its best groups in that position. I'm not actually doing that. The direction the projectile is actually heading in, is more dependant on where the last inch of bore is pointing, when the bullet exits, rather than where the mass of the barrel is pointing.

41.2. There is little doubt that vertical barrel oscillations can be detected when tuning a rifle, as best groups occur when they are printing either high or low on the target. Groups in between exhibit vertical dispersion, and we are looking to find the top or bottom of the barrels oscillation when we are trying to tune that vertical out. *So, one could rationalize that it would be a good thing to point the mass of the barrel either up or down, if you have that option, rather than off to the side.*

41.3. I prefer to turn the receiver in less than half a turn, so I am satisfied if the 'up' index mark lines up at the middle bottom of the receiver; that is with the mass of the barrel pointing down. In other words I will take the first indexing point that is within a half a turn or less of the original breeching position. *Just as long as the barrel doesn't point out to one side or the other.* As I said, I have no proof that it would be better one way or the other. It's just something I think I should do, so I am passing the information on. Make of it what you will.

Moving along, it's time for the next step. To simplify things for me I will describe chambering our barrel blank in 7mm Remington Short Action Ultra Magnum, which is the calibre I use with my Panda action. It's a good example because it is a little tricky to do dimension wise. You will see why.

42. Double check your setup with the range rod before proceeding. If you have not been aggressive with your turning, threading and receiver trying on there should be no change. If there is, it will be miniscule, but correct it before going any further.

43. Install a drill chuck in the tailstock. Now, select an appropriate diameter sharp twist drill, depending on the calibre you are going to be chambering. For my 7 Saum I will be using a 12mm twist drill. A couple of other examples I have used: 6x47 Lapua 10mm, .22ppc 8.5mm. Lay the drill along side a cartridge case with the point just behind the shoulder of the case, and mark it with a texta where the end of the barrel will be. Don't forget the case head may protrude from the end of the barrel, and don't get overly ambitious. We don't want to drill too deep here. Too shallow is better.

44. Install the drill in the chuck, and using plenty of lubricant, drill out the end of the barrel blank up to the mark that you made.

PHOTO 3-23.
Pre-drilling the rear of the barrel prior to taper boring it.

45. Now open up the hole you drilled with another appropriately sized twist drill, ½" for my 7 Saum (6x47–11mm, and .22ppc–10mm). Be careful not to increase the depth you cut previously. Your drill will cut closer to correct size doing it like this.

46. Select a small boring bar and mount it on the lathe tool post as you would for boring a small hole. Be sure the cutting edge is sharp.

47. Draw two texta marks on the flat face of your compound rest the same distance apart as the length your chamber will be. Adjust the angle of the compound rest so that it has about one half of a degree of taper towards the chamber.

48. Mount a dial indicator on the headstock of the lathe so that the probe is at the front mark on the compound rest, and zero the indicator. Now, using the carriage feed, advance the carriage until the indicator probe reaches the second mark. The indicator dial is now showing the amount of taper, in thousandths of an inch, of the compound rest over the length of the chamber you will be cutting. Photo 3-24 shows what I am talking about here.

PHOTO 3-24.

Adjusting the taper of the compound rest. You can see the two texta marks denoting the length of the body of my chamber. It is only a matter of moving the carriage back and forth with the carriage feed wheel from mark to mark, and adjusting the angle of the compound rest until you have the taper you require. Then lock it down and recheck.

The taper we want is chamber taper in thousands of an inch divided by two. In practice a thousandth or two extra taper won't hurt. Certainly, it is better than a thousandth or two less taper. The taper I use for my 7 Saum is .0075" over 1.400"—that is about .001" more than the actual chamber taper and works fine. Adjust the compound rest until you get the taper you want then lock it down and remove the dial indicator.

49. Wind the compound rest all the way forward until it stops. Using the cross-slide, and saddle travel, place the tip of the boring tool just inside the hole we drilled, and very close to the outside diameter of the hole. In other words about .005" back from where it would touch the side of the hole. Now advance it into the hole carefully with the saddle travel until it bumps into the end of the hole. Put a texta mark on the bar even with the back of the barrel for future reference, and lock the longitudinal travel stop down tight. Now move the cutting tool away from the edge of the hole with the cross-slide adjustment, around .020" to 030", and bring it out of the hole with the compound rest screw, until the tip of the tool is just at the end of the barrel. When we wind the tool back with the compound rest wheel we are bringing it out on the taper. We do not want it to run into the side of the hole half way out.

50. Start the lathe, running at about 570rpm, and using the compound rest wheel, and the cross-slide, place the tool tip just inside the drilled hole. Back out the cross-slide wheel, until the tool just touches the surface of the drilled hole, and zero the reading on the cross-slide dial.

51. What we are going to do now is taper bore the hole to size using the feed on the compound rest. What we will end up with is a hole that is tapered very closely to our reamer taper. It will be running perfectly true to the axis of the centre-line of the lathe spindle, *and of the 2" section of barrel just in front of the chamber,* which we will be reaming shortly.

51.1. Now we have to be very careful. My 7 Saum is a perfect example of how close to disaster we can find ourselves sailing when doing this job.

51.2. What we want to do is bore the hole to a diameter where *the pilot of the reamer is engaged in the bore of the barrel, and the shoulder of the reamer is engaged in the bored hole.* When we achieve this the reamer is fully supported in the barrel, and lined up perfectly with the centre-line of the lathe spindle.

PHOTO 3-25.

Taper boring the drilled hole in the rear of the barrel, to true it with the 2" section of bore, immediately in front of the chamber, and size it to accept the reamer as per the text.

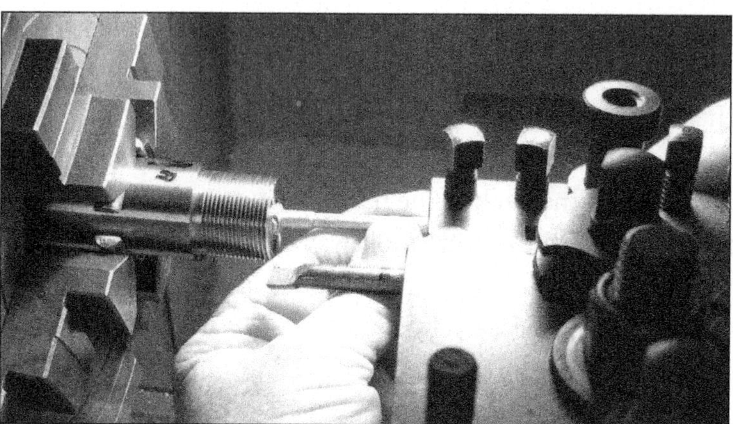

PHOTO 3-26.

Measuring the taper bored hole at the very rear prior to bringing it to size to accept the chambering reamer.

Time to digress! How are we going to feed the reamer into the barrel, or more importantly how are we going to feed it into the barrel accurately?

With our reamer fully supported in a taper bored hole lined up with the axis of the centre of the lathe spindle, an option would be to use a reamer pusher. A reamer pusher is a tool that fits in the tail-stock with a clearance of at least .020" around the reamer shank, and simply pushes against the reamer holder, not guiding the reamer at all but letting it find its own way into the barrel. Photo 3-29 (Page 116) shows one I made, and Photo 3-28 shows it mounted in the lathe. If you will go to Chapter Five, 'Reloading Dies', and have a look at Photo 5-10 (Page 204) you will see another shot of it that may show its operation a little clearer.

Conventional wisdom says that a reamer will always follow a hole. That may be true, but only up to a point. I would think it *very unlikely* that a reamer would follow a bore sized hole accurately, especially if it was started with a reamer pusher. However, I would think that given the way we have prepared to ream, as described above, there is a good chance that a reamer will follow our bored hole using a pusher, but I have never tried it out because I am not a fan of reamer pushers. I much prefer my reamer to be positively supported and guided on its way into the bored hole.

PHOTO 3-27.

The reamer is inserted, into the bored hole, with its pilot fully engaged in the bore of the barrel, and its shoulder fully engaged in the bored hole. There is no discernible movement at all when I try to wobble the reamer at its rear. *The reamer is positively held dead in line with that important 2" of bore just in front of where the chamber will end.* You can also see the tool I used to bore the hole.

We can support the reamer using a centre mounted in the tailstock of the lathe and engaged in the centre in the back of the reamer. However, if we are going to do it like this, we have to question how accurately aligned to the centre-line of the lathe spindle is our centre mounted in the tail-stock. The answer to that is mostly *not* accurate enough.

PHOTO 3-28.

A reamer pusher set up ready to chamber a barrel. The reamer is fully supported by its pilot in the bore and by its shoulder in the bored hole. The reamer holder has a groove at the back indicating that its rear face is perfectly square with the hole that the reamer is secured in. Note that the back of the reamer is inside the bore of the pusher with clearance all around. The end face of the Pusher will engage the reamer holder and apply force to push the reamer into the bored hole. The pusher *supposedly* exerts no influence on the reamer, which is free to find its own way into the hole.

The tail-stock on a lathe is able to be adjusted horizontally but not vertically, and they are manufactured to be a little high to allow for wear. If your lathe is old it may well be low. I guess at some time in its life it will be actually on centre. I use the tailstock with a centre installed to positively guide the reamer into the bored hole. It is one I made to be dead accurate with the centre-line of the spindle of the lathe, and I did it like this.

A. Set up a Morse taper between centres in the lathe and, using a dial indicator, adjust the angle of the compound rest until it is true to the Morse taper.

B. Chuck a piece of old barrel steel in the 4 jaw chuck and true it.

C. Taper turn the barrel steel, using the compound rest feed, to a diameter that will fit into the female Morse taper in your tailstock about 1.000", and polish it. If you have the taper right, 1.000" is plenty for the female Morse taper to hold it firm and square.

D. While it is still in the lathe, find the point where it exits the female Morse taper in the tail stock, and cut a groove about .020" in front of that point about .100" deep, and wide enough to accept a screw driver blade.

E. Remove the piece, cut it off about .200" in front of the groove, replace it in the chuck, face it off, and break the sharp edge with a file.

F. Notch it with a file to make a mark on the outside edge, and insert it into the Morse taper in the tailstock with the notch up. It doesn't need to be very tight, so don't over do it or it will be hard to extract.

G. We are going to bore this piece through with a boring bar held in the 4 jaw chuck, so select an appropriate sized boring bar. Mine just happened to bore a .447" diameter hole.

H. Mount a trued appropriate sized drill in the lathe chuck, and drill through the part to hog out the excess material.

I. Mount and true the boring bar in the chuck, and wind the tailstock into the position you will be using when reaming from now on. Whatever convenient position you want to use is ok, as long as you can return to it.

J. Bring the tailstock up to the boring bar, and using the tailstock feed bore the part right through. Remove the boring bar and remove the part from the tailstock. Lever it out with screwdrivers in the groove.

K. Now, we have to make a centre that will be a slip fit in the hole we bored in our part. Use oil hardening drill rod and turn the shank to be a very close fit in the bored hole in our part. You may want to lap it in with 400 grit lapping paste.

L. Reverse it in the chuck, and set it up true to the turned shank. Using the compound rest turn a 60° taper on it.

When installed, this part is lined up with the centre-line of the spindle in the headstock, and will positively support and guide the reamer accurately. When the reamer starts, it will be held in 3 places, all in line with the centre-line of the headstock spindle, and will give us our best possible chance of cutting a chamber that will start a projectile dead straight into the bore, directly in front of the chamber.

Another plus for this setup, is it will positively support and guide a separate throating reamer — *something a reamer pusher will not do.*

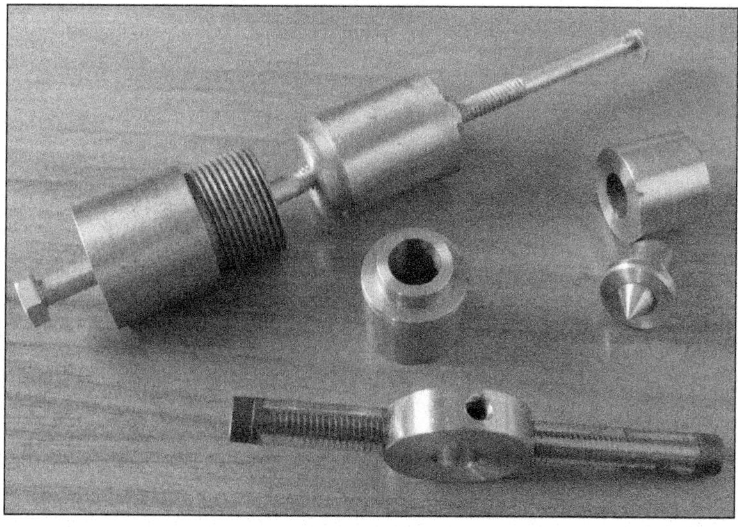

PHOTO 3-29.

From the top, the knockout tool I use to remove the Morse tapered pieces. You won't need this if you groove it as per my instructions. In the middle is the reamer pusher *I don't use*, and at the bottom my reamer holder. On the right are the centre and its Morse tapered holder that I prefer to use.

In use, I always set the tailstock feed in the same place to begin reaming, and advance it only .200". Then the carriage is moved forward .195", the tailstock feed backed out .200" and I start again. I am always reaming within the same .200" of tailstock travel. Back to the job at hand!

51.3. Typically my 7 Saum will go something like this. Remember the dial on the cross-slide is already zeroed. With the machine running, back the tool out of the hole, and back out the cross-slide adjustment .010" on the dial. Now get some cutting oil inside the hole. I put it in the mouth of the hole with a brush, and then blow it softly right into the hole with my compressed air gun. Now advance the compound rest, taking a tapered cut until the compound rest runs into the end of its travel. Wind the cross-slide wheel in .005", to clear the tip of the cutting tool from the surface of the hole, and wind the compound rest out until the tool clears the hole. Blow the chips out of the hole and measure the diameter at the very back of the hole.

51.4. If your drill was sharp and true you should have bored out any eccentricity. If not take another cut, just enough to make the hole run true.

51.5. Here's what you have to be aware of. My 7 Saum finish reamer, which is the only one I will be using (I'll discuss why shortly), is quite short from the pilot to the shoulder of the case, and the 7 Saum has very little taper over the length of its body. In order to have the reamer engage the pilot in the bore, and be supported at the shoulder inside the bored hole, I have to taper bore the hole to a diameter of .540" at the back of the barrel. Thus bored, the shoulder of the reamer will have to go into the hole nearly ½ way to allow the pilot to be engaged in the bore, and I will be left with only .007" (.0035" per side) of material to ream out, as my finish reamed chamber measures .547" diameter at the rear of the hole.

51.6. The upshot of the above is, until you know the characteristics of your reamer go very carefully with step 51 — you don't want to overdo it. Take small cuts and try the reamer in often. Once you know what to expect subsequent jobs will be less hair raising.

52. With the hole taper bored to size, remove the boring bar and wind the cross-slide all the way back. Zero the angle of the compound rest and wind it all the way forward. Place the centre parts we made previously in the tailstock, and a jar of reamer lubricant at a handy place on the saddle of the lathe. I have used BP Sevora 68 for over 45 years, having lucked upon it straight up when I first started fitting barrels. It's a terrific reamer oil — heavy consistency so it sticks to the reamer, and I have never needed to look for anything else. Be careful adding additives to it, however. When I discovered Rocol Ultracut it was so good I thought it could only enhance Sevora 68. Wrong! I mixed some up according to instructions and it very nearly seized the reamer in the chamber. Sevora 68 works fine on its own. You might want to put some padding on the flat surface of the compound rest, as you will be resting your arm on there for a bit.

53. Select your reamer, fit the -0001" pilot you found previously to it, and secure it into your reamer holder.

53.1. I mentioned previously that I only use a finishing reamer for the 7 Saum I am fitting. This is because I am only doing my own work these days, and I won't be cutting a lot of 7 Saum chambers, so I am saving a couple of hundred dollars by only having a finish reamer. However, if I were to still be a working gunsmith I would certainly have a matching roughing reamer to do the donkey work on a lot of chambers. The added advantage of a roughing reamer is you will be able to bore the hole in the rear of the barrel some .005" smaller. It will, however, add to the time it takes to do the job, but will ease the load on the finish reamer and keep it sharp for much longer.

53.2. I made my reamer holder from a piece of barrel steel and a couple of Allen head screws. You can see it in Photo 3-29. (Page 116) If you were to use a reamer pusher (*I don't*) the rear face of the holder needs to be square to the hole that has been bored through it. You will notice a groove on my holder. That denotes the square face. The other face doesn't matter. My reamer pusher can also be seen in Photo 3-29. (Page 116) The reamers I am using are in Photo 3-30.

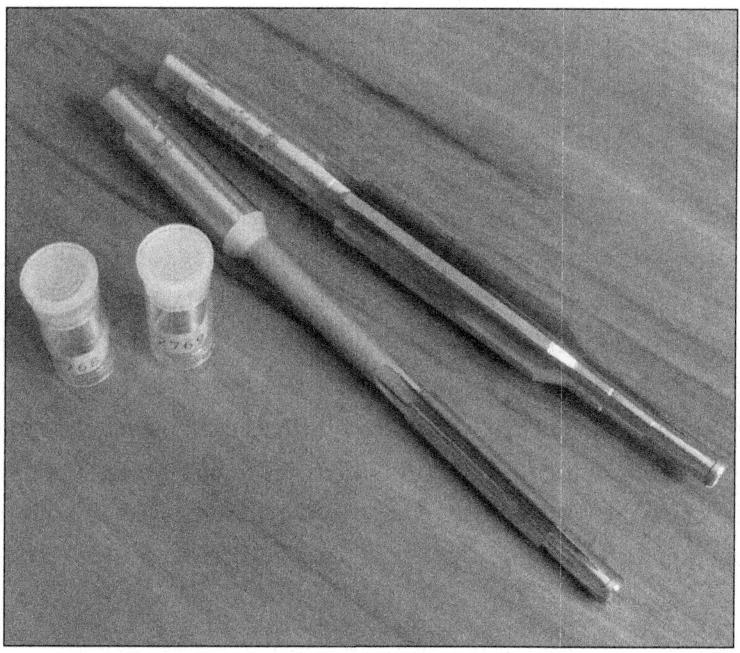

PHOTO 3-30.

The chambering reamer, throating reamer and pilots used on the 7 SAUM job described in the text. All made by Hugh Henriksen.

54. Set your lathe to run at slow speed. My slowest is 30RPM and this is fine. Run it fast if you like, but you will only be screwing the reamer over — false economy. Have your compressed air gun handy, blow out the hole in the end of the barrel, and the centre in the end of the reamer to clean them. Dip the reamer in the reaming oil, make sure your tail-stock ram is in the right position with the dial set at zero, and place the reamer centre in the centre in the tailstock. Bring the reamer carefully into the hole until it just begins to touch. Don't advance it any further yet. Lock the tail-stock in position.

55. Now with the machine still running wind the saddle back against the tailstock and lock it down so that it acts as a stop for the tailstock travel. Also, apply enough pressure to the lock down on your tailstock ram so that there is a little bit of resistance when you turn the wheel. You will need to change the position of your hand on the feed wheel while reaming, and this will prevent the wheel from rotating on its own when you let go of it. Pretty important, as you want to maintain a constant feed once you start reaming.

55.1. Depending on the makeup of your lathe, you may find your hand and arm holding the reamer a little cramped. If so use a spacer between the back of the saddle and the front of the tailstock. I need to use a spacer on my lathe to be comfortable. It is simply a block of aluminum about 2" long.

56. We are already running and lubed up, so we might as well take a cut. Feed the reamer into the barrel blank using the tailstock feed wheel. The feed rate you use will be variable depending on how the reamer feels as it is cutting, and depending on what stage of the chambering you are at.

PHOTO 3-31.

I have just removed the reamer after taking the first .200" cut. Note how well lubricated the reamer, and the rear of the chamber is. Your chambering reamers must be well lubricated at all times.

56.1. I have taken note when I have been chambering and have found that I am comfortable when the reamer is advancing at about .002" per revolution of the lathe. So I am advancing about .060" per minute.

56.2. How deep you should cut is also dependant on the results you are getting while the job is in progress. *Of utmost importance is to keep the reamer well lubricated at all times.* We want to avoid, at all cost, running the reamer dry, for obvious reasons. Some enterprising guys run oil through the bore, from the muzzle, under pressure to clear the chips away, and keep the reamer lubricated. Apart from the mess that creates, it's not an ideal fix. The oil will follow the path of least resistance, and if one reamer flute clogs with swarf it will bypass that flute and travel to the next clear flute, leaving the first flute dry, and in danger of scoring the chamber. I don't like that idea. You may well be of a different opinion.

56.3. Be careful to hold the reamer with even pressure, and advance it into the barrel smoothly.

56.4. This first cut will be skimming the body of the chamber at the shoulder only, actually removing very little material so, as the reamer is well lubed, we can make the cut a full .200" deep. This is the maximum amount I will advance the tailstock before resetting it.

57. With the cut at depth, hold the tailstock wheel in the 0 position for at least one and a half revolutions of the lathe, then back it out a bit, unlock the tailstock and slide it out all the way. Keep the reamer engaged in the tailstock center, and bring it out of the partially cut chamber with the tailstock. Remove the reamer and look at it, noting whether it is still sufficiently lubricated or not, and with your compressed air gun blow it off, and blow the chips out of the barrel.

57.1. There is going to be a lot of chips and atomized oil flying around during this operation, so you might want to consider using eye and breathing protection while doing this job.

57.2. I sit my reamer oil on a paper towel that also goes under the lathe chuck to catch any oil dripping from the reamer, or the end of the barrel. I also place a paper towel at the end of the muzzle to catch any oil and chips that will be flying out. Place it about one inch back from the muzzle, as you don't want to block it and prevent the air escaping. If you do, chips and oil will be trapped at the end of the chamber, and will cause problems.

57.3. Its not that you are using a lot of oil here, but more that a little bit goes a long way when blown around by compressed air. You'll get the picture quickly enough.

58. With the chamber cleaned up I wind my tailstock back .200" to zero. Zero the dial on my saddle wheel, unlock the saddle, move it forward .195", lock it again, and I am ready to take the next cut.

58.1. Typically, cutting the chamber for my 7 Saum will go something like this: 1 x .200", 1 x .200", 1 x .100", 1 x .100", (neck of the chamber begins to cut), 2 x .025", remainder .010" until the shoulder of the chamber takes up. The depth of cut then depends entirely on how well the reamer is lubed after each cut. I will end up taking only .005" cuts.

58.2. You need to feel what the reamer is doing and take note of its feed back. If you sense a problem back it out and check what is happening.

59. When the shoulder of the reamer is fully engaged in the barrel it is time to check the depth of the chamber you are making. We already know how much of the case we need to have sticking out of the chamber. Remember — measurement A minus measurement C, back in steps 18, 19 and 20, = measurement D. (Pages i)

59.1. If you are doing this professionally you would be making this measurement with a 'go' head-space gauge, and use head-space gauges to make a properly head-spaced commercial job.

59.2. However, I am doing this job for myself and want it to end up in a particular way. *I would be very freer of doing it like this for anyone else.* These days waivers are not worth the paper they are signed on, and if the customer who begs you to do it this way, even though he seems a good bloke, does something stupid, and blows himself up, its on the cards he will be looking to blame someone other than his own stupid self. That someone is likely to be you. Finally, I have no idea how extra tight head-space could ever cause a problem, but no doubt they will find a way.

59.3. I'll be using the cartridge case I selected earlier, using the case length gauge and head-space gauge we made — one with minimum head-space dimensions.

60. Blow the chips out of the chamber after your last pass, and then wipe it out with a cleaning patch held on a piece of split rod like the one you see in Photo 3-32. Pop the gauge in the chamber

(case in my case) and with a depth micrometer measure the distance from the rear of the gauge to the rear of the barrel blank. This is our protrusion measurement. We simply deduct measurement D from that measurement, and that is the amount we still need to ream the chamber to make head-space. If you did everything right you will still have something up to .100" to deepen the chamber by. I am measuring in Photo 3-33.

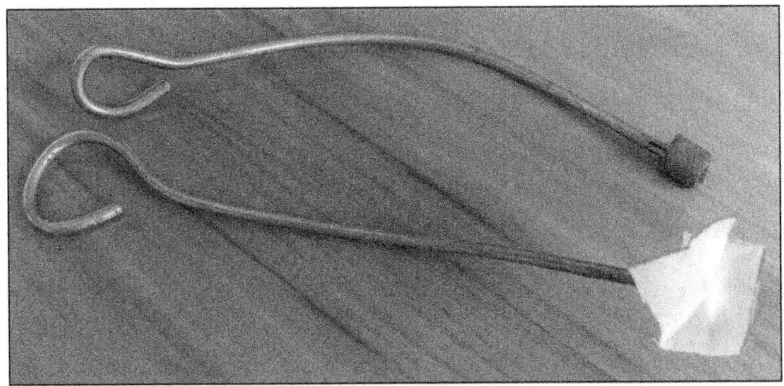

PHOTO 3-32.
Split rod chamber polishing and cleaning tools. The polishing rod has a short piece of 320 grit abrasive cloth on it from my last die polishing job. When polishing a rifle chamber I will use the full 1" width of abrasive cloth.

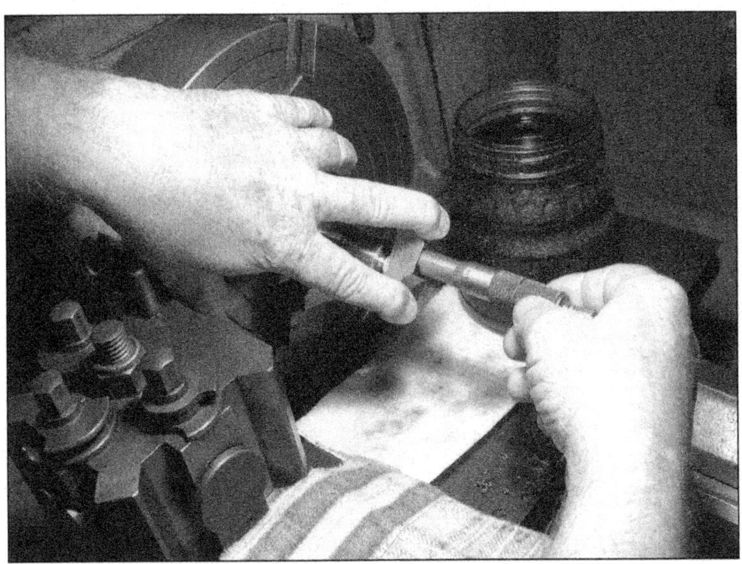

PHOTO 3-33.
Measuring case head protrusion for head-space. I have .016" left to ream here.

60.1. Heaven forbid if you have gone too far. If that happens go in to the minimum depth to make the chamber whole and stop. You will now have to adjust head-space by moving the barrel tenon (and the back of the barrel) forward the amount needed to make head-space, keeping in mind you want the barrel indexed up or down.

60.2. Proceed carefully now. I am taking my head-space measurement using my specially prepared case. If you are using head-space gauges you will find it very difficult to make a precise measurement from the back of the barrel, because the gauges are considerably undersize to the chamber. The rule of thumb here is be careful not to ream the chamber too deep. Measure carefully, and stop early. Your reamer will be making a lot of swarf that will be clogging the flutes, and removing the cutting oil away from the cutting surface. You will want to reduce the depth of each cut accordingly, depending on what you observe when you remove the reamer after the last cut. I am generally only making .010" cuts at this stage. If it takes me ten cuts to make .100" that's ok — I really like to look after my reamers.

61. When you think you are within about .015" from final depth, it's time to screw on the receiver, and start checking final dimensions.

61.1. Clean everything up, and screw the receiver on, to about half a turn before the breeching face. If your bolt has an ejector, remove it. My Panda doesn't.

61.2. Slip your 'go' gauge under the extractor of the bolt (case in my case — no pun intended), insert the bolt in the action, and close it. If there is interference when you try to close it, back the receiver out a little more.

61.3. Now screw the receiver in carefully until it stops. The 'go' gauge will now be centred in the chamber, and held firmly against the bolt face.

61.4. We can now measure the distance we need to deepen the chamber, by inserting feeler gauges in the gap between the breeching face and the front of the receiver. I am doing just that in Photo 3-34. In theory, if we can fit .015" of feeler gauge in that gap, and then, if we deepen the chamber .015", and reinstall the receiver fully up to the breeching face, the bolt should close on our 'go' gauge with zero clearance. Well, yes and no. Let's talk about head-space.

PHOTO 3-34.

Measuring head-space with a .006" feeler gauge inserted in the receiver breeching face. I can just feel the bolt tighten on my special head-spacing case, which tells me I have .006" left to ream.

Head-space is the gap between the shoulder of the case and the shoulder of the chamber, with the head of the cartridge case firmly against the bolt face. Given the world of tolerances in which we live, if you fit a barrel using SAAMI specification gauges you are guaranteed a degree of head-space. Remember our SAAMI specs for a maximum cartridge? +0 –.008". These tolerances guarantee that every cartridge will fit in every chamber, and the maximum head-space thus created will never be a dangerous condition.

The absolute minimum head-space, preferably zero, is very desirable provided flawless function is maintained. You really want every cartridge to fit in the chamber without any problem. Why is minimum head-space desirable?

When you fire the rifle the force of the primers ignition will try very hard to drive the case forward in the chamber. That little primer, you don't think much of, has a quite explosive force, and if there is any head-space in the chamber it will easily drive the case forward, at the same time pushing the primer cup out of the back of the case the corresponding amount. When the powder ignites and pressure builds, the thin walls of the case, at the front, expand and grip the walls of the chamber very tightly. This phenomenon is not generally understood, but it is an essential part of the overall system, and its function is to reduce the thrust load on the bolt caused by some 60,000psi of chamber pressure. If you want to be stupid and test it, simply get something like a 243 Winchester and lube your cartridges with case sizing lube before firing them. You will find it won't take very many shots before you blow the rifle up, even though the load is quite within safety parameters. I know this from hard experience. Seriously, *don't do it.* Just take my word for it.

Anyway, remember, we still have a gap between the case head and the bolt face. There is more than enough chamber pressure generated to stretch the case just in front of the solid head, which is strong enough to resist being forced against the chamber walls, and push the base back against the bolt face, at the same time re-seating the primer cup. When that case is full length re-sized, back to SAAMI specs, the head-space condition will have been recreated, and the same thing will happen. Do this several times and the solid head of that case may well crack off when fired, causing extreme pressure to be transferred to the bolt lugs, and possibly a catastrophic blow up. Obviously, *excess head-space is a condition to be avoided at all costs.*

There is another reason we want to avoid it when building a rifle for accuracy. There is certainly a distinct possibility that slamming the case violently forward in the chamber, then slamming the case head back against the bolt face violently, could have a detrimental effect on the characteristics of our barrel harmonics—especially considering that every case will not react, to the pressures of firing, in exactly the same way. Apart from that, if our chamber has excess head-space, then we need to deal with it. The usual way is by fire forming each case in the barrel, with a projectile jammed in the rifling—the idea being, that the projectile will hold the case against the bolt face, firmly enough, to resist the primers force. That will allow the shoulder of the case to blow forward, thus correcting the excess head-space condition.

Unfortunately barrels have a finite life, and depending on the calibre you are using, fire forming, say, 200 shells for no other purpose than to correct a little bit of head-space could well use up 20% of that valuable life.

The tolerance found in head-space gauges is generally .005". In other words, if the 'go' gauge is 0 then the 'no go' gauge is +.005". To head-space the chamber properly you should be able to shut the bolt on a 'go' gauge, but not be able to shut it on a 'no go' gauge. That's an additional .005" of gap we have over our allowable .008" in the SAAMI specs for a minimum cartridge, so you can see that, if you are using gauges, it is best to keep the head-space measurement as close to the 'go' gauge as possible. Preferably you should just 'feel' the bolt shut on the 'go' gauge.

Another consideration, when head-spacing the chamber, is that when the receiver is tightened up it will probably creep forward anything from .001" to .002", depending on how much you tighten it. This must be taken into consideration when you approach the final depth of your chamber. I tighten my Panda receiver to 100 foot pounds of torque, and experience has taught me that it will creep forward .001" when I do that.

When I head-space my barrel I will be eliminating head-space entirely by head-spacing it to be tight on the short case I selected previously. I will then select a long case that will not fit in the action and full length size it to be a perfect fit in the chamber (more on that in the FLS Die chapter), then FLS all of my cases the same. When I close the bolt on a case I will feel it tighten in the last bit of down swing of the bolt. That case will be firmly held in the chamber with no gap between shoulder and base which is exactly how I want it to be. Got that! Good — lets move on.

62. The dial on my tailstock wheel is perfectly accurate enough to make any head-space dimension I want, however I do not trust to measurements alone when approaching final head-space. I prefer to sneak up on it testing the fit often, with the receiver installed, until I can close the bolt on my head-spacing case feeling a bit of resistance as I do. I will then take a final .001" cut and that part of the reaming job is finished.

63. As I stated previously, I have Hugh grind my reamer throats short to allow me to cut a throat length suitable for any projectile I might want to use. The 7mm Saum reamer I use has a throat length of .100", which is not long enough to accept the Berger 180 grain Hybrid projectiles I use in this rifle. I have to lengthen the throat to accommodate them. This chore is accomplished with a special throating reamer that will cut only the throat itself at .2845" diameter, and the leade in front of the throat at 1½°. It must be supported accurately at the rear end, which it is in my special centre in the tailstock, and it will be supported accurately at the front end by the reamer pilot I was using on my chambering reamer.

63.1. Initially bring the reamer into engagement with the rifling lands as was described in steps 54, 55 and 56. I know I am over .100" short in the throat, on this job, so I will take a .050" cut initially.

PHOTO 3-35.

The throating reamer is well lubricated, and I am about to take a final .045" cut to bring the throat of the chamber to its final dimensions.

63.2. If you are not sure how much you need to lengthen the throat then just engage the reamer in the rifling until you can feel it cutting and stop. If you over cut the throat there is no way to replace the rifling you have removed. Until you know the characteristics of the chamber you are cutting stay on the safe side.

63.3. We do, here, have our carriage locked and our tailstock wheels zeroed don't we? We need to run a couple of patches through the barrel to clean it. Watch out — you will be pushing a deal of oil out of the muzzle with your first patch.

63.4. Take the projectile of your choice, slip it into the chamber, point first, and slide it in until it stops against the rifling. Now, with a depth micrometer, measure the distance from the rear of the projectile to the rear of the barrel. With this measurement in hand it is no problem to work out how much deeper you have to run the reamer in, to make the throat length you want. In my case I want a measurement of 1.400" from the rear of the barrel to the rear of the projectile. *Don't forget* to knock the projectile out before inserting the throating reamer. *Don't forget* to take case head protrusion into account.

63.5. You will be removing very little material when making this cut, and the throating reamer holds Sevora 68 well, so it's ok to take the full cut in one pass even if it is to the order of .100".

63.6. Put everything reamer wise away and prepare the lathe for machining.

64. We need to cut a bit of a leade in at the rear of the chamber to break the sharp edge and facilitate easy cartridge entry.

64.1. I use a crowning tool for this as shown in Photo 3-36, simply set it at a 45 degree angle to the axis of the centre-line of the bore, and with the lathe running, mine at 570RPM, bring it in to the sharp edge at the rear of the chamber, and make a chamfer of about .020" in width. Don't overdo it. We want to keep as much of the head of the case supported as possible.

PHOTO 3-36.

Chamfering the sharp edge at the back of the chamber to facilitate entry of a cartridge.

65. With the lathe running take a bit of worn .320 grit abrasive strip and give the back of the barrel and the chamfer you have just made a bit of a polish. It won't take much to make it bright and shiny.

66. Take another piece of worn 320 grit abrasive strip wrapped around a polishing shaft (Photo 3-32, Page 121) and give the chamber a light cross hatched polish to remove any slight reamer marks. This is just a light lick, probably about 15 to 20 seconds is all it takes to make the chamber shiny.

66.1. With very little effort we can make the chamber we have just cut mirror bright, *but that is the last thing we want to do.* It may look good, and some people might think you are right smart being able make a finish like chrome plating, but the opposite is true. Remember what I talked about previously—about the case being able to grip the chamber being a part of the overall system. Mirror polished surfaces are slippery, and that is not what we want in a chamber. Likewise, we don't want to see reamer marks on our cases, but with a quality reamer, well handled, a light polish, with worn 320 grit abrasive strip, will take care of that, and make a finish the case can still grip while looking the part. Our work at this end of the barrel is finished for now. Photo 3-37 shows the finished job.

PHOTO 3-37.
The completed work at the breech end of the barrel.

67. Reverse the barrel and set it up so that the muzzle is protruding from the chuck about 1½". Zero it with a pin gauge in the muzzle, and because there is a big hole at the other end, either indicate on the back of the chamber, or on the outside of the blank, just in front of the threads. It doesn't matter; your choice. Get it rotating at +/- 0 or at least a couple of tenths of a thou from that.

68. As described in step 4 insert our pieces of ½ round silver steel between the barrel and the chuck jaws, held in place but not tight.

69. Select a correctly fitting reamer pilot that will enter the bore at the muzzle, and will go in about 3". Fit the pilot to your range rod. Lay the rod along side the barrel so that the middle of the pilot is level with the middle of your ½ round pieces in the chuck, and mark the rod with a texta at the end of the barrel, that is, the muzzle. Mount the range rod in the drill chuck in the tailstock of the lathe.

> 69.1. Remember there will probably be a slight choke in the bore of your barrel, so the pilot you used to ream the chamber will no doubt be too tight for the muzzle by .0001" or so.
>
> 69.2. As a precaution always be sure a pilot will go further into the bore than you intend it to go. Otherwise, one day you will jam one in the bore very tightly. Best avoided, rather than dealt with when it happens.

70. Put a drop of oil on the pilot and in the end of the muzzle, and with the lathe rotating by hand, run the rod into the bore until the texta mark is level with the muzzle. Now mount a .0001" dial indicator, as we did in step #11, and adjust the chuck jaws while rotating the barrel, until the dial indicator reads +/- 0. Remember to be holding the barrel only lightly.

71. Still rotating the barrel, back the tailstock feed out until the pilot on the range rod is just inside the muzzle, and again bring the reading on the dial indicator to +/- 0, but this time using the screw adjustments on the spider at the other end of the headstock.

72. Wind the range rod in again, and repeat back and forth until the reading on the dial indicator is +/- 0, with the range rod in both places. Photo 3-38 shows that job in progress, on my 7 Saum. Double check the accuracy with the long probe dial indicator, as in Photo 3-39. (Page 129)

72.1. You will note that the barrel blank, at the chamber end, will be running out, maybe as much as .025". After trueing, the end of the muzzle on this blank ran out .0007" — so much for the accuracy of setup 2!

73. Remove the indicator and range rod, and mount a sharp facing tool on the tool post, and face the end of the muzzle off square. If you make your last cut .0015" deep with a slow feed towards the muzzle you will make a fine finish.

PHOTO 3-38.
Indicating the crown on my 7 SAUM.

PHOTO 3-39.

Double checking my crowning setup with the Interapid dial indicator to be sure it is right. (.30BR)

Ok, what have we done here? Well, the drill that made the hole in the barrel was still wandering around, like one of Brown's cows, when it headed on out of the muzzle. We have aligned the centre-line of that section of barrel, from around 2" behind the muzzle, out to the muzzle with the centre-line of the axis of the lathe spindle, and faced the end of the barrel square to that axis. Setting the barrel up like this for crowning gives us the best chance possible for the projectile to exit the barrel evenly. That is, every part of the circumference of the base of the projectile will exit the barrel at the same time; something that is very desirable. A projectile, exiting the barrel like this, will not have its stability disrupted by gas escaping from one side, while the other side of the projectile is still microscopically inside the bore.

74. I simply cut a recess in the end of the muzzle .035" deep and .200" larger in diameter than the caliber of barrel I am working with. My crowning tools both live on the one tool holder, one to cut the recess, and one to cut the crown. I make 3 x .010" passes and one .005" pass. I then chamfer the sharp outside edge of that recess 45° with the crowning tool, that is also on the tool holder. This recess provides some needed protection for the delicate crown, as its integrity is paramount to the maintenance of an accurate rifle. Photo 3-40 shows the recess being cut.

PHOTO 3-40.

Cutting the recess for the crown of my Shilen .30BR. This barrel will be fitted with a barrel tuner, hence the extra machining behind the muzzle.

PHOTO 3-41.

Here I am cutting the chamfer on the recess of the crown of my Shilen .30BR. The same tool is used to cut the crown itself. The crown, itself, will be cut in exactly the same manner.

PHOTO 3-42.

Drag a cotton bud along the bore and out of the muzzle. The newly cut crown should not pick up any fibers from the cotton bud. If it does your crown is faulty.

PHOTO 3-43.

The finished crown on my Panda 7 SAUM.

PHOTO 3-44.
The finished crown on my Shilen .30BR.

Photo 3-41 shows the recess, we have just made, being chamfered.

74.1. Now be sure the crowning tool is sharp, and break the sharp edge of the bore at a 45° angle, deep enough to break the edge past the grooves of the rifling. Photos 3-43 and 3-44 (Page 131) show two finished crowns. Be sure your cutting tool is sharp as you must make a cut that does not leave behind burrs. Check your job by inserting a cotton bud in the bore and pulling it out past the crown. The crown should not pick up any fibers from the cotton bud at all. If it does you will need to re do the job until you don't fail the cotton bud test. Photo 3-42 (Page 131) shows that.

74.2. Finally, break the sharp outside edge of the muzzle with a file, and give the flat face a lick with worn 320 grit strip to make it nice and shiny.

75. Clean everything up, and apply some anti seize paste to the barrel threads, and the receiver threads. This is very important, especially with stainless steel barrel blanks, and even more important when they are screwed into stainless steel actions. I use a product called Tru-Guard barrel thread protector.

75.1. Screw the receiver onto the barrel threads, and clamp the tenon of the barrel close to the receiver in a barrel vice. Barrel vices come in all shaped and sizes. I made mine about the same time the Dead Sea first reported sick, and it's a bit of overkill, but it has served ok. You can see it in Photo 3-45.

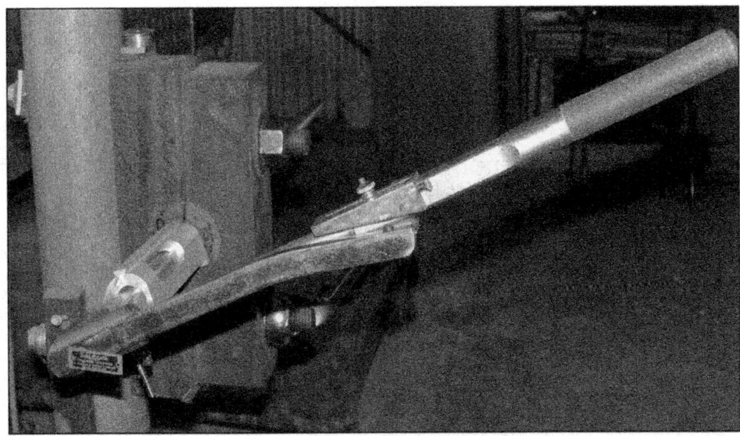

PHOTO 3-45.

I am about to torque the barrel on my 7 SAUM Panda to 100 foot pounds. I have already tightened and loosened it several times with an ordinary wrench to prepare the breeching surfaces to accept final torque correctly.

75.2. Place an appropriate action wrench in the rear of the receiver, and with a good breaker bar installed, tighten and loosen the receiver several times to mate the breeching surfaces. If you don't do this the receiver will not breech to its correct final position.

75.3. Loosen the receiver and fit a torque wrench onto the action wrench. Tension the receiver to 100 foot pounds torque.

76. Check the head-space, and if it is where you want it you have done a good job.

I don't bother doing anything to the outside of the barrel blank on my target rifles. If you want to make any cosmetic enhancements to the outside of the barrel you will have to remove the receiver to do so.

Because we took the trouble to mate the breeching surfaces (in step 75.2) the receiver will breech to the same place when you torque it up again.

What if you are not within correct head-space specifications when you breech the action? That is a good question. It can happen no matter how careful you are. If we have been very careful, our head-space dimensions will not be more than a thousandth of an inch or two out. Though that's not very much, it is enough to have to deal with none the less. The remedy goes something like this:–

Chamber too short (tight head-space). Remove the receiver and remove the barrel from the barrel vice. Don't do this with the barrel installed in the barrel vice as there will be a bit of squeeze on the chamber from the barrel vice tension, and you could very well ream the end of your chamber oval shaped. Don't risk it. Replace the barrel in the lathe, and have your reamer oil close by, as when you reamed the chamber. Get the reamer, fit the pilot you used when chambering the barrel, and fit your reamer holder on the end. Dip the reamer in the oil and carefully insert it in the chamber. Rotate it carefully, by hand, while applying a bit if forward pressure (a bit means not a lot!) for a couple of turns, and remove it. You will see what you have removed from the shoulder of the chamber on the flutes of the reamer. The reamer should not have cut anything from the body of the chamber, nor can you compromise the alignment of the chamber doing this, even if you try really hard to do so. Clean up, replace the receiver, torque it up and recheck your head-space. If it is still too short repeat the above steps until you have it where you want it.

Chamber too long. By having some small round pieces of shim steel stock of varying thickness (.001" to .010") you can easily determine by how much your chamber is too long and how much you need to shorten it by. To shorten the chamber we have to remove the correct amount from the breeching face of the barrel tenon, and a corresponding amount from the rear of the barrel to maintain bolt clearance. At the same time we must maintain the accuracy of our initial setup.

The really cool thing about setting a barrel up the way we did, to make this job, is that the setup is repeatable. If we took the trouble to check the run out of our chamber, at the rear, before we removed it from the lathe, we would have found it to be zero; no run out at all. We can now replace our barrel back in the lathe, set it up as we did before, and if we again indicate the rear of the chamber it will still indicate zero, meaning our second set up is exactly the same as our first set up. We can now face back the breeching face, and the rear of the barrel, maintaining the same accuracy we had in the initial setup, and that is what we have to do.

Be careful and you should make correct head-space in one go. The barrel will index a tiny bit further around, but you will just have to live with that. Also, be mindful of the .001" of sneak forward when you breech the barrel to final torque again.

That brings to an end our saga on barrel fitting and chambering. Our goal was to make the chamber so that the projectile starts dead straight in the bore, and the setup and machining methodology we have used will have achieved that goal, as much as is humanly possible. Further, we have made a setup that allows the projectile to leave the muzzle as square to the axis of the last bit of bore as is humanly possible. I can't think of anything (at this point in time) you can do to make it better, so for the time being, at least, one can be well satisfied.

OTHER ACTIONS

The fitting procedure I have described is probably the simplest you will be liable to undertake. Many actions you will encounter require extra work which I will touch on here. It's probably best if I list a couple of the actions I am familiar with and the extra attention they require.

Many factory rifles have the barrel secured in the receiver with some sort of glue, or loctite material, and are screwed in very tight, which makes them difficult to remove. Obviously, a good barrel vice, and wrench (and Wench) helps. However, don't get too aggressive when tightening your barrel vice, as it is very possible to deform the barrel, especially if you have to secure the barrel vice on the barrel some distance from the breech, as you have to when removing the barrel from a glued in action. It is easy to squeeze the bore permanently in that position, and that won't be doing you any favors.

Coating the surface of your vice inserts with Rosin will assist to grip the barrel, allowing you to apply less tension on the vice nuts to secure it. If you suspect the barrel has been secured with some sort of glue, apply some heat to the front bridge of the receiver with an LPG torch. Be sensible — it doesn't take much heat to break a glued bond — just enough to make it mildly uncomfortable to touch is all that is required. A good hair dryer would do the job, though it would take a while to heat the metal up.

Finally, and this is where I use my wench, have an off-sider take up pressure on the action wrench, and with a soft drift give the receiver a sharp whack at the bottom of the recoil lug, and the receiver should pop loose from the barrel thread. If you ever run up against an impossible to move one, the last straw is to set it up in the lathe and make a cut with a parting tool just in front of the receiver to relieve the breeching tension.

Sako 'L' series, 'A' series, and Tikka 'LSA' series. I can't remember if I have ever seen a re-barrel job on one of these actions that was done correctly. For some reason the guys doing these jobs ignore the factory example before their eyes, when they remove the old barrel, and fit the new barrel with a flat rear face which is a big *no, no*, because it exposes an excessive amount of unsupported case head.

Fitting the barrel like this exposes around .200" of case head which from a safety view point is marginal to say the least. If you do this and the case head lets go and injures someone, you might find yourself held accountable due to the faulty job you did. Photo 3-46 (Page 135) shows how it should *not* be done. Figure 3-4 (Page 88) shows the setup and dimensions needed, and Photo 3-47 (Page 136), the top barrel, shows what it should look like. The job only takes an additional ten minutes, so there is no excuse not to do it properly.

Sakos, along with some other actions, require a relief to be cut at the end of the thread to allow the action to reach the end of the thread. This is easily made with a parting tool when the threading job is completed.

PHOTO 3-46.

This barrel was from a re-barreled Sako L461. The flat rear face unshrouds the cartridge case head an excessive amount. *This is not the way it should be done.*

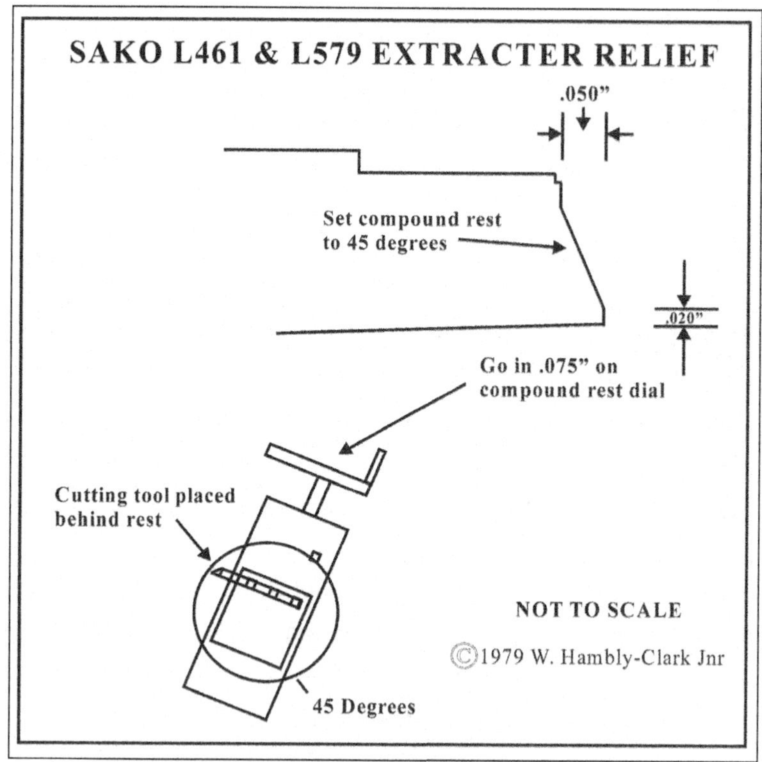

Figure 3-4.

This drawing shows the dimensions and setup needed to make the Sako extractor clearance properly.

Photo 3-47.

The top barrel shows the correct Sako L series extractor relief shape. The bottom barrel shows the bolt nose relief needed for Remington Model 700 actions.

I have never been a fan of Sako rifles. In fact it beats me how they ever work at all. I won't go into detail except to say be aware that their alignment is far from satisfactory. If you look closely at one and make a few measurements you will see what I am talking about. Don't assume their receiver thread size either. I had an L579 one time that was 1.020" in diameter rather than the usual 1.000" diameter.

When you run into that stupid late model trigger design with the ledge at the rear, convert it back to the old design by adding a screw just behind the retaining pin, and milling away the rear ledge — as it is, it's an accuracy killer. I discuss it in the bedding chapter. The small Sako actions just don't extract. The problem came about when they changed from the early long silver extractor to the short black extractor, sometime in the 1970s. It arose because the short black extractor required more clearance in front of the case rim to work, compared to the long silver extractor it replaced. What they should have done, when they changed the extractor, was increase the depth of the extraction cam to compensate for the increase in forward clearance. They neglected to do this, with the result that, when the bolt is lifted, it goes through the extraction cycle without breaking the case free from the chamber.

I quickly became aware of the problem and, being the good Samaritan I am, called the Sako agent out to show him. He just shrugged and said, "It doesn't cause us any problems." Go figure! I fixed the problem by drilling and tapping a 3MM hole just below the extraction cam, and installing a 3MM Unbrako cone head Allen screw. This was then shaped to blend into the existing cam, and increase its depth by about 100%. Every small Sako that came through my shop had this modification made to it.

Over the years I ran into several people, and witnessed them hammering their bolts back with the palm of their hands. When I questioned them about it, they thought that was the way it was supposed to be. Only a couple of years ago a mate had his Sako rebarreled to .223 for F Class. I spotted him at a club match soon after smacking the bolt back with the palm of his hand, and told him I could fix his problem. It's a pain in the ass job because the barrel has to be removed to do it, but he had done me many favors, so I bit the bullet and did it for him. He was surprised at how easy cases fell out of the chamber afterwards. Oh yeah, the factory never did address this problem.

Remington model 700. These actions require a recess in the back of the barrel to accept the nose of the bolt. This creates Remingtons famous (?) three rings of steel comprising the bolt nose, the barrel recess, and the receiver. Some reamer manufacturers market a reamer to cut this recess, but I always preferred to bore it to size.

If you have aligned the action you can make the recess a close fit to the bolt nose, .001" to .002" clearance, which will support the front of the bolt very close to the centre-line of the receiver. You must have a little clearance here, or it will end up seizing if a bit of grit finds its way in there. If you do not align the action, don't make the clearance so tight, or you won't be able to close the bolt. I always cut this recess after I have threaded the barrel, so that I can check that the bolt will fit before I cut the chamber. Photo 3-47 (Page 136), the bottom barrel, shows what it looks like. I am just finishing up the job in Photo 3-48 (Page 138).

Pre '64 Model 70 Winchester. These actions have a cone shaped bolt nose, and also require an extractor clearance cut on the end of the barrel. Again, some reamer manufacturers can supply a reamer to cut the cone shaped recess required, in the end of the barrel, to clear the bolt nose, and again I have always preferred to bore the recess to depth. The extractor cut is a complicated one because of the shape of the extractor claw. I used to cut it in the mill with a Woodruff key cutter, and finish the shape at the chamber with needle files. Photo 3-49 (Page 138) shows what it looks like.

PHOTO 3-48.

I have cut the bolt nose relief for my Shilen .30BR, and am making a chamfer on the sharp edge to facilitate entry of the bolt nose when the bolt is closed. The boring tool I used to make the recess can be seen still mounted on my tool post just to the right of the chamfering tool. This is one of the actions I aligned in Chapter one, so the bolt nose has only .001" clearance in this recess.

PHOTO 3-49.

PRE '64 Winchester Model 70 coned bolt nose and extractor relief.

There are a lot of specialty tools available to do various small jobs that we are faced with in this job, but you have to decide whether they are worthwhile economically. It would be nice to have a shaped milling cutter to cut the extractor relief on a PRE '64 Winchester; however you have to work out how many you are likely to be cutting. Such a cutter could cost $150.00 or more. You would need to be doing a number of jobs to make it worthwhile.

PHOTO 3-50.

Another coned bolt nose relief, this one for a Panda F Class action.

Back on Page 57 I referred to setup 1, being an option, if you needed to fit a barrel that was too short to reach through the hollow mandrel. *Don't even consider doing that.* Because the setup method, I have described, does not require you to indicate the muzzle of the barrel, all that is required to fit a short barrel, through the hollow mandrel of the lathe, is some means of supporting it at the end.

This is easily accomplished with a cat-head. I must have a barrel a minimum length of 24.8" to fit comfortably through the hollow mandrel of the Colchester lathe I use for fitting, and chambering. If I have to fit a 21" blank, the difference is easily made up by attaching a cat-head to the muzzle of the blank. You can see one attached in Photo 3-51.

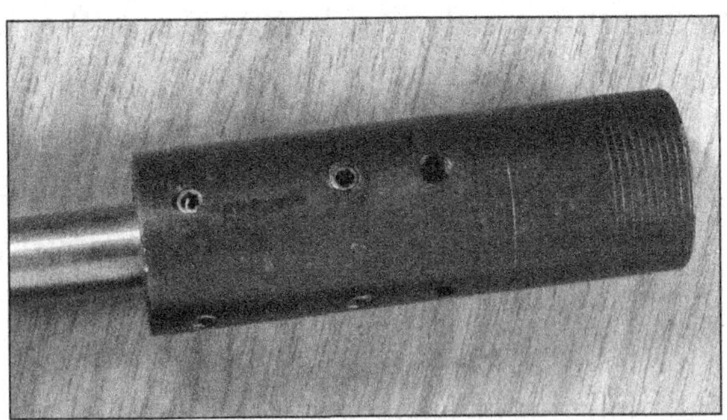

PHOTO 3-51.

This particular cat-head attached to the muzzle of a short barrel blank adds 2.4" to its length.

Often, the blank is long enough to fit through the hollow mandrel, for chambering, but you are required to cut it too short, to fit through, for crowning. To accommodate this I bored out the ends of my cat-heads, and threaded them for the most popular actions I was fitting barrels for. When I cut a barrel off to, say 22" long, I simply screw the cat-head onto the barrel thread to make up the difference. Photo 3-52 shows one of my cat-heads, with the internal thread, fitted onto a barrel blank.

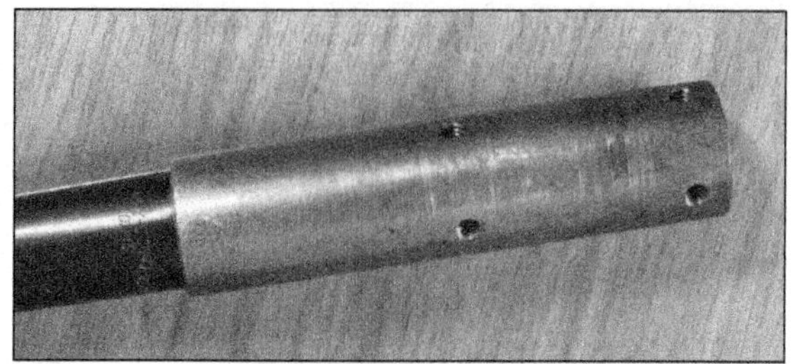

PHOTO 3-52.

This cat-head screwed onto the thread of a short barrel blank adds 4.2" to its length.

How do you know you have done, or have received a good job? A nice cosmetic finish is an indication a reasonable amount of skill and care has been applied when the job was done, but that is not the end of the story. Unfortunately I do not have the expensive equipment that would allow me to show you, so we will have to rely on words to get the message across.

You need a bore scope that will allow you to examine the throat of the chamber closely under magnification. Any discrepancy in the accuracy of the job will be evident in the throat and leade of the chamber. Even the smallest alignment error in the chamber will be easily seen in the throat. The dimensions and tolerances we are working with are very small, which makes any discrepancy stand out like dog nuts in moon light.

You will easily see the end of the throat, and the end of the leade, with a bore scope. Because the start and end of the leade are tapered, unless they are perfectly centred in the bore, you will easily see a variation in where the leade and throat end on each rifling land. The throat of the chamber should be .0005" over groove diameter, and where it ends in the bore it should be perfectly even, all round, in distance from the end of the chamber. If you can see that it is slightly longer on one side than the other, and you will easily see that, then you have a problem. Likewise, the end of the leade on each rifling land must be equidistant from the end of the chamber. Obviously, if one is right, then so will the other be. If there is any unevenness in the throat/leade the projectile will not start straight down the bore, and will not leave the muzzle gyroscopically stable.

What do you do if you find your throat/leade is uneven? I'm afraid there is nothing you can do. You've shot your bolt on that barrel. The only way it can be salvaged is to cut the entire chamber off and start again, and lose a couple of inches of barrel. *If you are wanting ultimate accuracy there is no other choice. You can not second fix a misaligned chamber.*

The fitting method I have described will give you the best possible chance to produce the most accurate job possible. *It's wrong to say a barrel won't shoot if it is not fitted as I described.* A good shooting factory rifle is a perfect example by which to refute that statement. By all means try it, as it may well be quite satisfactory.

I have never had a failure when fitting a barrel as I have described. If the rifle was mediocre it has been the barrel, not the fitting. My first 7 Saum barrel was mediocre because it was oversize in the grooves, and never shot really well, despite the barrel being fitted as perfectly as it could be.

In the appendix, at the rear of this book, you will find drawings of the pre-turn dimensions I used for most of the actions I worked with, along with any observations, or warnings, that were pertinent to each action. *Do not take these measurements as Gospel for they are a guide only.* You should always treat each action as an individual and determine its individual measurements before proceeding with the job. The drawings will, however, arm you with some knowledge of what to look for, and what you may expect to find in the individual actions I have listed.

Fitting a barrel to an action is a job that requires common sense, reasonable skill, and attention to detail. Always remember to put safety first, and don't quit until you get whatever part of the job you are on right. Oh, yes, and *never* refuse to buy a squirrel.

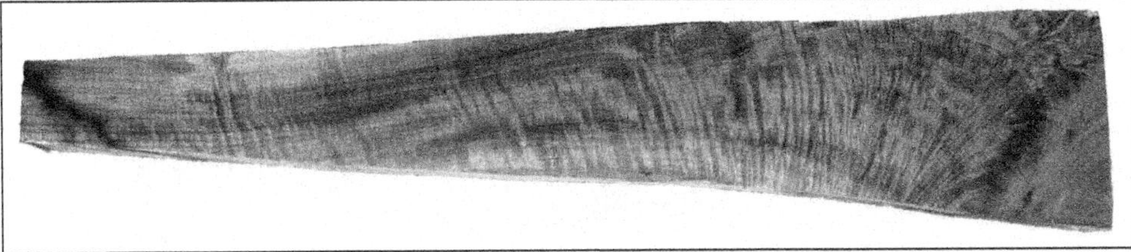

PHOTO C3-27.

This is the stick of California Claro Walnut that was used, in the creation of the stock, for the M'98 Mauser 6MM Remington rifle on the next page. One of the perks of this job was, you got to perve on a lot of really nice Walnut.

AN M'98 MAUSER IN 6mm REMINGTON

BUILT IN THE LATE 1970S

PHOTO C3-1.

The stick was a nice piece of Claro walnut (that's it on the left). The barrel was a #1 Douglas, stainless steel. I'll probably end up smoking a turd in hell for using an unblued stainless steel barrel on a rifle like this!

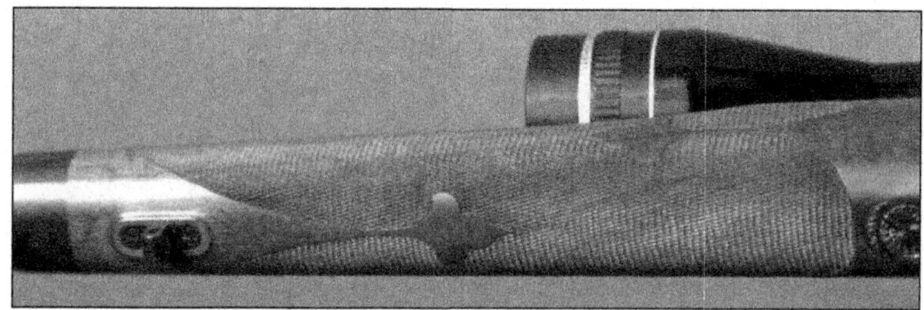

PHOTO C3-2.

The forend checkering was a Fleur-de-Lis pattern without ribbons. The forend tip was Rosewood, and the front sling swivel base was a 2 screw raised ledge design, popular at the time. Later I would move to barrel banded swivel bases.

PHOTO C3-3.

Phil Vinnicombe was using a larger scroll engraving design on my early rifles.

PHOTO C3-4.
The trigger guard assembly was made by me from solid steel.

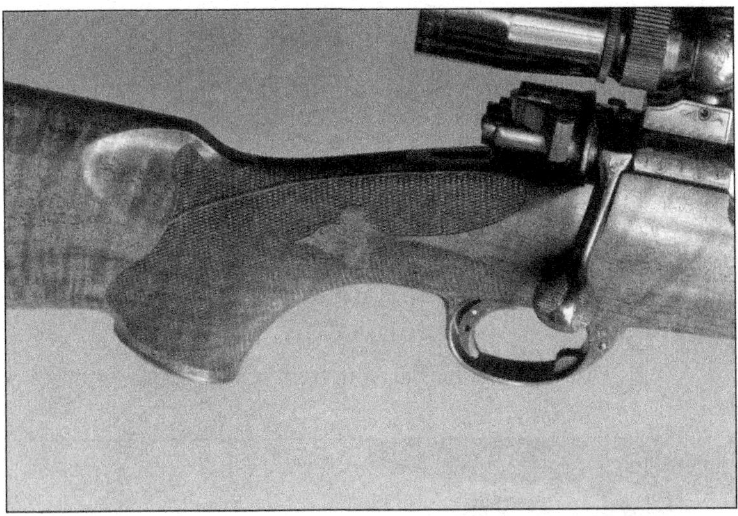

PHOTO C3-5.
The grip checkering went over the grip through two ribbons. The classic bolt handle had a three panel checkering pattern. The scope mounts were Conetrol Custum on Conetrol unmodified bases. The grip cap was one of Len Brownells. This rifle shot ½" groups at 100 yards. Beauty, handling, and accuracy, all in one package.

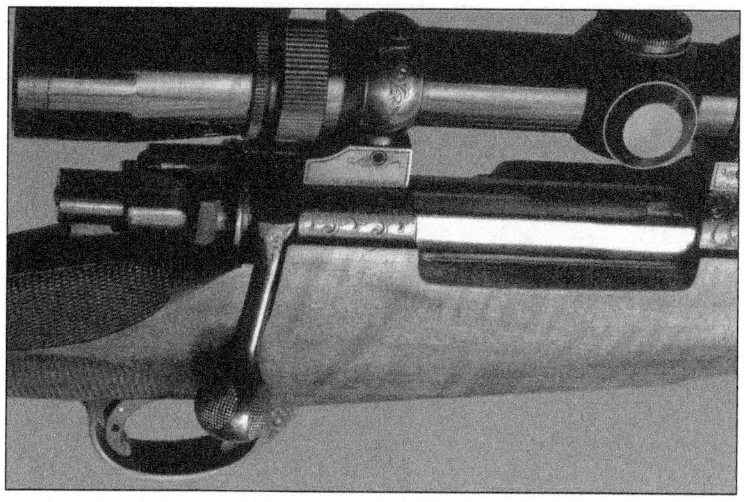

PHOTO C3-6.
The safety was of two position design made using the M'98 Mauser bolt shroud.

PHOTO C3-7.
Phil engraved the barrel in front of the action.

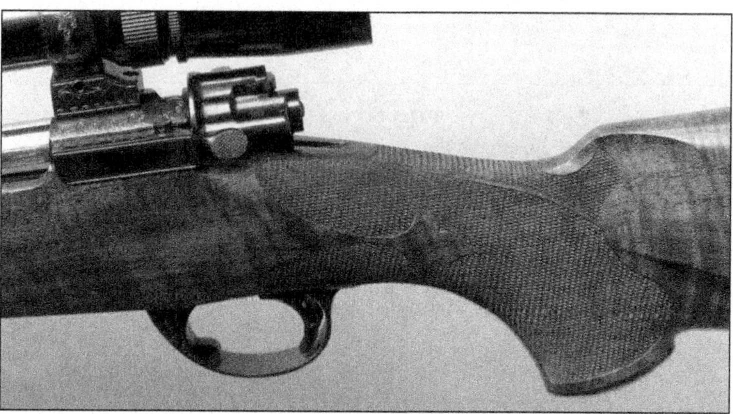

PHOTO **C3-8.**
The trigger was a Canjar MS–1/2 tuned to break at 1¼ pounds. The checkered Brownell bolt release tab was popular at the time, but lost favor with me later on.

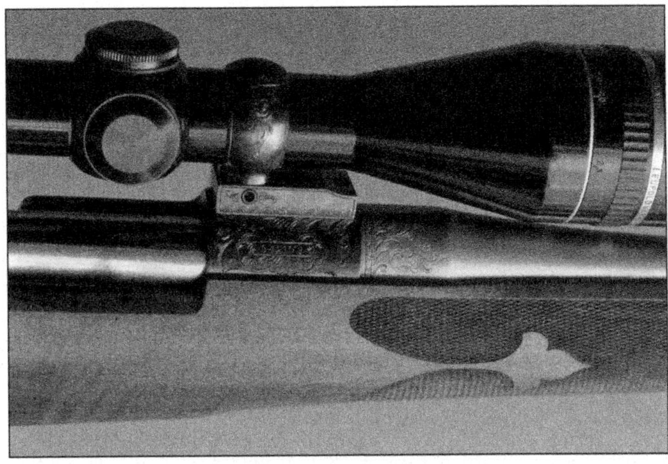

PHOTO C3-9.
The receiver was profile ground and polished throughout.

PHOTO C3-10.
The floorplate was made from a quite large piece of flat steel. Very time consuming.

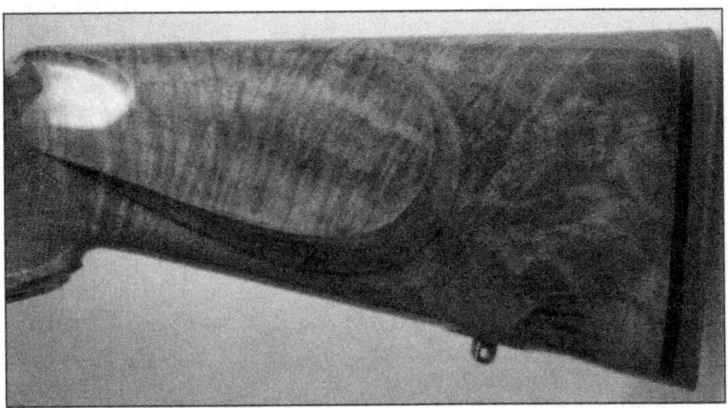

PHOTO C3-11.
Exhibition grade Claro Walnut with feathered crotch figure, as in this example, made a fantastic looking rifle. In sunlight the figure seemed alive.

AN M'98 MAUSER IN .270 WINCHESTER

BUILT IN THE LATE 1970S

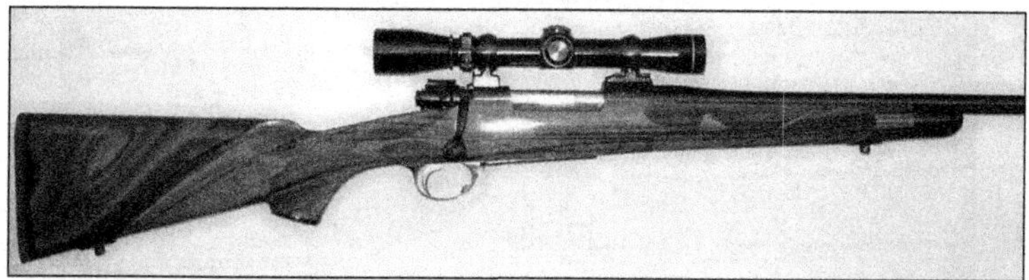

PHOTO C3-12.

The stock on this rifle was cut from a nice stick of well laid out California English Walnut

PHOTO C3-13.

It is a significant example, being built in the period just after shifting from using semi- inletted, semi-finished stock blanks. It shows the shape I was trying to achieve in a sporting rifle beginning to emerge.

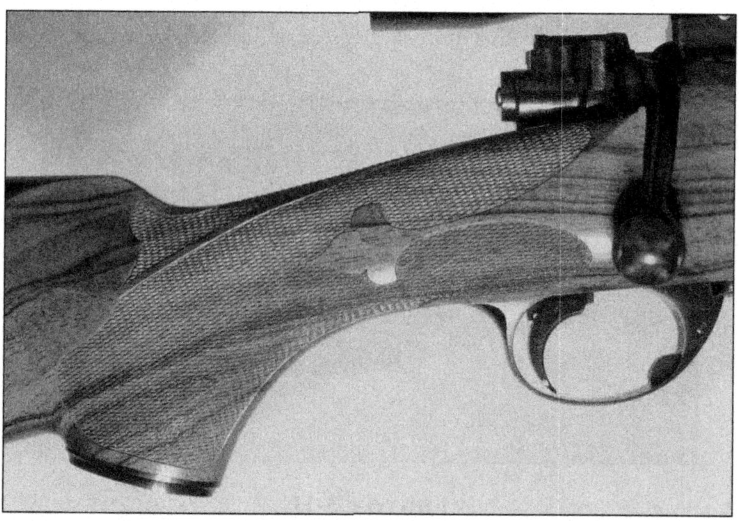

PHOTO C3-14.

Grip profile. The safety is of side swing two position design made on the M'98 Mauser bolt shroud. The trigger was a tuned Canjar M3-1/2.

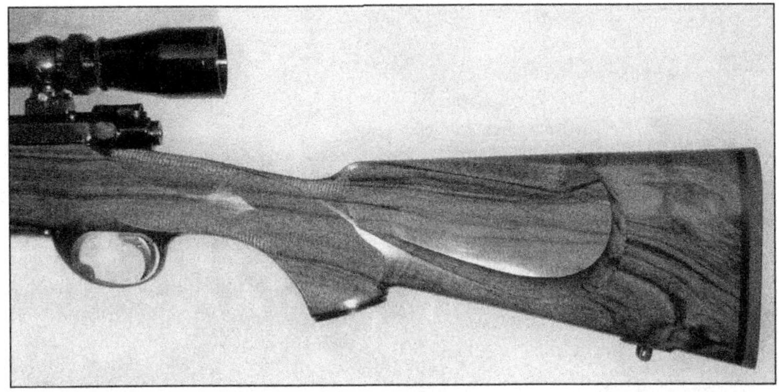

PHOTO C3-15.

LHS butt and cheekpiece profile. The rear swivel base was 2 screw raised ledge.

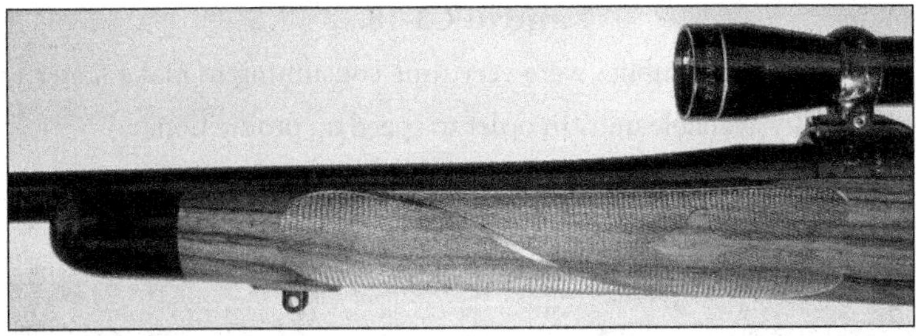

PHOTO C3-16.

The forend tip is African Ebony. The checkering pattern on the forend is wrap around, each line continuing through the ribbon at 28 lines per inch.

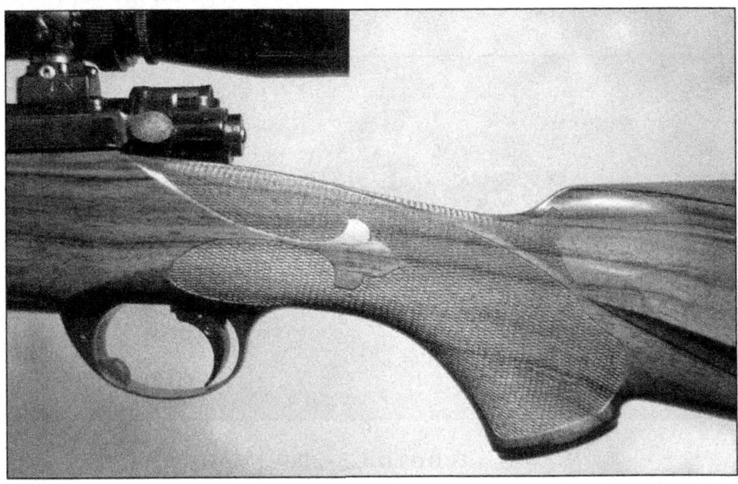

PHOTO C3-17.

LHS Grip profile. A checkered Lenard Brownell bolt stop pad is fitted.

PHOTO C3-18.

These trigger guard assemblies were very time consuming to make. Later I would use commercially available units in order to speed up production.

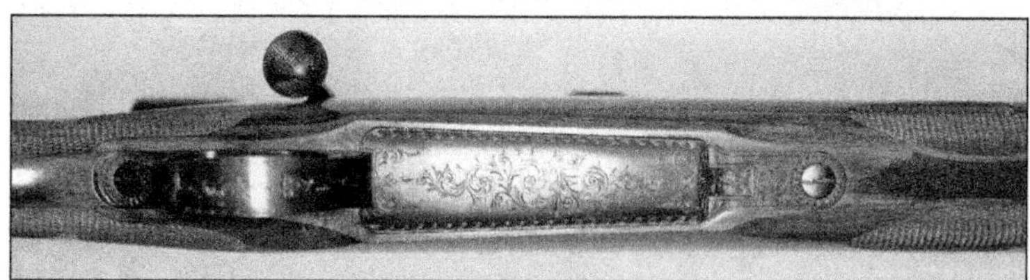

PHOTO C3-19.

Trigger guard and floor plate. Note the action screw slots pointing North and South.

PHOTO C3-20.

The raised ledge rear sling swivel base was popular at the time.

PHOTO C3-21.

The action was profile ground to remove the factory stamping and clean up its lines, and then polished all over. The barrel was a #1 profile Douglas premium grade chrome moly blank cut at 22" long. The sideswing safety was made on the original Mauser 98 bolt shroud, and was of two position design, fire or safe and locked. The classic bolt handle had the knob checkered in a five panel design.

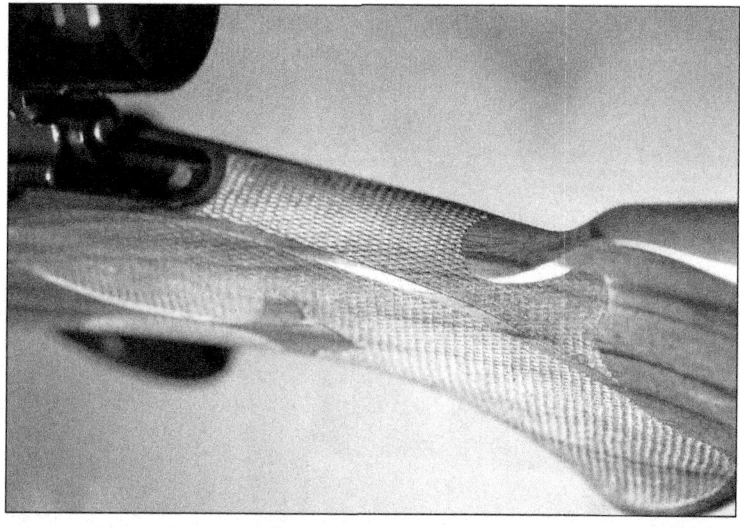

Photo C3-22.
The 28 LPI checkering pattern went through the ribbons and over the grip without a break in the lines.

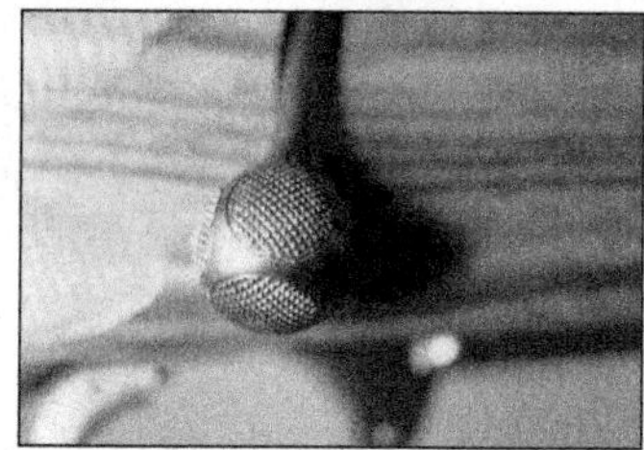

Photo C3-23a.

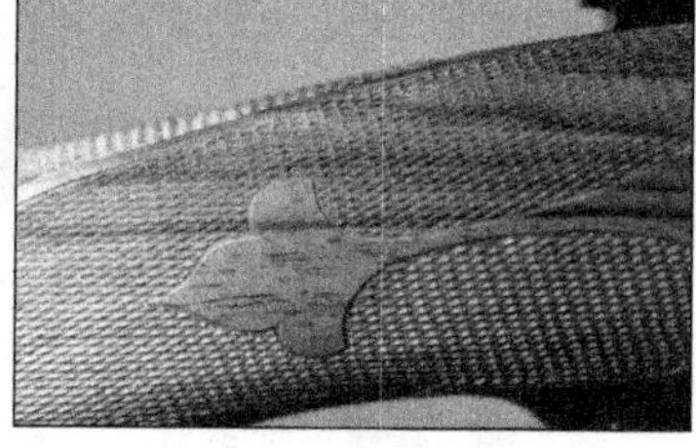

Photo C3-23b.

Photo C3-24.
I used Conetrol scope mounts and bases. The bases were milled around the tops for a custom look. I would continue with this theme on mount bases I would make later.

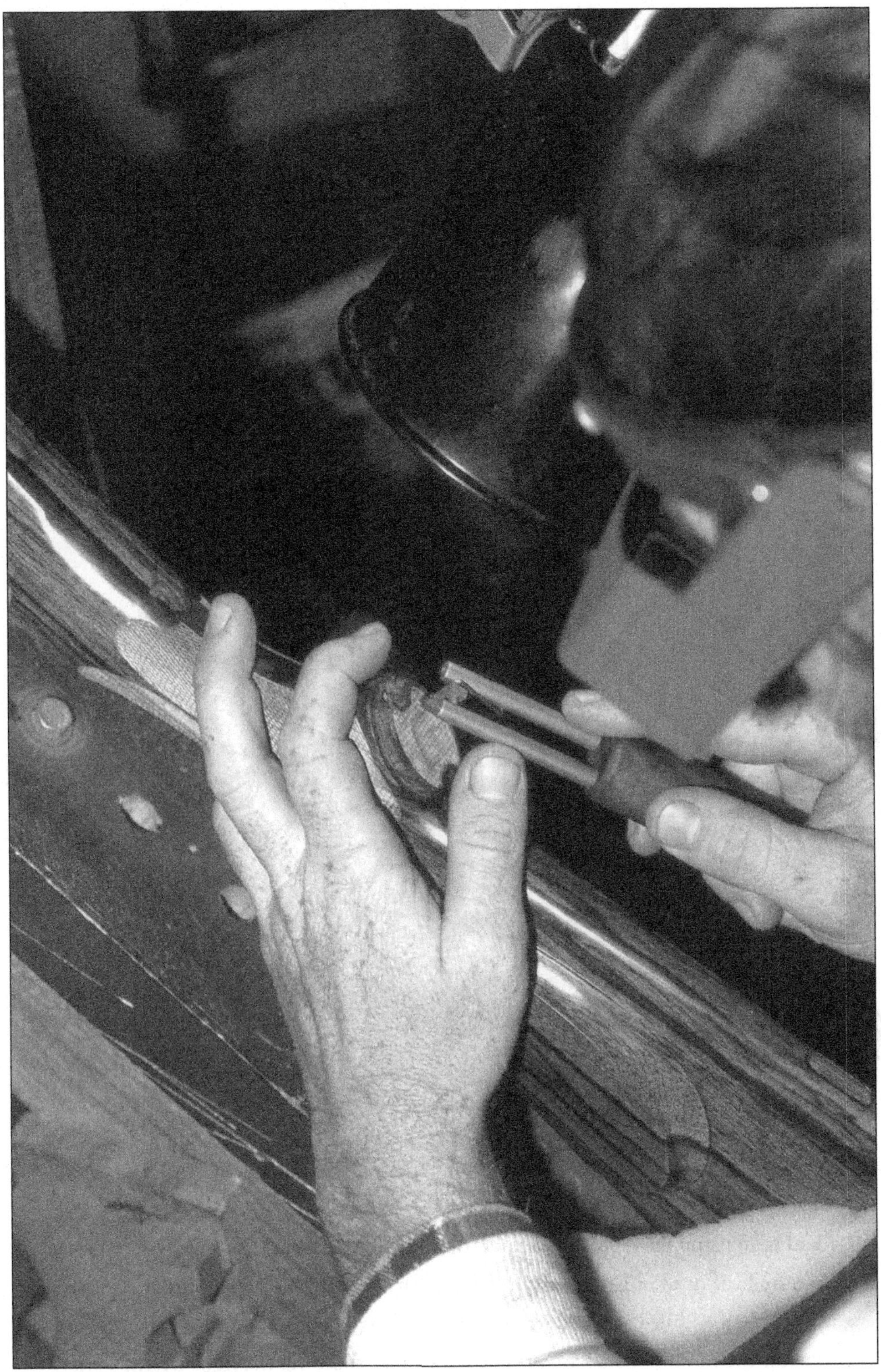

PHOTO C3-28.
Checkering the skeleton grip cap on a Mauser M'98 sporting rifle stock.

SIGNIFICANT RIFLES AND EVENTS

PART 3: THE 1980s (1)

PHOTO C3-25.

I had been using the .308 Winchester for a good many years, and had taken many thousands of head of game with it using both commercial projectiles and those I made myself. While it worked well enough, my experience with it led me to believe that, for the hunting I was doing, a larger caliber shooting the light weight bullets available for that caliber would work better. I had designed a Remington 700 fibre glass stock for Chet Brown (Brown Precision Inc.), which he put into production, so I had him send me one, and made up a rifle in .358 Winchester. It is seen here in the Victorian high country, with me examining a Sambar rub on a native cherry tree.

PHOTO C3-26.

I used the .358 Winchester for a few years, and it was very successful. My idea of using the light projectile in a large calibre for the game I was using it on was sound. The rifle was fitted with a #2 profile Douglas blank, which was a light profile for the calibre, and with my stock design it handled pretty well. The Remington action, however was not dependable enough for me. It had let me down a few times in .308 Winchester by miss feeding when I needed a fast second shot urgently, and I had the same problem with the .358. This is not a problem with the Remington brand per se, but a problem with all actions that do not feature controlled feed of the cartridges from the magazine into the chamber. They are fine in benign conditions, but when you are sprinting through the scrub, and reloading at the same time, they are just as likely to pop a cartridge into the left bolt raceway, or right out of the ejection port as they are to deliver it into the chamber. The final straw came when I was hunting pigs with my mate, Tom Buvac. The rifle had miss fed when I needed a fast second shot, so my mind was already working. We were walking along a channel, me trailing Tom, when I noticed that the fibreglass stock on my rifle was really hot—like burn your face hot. Tom was using a sweet little .308W wood stocked rifle, so I caught up to him and felt his stock. It was cool to the touch. I decided then my next hunting rifle was going to have an M'98 Mauser action and a wood stock.

CHAPTER FOUR
TRIGGER TUNING

Throughout this book I have been preaching alignment, alignment, alignment. Well now, for a break, I will change my tune, and begin preaching, SAFETY, SAFETY, SAFETY! There is nothing more dangerous than a malfunctioning trigger. It is a trap, just waiting to bite you in the ass big time. *It is only in your best interest to ensure that every trigger you come in contact with is 100% safe.*

A trigger is, sort of, like a spring set trap or snare. When we lift the bolt of our action (sometimes you have to pull it to the rear a little bit) spring pressure sets the trigger, so that when the bolt is closed the firing pin is trapped in the rearward position, with its spring compressed. The trap is released by squeezing the trigger bow, thus allowing the firing pin to move forward. Overall it seems a simple mechanism, but in reality it is more complicated than it would appear.

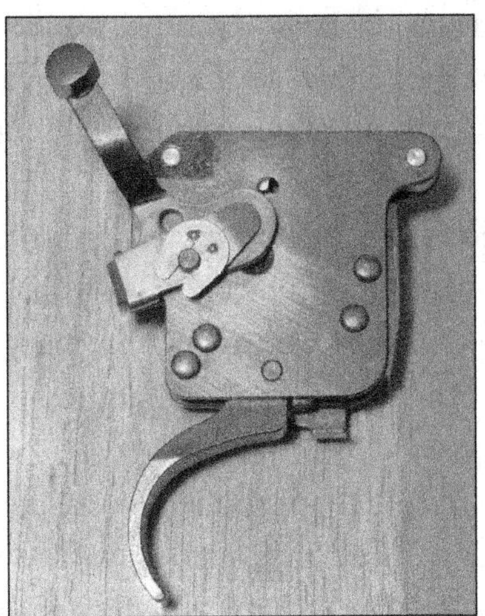

PHOTO 4-1.
A factory Remington Model 700 two lever trigger.

The trigger on factory sporting rifles is what is generally called a two lever design (Photo 4-1). Basically it consists of two levers; one is called the falling sear and the other is the trigger piece. The falling sear usually pivots on a pin and, as its name implies, it is free to fall away and release the firing pin. When the rifle is cocked the falling sear is held in place by the upper section of the trigger piece.

At the bottom of the trigger piece is the trigger bow, and moving it rearward pivots it on a pin, and moves the top of the piece forward, which releases the falling sear, and the rifle goes bang.

This design is perfectly adequate when used on hunting rifles that take mainly medium to large game, or in target competitions that specify a minimum trigger pressure of 2^{LBS} or thereabouts. Because of its design, and the pressure that design places on the trigger sears when the rifle is cocked, there is a limit to how light the trigger pull can be made and keep it safe. We will discuss why in a little bit. Bear with me for a while.

In order to make a design that will be safe at a lighter pull than the two lever trigger is capable of, we have to devise a way to reduce the loading on the trigger sears when the rifle is cocked. The way we do that is by introducing a third lever into the design, in such a way that the sear load is reduced considerably, thus allowing a lighter pull.

What are the pull weights I am talking about? Well, a two lever design will work from 1 pound pull weight to around 10^{LBS} or more pull weight. A 3 lever design will generally work from 2^{OZ} to 6^{OZ} pull weight, though there are some complicated designs that will work from 2^{OZ} to several pounds by installing an appropriate trigger weight spring.

Now I know some of you reading the above will be saying, "BS, this guy doesn't know what he's talking about. My Gunsmith made my Remchester trigger pull under a ¼^{LB,} no sweat!" Well, remember what I was preaching at the beginning of this chapter. I'll refresh. SAFETY, SAFETY, SAFETY! If you think I can't make a two lever trigger to break at 2^{OZ} you don't know me very well. The difference between me and your guy is, *I won't make a trigger like that,* because I know it's downright dangerous. My message to all you guys, who are doing things like this, is to stop and think. If the bloke you did it for, even though you think he's a good bloke, shoots someone with a rifle sporting an unsafe trigger you have worked on, *you will be the fall guy.* Believe it! He will turn on you like a Viper.

All of that aside, let's get into the mechanics of the system, and by the time you finish reading this you will have an understanding of what I am talking about.

Regardless of what design the trigger is, from the most simple to the most complicated, the whole system hinges around the sears and the contact they make with each other. Apart from ensuring that the sliding surfaces are smooth, virtually all of our attention is focused on that tiny area which makes up the contact point of the sears.

I have a rule that I have adhered to throughout my career. In fact it is the 12TH Commandment. It comes after the 11TH Commandment which is, I think, 'ROTATE YOUR TYRES'. My 12TH Commandment is: *'Every trigger, regardless of design, must be able to hold the firing pin, in the cocked position, without the trigger return spring installed'.* If you take that Commandment on board, and adhere to it, you will be on the road to making a safe trigger.

We need to deal with various forces that are applied to the parts within the system, one of which is friction. Specifically, we are looking to decrease friction within the system, and that is the primary reason for introducing a third lever into the design; to reduce the pull to ounces rather than pounds. Friction can be reduced by polishing the sear surfaces to a fine finish, but that will only work to a certain extent, so we have to work around it if we are to make the pull weight lighter.

Specifically, it is the angle of the sears we will use to tune our trigger pull, but before we get into the mechanics of the job we need to understand the theory.

If you will refer to Figure 4-1 (Page 157) you will see that the trigger sear can have 3 basic angle groups. They are climbing, level, and falling. A climbing sear can have any angle above the angle of the level sear, which will be 90° to a line drawn from the centre of its pivot pin. Obviously any deviation from that 90° angle will turn the sear angles into either climbing or falling. A falling sear can have any angle under the 90° of the level sear. The arrows in the drawings indicate the direction in which the parts will be moving when the trigger is pulled. Referring to the climbing sear drawing you can see, that moving the bottom sear in the direction of the arrow, will require it to push the top sear up before it can be released. The falling sear, on the other hand, is already facing down hill, allowing the bottom sear to slide out, from under the top sear, relatively easily.

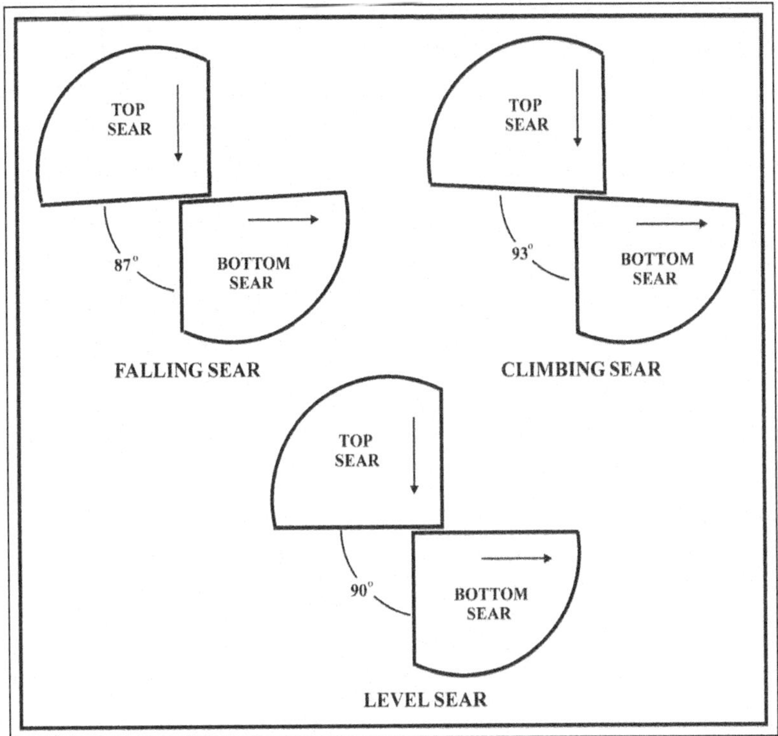

FIGURE 4-1.

The three possible sear angles one may encounter in a trigger.

You don't have to be a rocket scientist to realize that a trigger with a climbing sear will have a very hard pull indeed. Not only do we have to overcome the friction created in the sears, from the load that is applied to them when the rifle is cocked, we would also be trying to move the firing pin to the rear against the pressure exerted by the firing pin spring, so that the sear can climb up and be released. Depending on the design of the system, that can be really hard to do, and in some cases nearly impossible.

Obviously, we don't want a trigger with a 20^{LB} or more pull weight, so let's forget about the climbing sear angle as an option. Instead, let's consider the level, or 90° sear angle.

The level sear angle allows the bottom trigger sear to slide out of contact with the top trigger sear, releasing the firing pin, without any of the vertical movement associated with the climbing sear. It would seem to be the ideal sear angle, and it does probably make the safest usable trigger. However, it doesn't make an ideal trigger for sporting or target use. The load that is applied to sears with a level angle is considerable, and that load creates friction that, even on highly polished surfaces, is difficult to overcome. Triggers set up like this can have pull weights from 3^{LBS} to 7^{LBS} depending on the load applied to the sears. Such load is variable from action to action, and depends on firing pin spring strength, firing pin tail angle etc. If you are happy with something around a 5^{LB} trigger pull a flat sear is for you. Me, I like my hunting rifles to be between one pound and $1\frac{1}{4}^{LBS}$, so I need to look further if I want to achieve that.

To make a lighter pull than our flat seared trigger allows, requires that we adjust the angle of the trigger sears, thereby moving into the realm of the falling sear. When we discussed friction, associated with the flat sear angle, it was our enemy, and prevented us from achieving the weight of pull we wanted. Now we are working with a falling sear angle, friction is our friend. It will allow us to use a falling sear angle, *but there is a limit to its friendship.*

Remember Commandment #12! Never forget it. As we adjust the angle of the two trigger sears downward, friction will continue to hold them, but only up to a certain point. When that point is exceeded, friction is overcome by the load applied to the sears when the rifle is cocked, and the sears will not hold. Then you have violated Commandment #12, and eventually you will 'smoke a turd in hell' for doing that.

For all you blokes out there who think their guy is really smart because he can make a two lever trigger release at ¼LB, that's how he does it! *By altering the sear angles drastically, so that the only thing holding the action, in the cocked position, is the pressure of the trigger return spring.* "So what?" You say. Well — a trigger set up like this is in a very precarious condition. Because the trigger sears will not hold the action in the cocked position, without the assistance of the trigger return spring, *they are always in a state of trying to disengage.*

The upshot of this is, the slightest jar will start the sears sliding, and once they have started to slide they will not stop. Such triggers will not tolerate shutting the bolt on the action any way, but very carefully, without jarring the sears, and starting them moving. The end result of that is an accidental discharge. Hopefully the barrel is pointing in a safe direction when that happens. Really, though, there should be no potential for that to happen if the job is done correctly. You should be able to close the bolt smartly without the trigger releasing. You will never be able to do that if the trigger will not hold of its own accord, without the assistance of the trigger return spring, because the sears, having too much down angle, are always trying to disengage.

It would be nice if I were able to specify a sear angle for you to use, on every trigger, that would produce the results you want, but alas that is not possible. The sear loading developed by each action is unique, being made from varying degrees of spring tension and friction within the system. I use a jig to adjust sear angles, so you would think that once I had it set for a Remington 700 trigger I could do all Remington 700 triggers at that setting, but I have found that is not the case. It's more complicated than that, probably because the trigger pressure I aim for in a 2 lever trigger is at the very limit of its design parameters. Photo 4-2 shows my trigger tuning jig. The square stone in the photo is the only dry stone I had to take the photo with. I use triangular stones for the job, as I feel I get better control with them. There is a Remington Model 700 Slipper in the adjustable holding piece on the right. The stone rides on the ball bearing, which is also adjustable via its shaft.

PHOTO 4-2.

My trigger tuning jig.

Experience has taught me that I can make a safe two lever trigger that will break at between one and 1¼^{LBS}. Experience has also shown me that any pull weight under one pound will be prone to drop the sear when the bolt is closed, with even moderate speed.

Assuming I have tuned a trigger to break at 1¼^{LBS} (20^{OZ}), that weight will be made up of two parts. Part 1 will be a minimum of ¾^{LB} (12^{OZ}) of trigger pressure, that will be required to overcome sear friction, and break the trigger without the trigger return spring installed. Part 2, the remaining ½^{LB} (8^{OZ}), will be made up from tension supplied by the trigger return spring. Properly timed (more on that shortly) such a trigger will remain cocked when the bolt is closed smartly, will break crisply and cleanly, and be an asset on any sporting rifle.

To make a trigger like this requires some stoning, polishing, and much testing in the rifle it is destined for. It is not made by accident, but by intelligent effort.

Before we go any further we should discuss trigger timing. This is something that should be checked before you start work on any trigger, and if found to be wrong, corrected before you go any further.

I don't know about you, but when I'm running flat out after a pig, or whatever, and reload, I do it somewhat frantically. Likewise if I'm bombing up a mob, the bolt on the rifle is being operated at light speed. When you slam the bolt home, the first thing that it should contact at the end of its forward travel is the extraction cam. This has a two fold purpose. One, it halts the bolts forward travel effectively, and two, it starts the bolt rotating into its eventual locked position.

The position of the trigger in the receiver is very important. If it is positioned too far to the rear of the receiver, the first contact the bolt will have when it is slammed forward won't be the extraction cam, but the trigger itself. This will result in the trigger sears snapping together with considerable force. That might be acceptable if you are providing a 10^{LB} trigger with half a mile of engagement, which most factories do, but when we tune a trigger to break as we discussed, such a condition could well damage the sears, and cause an accidental discharge.

It would seem that some manufacturers either don't realize this is a problem, or don't care about it, because I have often had to deal with mistimed triggers. The test to check if your trigger is mistimed is simple and straight forward.

1. Remove the barreled action from the stock.

2. Hold the barreled action in soft jaws, in your bench vice, by the barrel with the trigger facing towards you. If you are lucky you will be able to observe the trigger sears through a sight hole in the side of the trigger housing. If not you will have to go by sound and feel.

3. Check that the chamber is clear, and insert the bolt, right into the action, with the bolt handle in the up position.

4. Holding the bolt up (that is, not letting it turn down) push it hard into the receiver against the extraction cam. If you can, observe what, if anything, is happening to the trigger top sear. Hopefully it will not move. If it doesn't move, the trigger is properly timed.

5. If the top trigger sear moves, keep the forward pressure on the bolt and see if there is a gap between the top and bottom trigger sears. If so we are still ok. While you are at it, keeping pressure

on the bolt, move the trigger bow back and forth. You should be able to move it through its full travel freely. If so we are still ok.

6. If you can't detect a gap between the sears, very likely when you pull the trigger, with forward pressure on the bolt, the top sear will be released to move down a fraction. Probably it will catch the bottom sear when the trigger bow is released, which will prevent it from returning to its original position. *The sears are doing duty as the bolt forward stop.*

That #6 condition is something we do not want to have with our tuned trigger. The trigger is not properly timed in the action, and we must address that fault before we proceed. Fortunately it's not that difficult. The fix is to remove a small amount of material from the surface, on the firing pin tail, that contacts the top sear of the trigger. You won't have to remove much, so go carefully. We only need a .005" gap between the trigger sears, when the bolt is fully against the extraction cam. I use a surface grinder, for this job, with the bolt tail held in a machine vice. It's another one of those jobs you sneak up on. I'll grind off .005", reassemble, and check for the clearance I want. When I first started tuning triggers I ground the tail carefully with a fine stone on a bench grinder, and cleaned it up with hand stones. If you do have to do it that way, just ensure to be ultra careful with the amount of material you remove, and to maintain the original angle and shape of the piece. A properly timed trigger is a beautiful thing. Photo 4-3 indicates where material must be removed to correct faulty trigger timing.

So, with that out of the way let's have a look at the mechanics of the job. As I said before, I use a jig with which to stone sears and make the angles I want. Having said that, though, I tuned many triggers successfully before I made the jig. You are not likely to have a jig, so I will describe the method I used pre jig. All a jig does is provide another way of holding the parts, and a more precise method of arriving at the angles we need to make the trigger work like we want it to.

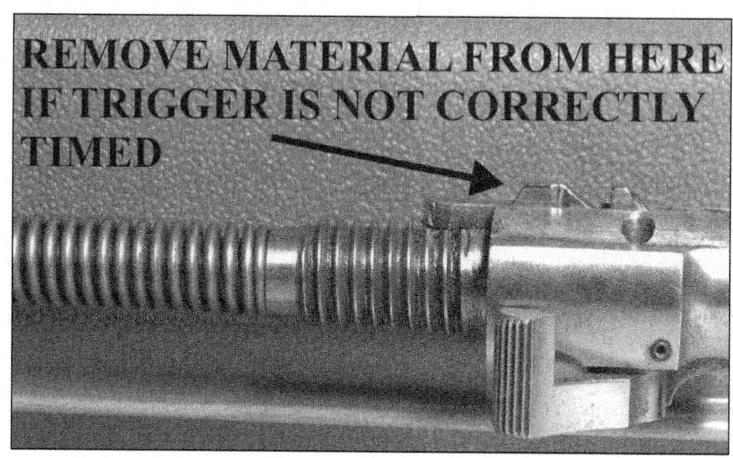

PHOTO 4-3.

The area from which material must be removed to time the trigger.

This is not a job for those who do not pay attention to fine detail. The amount of material we will be removing from the parts is miniscule, and it must be removed precisely. If you go too far you will create a lot more work for yourself, or possibly ruin the trigger.

The trigger tune I describe will be on a Remington model 700. The internal parts and their names can be seen in Photo 4-4 (Page 161). The Remington trigger is a good trigger to work on as it has what I call 'through sears'. In other words the sears are exposed, and you can make a good stroke with a stone when adjusting the sear angles. I detest working on triggers that have notched sears. They allow only a very small stroke of the honing stone, which makes the job very tedious, to say the least.

The parts in Photo 4-4 (Page 161) are approximately in the positions they would be if inserted straight into the trigger housing. If you look back at Photo 4-1 (Page 155), you will see the trigger sears peeking out through the sears sight hole, which I will be referring to later.

The only way I know how to do this job, is to sneak up on it. Make a small adjustment, polish the sear surfaces, reassemble and test to see what effect you have made. If it is not satisfactory, repeat the process until it is.

The tools I use for this job are as follows:

1. My drill press vice mounted on my drill press. It is the right height and has a flat top surface to work on.

2. A spacer about .012" thick. I used to use a Brownells flat mount base spacer.

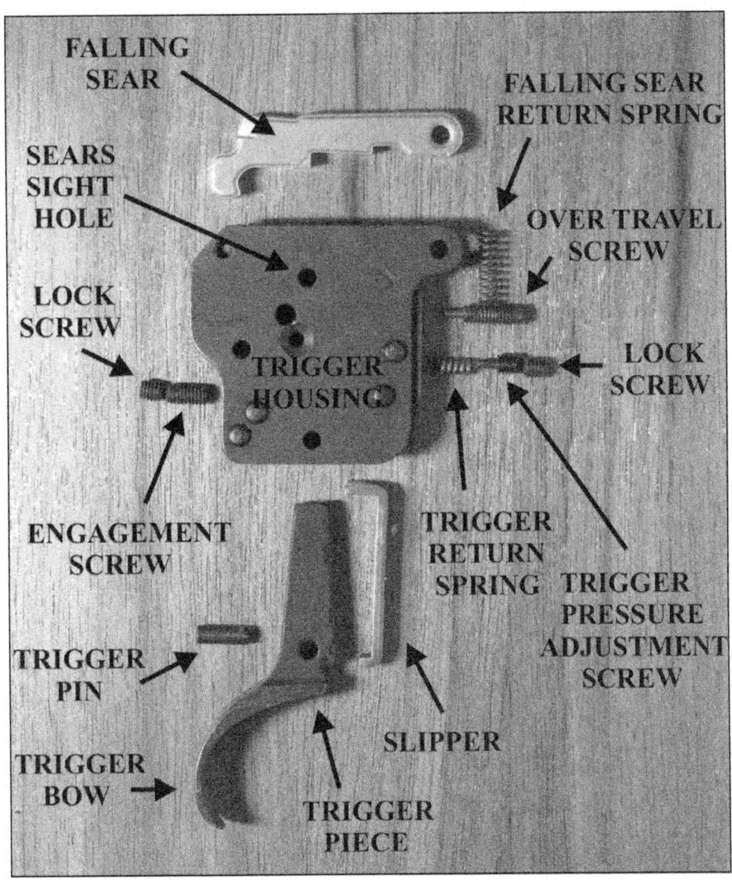

PHOTO 4-4.
A Remington Model 700 triggers internal parts.

3. Honing stones. I find triangular shaped stones are the easiest to control during the honing process. A 320 grit aluminum oxide stone, a soft Arkansas stone, and a hard Arkansas stone will do the job. I lubricate them with baby oil, which is good for my soft little pinkies, and store them in a container of baby oil when I am not using them. Photo 4-5 shows the container I store my stones in. There is a puddle of baby oil in the bottom of each compartment that keeps the stones charged while I am not using them. Baby oil works perfectly ok as a stoning lubricant, and is not toxic as are dedicated stoning oils.

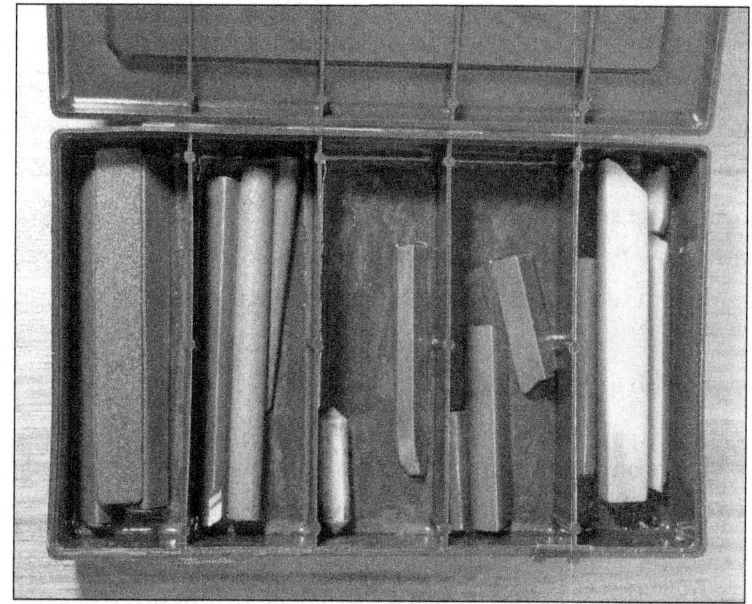

PHOTO 4-5.
Some honing stones in their container.

4. A light source that can be placed behind your work.

5. A 6" steel rule.

6. Some magnification. I use a pair of 4x chemist glasses that I put on over my reading glasses, and a 10x jewelers loupe.

7. A trigger gauge.

8. A Dremel tool with a couple of soft felt polishing wheels. One wheel I treat with a product called Summabrax polishing compound, and the other with white buffing compound.

9. Some suitable soft action trigger return springs.

Before we start, trigger sear surfaces must *not be* lubricated at all. The trigger housing may be protected against corrosion with a light film of hi-tech rust preventative, I use CLP Break Free, and the pivot pins may be lightly lubricated, but the sears themselves must *not be* oiled at all.

1. To start with we need to know what we are working with. Check that the chamber is clear, cock the rifle, shoulder the rifle and dry fire it, as if you were taking a precision shot at a distant critter. Do that a couple of times and take note of how the trigger feels.

    1.1. It's probably too heavy. Is it creepy or notchy? The feel of it will give you an idea of what to expect inside, and what you may need to do to fix it.

2. Remove the barreled action from the stock and hold it by the barrel in the soft jaws of your bench vice. Cock the action and test the weight of pull of the trigger with your gauge. It will probably

be somewhere between 3 and 7 pounds. Write the weight down for your own reference, or so you can pass the information on to the owner.

3. Remove the trigger return spring and put it and its screws in a safe place. The adjustment screws on Remington triggers are usually small Allen head grub screws locked in position with another small Allen head grub screw. The locking screw is covered with some sort of varnish. You must first scrape off the varnish and remove the locking grub screw before you can remove the adjusting grub screw. In Photo 4-4 (Page 161) you can see the screws and spring you should be removing.

Push against the rear of the trigger bow and re-cock the bolt. Release the pressure on the trigger bow — it should hold, and the action should remain cocked. Now, retest the weight of pull of the trigger with your gauge. Do it a few times to make sure your measurement is right.

> 3.1. The measurement will probably be somewhere between 1½^{LBS} to 5^{LBS}. Write it down so you don't forget and have a reference to refer to.

> 3.2. Sometimes with this test, the trigger will break close to the weight we are aiming for, ¾ pound (12^{OZ}) or an ounce or two more. What do you do then? Well, this means that the trigger sears are most probably fine just as they are. I would polish the sears, replace the trigger return spring with one of my soft action springs, adjust the pull weight to just under 1¼ pounds with the new spring, reassemble the rifle and see what it felt like. There is absolutely no point in trying to fix something that isn't broken. If the trigger breaks cleanly, has no discernible creep, and feels good, I'd simply give it a crash test by closing the bolt smartly, several times, to check that the sear doesn't drop. If it passes that test I'd call it a good trigger and say, 'job well done'. Speaking of soft action springs, I'd better digress and discuss them before we go any further.

When I started to study triggers, in the early 1960s, it quickly became apparent that it was impossible to tune a trigger, with the weight of pull and feel I was looking for, using the original trigger return spring.

I knew I would be doing a lot of this work, so I toddled off to a spring making works, and got them to make me several hundred soft action springs from stainless steel wire, in two lengths and two weights, with closed ends. The guy at the spring works did a really good job at a reasonable price, and I have used those springs all through my career.

When we tune the trigger, we are only looking to add 6 or so ounces to the 12 ounces of pull weight the trigger has without a return spring installed. 6 ounces is enough tension to ensure the trigger returns to position positively every time. The pressure springs exert increases as they are compressed, and they are rated by the amount of weight it takes to compress them. Ideally we would like a 10^{LB} spring to require 10^{LBS} of pressure to compress it to one half of its free length. In other words, if the spring was an inch long it would require 10^{LBS} of pressure to compress its length to one half inch long. So you can imagine (roughly, pretty roughly actually!) It will probably take only about 2^{LBS} of pressure to compress that spring one tenth of an inch, 4^{LBS} for two tenths of an inch, 6^{LBS} for ...... you get the picture!

Our 10^{LB} springs action, or working compressed length may be over two tenths of an inch, so its working weight will be from around 8 to 12^{LBS} of pressure which is probably quite acceptable over that range. But what if we want that spring to exert only one pound of pressure over the same two tenths of an inch of movement? Well, obviously it simply can't do that.

Its first one tenth of an inch compression will require 2^{LBS} of pressure and we are only half way to the action movement we want from that spring, so it is obviously completely unsuitable for our purpose. We need a different spring.

It is the same with trigger springs, except on a more miniscule scale.

Figure 4-2 (Page 164) is a table that lists the sizes and weights of the springs that I use, along with the same data for a factory Remington Model 700 trigger return spring. Photo 4-6 (Page 164) shows the springs themselves.

Typically a crisp no creep trigger will have close to .015" of sear engagement. The trigger return spring on a Remington is roughly ½ way between the pivot pin and the top of the sear, so the trigger spring will be required to move up to .0075" before the trigger breaks.

Doing the math from the table below you will see that in the first .005" of movement the factory spring will be at about 15^{OZ} of tension, more than double the tension we wanted. Simply put, it is totally unsuitable for the job. You just can't wind it out enough to make the weight you want, without disengaging it from the trigger slightly, and that is downright dangerous. *Don't do it!* Replace the spring with one that is suitable and is working within its action range.

Spring	Wire Diameter	Free length	Compressed length	Compression	Compressed weight
Remington Mod 700	.026"	.200"	.147"	.053"	More than 10 pounds
Short Soft	.0135"	.370"	.125"	.245"	8^{OZ}.
Long Soft	.0135"	.470"	.160"	.310"	11^{OZ}.
Short Inter	.016"	.320"	.155"	.165"	16^{OZ}.
Long Inter	.016"	.470"	.210"	.260"	26^{OZ}.

FIGURE 4-2.

The specifications of the trigger return springs I use.

PHOTO 4-6.

The trigger return springs I use. From the left, short and long soft, short and long medium. At the bottom is a factory Remington spring.

On the same note, don't use a spring in a trigger unless it has closed ends. The spring can be moving right into its hole in use, and a free sharp end can catch in the adjustment threads in the hole and stick. The result is no trigger return spring action, which could cause a serious accident. If you have to make a trigger return spring by cutting it from a longer length be sure to close the ends. Photo 4-7 shows what I am talking about here. Ok—back to the salt mine!

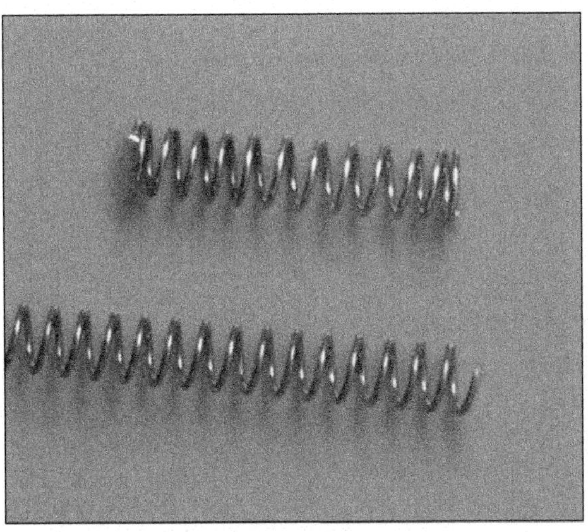

PHOTO 4-7.

At the top is a trigger spring with properly closed ends. At the bottom a spring with an open end. *Don't use open ended springs in triggers.*

4. Let's say our trigger breaks at 3^LBS^, so we have to work on it. This is a Remington trigger, so remove the bolt and secure the action in the soft jaws of your vice so you have access to the pins holding the trigger on the receiver.

4.1. I hope you aren't trying to do this job with a telescopic sight attached to the rifle. If so, smack yourself on the forehead and remove it!

4.2. Long 1/8" punches are best for this job if you have them. I get by with one long and one short. Make sure the safety catch is to the rear and then tap the rear pin through about 1/8", to release the bolt stop, and its spring, and give you access to the front trigger pin.

4.3. Tap the front trigger pin out with the long punch, and leave the punch through the hole to hold the top sear in place.

4.4. Tap out the rear trigger pin; leave the punch in the hole. Hold your hand under the receiver, with your finger pushing up on the top trigger sear, and remove the rear punch. There is a spring under the top sear you do not want to lose. It's a sneaky little booger so be careful!

4.5. Remove the long punch from the front pin hole, and take the trigger from the action. Remove the safety parts and bolt stop actuating slide, and place them in the tray with the trigger spring and screws.

5. Now I will want to examine the sear engagement closely. Ideally the two sears, top and bottom, will come together at exactly the same angle, but that is not always the case. If they are mismatched, bringing them into alignment may be all that is required to make the trigger good. On the other hand it may not, too. Anyway, I need to see if that is the case and decide which sear I will alter to bring them into line, in the event they are mismatched.

5.1. I don my 4x chemist glasses over my reading glasses. Install the top sear in the trigger housing with the front pin, but without the spring. Now I hold it up, with my bench light shining behind it so that it is back lit, and examine the sears in shadow relief with the 10x jewelers loupe. I don't know what the actual magnification power I have achieved is, with all of those optics, but it is enough.

5.2. The Remington trigger has a through hole in the housing so you can examine the sears. You will see what I am looking at when you give it a go. In Photo 4-1 (Page 155) you can see the sears in the sight hole, which is identified in Photo 4-4 (Page 161).

5.3. What sear would I adjust in the case of a mismatch? Well, remember we are aiming for a slight amount of rundown in the sear engagement, so I will be looking at which sear I can adjust to give me that. It can be either the top or bottom sear. Whichever one it is, I will make the adjustment, reassemble the trigger, and retest the weight before proceeding further. The procedure is exactly the same as we use when altering both sear angles, so for this exercise we'll pretend this trigger was ok.

6. Back out the trigger over travel screw and tap out the trigger bow retaining pin. This trigger is the older design with a separate shoe (slipper) that is the bottom sear. Triggers vary considerably in actual design, but they are all similar really, so I will leave you to work out the individual details for your unit. I am only giving you the general mechanics of the job, but you should be able to adapt that to your job easily enough. Place the parts in a tray for easy access.

7. The engagement screw on the trigger is much the same as the trigger return spring/weight adjustment screw. It is an adjustment screw locked in place with a lock screw, and that lock screw covered with varnish. *Leave this screw alone*, as we don't want to move it unless we really have to. Identify it in Photo 4-4, Page 161.

7.1. The only reason I will move this screw is if, when the sears are adjusted and I am final tuning, the trigger feels a bit creepy and requires a little less sear engagement. Once I am forced to move it though, I will make a modification to the system because I don't like that lock screw system on an engagement screw. The modification I make is to install a side lock screw in the trigger housing, which is a much more positive way to lock the engagement adjustment. It also allows it to be easily and precisely adjusted to boot. I always made that modification when I converted these triggers to a 3 lever, 2^{oz} design, so I will detail it later when I describe that. (Page 179)

Before we go any further I'd better discuss trigger reassembly. Make yourself a couple of pins, from #31 diameter drill rod, the same width as the trigger housing. Before you reassemble the trigger to the action, trap the top sear, with its spring, in the trigger housing with these pins (you can see them in action in Photo 4-1, Page 155). Line the trigger up in its recess in the action, and push the front pin through with your long punch. Leave the punch in the action, and push the rear pin through with your other punch. Leave it there too. Now you can tap the trigger pins through, at the same time removing the punches. Install the rear pin first, and the front pin second. When you install a Remington trigger always check that the sides of the housing are fully against the side of the trigger recess. Tap them lightly with a punch, to ensure that the internal parts are free to move, and are not binding. Photo 4-8 shows a trigger part way through reassembly.

PHOTO 4-8.

The front assembly pin has been pushed out of the housing, and can be seen sitting on the vice soft jaws. The punch will remain in the hole, and will be pushed out by the trigger retaining pin when it is tapped through the hole. I have pushed the rear assembly pin part way out here.

8. What we are going to do now involves a lot of eye ball engineering and precise guess work. I know that's a contradiction of terms, but that's exactly what it is. It would be really nice to have a comparator that would project our setup onto a large screen, complete with a grid, so that we could precisely adjust the angle of our piece. That just doesn't happen in my workshop, and I doubt it does in yours, so we just have to do the best we can. I've been doing this job for over 40 years and know, beyond any doubt, that eyeball engineering and precise guess work not withstanding, you can do an excellent job, and make a really good trigger, so don't despair.

8.1. We'll start with the bottom sear. Secure it lightly in the drill press vice, at the end, just like in Photo 4-9. Bring the spacer up to it and make the top of the sear straight and level with it. Move the spacer 2" away from the sear.

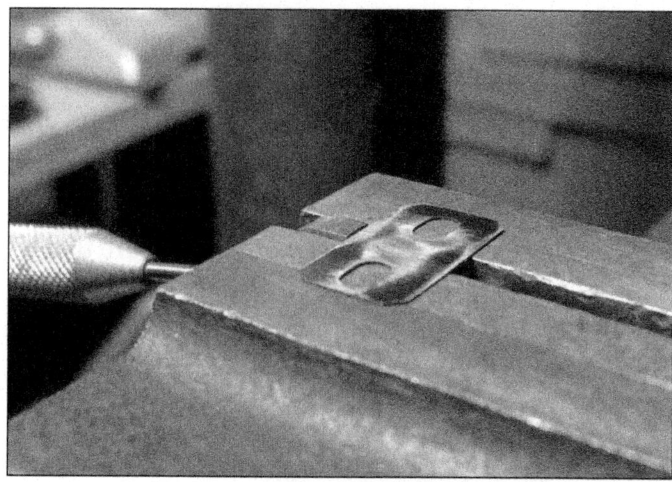

PHOTO 4-9.
I am about to level the sear surface with the spacer. The pin punch is placed through the hole in the part, and allows me to manipulate this small part into place more easily.

8.2. Lay the 6" straight edge on the spacer and the sear, and with magnification, and back lighting, adjust the sear so that it is level with the straight edge. See Photo 4-10.

8.3. Now move the rear of the sear part down about 1° and tighten the vice. Under magnification you will see the angle you have created. Don't over do it; better less than more. We are sneaking up on this, so go slowly and carefully, and don't make the angle too steep.

PHOTO 4-10.
Adjusting the angle of the sear surface.

8.4. Take the soft Arkansas stone and rest it on both the sear and the spacer. It should be wet with baby oil from being stored in a puddle of it. Be very careful to hold the stone flat and even on the sear and give it three *light*, one inch strokes back and forth, concentrating on keeping it level and straight.

8.5. Wipe the sear dry with a tissue and have a look at what you have done. The amount of material we need to remove here is miniscule, and a soft Arkansas stone will cut quickly and smoothly.

8.5.1. Remember, our sear engagement will end up being only about .015" or less, so we don't have to cut a very wide ledge here. About .030" will be plenty wide enough. Make sure you are cutting flat. We don't want this surface to be lopsided, otherwise both sears will not mate properly. If there is any unevenness, adjust the way you are holding the stone to compensate.

8.6. When you have created a suitable ledge, switch to the hard Arkansas stone and give it a few strokes to polish the surface even further. Remove the part from the vice and clean it up.

9. Repeat the exercise with the top sear. Try to make the angle as close as you can to the angle you made on the bottom sear. Again we need only around a .030" wide ledge. Photo 4-11 (Page 169) shows it in the drill vice.

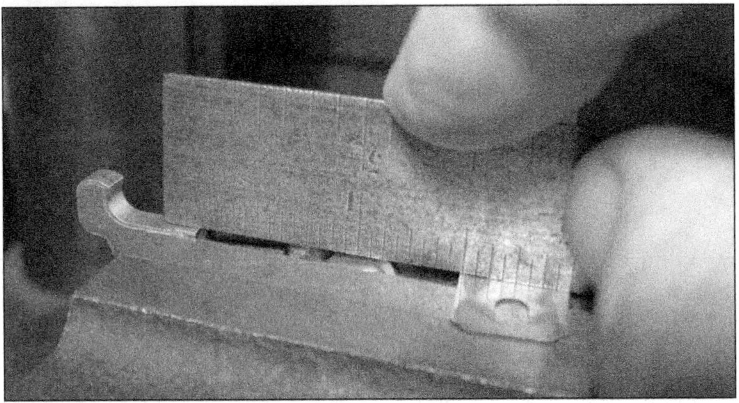

PHOTO 4-11.

Preparing to stone the top trigger sear.

10. Buff the two ledges on the sears with the Summabrax felt wheel on the Dremel tool, being careful not to round the edge, and then polish them with the white polish wheel. Photo 4-12 shows my Dremel tool and polishing wheels, and Photo 4-13 shows the method I use to polish a sear.

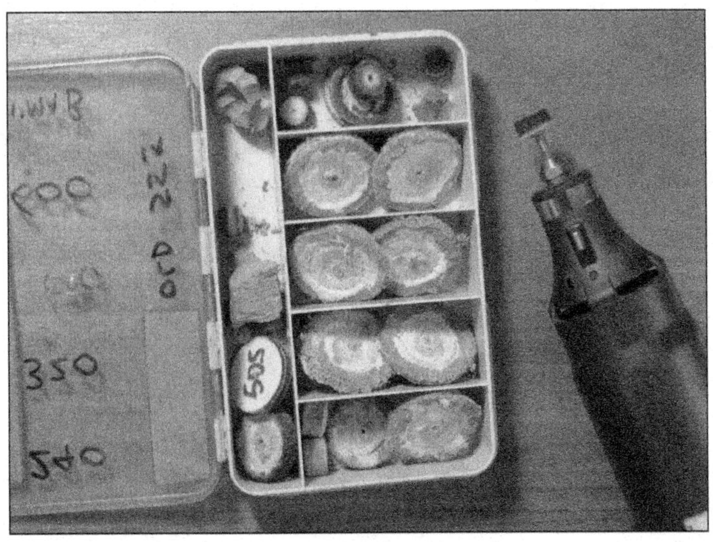

PHOTO 4-12.

For polishing stoned sears only the small wheels and compounds in the top and left compartments are needed.

10.1. Both of these operations take seconds to do, and when finished the sear surfaces will shine like a mirror. Clean the sears up.

PHOTO 4-13.

The method I use to polish the sears. Note how I steady my hands with my fingers touching. I draw the felt wheel across the flat sear surface paying attention not to round the 90° angle at the end.

11. Reassemble the trigger, replace it in the action and make the trigger pressure test again just like we did in step 3.

11.1. We are aiming for a pull weight of ¾^{LB} (12^{OZ}) to one pound (16^{OZ}) — somewhere in between would be excellent. If your trigger breaks within those weights, well and good, you need go no further.

11.2. Even if you did not make our target weight, you will have reduced the originally tested weight somewhat, so you should have an idea of what effect the angle you made has caused. Obviously if your weight is close to one pound, let's say 18^{OZ,} you don't need to adjust the sear angle much further, but you do still need to adjust it a little. Two ounces of trigger return pressure is not enough of a margin to ensure dependable trigger return. In that scenario be very careful not to overdo the angle.

12. Assuming we didn't make our target weight, we simply have to repeat step 8 through 11 until we do.

12.1. When we are restoning the sear surfaces we have an opportunity to gauge our angle and adjust it slightly if need be. Just take one light pass over the highly polished sear surface, clean and examine it carefully under magnification. You will easily see the mark the soft Arkansas stone has made on the highly polished surface. What I find, most of the time, is I am too conservative with my second angle, and have actually set the angle at the original angle, so need to sharpen it a tad. All I can say is to be careful, watch what you are doing and you will get there.

12.2. Sometimes I get the weight I want in one go, and sometimes it takes up to four goes.

13. We have arrived at an acceptable trigger pull weight, so install a soft action trigger return spring and adjust the screw to bring the trigger weight to just under 1¼LBS.

14. Reassemble the rifle, recheck that the chamber is clear, insert the bolt, shoulder it and dry fire it just like you would fire it out in the field. While you are doing this concentrate really hard on the feel of the trigger. Do it a few times to be sure of what you are feeling.

14.1. The trigger should break like a piece of glass rod. You should be concentrating on taking up the pressure, and then it should be gone. No discernible trigger movement at all.

14.2. If it feels good, shut the bolt smartly a few times to make sure it holds ok. If you did it right it should, and you can say, "Job well done."

15. If the trigger does have a bit of creep, that will have to be adjusted out with the sear engagement screw, located at the back of the trigger housing. I talked about this screw in step 7, so refer back to it now if you don't remember. (I will be testing you on this stuff later, you know!)

15.1. If you wish, jump forward to the 3 lever conversion section on page 179 for a description of this modification. There is not much sense in me describing it twice. Photo 4-22 (Page 179) shows the dimensions.

15.2. We'll proceed as if you have already made the modification.

16. Screwing the engagement screw in reduces sear engagement, and screwing it out increases it. The trick here is to adjust the screw to give us the *maximum* amount of engagement, at which the trigger still feels good.

16.1. We want as much engagement as possible. Make your screw adjustment, with the newly installed lock screw tightened lightly against the adjustment screw, so you can feel resistance when you adjust.

16.2. When you think you have it right, rig a dial indicator behind the trigger and see how much trigger movement you have before the trigger breaks. Aim for between .008" to .012", .010" being preferred.

PHOTO 4-14.
My setup for measuring trigger sear engagement.

16.2.1. To make this measurement you do it backwards. Drop the top sear, and as you slowly open the bolt observe the position of the sears through the sight hole. Just as the top sear reaches the tip of the bottom sear, note the reading on the dial indicator. When you lift the bolt the bottom sear will snap back into place, and you can read off the amount of movement on the dial indicator. Do it a few times to make sure your measurement is right.

16.2.2. Photo 4-14 shows how I hold the dial indicator to take the readings. Note that the probe is located in the middle of the trigger bow.

16.3. When you have the engagement right, tighten up the engagement screws lock screw and recheck. It doesn't take much movement to spoil the job. If it's still ok put ½ a drop of green Locktite Wick-In on the lock screw, and while you're at it, put the other ½ drop on the return spring adjustment screw. Pat yourself on the back, if you can reach that far.

17. You will notice that I did not mention adjusting the over travel screw so that the trigger had minimum movement after it broke. Modern conventional wisdom states that it is not a good idea to stop the trigger dead immediately after it has broken, as it will interfere with your hold and your follow through. This wisdom comes from champion marksmen far better and smarter than I am, and I am unable to disagree. I have set up my personal rifles, both hunting and target with maximum over travel for some 27 years now with no detriment to their performance, so suggest you do the same.

17.1. The over travel screw on the Remington 700 trigger is the top screw at the front of the trigger housing (Photo 4-4, Page 161). The top sear return spring sits on it, and also holds it from turning. Just ensure that it is deep enough in its hole to fully support that spring and no more.

18. There is a possibility that a screw or two may be sitting proud of the trigger housing after all of this, so check that you have clearance in the stock before you reassemble everything for the last time.

The work we have just completed created a really good trigger for use on a hunting rifle for medium or large game. The triggers on my hunting rifles are exactly like that, and work extremely well. However, it is not the sort of trigger I want for my varmint or target rifles. For them I would prefer something much lighter, 2^{OZ} weight of pull, rather than $1\frac{1}{4}^{LBS}$.

A novice might ask, "Well why don't you just use the 2^{OZ} version on all of your rifles?" The answer to that is, a 2^{OZ} trigger is something that must be used with precision and delicacy. You have to concentrate to feel the trigger bow. In short it is not the sort of trigger you want on a hunting rifle, where you are likely to be swinging the rifle, tracking running game, while shooting from the standing position after a hard sprint. Many shooters can't use a 2^{OZ} trigger at all, without a deal of practice.

The easiest way to go about this is to spring for the expense of a Jewel or Kelbly trigger, if you're that way inclined. However, the standard Remington 700 trigger can be made into a perfectly acceptable 3 lever design with a bit of effort. I have been using triggers I have converted for over 30 years, and they still provide sterling service. I currently have three in full time service, and keep one as a spare, that I take with me to away open F Class competitions, just in case. I have never had to use it. Photo 4-15 shows the internal parts and layout of the 2^{OZ} trigger design I use. Note that, when properly assembled, the 3RD lever return spring would be rotated one more turn, and its tail would bear on the flat surface on the bottom of the 3RD lever.

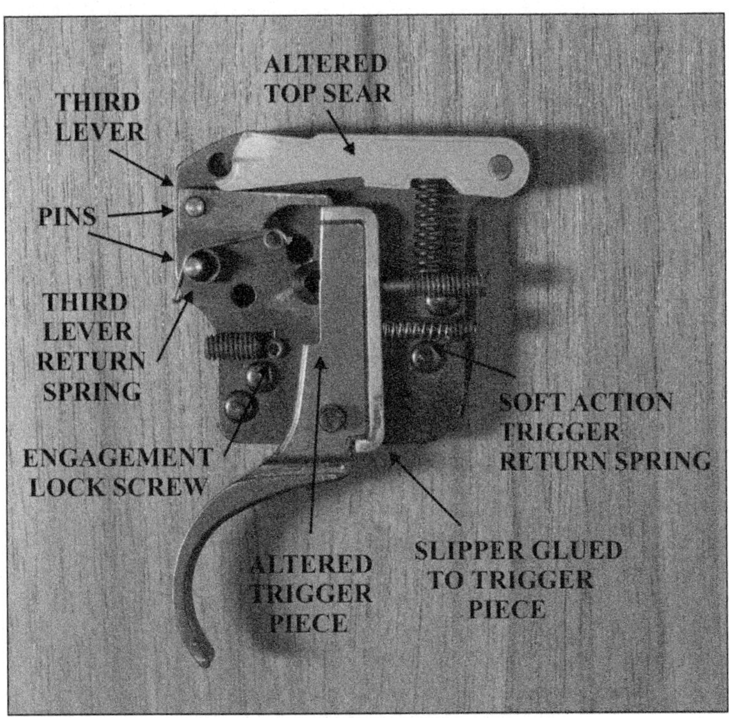

PHOTO 4-15.

The internals of a 2^{OZ} 3 lever trigger.

I won't bore you with the fine details of this triggers construction, but rather present the drawings and comment on details I think you should be aware of. You will tune the trigger exactly as I described the tuning of the 2 lever design, after all we are still dealing with sears. Sears are all basically the same, whatever trigger they are in. Often this trigger will work with a flat sear angle. The loading on the sear is very light with this design, so when tuning the sears *don't go grabbing a big chunk of angle* or you may well over do it.

To make this trigger we need some extra parts. We need to alter a couple of Remington's existing parts, and drill some precisely located holes. The extra parts we need are:–

1. A third lever (duh!).
2. A third lever return spring.
3. Two pins.
4. A 6BA grub screw.

Let's start with the third lever. I made them from 1010 mild steel and case hardened them .020" deep, by cooking them in Hardite case hardening powder, in a furnace I had suitable for small parts. To do this you must soak the parts in red hot molten Hardite for around 45 minutes. I used to put several pieces of mild steel wire in the container with the parts, withdraw one every 15 minutes, and quench it in water. Then cut ½" off the end, with an abrasive wheel in a Dremel tool, and polish the end to a fine finish. Under magnification you will easily see the depth of the case you have, by the difference in colour and grain between the hard outside skin, and the soft core. When you reach the desired depth quench the parts in room temperature water. When I was doing this work I lived hundreds of miles from a major centre, so made do with what I had on hand. As I said, these parts have served me well for over 30 years and many thousands of cycles, so they can't be too bad. If you are able make them from some exotic steel, and have them professionally hardened by all means do that. Remember, I am only providing information here, not a recommendation.

Referring to Figure 4-3, this is a straight forward milling job. To mill the sear surface itself I used a 3/8" diameter end mill, plunge cut to length then advanced it .005" and slowly wound it out of the piece to make a fine finish, and create the flat sear surface. Bevel the ends of the hole slightly with a 60° countersink, and make the bevels at the other end with a 6" fine hand file. Polish the part all over to a 400 grit finish to remove all tool marks before you harden it. It will be much more difficult to do that after hardening, and you will be eating into your case thickness as well.

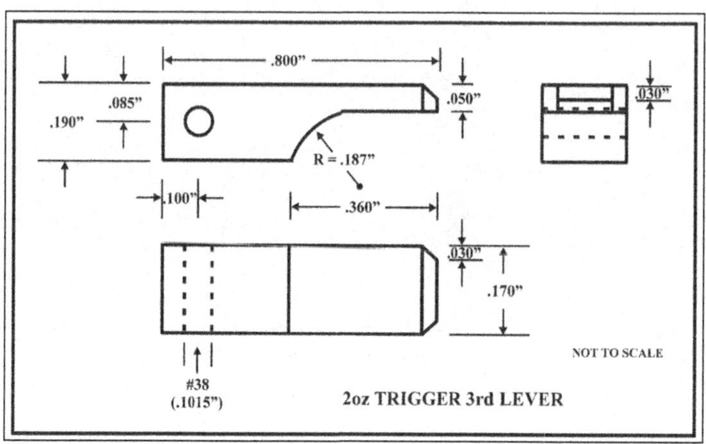

Figure 4-3.

The dimensions required for making the third lever.

After hardening give the sides a rub on a flat surface with 600 grit wet and dry paper to polish them, and give the pivot pin hole a bit of a polish to smooth it. The nose of the part will be sliding against the upper part of the trigger piece to retract, so it should also be polished. You can please yourself about the rest.

As with the parent Remington 700 trigger, this is a good through sear design that allows a long stone stroke length, unlike those notched designs I love to hate.

The third lever return spring looks complicated, but is actually pretty easy to make. I made a small jig, see Photos 4-16 and 4-17 (Page 175), that I use in the lathe for this job. I will detail the steps I take to make this spring so there will be no confusion in your mind. Photo 4-18 (Page 176) shows the dimensions of the spring, as well as the modification needed to the Remington bolt stop pin. We have to cut a groove in the pin to allow for the safety parts we won't be using, so that we can space the retaining circlip in, and continue to use the original bolt stop actuator. Cut the groove with a thin parting tool. Find the position needed by fitting up the parts.

1. Secure the jig in a 3 jaw chuck in your lathe.

2. Select a length of .020" diameter spring steel wire about 12" long. The minimum length required is 4".

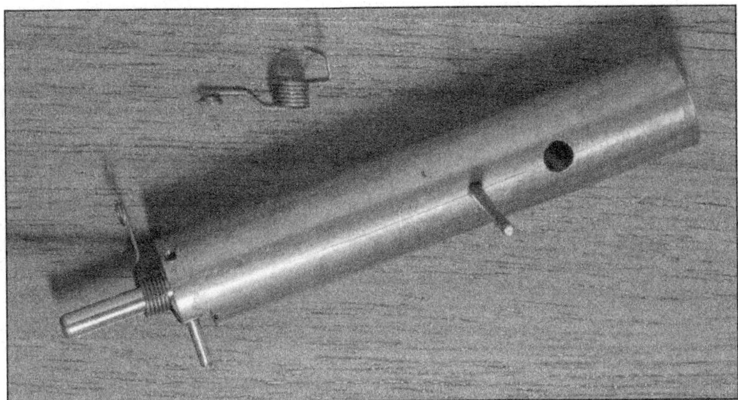

PHOTO 4-16.

My lathe driven spring making jig. The pin and hole on the body are for closing the tail end. See PHOTO 4-19 (PAGE 177).

PHOTO 4-17.

A close up of the head of my spring making jig.

3. Bend one end to make the square ended hook as in Photo 4-18.

4. Grip the other end of the spring wire with a pair of vice grips.

5. You will need an offsider to turn the lathe on and off, unless you have an extra arm, and hand, growing out of your rear end. Get him/her ready. Mine was a 'her'.

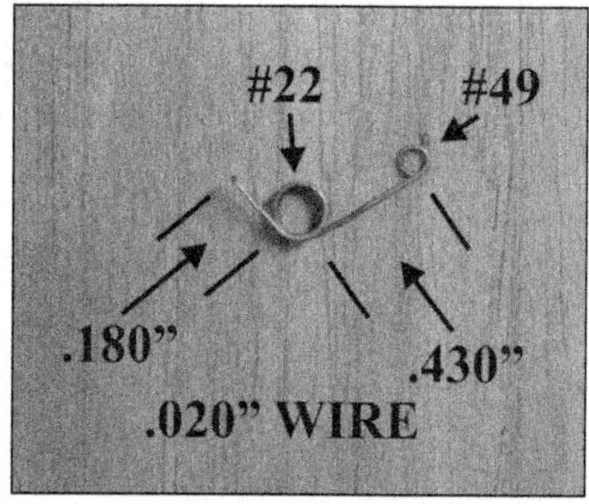

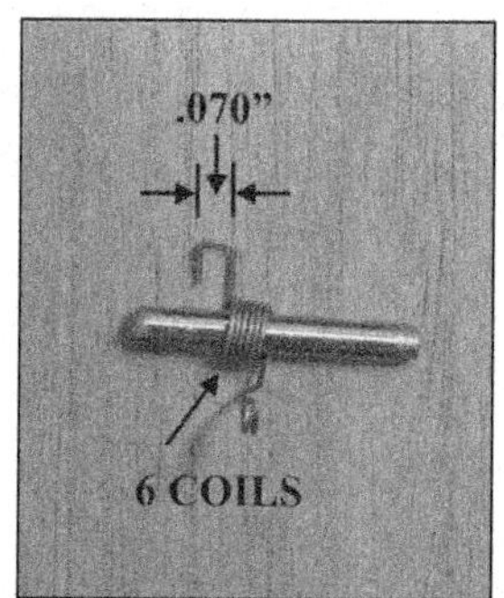

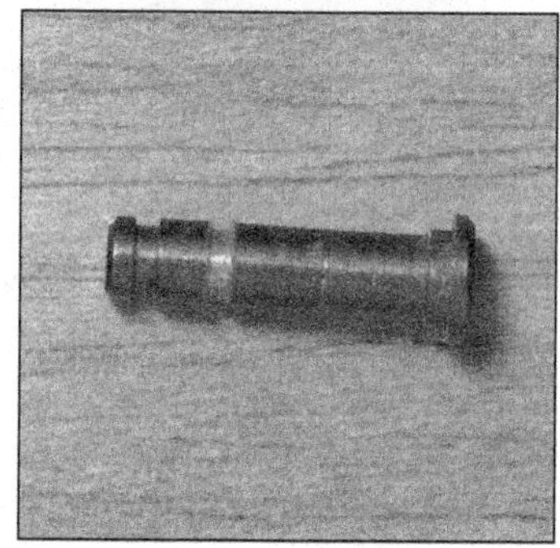

PHOTO 4-18.

The dimensions of the 3RD sear return spring. Also the alteration needed, for the bolt stop actuator retaining pin, to space the retaining circlip in.

6. Hook the square ended hook over the pin on the fixture, and hold the wire under a fair bit of tension with the vice grips.

7. Select the slowest speed your lather will turn at. Mine is 30RPM.

8. Keep the tension on the vice grips, and have your offsider turn on the lathe; Count off seven (7) turns, then, at the same time, release the tension on the vice grips, and tell your offsider to turn off the lathe.

8.1. While you are winding keep the coils tight, and right next to each other.

9. Remove the part from the fixture, and bend the long tail to centre as in Photo 4-18.

10. Hold the winding fixture in your bench vice, wind the round tail on the part, and cut off the excess wire. Photo 4-19 (Page 177) shows a spring on the jig.

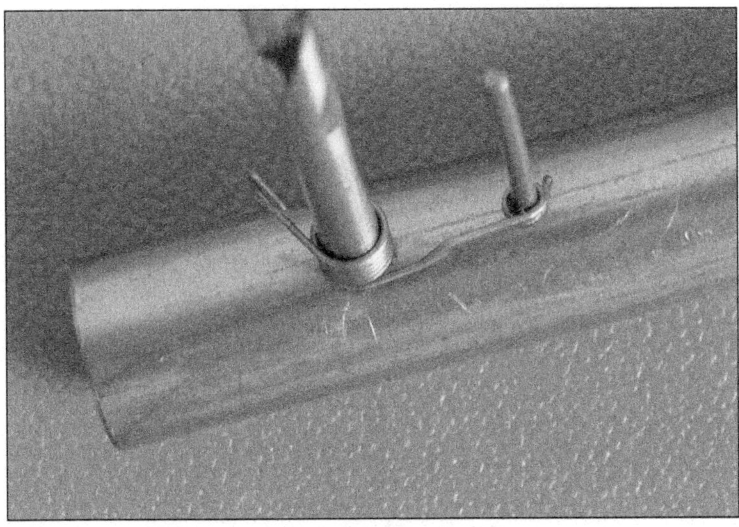

PHOTO 4-19.
The spring tail has been wound and cut off.

11. Make an adjustment to the angle of the spring if needed.

Pretty simple really; it took me about 10 minutes to make a spring in batches of ten when I was doing that job.

Remington's trigger bow has to be altered as per the drawing. It's handy if you have a mill to do this job with. You could also arrive at the same destination with a file and a bit of effort as well. There is not that much material to remove. The only caveat here is, don't go past the end of the sear slipper. Leave a couple of thousandths of an inch proud to be polished to a perfect fit later. Photo 4-20 shows the dimensions.

The sear slipper has to be glued in place — 24 hour Araldite is fine for this job. Epoxy glues need heat to cure properly, so after you rough up the parts, with coarse wet and dry, and clean them with alcohol, warm them up a bit under your bench light while you mix the glue. I hold the slipper in place with small vice grips, while the Epoxy hardens properly, under my bench light. Just be sure to get the slipper properly lined up when the vice grip is clamped on. After the Epoxy has hardened polish that rear surface to a high shine, and blend it into the rear of the slipper, so there is no ledge to catch the 3RD lever when it retracts. Photo 4-21 shows how I hold the pieces together for gluing.

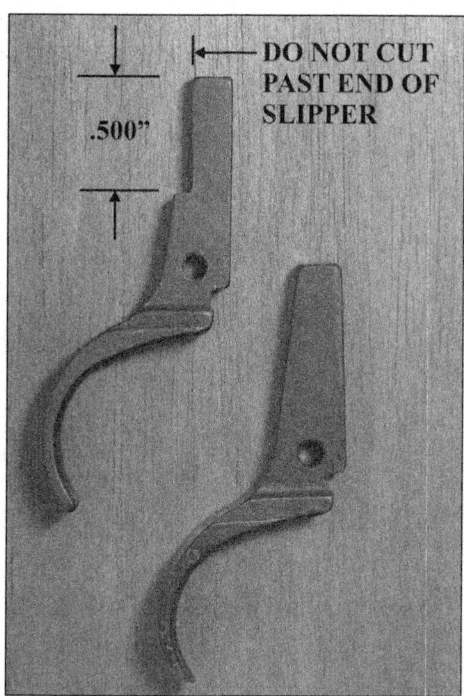

PHOTO 4-20.
The factory Remington trigger piece and an altered sample.

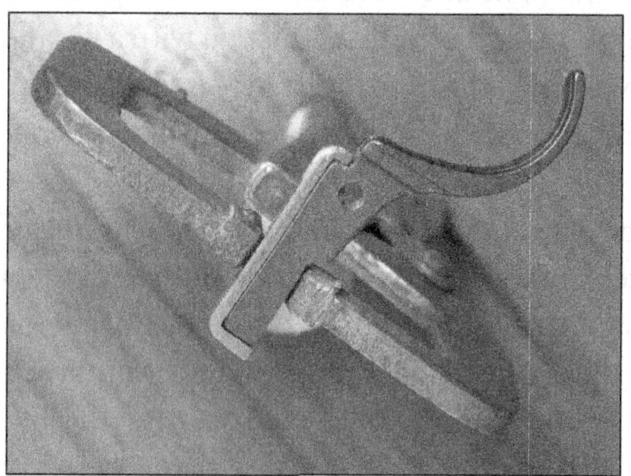

PHOTO 4-21.
Method of holding the pieces together for gluing.

The two cross pins can be made from drill rod. Make them the same width as the trigger housing, and chamfer the ends with a file, so they can be trapped in the trigger housing, with a prick punch, when tuning is complete.

We have to drill 3 holes in the trigger housing, and tap one to 6BA. Be sure you use sharp drills for this job, as these housings can be tough. I have found some that were too hard to drill, and had to be spot annealed. I used to do this with an oxy torch set to a very fine flame. When we had Solar electricity installed, the installer had a tiny little torch that produced the finest spot flame I have ever seen. That would be perfect for spot annealing the trigger housing. You don't have to get it very hot. If the part was shiny, heating the drill spots to just past straw colour would be fine, so *don't* go heating it red hot. We are just drawing the temper a bit, which takes no more than a second or two application of an oxy torch. Photo 4-22 gives you the dimensions for the drilling and tapping job. The trigger housing should not even be discoloured when you finish spot annealing it. The drilled and tapped hole is the one referred to on page 166, step 7.

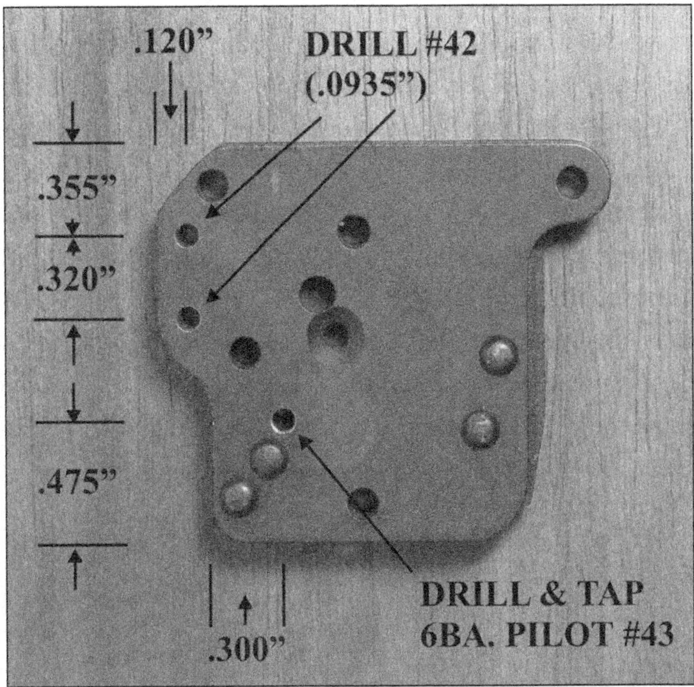

PHOTO 4-22.

The dimensions needed for altering the trigger housing. The hole to be drilled and tapped to 6BA is for the new lock screw that will secure the engagement screw. It must be installed if it is necessary to move the engagement screw to reduce creep in a two lever trigger tuning job, as described in step 7, on page 166.

Get yourself a piece of shiny flat steel 1/16TH of an inch thick, and practice before you commit yourself to the trigger housing. You will quickly see what is required.

I lay out the holes with a dial height gauge. Just be sure to lay them out and drill them accurately.

The top sear modification is also straight forward. This part is as hard as, and must be ground to size. I used to remove the excess material on my bench grinder by hand, being very careful not to overheat the part and draw the temper. I then finish ground it to size on a surface grinder. The rounded end was ground on a fine wheel by hand, stoned and polished to a fine finish. Photo 4-23 gives you the information you need.

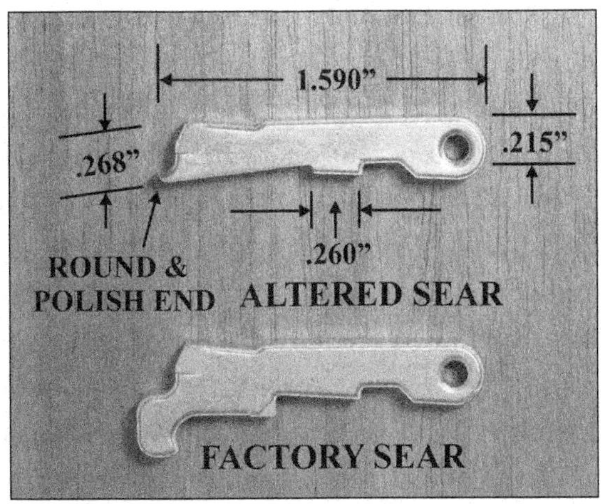

PHOTO 4-23.

The dimensions for the altered falling sear.

This trigger is tuned exactly as you tuned the two lever trigger, stoning the sears flat to start with, as that may well be satisfactory for you just like that. If not, carefully adjust the angles until it is satisfactory. As I said before, the sear loading is considerably reduced in this design, so you will not need much down angle to make it work. Photo 4-24 (Page 180) shows some tools I used to make the job easier. At the top left is the mount spacer I used when honing sears on my drill vice, before I made a jig with which to do that job. Next to the spacer is the dolly I use at my bench to knock pins out with. The pins fall into the hole and are captured.

Under the dolly is a fixture I made so that I could examine sear angles closely out of their trigger housing. It is far more convenient than reassembling the trigger every time you want to check sear relationship. Of course you must reassemble the trigger in the rifle to test weight and feel.

PHOTO 4-24.
Some of the tools I use in tuning triggers.

This trigger design is not suitable for a trigger pull much heavier than 6 ounces. To make, say, a one pound weight, will require a deal more tension on the trigger return spring, which will prevent the third lever from retracting, by jamming it against the back of the trigger piece. Getting this trigger to work is a bit of a balancing act due to the various forces that have to interact. Sometimes it will not want to break due to the accumulation of upward force on the top sear, generated by the top sear spring and the third lever return springs combined pressure, overcoming the power exerted by the firing pin spring. If this is the case try removing the top sear return spring, as there is plenty of power in the

3RD lever return spring, combined with the leverage between those two parts, to return the top sear into position when you lift the bolt. If the trigger will work with the top sear return spring installed I leave it there, but if it doesn't there is no problem in leaving it out, or replacing it with a lighter version.

Whenever you work on a trigger, that has a safety, it is incumbent upon you to ensure that the safety is operational before it leaves your possession. While you may not rely on a safety (I certainly don't) someone else who handles the rifle may, and if the safety is not functioning it can lead to a serious accident. The Remington 700 trigger is good in this regard, because its safety acts on the top sear, by raising it up, away from the bottom sear, so it is not affected by any adjustment made to the sears. Regardless, you should still test it before you let it out from your control.

Not all triggers are so obliging. Some safeties work by blocking the forward movement of the trigger piece, by jamming its top in the rearward position. You will find that, when you have adjusted the sears, you may have created a gap between the locking surface, and the trigger piece, that will allow the top sear to release with the safety engaged. The operation of this type of safety requires very close tolerances to be maintained. Quite frankly, it is a mongrel design that should not be used. The Sako L series triggers are examples, and there are others.

Sakos have no engagement adjustment, it being fixed in the design, so if the trigger is creepy, and you need to reduce the creep, you can only do it by grinding a bit from the face of the falling sear, immediately above the sear surface. If you overdo that, and have to increase the depth of the sear a smidgen, by again removing material from the falling sear, from that protrusion under the sear itself, to increase engagement, you may well find the safety will no longer work. So tread lightly if you are working on a Sako L series trigger.

In Photo 4-25, you can see how the safety rod will block the trigger piece when it is rotated. The notch in the rod provides clearance when the safety is in the off position. Looking at the photo, you can appreciate the fine tolerances needed for this design to work. If the tolerance is too tight, the safety will not engage fully or not at all, and if it is too loose it will allow the sears to disengage. Probably the best thing, certainly the easiest, is to replace it with a good aftermarket version. It can be made

into a good trigger with a bit of work, as I have described, but the job is tedious due to the shallow notched falling sear of the design. I have come across many terrible examples done by guys who should have known better. I have seen some other trigger designs with an adjustable screw, that bears against the trigger piece, to block it from moving when the safety is on, and that is certainly better than a fixed, no adjustment, design.

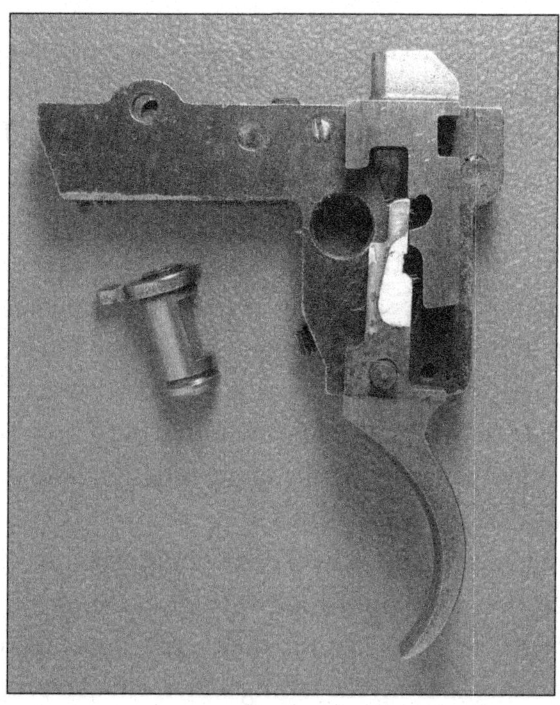

PHOTO 4-25.

You can see where the safety rod engages the trigger piece on this Sako L series trigger.

The safety on a Winchester M'70 acts directly on the firing pin, retracting the firing pin tail back, away from the top sear when it is applied. When you adjust the trigger sears you will find that the safety will not work, because the adjusted sears have allowed the firing pin to move forward, several thousandths of an inch, and out of reach of the safety cam. To make the safety work you will have to grind an amount away from the engaging surface at the firing pin tail. The Winchester M'70 safety is a three position design — safety off, safe on allowing the bolt to be operated, and safe on with the bolt locked down. It is a good design as far as safeties are concerned, and has been copied in aftermarket form for use on other action brands.

If your M'70 safety doesn't work, remove the bolt from the rifle and hold the bottom of the firing pin tail in a vice. Grasp the bolt body and pull it towards you until you can engage the safety lever to the middle position. Re-insert the bolt into the action, and you can now engage the safety into the third, or fully locked position. Now, with a dial caliper, measure the distance from the rear of the firing pin tail to the rear of the bolt shroud. Photo 4-26 is not a Winchester but shows the measurement being taken. Now push the safety lever to the 'fire' position and take another measurement. The difference, between the two measurements, is the amount that must be removed from the engaging surface, on the firing pin tail, to make the safety work.

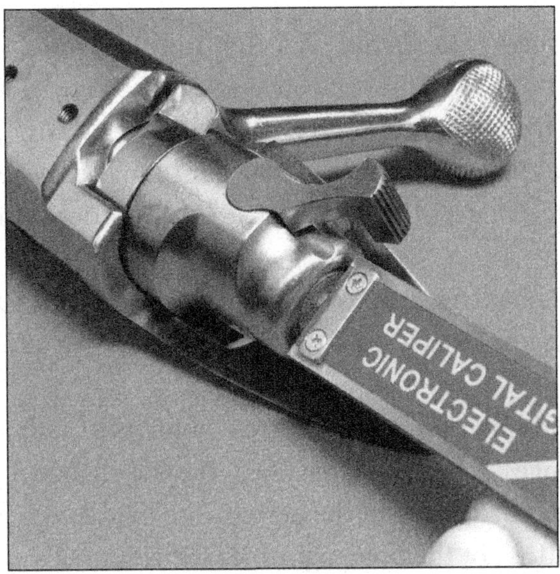

PHOTO 4-26.

The point where measurements must be taken, to determine the amount that must be ground, from the firing pin tail, to make the safety operational. This action is a Remington Model 700, but the Winchester M'70 is the same.

I used to adjust the firing pin tail with the firing pin held in a machine vice on my surface grinder. Photo 4-27 shows me doing that job, sometime in the 1980s. Be careful — you don't want to over cook it. If I had .010" to remove, I would remove .007", reassemble the bolt, and see how it went. If it still didn't work, I would re-measure, to confirm my measurement, and then take the remaining .003". It's relatively easy to remove material, and not so easy to put it back. Ideally, you want the safety to work with a bit of effort, and then you can polish the mating surface, to a fine finish, which will make the safety work easily, and smooth as silk.

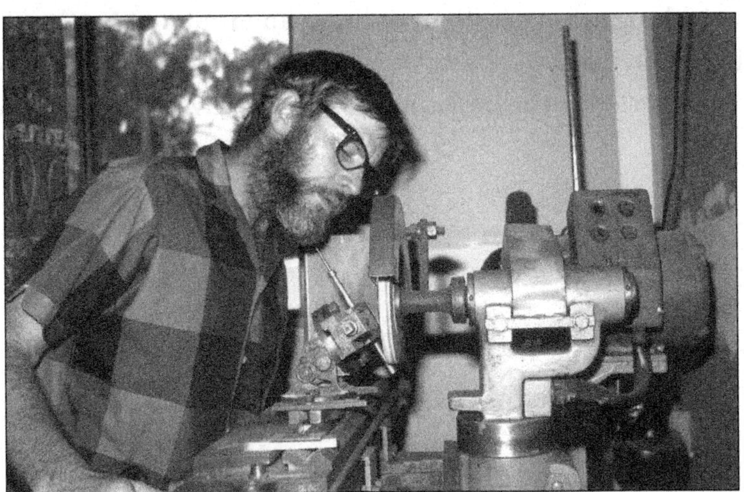

PHOTO 4-27.

Grinding a precise amount, from the firing pin tail of a Remington Model 700, in order to get a 3 position side-swing safety to work. The Winchester M'70 firing pin tail is adjusted in exactly the same way.

Just be aware that if you let a trigger out of your sight with a safety that is not working properly, you are setting a trap for an unwary player that could have tragic consequences.

Photo 4-4 (Page 161) shows the layout of a Remington Model 700 two lever trigger, and that design is a very good one. Whenever you work on a trigger, keep that design in mind, and use it as a reference. Often a manufacturer will change a design, not because they want to make it better, but because they want to make it easier to make. When you run across this sort of idiocy, don't be afraid to convert the part back to the old design if it is obvious to you that the old one was better.

I ran into this with the Canjar triggers I used a lot of years ago. It's a pity no one took that business over, as they were a good trigger — I have used them for over forty years, and still have two in service on my hunting rifles.

I guess it's a human condition that, when we are comfortable with something, we immediately notice when the feeling changes, especially if we don't like the change. I received a new shipment of triggers, and noticed that they had changed the design. The new design allowed the trigger pressure to be adjusted, from the bottom of the housing, while the rifle was assembled, which I guess they thought was a good thing.

To make the design work they transferred the trigger spring pressure from under the housing, 90° to the trigger piece, with two ball bearings. When the trigger was pulled it pushed against the ball that rested against it, which pushed the second ball down against the trigger spring. Even though the amount of movement was very small at that point, probably only to the order of .002" to .003", the two balls, rubbing against each other, made the trigger feel absolutely terrible.

I simply couldn't handle a trigger like that, so whenever I installed one of the new design Canjar triggers I converted it back to the old design, by drilling and tapping a new trigger return spring hole in the appropriate place, and installing one of my soft action springs, and a new grub screw. I left the existing grub screw in place, to block the hole, and removed the spring and two balls. Something to go play marbles with!

If you run across something like that, which is obviously not right, don't be afraid to change it. Many manufacturers design things with expediency in mind, not for their design to be correct.

So that's the ABC's of trigger work. Remember Commandment #12, and always put safety first. It is a far nicer experience to smoke a Cuban in Heaven, than that other thing in that other place!

Pretty rifles do get out into the field. My mate, Tom Buvac, is in the top photo with a Boar he took, right on dark, after we sneaked up on a tank, in central western Queensland. The rifle is the sweet little 308 Winchester, built on a Remington Model 700 action, that showed me how hot fibreglass stocks could be out in the hot sun (See page 153). In the bottom photo he is with a Dingo taken in far north South Australia. The rifle is a 25/06 Improved built on a Remington Model 700 action, with an electric trigger. It is deadly Dingo medicine.

AN M'98 MAUSER IN .270 WINCHESTER

STARTED AROUND 1977, NOT FINISHED UNTIL THE EARLY 1980S

PHOTO C4-1.

The stick was a nicely figured piece of California English walnut. This rifle was a bit of a hybrid. I started to build it around 1977 as a shop rifle to be sold when completed, but never finished it due to other pressures. Eventually my design had moved on, so I had no intention of finishing it without a compete stock design rework. Anyway, a guy saw it in the early 1980s, loved it and insisted I finish it for him as it was. Needing the finance I relented. I guess it didn't turn out too bad.

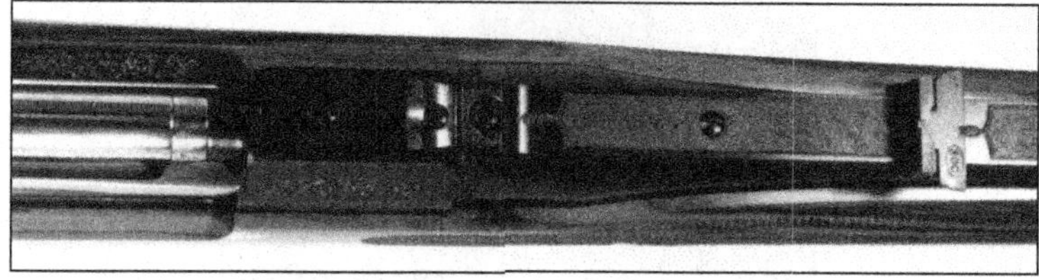

PHOTO C4-2.

I stippled the top of the custom made ¼ rib to reduce glare.

PHOTO C4-3.

While the stock is of my early design, the metalwork sports the fine English scroll engraving Phil Vinnicombe was doing on my later rifles.

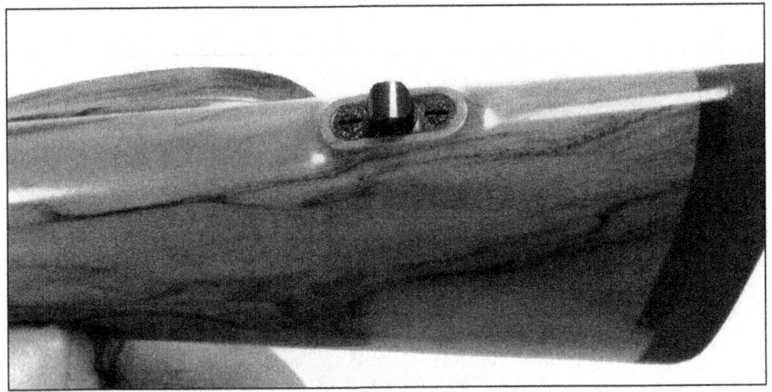

PHOTO C4-4.

The rear swivel base was of 2 screw raised ledge design.

PHOTO C4-5.

¼ rib profile. Scope mounts were side lever quick detachable on my custom bases.

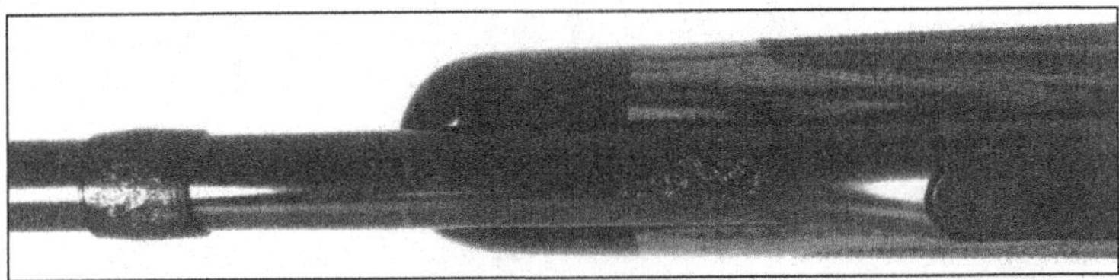

PHOTO C4-6.

Barrel banded front sling swivel, and African Ebony forend tip.

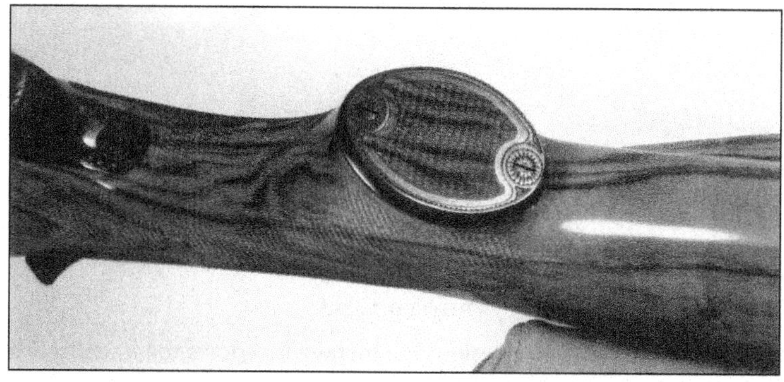

PHOTO C4-7.

The skeleton grip cap was a flat design from Dave Talley.

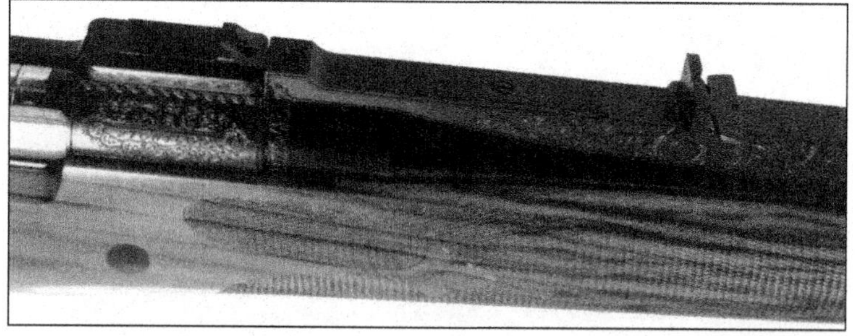

PHOTO C4-8.

¼ rib with one standing and one folding leaf rear sight. Note the recoil ledge at the front of the scope base. These bases were individually made for each rifle.

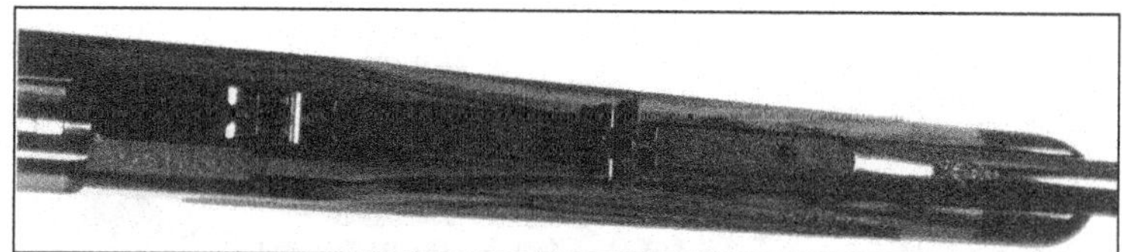

PHOTO C4-9.

I profile ground the receiver to reduce its width and weight.

PHOTO C4-23.

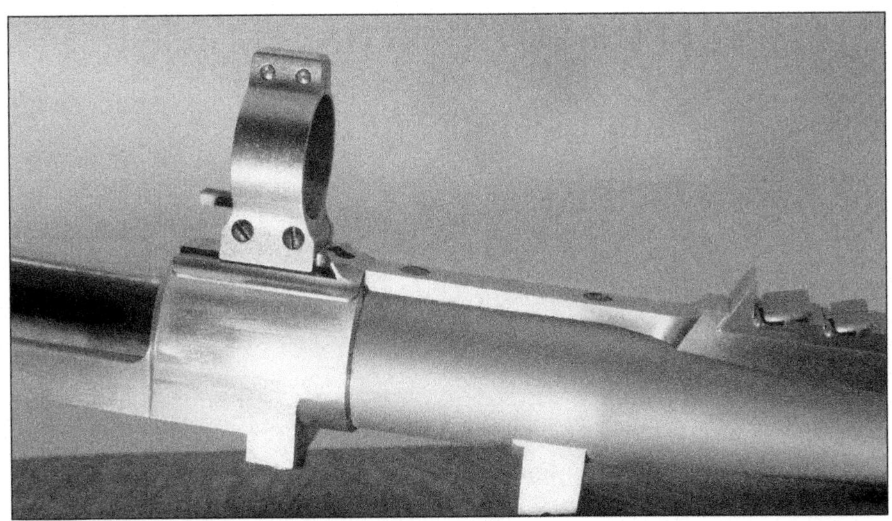

PHOTO C4-24.

PHOTOS C4-23 and C4-24, metalwork in process for a Mauser M'98 in .375 H&H Magnum. Note the second recoil lug. PHOTO C4-25, Setting up to machine a ¼ rib tail.

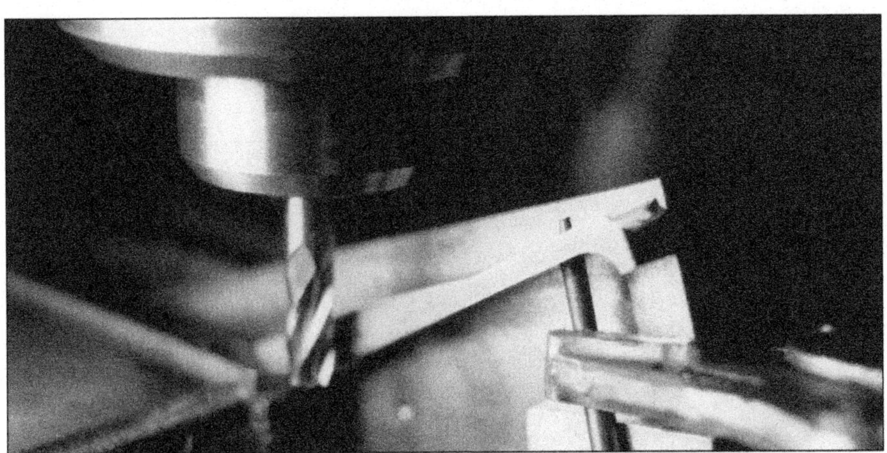

PHOTO C4-25.

A VZ24 MAUSER IN .375 H&H MAGNUM

BUILT IN THE EARLY 1980S

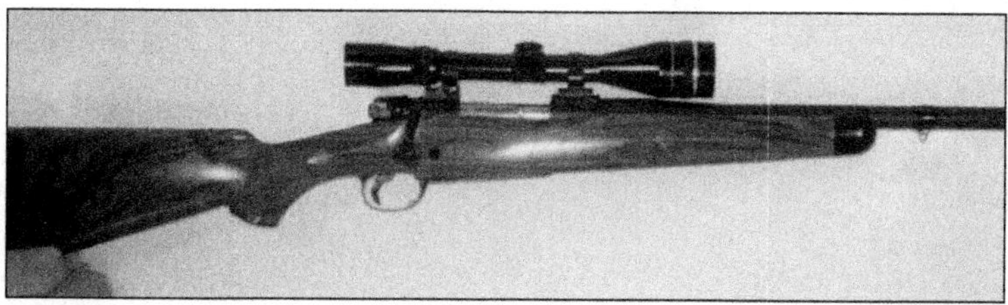

PHOTO C4-10.

The stick was a nicely figured piece of California English Walnut.

PHOTO C4-11.

The barrel was blued stainless steel. The forend tip is African Ebony.

PHOTO C4-12.

The telescopic sight mounts were 4 screw EAW in Leupold bases.

PHOTO C4-13.

This was a nicely laid out ¼ sawn piece of California English walnut.

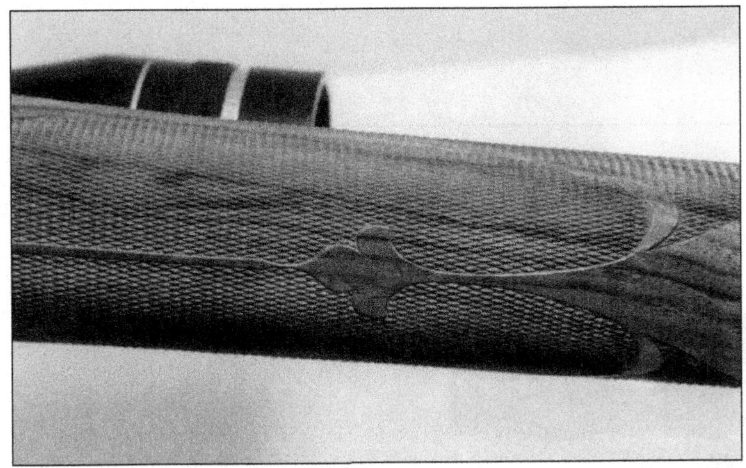

PHOTO C4-14.

The Fleur-de-Lis checkering was 26 lines per inch.

PHOTO C4-15.

Here the treatment of the stock line can be seen around the bolt stop.

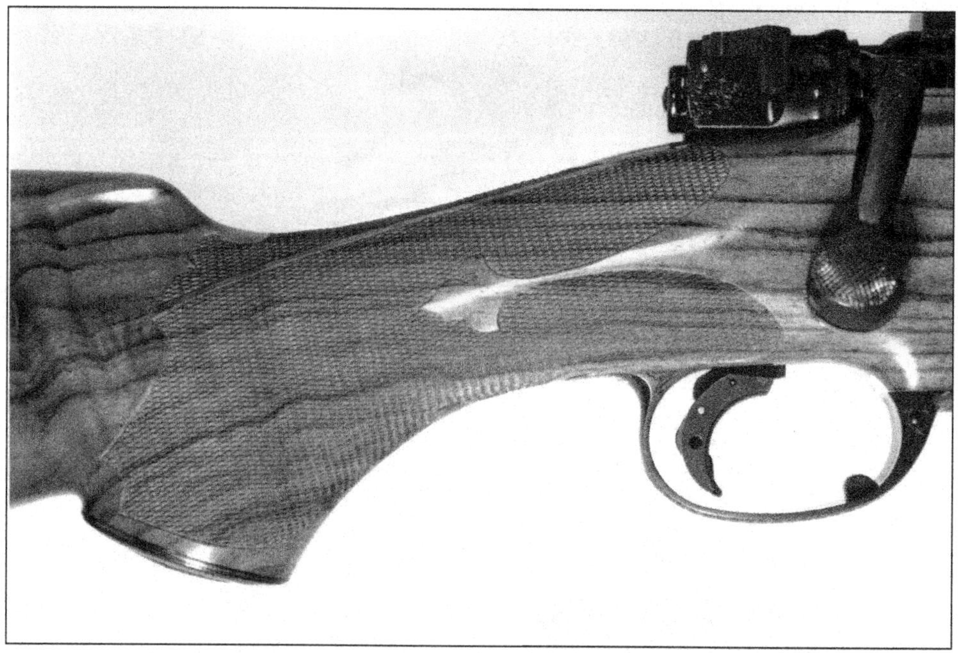

PHOTO C4-16.

The classic bolt handle was checkered with three panels in a teardrop pattern. The safety was a 3 position M'70 style. The trigger was a tuned Canjar M–1/2.

PHOTO C4-17.

The stock was double cross-bolted, and the holes filled with an Ebony plug.

PHOTO C4-18.

Checkering detail over the grip. The lines went through the ribbons without a break.

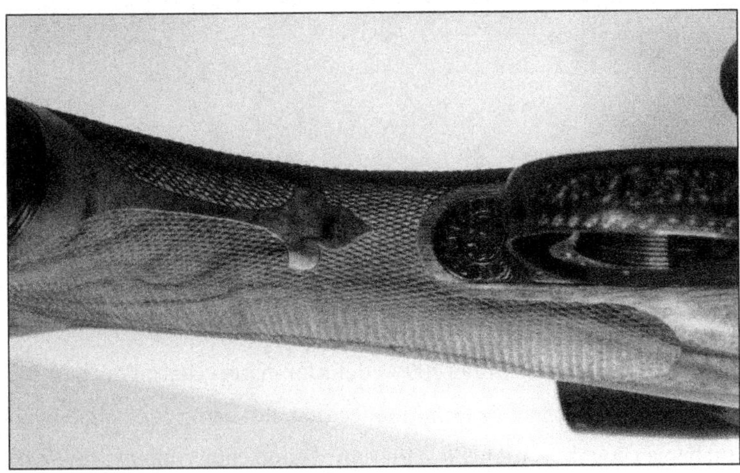

PHOTO C4-19.

Under the grip the checkering pattern met up thus creating a complete wrap around without a break

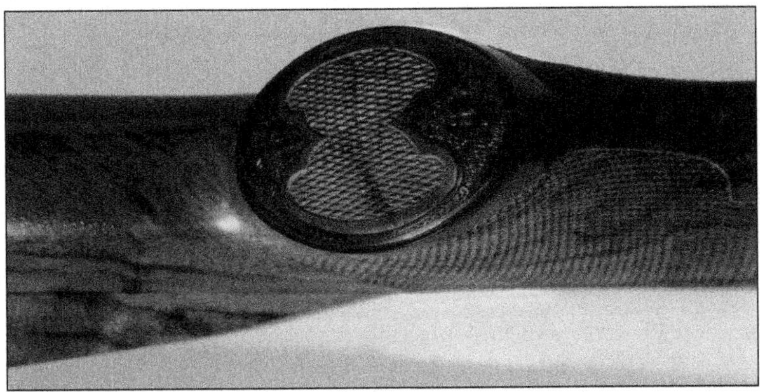

PHOTO C4-20.

The ever popular scalloped skeleton grip cap.

SIGNIFICANT RIFLES AND EVENTS

PART 4: THE 1980s (2)

PHOTO C4-21.

I had been using Remington Model 700 Actions for many years on my hunting rifles, but finally decided that their ammunition feeding, not being controlled in any way, was not reliable enough. I still believe they are a good choice for a varmint rifle, but their feeding system, which pops a cartridge out of the magazine, and leaves it to find its own way into the chamber was flawed. I was happy enough with the .358 Winchester cartridge shooting the 200^{GN} projectile, but it didn't seem right to use such a short cartridge in a 30/06 length magazine. My two options were either the .35 Whelen, simply a 30/06 necked up to .358 calibre, or a .338/06, a 30/06 necked up to .338 calibre. In the end I decided on the .338, as its trajectory would be a little bit flatter. Again, my intention was to use the lightest projectile available, which was 200^{GN}. I built the rifle on a good FN M'98 action, which I gave my usual treatment. The trigger guard/floorplate assembly I made myself. The barrel was a #1 Douglas that I reprofiled to super light, and cut off at 20". I used a stick of Roger Vardy's Australian English Walnut, that wasn't particularly fancy, but was perfectly quarter sawn and laid out. The wood was dense and hard, probably the best you could get for a gun stock. I fitted a cartridge trap, that held five shots, so the rifle always had ammunition with it, and a barrel banded front sling swivel base. The trigger was a Canjar M-3 tuned to break at just under $1\frac{1}{4}^{LBS}$. The stock was double cross-bolted, and the cross-bolt nuts covered with African Ebony. The forend tip was also African Ebony. The rifle was topped off with a Leupold 6X scope in Leupold rings. Later I changed the scope to a Leupold 2–8X variable.

PHOTO **C4-22.**

I got this 338/06 working in time for a pig hunting trip, and that's as far as I went with it. I had plans to finish it off, and have Phil Vinnicombe engrave it for me, but somehow that never came about. I guess I was too busy building our second house, which Lyn and I did, on our own, from the ground up, and by the time that was finished I had lost interest. The rifle is of my latest design with a 4" grip. I was doing three grip lengths on Mausers towards the end, depending on the size of my customers hand. The 4" grip length was right for me. This rifle literally handles like an extension of my body. What ever I want to aim it at, when I throw it up to my shoulder it is pointing straight at the target — there is no looking for the target — the cross-wire is right on it. This is so important, as it gives you extra time to make your lead on running game, and connect with your first shot. The 338/06 was also very good in heavy cover. If you could see an outline, you could put a bullet on it. One thing I can say about this rifle, emphatically, is I have never lost a pig to it, no matter where it was hit. I cannot say that about any other rifle I have used, and I have used a few.

This rifle was my #1 hunting rifle, and remains so today. It is a pity I never finished it off. I've pulled it apart a couple of times with the intention, but something always got in the way, and I ended up putting it back together for another trip. It might be more versatile if it were in .280 Remington, but I like it just as it is. Most importantly, it has never let me down, and that counts for something.

CHAPTER FIVE

RELOADING DIES

From a commercial point of view it doesn't make much sense to be making your own reloading dies, but from an accuracy point of view it makes a whole lot of sense. No doubt you have noticed I'm harping non stop about alignment, alignment, alignment. It follows, that having gone to all of that trouble to make everything as straight as humanly possible, it's pretty stupid to go and put crooked ammunition into the mix.

If you have some pieces of old barrel steel you have the makings of some very accurate dies, that will load straight ammunition, to go with your straight everything else. The dies can be made with whatever outside diameter steel you have on hand provided it will fit through your cathead. I prefer them to be around .850" diameter, just to make them a bit lighter to handle, compared to the 1¼" diameter of commercial dies.

We'll start with the bullet seating die because that is the simplest to make.

1. Make a piece of barrel steel, in the calibre of your choice, the diameter of your choice, turned parallel between centres, faced off at each end, with both internal and external sharp edges broken. In Photo 5-1 I am turning an old .308 stainless steel barrel to diameter for my .30BR dies.

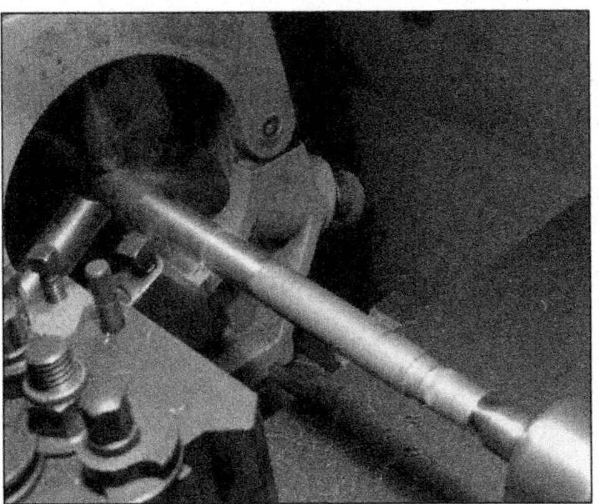

PHOTO 5-1.
Pre turning an old barrel. (.30BR)

1.1. The length of this die body should be the length of your cartridge with the longest projectile you will be using sitting on top of the neck, plus 1" to provide alignment and support for the bullet seating stem.

1.2. Run a couple of patches through the bore to clean it when you are finished. The die blank is ready to go in Photo 5-2.

PHOTO 5-2.

A finished die blank, and one of my Catheads. Note the texta mark indicating where the end of the chamber will be (6 X 47L). You may note the thread inside this cathead. They do double duty as a rebarreling aid when I need to fit a short barrel through the hollow mandrel of my lathe for crowning. Using the barrel fitting method I described in Chapter 3, the barrel only has to be supported at the spider end of the lathe. All that is needed is to have a surface that can be adjusted, as all alignment is taken from the 1½" of barrel just in front of the chamber, or just behind the muzzle.

2. I've been preaching, alignment, alignment, alignment all the way through this tome and the same applies here. We are using a piece of barrel steel, and we have already discussed, in Chapter 2, how the drill wanders on its way through the bar during manufacture. It follows that once again we will want to focus our attention on that section of bore just in front of the end of the cartridge case. If we can make the centre-line of that section run true with the centre-line of the lathe spindle, all we have to do is carry out all of our machining in line with that setup. Then, everything will be in perfect alignment.

2.1. It is not possible to make that setup by simply holding our piece of steel in the jaws of the lathe chuck. We need a way to be able to independently adjust the bore of the piece, which has no real relationship, concentricity wise, with the outside diameter. We do this with a cathead. One of mine is shown in Photo 5-2.

2.2. Lay your cartridge case alongside your die body and make a texta mark on the die at the end of the neck of the case. Now lay your die body alongside your cathead with the texta mark lined up with the rear screw on the cathead. Make a texta mark on the die body at the end of the cathead. Pivoting our die body at this point will make setup easier. Remember, we are only interested in the section of bore, in the die body, from this point (the rear screw) forward. Everything we do will be aligned with that short section of bore. Photo 5-3 refers.

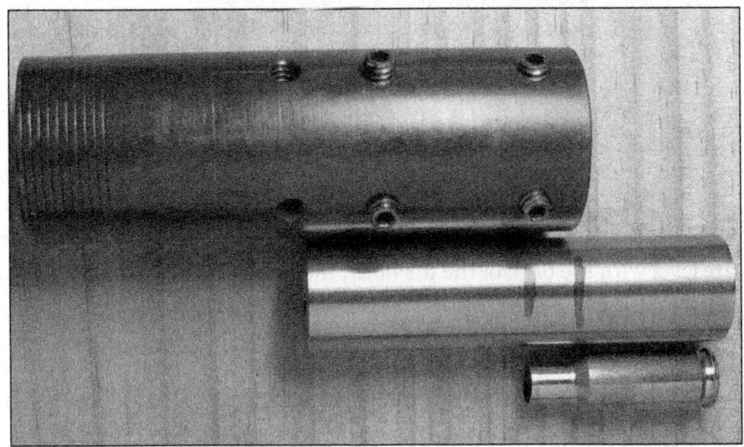

PHOTO 5-3.

The left texta mark indicates the end of the chamber, which is located at the rear screws on the cathead. The right texta mark needs to be level with the back of the cathead, so that the end of the chamber will pivot on the rear cathead screws. Set up like this, adjustments made at the front screws will affect rear screw adjustment less, and make set up a bit easier.

2.3. The amount of die body protruding from the cathead is not important provided you can face the end to square it when we are done.

2.4. Before we place our die body in the cathead, get the range rod we used when we chambered our barrel, and lay it alongside our die body with the pilot section level with the texta mark you made where the end of the case came to. Make a texta mark on the range rod at the back end of the die body.

Now, move the range rod forward to the front of the die body and make another texta mark on the range rod at the back end of the die body. These marks indicate where we will be indicating to bring that section of die body bore into alignment with the lathe spindle axis. Photo 5-4 refers.

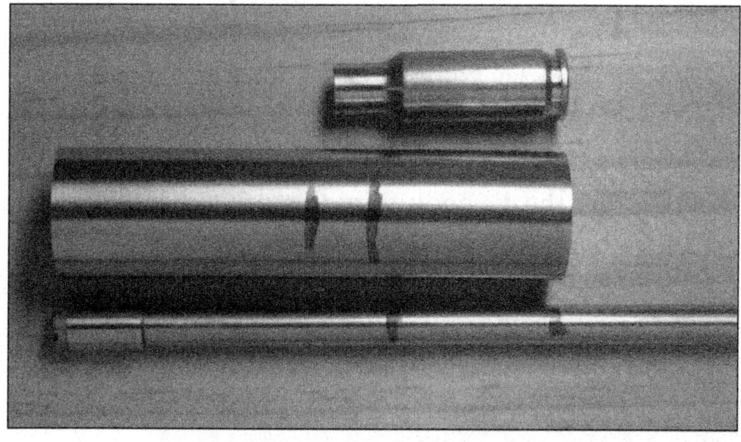

PHOTO 5-4.

We will be truing the die body using the range rod. When the left, and right, texta marks are level with the back of the die body, the range rod is within that section of bore we want to make in line with the centre-line of the lathe spindle.

2.5. Place the die body in the cathead with the texta mark lined up with the back of the cathead. Don't tighten it up. Tighten just enough to hold it there.

3. Hold the cathead in soft jaws in your bench vice and find a reamer pilot that will fit the bore of your die body. As with barrel fitting, aim for a pilot no more than .0002" under bore size, and make sure it will go right through the bore. Mount it on the range rod you used when you chambered your barrel.

4. Mount the cathead in the 4 jaw chuck in your lathe. Photo 5-5 shows that much better and easier than I can explain it. Notice that the adjusting screws on the cathead are easily accessible between the jaws of the 4 jaw chuck.

4.1. True the OD of the cathead in the chuck with a dial indicator to $^{+}$/- 0.

4.2. True the OD of the die body close to $^{+}$/- 0 as well, front and back, using the adjusting screws on the cathead. Anything under .005" is ok.

PHOTO 5-5.

Truing the Cathead in the 4 jaw chuck. The die body will also be trued on the outside diameter, front and back, using the Cathead screws, in preparation to truing the back of the bore with a range rod. (.30BR)

5. Lubricate the bore of the die body. Place the range rod in a drill chuck in the tailstock of the lathe. Lubricate the pilot on the range rod, and run it into the bore of the die body until the forward texta mark is level with its back. Set up a dial indicator with the probe bearing on the range rod at the back of the die body. See Photo 5-6 (Page 202).

6. We are going to true the bore of the die body with the axis of the centre-line of the lathe spindle, exactly the same way we did when we fitted our barrel. If you've forgotten how that went, refer back to Chapter 3 on fitting the barrel. (Page 94)

6.1. The only difference here is, we are using the adjusting screws on the Cathead, to bring the bore of the die body into alignment, instead of the adjustments on the lathe chuck and spider.

6.2. Adjust the cathead until the dial indicator reads $^{+}$/- 0 when the range rod is positioned with both texta marks level with the back of the die body.

7. Proceed exactly as you did when you originally chambered your barrel. Drill the excess material out, then taper bore the hole to true it. Photos 5-7, 5-8, and 5-9 (Page 202) sees me drilling, boring and measuring a die body. Refer back to Chapter 3 if you need refreshing.

PHOTO 5-6.

Setup to measure the eccentricity of the end of the bore with a range rod. (.30BR)

7.1. Now cut the chamber in the die body deep enough that a case will go into the die with its base .012" past the end of the die. Photo 5-10 (Page 204) is worth studying, as it has several features we have touched on before in Chapter 3, 'Fit the Barrel'. As when we chambered our barrel in Chapter 3, you can see the reamer is fully supported in the die body. The pilot has entered the bore, and the shoulder/body junction of the reamer is fully supported in our taper bored hole. The reamer is thus held with its centre-line exactly on the centre-line of the lathe spindle. There is no discernible wobble at the end of the reamer; it is positively held in place. Like this, the reamer has the best possible chance to follow the bored hole exactly, and make a chamber perfectly aligned with the short section of bore immediately in front of the chamber. This photo also shows the reamer pusher a little better than the photo in the barrel fitting chapter did. The back of the reamer will enter a clearance hole in the pusher when the tailstock is wound forward.

PHOTO 5-7.

Drilling a die body. Note the texta mark indicating where I should stop drilling. (6 X 47L)

PHOTO 5-8.

About to taper bore the drilled hole. (6 X 47L)

PHOTO 5-9.

Measuring the diameter at the back of the taper bored hole. (6 X 47L)

When the end of the pusher contacts the back of the reamer holder it will begin pushing the reamer into the bored hole, and make the chamber. There is a machined groove at the back of the outside diameter of the reamer holder which indicates that face is dead square with the bored hole the reamer is held in. I didn't cut the chamber with the pusher, as I prefer to use my custom made centre. This particular die was for my 6 x 47 Lapua.

PHOTO 5-10.
Preparing to chamber a die body. (6 X 47L)

7.2. Don't get smart here and speed things along. You are using your good chambering reamer for this job so look after it. Cut the chamber exactly the way you would if you were chambering a hummer barrel. In Photo 5-11 the chamber has been cut to depth.

PHOTO 5-11.
The chamber has been reamed to depth. (.30BR)

8. Change the chambering reamer for a throating reamer, and install the pilot from your chambering reamer onto it.

8.1. We have to increase the depth of the throat in our die to accept the longest projectile we will be using in our rifle, when it is sitting on top of the neck of the case.

8.2. Do the math, and work out how deep you need to deepen the throat to allow a case to fully enter the die, with the longest projectile you expect to use sitting on top of it. Then run the throating reamer in to depth. Measure your progress exactly as we did in Chapter 3.

8.3. In the past I have run the throating reamer right through the die creating a +.0005" calibre smooth bore for the seating stem to slide in. Lately, however, I have questioned the sense in that, and made my dies as described above. First up I have reduced the load on the throating reamer by using it only as much as needed. Secondly, the rifling is only a few thousandths of an inch deep, and the seating stem is not compromised by being that amount smaller in diameter. Thirdly, the rifling traps grease in the bore ensuring the seating stem is always lubricated.

9. Now we must cut a taper running from the back of the chamber to within a minimum of .050" from the edge of the die. At the chamber end the taper needs to be deep enough to expose the extractor groove of the case when it is fully inserted in the die. Its purpose is to allow you to use a screwdriver to extract a cartridge from the die, after you have seated the projectile, if needed. Cut it with a boring bar and set the angle to bore the taper on your compound rest.

9.1. The angle you need to use will depend on the diameter of the case you are making the die for, and the outside diameter of the die body. So, unless you have made this exact die before it will be a matter of trial and error. Just sneak up on it and you will get it exactly right. Photo 5-12 shows this in process.

PHOTO 5-12.

Cutting the extraction recess on the seating die. This taper will allow a screwdriver access to the front of the rim of the cartridge. This access may be needed in case you encounter a sticky case and need a bit of leverage to extract it from the die. Finger nails don't have a lot of power for removing even a slightly tight cartridge.(6 X 47L)

10. Skim face the back of the die to square it with the internal work we have been doing. It will clean up in less than a couple of thousandths. See Photo 5-13. Don't overdo it. The cartridge case must be able to go right into the die .010" past the end.

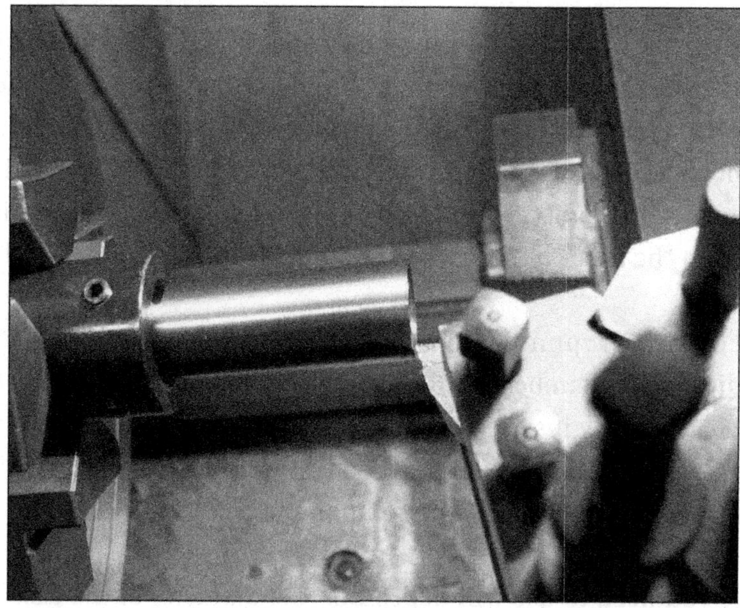

PHOTO 5-13.

Facing the rear of the die to square it with the centre-line. (6 X 47L)

11. Give the chamber a light polish with some worn 320 grit cloth strip. While you are at it polish the taper and rear of the die to make them nice and shiny.

12. I make the bullet seating stem from an Unbrako Allen head cap screw. They are convenient to use, the material is tough but easily turned, with sharp hi-speed cutting tools, and works fine. I use ¼" diameter for .22 CAL and 6MM, and 5/16" diameter for 7MM and .30 CAL. The trick is to do all of your machining in the one setup so that everything is concentric.

12.1. Set the cap screw up in your 4 jaw chuck with the Allen head out and true it to +/- 0 with your dial indicator. Turn the head of the screw to the diameter of the bolt body, and face it back to a square end. Centre drill the end of the screw with a #1 centre drill to form a 60° taper to within .060" of the outside diameter of the screw shank.

12.2. Deepen the parallel section of the centre drilled hole with a number drill. The diameter of the drill to use and the depth of the hole is dependant on the calibre and nose shape of the projectile you will be using. What we are doing here is providing end clearance for the nose of the projectile, and moving the point where the seater will contact the projectile further down the ogive. As a guide my .30BR die stem contacts a 115GN Berger match projectile .250" from the tip. My .22PPC stem contacts an 80GN Sierra match projectile .200" from the tip. You get the idea? You can make the clearance hole as deep as you like as long as it clears the tip of the sharpest projectile you are likely to use. Don't overdo the diameter though as we will be boring it out maybe as much as .005" later on. Remove it from the lathe.

13. Its handy to have a sample case with about 1/3RD cut away from the neck for this next step, like the ones in Photo 5-14. Actually it's a handy thing to have full stop, especially when you want to see what a projectile looks like in the case neck when you are selecting a seating depth.

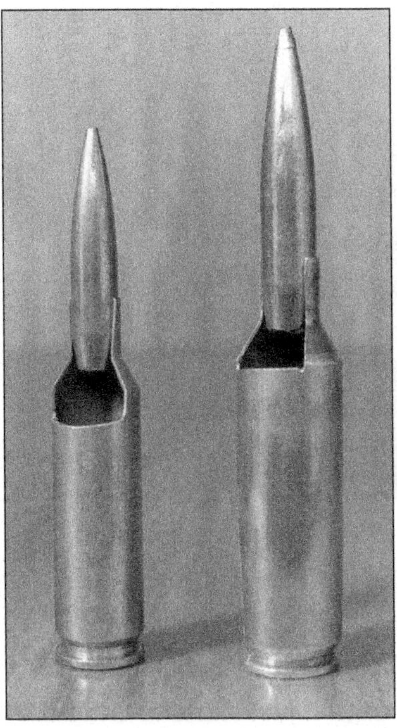

PHOTO 5-14.

These cutaway cases allow you to see exactly where the base of a projectile is situated in the case neck.

13.1. Slide the projectile of your choice into the neck of the cut away case with its base just above the junction of the shoulder and neck where a donut is likely to form. You should use the lightest (and therefore shortest) projectile you expect to use in this die. With boat tail bullets the junction of the body and boat tail should be just above the junction of the shoulder and neck of the case.

13.2. Lay the case alongside the die body with its base level with the end of the die. Slide the bullet seating stem over the top of the projectile until it stops and mark the stem with a texta where it is level with the other end of the die body.

14. Replace the seater stem in the 4 jaw chuck with the texta mark you made far enough from the chuck face, so that you can turn right up to it, and true it to $^{+}$/- 0.

15. You have a good idea of the diameter of the bore of the die from when you selected a pilot previously. Set your carriage stop with the turning tool at your texta mark and turn the shaft of the seating stem to diameter. In Photo 5-15 I have just started that job.

PHOTO 5-15.

Turning the seater stem to diameter. (7 SAUM)

15.1. Use a slow feed and a sharp tool. The fit we want is a slip fit with no wobble. I also like a polished surface, so will turn it until it just starts to enter the die body, then polish it with a piece of worn 320 grit abrasive cloth for a perfect fit.

15.2. When you are close to size take a few passes without advancing the cross-slide feed. This will take any taper out of the cut caused by the stem springing away from the tool. You may end up with a tenth or so of taper which is easily taken care of when you polish the stem.

15.3. If you are really close to size, or the stem has partially entered the hole and you feel that taking another cut will be too much, you can lap the stem in with 400 grit lapping compound for a perfect fit. It shouldn't be necessary but you have that option, so do as you please. Either way it will work fine.

16. Leave the stem set up in the 4 jaw chuck. Now, we want to true our seating surface — the part that contacts the bullet nose with the outside diameter of the seating stem.

16.1. Set the compound rest on your tool post to 60° and mount a very thin boring tool in the tool holder like the one shown in Photo 5-16.

PHOTO 5-16.

I have taper bored the seater stem true to the outside diameter. (7 SAUM)

16.2. Very carefully skim the surface of the 60° angle we made when we initially centre drilled the seater stem until it cleans up and is running perfectly true. It should not take more than around .005".

16.3. Set the compound rest back to zero, and bore the parallel hole you opened up with your selected number drill, for about 1/10", until it also cleans up and runs true with the outside of the seater stem. I am about to do this in Photo 5-17.

PHOTO 5-17.

I am about to bore the drilled hole parallel to the outside diameter of the seater stem. (7 SAUM)

16.4. Give the internal surfaces you have trued a polish to make them shine, and particularly to break the sharp corner at the junction of the bored tapered and parallel section.

16.5. Remove the seater stem from the chuck and clean it up.

17. You can go to a deal of trouble making a fancy cap for this die, but I just don't see the need. If you want to, go knock yourself out. You certainly won't do any harm, and it will look nicer. Me, I'd prefer to go shooting than spend time on trivialities. You make up your own mind. I simply use Nyloc nuts on my own seater stems. And they have worked fine for a long time. I make all seating adjustments with Skip's seating die shims for .22 and 6mm, and I have made shims for 7mm and .30 cal. In essence, once the nyloc nut is in place it stays put and all subsequent adjustments are made with washers and shims. Also I prefer the feel of seating projectiles with the smaller end of the screw rather than the large end of a custom made cap. Your choice!

17.1. Screw a nyloc nut onto the seater stem until its base is just past the end of the thread.

17.2. Place the stem in the 4 jaw chuck of your lathe. Leave enough room behind the nyloc nut so that you can get a thin turning tool between it and the bottom of the nut. True the seater stem to $^{+}/-$ 0.

17.3. Now take a shallow skimming cut across the bottom face of the nut to square it with the seater stem. Remove only enough material to clean the bottom face of the nut up and square it. I'm doing that in Photo 5-18.

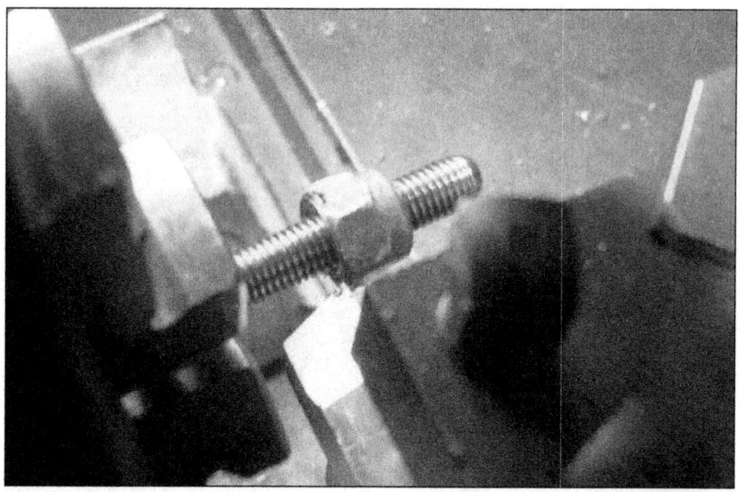

Photo 5-18.

Truing the bottom of the nyloc nut square to the seater stem. (7 SAUM)

17.4. Remove the stem from the lathe and place it in soft jaws in your bench vice. With a hacksaw cut a good screwdriver slot in the top of the seater stem.

18. Polish the outside of the die body until it gleams. Engrave it with the calibre, your name (that's important) and the date (month and year).

Now go sit down and grin at the wall for at least 30 minutes with a Rum and Pepsi Max in your hand, or whatever your poison is. You just made an accurate bullet seating die, second to none, and you deserve it.

Had a rest? Good! Let's start on a neck sizing die. This one is a bit more complicated than the seater die, but we'll get through it together. Commercial straight line neck sizing dies, at least the ones I am familiar with, all leave the case unsupported at the beginning of the neck sizing process. While they make the claim that the die is a chamber type die, if you stop and think about it, the only time the case is supported in the die is at the end of the sizing process. If you *really* think about it, the large tolerances commercial manufactures are forced to adopt, in order to ensure that every-ones case will fit in their neck die, pretty well ensures that the cartridge case is not even properly supported at the end of the sizing process.

I have never been happy with such straight line neck sizing dies as I could see the potential to start the sizing process out of line with the centre-line of the case. If the sizing process is started off line (crooked) then it will finish off line, and a projectile seated in that case will also seat off line, *no matter how straight the seating die is.*

I've given this problem a lot of thought over the years. The answer to the problem is actually as plain as the nose on your face. Support the case fully within the die before we begin the neck sizing process. Simple really! The trick is, how to make such a die with the perfect alignment we need to ensure the neck will be sized dead straight. This is how I do it.

I make these dies to use Wilson neck bushings. These bushings are readily available from various vendors in increments of .001" neck diameter. The nominal outside diameter of a Wilson bush is .500". I say nominal because that diameter can vary by a couple of thousandths of an inch, so it would be prudent to have a selection of bushes on hand before you start this job. The outside diameter of Wilson bushings is also compatible with the outside diameter of tungsten carbide bushings, which is a good thing. You can find the ideal diameter Wilson bushing to suite your rifle, and then purchase a much more expensive carbide bushing in that size. Of course, if you're well cashed up, go get all carbide bushings. Photo 5-19 is of the bushings I use in my dies.

PHOTO 5-19.

A selection of Wilson die bushings.

Why do I use Wilson bushings instead of making my own? Well, they are so cheap it's not worth my limited time, making things like this, unless it is impossible to obtain exactly what I want. Simple economics! You want to make your own, go right ahead. Just be sure to make them with the same nominal diameter as a Wilson bush, so that you can swap to carbide if you want to.

1. The length of our die body will be the length of our cartridge case plus the length of a Wilson bush plus one inch. Prepare it exactly as you did for the body of the bullet seating die.

2. We have done this before so there is no need to repeat it here. Follow steps one to seven in the bullet seat die instructions to make a chamber in the end of your die body that has its centre-line perfectly in line with the centre-line of that section of bore that is directly ahead of the end of the chamber.

3. Skim face the end of the die body to square it with our chamber; .002" should be more than enough to do this. While you're there cut a small 45° chamfer at the end of the chamber. I am doing that in Photo 5-20. We will be pushing the sized cases out of this die with a rod, so we don't need the extraction cone we made on the bullet seating die.

Photo 5-20.

Chamfering the end of the chamber on the neck die to provide a leade in for the shells. (.30BR)

4. Remove the die body from the cathead, reverse it and replace it back into the cathead.

   4.1. You will want that point where your chamber ends to be just behind the front screws of your cathead. Remember, pivoting at that point will make setup much easier.

5. Indicate our section of bore to +/- 0 exactly as we did when we trued it to cut the chamber, thus, again, bringing it into line with the centre-line of the spindle of the lathe. We are maintaining our perfect 'in line with the lathe spindle centre-line' setup here.

6. Now we want to make a recess in this end of the die body to accept our Wilson neck sizing bushing. The bottom of the recess should be .025" in front of the junction of the shoulder and neck of our chamber. Do the math to determine how deep it needs to be from the end of the die body.

6.1. We are leaving that .025" section, in front of the shoulder/neck junction of the chamber, to help support a full length sized case when it is fully inserted in the die body. The ledge, thus formed here, will also act as a stop for the Wilson bush at the end of the neck sizing stroke.

6.2. Drill the die body out with a 7/16" twist drill just short of final depth. I am doing that in Photo 5-21.

PHOTO 5-21.
Drilling out the top of the neck sizing die. (.30BR)

6.3. Bore the hole to diameter and depth, squaring it at the bottom in the process. Make a fine finish and polish it to .001" over bushing outside diameter to allow the bush to slide in and out freely. The diameter of your bore will probably be .501" or maybe .5015" depending on the diameter of your bushes. See Photo 5-22.

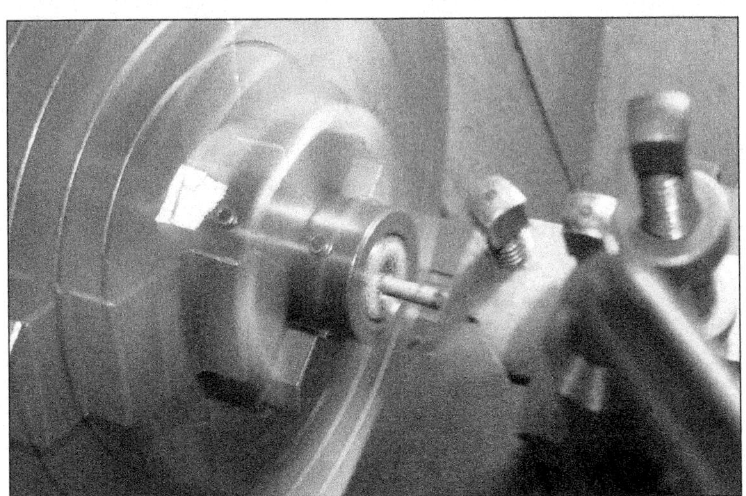

PHOTO 5-22.
Boring the Wilson bushing and plunger recess to diameter and depth.

7. Face the end of the die to square it. Take a small 45° cut on the inside diameter to chamfer it, and give the outside diameter a good chamfer with a file. I am cutting the inside chamfer in Photo 5-23.

8. Give the chamber a lick with worn 320 grit cloth tape just like you would a barrel chamber to polish it up a bit, and make the outside diameter of the die shine if that is your want. Remove the die from the cathead, and the cathead from the lathe. The die body is finished.

9. Now we need a plunger to push the Wilson bushing down to size the neck of the case.

9.1. I make the plunger from a piece of .22 calibre stainless barrel steel. Its length is simply from the top of the Wilson bush when it is fully in the die body to 1/10" above the top of the die. This is a simple turning job. Make it a slip fit in its hole and drill it out to accept the diameter of your de-cap rod. Mine are .200" in diameter, only because I had that diameter drill rod on hand. Make it whatever diameter you like, as long as it is compatible with the internal neck diameter of your case.

PHOTO 5-23.

Chamfering the bored hole. This particular die ended up with the top just inside the cathead, so I will chamfer the outside edge with a file when I polish the die body. I faced the end of the die square with my boring tool after I had bored the recess to size. It is more important to place the die in the cathead so that the front pivot point is at the front of the chamber to facilitate setup.

10. We also need a de-capping rod. I make two rods, one a de-capper, and the other a case remover. The de-capper has a trapped de-capping pin at the end, and the case remover is just a rod with no pin.

10.1. Drill the end of your de-capping rod to accept a suitable de-capping pin. You can use commercial de-capping pins or spring steel wire, whatever you have handy. Hold the pin in the rod with Locktite or Araldite.

10.2. Don't be stingy with the length of your de-cap rod. Make it so that it protrudes at least 1" above the top of the plunger, as you have to be able to easily grab it, after de-capping, to remove it from the die.

11. Finally we need one more part—a base. In use we slip the fired cartridge case into the die until its base is flush with the end of the die. When we do this the Wilson bush and the plunger are pushed out of the top of the die by an amount equal to the length of the neck (or thereabouts). Now we stand the die on the flat base of an Arbor press and push the plunger all the way in, thus sizing the neck of the case with the Wilson bush. Now the case is trapped within the die, and we need some way to remove it. That's why we need the base.

11.1. My die body's are around .850" diameter, so I made my base from a piece of 1" diameter stainless barrel steel. Your sizes may differ, but that's ok.

11.2. Refer to the drawing in Figure 5-1, and I'll try to explain it.

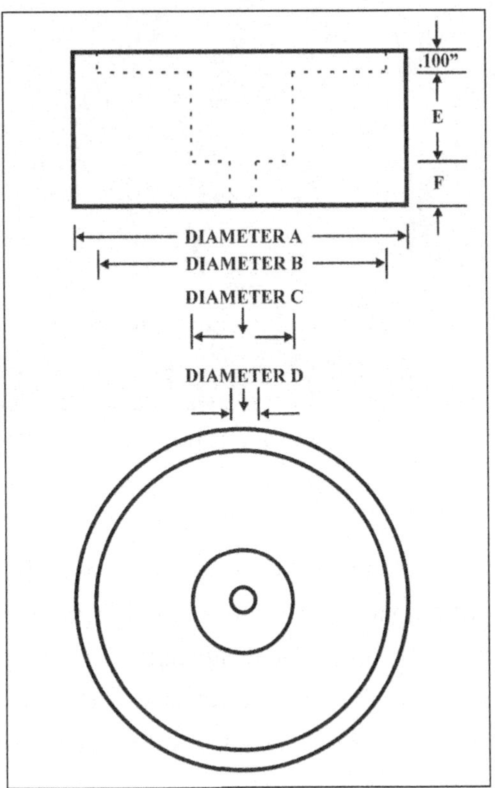

FIGURE 5-1.
The neck die base.

11.2.1. Diameter A should be the diameter of your die body plus .200" or thereabouts. It's not really critical. The top recess, diameter B, is a locator for the die body. It only needs to be deep enough to hold the die body in place and line it up with the base, .100" is plenty. Its diameter (B) should only be .002" over the diameter of your die body.

11.2.2. The second recess, diameter C, is to allow the case to be pushed out of the die. This one needs to be deep enough (E) so that the case neck will be released from the Wilson bushing when the base of the case reaches the bottom of the recess. If you size the neck .250" down, this recess will need to be .260" deep to release the neck from the Wilson bushing. This recess should be about .010" larger in diameter than your case head diameter.

11.2.3. The third recess, diameter D, is a through hole to allow the primer to be pushed from the primer pocket when the case reaches the bottom of its recess. Make its depth (F) twice that of a primer and that will be plenty to allow the primer to drop right out of the primer pocket. Make its diameter (D) .010" over the primer diameter.

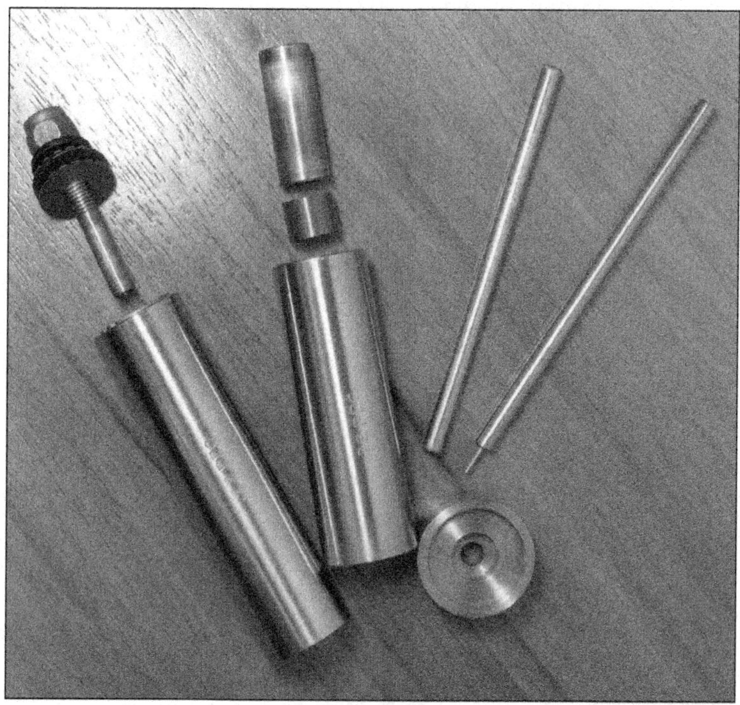

PHOTO 5-24.
My .22PPC reloading dies.

That's it, we have made a set of reloading dies that are as straight as humanly possible, and will load ammunition without introducing any runout error at all. Photo 5-24 shows my .22PPC dies disassembled. Note the Skips shims on the bullet seating stem. The sizing bush is tungsten carbide. The plunger above it pushes it down to size the neck of the case. The recesses in the neck die base can be seen, one to locate the die body, one to allow the case to be pushed out of the die, and the through hole so the spent primer may escape.

Your fired case will come out of the rifles chamber with zero run out. If it doesn't, better look for a problem; it's either a bad case or something misaligned in the barreled action. When you neck size the case in the neck die the run out will still be zero. When you seat a projectile in the case the odds are in your favor that it will still indicate a run out figure of zero. Not all of your cases will seat projectiles to zero run out because their necks will vary in their annealing. I'm not talking about from case to case, but rather about a variation around the circumference of some individual necks. I find that most of the ammunition I load with these dies indicates at zero, and a few may indicate at anything up to .0012" run out.

You will probably use these dies with a small short throw arbor press. At home I have a large, powerful arbor press with a long throw, but when I am away I use a small press marketed by Sinclair in the USA. When using the small press I clean the carbon from the outside of the case neck with steel wool, run a nylon brush through the neck, then push the case all the way into the die. I set the height of the press to suit the bullet seating die, which makes it too high for the neck sizing die. To make up the difference in height I simply turn the die base upside down on the base plate of the press, and sit the die with case inserted on top of the base. Now the height of the press is ok, and I press the plunger in which neck sizes the case. Take the die from the press and insert the decapping pin in the top, pin down of course. Turn the base right side up, place the die in its recess in the base and you're ready to press the case out of the die. The first movement moves the case back out of the die until it contacts the base of its recess, which stops it. The second movement of the press handle will decap the case leaving it ready to be removed from the die.

The bullet seating dies use is straight forward. Sit a projectile on the mouth of the case neck and insert it and the case fully into the die. You will note the bullet seating stem moves up out of the die as you do this. Sit the die on the base of the press, and push the seating stem all of the way home, and the bullet is seated. Do it twice to be sure. Even seating depth is very important in the accuracy equation.

You will notice that the neck die will size case necks to within about .050" of the bottom of the neck. This is because we left a .025" portion of the neck in the die, to assist lineup with a full length sized case, and there is about a .025" chamfer on the Wilson bushings bottom, to aid entry of the case neck into the sizing portion. You should not need to seat a projectile past that sized section, but if you do, you should really be looking at lengthening the throat in your chamber.

With the seating die I use a couple of .020" washers and Skip's or home made shims under the nyloc nut, and make all adjustments with the shims. Once the nyloc nut is set in a compatible position it is never moved again. These dies attack seated run-out at the very source. You made them so you know they are dead straight. If you encounter projectile run-out problems, look for the cause elsewhere. It's not in the dies.

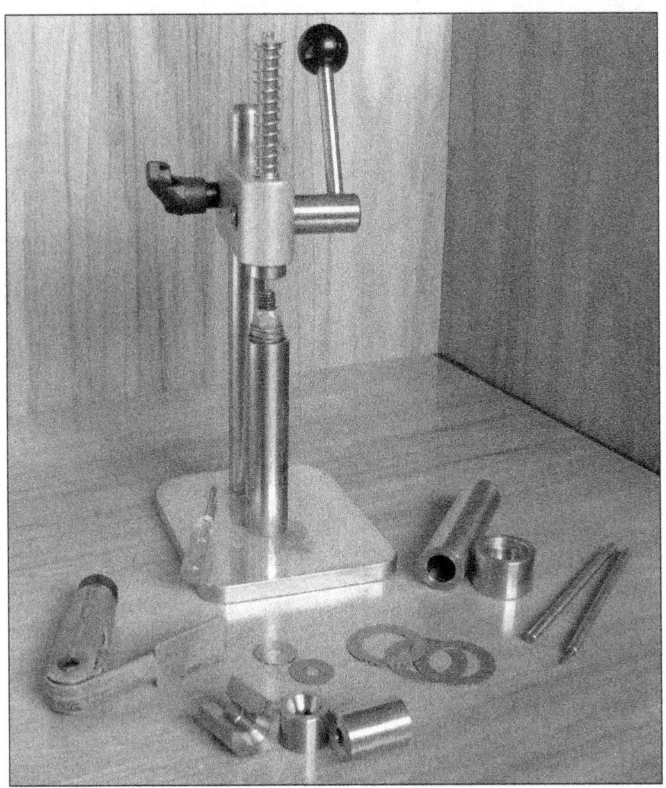

PHOTO 5-25.

The small Sinclair arbour press I take with me to away competitions, along with my 7 SAUM reloading dies. In front of the press can be seen some Skip's die shims, and some Skip's bullet seater shims. In front of the shims are the three tools we made before we fitted the barrel in Chapter 3. I use the old Lee priming tool, on the left because it has excellent 'feel', and I know exactly when the primer has bottomed.

PHOTO 5-25.

Machining a custom barrel banded foresight. Making 'one off' parts like this was very time consuming. This foresight has come from a quite large piece of steel that has first been drilled, and then taper bored to fit the barrel it was intended for. If I were an Electrician, Plumber, or Auto Mechanic I'd have charged ten times the amount I would have made on this job!

PHOTO 5-26.

I made these rear sling swivel bases to suite the cartridge traps I installed in the butt of many of the rifles I built. They came from a piece of 3/8" bright rod. The shank has been supported by a small centre for threading in the lathe. Here, I am milling the contour on the top. The part is rotated by hand to the stop I have rigged up. It's not a good idea to let it get away from you, which can happen easily!

A REMINGTON MODEL 700 IN 7MM REMINGTON MAGNUM

BUILT IN THE MID 1980S

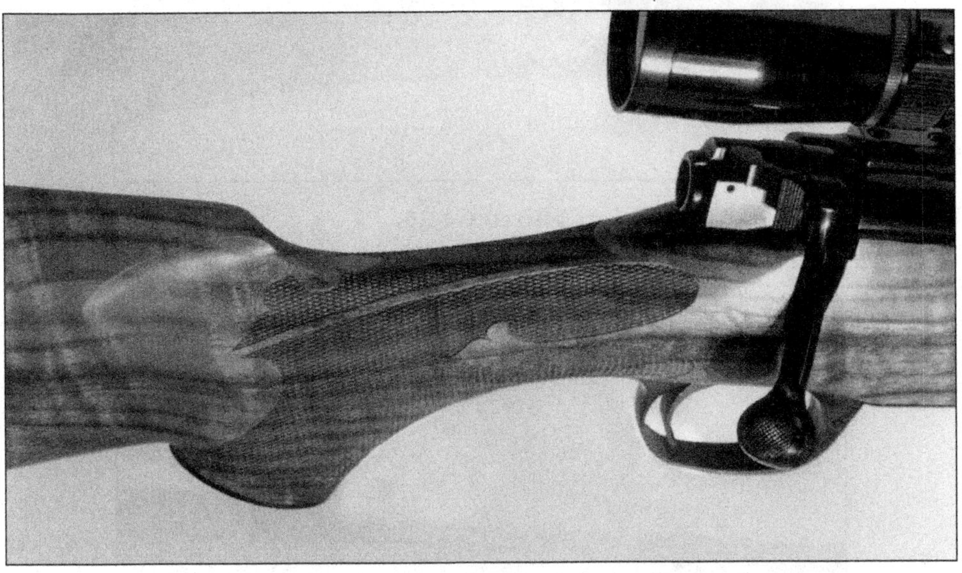

PHOTO C4-23.

The stick was a nice hard piece of Roger Vardy's Australian English Walnut. The safety was an M'70 style 3 position side swing design.

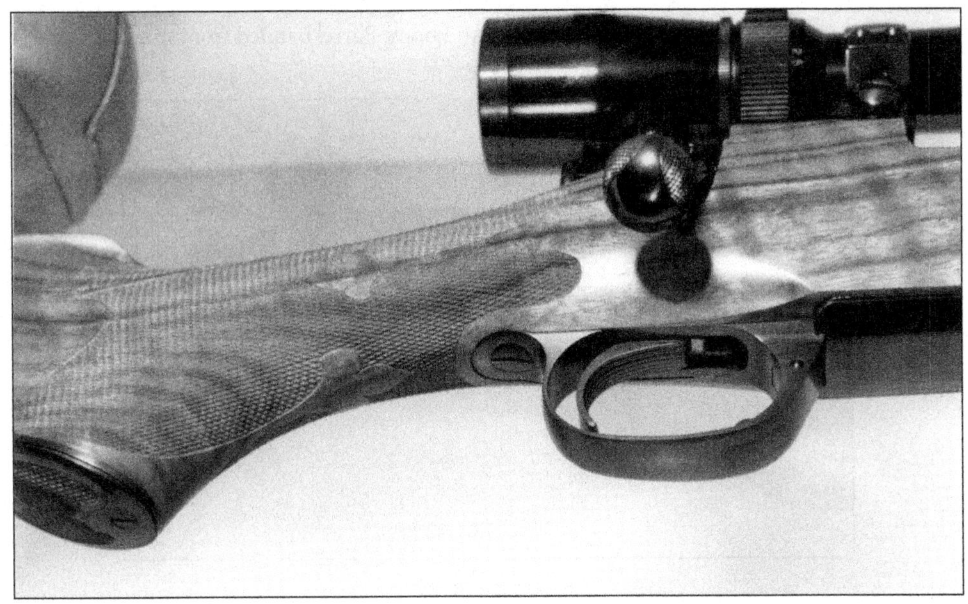

PHOTO C4-24.

The bolt knob checkering was a three panel teardrop design.

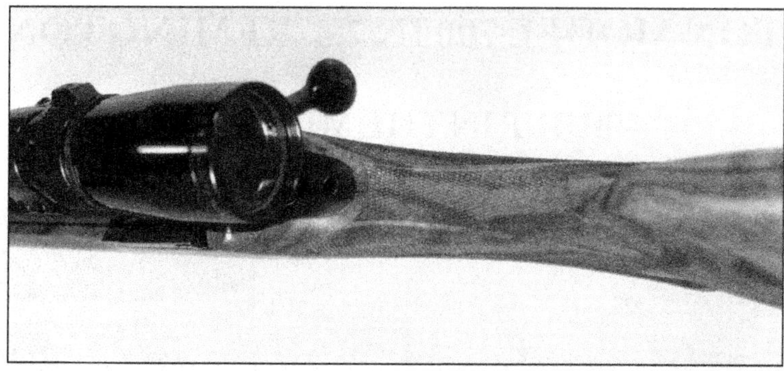

PHOTO C4-25.
Of note here is the reshaped rear tang treatment I had been doing for a while.

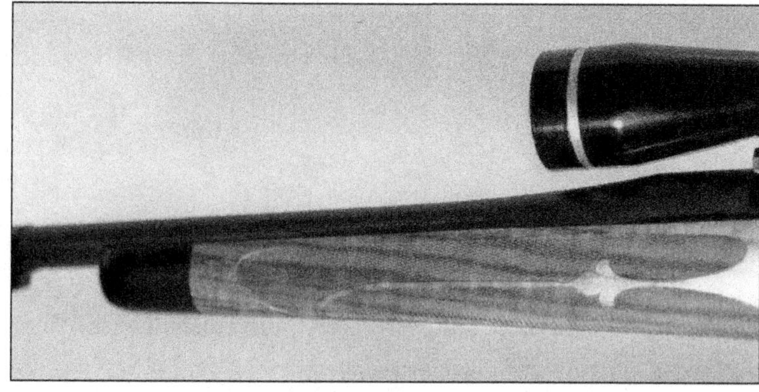

PHOTO C4-26.
Forend checkering. The forend tip was African Ebony. Barrel banded front sling swivel.

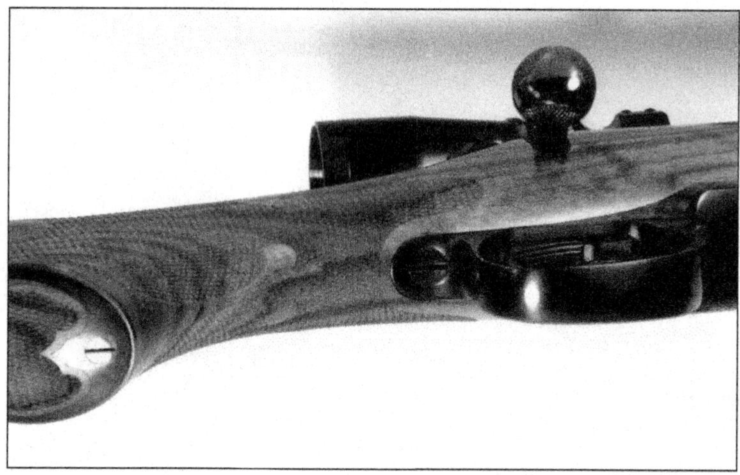

PHOTO C4-27.
The checkering detail under the grip can be easily seen here. The trigger guard was a Dakota. I was using these to help speed up production, which was slow!

PHOTO **C4-28.**

This rifle was custom in every respect. The action was fully worked over. The original Remington recoil lug was removed and an integral recoil lug welded on under the front of the receiver. The receiver and bolt were aligned, and threads recut, with all surfaces square and in line with the centre-line of the bolt hole. The receiver outside was profiled to remove Remingtons ugly stampings and to align it with the bolt hole. The rifle wasn't engraved (a shame) but I had Phil Vinnicombe engrave my name and the actions number on the receiver, and the calibre on the barrel.

The barrel was a #2 profile Douglas Premium Grade in stainless steel and blued. The scope rings are 4 screw EAW in Leupold bases.

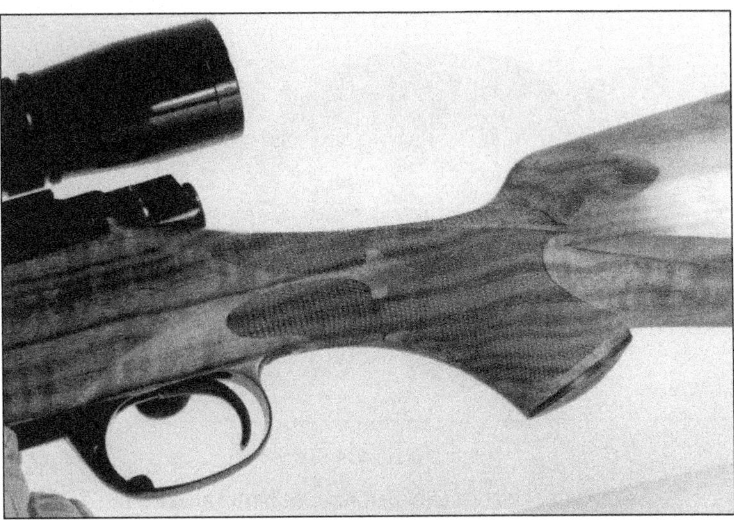

PHOTO C4-29.

The trigger was a standard Remington unit tuned for a 1¼ pound pull weight. When tuned, Remington triggers were every bit as good as any aftermarket replacement.

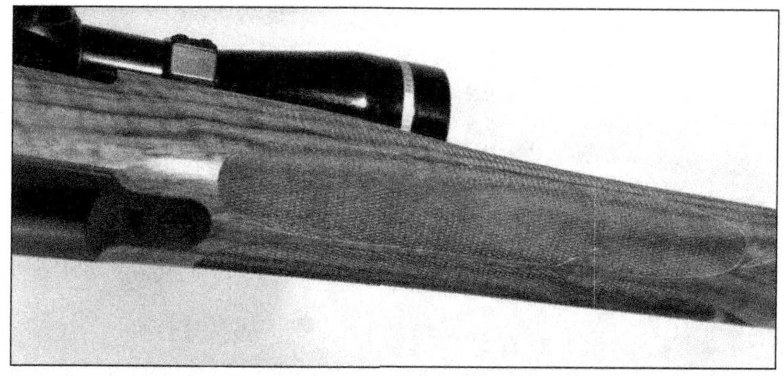

PHOTO C4-30.

Checkering was Fler-de-Lis with ribbons at 26 lines per inch.

PHOTO C4-31.

The rear swivel base was of oval 2 screw inletted design.

PHOTO C4-32.

Scalloped Skeleton grip cap with in panel checkering.

CHAPTER SIX

THE FULL LENGTH SIZING DIE

Full length sizing is a royal pain in the butt, but it does have some benefits that should not be ignored. Full length sizings main draw back is it requires us to make the cases sticky with sizing lube. The lube must then be cleaned off before any further operations can take place. They are extra operations I have to perform on my cases, and boring ones to boot.

Full length sizings major benefit is it pretty well ensures flawless chambering and extraction from an action, when it is done properly. This is pretty important if you want to shoot and reload quickly, without having to focus on getting cartridges into the chamber, and fired cases back out. Also, some matches we attend are week long events that either require us to have a lot of cartridge cases (some hundreds), or to reload cases several times during the course of the match. If you are full length sizing properly, your cartridges will fit the chamber equally from the start of the match to the finish.

Another possible benefit derives from the theory that chambers and cases are never straight but bent to a degree; banana shape or something like it. The theory says that cases that fit the chamber too tightly can be forced out of line and in tension in the chamber, thus being a possible cause of inaccuracy. Full length sizing prevents this alignment problem from occurring. That may or may not be true. I don't really know.

I full length size all of my cases for all of my rifles. With my bench-rest rifles I want to shoot as fast as I can, so I am looking for flawless functioning. I want to be able to get cartridges into the chamber easily, and fired cases out of the chamber easily, with no hiccups at all. With my F Class rifle I will reload cases every day, up to four times during a long match, so I want to ensure that I will not have to fight the rifle to chamber a round, or extract a case, at the end of the match.

In order to do this correctly you must have a full length die that fits your cases properly and is a good match to your chamber. What do we want in a full length die?

All full length dies are adjustable up and down in a reloading press, which allows the head-space of the case to be sized to very close dimensions fairly easily. Unfortunately they are generally considerably undersized in their body dimensions, and of course those dimensions are not adjustable. Well — not without a deal of effort.

Ideally a full length sizing die will size the body of the case between .0005" and .001" at the junction of the shoulder and body and .0005" just in front of the solid head of the case. If it sizes the case any more than that it is over sizing and needs to be altered or changed.

A die like that is not the sort of thing you buy off the shelf unless you are very lucky indeed. There are specialty suppliers that can make a custom die that may be suitably matched to your chamber, but these dies may cost around $500.00 to purchase (against $40.00 for a standard die). Add to that the cost of sending fired cases to the vendor, and getting the die and cases back to you. That's an easy option, if a bit expensive, or you can spend a bit of time and effort and alter a factory die to suite. If that is not possible, you can make a die from scratch.

A typical Full Length Sizing Die (FLD) from any of the several manufacturers will oversize the front half of a case, barely touch the next ¼ section behind that, and not touch the base at all. When full length sizing cases for only one chamber, it's not necessary to size the case at the base, as it tends not to expand enough there after initial fire forming, to tighten in the chamber at that point. It is only if you want to use that case in another rifle, of the same caliber, and run into chamber dimension variations, that you may need to squeeze the base of the case back to its original dimensions. To do that you will need a special small base die, that will reduce the diameter of the case right back to the solid head. Unfortunately small base dies are not made in many calibers, but if you can get one in the calibre you are using it may well be your best jump off point to make a custom die.

I have been able to alter many factory FLS dies to work perfectly with my chambers.

The job goes like this:–

1. Measure the diameter of your FLD in the mouth at the base. Use a small hole gauge and a .0001" micrometer for this measurement as it has to be accurate. A caliper will not be accurate enough.

2. Measure the diameter of your fired case at a point about .050" in front of the top of your shell holder when fitted to the case. That will be pretty close to where you measured the back of the die, close enough anyway.

3. Compare the measurements. Ideally the measurements will be the same. It would be excellent if the die was .0005" smaller than the case at that point, but that would be most uncommon. If you have either of those happy circumstances there's a good chance that die can be made exactly right for your chamber. If however, the die is oversize at that point (it can be anything up to .002"), depending on the taper of your case, that die may not be suitable.

4. Remove the de-capping assembly from the die, screw it into the press and have some fired cases handy along with your FL sizing lube. I use Imperial Die Wax and have found it to be the best I have used, though I confess I have not used them all.

5. Drop the press arm and screw the die all the way into the press until it contacts the shell holder. Back it out about one turn.

6. Take a case and measure the diameter of the body, about .020" behind the shoulder, with a .0001" micrometer, and write that measurement down. Also take a measurement about 1/10" in front of where the top of the shell holder would be and write that down.

7. Lube the case body (not the neck or shoulder), and run the case up into the die being careful to feel if you bump the shoulder of the case at the top of the stroke. You will easily feel the shoulder bump. If you do, stop and remove the case part way, and unscrew the die about ¼ turn and run it in again. We don't want to move the shoulder back here, but we do want to be very close to it, if not just touching. If you didn't feel the shoulder bump, back the case out and screw the die in ¼ turn and try again. You want to feel the shoulder bump and then back the die out a little bit so the shoulder just touches or just misses touching by a thousandth or two. When you get it right tighten the lock ring.

8. Remove the case, clean off the lube and re-measure it. You will probably find that the measurement just behind the shoulder is around .003" or more smaller than it was on the unsized case, and the measurement just in front of the head is unchanged. That's ok.

8.1. For those of you whose die was .002" or thereabouts larger than the case just in front of the solid head, we need to see if the die will size the case at least 2/3RDS of the way down. As I said, that depends on the case design, taper in particular, and how loose your chamber is.

8.2. Make two marks on the case you can easily identify, after sizing, about 1/3RD and 2/3RDS of the way down the body of the case. Measure the diameter of the case at these marks and jot the measurements down.

8.3. Run the case into the die (lube it first of course), remove it, clean it, and remeasure.

8.4. If the new measurements are .0005" smaller the die will probably be ok. If however, the new measurements have not changed that die is not good, and you should not proceed with it. You can sell it off to someone with a factory chamber, as it will probably work fine for that, but it is too big to work on a tight custom chamber.

9. With an over sizing die in hand we only have to polish the cavity out enough so that it sizes our cases to the perfect dimensions that are compatible with our rifles chamber. This isn't rocket science. All it requires, is that you be careful and test your progress often. During my career it has been a constant source of amazement to me how hard it is to remove .0001", yet how easy it is to remove .001". Be warned, slow and easy, and check often or you will regret it.

10. The tools you need are cutting oil (Baby Oil) and 1" abrasive cloth strip in 180, 240, and 320 grit. You can use the bent strip holder you used to polish your chamber when you fitted the barrel earlier. Measure the diameter of the die, just behind the shoulder of the chamber, with a small hole gauge, and write that measurement down. Photo 6-1 shows the abrasive cloth about to enter the rear of a full length die.

10.1. Abrasive cloth strip works best when it is soaked in cutting oil. I wet the back of the strip liberally with cutting oil, and when the oil has soaked through to the front it is ready to use. Use Baby Oil, it is not toxic.

10.2. Tear the strips in half, as we will only want a ½" wide or less abrasive surface.

11. We will be taking the die in and out of the lathe a few times (maybe more than a few, actually) so you may want to hold it in a three jaw chuck. The diameter of abrasive cloth we want on our holder is just under shoulder diameter. The grit you start with depends on how undersized your die is.

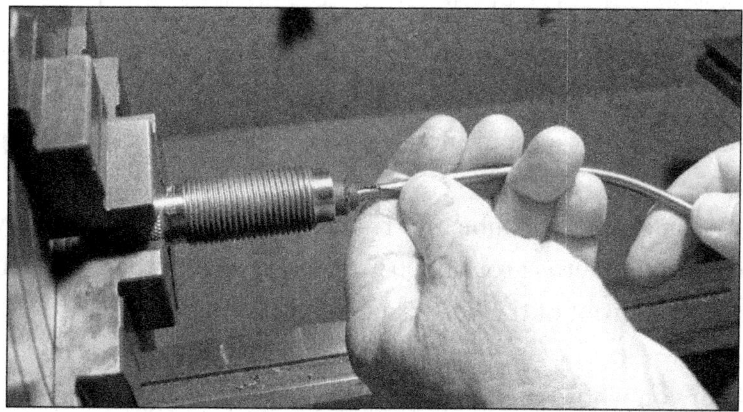

PHOTO 6-1.

I am about to polish out a die body. Most of my attention will be on the front third of the chamber with a little on the middle third if needed. It is rare to have to pay any attention to the rear third of the chamber, unless you started with a small base full length resizing die.

11.1. Keep in mind that the case will expand around .001" when it is removed from the die after sizing, and this must be taken into account when you are working out your sizes.

11.2. We don't want to polish the back 1/3RD of the die at all, except maybe to give it a fine grit lick to polish the surface a bit. That is why we are using only a ½" width cloth. Adjust the width, if necessary, when you are polishing a die for a very short case. Concentrate your attention on the front 1/3RD of the die with nearly no attention on the middle third.

11.3. If you have to open the die up .003" or more you will be fairly safe starting with 180 grit cloth. At .001" I would start with 320 grit and see what happens. These dies are very hard, around 60RC, so they can take a bit of polishing out, but remember what I said earlier about how hard it is to remove .0001", yet how easy it is to remove .001". If you go too far there's no easy way to put the material back.

12. Wrap a suitable length of abrasive cloth around your tool, spin the lathe up to 600-700RPM, dip the end of the cloth in cutting oil and insert it in the end of the die.

12.1. Move the tool back and forth in the front 2/3RDS of the die with more emphasis on the front 1/3RD than on the middle 1/3RD. While you are moving it back and forth put on side pressure all around the circumference of the die so that you are making the whole surface of your abrasive cloth roll cut.

12.2. The pattern you are making is a cross-hatch pattern that will make the job go quicker, because you are not allowing the abrasive grit to dwell in a groove it has just cut. Keep the cloth moving back and forth, but stay away from the back 1/3RD of the die.

13. This is a messy trail and error job, so don't polish for more than about a minute before checking how much progress you have made. Clean the die out with a couple of patches and measure it just behind the shoulder and compare that measurement with the one you took earlier.

13.1. You will quickly get an idea of how long you have to work at it to make an impression on the diameter of the die. Adjust the length of time you polish between diameter checks accordingly.

13.2. In theory you can polish to size with 180 grit, and refine the 180 grit surface with 240 grit and 320 grit, without increasing the diameter, however that doesn't work in real life. Leave yourself about .0005" to polish with the finer grits to be sure to remove all 180 grit scratches.

13.3. The die will work fine polished down to a worn 320 grit finish. If you want to go further than this by all means spend the extra time, but it is not necessary for other than aesthetic purposes.

14. Approach final dimension carefully and test the die by sizing a case in it at least .001" before you think you want your final dimensions to be. At this point I start checking how much the case has been sized with a dial caliper.

14.1. Take the case to be sized and clamp the caliper on the diameter of the body about .020" behind the shoulder and lock it. Now size the case, wipe it clean and try the caliper again for fit. Because the case has been sized to a smaller diameter the locked caliper can be moved down the case before it touches the new sized dimension. What we are wanting is for the caliper to move down the case 1/8" before tightening on the case diameter at that point. If it does that, the case is being full length sized correctly and you have done a good job. If it moves down ¼" you still have a bit of work to do, and if it moves down 1/16" you have over cooked it. It may still be ok, and you will soon find out when you test it.

14.2. Photo numbers 6-2, also 6-3, and 6-4 (Page 228) demonstrate the methodology of measuring the case in this way. It is difficult to obtain accurate measurements on the taper with a micrometer or caliper, and doing it like this is a valid procedure.

14.3. Doing the math, you can see, in this instance, the taper of my 7 SAUM is .013" over 1.350". Over 1/8" (.125") the taper is .0012", which is near enough to exactly the right amount I want to size the front half of the case, that being .0006" per side. Actually .0005" is perfect, but I won't quibble about an extra .0001". As long as your caliper moves down the case between 1/16" (.062") and 1/8" (.125") it will be excellent.

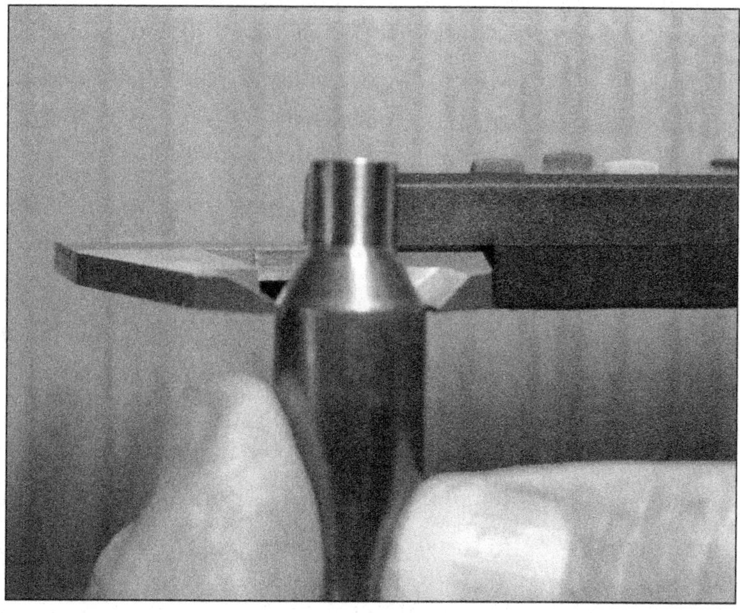

PHOTO 6-2.

The first measurement, taken before the case is full length sized. Lock the caliper at this measurement.

You may want to pay some attention to the neck section of the die unless you have a die that incorporates a neck sizing button. I don't like my FLD sizing the neck of my cases, preferring to do that in a separate operation in the straight line die we made in Chapter Five. *I know when I use that die it sizes necks with zero run out,* and that is what I want.

If you want to size the neck of the case in the FLD then it's a good idea to polish the neck portion of the die out to size the case neck, the minimum amount needed, to grip the projectile. As with the body go slow and check often. Me, I just polish it out so that it doesn't touch the case neck at all. Neck sizing will be a separate operation for me, but I am prepared to undertake the extra work in order to end up with sized cases that have zero run-out.

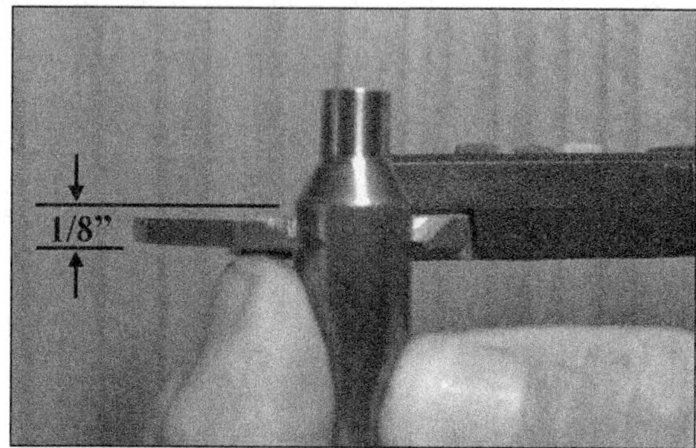

PHOTO 6-3.

The locked caliper should move down the case body a maximum of 1/8" after it has been full length sized. This is the maximum amount we want to size the case.

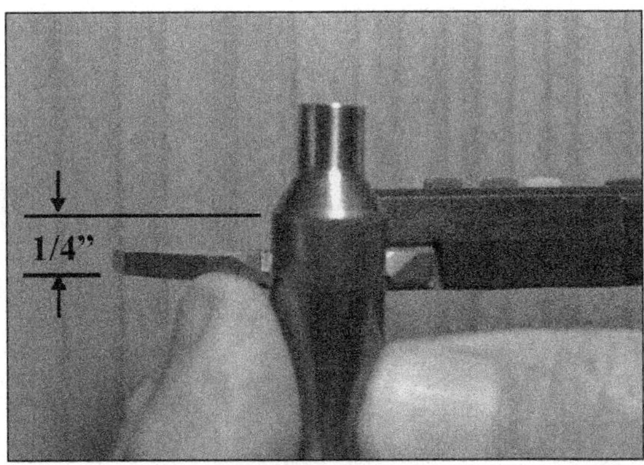

PHOTO 6-4.

The locked caliper has moved down the body of the case ¼" in this PHOTO, indicating that the die is undersized, and has full length sized the case twice as much as we want.

Once you have the die polished to the dimensions you want, wash it with solvent to remove the cutting oil and abrasive, and then oil it to prevent rusting. Now we will set it up properly to suite your chamber. To do this we need a set of Skip's die shims. These are available from various specialty vendors, and are simply steel shim material die cut to fit over the body of a standard 7/8 x 14TPI die in sizes of .003", .004", .005", .006", .007", .008", and .010". You will need the head-space gauge we made when we chambered the barrel, and a dial caliper. You can see some Skip's die shims in Photo 5-25 on Page 217. *You cannot set up a full length sizing die precisely without these shims.*

We do it like this:–

1. Loosen the lock ring on the die and screw it into the press with the .010" shim under the lock ring.

1.1. You adjusted the die prior to polishing it to size, so it should be fairly close to touching the shoulder of the case. The shim will move it away another .010".

2. Remove the firing pin assembly from the bolt of your rifle and also the ejector if it has one (*Super important*). Place the bolt in the action and cycle it a few times to see what it feels like. Basically there should be no resistance at all when closing it, and turning the bolt handle down.

3. Take a fired case *that is tight in the chamber*, fit the head-space gauge to it and measure the length from the top of the gauge to the base of the case. Write that measurement down. Photo 6-5 refers.

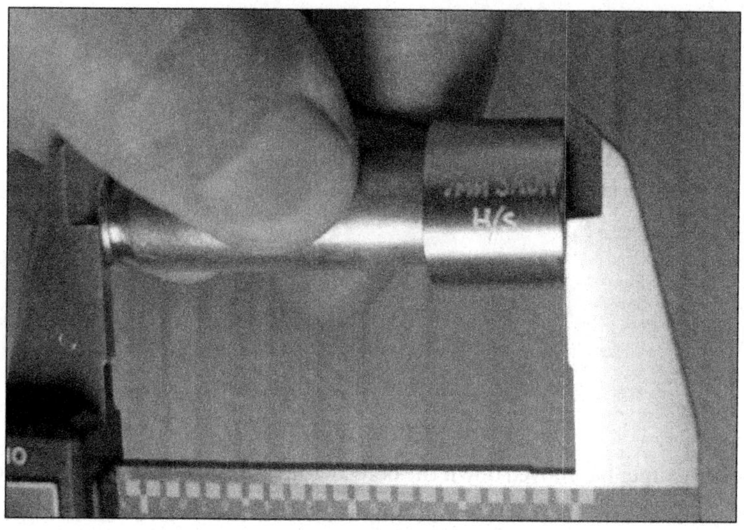

PHOTO 6-5.

Measuring the the distance from the top of the headspace guage, which is firmly against the shoulder of the case, to the base of the case with the case head-space tool we made in chapter 3.

3.1. *It is impossible to adjust the die properly unless you have a few cases that are tight in the chamber.* If you don't have them, go and do some testing with ½ a dozen cases until they get tight to chamber.

4. Apply case lube to the body only of the case and run it all the way into the die. Remove it, clean it and re-measure it with the head-space gauge.

5. If there is no change wind the die in about 1/16TH of a turn, relube the case and repeat.

5.1. What we are doing is making a coarse adjustment, and will no doubt oversize the case when we finally contact the shoulder. That's ok. The case isn't ruined. Just mark it with a texta so you know which one it is, and be sure to fire it and any others you oversize with a projectile seated well into the rifling lands so that it head-spaces correctly.

5.2. One rotation of a 7/8 x 14TPI die moves the die into the press by just over .071", so 1/16TH of a turn will move it in just under .005". So .005" will be our worse case scenario in creating excess head-space on that case. .005" excess head-space is not a dangerous amount.

6. Eventually you will make a change in the measurement and when that happens turn the die *almost* back to its last position and tighten the lock ring.

7. Select another case that is tight to chamber, measure it as before, lube it and run it up into the die. Extract it, clean it and re-measure. If there is no change in the measurement screw the die out, remove the .010" shim, replace it with the .008" shim, replace the die, relube the case and run it up into the die.

8. Continue sizing, measuring and reducing the shim thickness by .001" until you detect that the shoulder of the case has been moved back .001".

9. You already know what an empty chamber feels like when you shut the bolt. If not, re familiarize yourself.

9.1. What we are looking for is to feel very slight resistance when the bolt closes on the case. The case should chamber easily, and when the bolt is turned down you should feel a slight resistance when it reaches the end of the closing cam, and turns down.

10. Once you have reached that point, it is simply a matter of trying a few different settings until you find the perfect one. You will be making adjustments in .001" increments, so choose the shim that feels right. There will be very little difference in the resistance created by a .001" adjustment, so if I am faced with a bolt that closes too easily on a .004" shim, even though there may be more resistance with a .005" shim (I probably want a .0045" shim) I will opt for the slightly tighter bolt closure.

You want to have the case fully supported at the shoulder and base with a bit of pressure on the bolt holding it there. It is thus perfectly headspaced.

We are not finished yet though. If you are going to full length size your cases every time you fire them (I do), then we need to go a little further. Go ahead and FLS the rest of your *tight* cases, load them up and go fire some groups, or have a bit of wind practice with them so they are now once fired after full length sizing. Full length size one of them and test it in your rifle as we did before. It's on the cards that the bolt will close too easily, indicating the case has been oversized. Re-adjust the die with the next +.001" shim, size another case and test it. The distance you will need to move the die out depends on how tight the case was initially, and how hard the brass is. Once you have found the perfect head-space (you may have to move the die out up to .003") you can go ahead and FLS all of your cases, and the head-space will be right on.

You should recheck the head-space of your cases about every five shots and adjust the die, if needed, to maintain the perfect fit. Of course you should try and fire all of your cases an equal number of times so that they all react the same way to your die, and hence in your chamber. I am all too aware just how hard this is to do, so just be aware of it, and do the best you can without being too anal about it.

Correct head-space is very important to bench-rest shooters who have maybe 25 cases and reload them for each match. During the course of a big match those cases will be full length sized many times, and the shooter will keep a close eye on how they feel when they chamber, and adjust the die as needed to maintain the head-space at his preferred fit.

Polishing factory dies out has worked for me for more years than I care to remember. However, when I started shooting a 7MM Remington SAUM cartridge for F Class Open competition, I could not obtain a factory die that would not oversize the front 1/3RD of the case, yet not touch the back 2/3RDS of the case. If you run into this problem it's not a disaster, as you can make a perfectly adequate die in your lathe with a bit of effort. The only draw back is it will have to be hardened professionally, and those guys charge like a herd of wounded buffalo. The shop I used to harden this die billed me $85.00 minimum charge plus $25.00 (that's a 100% overcharge by itself!) to post it back to me. Add my cost to post it to them and the hardening cost came to $125.00. At least Ned Kelly wore a mask!

On the flip side you do end up with a die that sizes cases exactly right, and it is a one off expense, as it will out last you.

This is how I do it:-

The trick is to make the die in three parts, and when you do that its creation is basically a lathe boring job. I made my 7 Saum die from 1010 mild steel and had it case hardened. I have made many dies like this and they work fine. If you have something more exotic you want to use, go right ahead. Provided you work out the tolerances you need to allow for shrinking or expansion in hardening and tempering you should have no problems. Why did I use 1010 mild steel? It's all I had, and I know from past experience that it works ok.

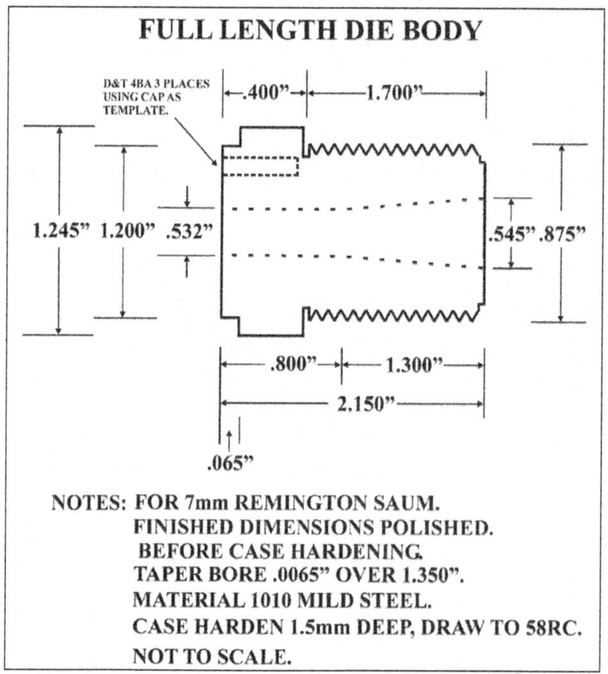

Figure 6-1.

The dimensions that I used when I made my 7 SAUM FLD body.

The drawing for the die I made for myself is shown in figure numbers 6-1, 6-2, and 6-3, and shows the dimensions that worked for my 7 Saum.

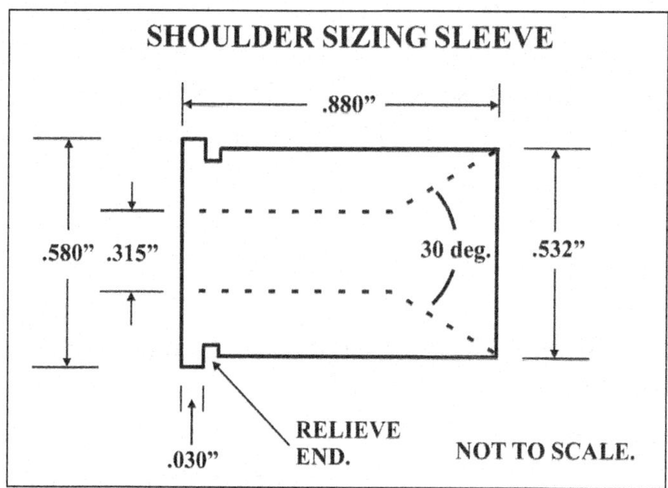

Figure 6-2.

The shoulder resizing sleeve dimensions for my 7 SAUM FLD.

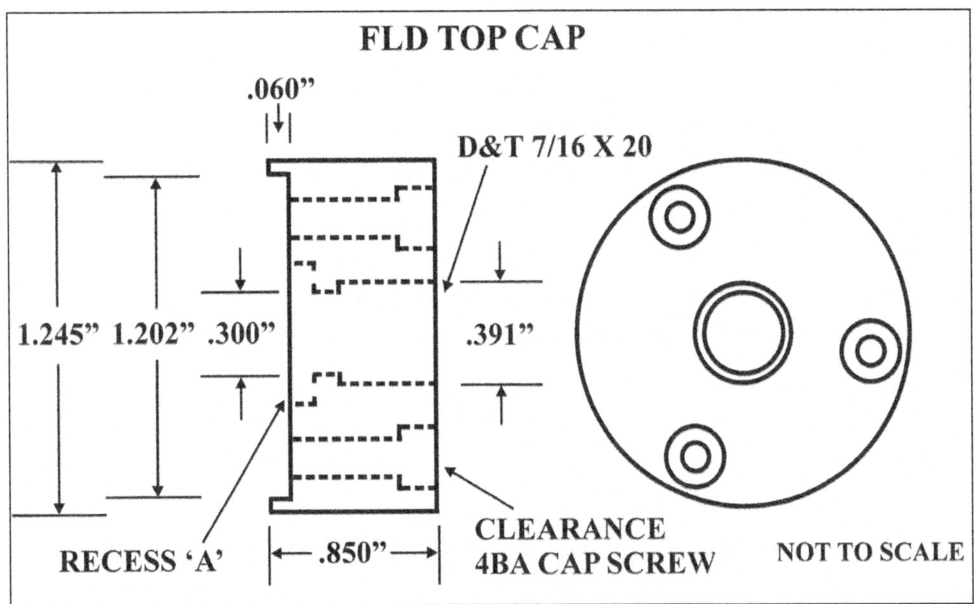

Figure 6-3.
The dimensions for the retaining cap on my 7 Saum FLD.

1. Secure your piece of round steel (mine was 1.250" diameter) in your 4 jaw chuck and true it.

2. Turn the shank to .875" diameter by 1.700" long or whatever length is needed to reach the shell holder in your reloading press. Don't forget to take into account the thickness of a locking ring.

3. Cut the 60° 14TPI thread just as described in chapter 3 (when we fitted the barrel). Relieve the thread at the end with a parting tool.

   3.1. Reloading dies are a good rattling fit in the press, and that fit should be maintained for alignment purposes. I simply use one of those split lock rings tightened onto a die, so it just screws on with resistance, as a gauge. Deepen the thread until the lock ring screws on with the same feeling it had on the die and it will be ok. If you want to go crazy with wires or thread micrometers etc, go knock yourself out.

4. Drill your steel right through to a diameter about .020" to .030" under the diameter of your chamber at the junction of the body and shoulder.

   4.1. I do this in several steps. Just be careful that your drill doesn't run out too much and that it drills to size.

5. Select a suitable boring bar, that will bore out the hole we drilled, to just under the diameter at the junction of the shoulder and body, both for diameter and length. Mount it in your tool post.

6. Bore the drilled hole, right through, to the diameter of your case at the shoulder/body junction, less an amount to allow for polishing before, and after, hardening. For my 7 Saum that was .531" diameter before hardening. I would have bored the hole to .530" diameter, and polished the last .001"out to bring it to size with a fine finish.

7. Set your compound rest at about ½⁰ but don't lock it down.

8. Measure the taper of a fired case over the length from the junction of the shoulder and body to the shiny mark you can see just in front of the solid head of the case. Write that down, along with the diameter of the case at that shiny mark.

8.1. That mark can be easily seen on all fired cases, and is well ahead of the shell holder top and represents the maximum expansion point at the back of the case.

8.2. The dimensions you should have written down will be something like .012" over 1.200", and .465", or whatever.

8.3. We have to halve the taper measurement because we are working only on one side of the case. As you can see on my rough drawing the measurement for my 7 SAUM was .0065" over 1.350". (Figure 6-1 Page 232)

8.4. Its ok to take this measurement from a case. Measure a few and see if there is a discrepancy. There shouldn't be. We are, after all, sizing a fired case, so those are the dimensions we want to base our final die dimensions on.

9. Set up a .0001" dial indicator on the headstock of the lathe. Mark your length dimension on the body of the compound rest (2 marks) and bring the probe of the dial indicator into contact at the first mark. Zero the dial on the indicator. Now wind the saddle wheel forward until the probe is on the second mark and read the taper off the dial. Adjust the compound rest and re measure back and forth until you achieve the taper you are after. We have already done this when we fitted a barrel in Chapter three. (Photo 3-24, Page 111)

9.1. Get this right to zero tolerance. Run the saddle back and forth a few times and make sure you always come up with the right measurement.

9.2. Once you are satisfied that it is right, lock down the compound rest and check it again. Adjust as necessary until it is right with the compound rest locked down. Remove the dial indicator and put it away.

10. Wind the travel of the compound rest all the way to its forward stop, and bring the tip of the boring tool level with the back of the die. Now, using the carriage feed, and reading off the carriage feed dial, run the boring tool into the drilled hole about ½" further than the length you worked out for your taper. For my 7 SAUM I would have moved the carriage forward 1.850" or thereabouts. This is simply to ensure that you bore the taper right through, and don't create a shoulder. Lock the carriage in place and wind the compound rest back bringing the boring tool out of the drilled hole, being careful not to let the tool drag on the side of the hole on the way out. Remember you are winding back with a taper.

11. You already have the measurement of your fired case at its maximum expansion point in the rear from when you determined the case taper. You did write it down didn't you? I told you to! Now

we are going to taper bore our drilled hole out to that dimension at the very back of the die less an amount to allow for polishing after hardening, and less an amount to allow for polishing the surface before hardening.

11.1. Referring to my rough drawing, for me, that was .545" diameter finally polished before hardening. (Page 232)

11.2. I lube the hole before each cut with cutting oil placed in the mouth of the hole, with a brush, and then blown right into the hole with a soft compressed air blow.

11.3. The compound rest will run into the end of its travel at the end of the cut. I'm assuming you were smart enough to bring the tool tip in contact with the hole and zero the dial on your cross-feed before starting to cut. At the end of the cut move the cross-feed in .010" or so to prevent the tip of the tool rubbing on the way out of the hole.

11.4. Make your last cut around .0015" deep with a slow feed to leave a fine finish inside the die. You should be able to make the die about .001" undersize at the back, and polish that last .001" out with 320 grit strip to produce a tool mark free bright surface inside the die.

11.5. Don't worry about the front dimension of the die, at the shoulder/ body junction. The taper will have taken care of that, if you got it right.

11.6. When polishing the bore to size be careful to polish it evenly or you will be compromising the dimensions of the taper.

12. Reverse the die body in the chuck and clean up the outside. At the same time I cut the recess on the end to locate the cap we will be making later on, and the die body is finished for the time being. Photo 6-6 shows my die body.

13. Now we turn our attention to the sleeve that will be a close fit inside the top of the die body and will eventually size the shoulder, and neck if you want it to. Again this is a simple job, all work being completed in the one step.

13.1. I made the sleeve a .001" interference fit to allow for possible expansion or contraction when hardened and tempered, and to allow it, and the bore it will fit in, to be polished to a close fit.

13.2. I left a small flange at the top of the sleeve to prevent it sliding through the die in case it was so inclined.

PHOTO 6-6.
The hardened die body for my 7 SAUM.

13.3. The neck of the sleeve will end up just over the diameter of my chamber when it is polished after hardening. I don't want to neck size in this die. You may want otherwise, so adjust as necessary.

13.4. The edge of the sleeve at the bottom is quite sharp and fragile until it is hardened and tempered. This edge will ultimately be supported inside the die body and will cause no problems. Photos 6-7 and 6-8 (274) show the sleeve for my 7 Saum.

14. The cap is again a straight forward turning and boring job, and tapping the hole in the end to accept a standard decapping assembly from another die.

14.1. The cap is located on the recess in the top of the die body and held to the body with three 4BA Allen head cap screws I happened to have on hand.

PHOTOS 6-7 AND 6-8.
The shoulder re-sizing sleeve for my 7 SAUM FLD.

14.2. The cap does not need to be hardened, and we will be machining it further once the other two parts are back from being hardened. Photos 6-9 and 6-10 show my finished cap.

14.3. Drill and tap the die body using the cap as a template once you have made it.

15. Send the die body and sleeve off for hardening. All you can do here is piss and moan like an impotent jerk, then bend over and take it up the tail pipe in regards to cost. Oh! that I could get so much money for doing so little!

15.1. For the 1010 mild steel I used, I specified a case hardness thickness of 1MM to 1.5MM thick and a tempered hardness of 58 Rockwell on the C scale (58RC).

16. When the parts are returned (and you've recovered from the shock of paying for the job) you will treat it exactly the same way we discussed altering a commercial FLD earlier in this chapter.

16.1. Start with the die body and give it a light polish to clean it up and smooth the bore. Probably a lick with 240 grit, followed with worn 320 grit will be all that is needed.

16.2. Once again you need to be testing with cases that are a little tight in the chamber. Screw the die body into the press until it is about .100" from touching the shell holder.

PHOTOS 6-9 AND 6-10.
The finished cap for my 7 SAUM FLD.

16.3. Select a case and measure the diameter at the shiny point near the base and just behind the shoulder/body junction. Also clamp a caliper and lock it just behind the shoulder/body junction like we did before.

16.4. Lube the case and run it right up into the die. Extract it, clean it and measure it. Also check whether the caliper moves down the body 1/8". If everything looks ok, wind the die in to within .050" of the shell holder, size a case and recheck the dimensions. Time to polish.

16.5. As before, go carefully and check often. Once you have determined that you have a little bit to polish out of the body you can fit a lock ring, slip a .010" Skip's die shim under it, screw the die down to its correct position in the press and lock the locking ring down.

16.6. Polish the die cavity until it sizes a case .0005" or a bit less at the base and .001" at the shoulder/body junction, finished with a worn 320 grit or better polish. It's hard to measure the case diameter at the body/ shoulder junction so use the caliper to determine ideal sized diameter. If it moves 1/8" down the body of the case after sizing you've got it just right.

17. You have already polished the bore in front of the taper. Now polish the shoulder and neck of the sleeve to the same finish as the body cavity. Then polish the outside diameter until it slides into the top of the die, all the way in. Polish the top of the sleeve as well to smooth it. If you want the die to be really slick, fit a 1/8" split rod to your Dremel tool, and insert some patch material into it. Charge the patch material with some Summabrax polishing compound, spin the lathe up, and polish the die cavity with the Dremel tool running. Repeat with white buffing compound, and the die cavity will shine like a mirror — very slick.

18. Screw the die body into the press and run a lubed case into it. Now slide the sleeve into the top of the body right down to the shoulder of the case. Give it a couple of taps with a soft hammer to ensure it is fully seated against the shoulder of the case.

19. Measure the distance from the top of the sleeve to the top of the die with a depth micrometer.

20. Now bore a recess in the cap the same depth to accept the protrusion of the sleeve from the die body.

20.1. I made the recess in my cap a large enough diameter to accept Skips seating die shims, in case I ever felt the need to adjust the depth of the sleeve independently from the die body. I haven't needed to do that, but the option is there just in case, by making the cavity diameter a little larger.

21. Assemble the die and adjust it in the press to full length size your cases to that perfect fit as we described earlier in this chapter. Photo 6-11 shows the finished, working die.

PHOTO 6-11.

The finished 7 SAUM FLD.

Full length dies like these whether altered from commercial products or made from scratch will ease the load on your action, and extractor in particular, as well as treat your cases as kindly as is possible. However it is imperative that they be adjusted properly and their adjustment monitored for best results.

AN M'98 MAUSER IN .375 H&H MAGNUM

BUILT IN THE MID 1980S

PHOTO C4-33.

The stick was a nice piece of hard Australian English walnut. Some photos are 'in the white' to better see detail.

PHOTO C4-34.

The barrel was stainless steel in #5A profile, fitted with a second recoil lug. It was blued for final finishing.

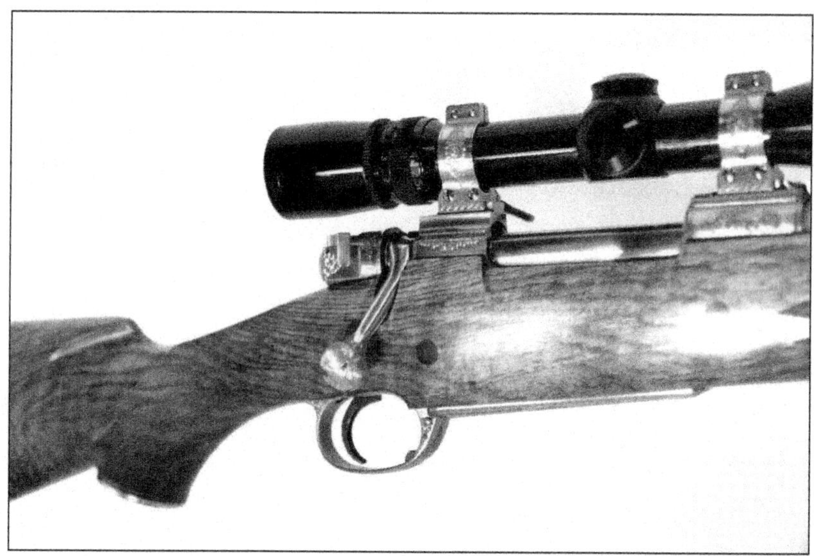

PHOTO C4-35.

Telescopic sight mount bases were custom made to suite side lever quick detachable rings. The trigger here is a tuned Canjar M-3.

PHOTO C4-36.
Classic bolt handle with 4 panels of checkering and engraving on the end.

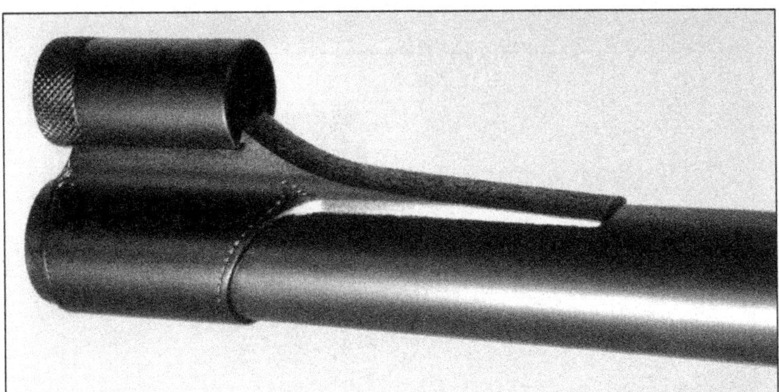

PHOTO C4-37.
Barrel banded foresight.

PHOTO C4-38.
Under grip showing detail around the trigger guard.

PHOTO C4-39.
The ¼ rib featured a one standing and three folding leaves express rear sight. The express sights were regulated by firing and machining to zero.

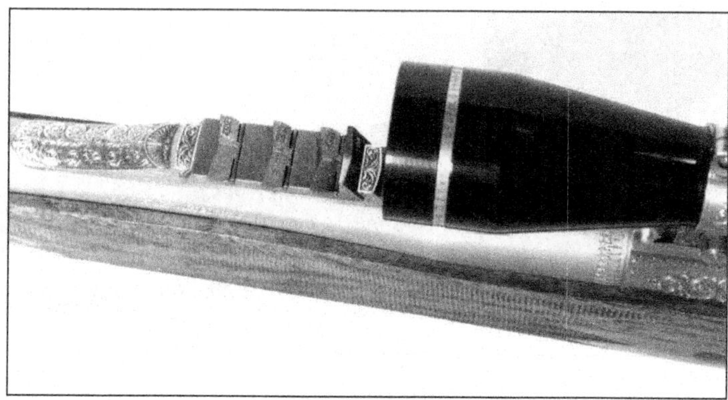

PHOTO C4-40.
The top stock line showing precise inletting. The barrel floated back to the reinforce.

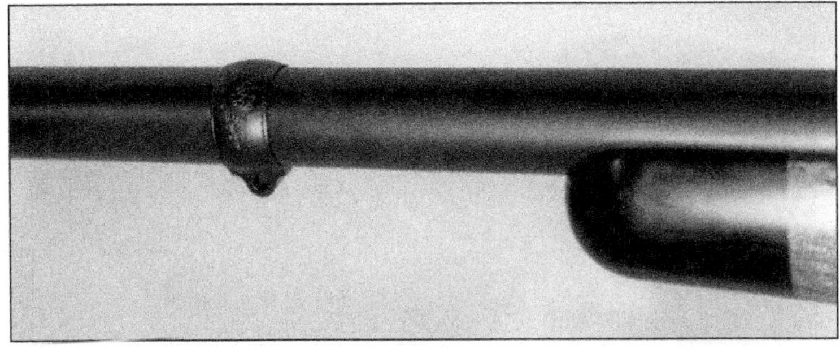

PHOTO C4-41.
African Ebony forend tip and barrel banded front sling swivel base.

PHOTO C4-42.
The stock was double cross-bolted, and the holes capped with African Ebony.

PHOTO C4-43.
The engraving was fine English Scroll masterfully executed by Phil Vinnicombe.

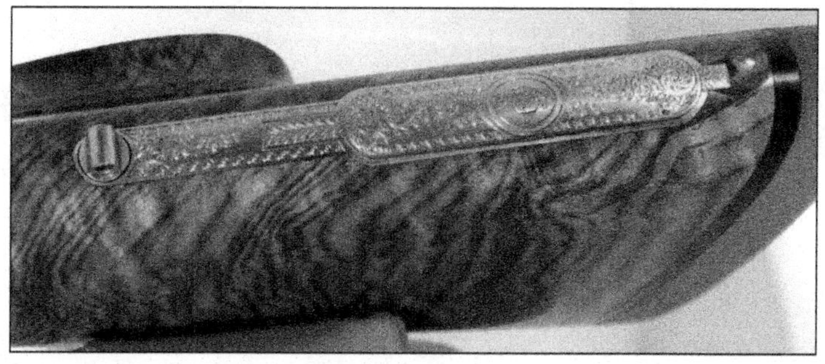

PHOTO C4-44.

The cartridge trap in the white with custom sling swivel base.

PHOTO C4-45.

The cartridge trap holds four .375 H&H cartridges.

PHOTO C4-46.

Close up of the front scope base, and shape at rear of the ¼ rib.

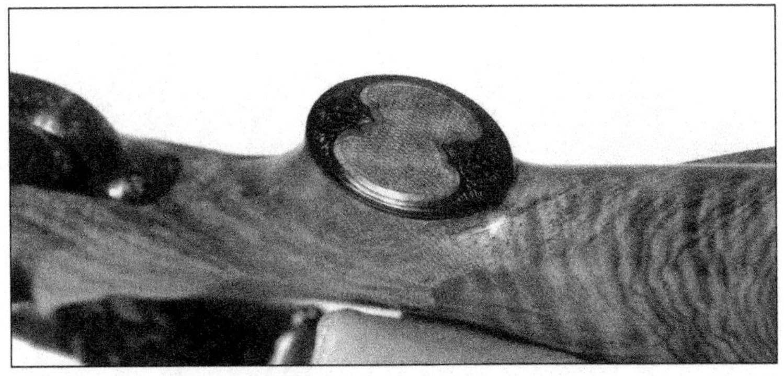

PHOTO C4-47.
The very popular scalloped skeleton grip cap.

PHOTO C4-48.
The classic point pattern checkering was 32 lines per inch.

PHOTO C4-49.
Side view of the ¼ rib.

PHOTO C4-50.

The action was profile ground all over before polishing.

PHOTO C4-51.

Side view of the very fine 32 lines per inch forend checkering.

PHOTO C4-52.

One standing leaf and three folding leaf express rear sight.

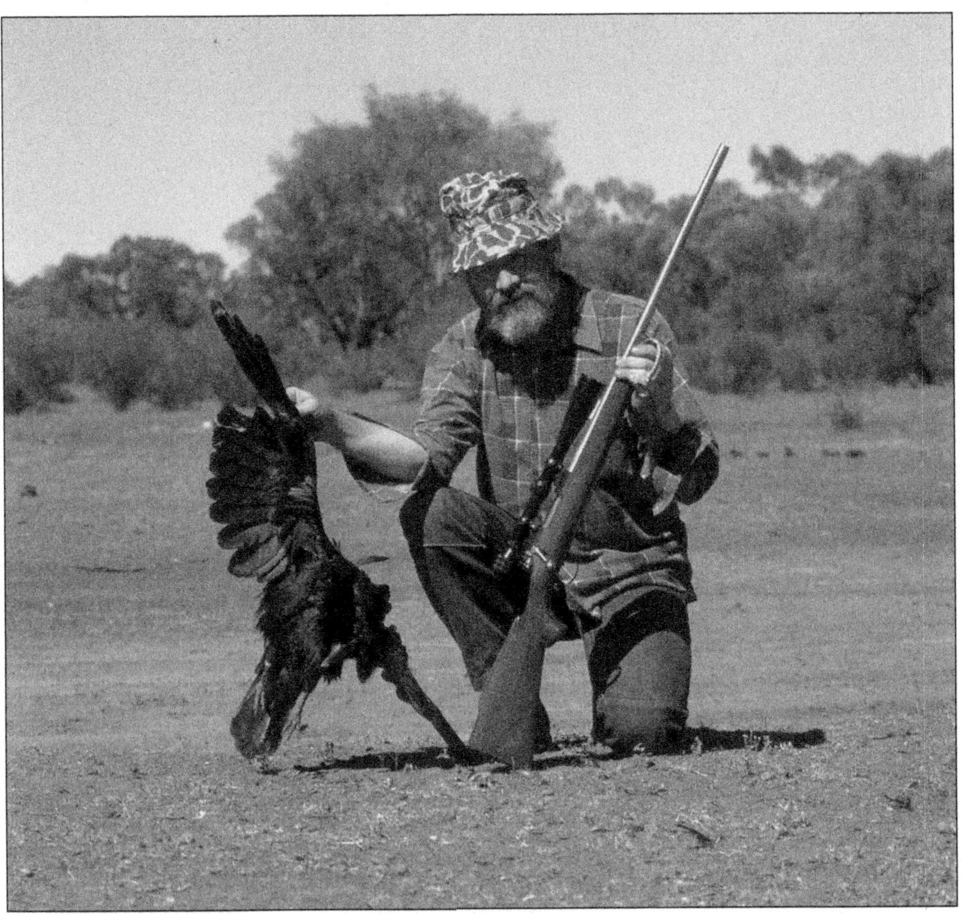

Photo C4-53.

In the early 1980s I needed a varmint rifle, so I fitted a Shilen #5A 1:12" pitch stainless steel barrel to a good 40X action, and bedded it into a Remington short ADL stock I had. The calibre I chose was .220 Ackley Improved Swift. I wanted a high intensity .22 calibre, and the Ackley Improved Swift was the easiest to feed, unlike many hotshot .22s that require a lot of case preparation. This rifle shot the 60^{GN} hollow point projectile out at just under 4000FPS, and was an accurate and very deadly combination. The 60^{GN} projectile was very explosive in the 12" pitch barrel. The scope is a very old 12X Redfield with the CH–Peep reticule in the old Redfield four screw per ring mounts. Pity they moved to that ugly angled design.

True to form, I started on a good stock for it, but never finished it. Oh, well!

CHAPTER SEVEN

STOCK BEDDING

Of all of the systems that go into making an accurate rifle, bedding is probably the most misunderstood. We need to get something straight, right from the outset. Just because you have some sort of fiberglass material in your stock, it does not follow that it is properly bedded. In fact quite the opposite is more than likely to be true.

I have been bedding rifles since the early 1960s, but more importantly have been thinking about the job ever since I started. The information I will be imparting here has been obtained through much trial and error, frustration, temper tantrums and heartache. It was a rocky road, but in the end I worked it out.

That correct bedding is absolutely mandatory, if you are to have an accurate rifle, has been a constant source of amazement to me. I have taken enough poorly shooting rifles, and turned them into tack drivers with a re-bed, over the years, to convince me that my bedding knowledge and practice is sound. Further, my methods rarely fail to produce a good bedding job. It does happen, but not very often.

Before we get into the nuts and bolts of the job we need to delve into a bit of theory, and try to understand exactly what it is we are trying to achieve. I have to say, that the theory I am going to discuss has absolutely no basis in proven fact. To attempt that sort of proof would be very costly, and time consuming, and no doubt beyond my expertise. Further, why do I need to prove the theory beyond doubt when what I am doing works, and the theory seems to fit the results very nicely? That having been said, you can judge for yourself whether you think I'm close to the mark, or completely bonkers. However, don't ignore the practice — I know that works.

When we break the trigger on a centrefire rifle we set in motion a whole series of events, mainly vibrations and movements, that in the end affect where each projectile will impact on the target. The event that concerns us the most here is recoil. We certainly feel the firearm recoil into our shoulder, when the shot is fired, and that is a fairly violent event. Where does it come from and how does it end up banging you in the shoulder?

Well, it is initially generated in the barreled action. A guy called Isaac Newton formulated a law, a long time ago, that states, 'For every action there is an equal and opposite reaction', or close to that. So, projectile goes out the front of the barrel, requiring an amount of energy to do so, and that same amount of energy pushes the barreled action to the rear, in the opposite direction. In our shooting system the barrelled actions rearward movement is mainly impeded by the recoil lug, being assisted by tension on the action screws. That energy is transferred through the recoil lug to the stock, and all of those parts, being essentially one unit, recoil to the rear, and ultimately into your shoulder.

If you think about it you will realize that there is no way that the violent rearward reaction, and energy caused by firing the barreled action, can be transferred into the stock without a small degree of deformation of the stock material behind the recoil lug. *It just isn't possible for the stock to instantly move to the rear.* There will be a small delay — it's called inertia. However, the barreled action is already moving, and can't be stopped, so it will compress the material behind the recoil lug slightly before the stock itself begins to move to the rear. How do I know this is what happens? It is evident by rub marks you can see in the inletting of the stock on all bearing surfaces, whether they be wood, metal or some sort of fiberglass material. These scuff marks do not appear for no reason at all. They have to be caused by movement between the barreled action and the stock, no matter how small the amount of movement is, and it is a small amount of movement.

This recoil movement within the stock is of great concern to us because it directly influences the harmonics of the barrel. In order for a centrefire rifle to be accurate the harmonics of the barrel must be, as close as possible, exactly the same from shot to shot. *Any external influence that changes the barrels harmonics, from shot to shot, will have an adverse effect on accuracy.* Bedding is certainly one of those external influences.

The material behind the recoil lug, regardless of what it is, is resilient. When compressed, provided the limits of its elasticity have not been exceeded, it will try to return to its former position when the force, that compressed it in the first place, dissipates. Sort of like a spring — you compress it, and when you remove the compressing force it springs back to where it was. The technical term for this is 'return to battery'.

Thinking of barrel harmonics, and the need to have them be exactly the same from shot to shot, it follows that unless the barreled action returns to exactly the same position, after recoil, that it was in before recoil started, harmonics will be affected detrimentally. How do we know that? Well, the diagnosis of a faulty bedding job is either double grouping, or vertical stringing. Actually, double grouping is simply a variation of vertical stringing, so you could really call vertical stringing the sole diagnosis. Vertical stringing is shots printing in a vertical line, either straight up and down, or obliquely on the target.

I will be discussing barrel harmonics and tuning more extensively in the tuning chapter, so I'll be brief here. Simply put, when the rifle is fired the barrel moves up and down at the muzzle (remember, I said 'simply put'). Given that the harmonics are exactly the same from shot to shot, our ideal condition would be for all of our projectiles to exit the muzzle at either the top, or bottom, of the barrels oscillation, as that is where the muzzle will move the least vertical distance over a given time period. It's a matter of timing. We adjust our powder weight and bullet seating depth to time our projectiles to exit the muzzle at that point in its travel.

Regardless of barrel oscillations, and regardless of what load we are using, if all of our projectiles are timed to reach the muzzle, and exit it at close to the same hypothetical time, it follows that anything that changes the harmonics of the barrel, from shot to shot, will change the exit point of each projectile. Each projectile reaches the exit point at close to the same time, but if the exit point is different for each projectile? You don't have to be a brain surgeon to figure that one out!

Anything that prevents the barreled action from recoiling smoothly within the stock, and then prevents it from returning to battery smoothly and fully, will interfere with the harmonics of the barrel. With bedding, interference is caused by cramping, or stress, applied to the receiver when the barreled action is tightened into the inletting. This prevents smooth and consistent recoil, as well as a complete return to battery for every shot.

To make matters worse, bad bedding has a far larger impact on group size and configuration than does simple 'out of tune'. A rifle that shoots, say in the .200s at 100 yards consistently, when in tune, would probably increase its groups by a tenth of an inch when it went out of tune, that extra tenth being in vertical displacement of the shots. However, that same rifle with bad bedding would be struggling to print groups less than one inch, and with very noticeable vertical displacement. It would appear that bad bedding causes barrel harmonic variations to be modified considerably, thus causing the extreme dispersion we see on our targets.

Such a rifle, even though it has the potential to be very accurate, will never be able to be tuned to anything, even close to its full accuracy potential, until the bedding fault is corrected. *Bad bedding is an accuracy killer*, pure and simple.

A straight vertical string is caused by the barreled action coming to rest in random positions in the bedding after every shot. Sometimes it may return fully to battery, but essentially it is never at rest in the same place twice, or rarely. Double grouping is caused when the barreled action has two places where it would prefer to stop when trying to return to battery. As I said early on, not proven, but it certainly fits.

Figure 7-1 is a much simplified visual example of what I am getting at here. The squiggly line represents the barrels vertical oscillations. A rifle in good tune, and with good bedding, will release the projectiles from the muzzle when the barrel is either at the top or bottom phase of its oscillation, represented by the green zones in the figure. If the barrel releases the projectiles in the red zone the rifle will be out of tune, which will be exhibited by some vertical dispersion in the group.

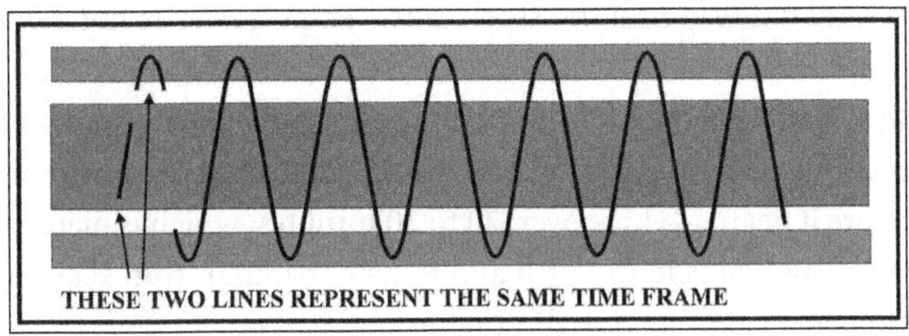
THESE TWO LINES REPRESENT THE SAME TIME FRAME

FIGURE 7-1.

An in tune rifle will release all of its projectiles from the muzzle in the green zone.

Figure 7-2 is a simplified visual example of the effect we see printed on the target when bad bedding is causing the barreled action to stop in two distinct places in the bedding, during return to battery, after the recoil force has dissipated. It demonstrates classic double grouping most often seen with bad bedding. Because the recoil within the stock starts from two different places, there will be two different oscillation patterns, represented by the different colored squiggly lines.

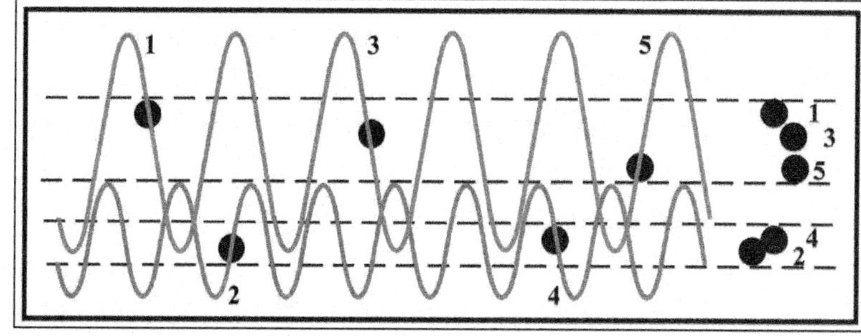

Figure 7-2.

Double grouping caused by bad bedding. The numbers above, and below, the dots represent the shot sequence of the 5 shot group.

Given all of this, what exactly are we trying to do? Obviously we want the barreled action to return to battery in exactly the same place for every shot we fire. How can we achieve that? By providing a straight, flat, stress free bedding platform, *tested and known to be correct.*

I have seen rifles bedded in many different mediums over the years. Silicon sealer, window putty coloured with black texta, various different polyester materials, Araldite, and some others that don't immediately come to mind. I began bedding rifles in the early 1960s using a polyester material called Plastebond. I believe it is still available today, but don't rush out and buy some because, as a bedding compound, it is totally unsuitable. Without going into a long discourse on the properties of various materials, let me just say, that it has been long established, that the best material for this job is some sort of epoxy material. Polyester materials are not suitable. They have too much shrinkage, and harden too quickly, leaving the operator exposed to the disaster of having the material kick over (go off) when the barreled action is only halfway into the stock. Further, polyester is not a good glue, and is very fragile in thin sections.

Epoxy, on the other hand, is perfect for the job. It is very good glue indeed, and will stick, like that proverbial substance to a blanket, to darn near anything. It exhibits very little shrinkage and gives a good working time before it begins to kick over; 20 to 30 minutes, which is plenty of time to get the job done and clean up. It has high tensile strength and is very strong in thin sections. There is no better material with which to bed a rifle — end of discussion.

I have tried many materials over the years, especially in the early years, and settled on two brands that I ended up using exclusively. For factory, and target rifles, I use Devcon Plastic Steel type A. Devcon is an epoxy material that has been mixed with atomized steel to create a material of soft butter like consistency that flows readily, but has good slump characteristics. It will pretty well stay where you put it in the stock, and not all run out the magazine mortise. It is very strong, and when used properly, sets up very hard and provides an ideal bedding platform. Photo 7-1 shows the products I use exclusively.

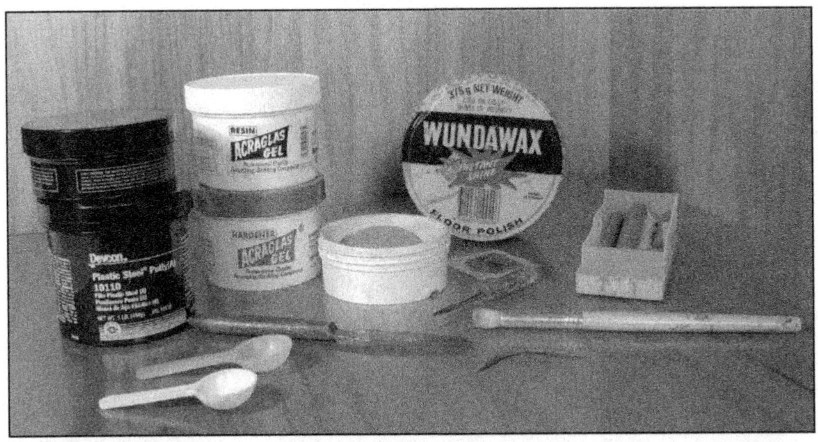

PHOTO 7-1.

The bedding materials I have used for a long, long time. The white dish contains atomized stainless steel, and just along side of it brown dye, both used with Acraglas Gel. On the right is a container of plasticine, and in front of the Wundawax application brush a thin worm of plasticine. I will use that to blend the sharp corners on the action to prevent the bedding breaking out when the barreled action is removed.

Devcon makes the material with several different atomized materials mixed in, such as aluminum, stainless steel, bronze, ceramic etc, etc. I have seen many jobs bedded in aluminum that were unsatisfactory and would suggest you do not use it. I will explain why later on. As far as the other atomized materials go, stainless steel would be ok and probably ceramic, though they are much more expensive than steel, and steel is expensive enough. My rule would be *not to use* anything that is more conductive than steel.

If Devcon has a problem, it is that it does not easily escape through small orifices. The way this job goes is to over fill the bedding cavity, and squeeze the barreled action in. The barreled action won't go in if the Devcon has no where to escape through. That is why I said I use it for factory rifles and target rifles, as those types usually have pretty sloppy inletting, with plenty of gaps, to allow the material to escape as the barreled action is lowered into place.

For the quality custom sporting rifles I made for many years I used Brownells Acraglas Gel. This is a white soft butter like consistency material without any atomized additives. It could be coloured with brown dye (or whatever colour) and could escape the hairline inletting that was a feature of those quality rifles. I used to mix in some atomized stainless steel, in a portion of the material, for behind the recoil lug and at the rear tang to provide extra strength at those points. Photos 7-2 and 7-3 (Page 254) show an Acraglass Gel bedding job.

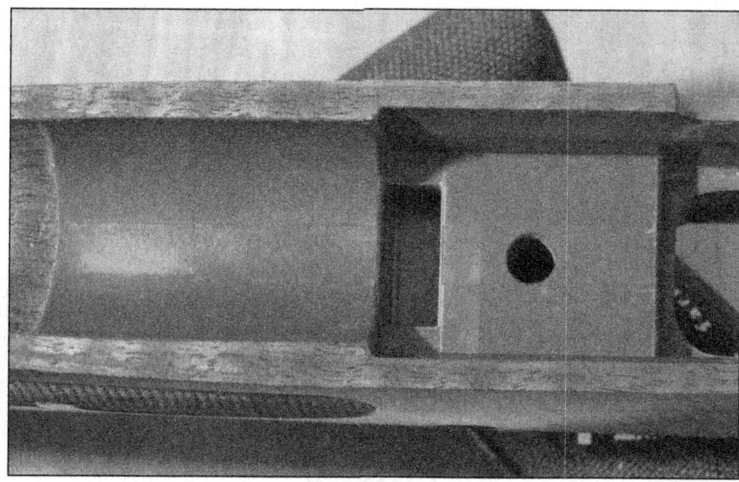

PHOTO 7-2.

This is the receiver section of a custom stock bedded in dyed Acraglass Gel. This stock has a second recoil lug fitted and encapsulated within the epoxy, as the rifle is a heavy kicker. The 2ND recoil lug surrounds the receivers recoil lug and transfers recoil from the relatively weak area behind the existing recoil lug to 2" forward in the forend. It can be just seen through the bedding. Also note the colour of the atomized stainless steel added to the mix behind the recoil lug and the breaking of sharp corners with play putty (Plasticine).

As a bedding material, Devcon is by far the superior of the two, but is totally unsuitable for use with hairline custom inletting. It's a case of "horses for courses."

Before we start we have to get something straight. *It is impossible to bed a rifle properly if the inletting is not correct.* When I was making those fancy custom rifles, years ago, much time was spent making sure the inletting was perfect before attempting to bed the barreled action. I cannot stress this enough. *The inletting must be correct.* Do not attempt the job if it is not.

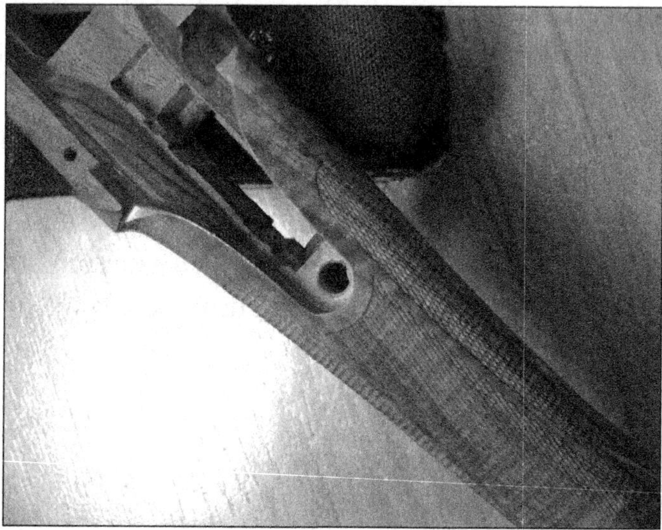

PHOTO 7-3.

The rear tang bedding of the same stock. The Acraglas Gel has atomized stainless steel added to increase its strength in this critical area. Even though this stock is made of very strong Australian English Walnut, the small rear tang bedding area of actions like this must be treated with care.

By correct, I mean that the inletting must not cramp or hold the barreled action in any way. *The barreled action must be seated, in its correct position in the stock, without any stress or pressure acting on it at all.* If this is not the case, find out where it is cramped and fix it, by removing material from the inletting. You should be able to lift the barreled action in and out of the inletting, with no resistance whatsoever. It should literally fall in and out of the stock.

Even on my custom rifles, with inletting so fine you were hard pressed to see a gap with a magnifying glass, the barreled action would literally fall in and out of the stock. I don't even want to remember how much pain those jobs caused me to get right, but they had to be right or the bedding job would never work.

We will only be bedding the front bridge and the rear tang of the receiver, so the area between those two points will be floating with no contact in the inletting. Getting the inletting right before we start will ensure that important clearance is maintained when the job is completed.

Ok! No compromises. Get it right, or don't bother with the bedding job, because you will never get that right if the inletting is not right. 'Nuff said.

When we have the inletting right, examine the barreled action with a critical eye looking for reverse tapers, cavities, or anything that may trap it in the stock when it is bedded. It is critical that anything like this is found and dealt with. We have to be able to remove the barreled action from the stock after the material has hardened, and any of the above features will make that extremely difficult, and pose a real threat of splitting the stock or breaking something.

For instance, Brno 600 series actions have a concave milling cut along each side of the receiver that I know, for a fact, has trapped many budding Bedders, and split stocks. Anschutz 222s and .22 Hornets have a groove on each side of the front of the receiver that is, likewise, a trap for young players. Examine your barreled action carefully, identify these problem areas before you begin, and deal with them by filling them in with play putty or duct tape, several layers if necessary.

In order for our bedding job to work correctly the barreled action must be free to move backwards, with the force of recoil, and forwards again, freely, once recoil force has dissipated. In order to do that it must not be impeded in any way. It always brought a smile to my face when some guy told me what a perfect bedding job he had, because you could see the writing on the side of the receiver, in relief, in the bedding job. The simple fact is, that's the worst thing you can have, as it will impede the proper recoil movement of the barreled action within the bedding, guaranteeing vertical stringing, and double grouping. If you can see any raised lettering in a bedding job it is guaranteed to be a bad job.

We will need to collect some bits and pieces together and have them close at hand, before we begin the job, as follows:–

1. The bedding medium of your choice.
2. Something to mix it on. A small plastic box is best for me. The bedding material is fairly stiff until the hardener is mixed in. It helps to be able to hold onto the box with one hand while mixing it with the other. Plastic is non conductive so it is the best material to mix on. Don't use tin, you'll see why later.
3. A screwdriver to mix the two parts of the material together.
4. A small spatula to apply the mixed material.
5. A roll of duct tape.
6. A pair of scissors.
7. A sharp craft knife (Exacto is a good one).

8. A roll of masking tape.
9. Some play putty (Plasticine).
10. A very small screwdriver with a rounded blade (you can't guess what that's for huh!).
11. A bottle of methylated spirits (alcohol).
12. A packet of tissues (you can also use them to blow your nose).
13. An electric radiator, or similar heat source.
14. A cradle, that will hold the rifle level with the barrel slightly elevated.
15. A dial or digital caliper.
16. A pair of long action screws. See page 287 for a description.
17. An intermediate thread tap, in the thread diameter and pitch of your actions take down screws.
18. A tap handle.
19. If you are bedding a single shot rifle, a piece of drill rod that will fit through the front take down screw hole of the receiver, about 3" long, and a piece of round barrel steel that will fit in the bolt hole of your action right up to the end of the barrel. That can also be as short as 3", or you can use an action mandrel.
20. If you are bedding a magazine equipped rifle, a piece of soft material; 1" x ¼" x 6" aluminum bar is fine, and is what I have used for over 30 years.
21. If you have a mega barrel channel gap, some polyester fiberglass material. Body filler bog is fine. Really, anything that goes hard quickly is ok. Plastibond is excellent here.
22. A length of light chain, a small 'D', and a long Tyre lever.
23. Release agent. More on that as we go along.
24. A strip of heavy shiny backed paper between .005" to .007" thick and about 1" wide. This sort of paper can be found as backing on various sticky backed materials. Most recently I found perfect stuff on the back of sticky abrasive tape used on boats or other walkways that need to be non slip.
25. A Dremel tool with a ¼" round square bottomed tungsten carbide cutter.

I have already discussed the theory associated with why a bedding job needs to be the way it should be. Perhaps we should talk about why we need to bed our rifles at all.

In the good old days gun stocks were made of wood. English Walnut (Juglans Regea) is widely considered to be the best stock wood available, though many other varieties are used in gun stocks. Factory rifles from the U.S.A., for instance, may well have stocks made from Claro Walnut.

Claro Walnut is simply another variety of walnut, native to California, that is inferior to English Walnut, though still suitable for gun stocks. I've seen gun stocks made from every kind of wood imaginable.

In those days barreled actions were inletted tight into the stock inletting, and it was quickly discovered that these rifles gave their best accuracy when they were inletted with upward pressure, on the barrel, at just behind the forend tip. It was also discovered that the amount of upward pressure, near the forend tip, had a bearing on accuracy. By increasing, or decreasing, the pressure, one could witness an increase or decrease in accuracy, depending on the needs of the overall unit. Many experiments were conducted with forend pressure in the early 1960s, and I can remember conducting a lot of them myself. Bench-rest shooting was in its infancy, and the drive was on to find out what made rifles tick; what were the secrets of real accuracy?

However, forend pressure is a fickle mistress, especially when combined with gun stocks made of wood. The problem hinges around woods basic instability when subjected to varying atmospheric conditions, mainly humidity. Wood will take on or lose moisture from within the fibers of its construct, depending on the relative humidity of the atmosphere. For example, if we were to experience a long period of time with an atmospheric relative humidity of 65%, eventually the moisture content within the gun stock (or any wood for that matter) would stabilize at the same 65%. If the atmospheric relative humidity were to increase to, say 70%, the gun stock would begin to absorb moisture until it stabilized at 70% moisture content.

Likewise, if the relative humidity of the atmosphere reduced to 50%, yes you guessed it, the stock would lose moisture until it stabilized at the 50% figure.

Of course the atmosphere doesn't act like that. Relative humidity is up and down all over the place from day to day, even hour to hour, with the result that the gun stock is always in a state of flux, either taking on or losing moisture. It is rarely, if ever, stable for long.

Unfortunately the stock does not gain and lose moisture benignly, and therein lays the problem. Probably, because moisture acquisition, and loss, is not evenly distributed over the entire mass of the gun stock, the stock material moves around — we call it warping — during said moisture acquisition and loss. Such movement in the butt stock behind the action is of no consequence, however movement in the forend in front of the action has a direct effect on the barrel of the rifle. You should, by now, be aware that barrels are very easily bent, or displaced. A warping forend has more than enough power to deflect a barrel.

The upshot of all this is, not only is accuracy affected by a change in forend pressure, but so is zero, and having been one that has experienced that in all it's glory, I can tell you that it is the absolute pits. In those days you could never depend on the zero of your rifle. Honestly, I used to bed the forend of my target rifles in the morning before I went to a match (the quick hardening time of plastibond was useful for that job), and a good amount of time was spent checking the zero of my rifles during a hunt.

It didn't take long for some bright spark to realize, that if forend contact with the barrel caused so many problems, why don't we just remove that contact completely, thereby floating the barrel? Seems reasonable doesn't it? Actually the light bulb probably shone over a dozen or more heads simultaneously all over the globe, like many ideas do. But that created a whole new problem. Rifles that had their barrels floated rarely shot well because they had faulty action inletting and bedding.

You see, *upward forend pressure on the barrel cancels out the consequences of bad action bedding.* It probably does this by cramping the barreled action in the stock so that it is stuck in one place from shot to shot. Essentially, the barreled action does not move with recoil as it is jammed tightly in the rearward or recoiled position, and the compression behind the recoil lug does not have the power to move it forward. Whatever the reason, and that one seems to fit, it's a fact and it works. You will see lumps of wood left in the forends of factory rifles, even today, that are designed to put upward pressure on the barrel in order to cancel out the bad effects of less than perfect bedding.

It didn't take long to work out what the problem was, but the cure was very painful and time consuming. What was needed was to make the bedding platform straight, and flat, so that the barreled action could be tightened, into the inletting, without being stressed, bent or cramped. It sounds easy, but it's not. It takes a great degree of skill, and a long time to create a perfect bedding platform in wood. This is a job that is simply beyond most people, even beyond most experienced craftsman, the tolerance required being so miniscule; to the order of less than tenths of a thousandth of an inch.

Fortunately, around the time all of this was happening, fiberglass materials began to appear on the market, and these offered a solution to those of us who had difficulty making a perfect bedding platform in wood.

So that is the reason we have to bed our rifles. It is simply to allow us to enjoy the benefits of a floating barrel, those benefits being to realize best accuracy along with a stable zero.

In order to be able to move freely within the inletting of the stock the barreled action needs clearance between itself and the inletting. This clearance should be in the following places.

1. In front of the recoil lug.
2. At both sides of the recoil lug.
3. At the bottom of the recoil lug.
4. At any flat sides on the receiver.
5. Behind the rear tang.
6. At the sides of the rear tang.
7. At the front of the rear tang, if it is of a step design (Sako L series).
8. At any point between the front bridge and rear tang of the receiver that is not bedded.

This clearance is easily and accurately provided by the application of duct tape in the appropriate places. The clearance in #8 is provided when we condition the inletting properly, and will be maintained throughout the job. There is no need to use duct tape there.

Something you should be aware of, before we get started. It is very easy to bend a receiver, especially one with the large magazine, and ejection port, cutouts common to most sporting rifles. It took me a while, and a lot of failed bedding jobs, before I worked this out, and modified my procedures to allow for it. Oh, you won't bend it much, but you will bend it enough that the bedding job will test out of spec, and will need to be done again. Take this fact on board. *Very little external pressure applied to a receiver will displace its straightness.* If you ignore that it will cause you much grief.

Ok, let's bed a rifle.

1. Examine how the barreled action is sitting in the stock. We want it to be nice and level, and in its correct place. If it looks good, note its position in the stock relative to the ejection port, receiver lettering etc. *You will want this information for future reference.*

    1.1. Stocks with barrel pressure lumps in the forend may have the barreled action sitting up at the front. If so remove the lump until the barreled action is sitting straight. There is no need to float the barrel yet, so remove only enough material to get the metal work sitting properly in the inletting.

    1.2. If your barrel has already been floated it may drop into the forend creating a 'down barrel' situation. If so stick a few layers of duct tape in the bottom 1/3RD of the forend to support it in its correct position.

    1.3. In some cases there is a gap between barrel and forend you could drive a truck through. In such cases I stick a piece of duct tape in the forend, paint some release agent on the barrel, and make a pad for the barrel to sit on with polyester fiberglass (body bog is fine). If the barreled action sits in the stock properly, when screwed down with the action screws, simply put a little premixed bog on the duct tape, and screw the barreled action into the stock. Wait an hour, remove the barreled action and you're ready to move on. If not you will need to prop it up somehow, in its proper place, while the bog hardens. *No, don't prop it up to do the bedding job!* You will come to grief. We want a secure pad for the barrel to rest on, in its proper place, in the stock.

2. Remove any stock finish in the inletting where you will be applying the bedding material. This is easily done with scrapers and chisels.

2.1. Don't go hogging out material from within the inletting, with the notion that you will be replacing it with stronger bedding material. The material in your inletting is fine. Leave it there.

2.2. On magazine rifles we will be bedding from the recoil lug to a point about 1/8" past the magazine mortise. At the rear tang we will be bedding to a point about 1/8" past the trigger cutout.

2.3. On single shot rifles we will be bedding behind the front receiver screw an equal distance, as there is, from the front receiver screw to the recoil lug. At the rear tang we will be bedding the same as in 2.2.

2.4. On actions that have no support in front of the front action screw (Sako L series actions are a prime example) we will have to bed about 1¼" of the rear of the barrel to provide equal support in front of, and behind, the front action screw when it is tightened down. Photo 7-4 is not a Sako, but does show the reinforce bedding I am talking about here.

You can see the demarcation line where a double layer of duct tape was applied to the barrel, where the parallel section started its taper, in order to float the barrel from that point forward.

PHOTO 7-4.

I bedded this Remington Model 700ADL in 1985 with dyed Acraglas Gel. At the time I was bedding the barrel reinforce as well, which is *not needed* on a Remington. It is needed, however, on actions without support in front of the front receiver screw, such as Sako L and A series actions.

2.5. There is absolutely no need to bed the action over its full length. In fact doing so will probably be detrimental.

3. As I mentioned earlier, the bedding material has to have a means of escaping the action inletting, if you are to be able to locate the barreled action in its proper place. This is important as, of necessity, we need to overfill the bedding areas we have chosen to bed. Some material will escape out of the top of the stock initially, but as the barreled action is lowered into the inletting, that gap becomes small and it is harder for the material to get away. On magazine rifles bedding material can escape through the magazine mortise fairly easily. On single shot rifles, however, no such facility exists, and this is a problem. The solution is to provide a cavity behind the bedding platform that will allow the bedding material to escape. Such a cavity can be seen in Photo 7-5 (Page 260).

The cavity needs to be only the width of the inletting x 1" long x ¼" deep to do the job. If you have a milling machine, that will be an easy way to make it, otherwise worry it out with chisels and scrapers. If you neglect to make it you will find it almost impossible to squeeze the barreled action into its correct position in the inletting, and the power you will be exerting, trying to do so, will without doubt compromise the final result. Photo 7-6 shows the same stock after the bedding job so you can see how the Devcon A has flowed into the provided cavity. If this cavity was not provided the Devcon would have had to try to find its way along the length of the receiver towards the rear tang. This it can do to an extent, but once the bottom section starts to thin out, the atomized steel in the mix will begin to bunch up, and will cease to flow, no matter how much pressure you apply to the receiver. This is a characteristic of atomized metal/epoxy mixes that must be taken into consideration. *The material must have an escape route.*

PHOTO 7-5.

There are a few things to note here. At the end of the forend can be seen the polyester pad the barrel will sit in for the job. It, in turn, is glued to duct tape stuck in the forend. The stainless steel pillars are glued into the stock with Devcon. The recess behind the bedding surface to allow the Devcon to escape. Taping of the stock. Finally, the relief allowed for the front trigger housing screw.

4. Take your trusty battery operated drill with a ¼" twist drill installed and drill a series of holes in the inletting to act as anchors for the epoxy material to key into.

4.1. Epoxy is terrific glue, probably one of the best available to we mere mortals, so possibly this step isn't really necessary unless you need to provide an anchor into clean wood under oil damaged wood (or fiberglass). It probably stems from my early days bedding in polyester material (which was and is a lousy glue), however I still do it. Think of it as extra insurance. It certainly does no harm.

PHOTO 7-6.

Here can be seen where the Devcon has flowed into the prepared cavity as the barreled action was lowered into its correct position in the inletting. Note also, there is clearance under the receiver here provided by duct tape. This overflow stays in the stock; don't bother removing it unless you need to save weight.

4.2. The holes need only to be about 1/8" deep. I'll drill 14 in the front bedding section holding the drill at a different angle for every hole. I'll also drill two holes into the material behind the recoil lug about ¼" deep. The epoxy section behind the lug is thin and those holes are to provide extra support. Photo 7-7 (Page 262) shows the preparation I made to bed my Remington Model 700 rifle. Note the loop of masking tape in the magazine mortise to catch extruded epoxy, thus preventing it from gluing itself to the stock. There are two holes drilled in the recoil lug mortise to provide an anchor for that thin section. The top of the take down screw hole has been chamfered, and the holes on the bedding platform have been drilled at different angles.

4.3. At the rear tang on sporting rifles you will probably have to use a smaller drill bit, more like 3/16" diameter, or even smaller on some actions with slim rear tangs (M'98 Mauser comes to mind). Many stocks are oil soaked in the rear tang area, thanks to our habit of storing our rifles in the butt down position. Gravity sends all of the oil, we put on the metal work, straight to the rear tang. You will spot the dark oil soaked wood/ fiberglass easily enough, and it is very important that you drill at least 4 holes right through the oil soaked section at least ¼" into good clean material. Epoxy will not stick to anything coated in oil, as the oil is a release agent. No, it's not a good enough release agent with which to do the bedding job. We'll get to that later. You must provide a clean oil, and dust, free surface for the epoxy to adhere to. Photo 7-8 shows the preparation at the rear tang for bedding a Remington Model 700 rifle.

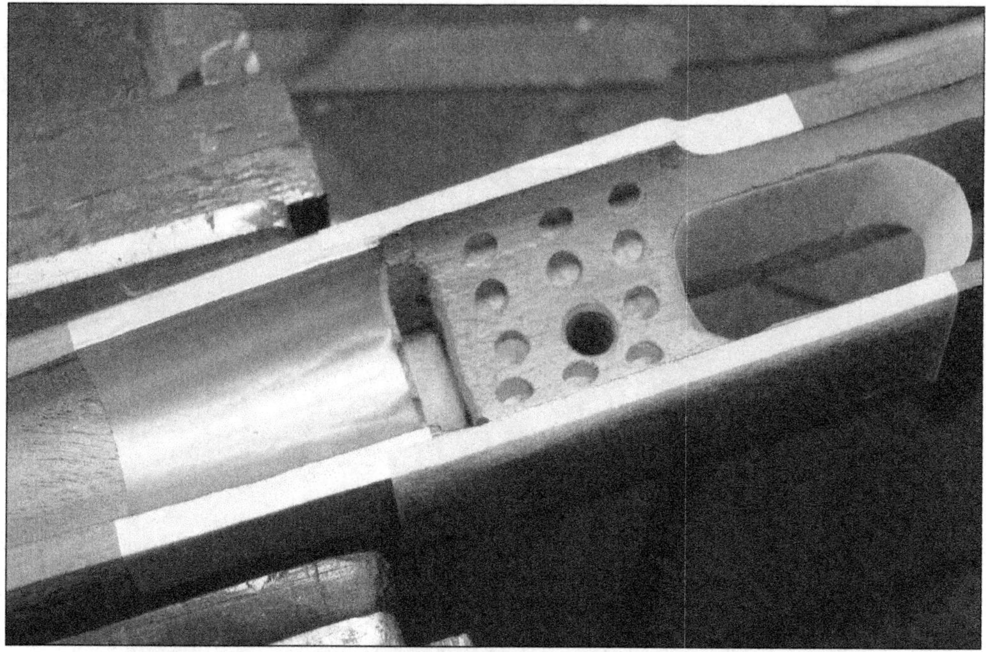

PHOTO 7-7.

The preparation needed at the front bridge for bedding my Remington Model 700 .25/06 Ackley Improved varmint rifle. Note the chamfer behind the recoil lug slot, to clear the little triangle of play putty, I use to break the sharp corner. Also, the tape in the magazine well to catch excess Devcon, and the duct tape to prevent Devcon sticking in the barrel channel where I don't want it.

4.4. If the area at the rear tang is very oil damaged you may want to cut it away down to fresh material, and rebuild it with Devcon. This is ok, but if you do that you will have to re-establish the rear tang bedding area before continuing with the bedding job proper. The rear tang area is one of our important location points. Even then, when preparing the bedding job I would still drill through the newly made Devcon bedding platform and into the grip where there is clean material to key into.

4.5. If it is necessary to bed under the rear of the barrel I drill a few holes there also.

4.6. Finally I replace the drill bit with a chamfering bit and chamfer the tops of the receiver screw holes a little.

PHOTO 7-8.

The rear tang preparation for my .25/06 Ackley Improved varmint rifle.

5. Now we can tape up the barreled action to provide the clearance in various places that I listed a while back. Duct tape is ideal for this job but being only .005" thick will require multiple layers on some places. It might be more understandable if I describe how I would tape up a Remington Model 700 action with additional comments on how the job would vary with some other action types. It is very important that every time you apply a piece of tape to the action you try the fit of the barreled action in the stock. Only by doing this will you know exactly where the cramping is coming from, and be in a position to rectify it immediately, then move on. Believe me, I learned this the hard way, and it is a great time and frustration saver. Tape, check, remove the tight spot and move on. When we are finished we want the barreled action sitting correctly in the inletting without any tight spots. Even with hairline inletting the barreled action should fall in and out of the stock with zero binding.

5.1. I start with the recoil lug front, #1 on the list. Fancy that! Cut off a strip of duct tape about 1½" long. Fold it in half length wise (sticky side out), and cut a half circle out of it, about the diameter of the barrel where it butts onto the action. Apply the tape so that it covers the front of the recoil lug completely; no doubt some of it will be stuck to the barrel as well. The tape will be long enough to fold over the bottom of the recoil lug as well, so we can take care of #3 on our list at the same time. Kill two birds with one stone as it were. Now trim the excess tape from the barrel, sides and the back of the recoil lug with your sharp exacto knife. I like to have a bit of extra clearance here, so let's do it again, so that we have two layers of tape on the front and bottom of the recoil lug. Now test fit the barreled action in the stock. If there is any binding, or if it doesn't go all the way in we know exactly where the problem is, so clear the front and/or bottom of the recoil lug until the barreled action fits properly before moving on. Photo 7-9 shows me starting that job.

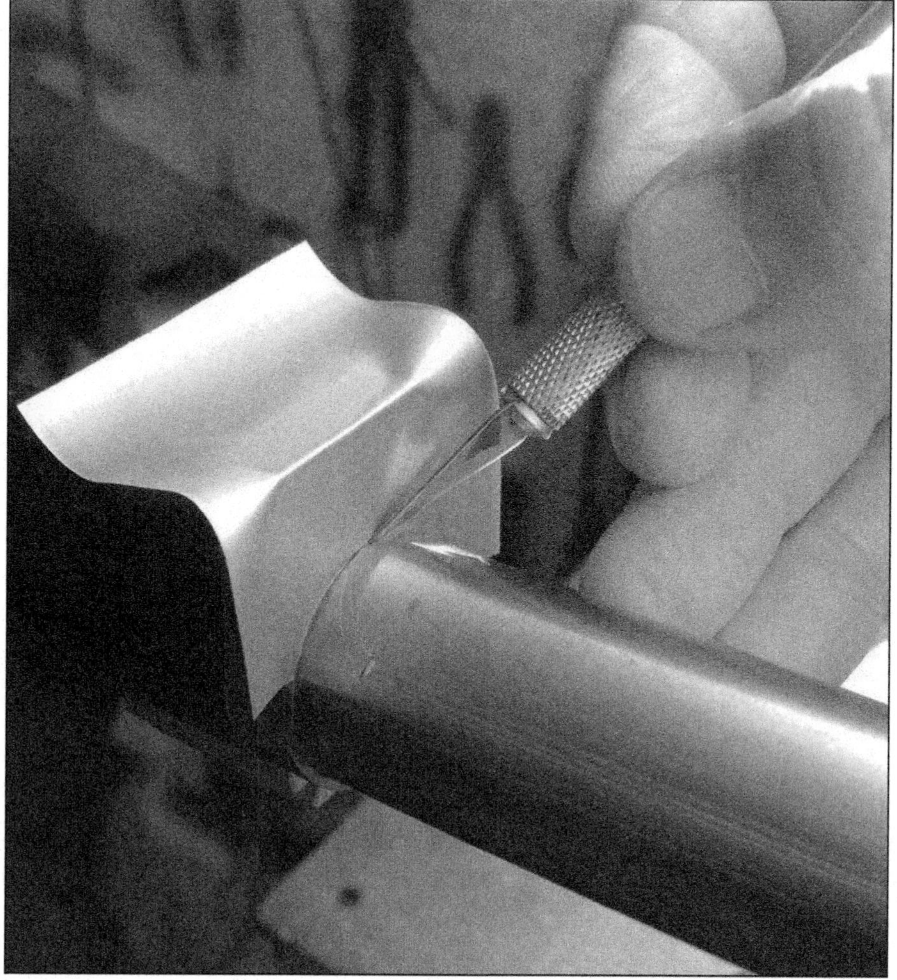

PHOTO 7-9.

Taping the front and bottom of the recoil lug. Use a very sharp Exacto knife to trim the tape. Two thicknesses are needed here.

5.2. The Remington 700 front receiver ring is supported both in front and behind the front action take-down screw, so there is no need to bed the barrel reinforce in front of the receiver. We do need clearance here though, so apply two layers of tape, the full width of the duct tape roll, being sure that they extend around each side of the barrel up past the top line of the stock. As extra insurance I always put two sections of tape here in case the bedding material finds its way up the forend past the first length. It's just that an 'off the tape' epoxy finish is much neater than a ground away epoxy finish. You can make up your own mind on that. Check the fit in the stock etc, etc. You should have the picture by now. Photo 7-10 sees me applying the tape.

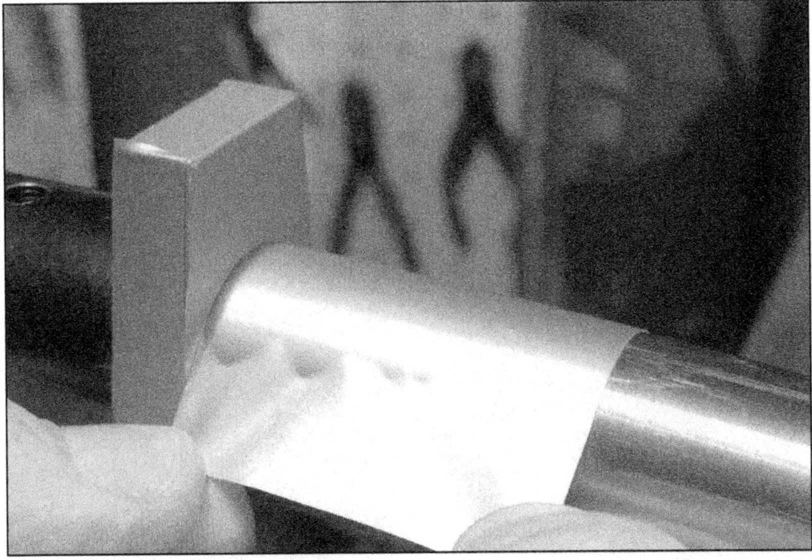

PHOTO 7-10.

Applying the tape to the barrel in front of the recoil lug to provide clearance and float the barrel right back to the lug. Two layers should be applied here. If you are unsure whether the epoxy will extrude past the end of the tape apply another two layers in front of these ones.

5.3. Cut a thin strip of tape and apply it to the side of the recoil lug. The width of the tape is the correct length for the recoil lug, so if you start it at, or just under, the bottom of the recoil lug it will finish above the stock line, which is where we want it. Trim it with the Exacto knife and then apply another layer and trim that too. We also want extra clearance here. Do the same to the other side of the recoil lug, and then check the fit of the barreled action in the stock and modify, if necessary, by removing stock material to allow it to fit properly. Photo 7-11 shows me applying the tape (Page 266). My left thumb is holding about 1/16" of tape under the recoil lug, and the width of the roll is plenty to reach past the top line of the stock.

5.3.1. At this point we should make an additional check. Have your dial or digital caliper handy, and sitting on your bench stool, hold the barreled action into the stock with one hand. Stand the rifle up with its butt resting on the stool between your legs, and the trigger facing towards you. Now see if you can move the trigger left and right past centre. Sometimes it looks right but isn't, so use the caliper to measure the gap each side of the trigger housing to be sure. If you can't do this, the recoil lug needs extra clearance on the relevant side to allow you to. Remember what I said about the atomized steel in the epoxy bunching up and not allowing any further compression — well, that happens here too. If you can only move the trigger to centre now, when the epoxy goes into the recoil lug mortise, you will not be able to make centre, and it will be too late to do anything about it. *Now is the time to fix it, so make sure you have plenty of clearance each side of the recoil lug so the trigger is free to be moved well past its centre either side.*

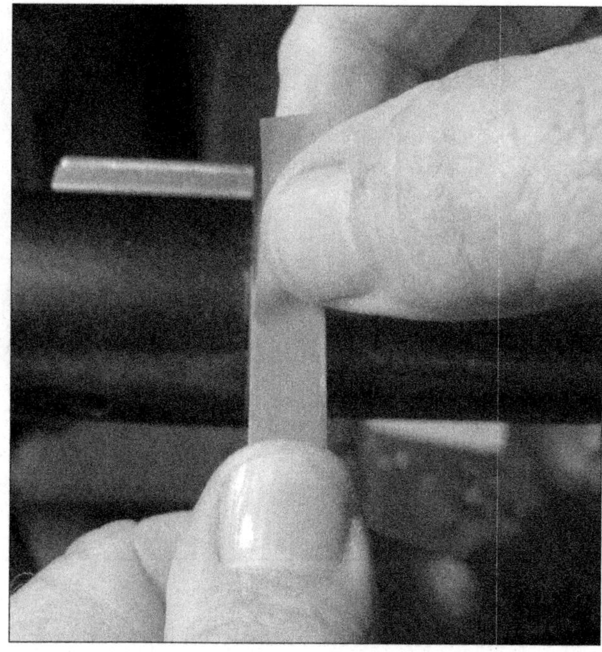

PHOTO 7-11.

Taping the side of the recoil lug. This recoil lug is one of David Tubb's extra wide stainless steel parts. Again, two thicknesses are needed here.

6. Snip off a piece of tape a little wider than ¼" (which is the diameter of the action screws) and stick it on the bottom of the receiver running from the middle of the recoil lug, over the front action screw hole right up to the front of the magazine box cutout. If there is any surplus at the end just stick it on the feed ramp. Take your trusty Exacto knife and cut the tape away from the front action screw hole thus exposing it. See Photo 7-12.

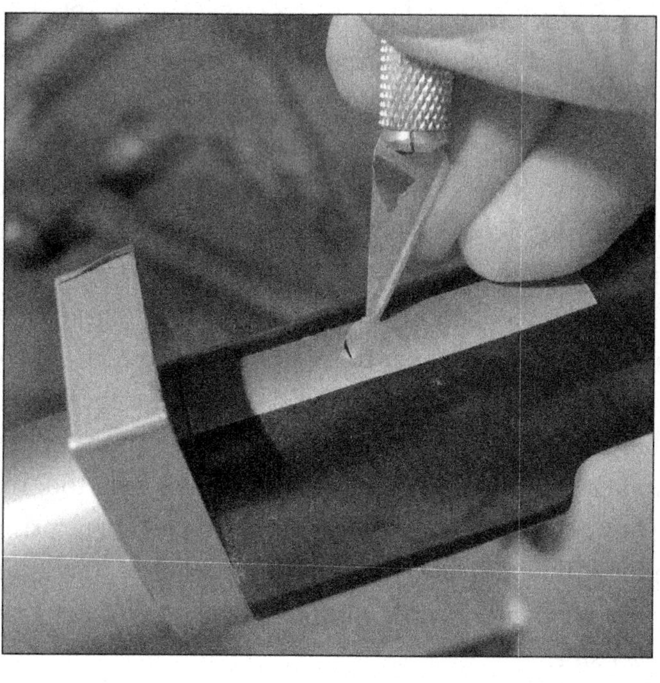

PHOTO 7-12.

Exposing the front takedown screw hole by cutting the duct tape away with a sharp Exacto knife.

6.1. This tape will provide .005" of clearance along the length of, and under, the front bridge, and prevent the action from bottoming out in the bedding. What we are doing here is creating a V block for the receiver to slide back and forth in, and the clearance ensures that it will be pulled into the bedding evenly, by the action screws, when they are tightened. Check for fit etc, etc, and we are done at the front of the action.

6.2. For those of you who are bedding single shot actions refer to Photo 7-5 (Page 260) and step #3 (Page 260), and you will know what to do. Clearance is needed behind the front ring bedded area on single shots, and this is provided by a strip applied as in Photo 7-13 (Page 267). No tape is needed here on magazine rifles.

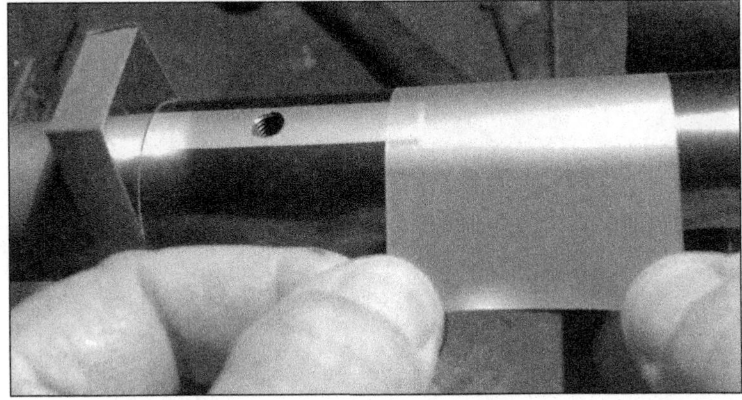

PHOTO 7-13.

Applying a piece of duct tape to provide clearance, between the front and rear bedding surfaces of the action, on my Remington 40X single shot.

7. Turning our attention to the rear of the action, remove the safety parts from the trigger along with the bolt stop. We don't need them getting in our way. When I was doing this work for a living, (not much of one I might add) I had spare triggers I used only for bedding, so I didn't have to dismantle my customers trigger. You need a trigger on the action for line up when you are bedding it. I notice that new Remingtons now have one way fasteners in the trigger parts, so lots of luck there. Maybe you have a mate with a spare trigger sans safety parts.

8. Stick a piece of duct tape on the rear of the trigger to block the slot there, then block the hole at the rear of the trigger mortise with a bit of tissue or cleaning rag and fill the hole level with play putty. You can also fill the slot for the bolt stop with play putty (Plasticine) while you're at it.

8.1. You can see why you don't want those safety parts or bolt stop parts getting in your way here. The job is much easier without them.

9. I still want to create a V block effect at the rear tang, but the bedding area here is small. Make your strip of duct tape only 3/16" wide and stick it from the rear of the trigger, over the rear action screw hole, and if there is any surplus, just stick it over the top of the rear tang. Again cut the tape to expose the screw hole with your exacto knife. That's all we need at the rear of the action. Check, etc, etc. Photo 7-14 shows the rear tang of my 40x taped and ready to bed. Note that the rear of the bolt stop slot has been filled with Plasticine, as is the rear of the trigger recess.

PHOTO 7-14.

The rear tang of my 40X Remington taped for bedding.

10. I said that we were done at the front of the action. I lied! We could bed the barreled action like this. If we do, there is a very good chance that we will break some good sized chunks out of the bedding material, in front of and behind the recoil lug, when we remove it from the stock, once the bedding has hardened. To prevent this happening we have to break the very sharp 90° angle, both in front of, and behind the recoil lug. To do that we need some Plasticine, and that very small screwdriver with the rounded blade I mentioned in #10 on the needed tools list. Roll a small piece of Plasticine between your hands, to create a long thin round piece. Work it into the bottom third of the circumference at the bottom of where the barrel and recoil lug butt up at the front, and where the recoil lug and action butt up at the back. Jam it in there so it sticks. Then, sort of run the screwdriver blade around the circumference, removing excess Plasticine, and leaving a small triangular section of putty in the corner, front and back. Photo 7-15 shows me applying the Plasticine, and Photo 7-16 shows the finished job. Photo 7-17 shows my Panda F Class action taped up and ready to bed.

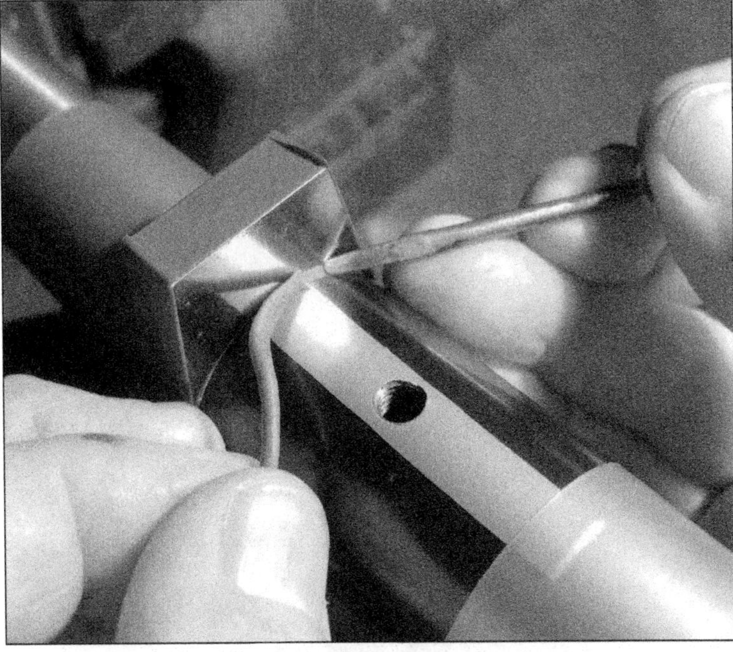

PHOTO 7-15.

I am jamming a thin worm of Plasticine into the corner of the recoil lug and receiver of my 40X. This will prevent the sharp edge created in the bedding from breaking out when the barreled action is removed. The same procedure should also be carried out at the 90° corner in front of the recoil lug, and any other 90° corner on the action.

10.1. You will have to provide clearance for the putty in the inletting, so make corresponding chamfers both behind, and in front of the recoil lug to provide that.

10.2. When the barreled action is removed from the bedding the putty will be left behind. You can remove it with the back of your exacto knife to reveal a nice clean finish; far better looking than a broken out piece of bedding that would be the case otherwise.

10.3. Whatever brand of barreled action you will be working on, look for these sharp 90° angles that will end up in the bedding and break them like this with play putty (Plasticine). It is cheap insurance against a piece of bedding being broken out when the barreled action is removed from the stock.

PHOTO 7-16.

The job I started in PHOTO 7-15 finished. Removing the sharp edge from the bedding, like this, also removes a potential for the sharp corner to prevent the barreled action from seating fully in the bedding. Any sharp corner in the metalwork should be chamfered like this.

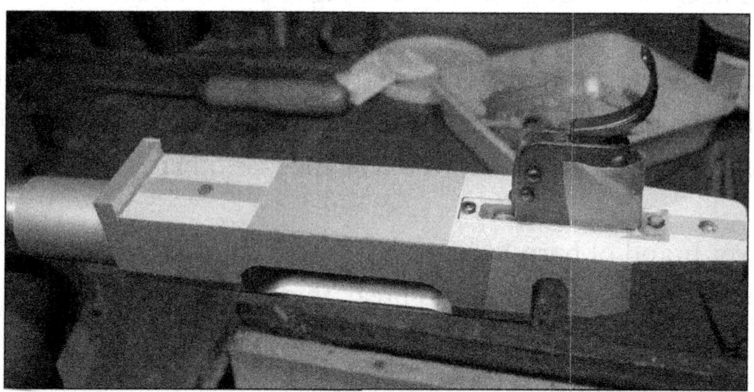

PHOTO 7-17.

A taped Panda action ready to bed. Note the small triangle of play putty (Plasticine) behind the recoil lug. Play putty is also placed similarly at the front of the recoil lug, also in the bottom of the rear screw hole, and in the Allen head cavity of the rear trigger housing screw. Duct tape provides clearance at all of the areas mentioned in the text.

Before we go any further I'd better discuss the taping of a couple of other action types. Any action that has its front take-down screw at the front of the receiver will need to have the rear of the barrel bedded for at least 1" in front of the receiver. Sako L and A series actions are classic examples. Because we must have clearance under the recoil lug, and these actions are unsupported in front of the action screw, when we tighten the front screw we will be causing a bending moment, or stress, in the receiver that will interfere with its correct return to battery when recoil forces have abated. My practice with these actions is to again create a V block by sticking a piece of 3/16" wide tape longitudinally under the barrel. I will bed the length of the parallel section of barrel in front of the receiver or 1¼", whichever is the shortest. A double thickness of duct tape in front of the bedding section, to provide clearance between the barrel and barrel channel (two lengths is advisable), is all the preparation we need. Be sure the barreled action fits into the stock properly after you've taped it, as before. When the job is finished the front screw can be tightened without stressing the action because it has proper support, both behind and in front of the screw. The only draw back with these actions is, when they are rebarreled, they must be rebedded. I could never bed the reinforce only without compromising the rest of the job, requiring a complete rebed. My recommendation is to do the complete rebed — don't waste time trying to short cut. Refer back to Photo 7-4. (Page 259)

With straight sided flat bottomed actions such as my Stolle Panda (and the Sako L and A series are a variation of this) I still stick the tape longitudinally under the action, this time to provide, like, two rails for the receiver to slide on. These action types need side clearance and one thickness of duct tape stuck on each side is plenty. Photo 7-17 (Page 270) shows my Panda taped up prior to bedding. Those Sakos also have flat sides with 'Made in Finland' deeply stamped on one side that needs to be covered with a piece of tape (both sides). I don't bother with the rounded section above the flat sides. It's ok to bed it as it won't cramp the action, thus interfering with recoil and return to battery.

These actions also have flat sides at the rear tang and behind it. We must provide clearance at those points, so stick a double thickness of duct tape on those areas to provide it. Again check for proper fit, yadda, yadda, yadda.

There are other considerations we must allow for with various other actions, and I will discuss them at the end of this chapter. In the meantime let's move on.

11. We don't want Devcon stuck all over our stock, so we will need to cover it to protect it. Masking tape is ok for this job as it is easily applied and easily removed. A roll 1" wide is fine, stick it along the top of the stock and go at least 1½" past where you think the bedding will end front and back. At the rear tang stick it around the area to be bedded. You could go overboard with this and tape up the whole stock, but that isn't necessary. If you have any doubts use a bit extra, it's cheap enough.

11.1. Make a loop that will fit inside the magazine cutout and stick it at the front of the mortise and to both sides. Cut out the ½ moon piece that protrudes into the bedding area with an Exacto knife. When we bed the rifle a deal of bedding material is going to come out into the magazine cutout and this loop of masking tape will catch it for you, and maybe prevent it falling onto the pistol grip of the stock, or in your lap. Last check — does the barreled action fit into the stock properly?

12. Now that all of that is finished we can apply the release agent to the barreled action and stock. When I first started using Devcon they supplied an excellent release agent with their epoxy kit, then some years later they changed it to something that wasn't so good, and now they don't supply anything at all. Progress! When their release agent changed I went on a hunt for a suitable replacement, but it was my wife who came up with the product I have been using for over 40 years, Wundawax Floor Polish. A release agent needs to possess several important properties if it is to be suitable for this job.

1. It must be easy to apply.
2. It must be easy to remove.
3. It must be microscopically thin when applied.
4. It must *not* be easily disturbed, thereby leaving the surface unprotected.
5. The epoxy must *not* be able to stick to any surface treated with it at all.

Wundawax Floor Polish has certainly met all of those criteria.

I apply it with a fairly stiff art work painters brush, with the bristles shortened, being sure to cover all surfaces well past where I think the bedding material will reach. Make sure to get full coverage in a very thin layer. I also apply it to the tape on the stock, and on the stock finish itself wherever there is a chance that bedding material may lodge. It won't do any harm to the finish, so knock yourself out. The Remington front guard screw hole is a through hole, so bedding material is going to be squirting through that hole. Get some wax onto the back of the barrel, around the inside of the screw hole, on the bottom of the recoil lug, and on the feed ramp. When the material has hardened there will be an inch long x ¼" diameter piece of hardened Devcon, hanging over the feed ramp, that will fall away when the front screw is inserted, if everything is released properly. Get that little screwdriver we used earlier, and use it to put release agent inside the front and rear take-down screw threads. Use the brush to apply release agent to your long bedding screw threads. Anything or any area you don't want Devcon to stick to must be properly released.

Before we start mixing things together we'd better discuss some important information, and get a few things straight. Epoxies come in two parts, typically called part A and part B. Part A is usually the filler material, and part B is the hardener. You mix the two parts together, and a chemical reaction occurs that causes the mixture to harden. In order to harden properly Epoxy needs heat, and that heat is generated from within itself, during the chemical reaction that takes place, after the two parts have mixed together. Epoxy that has been deprived of that heat does not harden to its full specification. After the hardening process is finished it will be malleable, easily deformed, and not a very suitable bedding platform. Properly hardened, Devcon in thin sections will snap if you try to bend it. If it hasn't hardened correctly it will bend.

The problem is, when we do this job, we are not providing a very good environment for the Epoxy to harden properly in. The wood or fiberglass stock is fine, as it is not conductive, however the metalwork, being fairly conductive, is a problem. What happens is the epoxy begins its chemical reaction, generating the heat it needs to harden, but as fast as it generates that critical heat the barreled action sucks it up, conducts it away from the epoxy, and releases it into the atmosphere. I think that is why I have never seen a properly hardened Devcon aluminum bedding job. Aluminum is a terrific conductor, so it does an excellent job of getting heat out of the epoxy mix into the atmosphere via the barreled action. Remember, the epoxy mix is full of atomized particles touching each other, so heat transfer is guaranteed. That is the reason I don't recommend aluminum mixes.

Being aware of the problem gives us the chance to do something about it. Heat flows to cold. Even on a warm summer day the metalwork on a rifle stored indoors will be cool to the touch, so the problem is always present no matter what the temperature. If there is a differential in temperature the heat the epoxy needs will be sucked from it.

The cure, of course, is simple. Make sure the metalwork is warm to the touch when you lower it into the bedding mix, and provide a heat source to keep it warm for a couple of hours while the epoxy hardens. That's why we had a radiator on our list.

The key word here is 'warm'. We don't want the metalwork to be hot, quite apart from the fact that would make it hard to handle. Excess heat, applied to epoxy, speeds up the chemical reaction considerably, causing the material to kick over, or begin to harden, very fast. This is to be avoided, as we need a bit of time in order to do the job, and, all in all, epoxy really provides just enough time to get the job done comfortably. We don't need any accelerated hardening to speed things along. *All we want to do is assist the epoxy to retain its chemically generated heat*, and that will allow it to harden to its full specification. By warming the metalwork, and keeping it warm for a couple of hours, we are actually only slowing the heat transfer from the epoxy material to metalwork to atmosphere, but that is enough to allow the epoxy to harden properly.

If I can, I put the barreled action out in the sun for a while to warm up before I do the job, then use the heater to maintain some temperature once the metalwork is in the stock. In the winter the metalwork will need to be pre-warmed with the heater.

In the old days Devcon was a reasonable price and seemed to last forever, but now the new stuff with the white hardener has a use by date on it, and that date is fair dinkum, believe me. *Don't use Devcon past its use by date for any critical job.* It will still be fine for non critical filling jobs or such like. The problem is, once past its use by date, it will begin to harden very fast; much too fast to be used in a bedding job. So if you have some sort of job where you can get it mixed and applied in ten minutes go ahead and use it up. For a bedding job you'll be just applying it to the inletting when it kicks over, and that's a world of hurt. Fortunately I discovered this doing a non critical filling job. Phew! That was close.

When you read the chapter on barrel fitting you will have seen how easy it is to bend seemingly massively strong pieces of steel, like barrels and actions. Bending is probably not the best choice of word; deflecting would be better. Regardless, take it on board, as it is critical with this job. This job, being the way it is, will more often than not have the barreled action suspended between the forend tip, and the rear tang, with the centre section sitting slightly above the inletting when properly positioned in the stock. In that situation it takes only miniscule pressure, applied at the midpoint of the two supports, to deflect the metalwork. I have observed this over many years through many failed bedding jobs, and that is why I adopted the procedures I will now describe. If you follow them closely you will make a good job. If you don't follow them, the result will mainly be up to the Gods, and they 'aint kind!

13. It is important to mix the two parts of the epoxy material together thoroughly and in the right proportions. Brownells Acraglas Gel is straight forward in this regard being a 50/50 mix; however Devcon is a bit esoterical being either 9:1 by weight or 2.5:1 by volume. I find it simpler to dispense the Devcon proportions by weight, and thereby obtain the correct mix.

13.1. I use a plastic box as a mixing surface. It is easy to hold onto while mixing, unlike flat pieces of mixing surface. I use plastic because it is non conductive, so the heat the epoxy begins to generate stays put. If you use tin or other metal mixing surface you will have started heat erosion right from the beginning.

13.2. I warm the surface of the box up by putting it under my bench light while I go into my man cave and weigh out the two components of the mix. I happen to have an Acculab electronic scale I use for this, but I would think any powder scale would be fine. Heating the mixing surface assists the epoxy to maintain its self generated heat.

13.3. Use a 3" screwdriver to initially mix the two components together. I mix for at least 3 minutes being sure to blend every bit of the material over and over again. About a minute or so into the job, when the mix has become a soft buttery consistency, I switch over to a small spatula, and pay attention to scraping the surface of the box to be sure every bit of part A is mixed with part B. You don't want to risk any soft spots on the finished job from insufficient mixing.

13.4. Once I am satisfied that the material is blended sufficiently I let it stand under my bench light (60 watt) for 2 or 3 minutes to give it a bit of time to start working. By standing it under the bench light I keep a bit of heat up to it while I get the stock ready.

13.5. Now, we don't need to rush madly, but on the other hand we shouldn't dawdle either. Both Acraglas and Devcon will give you enough time to do the job if you work briskly, so have everything you need close at hand before you mix the components, and be positive in your actions. When the material kicks over it begins to stiffen and we have to be finished before that happens. We want the barreled action in position, in the stock, while the material is still in the thick creamy buttery state.

14. Ok, sitting at the bench with the stock in your lap, epoxy close by, bench light in position so you can see, and a 3" screwdriver in hand. Ready, set, go!

14.1. Pick up some epoxy with the blade of the screwdriver and quickly fill all the holes you drilled in the inletting. Be sure the ones behind the recoil lug and at the rear tang are fully filled.

14.2. Stay with the screwdriver and fill the recoil lug slot. This is a narrow slot on Remingtons and the screwdriver lets you get right to the bottom. Make sure it is full without any air bubbles.

14.3. Now switch to the spatula and coat the front receiver ring bedding at least 1/8" thick or a little more. If you are unsure put in a little more rather than a little less. We don't want to leave sections not supported by bedding material in the finished job. Just looks ugly. (If we were bedding a Sako, or something similar, we would coat the back of the barrel channel at the same time.)

14.4. Now coat the rear tang area at least 1/8" thick or a little more. Make sure you have full coverage without any voids or air bubbles.

14.5. Still with the spatula move to the metalwork and place a layer of material around the bottom 1/3RD of the 90° angle at the front, and rear, of the recoil lug. You, sort of, get a dob of material on the end of the spatula, stick it on the edge of the recoil lug in the 90° angle, and swoop the spatula around the circumference of the join, leaving the material behind and filling the angle with epoxy. Got that? I hope so! Doing this will ensure that you won't have any air bubbles in your finished job, either in front of, or behind the recoil lug.

14.6. Any bedded 90° angle on the action should be filled as in 14.5, such as behind the recoil lug of flat bottomed actions. Air will trap in these places leaving behind half a bubble in the job when the metalwork is removed unless you attend to it.

15. Without wasting any time, stand the stock on its butt on your stool (between your legs). Take the metalwork by the barrel and bring the two together.

15.1. Your lineup here is initially the trigger, and then the recoil lug. Line up the trigger and bring the metalwork straight into the stock, and then line up the recoil lug. Continue bringing them together and the recoil lug will enter its mortise pretty easily. Lean the stock forward a little, and when the metalwork is about ½ way in, transfer your guiding hand to the front of the receiver.

15.2. Watch what is happening to the epoxy. You have your spatula and screwdriver handy — it's better to remove excess epoxy that squeezes out of the job as you go, rather than wait until it falls off and makes a mess on the stock, stool, floor or you. Just scrape it off and deposit it on your mixing surface.

15.3. As you bring the metalwork into the stock, check that you are bringing it in straight, by keeping an eye on the position of the trigger in its mortise. Try to keep it as even as possible.

15.4. When the metalwork is a bit more than ¾ of the way into the stock it is time to install the long action screws we released earlier. Screw them in 1 or 2 turns. There will probably be a lump of epoxy protruding out of the rear tang hole, so pick it off with the screwdriver and stick it on the mixing surface. Don't worry about the worm in the locking lug area. It will come away easily once it has hardened, if you have released that area properly. If you try to remove it you will smear it and make a mess, as well as waste time.

15.5. Continue squeezing the parts together gently. It should not require very much pressure to do this. As the two parts come together keep on eye on the triggers position in its mortise, and remove excess epoxy before it falls off and becomes a nuisance. From your previous work you will know where the metalwork should be in the stock. You should have observed visual indicators, like the relationship of the ejection port to its cutout in the stock, or perhaps the distance from the lettering on the left hand side of the action to the top line of the wood work etc. Whatever reference you are using, stop squeezing as soon as you reach it. *If you squeeze it past that point you will deflect the metalwork and run a chance of causing a low spot in the bedding.* I did tell you to take note of the metalworks position in the stock on page "1. Examine how the barreled action is sitting in the stock. We want it to be nice and level, and in its correct place. If it looks good, note its position in the stock relative to the ejection port, receiver lettering etc. You will want this information for future reference." on page 258.

15.6. Clean away any remaining excess epoxy, and check that the trigger is in the centre of its mortise with the dial or digital caliper. Adjust it if necessary while keeping light pressure on the metalwork to keep it all together, and then place the job in the cradle for curing. Photo 7-18 shows my curing setup.

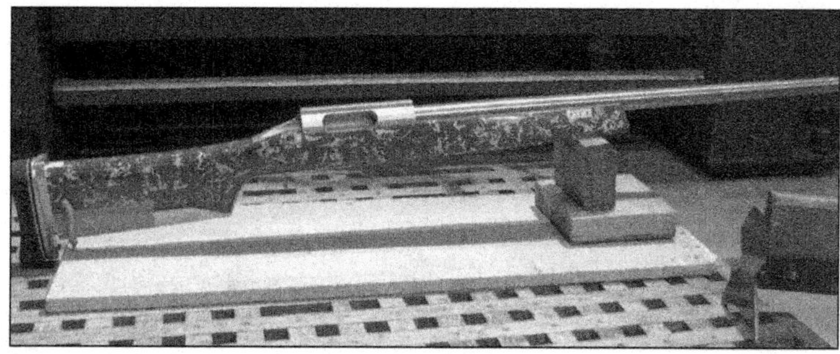

PHOTO 7-18.

Nothing special required here. The plastic covered U screw at the butt holds the stock securely. This is a flat forend stock, so I don't need another U screw up front, but I will use one on a rounded forend stock. The barrel is slightly elevated, and the radiator is pointing at the barrel and away from the forend of the stock. You can't see masking tape because this is a mock up.

15.7. While it is in the cradle run the screwdriver around the outside of the rear tang to remove any epoxy there back to the tang line. Set up your heater a foot or so from the side of the barrel (but not aimed at the stock) and turn it on for a couple of hours to keep some heat in the metalwork and assist the epoxy not to lose heat. Don't get the metalwork too hot. Lukewarm is what we want. Clean up your tools and mixing box with tissues, wet with alcohol, and we are done for the day.

16. I scraped the epoxy away from the sides of the rear tang for a reason. Hopefully, what we have achieved here, is to have inserted the metalwork into the epoxy compound in the stock, in a totally stress free attitude. The metalwork is in its relaxed straight state, and is floating on a bed of epoxy, supported at the forend of the stock, and sitting straight in the inletting. *What I want to happen is for the metalwork to sink into the epoxy a tiny bit, of its own accord, before the epoxy kicks over.* I will see that has happened by the extrusion of a small amount of epoxy around the rear tang. When I see that I get a big grin on my face, as I know I have done this part of the job as well as it can be done.

16.1. I prefer to do my bedding job in the morning, as ambient temperature will be higher during the day than if I had done the job in the afternoon, and the epoxy had to cure through the night. I leave the heater on the barrel for 2 or 3 hours, maybe longer if it's cold in the winter. There's not much point leaving it on past 4 hours as the epoxy will be well set by then. I leave the job alone for 24 hours, and then its time to start thinking about pulling it apart.

17. How we separate the metalwork from the stock has a direct effect on the accuracy of the job, and has the potential to ruin it completely. It is ultra important that the metalwork be removed without applying any force whatsoever that could potentially deflect (read: bend) it in any way. We have already touched on how easy it is to bend a barreled action. This is where you can do it big time. The smallest deflection, which could cause the metalwork to take a set of only .0003" from where it was originally bedded, will ruin the integrity of the job. We don't want that to happen. I use two methods, one for single shot rifles, and one for magazine rifles. Actually the single shot method can be used for magazine rifles also, if you prefer. Both methods will remove the metalwork from the bedding without stressing it, thereby preserving its straightness, and the integrity of your bedding job.

17.1. Remove your long bedding screws. Check that some excess material has not intruded too far above the stock line so that it is past the centre-line of the receiver. Sometimes this happens at the recoil lug. If you do have excess there chip it away with a chisel. Don't get over zealous here. I have seen jobs where the guy left a line of chisel marks right along the side of the receiver above the stock line. Not a popular chappie! Have a look for any other areas where the hardened epoxy may be trapping the metalwork in the wood. The front of the ejection port is a good place. If you do not find them now, and attend to them, they will be broken out when we remove the metalwork, and worse, probably take a piece of the stock with them. All Clear! Good! Let's move on.

17.2. Get a couple of strong rubber bands and put one around the forend and barrel, up near the forend tip, and one around the pistol grip so that it goes over the rear tang. Their purpose is to support the metalwork when it comes free of the bedding.

17.3. Hold the forend of the stock, not too tightly, just in front of the action in the soft jaws of your vice, metalwork facing down, and slide that piece of round steel into the bolt hole right up to the back of the barrel. Now it helps here if you have an extra pair of arms and hands growing out of your chest. For those of you who don't, just do the best you can. Support the butt stock as best you can, with your hip or your knee, or get a mate to hold it. Take the aluminum drift and place it on the piece of round steel right up against the front of the magazine well. Now give it a sharp whack with a hammer. How hard should you hit it? I know from experience. You have to learn, so there will be no problem in sneaking up on it. It does take a few pretty good whacks though.

17.4. When you whack it hard enough the metalwork will break free from the bedding and hang down on the rubber bands. Don't stop there though. Support the metalwork evenly so it's coming straight out of the bedding and tap it until it is about half way out.

17.5. Keeping the metalwork as straight as you can, turn the rifle over, secure it in the vice and remove the rubber bands. Now, applying as little pressure as possible, wriggle the metalwork back and forth, and ease it out of the recoil lug mortise. It will come out pretty easily.

17.6. For single shot rifles install the two rubber bands and the round piece of steel as we did for the repeater. Now insert that 3" long piece of drill rod through the front take-down screw hole until it bottoms on the round piece of steel. We need a piece of light chain about 18" long, a 'D' to fit it and a long Tyre lever or short crowbar (this is getting interesting huh!). Place a pair of soft jaws in the vice that won't mar the stock finish, balance the rifle upside down with the drill rod in the middle of the vice jaws, and tighten the vice just enough to allow the action to slide through, leaving the stock sitting on the vice. Now loop the chain under the tail of the vice, install the 'D' so that you can slip the Tyre lever through the chain and have it resting on the drill rod with its end slightly elevated. Apply pressure to the end of the tyre lever and you will hear a loud '*crack*' as the metalwork releases from the bedding. As with the repeater, push it out about half way, remove the tyre lever, turn it right side up, secure it in the vice and ease the metalwork all the way out of the bedding. Easy! Photo 7-19 (Page "photo 7-19." on page 278) shows the setup. Both of the above methods will remove the metalwork without deflecting (bending) it.

18. Remove the duct tape from the receiver and wipe it over with fine steel wool to remove any release agent. Screw the special long bedding screws through the take-down screw holes, to drive out the hardened epoxy, and clean the threads out. If there is any putty left in the corners of the recoil lug, remove it.

19. Dress any hardened epoxy above the top line of the stock down to the level of the masking tape, either with a sharp chisel or a file. Be careful not to cut into the stock finish.

19.1. You will probably have some sizeable hardened epoxy excess at the front of the magazine well and in front of the rear tang bedding. You can break away most of the excess with a few judicious taps with a chisel and mallet, but don't get too ambitious as we don't want to crack into the bedding proper and make it look untidy. Once you knock away the excess epoxy your Dremel tool will make short work of removing the remainder back to the wood line very neatly. Use that flat bottomed tungsten carbide cutter (#25 on the list).

PHOTO 7-19.

This is how I extract the metalwork on a single shot rifle and blind magazine designs. The same method can be used with a repeater if you don't want to hammer it out as per the text. The rubber bands support the metalwork as it comes out of the stock. The drill rod in the front takedown screw hole is pushing against the mandrel inserted in the bolt hole of the receiver. The Tyre lever is cantilevered by the chain around the tail of the vice and the drill rod. Applying pressure to the end of the Tyre lever pushes the metalwork through the vice soft jaws leaving the stock behind. The barrelled action is not stressed (bent) when removed like this.

19.2. Now, *this is important.* Take a sharp ¼" wide chisel and a sharp ⅛" wide chisel and relieve every corner you can see in the bedding. Have a look at the barreled action and you will see the little front facing flats around the recoil lug. Most actions will have these little flat areas that must be relieved, as, if they are not attended to, they will cramp the barrelled action in the stock, and interfere with the test we must make shortly, to ensure bedding integrity. On Remingtons, there are none at the rear tang, so all you have to do there is remove the little raised ledge, around the rear tang, that was formed when the metalwork relaxed into the bedding. You don't have to cut deeply into the bedding material here, just be sure that the corners are clean by squaring them off, and the flats do not bind the metalwork.

19.3. Chamfer the screw holes in the stock, so they will not chip out when you drill them through, and then drill them through with a 17/64" twist drill (just larger than ¼").

19.3.1. The best way to do this is to drill to a centre. To do that you need a short 60° centre that will be held in your bench drill vice. Secure it at one end of your vice high enough that you can sit the stock straight on it, and check for clearance with the centre in both stock holes. Now place another centre in your drill chuck, and adjust the table until both centres come together exactly. Now replace the chuck centre with the 17/64" drill, and adjust the travel stop on your drill press so the drill just doesn't quite reach the centre in the vice. Hold the stock with the screw hole in the vice centre, to drill the hole out. Drill both holes, then turn the stock over and repeat. This will drill the holes accurately; much better than by eyeball engineering. Photos 7-20, 7-21 and 7-22 show the method.

PHOTO 7-20.

The centre in the drill Vice is lined up with the centre in the drill chuck.

PHOTO 7-21.

The drill depth stop is locked just before the drill hits the centre.

20. Turning our attention to the forend, we need to make the barrel floating.

20.1. If we left a knob of wood at the forend tip remove it with a scraper or half round chisel.

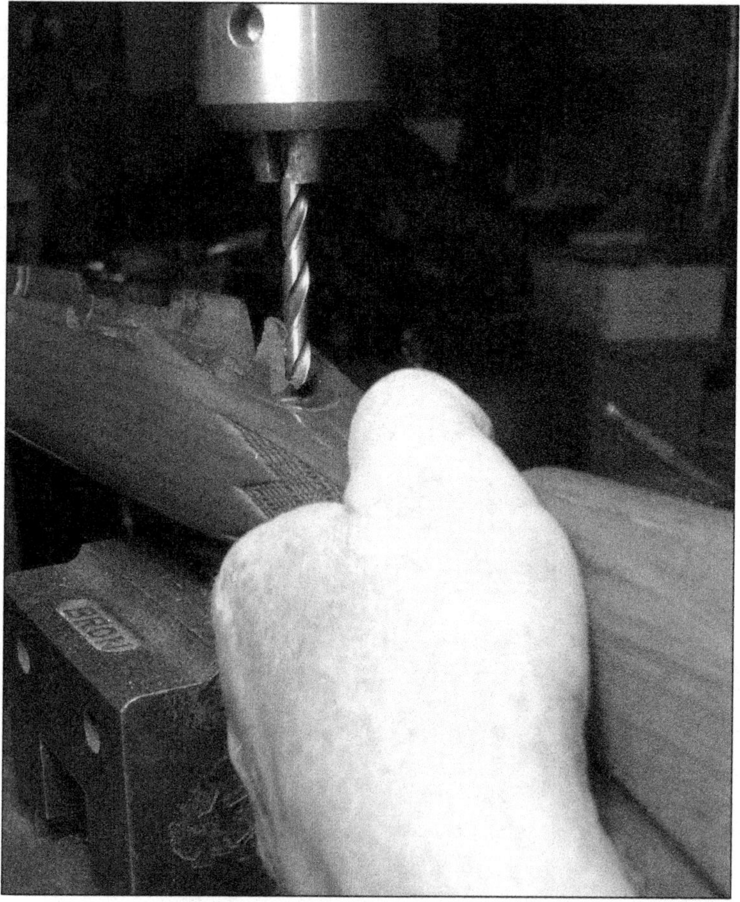

PHOTO 7-22.

The bottom of the take-down screw hole is placed onto the vice centre, and the hole is drilled through while holding the stock down. Drilling the stock take-down screw holes like this prevents the drill from wandering.

20.2. If we made a polyester platform in the forend channel to support the metalwork remove it. Of course, if you supported the barrel with duct tape, remove that as well.

20.3. Install the metalwork in the stock, take that heavy shiny back paper, #24 on the list, and try to slide it between the forend and barrel right back to the front of the receiver. Of course, if you needed to bed the barrel reinforce it will only slide back to the bedded surface.

20.4. If it catches at all on the way back, note the area, remove the metalwork, clear some forend material out with a scraper, reassemble and try again. Keep at it until the paper slides all the way back freely. If you are bedding a wooden stock, seal the raw wood with some stock finish. Photo 7-23 shows some of the tools I use.

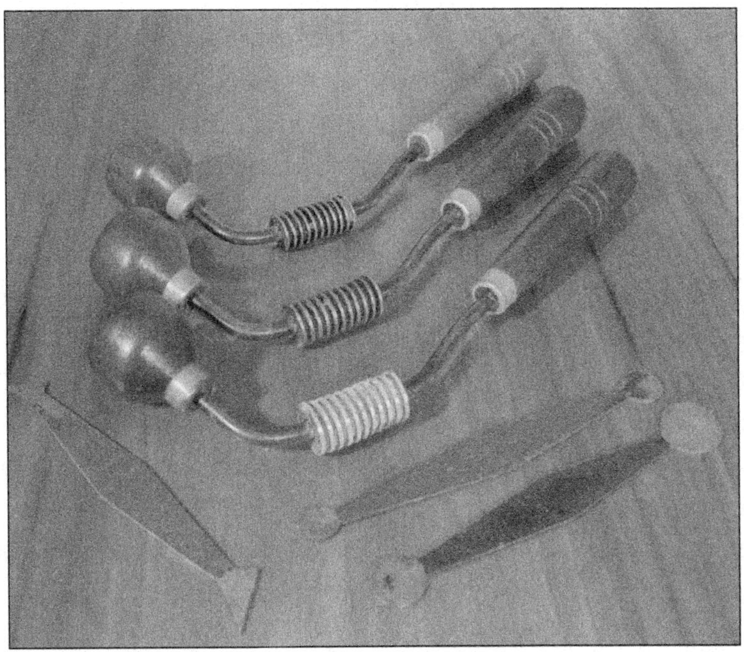

PHOTO 7-23.
Barrel channel and inletting scrapers.

21. Remove the masking tape from the stock and the bedding part is done.

If we did the job properly the bedding should be right, but it would be foolish to assume that. You remember what our mission was when we embarked on this job? To provide a true, flat, stress free platform that would allow the metalwork to slide freely to the rear under recoil, and return freely to its original position when recoil has ceased. If the bedding platform is not straight it will, via the tightened action screws, hold the barreled action in a stressed, or bent, condition, not unlike a bent leaf spring. So it follows that if we release one action screw, or the other, the bent, deflected actually, metalwork will spring back to its original position. It is this property we will use to measure the correctness of our bedding job.

Naturally, a perfect bedding job will be dead straight, and when the action screws are tightened, the metalwork will be held on the bedding platform in a totally relaxed stress free attitude. That is what we are aiming for, and this is how we test for it.

All we need for this job is a dial indicator that measures to .0001" and a magnetic stand for it. The one you use on your lathe is fine. You can use your existing action screws along with a few ¼" flat washers to space them out a little, but I prefer to use appropriate length Allen head cap screws. With cap screws I can more easily apply torquing motion, to the screws, without any forward force needed to keep a screwdriver blade engaged in its slot. With your original screws you will just have to be more careful not to push on the screwdriver when you perform the test.

It is ultra important that, when we make this test, the barreled action is free in the bedding. If there is any binding or cramping at all the test will not be valid. You should be able to stand the rifle on its butt, tighten the action screws, and with the rifle leaning slightly forward, loosen the action screws a couple of turns, and when you lean the rifle back a bit, the metalwork should fall out of the inletting. If it doesn't, find out why and relieve that area until it does. On Remingtons you may have bedded the metalwork a fraction below the centre-line of the receiver so that it is captured by the slight reverse circumference. That's ok; just take a scraper and relieve the bedding material, at the top line of the stock, until the receiver is free to fall in and out of the bedding with no restriction.

Also, start testing with only the barreled receiver, with nothing attached other than the trigger. We don't want anything interfering with our initial test. Once we have established that our job is right, we can add things like magazine boxes, trigger guards, mounts and scopes and see if they affect the job. If any of them do we know the culprit immediately, and can work out a fix.

Guard screw tension. If you question ten people on this you will probably get ten answers. Personally, I have always tightened my action screws snug for the front one, and not quite so snug for the rear one, especially if the rear tang bedding area is small, such as on the M'98 Mauser. I've never felt the need to spring the cash for an inch pound tension wrench, but if you do, go right ahead. You certainly won't do any harm. As I said, not tight, just snug. Medium pressure on an ordinary 6" screwdriver is fine. If you overdo it at the rear tang, even on a Remington, you will crush the material slightly and wreck the integrity of your bedding job. You'll probably wonder where the accuracy went too.

Ok, we only want our barreled receiver, stock, two action screws and some ¼" flat washers to start with. Screw the bits together and use enough flat washers to space the screws out to about their normal position. Snug the screws up to working tension. Release them and check that the metalwork falls out of the inletting. It does? Good. Retension them. Stand the rifle on its butt and attach the magnetic base of the dial indicator under the barrel, just in front of the forend tip. Adjust the dial indicator so that its probe is bearing just behind, and on the bottom of the forend tip, in about half the way of its travel.

Now, with the rifle leaning slightly forward, and without pushing against the front action screw, alternately loosen and tighten the front screw, and see what that does to the needle of the dial indicator. You can hold the parts with your hand over the front receiver bridge to do this, but don't apply any pressure holding the metalwork in the stock. If the bedding job is perfect the dial indicator will not move. If the bedding job is not perfect the dial indicator needle will move. Don't panic yet. Photo 7-24 (Page 283) shows the method.

A certain amount of movement, which indicates an uneven bedding platform that is applying stress or tension in the barreled receiver, can be tolerated. Also we can tell what has happened with the integrity of the job by observing the dial indicator. When you release the tension on the front screw and the dial indicator probe moves in, moving the needle in the '+' direction, the barrel is springing out of the forend. This usually indicates a low rear tang bedding condition, and that condition is probably the most common in bad bedding jobs. You can mount a dial indicator on the grip of the stock, with the probe bearing at the end of the rear tang, if you wish. By loosening and tightening the rear screw you will find out exactly how low the tang is. That is a fairly redundant test, however, as the first test has already told us all we really need to know.

The dial indicator probe can also move out, with the needle moving in the '–' direction, which tells us the barrel is moving into the forend when the front screw is loosened. This indicates that there is a low spot at the front receiver ring, possibly caused by over squeezing the barreled action during the bedding job. This bedding condition caused me much grief, until I finally realized that I was causing it by applying pressure on the front of the receiver, with elastic, to hold the parts together while the Epoxy cured. When I woke up, and stopped that practice, my low receiver ring conditions all disappeared. It takes very little pressure at this point to deflect the metalwork. Just the pressure from a rubber band is enough. If the metalwork is deflected while the Epoxy hardens; well, I don't need to go into detail do I!

Of these two conditions the low rear tang is the better of two evils. If your job has a low front receiver ring my suggestion is, don't fool around with it. Bite the bullet and re bed it. *It is an accuracy killer.*

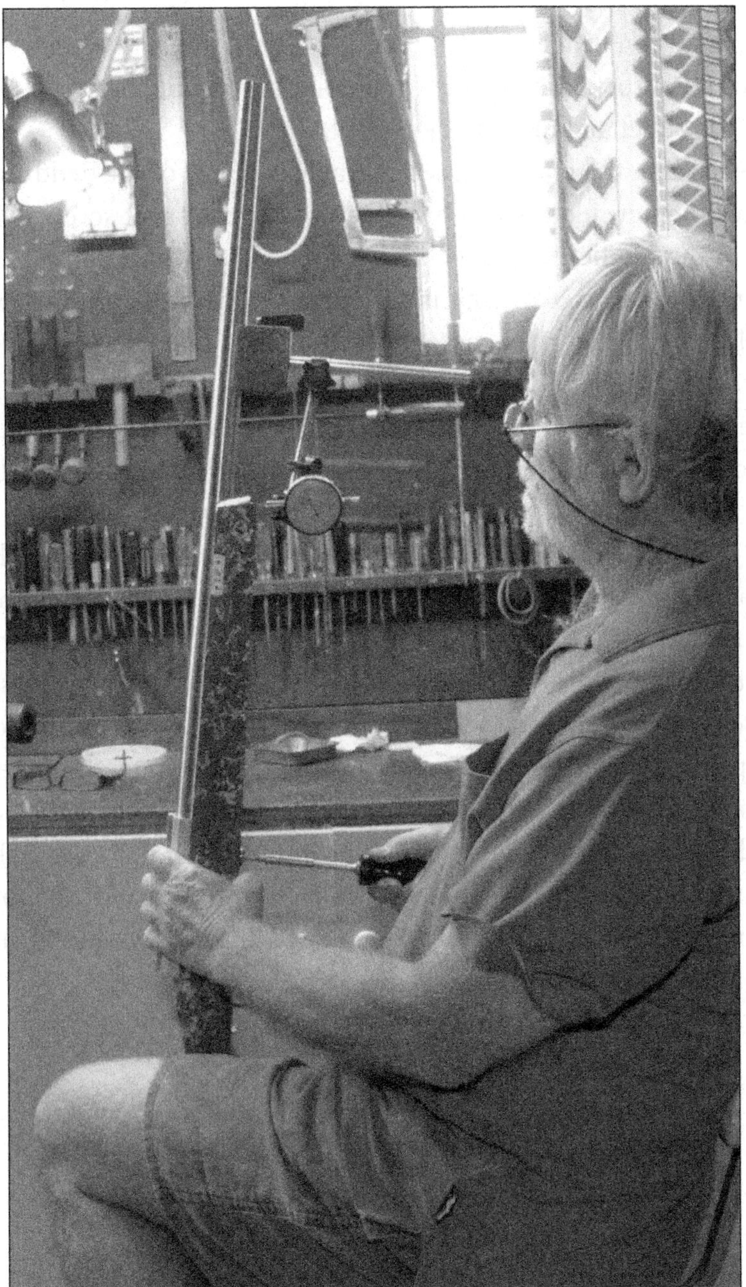

PHOTO 7-24.

Testing the accuracy of the bedding with a dial indicator. My left hand is not applying any pressure to the top of the receiver. I am holding the stock with my thumb on the underside and with my fingers on the far topside of the stock.

Experience has shown that a degree of low rear tang inaccuracy can be tolerated, at least on a sporting rifle. *On a bench-rest rifle I would say no inaccuracy could be tolerated at all.* The needle should not move. For sporting rifles any job that moves the needle .002" or more will probably not be capable of shooting 1MOA five shot groups. For sub 1MOA accuracy I think the upper limit is .0015". When I was doing this work for a living, I failed any job that tested at more than .00075" of movement. You just bite the bullet and do the job again, and keep doing it until you get it right.

I am only talking about low rear tang inaccuracy here. *I don't think any movement indicating a low front receiver ring can be tolerated at all.* If you have bedded a sporting rifle and ended up with, say, .002" of low rear tang it may be worthwhile rebedding just the rear tang, and see if you can pick it up.

Rebedding a job that has been bedded is, quite frankly, a pain in the ass because Devcon is hard and messy to remove from the stock, even though you don't have to remove it all. Sometimes, however, you just have to bite the bullet and make the job right.

If you are just rebedding the rear tang, remove at least 3/32" of the bedding material, and drill some holes to anchor the new platform. This time tighten the front screw to its working tension and place the rifle in the cradle exactly as before. Of course, you don't need any support under the barrel at the forend. The receiver ring is supported in front of, and behind, the front screw, and this should hold everything in its correct position. The rear screw should, of course, not be tightened.

Once you have established that your bedding platform is correct you can add the extras onto the barreled action, checking as you go that they do not stress the receiver, and thereby compromise your perfect job.

You don't have to use the dial indicator to check if adding parts to the barreled action has affected the accuracy of the bedding job. You can make a spot check by holding your thumb, bearing lightly, on the side of the barrel, and the top line of the stock near the forend tip. Stand the rifle on its butt leaning slightly forward, as before, and alternately loosen and tighten the front screw. If there is any inaccuracy you will feel the barrel move in the forend. With a little experience it is surprising how little movement you can feel when testing like this. I can feel less than .0005" easily, so it's a valid test to make while you are adding bits and pieces to the assembly. Only resort to the dial indicator if you detect movement on a job that originally tested at zero, or the movement seems excessive on a job, that tested originally, with a little movement. Photo 7-25 (Page 285) shows me doing this, and Photo 7-26 (Page 286) shows the ideal position for your thumb in the gap between the barrel and forend.

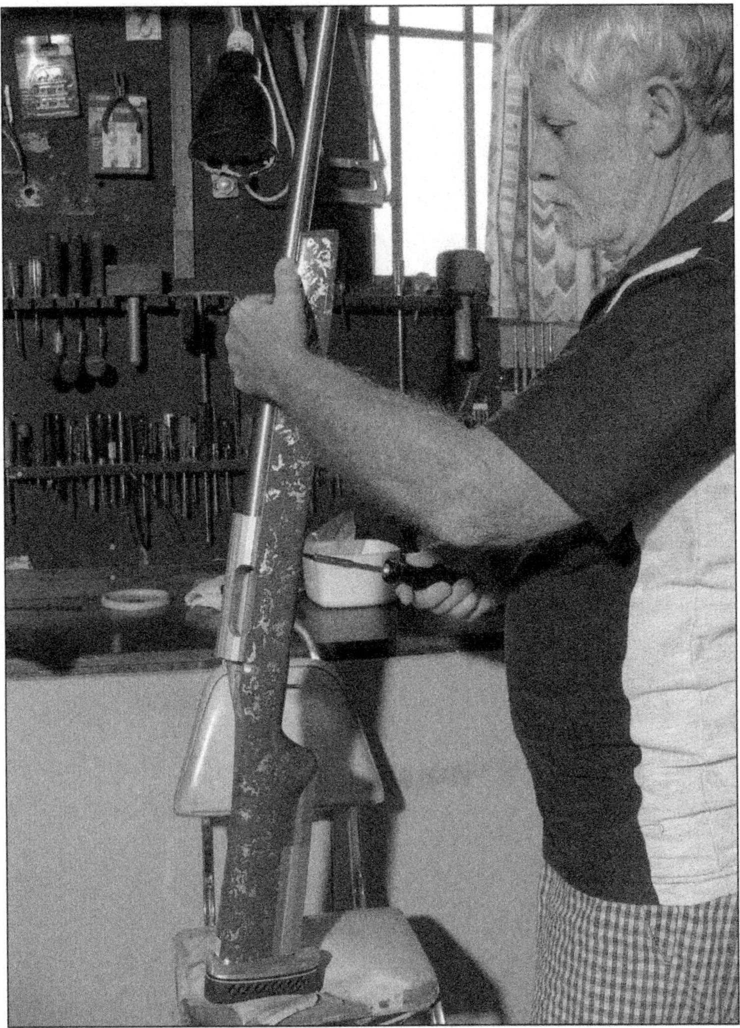

PHOTO 7-25.

Testing the bedding by feel. Again, I am not applying any pressure to the top of the barrel, but gripping the stock by its sides. My thumb rests lightly at the gap between the barrel and forend, and I am concentrating on feeling any perceptible movement of the barrel in the forend at that point.

If you don't have a dial indicator you can still test by thumb. Just be aware that any movement you feel should be miniscule. Movement of say .005" feels like a stallion rearing to me, though an inexperienced person may think it acceptable. Until you gain the experience to know the difference you feel with the thumb test, beg borrow, or steal a dial indicator to confirm the amount of movement you can feel. Of course, if you can feel no movement at all, you are probably safe.

PHOTO 7-26.

This is the ideal position for your thumb to feel the smallest amount of movement between the barrel and forend.

You can also place your thumb lightly over the rear tang, right at the back, so your thumb is resting on both the back of the tang and the top of the pistol grip. By alternately loosening, and tightening, the rear screw you will easily feel any movement of the rear tang moving away from its bedding surface. If you have a problem you will feel it there too.

The bedding test thus described is a valid test for any conventionally bedded rifle. By conventionally bedded, I mean any rifle that has a barreled action, held into the inletting, with screws at the front bridge and rear tang of the receiver. Whether the inletting be of wood, fiberglass, aluminum V block, or aluminum chassis, if the barreled action is secured by two screws it will move under recoil, and its correct return to battery is paramount to accuracy.

Remember, if your rifle is already bedded, and you want to test the integrity of the job, it must be free to fall in and out of the stock, so the test will be valid. If it doesn't, you will have to provide the clearances I have detailed on page 258 before you make the test. Only by making this test can you be in a position to know, with certainly, that bedding is, or is not the problem, if your rifle is not accurate.

Some considerations you may want to think about.

Long bedding screws: 3" Allen head cap screws are ideal for this job. I have a few extras and treat the ends as shown in Photo 7-28 (Page 288). Simply form the coarse screwdriver blade end and the notched end on the screws with a sharp 6" or 8" mill saw or hand file, or cut them in with an abrasive wheel on a Dremel tool; your choice. These treated screws are very handy when bedding actions with a blind end take-down screw hole. Examples are Sako and Tikka front screw, and Panda rear screw.

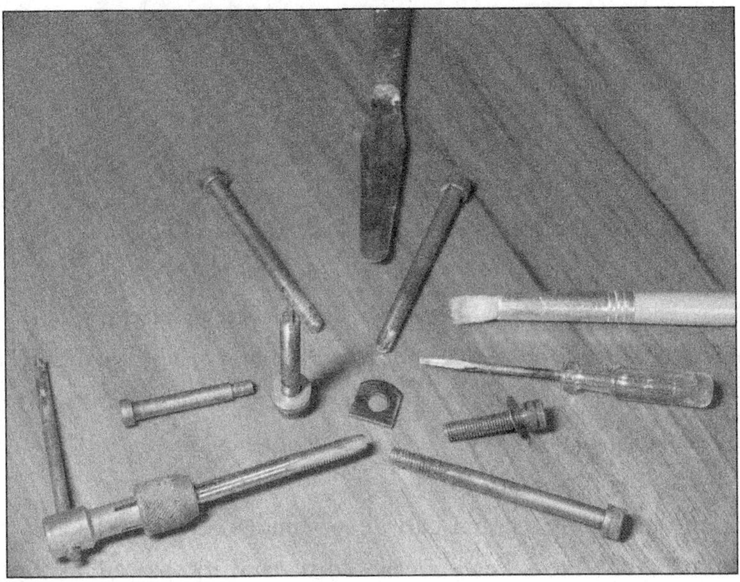

PHOTO 7-27.

Long bedding screws, a small spatula, my small round blade screwdriver, receiver screw tap and holder, and my artists brush with shortened bristles I use to apply the Wundawax release agent. The plate in the middle is used to provide relief for the magazine guide on Tikka LSA series actions.

When bedding actions with blind screw holes place some Plasticine in the bottom of the hole, enough to fill about 2 threads, and squeeze it flat in the bottom of the hole with a flat bottomed guard screw. When you bed the job make sure you use the spade bottomed bedding screw in this hole. Be sure to coat the thread in the hole with release agent, of course. When the epoxy has hardened and you remove the screw, the plug of hardened epoxy that is inside the hole will come right out with the screw. It won't be stuck in the bottom of the hole because you had Plasticine spacing it out a couple of threads. The Plasticine is easily removed by screwing the bedding screw, with the groove in the end, into the hole.

The notched bedding screw will clean the hardened epoxy out of the screw threads in the receiver pretty well, however, be aware that your receiver screws should screw into their threaded holes freely. If there is any binding at all run the appropriate intermediate tap through the hole to ensure all of the epoxy is removed and the screw goes right in freely. Personally, I prefer to do that with the metalwork installed in the stock, and run the tap through the stock screw holes into the receiver threads.

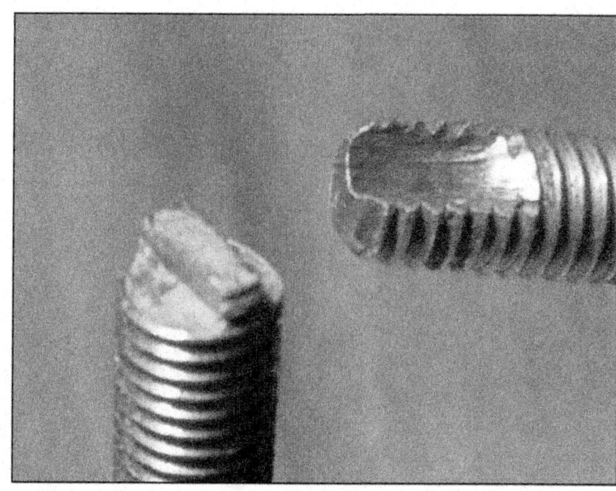

PHOTO 7-28.

The altered ends on some bedding screws. The left screw is useful when bedding actions with blind screw holes, as it will remove the epoxy plug from the hole as it is screwed out. The right screw is useful for cleaning epoxy out of screw hole threads, and for removing play putty from the bottom of blind holes.

If you have an action with a trigger that cantilevers near the end of the rear tang *you will not be able to bed it successfully.* Later Sako L and A series come to mind as well as Howas. Early Sako triggers were held with a cross-pin to the action. They were tensioned with an angled lock screw, at the front, against an adjustable screw, that bore against the bottom of the receiver, at the rear of the rear bridge. Some bright spark at the factory decided it was easier to delete the locating screw behind the cross-pin. He left some metal at the rear of the trigger housing, so the front tensioning screw could put pressure on it, thus locking the trigger in place. The only problem with that stroke of genius is, when you tension the front screw, you bend the rear tang. Very helpful!

Howa actually did this on purpose! Their trigger has two crosswise protuberances of metal at the front and rear of the trigger housing. The housing is held to the action with a counter sunk screw, and located in place with a crosswise groove in the bottom of the receiver, just in front of the hold down screw. Of course, the cantilever is close to the rear tang bedding area so when the screw is tightened the rear tang is bent up.

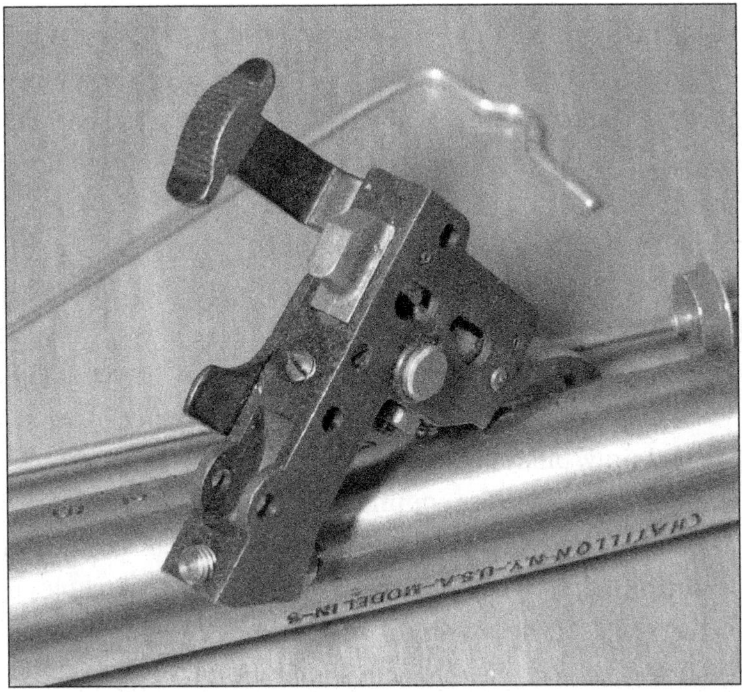

PHOTO 7-29.

This is the old design of Sako L and A series triggers. The front screw is the tensioning screw. The trigger is held to the action by a cross-pin through the holes behind the front tensioning screw. The small screw behind the holes is the trigger spacing screw. It bears at the rear of the rear bridge on the receiver. On later triggers this screw was omitted in favor of a strip of metal, left at the rear of the housing, which bends the rear tang when the tensioning screw is tightened. When bedding these actions the trigger must be modified to the early version shown here, *or your bedding job will never work.*

The fix is to convert the Sako trigger back to the original design by drilling, tapping, installing a grub screw, and removing the offending lump of metal at the rear of the trigger housing. With the Howa, do the same thing. Convert it to the old Sako design. Then you will be able to bed them successfully. Photo 7-29 shows the old Sako trigger.

There are some who would tell you that the only way to get a rifle to shoot to bench-rest standards is to glue the barrelled action into the stock. In no way do I believe that to be true. In fact, I view glue jobs as a crutch to be used by those who do not know how to make a proper, stress free, conventional bedding job.

I first started gluing barreled actions into stocks in the early 1970s when I wanted to make a very light rifle. In that case I would use a fiberglass shell filled only with Urethane and, by gluing the barreled action into the stock, could make a Remington 700 actioned rifle that weighed only 6^{LBS} with a 6x Leupold scope, full magazine and sling.

While I admit the process works I am not a fan, mostly because I like to be able to take things apart for maintenance, etc. If I get caught out in the rain and my rifle gets a good soaking, I like to be able to take everything apart for drying and oiling. To get the metalwork out of the stock is a federal case with a glue in, compared to a conventionally bedded rifle, and if you leave the moisture trapped under the metalwork of your glue in, it certainly isn't going to be doing you any favors.

If you can bed a rifle properly there is no need to be gluing it in. Properly bedded, it will be every bit as accurate. If your guy is gluing, it is because he can't get the conventional job to work for him, and he's adopting a quick fix. A glue job works much the same as upward barrel pressure, by jamming the metalwork in the stock, and not allowing it to recoil. Just be aware that it can shoot loose, and there is no test for integrity.

Some people advocate the use of steel or aluminum pillars glued into the stock to supposedly add strength between the bottom of the receiver, and top of the trigger guard assembly, with the claim that they are miracle bedding fixers. Personally, unless your stock is made of very soft spongy material, I don't see the need. Some commercial injection molded stocks are very weak, and some stock woods can be weak enough to be displaced when the guard screws are tightened, especially at the rear tang of the action. If so, then certainly, pillar bedding would be beneficial.

You can make them yourself or there are commercially made units available. They should be glued into place before you do the bedding job. The only caveat is to get them straight and at the right height. Drilling the stock to size to a centre, as I described for opening the screw holes up after bedding, will help. Devcon is fine to glue them in with. As I said make sure they go in straight if you use them.

On two of my target rifles I needed a front escutcheon for the front screw, so decided to make it in one piece out of stainless barrel steel, and incorporate a pillar into the design. See Photo 7-30. While I was at it I also made pillars for the rear screws. My Remington 40x practice rifle has a one piece full length trigger guard rail, so I didn't bother with the pillars. The bedding on all 3 of my target rifles tests to +/- 0 and all will print bug holes, if I do my part, which I don't often do!

As I said, if you want to use them go right ahead, as they certainly won't do any harm, properly installed, and may be beneficial if your stock is prone to collapse the bedding area, at the rear tang, when the rear screw is tightened.

PHOTO 7-30

The escutcheon/pillars I made for my target rifles from stainless barrel steel. They can be seen installed in PHOTO 7-5 (Page 260).

Sometimes you will find it expedient to make something like a spacer, or whatever, to provide clearance for a part that should be removed to bed the metalwork. There should be no extra parts on the receiver when you bed it. One piece scope bases (especially), bolt stops, magazine guides or anything else. The baseline is the barrel, receiver and trigger. Once you know that is right you can look for any, deterioration in bedding accuracy, as you add other bits. In particular look for trouble when you add the magazine box to the system. Many of them are too high.

In Photo 7-27 (page 287) you can see a spacer I used, when bedding Tikka LSA series actions, that provided clearance in the bedding for the box magazine guide and its screw. It is much easier to provide clearance within the bedding, when making it, rather than by grinding away excess material afterwards. Also it is much neater. Photo 7-31 shows some other parts I used to assist with the job. The round ferrule is for a Mauser M'98 front screw, that provided the correct clearance in the stock for the front take-down screw housing, which is integral on the trigger guard assembly. I used a short screw to attach it to the bottom of the action, and filled any gaps between it, and the bottom of the receiver, with Plasticine. When the bedding had hardened I removed the screw, and then removed the barreled receiver, after which the ferrule could be tapped, out of the bottom of the stock, leaving behind the correct clearance for the trigger guard assembly.

PHOTO 7-31.
Some bedding aids

Some actions you will encounter will have spring loaded triggers, that will make it very difficult to ensure that your barreled receiver is centered properly in the inletting. This is because it is hard to get a good measurement, from the trigger bow to the side of the trigger guard inlet, due to the spring away in the trigger. The Winchester M'70 is a classic example of this type of trigger, and the small block in Photo 7-31 is designed to replace the trigger spring on the trigger, and lock it firmly into place for bedding. You can see its placement in Photos 7-32 and 7-33.

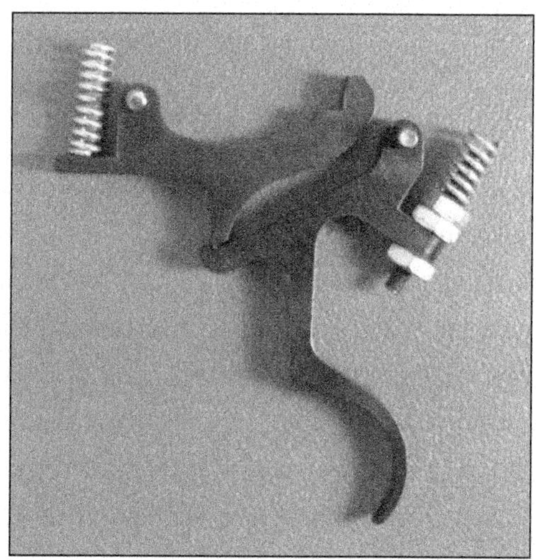
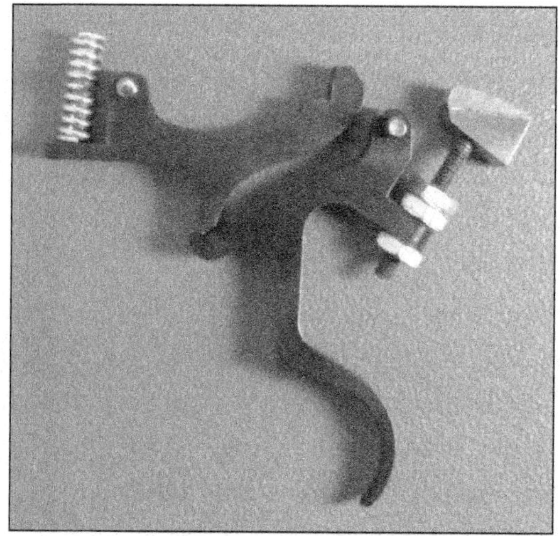

Photos 7-32 (Left) and 7-33 (Right).
The position of the spacing block used on a Winchester M'70 for bedding.

In use, I removed the trigger, the trigger spring, and the bottom locking nut on the trigger. Don't disturb the tension adjustment, but do measure its distance from the top of the nut to the trigger, so that we can set the trigger pull back, to what it was, when we are finished, unless you have to do a trigger job, in which case don't bother. Replace the trigger, insert the block, and wind the adjusting screw in so that it engages the hole, in the block, and tightens the trigger, so that it doesn't move. Then, as a precaution fill any gaps between the receiver and block with Plasticine, and surround the screw with Plasticine as well. The trigger is thus held firmly and straight, and you can get a positive measurement between it, and the inlet, to get the barreled receiver straight in the inletting.

The small truss in Photo 7-31 was another trick I used to secure a spring loaded trigger assembly, for bedding, but for the life of me I can't remember what trigger I used it on. Maybe Mk X Mauser or Husqvarna.

So there you have it! Epoxy bedding is not a hit or miss affair. It must be made correctly, to a measurable standard, and when that standard is met bedding can be discounted as a possible source of inaccuracy.

A RUGER #1 IN .240 WEATHERBY MAGNUM

BUILT IN THE EARLY 1980S

PHOTO C4-54.

I saw this stick some time in the late 1970s at Roger Vardy's house, when he lived in Melbourne, and had not a clue that some years later I would be using it to create a stock for a fine sporting rifle.

PHOTO C4-55.

A collection of the bits and pieces that make up a Custom Sporting Rifle. I have cut the blank out, and it is ready to be fitted to the receiver. The ¼ rib is completed, as is the custom steel trigger, safety and barrel.

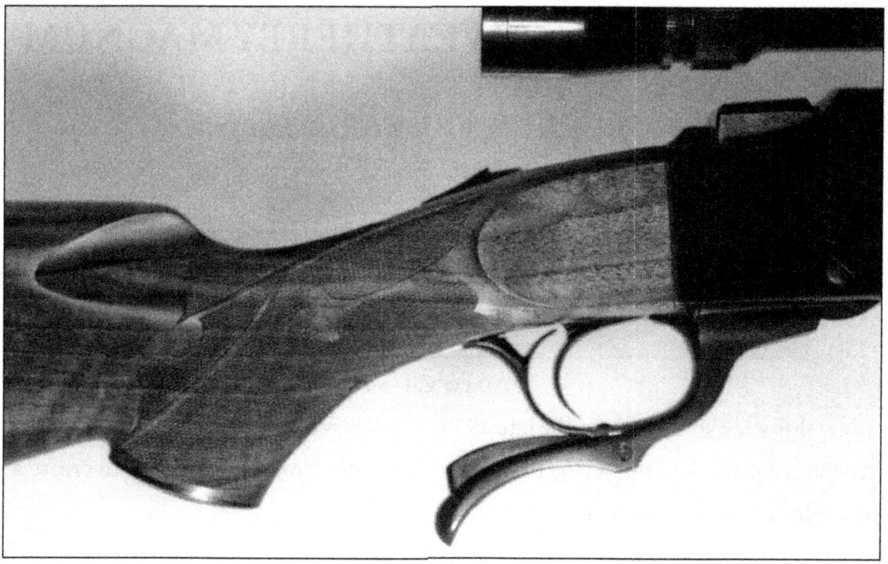

PHOTO C4-56.

Of note is the safety and trigger, which are made from solid steel blocks. The rather complicated checkering pattern goes right around the grip, and through the ribbons without a break. That Fler design became a trademark of mine.

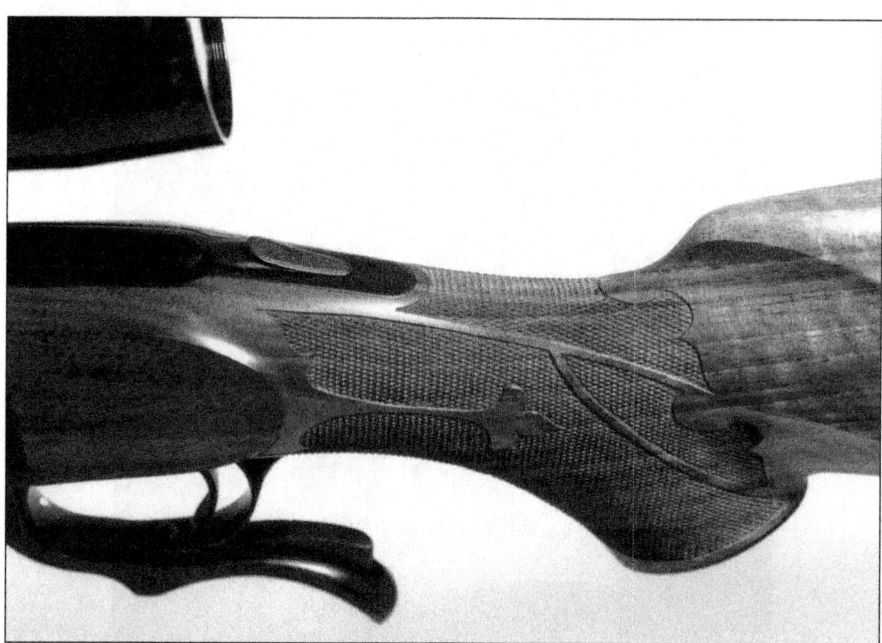

PHOTO C4-57.

Over the grip checkering detail and a better look at the custom made safety. The action on this rifle was fully polished inside and out, a new quarter rib made from a solid block of steel, and fitted to suite Leonard Brownell's side lever quick detachable mounts.

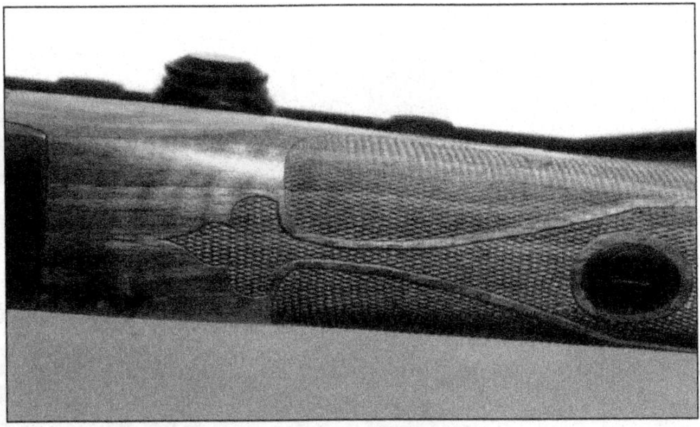

PHOTO C4-58.
Under forend checkering detail, with a trapped and covered front screw escutcheon.

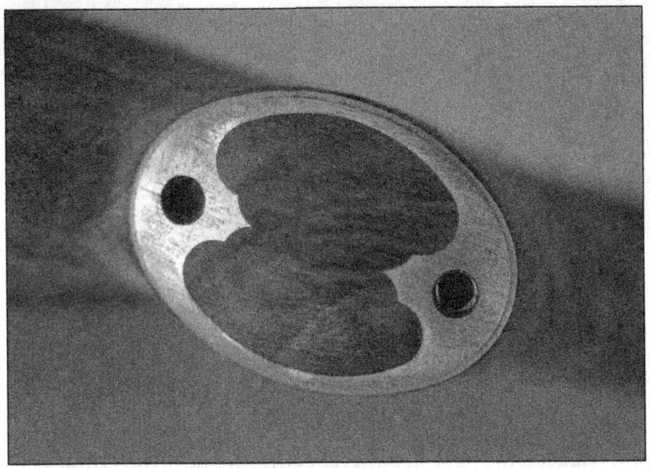

PHOTO C4-59.
Scalloped skeleton grip cap newly inletted.

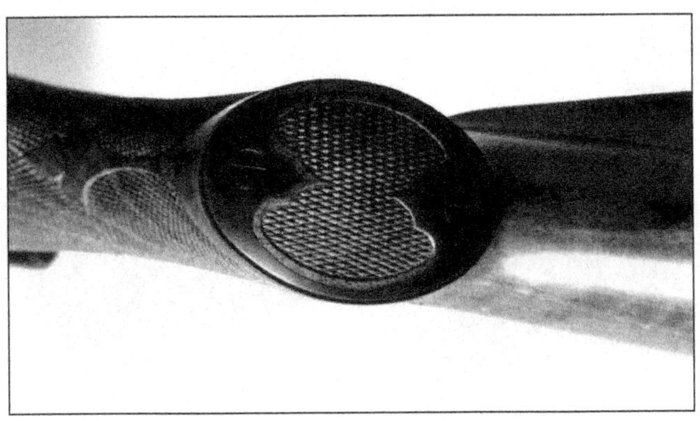

PHOTO C4-60.
Scalloped skeleton grip cap finished and checkered.

photo C4-61.

The safety and trigger shoe were in panel checkered. The receiver was profile ground, to flatten its surface, and all internal parts polished to smooth operation.

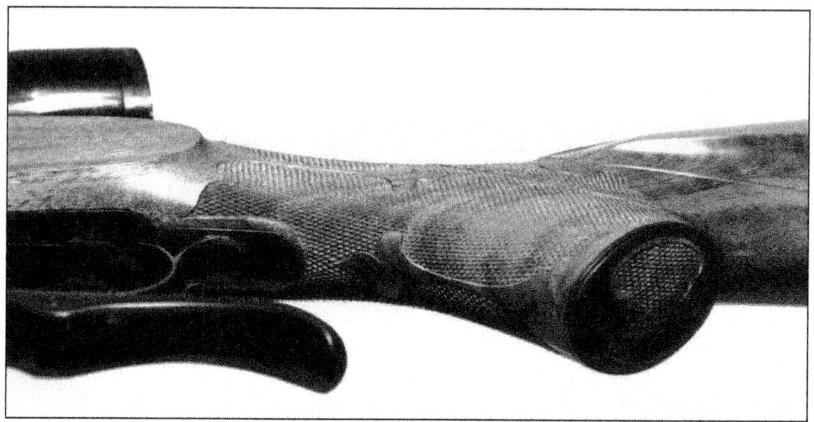

photo C4-62.

Under grip profile.

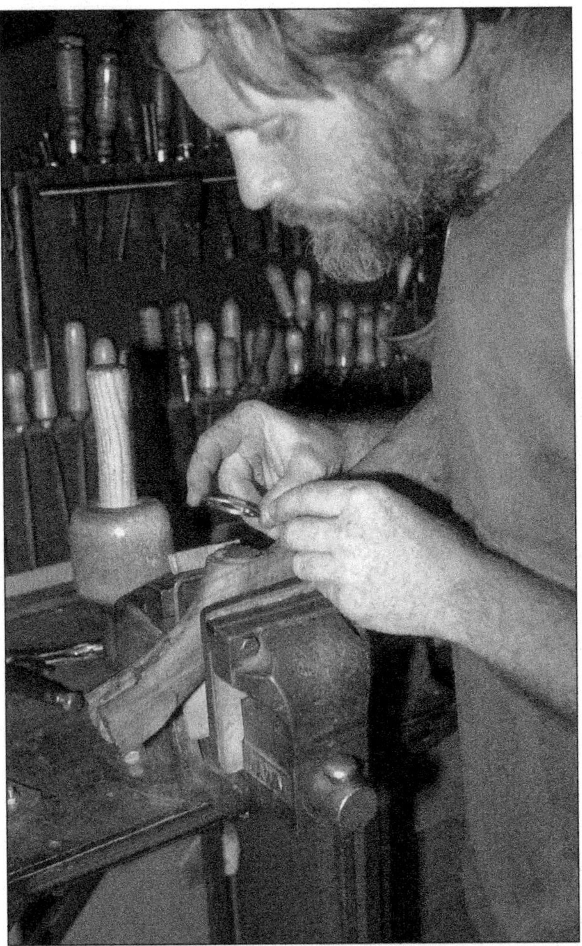

PHOTO C4-63.

Spotting in the scalloped skeleton grip cap for this Ruger #1. This was one of the first jobs to do, when the stock was cut out, to protect the delicate edge of the grip.

PHOTO C4-64.

The Ruger #1 forend is attached to a hanger, welded to the front of the receiver, which is very flexible. In order to stabilise the forend I installed a screw in the hanger, that pushed a V block against the barrel, just in front of the angled forend screw. This upward pressure on the barrel was an accuracy fix for these Ruger #1s.

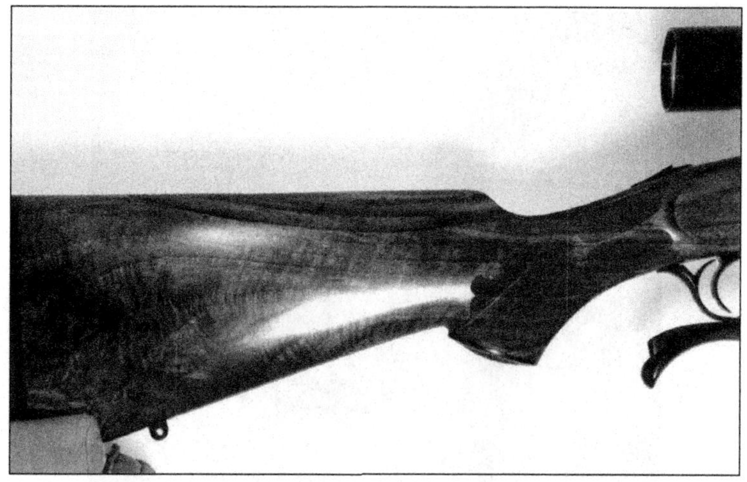

PHOTO C4-65.

This was a lovely piece of Roger Vardy's Australian English Walnut.

PHOTO C4-66.

Beginning to apply the first coat of stock finish. This was probably the best part of the whole job, as I am about to see what the grain in the stock is really going to look like. It's never disappointing!

SIGNIFICANT RIFLES AND EVENTS

PART 5: THE 1980s (3)

PHOTO C4-67.

In the mid 1980s I decided I needed a light kicking rifle that Lyn could use. My .338/06 was far too violent for her. I had come by a very good commercial Mexican Mauser action that was perfectly suited for the 7X57 Mauser cartridge. I reprofiled a #1 Douglas chrome moly blank I had to super light profile, fitted it to the action, and cut it off 20" long. The classic bolt handle was welded on, and a Canjar M-3 tuned trigger fitted. The trigger guard assembly was completed to useable stage. I made the stock pattern with a 3¾" grip, and fitted the barreled action to it with the intention of trying it out before making a 'real' stock for it. I had picked out a very nice stick to put on it, intending to give it the full treatment, but that never happened. I guess the road to hell is paved with good intentions! PHOTO C4-67 sees Lyn with it and a small boar she shot, all on her own, while the boys were away from camp unsuccessfully hunting. That accounts for the big grin.

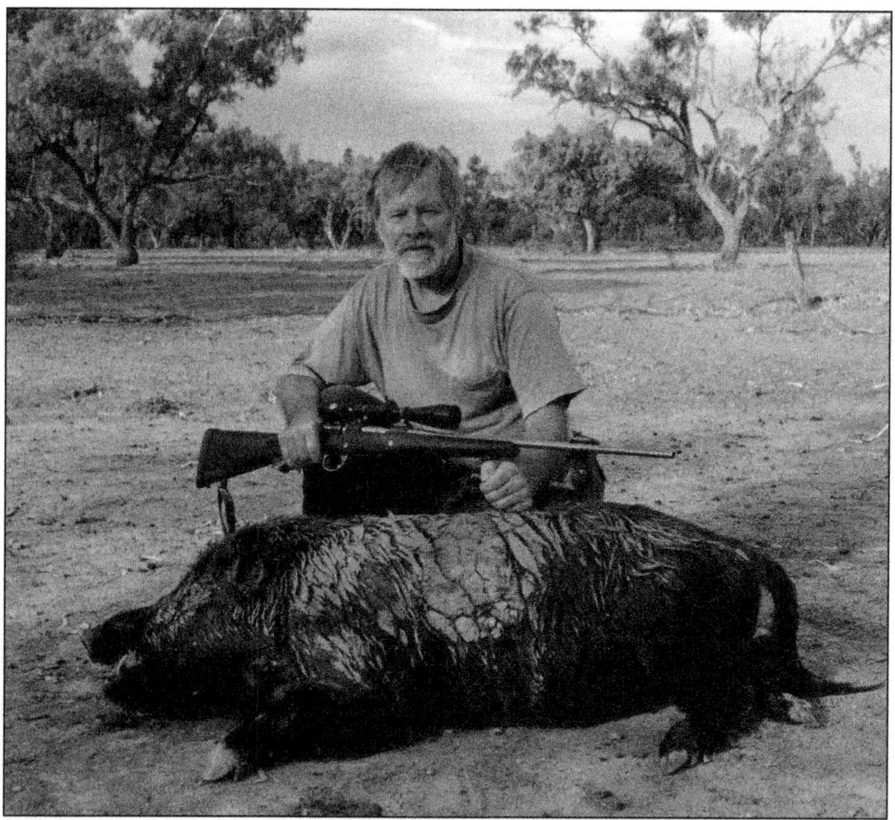

PHOTO C4-68.

It's a pity I didn't get to finish this little Mexican 7x57 Mauser. I have taken a lot of game with it, so have a good idea of its capabilities. I can shoot it much faster than my 338/06. I would guess I can get off 5 shots with the 7MM in the time I get off 3 shots with the 338. The recoil of the 338 accounts for that. This rifle absolutely points like a laser beam. When I was healthier, and active, a mob of pigs was in mortal danger if they got anywhere near me and this rifle, down to the last pig. I still have it in the cupboard, and when I get away again it will be coming along too.

CHAPTER EIGHT

TELESCOPIC SIGHT MOUNTING

Correct telescopic sight mounting is an important part of the over all accuracy equation, and should not be ignored. Basically, what we want is to have the scope mounted on the rifle, in a totally stress free condition, with its adjustments in the optical centre of the instrument. That is not necessarily in the centre of their travel.

If you think that is easy to achieve you are dead wrong. In most cases it will be virtually impossible to achieve, unless you are willing to expend an inordinate amount of money, and time, to make it happen. For most of us, me included, that is not feasible, and so we have to settle for the best we can reasonably do.

You have to be aware of something before we start, and that is, the thin aluminum, or steel, tubes these instruments are made from are extremely easily displaced (read: bent). They are fragile - don't forget it. The high powered variables, we use these days, do not like to be operated in any condition that is not totally stress free, and that condition is not achieved without a deal of effort. (*Crikey — is anything not easily bent!*)

What I'll do here is detail the steps I take in mounting my own telescopic sights, with a few observations along the way.

To check that our adjustments are set at the optical centre of the scope, and correct them if they are not, you need a couple of V blocks. If you don't have V blocks you can get by with a stiff narrow cardboard box with a couple of Vs cut in it. Photos 8-1, 8-2, and 8-3 (Page 302) show the setup. You can do this at home, but you need to set it up so you can sight on something at least 100 yards away. The insulator on an electric light pole is ideal, or something like it.

I have screwed the cardboard box to a piece of wood, with a screw and washer in each corner. This adds considerable stiffness to the setup. I have also installed three wood screws under the piece of wood, to act as a tripod, and give me a way to adjust the scope reticule, to aim at a target. With a set up like this, our cardboard 'V' box is every bit as stable as regular V blocks, and will do the job without any hassles.

PHOTO 8-1.

The scope is placed in V blocks and rotated to check for an out of centre reticule. These V blocks will have to be raised on spacers to make clearance for the high adjustment turrets and allow the scope to rotate 360 degrees. Note the duct tape in the Vs to protect the fragile matte finish on the tube.

PHOTO 8-2.

If you haven't got a set of V blocks you can still do the job with a cardboard box like this.

PHOTO 8-3.

The box is reinforced with a layer of tape around it, and I have applied duct tape to the cut out Vs, to strengthen them and protect the scope finish. In use, hold the box steady and rotate the scope. This setup is as solid as regular Vs, and will do the job adequately.

Place the scope in the V blocks, steel or cardboard, and line it up on your target. If you're using steel V blocks put a piece of duct tape in the Vs so you don't scratch the scope. Now rotate the scope and observe what happens with the reticule? If the reticule is in the optical centre of the scope it will simply rotate with no displacement at all. If not it will rotate in a circular arc around the target. If this happens you have to move the adjustments until the reticule rotates on its axis. Figures 8-1 and 8-2 show what I mean.

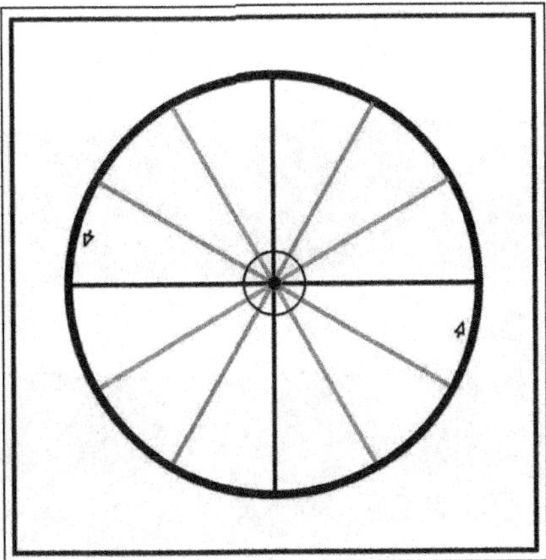

FIGURE 8-1.

The circle in the middle represents the target. The black reticule is horizontal. The green reticule is rotated 30 degrees. The red reticule is rotated 60 degrees. If the reticule is optically centred the dot will remain on target, during rotation, as it is in this drawing. The small arrows indicate the direction of rotation.

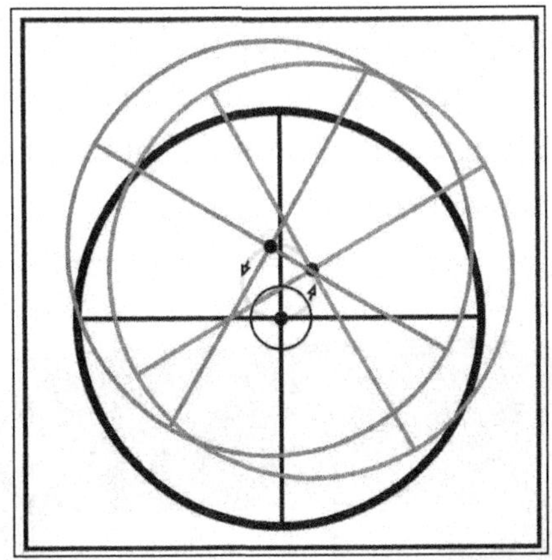

FIGURE 8-2.

Here the scope reticule is not centred. Again, the green and red reticules represent degrees of scope rotation. The yellow circle represents the track the dot will follow as the scope is rotated. It is necessary to adjust the scope adjustments until the reticule dot rotates on its axis, as in FIGURE 8-1 to centre the reticule in the optical centre of the scope.

Ok, we know how to optically centre our scope, let's talk about scope mounts.

For starters, there is no such thing as a perfect scope mount. They all suck to a degree, some more than others. If you have a bridge mount base on a hunting rifle I would dump it. All it is doing is cluttering up the ejection port, which is an area I want to be clutter free, in case I need to get at it in a hurry. It may be tolerable on a varmint or target rifle, but be aware that, as it comes out of the packet, it will not fit the action properly; more on that later. Yes, I know they say a bridge mount adds stiffness to the action. Frankly, the stiffness it adds is negligible, and the problems it can cause far out weigh any perceived benefits. Of course, their fit up is not helped by the tolerances found in the external dimensions of the receivers we have to mount them on. Stop and think about it and you will agree, that you are living in fairy land, if you think there is any chance of any scope mount base fitting the action it is intended for properly. The good news is we can do something about it and make it right.

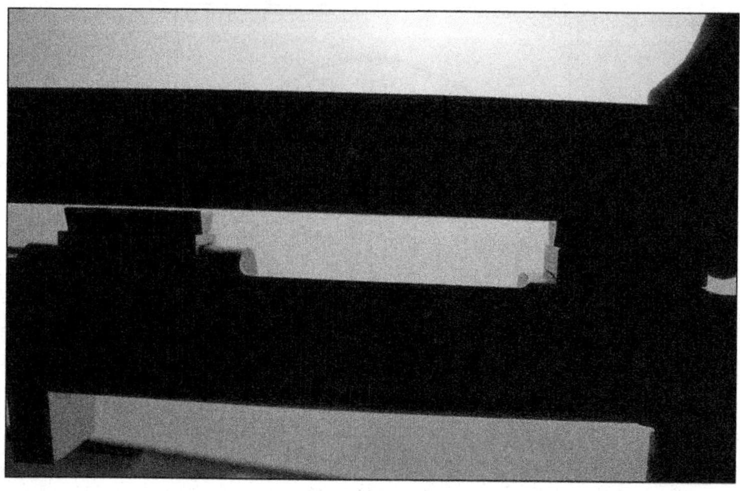

PHOTO 8-4.

The misalignment on this pair of Davidson bases fitted to my 40X can easily be seen. The front base is low.

Probably the system with the best chance of working out of the box would be that on the Kelbly Panda actions. That's a dovetail integrally machined on top of the receiver, and the scope rings are machined in one long unit, cut off in pairs right next to each other and numbered 1-2, 3-4, etc. You'd think that system would be right, straight out of the box, but think again. They still need to be lapped in to be perfectly aligned. It's a crazy world.

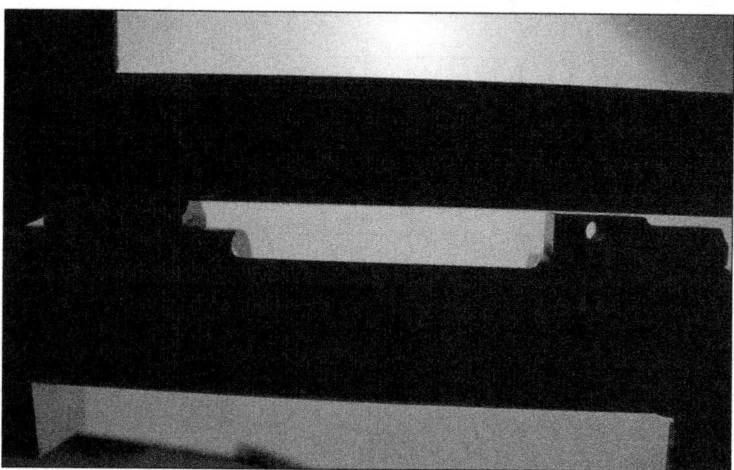

PHOTO 8-5.

The same 40X, with a pair of Leupold bases fitted. This time it is the rear base that is low. Given the tolerances found on receiver externals, it is pretty well impossible for a commercial base manufacturer to make bases that fit properly. They must be custom fitted, or custom made from scratch.

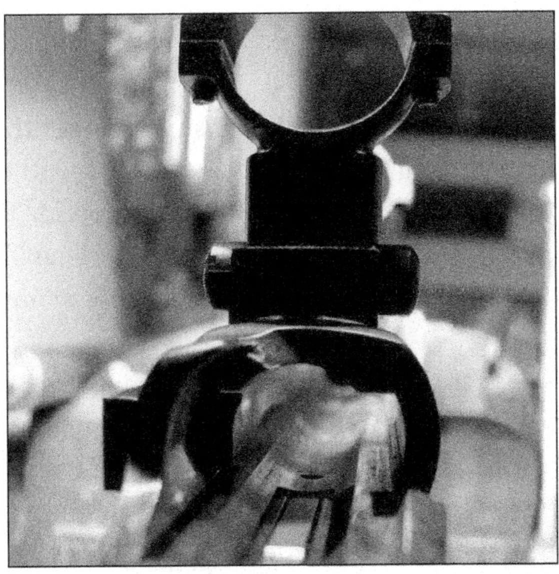

PHOTO 8-6.

As if height misalignment is not bad enough, often there is diameter mismatch to contend with as well. Here a rear base, fitted to my 40X, is not even remotely sized to fit the diameter of the rear bridge. It is sitting on two sharp edges leaving a large gap everywhere else. Set up like this it is guaranteed to shoot loose. The good news is, if it is too high it can be machined to correct the height, and diameter, and be made to fit properly. Failing that, it will be fixed when fitted as per the text.

The Panda system has its drawbacks, mainly because there is no provision to correct any windage or elevation misalignment in the system. We have already discussed the straightness of the bore in a barrel blank, and seen that ultimately the direction a projectile is heading in, when it exits the muzzle, depends on what direction the last inch of the muzzle is pointing. If that happens to be out to one side, or the other, the deviation from the centre-line of the mount system can be considerable.

When I made scope bases for the custom rifles you see in these pages, I shot the rifle to determine the line up of the bases before machining the dovetails to get the windage and elevation right. Those bases were machined on the action they were intended for.

A windage mount would seem to be the way to go, but they all suck too, some more than others. Probably the most ubiquitous windage mount design out there would be the Redfield design, with a front dovetail and two coned adjusting screws at the rear. This would appear to be a good system, but it has problems. To be effective, the front dovetail has to be tight — no looseness can be tolerated if consistent zero is to be maintained. With a tight front dovetail, when you move the rear windage screws you are only bending the scope tube to make the adjustment. There isn't a strong enough scope tube made to move that dovetail, a small amount, if it is at its proper tension. The rear ring on these mounts does little to hold the scope in place from recoil. This doesn't rear its ugly head until you use these mounts on heavy kicking rifles, from the big .338s up. On those rifles you quickly learn that the only ring pulling its weight is the front ring, and if it slips, the rear ring will pull straight through its windage adjustment screws.

These mounts need a strong front ring to hold firm with a heavy kicking rifle. The old original Redfield design with four 4–48 screws per ring was good, but the later Redfield design, and Leupold, with two 8–40 screws per ring is not good enough. If it were up to me I would make the ring half as wide again and use six 6–48 screws — with that extra bearing surface it wouldn't move then!

As for the dovetail, I had some EAW bases and rings with the Redfield design back in the late 80s. They had four screws per ring and interestingly, the cunning Germans had split the front base at the side and included a screw so that it could be tensioned. With that design the tension could be released on the dovetail for adjusting the rear windage screws, without bending the scope tube, and then retensioned once the optimum windage setting was found. That was a good system that addressed the inherent problem of the original Redfield design. Leupold and Redfield should take it on. That system would be my choice for a windage adjustable mount, though its appearance is not as pleasing.

Just be aware that there is no such thing as a perfect scope mounting system. Choose the strongest mount you can find, examine the design carefully, and work around its faults.

Windage is a bigger problem than elevation. By comparison elevation is easily adjusted. I should mention here that taking the trouble to correct elevation problems is only of concern to anyone who uses their rifle at close distance, and adjusts their telescopic sight rarely, or not at all. That would be short range bench-rest shooters and hunters. Those who indulge in long range shooting that requires often, and large, elevation adjustments need not be overly concerned, except to check that they can make zero at the longest range they will be competing in.

We've already talked about how to get our adjustments on optical centre. Don't do that yet. First we need to get in a little range time. The first job to do is to zero the rifle at the midpoint of the distance we expect to be using it. For a short range bench-rest shooter that would be 150 yards. For a hunter that would probably be 200 yards. Get a good no wind zero with at least 2 or 3, three shot groups. Having obtained a good no wind zero go home!

Now we need a good bore sighter to go further. When it is installed on, or in, the muzzle of the rifle, you need to be able to crawl around it without bumping it. There's nothing much you can do here except be ultra careful. Nothing short of making a purpose built truss to clamp on the barrel and bore sighter, and hold it securely on the end of the barrel, will be worth anything, so just be careful. Have everything you need close at hand before you begin.

I use a Leupold bore sighter, and find it to be simply amazing. How something can zero a rifle to print so close to centre, when it is only magnetically clamped onto the end of the barrel, is quite beyond my understanding. Someone really clever worked that out. One caveat, though. It only works if the muzzle is dead square to the bore. Also, it is possible to move it around to a degree on the end of the barrel and the reticule dot stays in the same place on the grid. I repeat, simply amazing! Photo 8-7 shows a trick I use to hold it a little firmer to the barrel that helps me to turn it on and off without disturbing it.

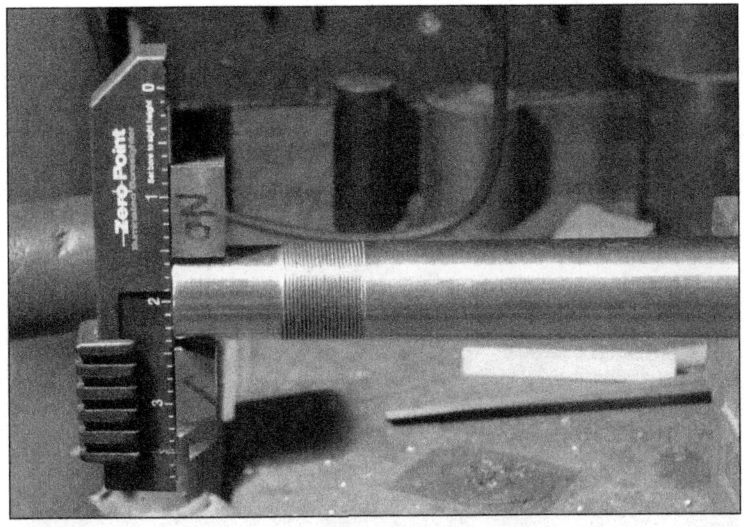

PHOTO 8-7.

Two pieces of steel magnetically clamped to the bore sighter, above and below the barrel, assist me to turn it on and off without disturbing it.

Make a drawing of the grid in your bore sighter, and mark on it where your cross-hairs reside. Remove the top halves of your scope rings, and put them aside. Now remove your scope, and centre the adjustments as we discussed at the beginning of this chapter. When you have the adjustments centred, if you can, zero the scale on them. If that's not possible stick some tape on the turret, and make a mark next to the zero on the adjustment.

Replace the scope in the rings, reinstall the top halves and check where the reticule is on the grid. In a perfect world you would not have had to move the adjustments and the reticule would have remained in place. Yeah — Tell him he's dreaming luv!

Of course, the ideal is to aim for perfection. How close you can come to that will depend on how anal you are, I guess. At the very least I think you should aim for making zero within ¼ of a turn of adjustment centre. On most scopes that will give you at least 2-3 minutes of leeway, or a bit more. Less would be better.

So how do we do that? Let's discuss elevation first.

Mount bases that screw on are the easiest to correct. Remove the top ring halves and determine which mount needs adjusting by lifting each end of the scope. The best way to determine the amount of error is to use shims cut from an aluminum beer/soft drink can. These run around .006" thick which will get you close to the mark, and they are soft enough to conform to the circumference of your receiver. Cut them as in Photo 8-8, and be sure there are no burrs present to bunch up and cause an error. Let's say you had to lift the rear of the scope to make zero. Place shims under the rear base until the reticule is on the spot. The number of shims x .006" equals the amount you have to remove from the bottom of the front mount base to bring it into line.

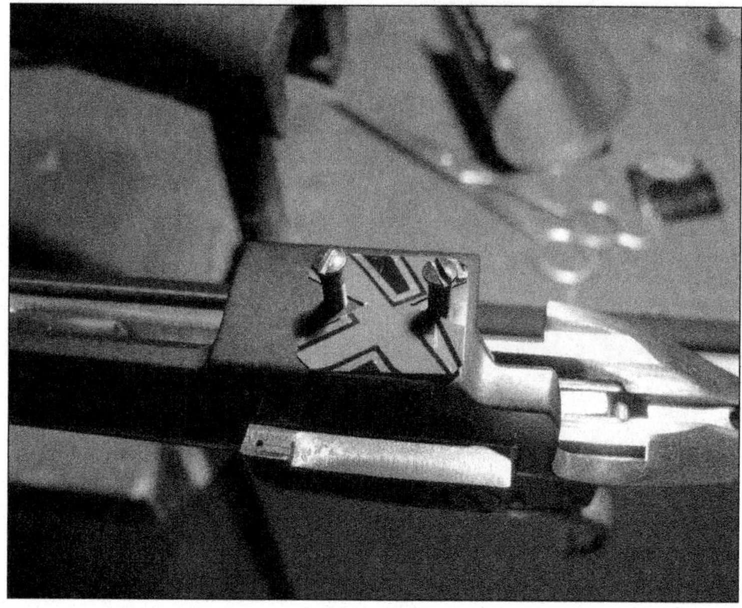

PHOTO 8-8.

This shim was cut from a Pepsi Max aluminium can (after I emptied its contents over a shot of Rum), which was .004" thick, ideal for our purpose. Cut the shims length ways from the can, and they have the right set to fit the contour of the receiver.

I do this job in my milling machine with a boring bar sized to the diameter of the action front, or rear bridge, which ever one needs to be adjusted. You can see the bar in Photo 8-9, and the setup in Photos 8-10 (Page 309), 8-11, and 8-12 (Page 310). Adjusting scope bases like this will make the top of the bases an uneven height, which you may want to take into account when you set up the base for machining to height. You will get an idea of the amount of taper needed if you lay a straight edge over the two bases, and measure the gap at the end of the packed base with feeler gauges. Don't bother getting too anal about this, as we will be compensating, when the bases are finally fitted up, by filling any mismatch with a strong epoxy pad for the bases to sit on. Further, the bases will be glued to the receiver, adding more stability and strength.

PHOTO 8-9.

The boring bar I use, in my milling machine, to make the contour on the bottom of scope bases. The measurements on the bottom of the bar remind me of the diameter of the machined portion at the end of the bar. It's simple math to work out the protrusion my cutting tool needs to make a properly sized contour. For instance the diameter of my Remington 40X rear bridge is 3.900" (pity the guy who made the mount in Photo 8-6 didn't know that!). ½ of 3.900 is 1.950. ½ of the diameter of the bar is .361. Take .361 from 1.950, and the tip of my cutting tool has to protrude 1.589" from the machined section of my boring bar to make a 3.900" diameter hole. Got that!

Locate the base straight in the mill vice, using a square piece of steel, with enough protruding from the edge of the vice to machine it to size. Find the edge with an edge finder, and wind the cross-feed to centre. Mount a dial indicator in the quill of the mill, and use it to check that the base bottom is parallel to the quill travel. Adjust it, if necessary, by tapping the base lightly into place with a soft hammer to get it straight. If you want to make a taper on the base use the dial indicator to get it right. Once you have it how you want, tighten the mill vice.

PHOTO 8-10.

Initially use a large squared spacer block to secure the mount base in the mill vice square to the quill. Do not tighten the mill vice to final tension at this stage.

PHOTO 8-11.

With a dial indicator mounted in the quill of the mill, adjust the base for zero runout, or to a predetermined taper, if that is what you need.

PHOTO 8-12.

The boring bar has been set to bore a 3.900" diameter hole to size this Remington 700 rear base. The cut is intermittent, and made using the automatic feed on the quill of the mill. The height of the base is measured with a tubing micrometer. Paint the base bottom with cutting oil prior to each cut.

I know the diameter of my boring bar so, knowing the diameter of the cut I have to make, its easy enough to work out the protrusion I need in the cutting tool to make the right diameter. It's then a simple matter to bore the base to make the correct height.

This could also be accomplished on a lathe, with a bit of extra fooling around, if you have an adjustable height tool post to get the base centred on the spindle.

Mount the scope up and check that your adjustment was correct. If not make another one and get it right. If it is right remove the scope and the mount bases.

What we are going to do, is glue the bases on the action with the scope in place, which will take care of any taper, and mismatch, of the bases to the receiver at the same time. To do this we need glue with a bit of body, especially if there is a bit of a gap, between the bases and the receiver, otherwise the glue will run away before it hardens. Obviously the glue needs to be an epoxy. Devon Plastic Steel A, JB weld, or 24 hour Araldite mixed with some atomized steel will be ok. Just as long as the glue has some body and is not thin. I would *not* use Brownell's Acraglas Gel for this job as I don't think it makes a hard enough base.

We must find a way to locate the mount base in order to ensure it is properly aligned. The way to do that is to turn the heads off some mount base screws, so that they are a slip fit in the clearance holes of the mount bases, and use them as locators. Photo 8-13 shows a screw head being turned to size, and Photo 8-14 shows the locating screws in position on the receiver.

PHOTO 8-13.

Turning a 6–48 short mount base screw head to size to act as a locator. The diameter will be close to #28 (.1405"). Don't make it too tight, as it will need a little clearance to allow the base to fit right down onto the receiver at a slight angle. That angle is, of course, caused by the height misalignment between the front and rear bases.

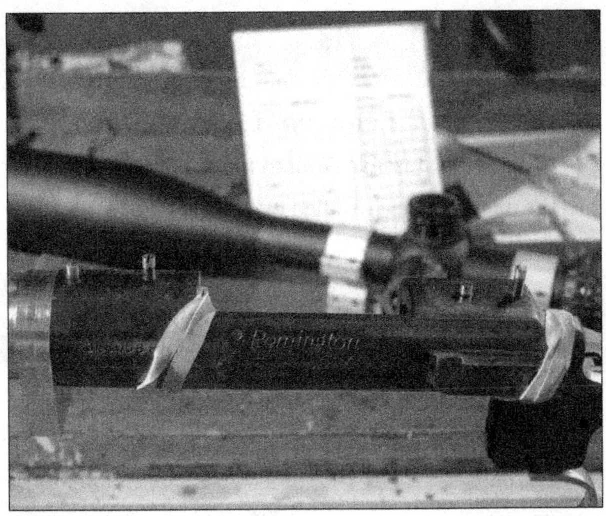

PHOTO 8-14.

The locator screws in position on my 40X Remington. The heavy duty rubber bands are also in position, for when they are needed, to hold the unit in place. They will be placed after the initial extrusion of epoxy has been removed. Another rubber band will hold the assembly in position, during initial cleanup.

When the glue has hardened, the screws will be removed through the top of the bases, the hole cleared of any intruding hardened glue, and then the original screws installed.

Install two heavy rubber bands on the receiver, positioned so that they can be placed over the bases later on. Photo 8-14 shows them in position. Test fit the assembly, and check that you can make whatever alignment adjustment you need with your bore sighter. In my instance, because I use this rifle for long range practice, I had no vertical concerns, and with my horizontal error there was enough clearance, in the mount base holes, to allow me to bring the scope into perfect horizontal zero with the adjustment centred. I am making that check in Photo 8-15 (Page 312). Note that the rubber bands are installed in place for this check.

Clean the top of the receiver and the bottom of the mount bases with alcohol. Apply release agent to the screw holes in the bases, to the threaded holes in the receiver, and to the screws. Stick the parts and receiver under your bench light to warm up a bit while you mix the glue. We've discussed the conductivity of metal, and epoxys need for heat in order to cure properly before, so you should be well aware of that by now. Photo 8-16 (Page 312) sees me releasing a screw hole.

PHOTO 8-15.

I am checking to see that it is possible to align the scope reticule to zero on the bore sighter grid with the mount bases installed over the locator screws.

PHOTO 8-16.

Applying release agent to the mount base screw holes of my 40X Remington.

You need to be nifty here. The idea is to apply enough glue to the receiver to fill all voids, and get the parts together without getting glue into the screw holes, in the receiver, or the mount base holes.

Apply a thin layer of glue to both base bottoms and the top of the receiver. I screw some long screws into the receiver so I don't get glue in the holes. Just be careful with the mount bases. Be sure to rub the glue well in—just a thin coat. When you have done that, install the locator screws in their respective holes, and then add a little extra glue to the top of the receiver, but keep it well away from the screw holes. I've done that in Photo 8-17.

PHOTO 8-17.

Devcon Plastic Steel A has been rubbed well in to the base bottoms and the receiver top, but kept well away from the screw holes. The mount base locator screws are in place ready for assembly.

Hold the scope with the mounts attached above the receiver, and guide it into place above the glue so you can engage the mount base holes, on their respective locator screws, without getting glue on them. Slide the mount bases down the locator screws to the top of the receiver. The epoxy will extrude from under the bases. At this stage it will be helpful to place a medium strength rubber band, so that it goes over the scope, and under the receiver, to hold the parts together while you clean up the excess extruded epoxy from the sides of the mount bases. Clean the excess away with a small screwdriver, and finish up with cotton buds. I'm doing that in Photo 8-18 (Page 313).

PHOTO 8-18.

The temporary rubber band is in place to hold the parts while I clean up the excess epoxy extrusion with a screwdriver, tissues, and cotton buds.

Install the heavy rubber bands over the mount bases, and remove the medium strength one. Turn the bore sighter back on and gently make the lineup, you need, to zero your scope on the bore sighter grid. A little more epoxy will extrude, so carefully clean it up, without disturbing your setup, and finish up with cotton buds dampened with alcohol. A final check to be sure the scope is pointing where you want it to be, and then bring your bench light close to the bases, for a couple of hours, to keep a bit of heat in them, while the epoxy hardens. Leave it alone for at least 24 hours. Photo 8-19, and Photos 8-20 and 8-21 refer.

PHOTO 8-19.

Making the final lineup on the bore sighter grid.

PHOTO 8-20.

Finally clean up the last bits of epoxy with cotton buds dampened with alcohol. One last check that our alignment is right, and we are sweet.

PHOTO 8-21.

To be sure the epoxy hardens properly, it is necessary to maintain a bit of heat around the scope bases. A couple of bench lights do this nicely, as will an electric bar heater placed a little distance under the receiver. We want the receiver to be warm, not hot.

After 24 hours remove the scope, mounts, and the locator screws from the bases. Select a number drill that just fits through the screw holes in the bases (usually #28 for 6–48 screws) and carefully, by hand, ream any epoxy out of the screw holes. Be careful not to bite into the threaded holes in the receiver. Clean the screw threads with alcohol, apply a drop of Locktite to them, and screw them into their holes good and tight.

All that remains is to lap the rings (more on that later), and we have taken care of our elevation and base misalignment problem (a windage and base misalignment problem in my case). The bases are glued to the receiver, but if you ever need to remove them, don't panic. Some heat applied to the bases with a good hair dryer will beak them free, without any trouble. Once removed, the same heat applied to the epoxy will allow you to peel it away from the surface it is stuck to, receiver or base, easily. Epoxy does not like heat, even not much of it.

Windage is another matter. If you are using a windage mount, such as a Redfield, or Leupold, we have already discussed how they can bend the scope tube, when you move the cone screws, to adjust windage. These mounts, and others like them are problem children compared to conventional dovetail bases, like the Davidson bases I fitted to my 40x Remington, and as such they require special handling.

You really need to get the rings, and scope, mounted on the bases with as little stress/bend as possible before you begin to work out what you need to do to bring the system into alignment. If you have the scope already mounted, and sighted in, you can bet, with confidence, that the system is well stressed before you start. If you go back to page 304, and look at Photo 8-5, you will see that the rear Leupold base is considerably low. I can't mount a scope on those bases without bending the tube down, at the back, in order to tighten the cone screws on the rear mount ring properly. It's a mish mash. When I loosen one cone screw, to make an adjustment, the scope will ride up, and when I tighten the other cone screw it will have to bend the scope back down again. If I am not careful it could even make a new groove in its mating surface, and not pull the ring down onto the base properly.

Remember, the front ring must be tight in its dovetail. If there is any looseness, or if there is not enough resistance when you rotate it into position, you should tighten it before you begin the job. Do this by lightly peening the dovetail, as in Photo 8-22. This will upset the metal slightly, and force a tighter fit into the dovetail cavity. Don't overdo it — test the fit often. You may have to dress the sides of the dovetail with a fine hand file afterwards, so it will enter the cavity in the front base. *Don't* have the scope fitted to the ring when you peen it, unless you need a new scope! Do the job with the ring secured to a scope tube sized mandrel. When attaching a new front ring, for the first time, I prefer to make a small chamfer on the leading edges of the male dovetail, with a fine needle file, and apply a bit of extra grease to both dovetail surfaces.

It is very likely that the male dovetail will shave a piece off both sides of the female dovetail if you don't do this. I know this from personal experience.

Photo 8-22.

A few light taps with a hammer around the periphery of the dovetail, front and back, of the front scope ring will tighten it in its mount base. Go carefully, and don't overdo it.

Also, be aware that the cone screws, on the rear base, are prone to upsetting the material at the edges of the mating surface, on the bottom of the rear mount ring, if they are over tightened. This prevents the ring from sitting properly, flat on the top of the base. Photo 8-23 shows this. You can peen the material lightly back into place, and then dress the surface flat with a fine hand file. Don't have the scope attached to the ring when you peen it, unless you *really* need that new scope! As before, fit it to a mandrel.

We must attend to the discrepancy in height, between the front and rear bases, so that we can make adjustments to the front ring with the rear ring not sitting up in the air, or under a lot of tension in the other direction. We do this by employing the shims I described on page 308 (Photo 8-8). Use a straight edge and place shims under the offending base until the bases are level. You won't get them perfect, so aim for a thousandth or two of an inch more height in the rear base, rather than the other way around to ensure the ring sits flat on the base.

PHOTO 8-23.

Note the upset material at the edges of the cone screw slots on this rear ring. The material can be lightly peened back into place, and then dressed flat with a fine hand file. Then, be careful not to over tighten the screws again. Fingers and 10 cent coin only.

With the bases, sort of, in line we can mount the scope in a less stress free attitude on the rifle. Install the front ring, in the front base, square with the side of the base. Use a small set square to get it in the correct position. It's best to twist it into the base with a scope tube sized mandrel. If you don't have one, a close fitting screwdriver handle will do. Install the rear ring on the scope, but leave it loose. Remove both cone screws from the rear mount base, and secure the scope *in the front ring only* with the reticule straight. Don't worry about the rear ring at this stage.

Place your bore sighter either in or on the muzzle of the rifle. Now we want to twist the front ring in its dovetail to bring the scope reticule vertical wire to the middle of the collimator grid. The best way to do that is with a spanner applied to the front ring, if it is possible to fit one between the mount base and the bottom of the scope tube, as in Photo 8-25.

PHOTO 8-24.

Adjusting the telescopic sight to zero on the Collimator with a spanner. The scope is not stressed in the mounts doing it like this. The rear windage cone screws are not installed at this stage.

PHOTO 8-25.

Protect the finish of the front ring by sticking duct tape to the jaws of the spanner. This spanner would not fit on the other side of the mount, due to interference from the adjustment housing.

For medium height, or higher bases an ordinary open ended spanner will usually fit, but for low bases you will need a thin spanner, something under 1/8" thick to fit in. a 5/8" spanner will fit Redfield rings and a 15mm spanner will fit Leupold rings. Protect the finish on the scope ring with duct tape applied to the spanner jaws. With super low rings, or rings with an extension, you will have to employ a mandrel to move the ring as discussed on page 322 (Photo 8-30).

Once the vertical wire is zeroed, fit the two cone screws to the rear base and bring them into contact with the rear ring. Keeping on eye on the collimator, tighten the cone screws, a bit at a time, so that they arrive at final tension holding the rear ring in place, with the scope vertical reticule wire zeroed in the centre of the collimator. All tightening must be done with the vertical wire centered as much as possible. By the way, these cone screws should be tightened with a 10 cent piece, not a large screwdriver. That's why they have that large round bottomed slot in them. Photo 8-26 shows me doing that. Now tighten the top half of the rear ring to final tension, and we are ready to go and sight in the rifle in preparation for adjusting the bases, as detailed, starting on page 306. The rear ring will stay in position on the scope from now on. *When you sight in the rifle do not touch the cone screws.* Do all of your adjustment with the scope adjustments only. If you move a cone screw you will stress the scope, and we just did a deal of frigging around to get our scope on the rifle as close to stress free as possible.

PHOTO 8-26.

Tightening the windage adjustment cone screws, while keeping the scope reticule centred as close as possible to the centre of the collimator grid. I am using a purpose made cone screw adjuster that will not allow me to overtighten the screws.

Having zeroed the rifle, re-mount the collimator, and note the position of the scope reticule on the grid. Make a drawing of the collimator grid and mark the position of the reticule on it, or you will forget. Make a texta mark on the left hand cone screw so you can identify its location and return it to the mark in case you inadvertently move it. Remove the right hand cone screw, and remove the top half of the front ring. Now remove the scope, leaving the front mount ring bottom half in place on the front mount base. Adjust the scope reticule to optical zero as discussed, starting on page 301. Remove the mount bases and shims, and install the locating screws I mentioned on page 311, in place, on the receiver. Sit the mount bases on the screws and reinstall the scope. Secure the rear ring in the cone screws first to locate the scope in position, and the top half of the front ring second. Keep everything as straight as possible when you do this, paying special attention that the front base is in position correctly, and not leaning over.

Now you can look through the scope at the collimator, and see what you have to do to bring the reticule into its proper elevation zero. Don't worry about windage — we are only concerned with elevation at this stage. These mount systems do not give you much to work with, if you have to remove material, from under the front base, to make elevation zero. You will not able to remove more than .020" without having the bottom of the front ring dovetail hit the top of the receiver.

PHOTO 8-27.

Spacing shims to pack the rear mount base to correct height, prior to gluing it onto the receiver, and the panel drill that cut the holes cleanly through the thin shim material.

You need a safety margin, so if you need to remove more than .015" from the front base you will have to make up the extra by packing the rear base. To do this you can make small shims from a .004" thick Pepsi Max aluminum drink can. Better would be to make them from shim brass if you have it. Cut the holes out with a panel drill like the one in Photo 8-27. Make the drill from a 9/64" twist drill. Grind it flat, and make the cutting edges with an abrasive cut off wheel on a Dremel tool. The centre point must protrude past the cutting edges. If I had, say, a .025" discrepancy, between the front and rear base, I would still take the .015" I can from the front base, and sit the rear base up .008" with 2 x .004" shims, or better, with a .010" brass shim. It's just that sitting the rear base up the full .025" won't look as nice. You will hardly see the .008"–.010" elevation, but the .025" will be very visible. Your choice of course.

Before you glue the bases on, fill the cavity around the front ring dovetail with plasticine (play Putty) like you see in Photo 8-28. Likewise fill the cavities under the rear windage screws. We will probably (read: definitely) want to move this dovetail for final zeroing, and if it is full of Devcon or whatever you are using, it won't be very co-operative. The plasticine will stay in the dovetail cavity — it will not cause any problems. When the rear windage screws are removed for final fit up, the plasticine in those cavities will be accessible, and can be removed.

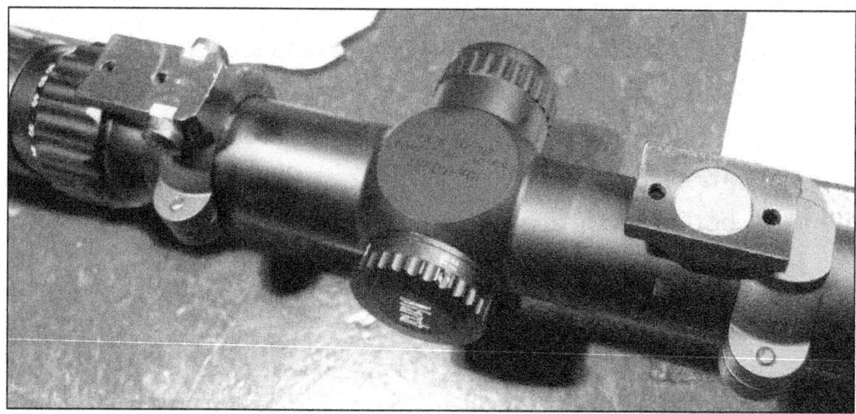

PHOTO 8-28.

Fill the cavity under the front Redfield/Leupold base, and under the rear windage screws with plasticine before gluing it onto the receiver. We don't want Devcon to fill the cavity, and lock the front ring or windage screws in place. We will want to move the front ring when we make our final windage adjustment.

If you are using an extension front ring, as I do on my .25/06 Ackley Improved varmint rifle, you will have to drill a hole in the bottom half of the ring as shown in Photo 8-29 to allow access to the front mount base screw with a screwdriver, or allen key.

PHOTO 8-29

This hole drilled in a front extension ring allows me access to the front mount base screw with a screwdriver.

Square the ring bottom on the base, and locate the hole by drilling through the base from the bottom with a #28 drill, then remove the ring bottom and open up the drilled hole with a #4 drill, or whatever size will give clearance to the head of the screws you are using. Elongate the hole .020" or so on the sides to allow the ring to be rotated slightly when you are adjusting it, and still provide clearance for the screw head and screwdriver. Finally, recheck that you still have enough clearance to install the front screw, with the scope windage zeroed, before you glue it in place.

Glue the bases onto the receiver as we did starting on page 311, and when the glue has set, remove the right hand cone screw, front ring top half, and scope. Replace the mount base screws, as detailed on page 315, and replace the scope, right hand cone screw first, followed by the front ring top half. Remove both cone screws and bring your windage to the zero you obtained earlier, at the range, on your collimator, using the spanner, as we did before. If you are unable to fit a spanner in you will have to use a mandrill, and do it by stages, which will take some extra time and effort, as detailed below. Finally, re-install the cone screws in the rear base, keeping the reticule as close as possible to zero, on the collimator, as you bring them to correct tension, and your scope is mounted as close to stress free as possible with the reticule optically centred. *The cone screws will not be moved again*—all future sighting in adjustments will be made with the scope adjustments only.

If you cannot fit a spanner under the front ring, then you will have to make your initial, and final adjustment by stages, using a scope tube sized mandrel, which is a bit of a pain, to say the least. It's simply a case of trial and error. The idea, is to arrive at windage zero with the scope tightened in the front ring only. All twisting of the front ring, on its dovetail, should be done with the mandrel, not the scope. It will help to rig a dial indicator, on the action, so you can measure the amount you move the front ring, and correlate that with the distance the reticule moves on the grid of the bore sighter. That way you will find your windage zero reasonably quickly. The job goes exactly as before, except it's a bit more long winded getting the front ring properly lined up. See Photo 8-30.

PHOTO 8-30.

Making an adjustment to a Redfield design windage mount. The Leupold bore sighter can be seen on the end of the barrel. The magnetic base is clamped onto the front receiver ring, and is supported to prevent it rotating, as it does not have the power to stay put in this situation. The dial indicator probe is located at the rear base. There is about .010" of flex to consider when making this adjustment, though the mandrel will return to centre within a thousandth or two consistently.

When zero has been found, install the rear ring on the scope, but not tight. Bring the two coned windage screws carefully into contact with their grooves, and tighten them up enough to locate the rear ring properly on the base. Now tighten the ring onto the scope with final screw tension. Back out the two windage screws and check that your windage zero is still ok on the bore sighter, and if so, keeping an eye on the grid, tighten the two windage screws to final tension, with the reticule on zero.

Remove the scope, lap the rings (yes, we'll get to that) and the job is complete.

If you have a non windage mount your options are very limited. Basically all you can do, apart from having custom bases made, that will compensate for the discrepancy, is mix and match components and see what result you get. If you can, try reversing the bases or the rings. There may be excessive clearance in the base screw holes, so tighten the base with it twisted to one side and see what effect that has on the bore sighter grid. The bases on my 40x could be moved 1.750moa by doing this. Try reversing the rings one at a time, and then both together. Try another set of rings.

In the end it will depend on how anal you are prepared to be to get this right. However far you go with it, your scope will work better if its windage adjustments are close to centre. The closer the better. If you have to have custom bases made, don't expect them to cost the same as factory bases. Making properly fitted and aligned bases is expensive.

When I did this for the custom rifles I built, the first step was to fit the blocks to the receiver. The receiver was then held in a jig, in the milling machine, and a single cut taken, that went down the side of each base. I used a special set of scope rings, that located on the machined surface, and fired the rifle at 100 yards on target. The impact deviation was noted, the amount of offset needed calculated, and the mill vice was rotated, to compensate, before taking another cut along the side of the bases. Firing the rifle at 100 yards, again, confirmed the correctness of the alignment, and if it was right I then completed the machining work to create the bases. It is quite time consuming, *and little appreciated.* You can see them in Photos 8-31, 8-32, and 8-33. Partially made blanks in Photo 8-31, and finished, in the white, bases in Photos 8-32 and 8-33.

PHOTO 8-31.
Custom Scope bases in varying stages of manufacture.

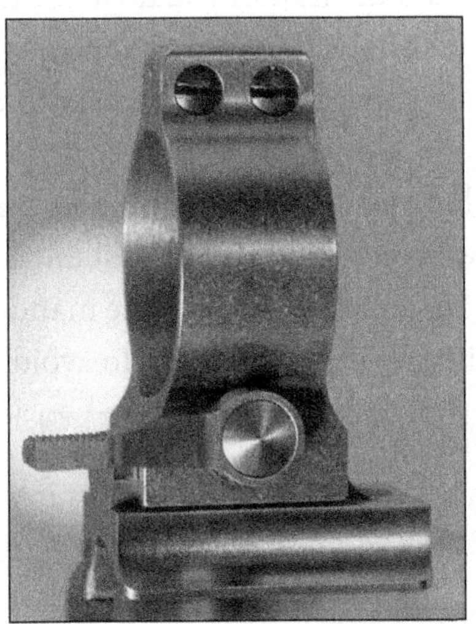

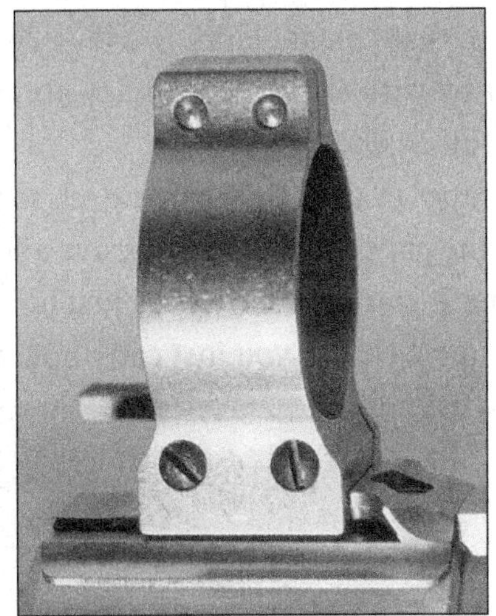

PHOTOS 8-32 AND 8-33.
Custom scope mount bases like these are very time consuming to make, so don't expect them to be cheap. These are on an M'98 Mauser, the rear base on the left, and the front base on the right.

With our scope bases and mounts lined up, as good as we can get them, it is time to attend to the last bit of stress inducing misalignment in the system, and we do that by lapping in the scope rings. Which ever way you do this job it's messy so you will have to take precautions to protect your barreled action from grit and/or abrasive dust. I tape newspaper over the whole works and jerks, as you will see in the following photographs.

There are kits that you can purchase, or if you have the facilities you can make your own lapping bar. Basically all the process involves is applying an abrasive to the bottom halves of the scope rings, via a straight, correctly sized, mandrel until the surfaces of both ring halves are aligned with each other. Their alignment is evident by the witness marks the lapping abrasive leaves behind. You can accomplish this by hand, or if your lapping bar will accept it, with a power source such as a battery drill set on slow. Really, you shouldn't need a battery drill.

The idea is to move the lapping bar so that it rotates, and moves back and forth, to create a cross-hatched pattern in the ring halves. If you are using lapping paste, 320 grit is as fine as you need to go. *We don't want a shiny (and slippery) surface in the rings.* 320 grit will make a perfect gripping surface that won't harm the scope tube. I have found no need to use coarser grits than 320, but then I may not have run into severe enough misalignment to warrant moving to something like 180 grit. If you do run into that, perhaps you should be attending to the alignment of the scope mount bases, as detailed a ways back.

Be aware that scope rings will not stand a lot of lapping. It is a process that should be used to correct the last few tenths of a thousandth of misalignment, after the major problem has been cured at its source, namely the scope bases.

The mandrel, to use with lapping paste, will be the same size as your scope tube, or a thousandth or two larger. The problem with this system is, if you are doing several scope setups, the mandrel doesn't stay at correct diameter for very long. Friends were borrowing my mandrels, so they received a deal of work, and when they wore down I did something different. I turned them undersize to accept sticky backed aluminum oxide abrasive paper, and that is what I use now. If you do it like this you need to use sticky back paper so that you are lapping a true circular hole. If you can't source sticky back abrasive paper, you can get by with sticking ordinary abrasive paper to the mandrel with shearers adhesive. You can see that stuff in Photo 8-34.

You want the paper to stick to the mandrel, so that you can lap a true circle, but you also want to be able to remove the paper. Shearer's adhesive allows you to do this without any hassles, as does the sticky backed paper. If you lap the rings by just holding abrasive paper to the mandrel you will lap the rings to an oval shape, because you just can't hold the paper tight enough to avoid that happening.

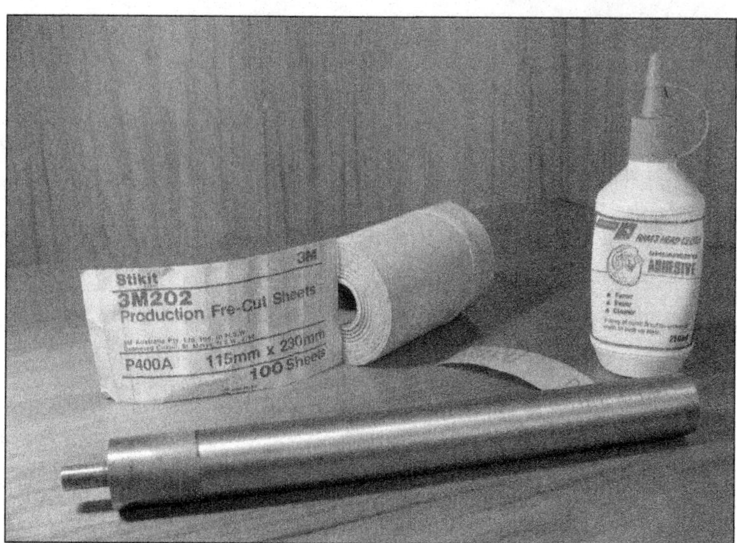

PHOTO 8-34.

The aluminium oxide sticky back paper, I use on my lapping mandrel, and a bottle of shearers adhesive, that can be used with ordinary abrasive paper, to secure it to the mandrel.

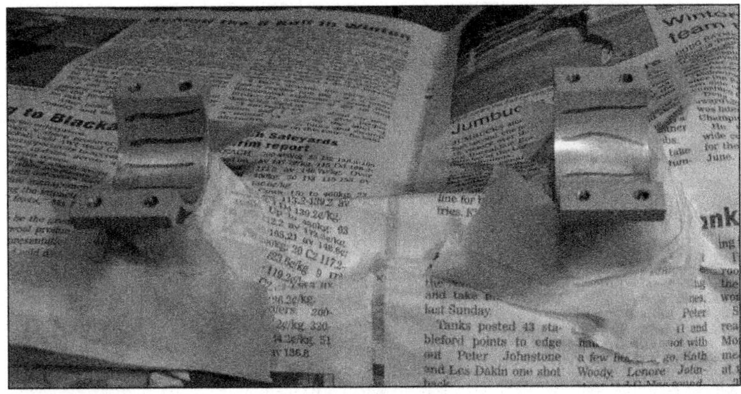

PHOTO 8-35.

I have marked the Kelbly rings I am about to lap with texta to better see my progress.

If you can't source either of the above, you can stick the abrasive paper to the mandrel with a thin strip of contact adhesive on each end. Apply the first end, and let it dry before applying the second. Pull the abrasive paper good and tight around the mandrel when you stick the other end. This works ok, and is the method I used in the accompanying photos, so you can see that it works. Get a sharp Exacto knife under the adhesive and it will come right off. You must have the abrasive paper held positively to the mandrel, or you will not lap a true circle. You can see this in Photo 8-36.

PHOTO 8-36.

The action has been covered in paper to prevent abrasive dust from getting all over it. I have glued 320 grit abrasive paper to the mandrel with contact adhesive along the butting edges only. This holds the paper good and tight to the mandrel.

When you size the mandrel make it a thousandth or two over the diameter of your scope tube with the attached abrasive paper. This will make no difference to the clamping ability of your mounts, but will allow you to rotate the scope to straighten the reticule. If you size it exactly, or heaven forbid .001" smaller, you will have great difficulty rotating the scope.

It's simply a matter of rotating the lap, while moving it back and forth in the bottom of the rings, while keeping it straight, thereby creating a cross-hatched finish. Check your progress now and then, and stop as soon as the witness marks in the bottom of the rings indicate the job is done. Photo 8-37 refers.

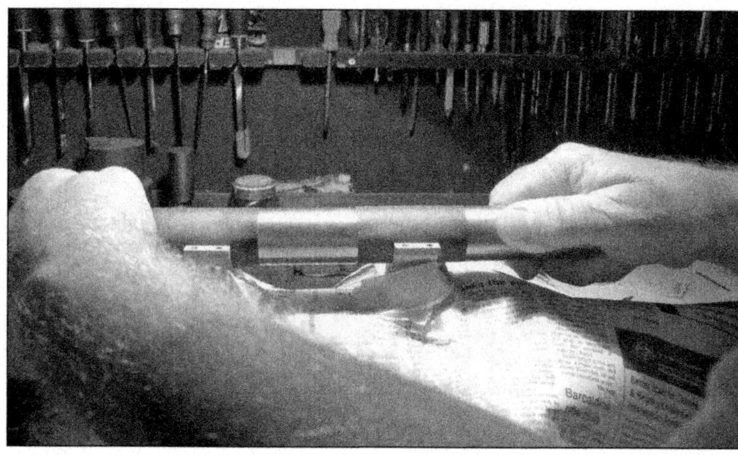

PHOTO 8-37.

When lapping the rings keep an even pressure on the front and back of the mandrel. Rotate the mandrel about ¼ of a turn with each stroke, each turn in a different direction with each stoke, to create the cross-hatched surface. These rings were lapped in with only 5 strokes of the mandrel.

Clean everything up, and it is time to mount the scope for the final time. Photo 8-38 shows the cross-hatch pattern you will achieve by lapping as described.

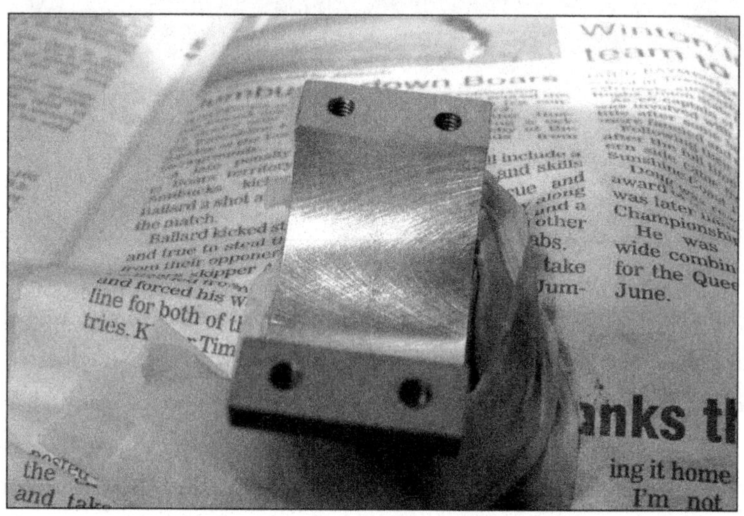

PHOTO 8-38.

This is the cross-hatch pattern you will lap into the rings. It will provide a firm grip on the scope precluding the need to tighten the rings excessively.

This final job, too, requires a bit of attention. It's important that the vertical wire in the reticule should, if extended, run through the centre of the bolt hole in the receiver. When you mount the rifle, or set it up in sand bags, your eye will automatically level the horizontal wire, and it being at 90° to the vertical wire, will mean the rifle is being held without any zero compromising cant. This is especially important for long range shooters, as even a small amount of cant can cause a considerable sighting error at long distance.

The best way I have found to do this is to level the horizontal wire parallel with the bolt raceway in my two lugged actions. I do this by placing a small spirit level in the back of the bolt raceway of the receiver, and a 3 foot spirit level, usually suspended on a fence, leveled at least 60 yards from the rifle. I level the one in the receiver using the adjustable feet on my rest, and aim the reticule at the distant level. Now it's simply a matter of lining up the horizontal wire with the top of the distant spirit level, and tightening the scope rings, keeping the horizontal wire lined up. If the horizontal wire is lined up, so is the vertical wire. Photo 8-39 shows the spirit level in place on the locking lugs of the receiver.

PHOTO 8-39.

A small spirit level placed across the bolt lug raceways allows me to make the rifle level. Then it is a simple matter to line up the horizontal reticule wire with a leveled 3 foot spirit level hanging on my back fence, 60 meters away.

You could also do this job with the vertical wire lined up on a builders plumb bob, and that would be ok. It wouldn't work where I live, as the wind would have it swinging like a metronome. We don't get many calm days here.

If you have a 3 or 4 lugged action you will have to find a similar flat surface to level the receiver with. Perhaps the top of a scope base, if it is a round top receiver, or the receiver itself if it is octagonal.

Once that job is done it's time for another Rum and Pepsi Max (substitute your personal poison), and be happy you've made another contribution in creating an accurate rifle.

PHOTO 8-40.

Lyn with a Dingo taken on the Birdsville Track in 1981, using a .25/222 Magnum I put together for my son, using the Shilen DGA action we aligned in Chapter 1.

PHOTO 8-41.

Lyn sighting my .25/06 Ackley Improved, sometime in the mid 1970s. This rifle and scope was a typical varmint rifle of its time. The telescopic sight was a Unertl, with a 14X eyepiece. You can see the scope block still on the barrel from when I was using a long Unertl scope on it, in the same power. It was built on a long Remington Action. The barrel was a Shilen 5A stainless steel. I figured out how to use a 100 watt Halogen globe in my spotlight, that allowed me to use the 14X scope, but it would have cost, at the time, $65.00 to produce them. I didn't think anyone would pay $65.00 for a spotlight. More fool me. Nowadays they pay over $1200.00!

A REMINGTON MODEL 700 IN 5.6X50 RWS

BUILT IN THE MID 1980S

PHOTO C5-1.

The stick was a piece of Australian English Walnut. My wife, Lyn, created the engine turning on the bolt body for me.

PHOTO C5-2.

The bolt knob checkering was a four panel teardrop with ribbons design. The trigger was a tuned Remington.

PHOTO C5-3.

Phil Vinnicombe's exquisite engraving.

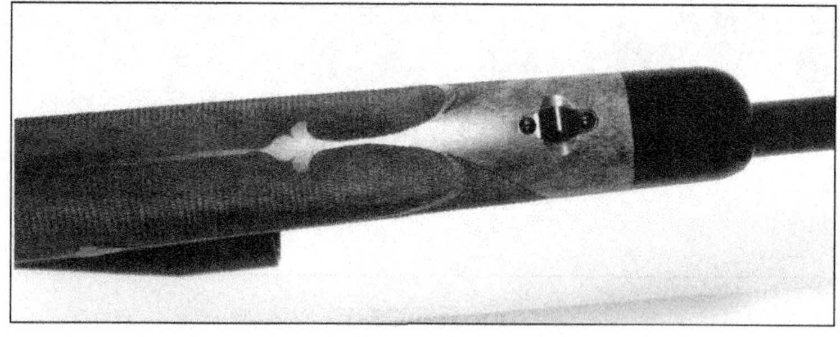

PHOTO C5-4.

The front sling swivel base was a two screw oval inletted design.

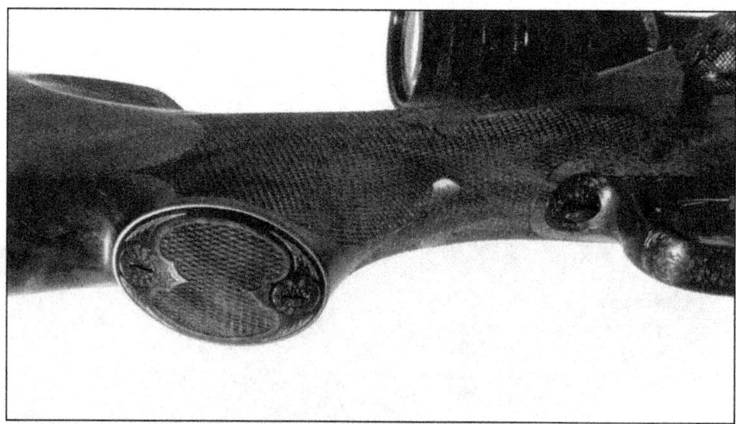

PHOTO C5-5.

Scalloped skeleton grip cap with in panel checkering. Note rear screw slot facing North/South.

PHOTO C5-6.

I fitted these Ruger bolt stops to all of the Remington Model 700s I built in order to break up the slab sided look of the left hand side of the stock at the rear of the action. Of note is the absence of the original recoil lug, an integral one having been fitted. The action has been fully accurised, and the receiver externals profiled.

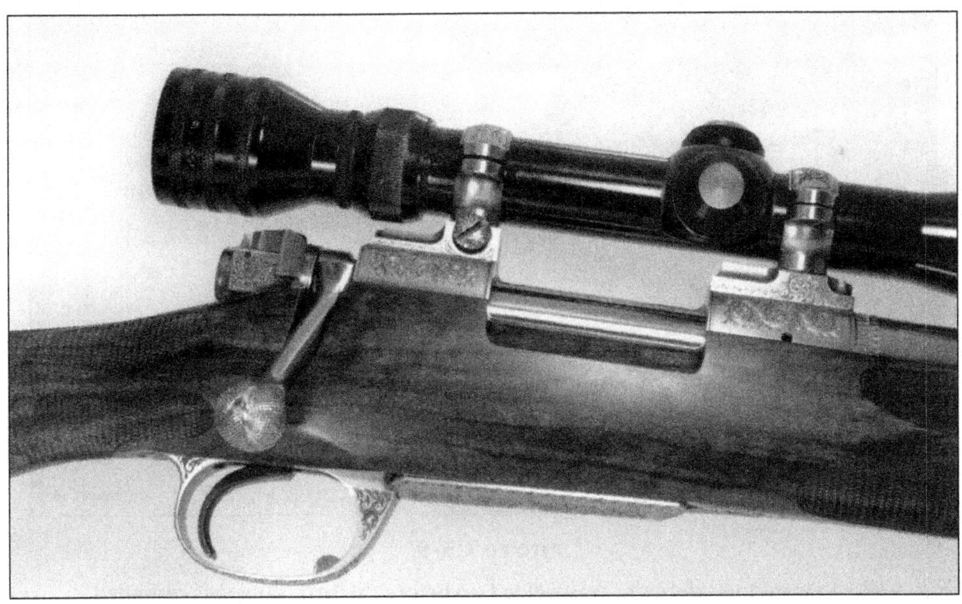

PHOTO C5-7.

Three position M'70 style safety. The telescopic sight mount bases are custom made to fit the action properly. Lyn will not engine turn the bolt until it has been blued.

PHOTO C5-8.
Of interest here is the reshaping of the rear tang so that it blends nicely into the top line of the grip.

PHOTO C5-9.
The Remington safety slot was welded up before the rear Tang was reshaped.

CHAPTER NINE

JAM & TOUCH

Jam and Touch! Sounds like a couple of Miami Vice Cops. These are terms that shooters use that you should be familiar with, but not fixated on. So what are they?

Touch is the point in the barrel where the projectile is just resting against the rifling lands. If you slide a projectile into the chamber point first until it stops at the end of the chamber, just resting against the leade of the rifling, it is said to be in Touch or Touching.

Jam comes in two flavors — Raspberry and Strawberry. Just kidding! Any projectile that is forced into the rifling past the Touch point is said to be Jammed.

Full Jam is the *maximum length* a projectile can be seated out of a case without being pushed back into the case when chambered. The projectile is, thus, jammed into the rifling as far as it can physically go.

Essentially, Jam and Touch are parameters — jump off points as it were, that are useful to know when we begin to tune a rifle. Bullet seating depth is the main fine tuning tool we have to successfully tune a barrel, so it is handy to have a measurement to start from. Sort of narrow things down a bit, so we can expend less useless shots arriving at the result we want.

To do this we need to be able to initially measure these parameters with a reasonable degree of accuracy. There are many tools on the market designed to measure Touch, but I have never felt the need for them. I already have something, I use regularly, that is perfectly adequate for the job. I am talking about a cleaning rod. I will go though the procedure of finding Jam and Touch measurements, and then discuss the pit falls you need to be aware of.

The tools we will need are as follows:-

1. A cleaning rod in your calibre.
2. A screw on end that has a flat surface to fit your cleaning rod. This can usually be made from an old brush ferrule.
3. A dial caliper or a digital caliper.
4. Some good sticky masking tape.
5. A wood chisel or a sharp pencil, your choice.
6. The throat and leade tool you made when you first chambered the barrel.
7. A projectile — obviously of the exact type you will be using.

8. If available, a micrometer depth gauge.

If we follow the correct sequence of steps we will arrive at the measurements, we are looking for, using the same projectile. I do it like this.

Before you take these measurements it is important that the surface of the barrel in the throat and leade be chemically clean, especially if the barrel has been used, even for only 20 shots. The smallest film of carbon fouling will compromise your measurement, so before I make these measurements, I clean the bore with JB Non Imbedding Bore Cleaning Compound to remove any accumulated carbon. More on that subject a bit later.

1. Remove the extractor (if you can) and the ejector from the bolt (if it has one).

2. Screw the flat surfaced end onto your cleaning rod. Photo 9-1 shows the one I use for .270 calibre up to .30 calibre.

PHOTO 9-1.

The flat end on my cleaning rod is made from an old brush ferrule with a flattened screw inserted in the end. The screw was necessary because this ferrule had a through hole in it. The ferrule I use for .22/6MM calibre had a blind hole, so I only needed to face the end off square to make it work.

3. Take one of the projectiles you will be using, drop it point first into the chamber and push it in with a cleaning rod, (I use a short pistol rod) until it engages the rifling. You don't need much forward pressure here, just a little bit. See Photo 9-2.

PHOTO 9-2.

Here I am pushing the projectile to just stick in the rifling lands. Very little pressure is needed.

4. Insert the cleaning rod, with the flat ferrule on the end, into the muzzle, and run it right down the barrel, carefully, until it touches the tip of the projectile you inserted in the throat of the chamber.

   4.1. You will feel the rod bump the projectile when you reach it.

   4.2. If you knock the projectile back from the lands don't worry. Simply reinsert it and try again.

   4.3. You can get pretty aggressive pushing the projectile into the lands without making much headway. *Don't do that.* We want the projectile to be barely held in the leade of the chamber. Just stuck, not engaged.

5. Cut a couple of strips of masking tape about 1" long and ¼" wide, and stick one of them on the cleaning rod. Position it so that it is half in the muzzle, and half out, with the ferrule on the rod resting against the tip of the projectile. See Photo 9-3.

PHOTO 9-3.
The rod has been withdrawn from the tip of the projectile and a piece of sticky masking tape installed.

6. I use a straight steel (not covered with plastic) cleaning rod for this job. Now I take a flat 1" wood chisel and lay the flat back against the flat end of the muzzle, and with the cleaning rod held against the projectile tip, rotate the rod against the chisel thus cutting the masking tape. I then remove the piece of tape that is inside the muzzle, and mark the end of the tape, with a pen, so that I don't forget which end it was. See Photos 9-4 and 9-5.

6.1. You have to be careful to hold the chisel dead flat against the muzzle and the cleaning rod against the projectile while you cut the tape.

6.2. If you have a plastic covered cleaning rod it would probably be best to use a sharp pencil instead of a chisel to mark, rather than cut the tape. Try to mark the tape right at the mouth of the crown. You will be doing this twice, so however you do it, do it the same way each time.

7. Give the projectile a little bump with the cleaning rod to knock it out of the bore, and remove it from the barrel. It won't take much of a bump to loosen it, as it should not be tight to start with.

8. Insert the bolt in the action in the cocked position.

9. Run the cleaning rod into the barrel until it stops against the bolt face.

10. Stick the second piece of masking tape on the barrel, like we did before, half in the muzzle and half out.

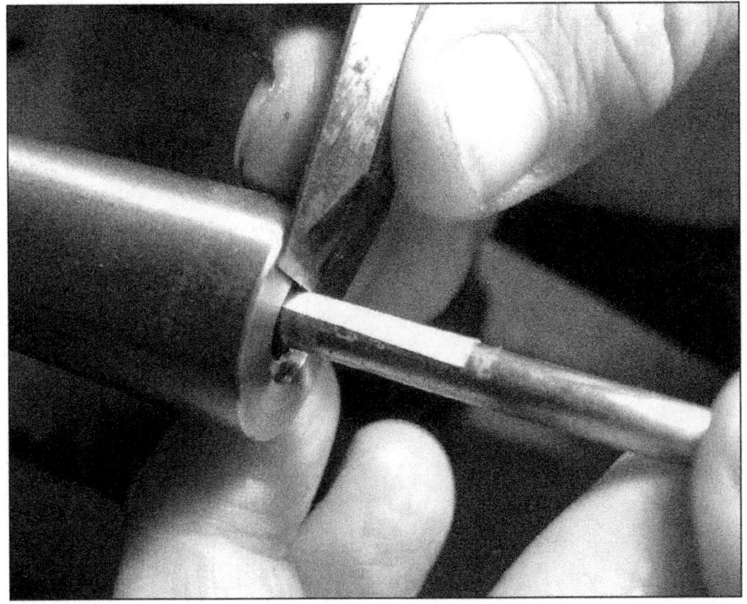

PHOTO 9-4.
Cutting the tape with a chisel. The rod is held against the tip of the projectile, and the chisel flat against the muzzle.

PHOTO 9-5.
The tape has been cut and marked. I have peeled it halfway off here.

11. Repeat step 6. Now we have two pieces of tape with two marks on the cleaning rod.

12. Back the cleaning rod out of the bore, and with your caliper, measure the distance between the ends of the two pieces of tape, with the two marks, on the rod. Write that measurement down. Photo 9-6 shows this.

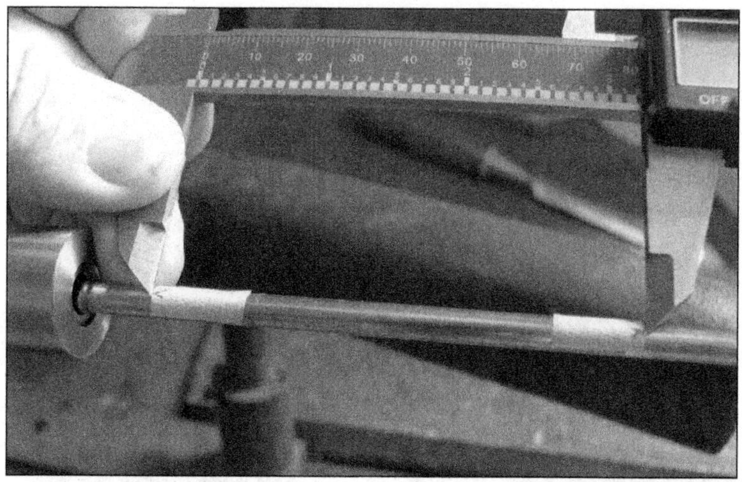

PHOTO 9-6.

Taking the measurement from each end of the tape.

12.1. The measurement, we have made, is the length from the bolt face to the end of the projectile, when the projectile is just touching the rifling lands or leade. In other words it is the overall length we should make a cartridge, loaded with *that particular individual projectile*, if we want it to touch the rifling lands, measured from the base of the cartridge case to the tip of the projectile.

12.2. The measurement will be more than accurate enough for this purpose.

12.3. If you want to use another projectile, weight or shape, you will have to re-measure to get the length for that individual projectile.

12.4. Projectiles vary considerably in length, sometimes as much as .10" or more. Therefore, this measurement is *not* one we can rely on to use, in measuring seating depth, with any other projectile, even from the same box — let's move on.

13. Take the throat and leade tool you made earlier (on page 87), and insert the projectile you used, to make the measurement, in the correct end. Push it in until it stops against the leade, that was cut by the reamer, that cut the leade in your barrel.

14. Now, with the micrometer depth gauge (or your caliper) measure the distance from the top of the gauge to the tip of the projectile. Photo 9-7 refers.

PHOTO 9-7.

Measuring the distance from the top of my throat and leade tool to the tip of my projectile.

15. Add the measurement, we obtained in step 14, to the measurement we obtained in step 12, and we have a measurement we can use to set up a bullet seating die, *with any projectile of the same make, weight, and shape as the projectile we used to make the initial measurement.* In other words, any projectile from the same box, or same batch, the projectile we made that measurement came from.

15.1. This works because we are now measuring the overall length, *using the tool*, from the ogive of the projectile, where it contacts the leade of the rifling. This is the point on the projectile that is critical, and must be repeatable, *even if it varies a little bit in length to the tip or to the base.* We want all of our projectiles to be seated the same length into the bore *relative to the ogives contact point with the leade.*

15.2. With that in mind, all of my records list overall length measurements as *'X.XXX" with tool'* to indicate that I have used the tool to obtain the initial measurement. Lest we forget!

Touch measurement is very repeatable. If you were to make the measurement ten times (using the same projectile, of course) you will obtain measurements within a thousandth of an inch or two — more than accurate enough for our purpose. Jam, however, is something else again, and we should discuss it a little further before we measure it.

There are several factors that affect how far a projectile can be jammed into the leade of a chamber, some of which preclude ever being able to obtain a truly repeatable measurement, when finding maximum Jam length. They are as follows:

1. Lubricity of the bore.
2. Lubricity of the individual case neck.
3. Lubricity of the individual projectile.
4. Individual case neck hardness.
5. Individual case neck tension.

These factors are all constant variables. In other words they are never *exactly* the same from cartridge case to cartridge case. That property precludes truly repeatable measurements, but, in the end, that doesn't matter. Remember, *we don't need to be fixated on this measurement*; it is only a jump off point.

I do not think it is a good idea to use maximum Jam length as a reference point, because of these variables. If you were to make the measurement using 5 different cases, and five different projectiles, you would end up with 5 different maximum Jam measurements. For reference I much prefer to use Touch, as I can repeat that measurement to within .001" easily — more on that later.

We need to consider a few things before we start. If the bore has any oil in it, or we apply lubricant to the projectile, the projectile will be jammed considerably further into the bore than it would if the bore is lubricant free. *We should avoid this,* or we will be testing many overall lengths, that will never be achieved in the real world, where the barrel and projectile are not lubricated. This will avoid wasting ammunition and barrel life.

Case neck tension has a direct bearing on how far the projectile will be jammed into the rifling. The more tension you size the case necks with, the further the projectile will jam into the rifling.

Case neck hardness also has a direct bearing on maximum Jam length, much the same way as case neck tension has. Probably the best thing to do here is to anneal the case necks after you have finished all of your case preparation (neck turning etc), which is what I do. Just be aware that maximum Jam will be much deeper with a work hardened sized neck than it will be with a newly annealed sized neck.

Jam length is best measured after the new barrel has fired twenty or more shots, to round off the sharp edges in the leade left by the throating reamer. That is also when you should take another Touch measurement, as it will likely be a little bit longer than the initial measurement you made on the new un-fired chamber. You have to make a Touch measurement with the un-fired barrel, so that you can determine a suitable bullet seating depth for your initial testing. This will be mainly focused on working up a suitable powder load to produce the velocity you are looking for. During this phase of tuning, bullet seating depth is important, only in that, best practice dictates that the projectile be seated into the rifling lands. This is needed to hold the case firmly against the bolt face for the initial fire forming load. You can't do that unless you know exactly where the projectile engages the rifling lands.

Let's assume that you have fired those twenty or so shots, found a suitable powder load/velocity/accuracy combination, and now want to find your starting point Jam and Touch measurements.

Before starting be sure that the barrel is clean and dry! I have already described how to make your Touch measurement, so select a projectile the same as the ones you intend to use, and make that measurement as described previously. (Page 333)

With that measurement in hand, you must now prepare a cartridge case exactly the way you would if you were going to reload it. For me that would be:–

1. Full length size the case.
2. Run a nylon brush through the neck of the case.
3. Neck size the case using the smallest neck sizing bush I am likely to use to give me the tightest neck, and therefore longest Jam.
4. With that case in hand let's find our maximum Jam measurement.

1. Seat the projectile you used when you found your Touch measurement, just a while ago, in the case you prepared, to that Touch measurement plus .050". See Photo 9-8.

1.1. You are very unlikely to want to (let alone be able to) Jam a projectile more than .050". Seating the projectile longer is superfluous and will only make it harder to close the bolt.

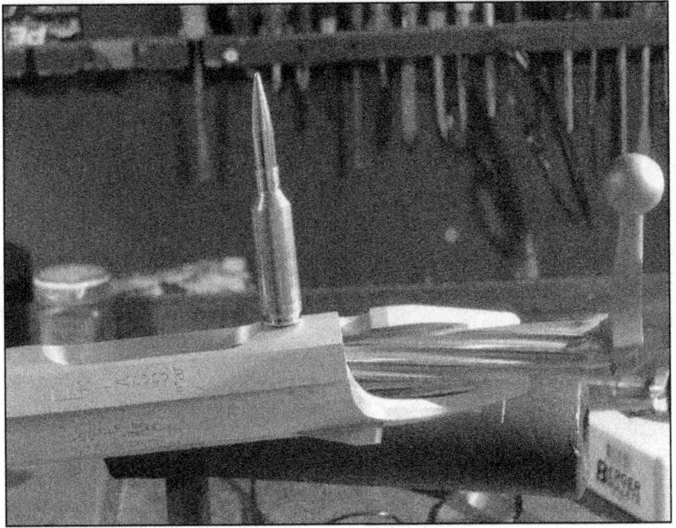

PHOTO 9-8.
This dummy cartridge has been prepared as per the text.

2. Place the case with seated projectile in the chamber and carefully try to close the bolt.

2.1. The firing pin assembly, ejector, and extractor must be removed from the bolt for this measurement. You must be able to feel what is happening.

2.2. What you want here, is to feel the bolt ride down on the closing cams, in the receiver, so that it ends up with no forward movement when closed. That is, the cartridge case is held firmly against the bolt face by the projectile that is engaged (Jammed) in the rifling lands.

2.3. If you cannot engage the closing cam on the action, get a soft hammer and tap lightly on the back of the bolt, with a bit of down pressure on the bolt handle, until you can feel the cams engage. Then finish the downward stroke *without* using the soft hammer.

3. If you do not have an extractor in the bolt, remove the bolt from the action. If you have a non removable extractor, go to step 5.

4. Place your cleaning rod in the muzzle and lightly tap on the end of the projectile to remove the case with its projectile from the barrel.

4.1. *This will not work if you are using a case that is tight to chamber.* Common sense dictates that you use a case that is easily removed from the chamber — that is a properly full length sized case.

5. For those of you with non removable extractors:–

5.1. Lift the bolt, only until it just touches the extraction cam. See Photo 9-9.

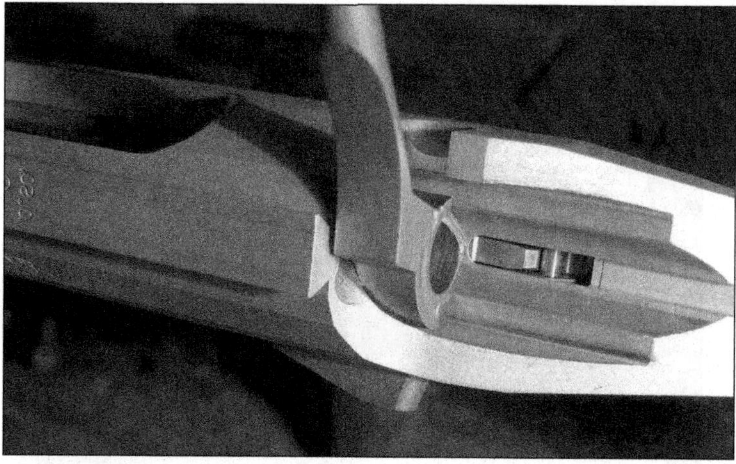

PHOTO 9-9.

The bolt on this Panda action is just resting against the extraction cam.

5.1.1. The extraction cam is usually located near the top of the bolt stroke, and is engaged by the root of the bolt handle. See Photo 9-10.

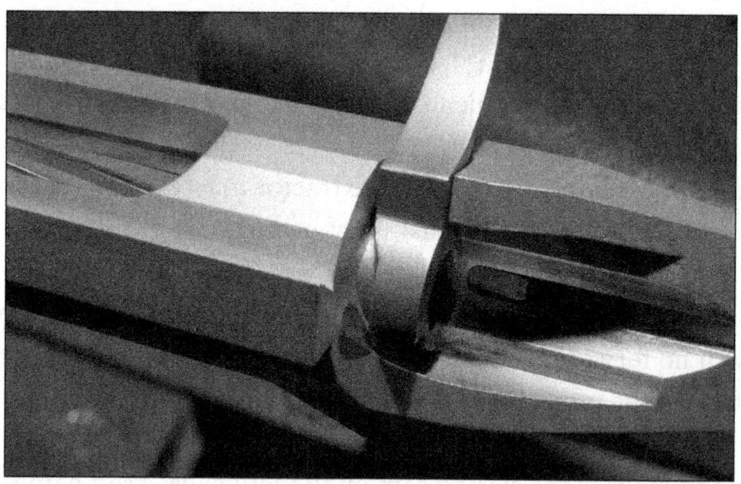

PHOTO 9-10.

The extraction cam can be easily seen on the bolt handle here. It will engage the steel disc inletted into this aluminum Panda action.

5.1.2. The initial bolt handle movement is straight up. Do *not* engage the extraction cam so that the bolt handle begins to move to the rear.

5.1.3. Slide the cleaning rod, with the flat end installed (see Photo 9-1, Page 334), in the muzzle until it touches the tip of the projectile.

5.1.4. Now, apply a little bit of upward pressure on the bolt as you tap lightly on the tip of the projectile with the cleaning rod.

5.1.5. What we want, is to tap the shell, with seated projectile, out of the chamber, with the cleaning rod, without pulling it back with the extraction cam on the bolt.

5.1.6. We need to keep a bit of upward pressure on the bolt because it will not move to the rear until it has completed the full up stroke.

5.1.7. By the time the bolts up stroke has been completed, the projectile may well be disengaged from the rifling lands, and the bolt can be slid backwards, thus removing the case with seated projectile from the action. If, however, you still feel resistance simply apply a little bit of rearward pressure on the bolt, while tapping on the tip of the projectile, with the cleaning rod, until the projectile releases from the rifling. Then withdraw the case with its seated projectile. See Photo 9-11.

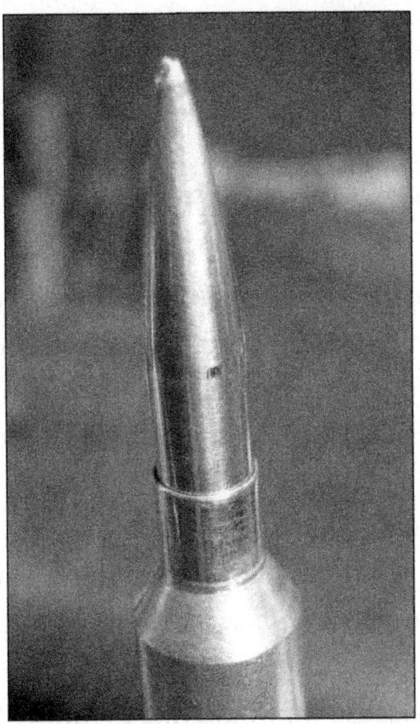

PHOTO 9-11.

The dummy cartridge has been extracted. The amount of Jam (.0115") can be seen by the mark engraved on the projectile. Neck tension in this instance was .002". I left the extractor on the bolt, and removed the case as per the text in step 5.

Ok, what have we done here? When we chambered the case, with the projectile seated, (dummy cartridge) its overall length was .050" too long to fit in the chamber. As the dummy cartridge was pushed into the chamber the projectile entered the throat of the chamber, and was pushed past the leade, thereby being engraved by the rifling as it was pushed into the barrel. Eventually a point was reached where friction in the barrel was built up, to an extent, where it overcame the friction holding the projectile in the case neck. At that point the projectile ceased moving forward in the barrel, and stopped, allowing the case neck to slide forward along its length. When the bolt was fully closed, thus ending all forward movement of the case, the projectile was at full Jam, *with the neck tension and lubricity characteristics of the neck of that particular case, and the characteristics of the throat and leade of that particular chamber.*

If we simply extracted the dummy round there is a good possibility that the projectile may be pulled all of the way, or part of the way, out of the case neck — something we want to avoid. That is why it is necessary to tap the dummy cartridge out of the chamber from the tip of the projectile. With the dummy cartridge thus obtained we can fit our throat and leade tool onto the projectile, and using a caliper, measure from the end of the tool to the base of the case to obtain our maximum Jam measurement *with tool.* See Photo 9-12.

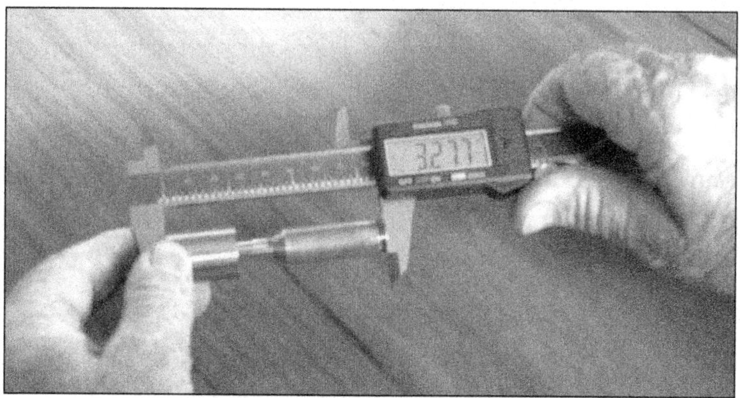

PHOTO 9-12.
Measuring the overall cartridge length with the tool installed.

Why do we want to obtain these measurements? Well, there's no point in testing ammunition with projectiles seated past the maximum Jam measurement. They will only be pushed back to *approximately* that measurement when chambered. Because of factors already discussed they will not all be pushed back to the same overall length. Cartridges loaded with varying overall lengths are very unlikely to be, even remotely, accurate.

The Jam measurement we end up using will be somewhat less than the maximum Jam measurement we have obtained. As such it will not be long enough for the projectile to be pushed back into the case, so *the working Jam measurement will be constant,* from cartridge to cartridge, regardless of neck hardness or lubricity factors.

Touch length is good to know because we would like to know at what point the projectiles cease to be Jammed, and begin to Jump. Jump is a term used for any projectile that is seated behind engagement with the leade of the rifling, and must move forward before engaging the leade. Such a projectile is said to be Jumped or Jumping.

As I said, you do not need to be fixated on these measurements. Many shooters are, for no sensible reason. They are only a jump off point to define the parameters, within which you will be seating projectiles, to fine tune your barrel *initially.* Your barrel will tell you what seating depth it prefers, and once you have found that, those measurements will not be needed again. In fact as the barrel wears, in very few shots, they will no longer be relevant.

When tuning your barrel you will test seating depths from maximum Jam to probably up to .060", or even more back, from Touch to find the overall length where your barrel is most accurate. We will discuss more on that in the next chapter on tuning.

Eventually, (hopefully sooner than later) you will find the perfect seating depth (overall cartridge length, or OAL) where your barrel shoots at its most accurate. When you have found that OAL, measure it using your throat and leade tool and record the measurement, along with the amount of Jam or Jump, the projectile has at that OAL. If you are adjusting seating depth with shims (I do), note the number of shims and their thickness, and write that down. If you are using a micrometer seating die note down the reading on the micrometer. If you are using a seat die with no precision means of adjustment you'll just be in a bit of trial and error, when it comes time to adjust seated depth, and, frankly, that isn't the way to do it. *Get a set of Skip's shims!*

Once I have found my most accurate OAL I am thereafter only concerned with monitoring barrel wear, and the relationship of that to the amount of Jam, or Jump, I need to maintain, to preserve the barrels accuracy during its life cycle. I monitor barrel wear with a simple tool I made which can be seen in Photo 9-13.

PHOTO 9-13.
The simple tool I use to monitor throat length.

The tool is simply a piece of barrel steel that has been turned, between centres, to fit closely through the bolt hole of my action, and protrude out of the rear bridge enough, so that I can comfortably get a caliper on to its end. A length of bright steel rod fits into the bore of the tool body. It's difficult to find a piece of rod that is a close fit to the bore of most calibers, so you can make up the difference with a couple of sleeves on the rod to make it a more precision fit if necessary. The tried and true method of try and see determines the length of the rod.

I use it like this:–

1. Make sure the surface at the end of the barrel is good and clean.

2. Insert a test projectile into the chamber. Push it into the throat but not into the leade.

    2.1. You will be keeping this projectile as your 'standard' and using it to make all future measurements. Look after it.

3. Insert the body of the tool in the action and run it right up against the back of the barrel.

4. Insert the rod into the body of the tool and push it in until it contacts the rear of the projectile, and pushes it up to the leade in the rifling. There will be about 1" of rod protruding from the end of the tool.

5. Open the dial caliper a bit over 1" and lay it alongside the rod with the end of the probe, protruding from the end, against the back of the tool.

6. Carefully push the caliper forward until its rear measuring face stops against the end of the rod.

7. Record that measurement, and keep it and the test projectile together for future reference. See Photo 9-14. Photo 9-15 is a close up of another measurement.

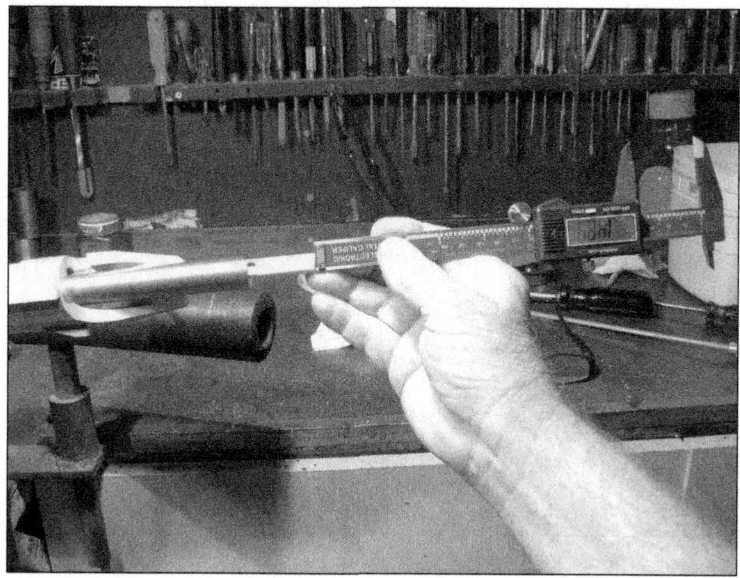

PHOTO 9-14.

The projectile is resting against the leade in the chamber, and the outer sleeve is resting against the end of the barrel. The rod is resting against the end of the projectile. The measurement from the rear of the sleeve to the rear of the rod is recorded and stored with the projectile that the measurement was taken with.

The measurement taken in this way is repeatable within better than .001" of accuracy. There is a caveat, though, and that is it must be taken on a pristinely clean barrel to be accurate. The reason for this is *the leade in the chamber doesn't wear forward* as you would think, but rather *increases in diameter,* thus letting the projectile move further into the bore. This I have observed while wearing out a lot of barrels. The throat and leade may look tatty and fire cracked, when viewed through a bore scope, but the length of the throat, and leade, remain very close to the original form and length dimensions they had when the barrel was new.

PHOTO 9-15.

A close up of taking the measurement of relative throat/leade length.

When the barrel is fired the high pressure generated expands the diameter of the barrel microscopically. This expansion can be used for determining chamber pressure, by attaching a strain gauge to the outside of the barrel to measure the expansion, and then correlate that measurement to chamber pressure in P.S.I. The barrel expands, but does not contract back to its original size completely. Sort of, expand .000020" and contract .000019". At each firing the diameter of the barrel will increase a tiny amount, that amount depending on the pressure generated, and the duration of the pressure peak. Twenty shots are enough to cause a permanent increase in bore diameter, that can allow the projectiles Touch to move around .001" into the bore in a high pressure load of the intensity we normally use.

Because it is the bores increase in diameter, rather than forward wear of the lead that increases Touch OAL, the tiniest amount of reduction in the diameter of the bore results in a significant change in Touch OAL. I noticed this when I was closely monitoring OAL increases on a 6x47 Lapua rifle I was using. The rifle had about 1600 shots on the barrel and I had measured a Touch OAL increase of .031" in 425 shots, equal to .0073" increase per 100 shots. At our local club we fire 2x12 shot rounds at a club shoot, so I figured it was reasonable to look for .0018" of Touch OAL increase after a club shoot.

I had cleaned the bore with JB non imbedding bore paste, and inspected it with a bore scope, to ascertain that it was free of any powder or copper fouling before I made my pre shoot measurement. The bore was bright and shiny, with the heat cracking expected of a barrel with that many shots on it, and the throat and leade still looked very good.

After the match I cleaned the bore in my normal manner, and made the OAL measurement, only to find it had not lengthened at all, but still measured the same as it did pre-match. That didn't make any sense to me. What! Was the barrel getting better? So I had a look at it with the bore scope, and saw a thin film of powder fouling in the bore — the glazed on powder fouling that solvents and brushes just don't remove. An application of JB removed that powder fouling, returning the bore to a bright shiny condition, and my next measurement revealed the .0018" amount of Touch OAL increase I was expecting.

The moral of the story is, the bore must be bright and shiny clean before you make these measurements, or they will not mean anything. The only way I have been able to remove glazed powder fouling from my rifles is with JB. I use it every 100 shots or so, or before I make an OAL measurement.

As a side bar, I measured the outside diameter of the barrel blank on my 7 SAUM at the point where the chamber ends, and marked it under the barrel when it was first chambered. At 908 shots, when viewed with a bore scope, the leade and throat are still in the same place they were when the barrel was first chambered. However, the diameter of the barrel has increased .0002", and my Touch measurement has moved forward .010".

It is the increase in diameter of the bore in front of the chamber that is the cause of inaccuracy with age. I have seen barrels with a bore diameter increase of up to .006", that diameter tapering evenly back to original bore diameter about 4" or so down the barrel. My last .22PPC barrel was .003" over its new .218" bore diameter when I retired it. I had to cut 4" from the end to get back to the original .218" diameter before fitting it to my practice rifle, where its accuracy was mostly restored.

Even 4" down the bore, of a well used barrel, the rifling is not in a pristine condition. This I have observed in the barrels I have set back, it being apparent in the throat of the newly cut chamber. Figure 9–1 is a drawing of the cross section of a new barrel, and shows the form and shape of the rifling, or very close to it. When the throat is cut, by the chambering reamer, the diameter of the grooves in the rifling will be over cut by .0005", or .00025" (at least on my reamers) per side, to allow a projectile access to the leade at the end of the throat.

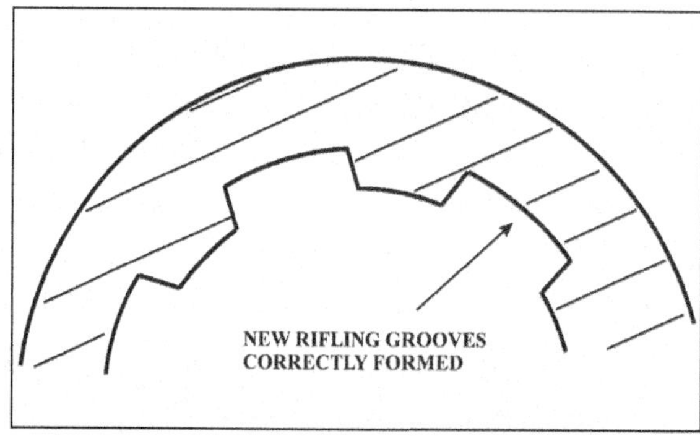
NEW RIFLING GROOVES
CORRECTLY FORMED

Figure 9-1.

This drawing represents the cross section shape of a new barrel.

Figure 9–2 is a drawing, of the cross section of a barrel, which has had around 1000 shots through it, and shows the form and shape the rifling has assumed. I don't have the instruments required to measure it, but the hollow formed at the bottom of the rifling lands is quite deep (relatively speaking). My throating reamer cuts away the lands themselves, and maybe .010", or thereabouts, each side of the lands, but does not touch the hollow that had been formed between them. That suggests to me that the bottom of the hollow could be considerably more than .0025" deep — maybe more like something around .001"

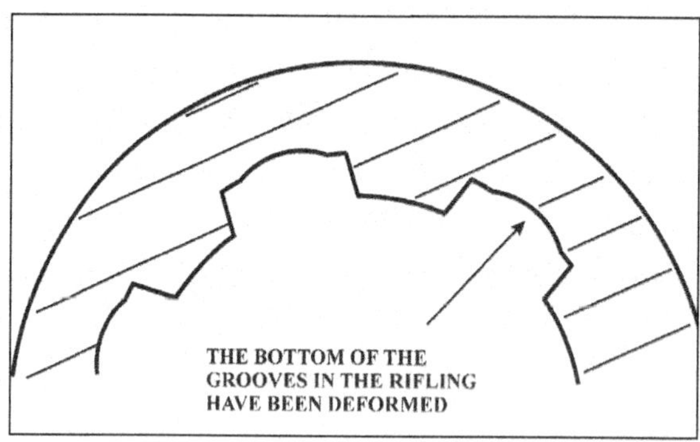
THE BOTTOM OF THE
GROOVES IN THE RIFLING
HAVE BEEN DEFORMED

Figure 9-2.

This drawing represents the cross section shape of a used barrel after throating.

You don't need much imagination to see that a projectile doesn't have much chance to start straight into a bore that is .003" oversize. Added to that, its crooked start can be anywhere in the 360° of the periphery of the bore, so inaccuracy is pretty much guaranteed.

The older a barrel is the less elastic the steel will be due to work hardening, and the less it will return to its former dimension after each shot, resulting in a greater increase in Touch OAL per shot.

All this begs the question? What in the Sam Hill are we doing all of this for?

Well:—

1. We know our Touch OAL measurement when the barrel was at its most accurate tune.

2. We know the OAL measurement at which the barrel was in its most accurate tune.

3. We have a Touch measurement that we can monitor with a test projectile.

4. Given the above measurements we can work out that the barrel is in its best tune with the projectile Jammed .xxx" forward of Touch or Jumped .xxx" back from Touch.

So if we detect, say a .005" increase in Touch OAL we can maintain our Jam or Jump OAL by adding a .005" shim to our seating die, or winding the dial of our micrometer seater out .005".

It would be nice if your barrel always shot its best at the Jam or Jump measurement you first worked out, but that may or may not be the case. Ultimately your barrel will tell you where it wants the projectile to be seated, as it ages, and that can only be determined by observation or testing. However it is very useful to know where your projectile is seated, in relation to a repeatable Touch measurement, so that any adjustments you make are incremental and refer to a base measurement.

Once I have tuned the barrel to its best seating depth accuracy, I measure the cartridges overall length using the measuring tool I made, note down that measurement, and note it every time I make an entry in the running sheet for that barrel. When I feel the need to retest seating depth, the seating die setting (the number of shims under the stem) becomes my zero point. I only note, on each target, the amount of shims I add, or remove, from the seating stem; +.005", –.010" or whatever I remove, or replace, at the range while I am testing.

If I arrive at a new OAL, where the rifle is more accurate, I measure that using the overall length tool I made, and it then becomes my new zero, along with the thickness of the shims, under the seating stem, of my bullet seating die. Because all of my measurements are taken on the ogive of the projectile, I can always know where my most accurate seated length is, in relation to the Touch measurement that is current, at whatever point the barrel is in its wear cycle, if I want that information, by re-measuring Touch.

Quite frankly, I view that as a piece of useless information, because in reality I never refer to the relationship between where Touch is, compared to my OAL. All I am interested in is how far Touch moves forward, as I begin to accumulate a number of shots on the barrel, so that I know how far forward to move the projectile out to maintain the Jump or Jam that was originally right for that barrel. In other words I keep track of barrel wear in real time with my measuring tool, and chase the leades movement by adding shims to my seating die, and checking, occasionally, if the barrel is happy with that seating depth. If I find the barrel is not happy I will then test different seating depths, and track the movements I make as +/- .xxx" (+/- the shim thickness on the seating die stem) from the seating depth where I started the test. If I find a new seating depth that works better, that becomes my new 'zero', and I again just monitor leade movement as before, and adjust the seating die as necessary to maintain a relationship that, in effect, I don't even know.

If that sounds confusing, I'm sorry. What I'm saying is, you don't have to know the actual Touch measurement in order to maintain your projectiles Jump or Jam relationship to it. As long as you have a way to know the amount that Touch measurement has changed you have enough information to run with.

My measuring tool gives me that precise information very accurately, very easily, and very quickly. You should make one. I'm sure you will find it as useful as I do.

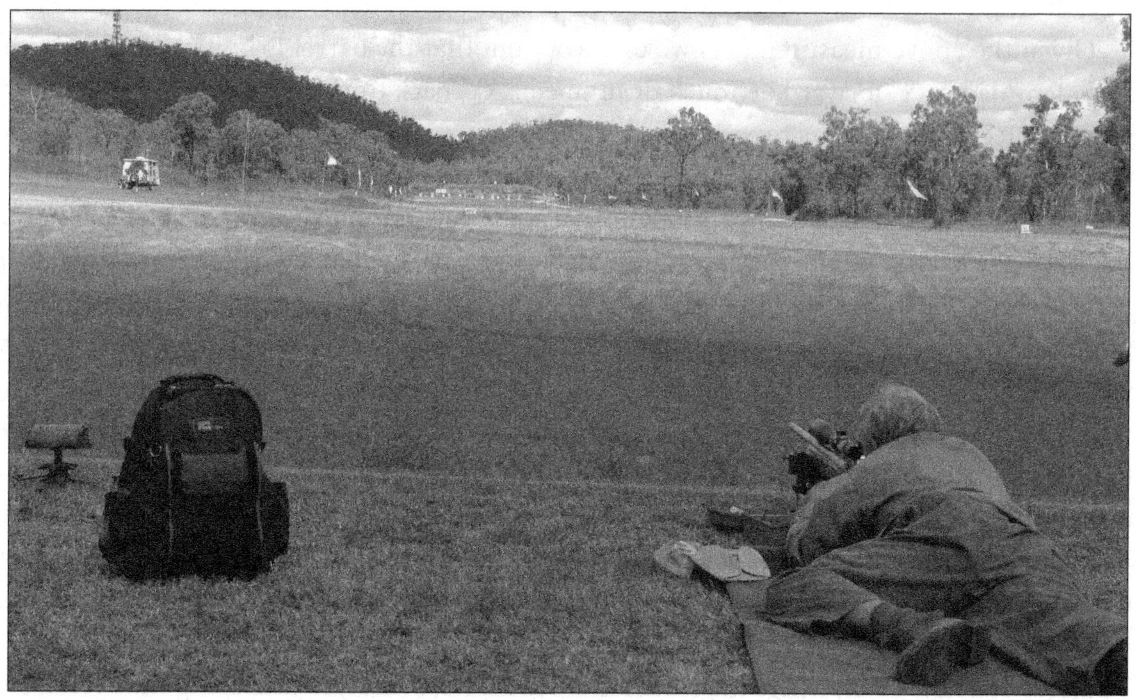

PHOTO 9-16.
The cover photo of the Author, on the 1210 yard (1100 meter) mound, competing in the 2012 Queensland Long Range Championships, held at the Raglan Shooting Complex, 50Km south of Rockhampton, in Queensland.

A REMINGTON MODEL 700 LONG ACTIONED RIFLE

BUILT IN THE LATE 1980S

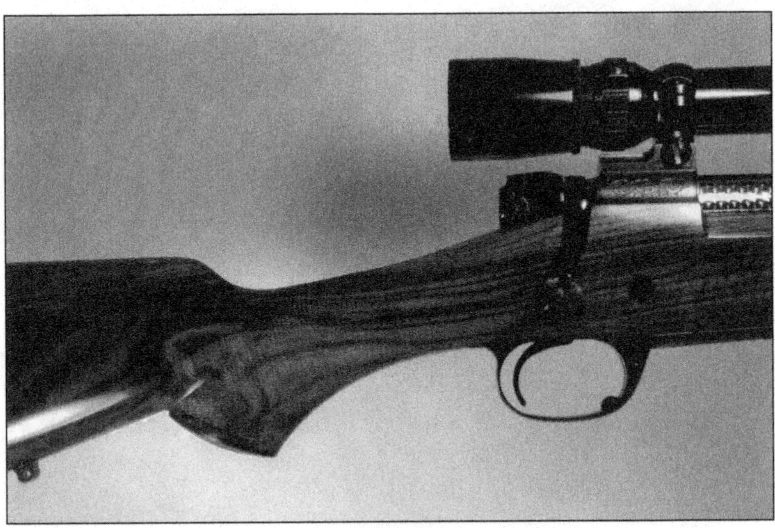

PHOTO C5-10.

I have no recollection of this particular rifle, but the rear cross-bolt and cartridge trap would suggest that it was in a heavy recoiling caliber. This rifle is a good example of the clean lines and shape I had been aiming for throughout my career, and had arrived at in the late 1980s. Unfortunately these are the only photos I have of it.

PHOTO C5-11.

Of particular note here is my treatment around the Ruger bolt stop, which was a bit of a trademark of mine when I built rifles using the Remington Model 700 action. Also note the blending of the rear tang into the line of the grip.

PHOTO C5-12.

The classic bolt handle has four panels of checkering separated by ribbons. The trigger guard was a Dakota. I used quite a few of these in the 1980s, as I needed to cut down my production time, and making trigger guard assemblies from the solid is very time consuming. As is was it took me a long time to deliver a rifle because this work was not commercially viable, and had to take second place to my 'bread and butter work', which was rebarreling, bedding and accurising. The engine turning of the bolt body was carried out by my wife, Lyn, who was very helpful and supportive throughout my career. The scope mount bases are custom made.

CHAPTER TEN

BARREL TUNING

There's a basic truth you need to believe before getting into this chapter. I have observed this over a good many years with a good number of rifles.

Simply put—*a rifle in perfect tune is a transient thing.* It is not even a remotely permanent condition. A rifle that is in not so perfect a tune probably has as much chance of moving into perfect tune as it does of moving into a worse tuned condition. You need to get your head around this very important fact to fully appreciate what is going on with your equipment.

I do not often go to the range for practice and find my rifle in perfect tune. The advent of barrel tuners (I will discuss them in the next chapter) has made this all the more glaringly obvious. Probably 8 times out of 10 the tune of my bench-rest rifle will be improved with a change in tuner setting.

I should hasten to explain to those of you who are thinking, "You beaut, all I need is a barrel tuner" that the tuner is *not* a magic bullet. It simply makes small changes in tune possible quickly and easily. Those changes would ordinarily be made by adjusting powder load or seating depth. Changes like those are far more difficult to make during a match, but lets forget about tuners for a while and concentrate on tuning.

Once you understand that basic fact, it will become apparent that to tune a rifle to shoot its very smallest group on a given day, and settle on that load for future use, is a fatal mistake. While that tune may be fantastic at the moment and shoot very tight groups, in an hour or two it may well shoot a monster. Over the course of the next few days, weeks or months, the only time the rifle will return to perfect tune, is if atmospheric conditions parallel those that were current when you first tuned the rifle. Eventually, barrel wear may be requiring a new tuning point. In essence the worn barrel will be in tune in a different set of atmospheric parameters, of which you are not aware. Not that any of us are actually aware of the precise conditions that have combined to produce the tune we originally arrived at.

Short range bench-rest shooters are aware of this only too well. An out of tune rifle in bench-rest competition can be readily spotted, because all of their shots are printed on one easily seen target, and the shot dispersion can be observed and analyzed in real time. Primarily they look for vertical dispersion in the group, and shots that go against the wind rather than with it. During the course of a match they will adjust tune by altering their powder load slightly, basing their adjustments on the results of their last group, and what they think the atmospheric conditions may be doing when it is time to start the next group. These adjustments are based on experience gained by careful observation of the barrels requirements, knowledge of the characteristics of the powder they are using, and the results they have seen during practice prior to the match.

In bench-rest shooting it is not the small groups that win matches, but rather the absence of large groups. The same can be said about long range competition. It isn't the centres that win matches, but the absence of outers and worse. Name your shooting discipline and the same adage can be applied. I think you get the idea.

So it follows that the best way to tune your barrel is to its best accuracy over a wide range of conditions. In short, its best average accuracy. By tuning to best average accuracy you probably won't shoot your smallest group, but you will shoot the smallest aggregate the barrel is capable of. Likewise, long range competitors may not have their highest x count for the match, but the barrel will shoot the highest aggregate score it is capable of. You don't often win a match by winning one range only with a high x count.

Unfortunately barrels have a finite life, some more than others, and unless you have an impressive budget to spend on barrels and components, you will want your barrel to last at least one season, or hopefully two. Their best accuracy potential is early in their life, probably within the first 500 shots, so it figures that we shouldn't be blowing off 500 odd shots finding the barrels tune. We need to be methodical, and find it quickly, so as much as possible of that most accurate barrel life can be used for winning matches (or trying to!).

We have a few tools at our disposal we can use to obtain best tune.

They are:

1. Primer selection.
2. Projectile selection.
3. Powder selection.
4. Powder weight.
5. Projectile seating depth.
6. Neck tension.

Let's look at these tools more closely.

PRIMER SELECTION: There are a variety of primers available on the market, for centrefire rifles, in standard and magnum strengths. Broadly speaking, standard primers are designed for use in smaller capacity cases that use the faster burning, easily ignited, powders. Magnum primers are designed for use in larger capacity cases, that use the slower burning, harder to ignite, powders. Magnum primers utilize a tougher disk resisting cup, that is needed for cases that run at high and prolonged pressure.

As an aside, a case doesn't have to be of high capacity, using slow burning powder, to require a magnum primer. When I started experimenting with the .17 Ackley Hornet, in the mid 1960s, I found it to be a primer disker par excellence. There was no way we were running high pressure in that cartridge; .22 Hornet cases blow primer pockets at very low pressure. The culprit was the prolonged pressure peak, caused by the reduction in bore diameter, overcoming the inertia of the firing pin and spring. A simple change to a magnum primer, with its stronger cup, coupled with a stronger firing pin spring to provide enough energy to set it off, cured the problem. But I digress.

There are bench-rest primers available that are said to be of higher quality; that is, more consistent than the non bench-rest variety. That may be true. I guess you pay your money and make your choice.

I use them, and consider the added cost worthwhile for the promise of more shot to shot consistency, even though I can't prove they actually do that.

I have never had a rifle 'come alive' with a change in primer. I have had acquaintances tell me their rifles improved with a primer change, so it may be an option to try if you have run up against a brick wall. For me that would be desperation time.

PROJECTILE SELECTION: Projectile selection can have a dramatic effect on rifle performance, so much so that I have always avoided rifles that are of the one trick pony variety; that is designed to use only one brand, weight, and shape of projectile. I have seen too many rifles that would refuse to shoot one projectile accurately, yet be a tack driver with another of the same weight to discount this. Why this happens I don't know, but I have seen it occur enough to believe in it, and always have options available in case my primary choice doesn't work out. Your choice may be narrow, but anything is better than nothing.

POWDER SELECTION: Ideally your powder selection should be aimed at filling the case to 100% density, or close to it, with the projectile weight you are using. That simply means that at working pressure, the powder load in the case will fill the case right up to the base of the projectile, or close to it, when it is fully seated. This is ideal, but requires the capacity of the case to be matched to the burning rate of the available powder, and the weight of the projectile you are using, which they seldom are. Fortunately this rule is not engraved in stone.

Cases that are balanced like this are our most inherently accurate cartridges. The 30BR is a classic example. Using AR2207 powder and a 115GN or 118GN projectile, the optimum load will fill the case right up to the base of the seated projectile, and that little cartridges accuracy, easy tuneability, and maintenance of tune over widely variable conditions is legendary.

Such perfect balance is not often seen in contemporary cartridges, but overall, you should be looking for the slowest powder you can use in the case, without compressing the load excessively, when you seat the projectile. That limits your selection of powders for a particular case, but there is nothing we can do about that. Any good reloading manual will point you in the right direction here.

POWDER WEIGHT: Powder weight could be considered a coarse tuning tool, though short range bench-rest shooters also use it as a fine tuning tool during the course of a match. In long range competition its use as a tuning tool is largely limited by the velocity you wish to achieve in the case you are using, along with the velocity reduction you are willing to accept at a reduced powder charge. As an example, finding a really accurate powder load in a 7MM Magnum that drove a 140GN bullet at 2600FPS would be pretty pointless. You can get that sort of performance from a 7x57 Mauser. A 7MAG should be able to do much better; more like 3000FPS.

In the main, we want our velocity level to be right up there, and we achieve that velocity level with powder load. If we want to maintain that velocity level, there is not a lot of room to move in tuning with powder load. For instance, a 155GN .308 projectile will drift 6" more at 1000YDS if it leaves the muzzle at 2800FPS, instead of 2900FPS. It doesn't sound much, but constantly missing the bulleye by 1" makes 6" less wind drift pretty attractive.

PROJECTILE SEATING DEPTH: This would have to be the main fine tuning tool we have at our disposal. A centrefire rifle will react considerably to a change in bullet seating depth. If your powder is of a suitable burning rate, and its working load is close to 100% loading density, you will find perfect tune for that barrel by varying bullet seating depth. The level of accuracy you achieve may not be what you are wanting, but it will be the best the barrel is capable of, provided everything else in the system is working correctly.

Neck tension: This should not be overlooked as a tuning tool. In general it is useful to try if you have tuned a load that exhibits some characteristics you can't seem to cure by any other method. As an example, when I first tuned my 7 Saum, it shot fine at 200 yards, but at 500 yards it exhibited a bit too much vertical. I tested neck tension, and found that a reduction (I ended up – .002") made those vertical shots go away. There is no need to fiddle with neck tension until you have a working accurate load.

All of the above factors will affect tuning to some extent, some more than others. Given the plethora of component brands, weights, burning rates, etc, etc, there is an almost infinite number of possible combinations to test. You can appreciate the need to have a very good idea of the direction you want to go in, and be very methodical in your approach. *You don't want to burn the barrel out finding tune.*

Why does one load combination work when another doesn't?

As far as I know, the answer to that is theoretical, rather than hard proven fact. The theory, though, seems to fit the observed results very well, and is probably very close to the mark. It goes something like this. By the way, this is the short, short version!

When a rifle is fired, a whole lot of things happen in a very short space of time, including a series of very complex vibration patterns, or harmonics, that occur over the length of the barrel. The harmonics in the barrel are probably moving it in every direction, but it would appear, that chiefly, its oscillations are in the vertical plane. This is, possibly, because the barrels weight, or mass, is in a downward direction, thanks to gravity.

These harmonics, in the barrel, run over its full length. They beat the bullet to the muzzle, of the barrel, with the effect that, before the bullet exits the muzzle, the exit hole is moving, mainly up and down. If you think about it you will realize that, as the barrel reaches the zenith of its up and down movement, it will be at its period of least amount of *vertical* movement within a given time frame. Figure 10-1 is a greatly simplified drawing that demonstrates what I am talking about. The wavy line represents the up and down oscillations of the barrel.

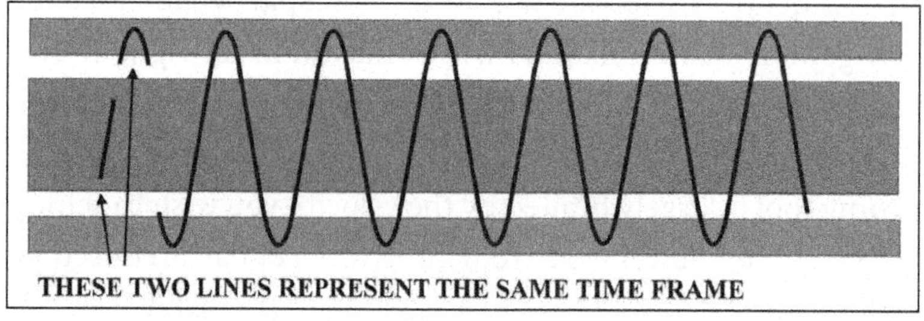
THESE TWO LINES REPRESENT THE SAME TIME FRAME

Figure 10-1.

We want all of our projectiles to exit the muzzle of the barrel in the green zone.
Projectiles exiting in the red zone will print with vertical on the target.

When the barrel is between the two extremes, top and bottom of its oscillation, it will be moving the most vertical distance in a given time frame. That is, it will be moving vertically through the red zone in Figure 10-1 relatively quickly, compared to its vertical movement through the green zone. Our ammunition does not have the exact same in barrel time, from shot to shot, as exhibited, by the shot to shot variations in velocity, that we note as a matter of course. If it did have the exact same in barrel time, tuning would probably not be necessary.

This is an important fact to consider. Very few, if any, projectiles travel from the leade, in the chamber, to the muzzle, in the exact same elapsed time. Each projectiles arrival time varies infinitesimally. So, it follows that projectiles exiting the muzzle at the mid point of its up and down oscillation (red zone, Figure 10-1) are going to leave the muzzle at a wider variation of exit points than projectiles that exit the muzzle, at either the top or bottom of its oscillation, where it is more dormant for a time (green zone, Figure 10-1).

That is the theory and, as I said, the practice seems to support it pretty well. To see it in action you need a rifle that shoots dots (one hole groups), and the phenomena will be readily seen on the target. In perfect tune the rifle will print to a point on the target, let's say right on the top of the mothball of a 100 yard bench-rest target. We are shooting at 100 yards. If we take the rifle out of tune by adjusting powder load down, in small increments, we will note the rifle exhibits its out of tune condition, with small amounts of vertical dispersion appearing in the group. The group will also be moving up or down the target from the original impact point. At some point the impact point will be much lower or higher than it originally was, probably at or close to the middle of the mothball, or somewhere above the top, and at that point the vertical will disappear.

What has been demonstrated here, is that the barrel has two in tune points, one near the top of the mothball (representing the limit of its upward travel) and another near the bottom of the mothball (representing the limit of its downward travel). The grouping capability at the top may be slightly better than that at the bottom, or vice versa. It will be obvious that the barrel is in tune at both points, by the absence of vertical, that is very apparent in all groups between these two points (they are called accuracy nodes).

It is these accuracy nodes we are looking for when we tune our barrel; to have every projectile exit the muzzle when it is as close as possible to the top or bottom of its oscillation. Figure 10-2 demonstrates what I am on about here. It is, of course, simplified, but you should get the picture.

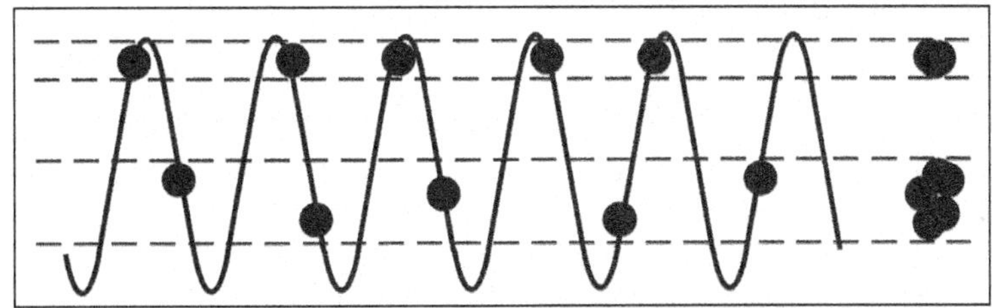

Figure 10-2.

The distance between the two lots of dotted lines represents an equal amount of elapsed time. The squiggly line represents the barrels oscillations. Although all of these projectiles arrive at the muzzle within the same time frame, those that arrive when the barrel is in the middle of its oscillations and is therefore moving at its fastest, will have considerably more vertical dispersion.

In reality, tuning is a matter of timing. What we are actually doing is adjusting load parameters, in order to cause our projectiles to arrive at the muzzle of the rifle when the barrel is either at the top, or bottom, of its oscillation cycle.

Our first parameter to consider is powder weight. By adjusting powder weight we can time the projectile to arrive at the muzzle of the rifle, at many different points in the barrels oscillation. A very simple graph, of the relationship of powder weight to projectile arrival time, at the muzzle, during the barrels oscillations, would look something like Figure 10-3.

Don't take any notice of the actual figures, as they are only hypothetical, however, they are representative of what occurs in the real world. You will note, that as the powder load increases, the projectile arrives at the muzzle at different points in the oscillation of the barrel, depending on the powder load, and therefore speed of the projectile. Also, the effect is fairly linear.

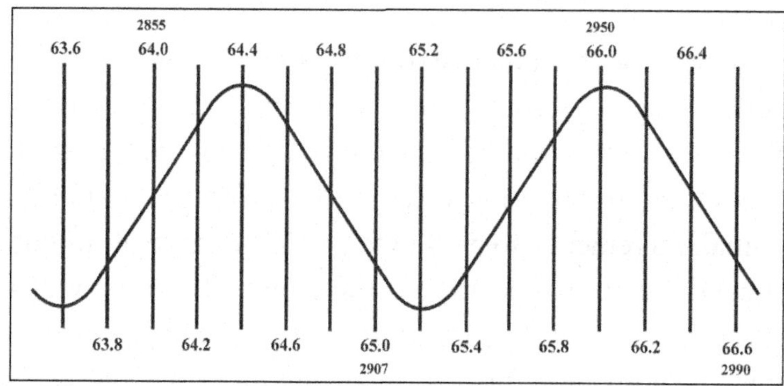

Figure 10-3.

A hypothetical graph showing the relationship between powder load, projectile speed, and barrel oscillations.

Looking at the hypothetical graph in Figure 10-3 we have started with a powder load of 63.6 grains, which has the projectile arriving at the muzzle of the barrel, at the bottom of its oscillation cycle, at a point where the barrel is moving its minimum vertical distance in a given time frame. When we increase the powder load to 64.0 grains, thereby increasing the speed of the projectile, we see that it now arrives at the muzzle when it is at the mid point of its oscillation, and therefore moving its maximum vertical distance in a given time frame.

We have already discussed the desirability of finding a load combination that allows our projectiles to exit the muzzle of the barrel when it is either at the top, or bottom, extremes of its oscillation, and here we found one. Theoretically the 63.6 grain load will be more accurate than the 64.0 grain load, however the velocity it produces may not be satisfactory, at around 2834FPS, when I am looking to realize 3000FPS.

As we increase the load .2 of a grain at a time, our projectile begins to arrive at the muzzle closer to the top of its oscillation, and is eventually arriving when the muzzle is moving the minimum vertical distance, in a given time frame, at the 64.4 grain load. Increasing the load further has the projectile moving faster and faster, and eventually it is arriving at the muzzle when it is again at the mid point of its oscillation.

If we continue to increase the powder load, the same thing will happen. We will continue to arrive at, pass, and arrive at those points where the barrel is at the limit of its oscillation. Low, high, low, high, and so on, until we reach the maximum pressure that cartridge is safe to work with.

If the projectiles are exiting the muzzle when it is at either a high or low point, we have a powder load that has the *potential* to produce the best accuracy the rifle is capable of. Those points are called accuracy nodes. A powder load that has the projectile timed to exit the muzzle, at an accuracy node, only has the *potential* to be the most accurate load, because other factors must be considered.

Referring to our hypothetical graph, the 63.6 grain load is at an accuracy node, but would not be the best choice because it is too light, and will not allow the powder to operate within its design parameters. A reduced powder load will generate reduced pressure in the case, and it is unlikely that the pressure will be consistent, from shot to shot. While the load may in fact be centred on an accuracy node, a large shot to shot velocity variation will cause its spread, around the centre of the node, to be large, so that best accuracy is not achieved. We can do better!

It would be unusual if we didn't have a velocity expectation for any cartridge we are working with, and that gives us something to aim for. I don't know about you, but usually, my expectations are on the high side, and that is where the powder will be operating most consistently. So our first goal when we begin tuning will be to find an accuracy node close to the velocity we are hoping to achieve from that cartridge.

Assuming we have a calibre, or powder, we haven't used before, the first order of business is to find the maximum load the barrel will accept, and the velocity it will produce with that load. To do this we need a chronograph, or are able to borrow one. I don't take a lot of notice of chronographs, so don't tend to bother putting very many shots over one. If the machine has a +/- .5% accuracy specification, at 3000 feet per second the velocity will read anywhere from 2985FPS to 3015FPS which is a considerable variance. I prefer to save my barrel life for use in competition, or hunting, rather than collecting reams of figures that aren't that accurate anyway. Once I have the powder load/ velocity combination I am looking for I put the chronograph away, and don't bother with the extra hassle it would add to my range work.

It would be unusual if we didn't want our rifle to be operating at its velocity peak, so the next step is to shoot it for group. For starters, we have to find the closest accuracy node we can to the maximum *usable* load we can use in our barrel. Referring back to Figure 10-3 (Page 358), we see that our maximum working load was 66.6 grains of powder. In our hypothetical example this is not quite at an accuracy node, but we cannot reach the higher accuracy node without running at unacceptable pressure levels. We must decrease the powder load and find the next node down. Years ago that would involve loading up a wedge of cartridges, with incremental powder loads, going out to the range, and firing them all off to obtain the necessary data. These days I have a better system that allows me to use fewer shots, and save unnecessary wear on my barrels.

What I do is take at least 50 prepared and primed cases to the range with my projectiles, bullet seating die, and arbor press. My powder is loaded into blood sample vials, six loads of each increment I think I will want to test.

These vials can be seen in Photo 10-1. They will hold 70 grains of AR2225 easily, have a screw top that seals, and are available from medical supply businesses. However, there is a trick to their use. As you receive them they are nearly impossible to use, due to static electricity, that causes powder granules to stick to the sides of the vial, making them very difficult to dislodge. The cure is to fill the kitchen sink, exactly as you would for washing up the dishes, with detergent and warm water. Dunk the vials in the water, get them good and wet, then set them out to dry (do not rinse them). The washing up detergent will kill the static electricity and the vials will be usable.

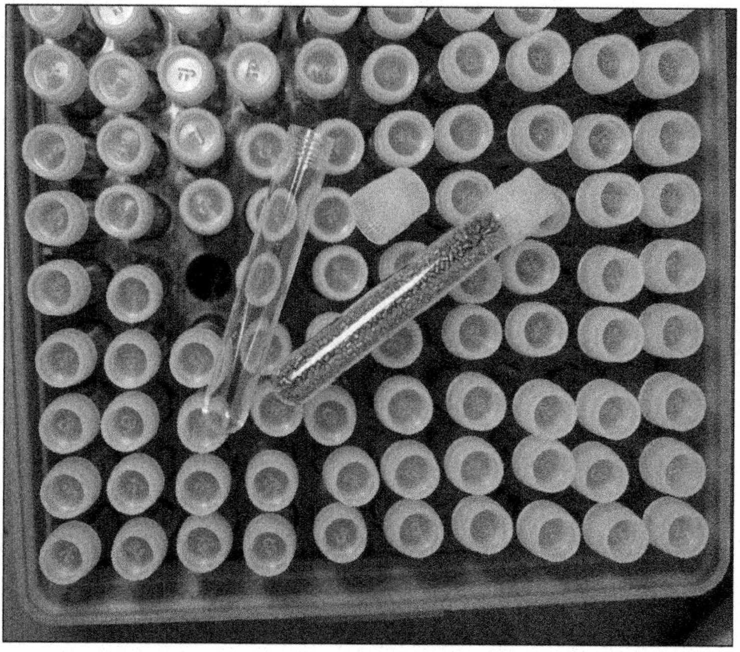

PHOTO 10-1.

The vials I use for powder loads when tuning. There is 66 grains of AR2225 in the right hand vial. I also preload my powder in them for away competitions.

Tuning is not practice. When we practice we should simulate match conditions as much as possible. Our aim should be to learn the hold off, or the sight adjustment needed, to compensate for whatever wind conditions we encounter, so that we can employ that knowledge during a match, and hopefully save a point. With tuning, however, our aim is quite different.

When we tune a barrel, we should aim at the same mark on the target for every shot, note the conditions the shot was fired in, and the effect they had on the projectiles impact on the target. To do this you must deploy wind flags on the range and keep notes for every shot you fire. You don't shoot fast. Observation is what is required, not speed.

You must have good wind information to do this job.

Whether you buy wind flags or make your own is up to you, but whatever you do, don't neglect them. Commercially made wind flags can cost around $140.00 each with a stand, and no doubt will work really well if you are cashed up enough to afford them. I get by with home made ones that give me all of the information I can handle.

My flags are made from 5MM plastic core flute material — the sort of stuff they make political advertising signs from. You can usually find it at the local hardware store. The sail is 21" long by 7" high with a triangular piece cut off one end 3½" x 3½". It is painted dayglo red on the right hand side, and dayglo yellow on the left hand side, to easily distinguish in which direction it is pointing. A dayglo red surveyor's tape tail 37" long is attached to the rear of the sail with a paperclip. The swivel is a piece of #8 drill rod pointed at one end. It is held in a 1" dia x 1.375" long aluminum hub with a grub screw. The hub also holds a piece of bent fencing wire, which inserts into two of the flutes of the sail. The stand is simply a tomato stake with a hole drilled in the end.

These flags are cheap to make, quick to set up, and give me as much wind information as my addled brain can handle. You can see one in Photo numbers 10-2, and 10-3, and the construction of it in Photo numbers 10-4, and 10-5.

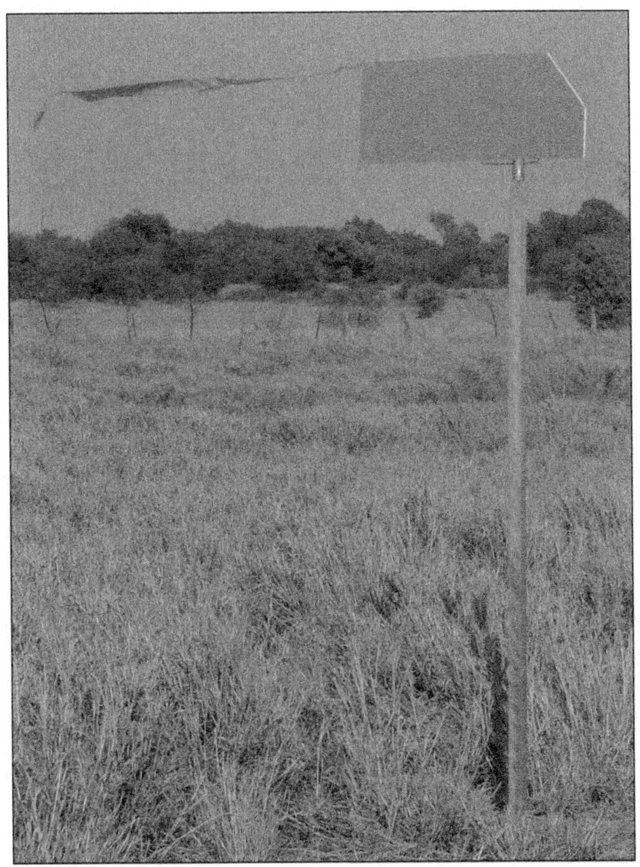

PHOTO 10-2.
One of my wind flags on a calm Barcaldine day.

PHOTO 10-3.
A close up of the sail.

PHOTO 10-4.
The simple frame and swivel mechanism.

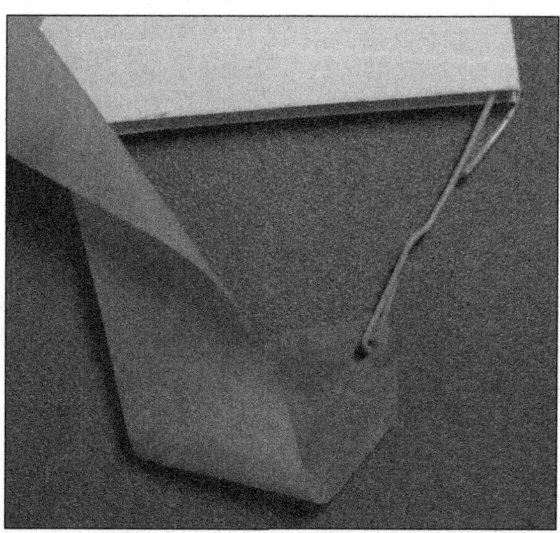

PHOTO 10-5.
A close up of the simple tail attachment.

How many flags should you deploy? That is entirely up to you, and in the end will be an informed decision. If you have ever been to a bench rest match, or seen photos of one, you will note that they literally deploy a sea of wind flags. You would think that many flags would cause sensory overload, but that isn't the case. If you had 8 flags deployed on your 200 yard range, that would, more than likely, be more of a sensory overload — it certainly would be for me.

The reason for this is, when so many flags are deployed, your focus should change from each individual flag to global flag watching. Imagine the flags are a field of wheat, and you will understand what I mean. While I can look at 100 flags globally, I can't do that with ten flags in a line to the target. The flags provide too much information for me to decipher. Five is as many as I can handle, and three is better. You may well be able to handle ten easily, and if so that is good. It's an individual thing you will have to work out for yourself.

Whatever you do though, do not ignore my advice. You cannot tune a barrel effectively without good wind information. I'm a lazy, cheap B@$#@*d, and would not use them if I thought I didn't need them. *Take a lesson, and don't leave home without them.*

Perfect tuning weather is a cloudy overcast day, with anything up to a 5MPH wind, coming from either 3:00 or 9:00. Such a day will have no mirage, to play merry hell with your aiming point, and the variable side wind will move your projectiles with only a little vertical displacement. You will only have to contend with wind speed, which will be easily observed in the attitude of the tails on your wind flags.

The worst possible condition, in which to tune your barrel, would be a hot day with a wind quartering from behind, or in front of you, with varying speed and direction. On such a day mirage will make your aiming point very hard, or impossible, to define precisely. The combination of wind speed and direction, with a quartering wind, will be very difficult to read correctly, and will cause considerable vertical dispersion in the shots.

If you are able to tune your barrel in ideal conditions you are indeed lucky. At my local range we rarely get that condition. Our prevailing condition is the worst possible condition. If you are faced with that, too, you will have to do what they do in Barcaldine — live with it and do the best you can. In conditions like those you must be very attentive to wind speed and angle. At our range there is a curfew before 8:00AM and by 9:00AM severe mirage makes further testing impossible. In the summer months it's hopeless even at 8:00AM. Life's a bitch, and then you die!

My method is to fire a shot, note its position on the target and give the wind a value for that shot, from 1 to 5. I observe my wind flags while setting up and have an idea of the parameters I will be shooting in by the varying angles of the tails, and sails, of my flags. I am no expert wind reader—I simply do not have the eyes to resolve small changes in angle or tail, but in reality what we are looking for here is relativity.

It's a case of more or less. Every shot in each group I fire is assigned a wind number from 1 to 5. I give shot #1 a wind value, let's say 3/5. When I fire shot #2 I say to myself, "Was the wind more or less for that shot?" If it's more, "Was it a lot more or a bit more?" If it was a little more I give it a value of 4/5, and if it is a lot more I give it a value of 5/5. That is how I assign my value to the wind for that shot. In this way I keep tabs on whether the shot went with the wind or against it. A shot that goes against the wind is not a good sign. If your load is good all of your shots should go with the wind. With wind coming from the left, a shot with a value of 5 should print further to the right than a shot with a value of 1.

Why am I so concerned about shots that have gone against the wind? I am concerned because a shot that goes against the wind has effectively doubled the group size or worse. If the wind it was fired in should have blown it ½" to the right of the group, but it printed ½" to the left of the group, you don't have a ½" group—you have a 1" group. This is because, if the wind that should have moved the projectile ½" to the right was not present, the shot would have printed the full 1" to the left. That is why having shots go against the wind is a positive indication of a bad load. All of your shots should move predictably with the wind.

When you start tuning like this you will quickly begin to gain knowledge of how your rifle will be pushed around by the wind. If you have, or can beg, borrow, or steal a wind gauge, such as a Kestrel or similar, you will see that the tails on your flags can tell you the speed of the wind pretty accurately by their angle. The tails on my flags equate to 8MPH if the wind is just holding the tail at 90 degrees, or horizontal to the ground. At 45 degrees they indicate 4MPH. So I have a good indication if the wind is running at 2MPH (22.5degrees), 4MPH (45degrees), 6MPH (67.5degrees) or 8MPH (hovering at 90 degrees). In Photo 10-2 the tail on that flag is being held violently at 90 degrees, which indicates wind somewhat in excess of 8MPH (Page 361).

It can be really perplexing if you have 5 flags out at say, 200 yards, and every flag points in a different direction, and every tail is a different angle. That happens pretty often at my place. If the wind isn't going to settle down into some sort of pattern you can read, go home. You will not be gathering any meaningful data tuning in those conditions. By all means practice in those conditions, but forget about tuning.

Photo 10-6 shows an early tuning target from my .30BR that demonstrates my method.

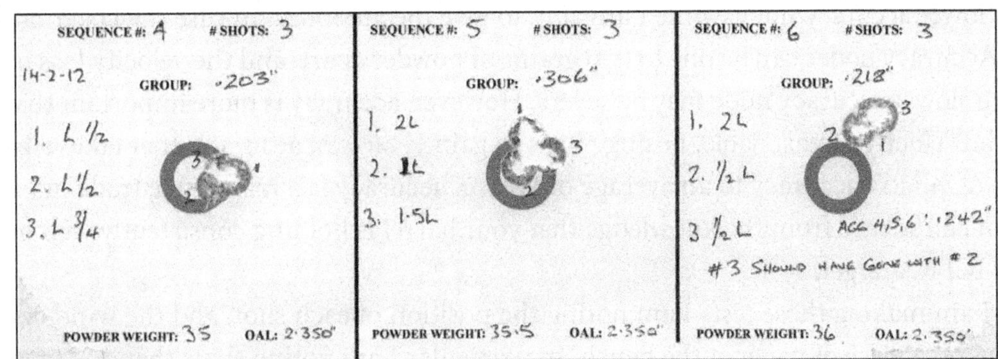

PHOTO 10-6.

Part of a tuning sequence from my .30BR, fired when the wind was somewhat more benevolent.

Every shot I fire is numbered on a mock up target back at the bench, and its wind value recorded along with any other relevant data. All of these observations are transferred to the target when I get home. I make further entries on a running sheet, that I keep for that barrel. You can see a portion of that running sheet in Photo 10-7.

	CALIBRE	.30 BR								PAGE # 1	RUNNING SHEET
DATE	POWDER	LOAD Gns.	BULLET	PRIMER	BRASS	O.A.L.	# SHOTS / RANGE	TGT #	GROUP SIZE / SCORE	CONDITIONS	COMMENTS
9-2-12	AR2207	30 TO 35.7	BERGER 115GN MATCH BUSH: .321	REM 7½	LAPUA	JAMMED FOR FIREFORMING	100YDS SEE TARGET SIGHTER: →	1	SEE TARGET	27°C CLEAR WIND FROM 3:00 2-8MPH SCOPE: NXS 42	FIREFORMING - RUNNING IN + WORKING UP TO VELOCITY. 35.7/2207 GAVE 3002 FPS WITH EASY EXTRACTION AND ONLY A LITTLE EXTENSION ON PRIMER. LOAD RANGE SHOULD BE FROM 35GNS TO 36GNS AR2207 TF: 21
13-2-12	AR2207	35 35.5 36	BERGER 115GN MATCH BUSH: 321	REM 7½	LAPUA	VARIOUS SEE TARGET	46×100 SIGHTER: 4	2 3	SEE TARGET	28°C CLEAR WIND FROM 9:00 0-3MPH SCOPE: NXS 42	TESTING SEATING DEPTH. BEST WAS 2.350" - .008" OFF JAM (SHIMS .045"). WILL RETEST WITH 3 SHOT GROUPS AND RUN A MATCH TARGET. TF: 71
14-2-12	AR2207	35 35.5 36	BERGER 115GN MATCH BUSH: 321	REM 7½	LAPUA	2.350" .008" OFF JAM	23×100 SIGHTER: 5	3	AGG .193" AGG .247" AGG .275"	27°C CLEAR SOME MIRAGE WIND FROM 9:00 SCOPE: TO 6:00, 0-4MPH	TESTING .008" OFF JAM - 3 SHOT GROUPS. SEEMS TO WORK BETTER AROUND 2950 FPS THAN JUST OVER 3000 FPS. TRY 34.7, 35, 35.3 GN SPREAD AND SEE IF GROUPS ARE BETTER. KEEP OAL AT 2.350". NB: STILL FIREFORMING SHELLS. TF: 99

PHOTO 10-7.

Entries from the running sheet for my .30BR barrel. The entry that refers to Photo 10-6 is the bottom entry.

You can see, in sequence #6, that I have noted a shot that did not go with the wind. Also note that the centre of each group is moving higher on the target as the load is increased, ½ a grain of powder, at a time. I am aiming at the middle of the mothball for every shot.

I fire 2 shot groups. If the rifle won't put 2 shots close together, a third certainly isn't going to improve the group. I test at 200 yards, and if I already know what my maximum load is for the current barrel, I fire 2 shots and work down from that in .5 grain increments. Otherwise, I work up in .5 grain increments. When I come to a load that prints its two shots close together I will load a third shot and fire that into the group.

If the group is still good I may confirm it with another 3 shot group at the same powder load. I don't stop there though, but continue reducing (or increasing) the powder load, until I reach the next accuracy node, which I again confirm with a third shot, and may fire a conformation extra group. That depends on how I am going with time.

By examining the targets and noting where the centre of the groups formed on the target, I will be able to determine if my node is at the top, or the bottom, of the barrels oscillation. It probably doesn't make any difference, but I prefer my faster node to be at the top oscillation. I continue the test to find the lower accuracy node, while I am at it, to give me an option in case the faster node doesn't work out. Accuracy nodes can be one to two grains of powder apart, and the velocity loss incurred by moving to a slower accuracy node may be severe. However, accuracy is more important than velocity, provided the velocity is reasonable. Losing 60FPS to gain ¼ MOA of accuracy, that takes a barrel from an average of ½ MOA accuracy to an average of ¼ MOA accuracy is a reasonable trade off, as you will gain a lot of confidence from the knowledge that your barrel is holding consistently well inside the X ring of the ICFRA target.

While I am making these tests I am noting the position of each shot, and the wind conditions it was fired in, on a piece of paper at the bench. In particular I am noting shots that do not go with the wind. Such shots are a good indication of a bad load. If the load is a good one all of your shots should react predictably with the strength of the wind. If there is an increase in wind velocity from the left, then your shot should be blown to the right. If it isn't the load is suspect.

It will be convenient to refer to the tuning of my second 7 Saum barrel while I am rambling on here, as you will be seeing something from the real world (warts and all), and be privy to my thinking during the process.

Often, things don't work out the way you expect them to, and this barrel was one of those things. I had a little bit of experience with the 7 Saum from my first barrel, which led me to pick up from where I left off. I thought I knew the range in which I would be loading powder, so loaded a series of vials from 64 grains to 67.5 grains of powder, which was the maximum load in my previous barrel. I intended to kill three birds with one stone — 1. Run the barrel in, 2. Test the powder load for group, and 3. Test the velocity and pressure at the same time. I intended to have this barrel tuned quick smart. Hah! You shouldn't tell God your plans — it only makes Him laugh.

I used Berger's 180[GN] Hybrid projectiles, and started with .010" Jump for my initial testing. Referring to Photo 10-8 you will see the progress of the test.

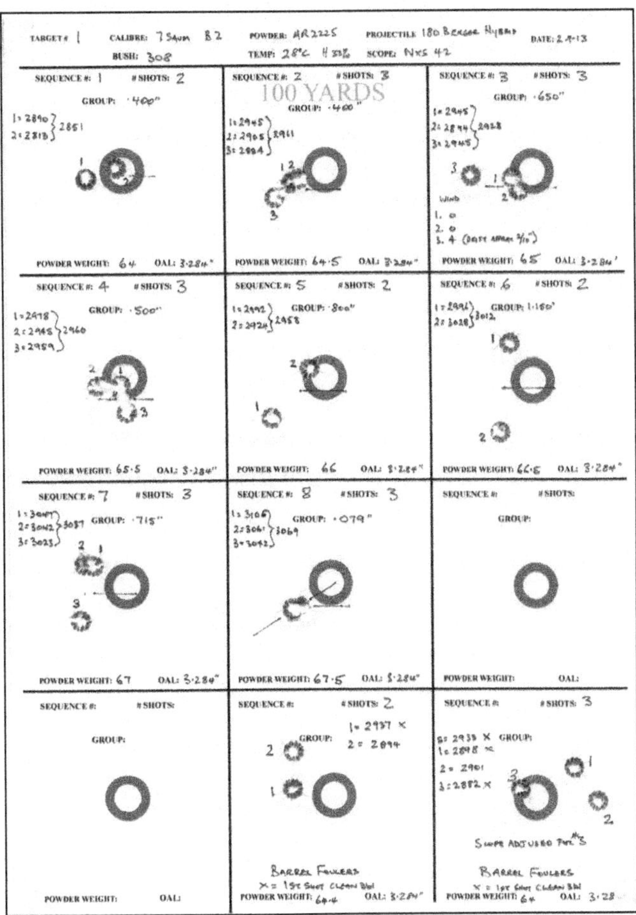

PHOTO 10-8.

The initial test to find velocity/pressure/and a potential accuracy node, while running in the new barrel.

This initial test was carried out at 100 yards in a wind that was coming from 6:00 at 4–8mph. Looking at the two targets, on the bottom right of the photo, you will see I fire two fouling shots after I clean the rifle. I do this while I am tuning a new barrel to see if there is any consistent pattern as to where the barrel will print its second shot, after the first fouling shot, from a clean barrel. If I can find a repeating pattern I will keep that knowledge in mind come match time. For instance, my 6x47 Lapua consistently printed its second shot 1 minute high and left, and knowing that kept my second shot in the x or 6 ring many times. There's nothing worse than shooting a 5 after sticking your first sighter in the x — it really sucks.

Before I go any further, I must warn you not to try and duplicate the powder loads, I will be discussing, in your own rifle, as it is more than likely they will be excessive enough to blow the rifle up. For this reason I am not mentioning the powder types I am using. With powder, you must always be safe, and start at a low manufacturers recommended load to begin with. Work the load up carefully looking all the time for signs of pressure building, such as a slightly tight bolt lift, and a change in the appearance of the firing pin indentation on the primer. When you consider you have reached a safe working load, thereafter monitor the life you get from your cartridge cases. A good safe working load should allow you to use a case at least 10 times before the primer pocket loosens. If you don't make 10 reloads or more from a case, you are running with pressure too high.

You can see I found two nodes. The high muzzle node at 64.5 grains of powder, and the low muzzle node at 67.5 grains of powder. You can also see in sequence #3 where I was caught out big time by not watching the wind when I returned to the bench after loading my third shot. As soon as I saw the shot print way to the left I looked at the flags and saw why — the 6:00 wind I shot #1 and #2 in was a 3:00 wind at 8mph, and worth at least .2moa for shot #3. Some mothers have dumb kids.

Everything looked promising apart from one major problem. Even at the 67.5 grain load I had absolutely no pressure signs. Cases just fell out of the chamber, and primers showed no protrusion at all. This barrel was very hungry for powder, and that was a problem. I needed to find its maximum load by testing further before making a decision.

Photo 10-9 shows that test. I conducted it at 200 yards and worked up to 68.5 grains still without any signs of excess pressure. As you can see the up and down muzzle accuracy nodes are more distinct at 200 yards than they are at 100 yards, the 64.5 grain load in sequence #1 printing much higher than the 67.5 grain load in sequence #3. The load I would want to pursue further, from these tests, would have been the 67.5 grain load, and that was a problem. At the seating depth I was using (.010" Jump) the loading density for that powder was 102%, which doesn't sound like much of a compressed load, but in practice the powder, poured through a drop tube, filled the case nearly to the top of the neck, requiring it to be crushed nearly 3/10" when seating the projectile. Even at 68.5 grains I had not reached maximum operating pressure.

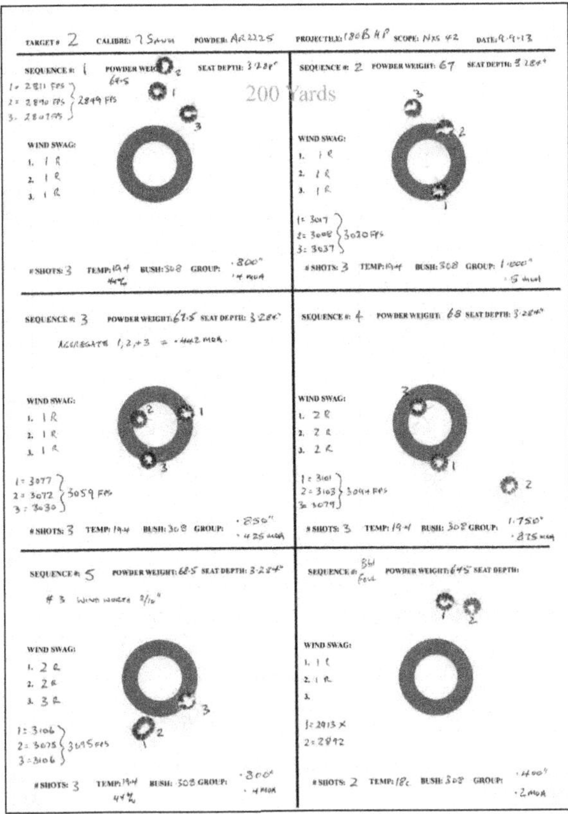

PHOTO 10-9.

The continuation of the test started in PHOTO 10-8.

When seating boat tail projectiles on a compressed powder load, most of the loaded ammunition will have excessive run out, caused by the boat tail being forced off line, when crushing the powder, as the projectile is seated. The loading density with this powder, in my first barrel, was 101%, and I solved the alignment problem by cobbling up a die that compressed the powder, before I seated the projectiles, that worked ok. But 102% was too much to cope with, and that loading density would only get worse if I needed to seat projectiles deeper to make more Jump. 44 shots gone to find out I needed another powder.

I had tried the next faster powder in my first barrel and found it to be nearly the same as the existing lot. The only other powder I had was, in my estimation, a bit fast for the 7 SAUM case, but was reputed to do very well in it, so I decided to give it a try.

Photo 10-10 shows the results of that test, fired at 100 yards, and conducted in the same way as the test in Photo 10-8 (Page 365). From this test I figured I had an up muzzle node at 55.5 grains for 2901FPS and a down muzzle node at 57.5 grains for 2959FPS. 2959FPS was ok, velocity wise, so I decided to pursue the 57.5 grains load further.

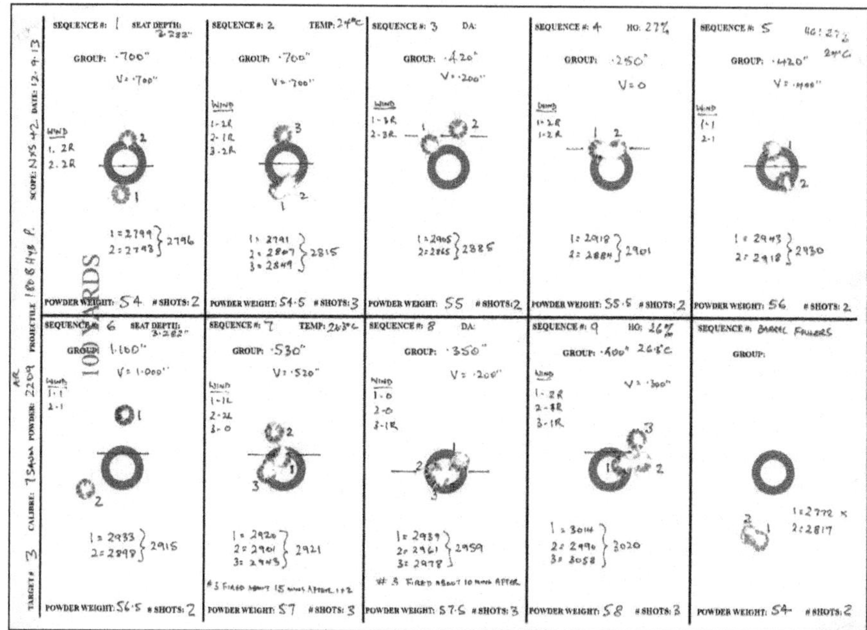

PHOTO 10-10.
The initial test to find velocity/pressure/and a potential accuracy node with the new powder.

Having found the powder load I will be using, the next step is to fine tune the accuracy of the barrel with projectile seating depth. I will now determine Jam and Touch parameters, after I have found my optimum powder load, because by then the leade in the throat of the chamber will be sufficiently conditioned to give a true reading. If I am using VLD or bench-rest projectiles I will be testing seated length from full Jam to Touch, and if I am using Hybrid, or hunting projectiles, from Touch up to .100" back from Touch. These tests will be initially made in .005" increments and fine tuned to .002" increments if needed.

I will start the test with my bullet seating die set at maximum Jam for a VLD projectile, or set at Touch with a Hybrid. I conduct it in the same way I did for the powder weight test. Take prepared cases, weighed powder in vials etc, to the range and load only the ammunition I need to conduct each phase of the test.

I will fire two shot groups at 200 yards until I find a seating depth that prints its two shots close together, at which point I will load and fire a third shot into the group. If the third shot prints in the group I may confirm it with another 3 shot group at the same seating depth. Then I will move on with two shot groups and see if I can find a second accuracy node, where two shots print close together, and again confirm with a third shot, and possibly another 3 shot group at the same seating depth. That may or may not happen, but if it does I have doubled my options for further testing.

The position where those two accuracy nodes print their groups on the target and their group sizes will determine which one I will test further.

Photo 10-11 shows the results of my first bullet seat depth test with the #2 barrel. Again the test was carried out at 200 yards, and I started with a control group of 3 shots at 57.5 grains of powder and .010" of projectile Jump. The group looked ok, and was in keeping with the group the rifle shot at 100 yards while velocity/pressure testing. I expected that it would not take much to improve it — which only shows how much I know!

For the subsequent targets I didn't bother with a third shot because I was not improving on the sequence #1 group with my first 2 shots. It's pretty pointless to throw another $1.30 down the range if you are not going to improve on what you have already done. Before I do that I want my first two shots to be nearly touching. The more Jump I gave the projectiles the further apart my 2 shots were until I pulled up at –.015" from my 0 setting, which equated to .025" of Jump, and paused to scratch my head and ponder. The more Jump I gave the projectile the worse it shot. I had already tried +.005" and –.005" in sequences #2 and #3 with similar results as the 0 setting, so decided to try +.010", which was just on Touch. That didn't work either. I decided to try 3 shots with a setting of –.005" (.015" Jump), which didn't work, then decided to see if I could duplicate the control load (sequence #8), and found I couldn't.

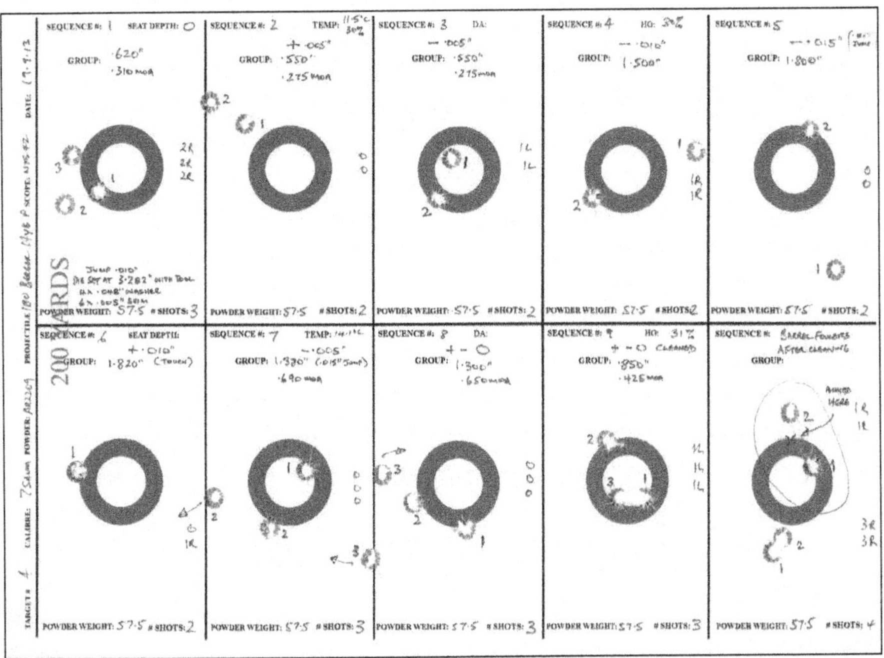

PHOTO 10-11.

The first bullet seat depth test with the #2 barrel.

Ok, what to do? I had 21 shots from clean already, so I gave the barrel a clean, fired two foulers, and a control group again, in sequence #9 at the 0 setting, which didn't do anything for me. Moving on to Photo 10-11A, I tried 3 shots at +.002" (.008" Jump) which was even worse. Finally, with the powder I had left I tried something radical, and fired sequence #11 at +.030" (.020" Jam) which was so bad I didn't bother with a third shot, and sequence #12 at –.030" (.040" Jump) wasn't much of an improvement. Because the first two shots were so close together and the third shot so far away, I fired the fourth shot to confirm that the two close shots were an aberration.

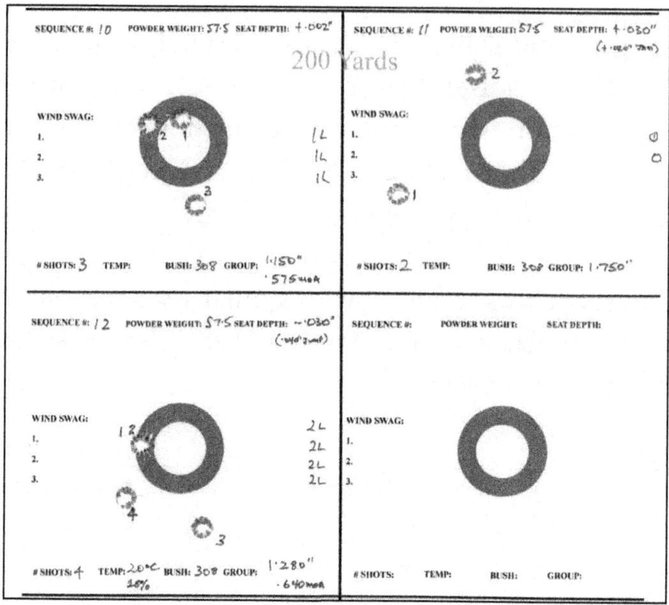

PHOTO 10-11A.

Continuing the PHOTO 10-11 test.

Obviously, this barrel didn't like projectiles Jammed, Touching, or close to the leade. I guess you could call the 0 setting a tuning node, but it wasn't a very good/accurate/repeatable one. It is a problem with these Berger Hybrid projectiles that they are liable to work at any point over a wide range of seating depths. In that regard VLD or bench-rest style projectiles, that prefer to be jammed into the leade, require many fewer seating depths to test, which speeds the job along, and subjects the barrel to less tuning shots. However, I much prefer to use projectiles that shoot best when Jumped. Often I have to unload my rifle on the line because I have had to wait too long for a condition, I would prefer to shoot in to return, and the cartridge has been cooking in the chamber. I have seen fellow competitors have to do this, with Jammed projectiles, many times, and it ain't much fun with a projectile Jammed in the bore, and an action full of powder half way through a string. Guaranteed to spoil your day.

Photo 10-12 shows the continuation of my seating depth test a couple of days later. This time I worked from the other direction starting the test at a new zero, which was Touch –.100", or .100" of Jump. Because shots through the barrel were accumulating (102 so far with no result) I tested initially in +.010" changes, hoping to narrow things down a little quicker. By the time I arrived at sequence #5 it seemed to me that the barrel was not going to behave unless the projectile was seated with .100" of Jump. The only depth I didn't test was +.050" (.050" of Jump), but I didn't figure there would be any miracles happening with it, so I didn't bother. Sequence #1 had its two projectiles nearly touching, so I returned to that setting and shot sequence #6, for 3 shots that printed in a group of .400" (.2MOA). I decided this would be the load that I would pursue further — 57.5GNS of powder and .100" of jump.

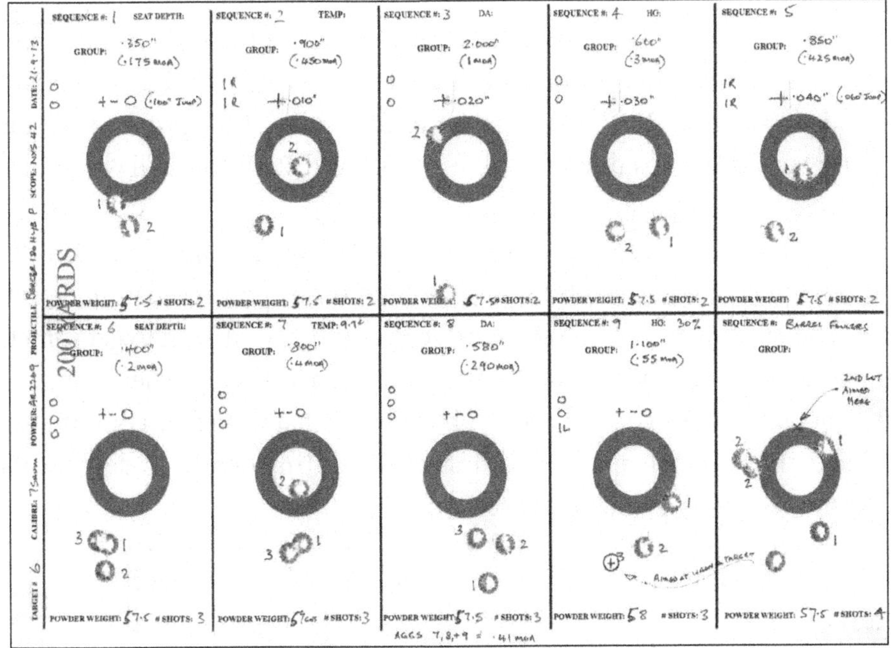

PHOTO 10-12.

The continuation of my seating depth test started in PHOTO 10-11.

Having found the optimum powder load, and optimum seating depth, for the barrel, I now test for the best average accuracy over a range of conditions. This I do by testing my best seating depth with powder loads ½ a grain each side of my optimum powder load. For instance, if my optimum powder load is 66 grains of powder, I will test at 65.5 grains, 66 grains, and 66.5 grains. In the case of a long range rifle I will be looking for an aggregate of the 3 x 3 shot groups, with 3 different powder loads, of .3MOA or less.

If I don't realize my less than .3MOA target, I will make the same test with my other seating depth accuracy node — if I have a suitable one. If I don't make the accuracy I want there, then I will move back to the first node and test seating depths either side of the optimum seating depth to find the best average accuracy.

By testing with three powder loads I am simulating variations in temperature I am likely to experience from day to day during a match. While my optimum seating depth may give me the best group in the condition in which it was shot, it may well shoot a monster when the conditions change. Testing that seating depth with powder loads a half a grain each side of the optimum powder load, gives me an indication of how that seating depth will react to a change in conditions. To my mind it is far better to have a combination that shoots three .3MOA groups, than one that shoots a 1MOA group on the low side, a .1MOA group in the middle and a .730MOA group on the high side. Were I testing with a single powder load only, I would no doubt seize on that .1MOA group as the best tune point, and it is *at that very moment*. But by testing powder loads either side of it I will see that it is, in fact, not ideal.

Before we finish with Photo 10-12 I decided, before I packed up to go home, to get a little bit of advanced information from the powder, I had left, before the next series of tests. Sequences #7, #8, and #9 were fired at .100" Jump with a one grain spread of powder to give me an idea of what to expect with my averaging tests.

While I was at it I also shot sequence #10 and #11 (Photo 10-12A) at –.005" and +.005" from 0, (.105" and .095" Jump) to again give me something to think about in the interim. Again the 57.5 grain load with .100" of Jump was satisfactory (sequence #8 Photo 10-12), the third time it had worked for me, and the spread was nearly there. It still needed a bit of work, but it showed promise. My thoughts from sequence #10 and #11 were that the optimum seating depth for this barrel would be somewhere between –.004" and +.004" from .100" of Jump. Hopefully finding the optimum seating depth would trim the +/- .5 grain spread groups down a tad also. I should stick to my day job, and forget about prediction as a career!

Photo 10-13 shows the next test shot at 200 yards in still early morning conditions. Up to this point this barrel has given me nothing to fall back on. My high travel powder load node is too slow, and I don't have a second bullet seating depth node worth considering, so if I am to get something from this barrel I need to make the +.5 grain load work with a seating depth somewhere from –.004" to +.004". I tested it in .002" increments. As you can see in Photo 10-13 that didn't pan out. It just didn't want to put two bullets closer than an inch apart regardless of the seating depth. In desperation, in sequence #6, I tried .002" less neck tension which was even worse.

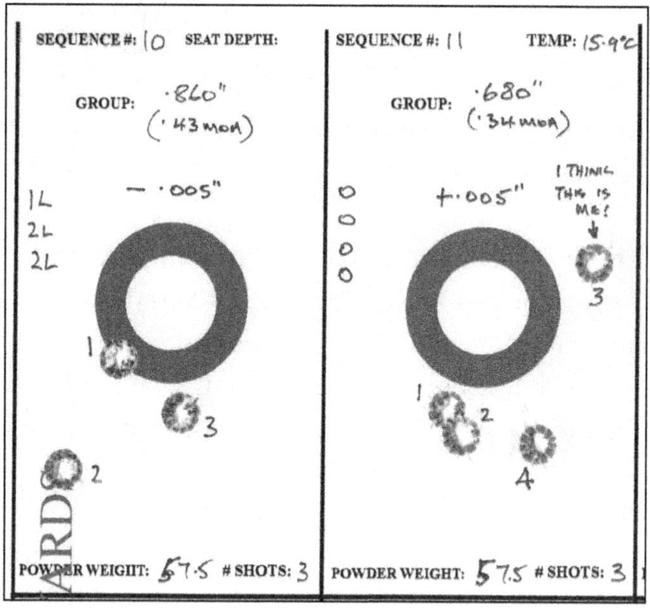

PHOTO 10-12A.

The final groups from the test in PHOTO 10-12.

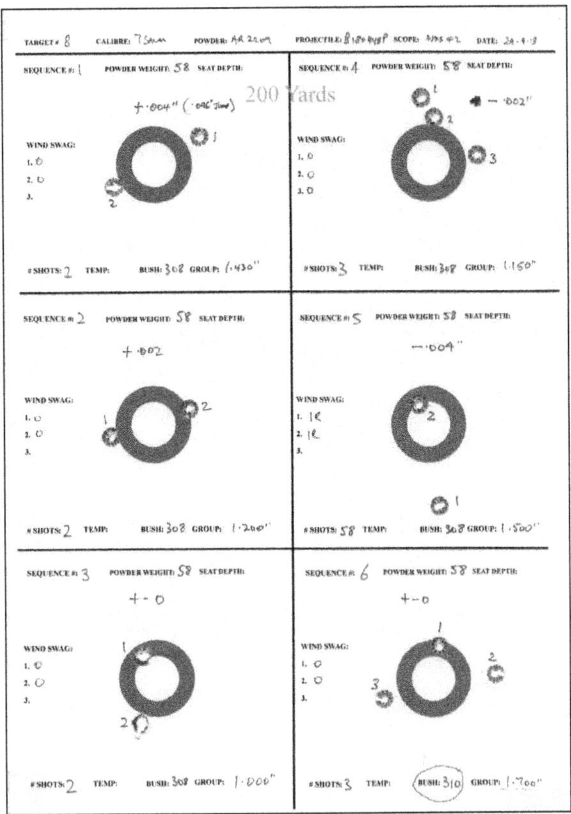

PHOTO 10-13.

Looking for the optimum seating depth with the +.5 grain load.

Finally I decided to check the primary load, 57.5 grains, at –.002", which showed me that only .002" of throat extension increased the group size considerably (+42%), and then retested my control load, 57.5 grains with .100" of Jump. Again the control load printed its three shots in a .600" (.3MOA) group. See Photo 10-13A.

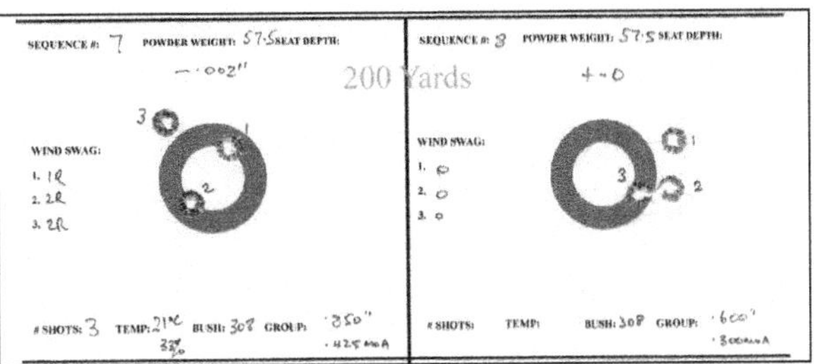

PHOTO 10-13A.

The final groups in the test from Photo 10-13.

What does all of the above tell me so far? Well — *this is not a competitive barrel,* but it does demonstrate very well what I have been talking about in this tuning chapter, namely tuning for best average accuracy, rather than best single group accuracy. Had I seized on the sequence #6 group in Photo 10-12 (Page 371), I would have fired several groups with it to prove it was a good setting, and all of those groups would have been .3MOA or just under. I would have moved to 500 yards and I am confident the good accuracy would have been repeated, and I would have been pleased with myself and the barrel. See Photo 10-14.

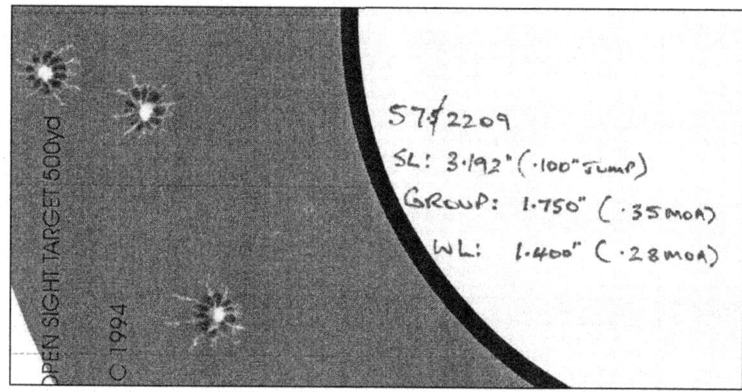

PHOTO 10-14.

A 500 yard 3 shot group fired with the control load in very ordinary mid morning conditions.

However — there is always a 'however' — by testing further with a load and seating depth spread I have discovered that the barrel is in fact a one trick pony. It has:–

A. No load window at all.
B. No seated depth window, and therefore no wear window at all.

What this means is, it is a barrel that will lose its tune easily, and will not be in good tune very often. As the throat, and leade, expand slightly with use, during the course of a two or three day competition, the throat will lengthen. The barrel will lose its tune requiring constant overall length adjustment to maintain optimum Jump. Adjusting overall length may or may not be beneficial, and it is not normally possible to test its effect during the competition. I would class it as a .5MOA barrel — good enough to straddle the X ring most of the time, but not good enough to stay inside the X ring throughout the day. As such it's a good barrel for small open matches, such as lead ups, or for club/practice matches, but not quite good enough if I want to be in the hunt in a big match, such as a Queens. There will be guys competing in those big matches with barrels that will hold well inside the X ring all through the day and week. If you want to finish at, or near the pointy end in those matches you need a barrel like they have — not this one.

Discounting that my first powder was unsatisfactory for this barrel, due to it being so hungry for powder, and considering the wide range of tuning possibilities, between touch and .100" of jump, I have found the barrels full potential in only 121 shots. It would have been less if the tune point was closer to where I started.

Unless you test the load like this you will not know how it is likely to react to condition changes. By tuning your barrel in this way you will have found the true potential of your barrel, and identified whether you can rely on it over the long haul, or whether the load you have settled on is a one trick pony load that shoots brilliantly one hour, and like a dog on the next.

Armed with the information I have obtained, by testing as I have, I know what to expect from this barrel. I will not be surprised when it doesn't perform as I would have expected had I tuned it only to its best single group. I won't be wondering what the Sam Hills happened, and suspect everything, but the barrel, when the accuracy has deteriorated during the day, ultimately, from nothing but a change in atmospherics.

Further testing with the #2 barrel, with yet another powder, confirmed what I had already worked out. It is an honest .5MOA barrel in any conditions, and will do better than that when conditions favor its working load. Certainly, not a hummer by any means, but not a dog either. It will hover around the X ring all day long, and when conditions favour its working load, may hammer that X ring. I have to live with that. Now—if only I could get that big nut behind the butt to work properly......

Often, you may very well not achieve the accuracy you are looking for, simply because the particular barrel you are testing is not capable of it. If you have followed the procedure I have outlined, you will know your barrel is tuned to the best accuracy it is capable of producing. If that is not satisfactory you will only be flogging a dead horse by pursuing it further. You have only two options. Live with it or get yourself another barrel. This one is no good!

I'm being harsh here, as it isn't so much that the barrel is no good, it's just that, more likely than not, it is not *completely* satisfactory for our purpose. The first barrel I had on my 7 SAUM was also just such a barrel, as is the #2 barrel, and at a cost of $600 for the blank, I have little choice but to live with it. In the real world you don't often get what you want. Some people are cashed up enough to have no problems dumping a mediocre barrel with only a hundred or so shots on it, but I am certainly not one of them. I just have to live with the handicap.

Why do barrels differ in quality? What makes one barrel blank a hummer, and the one right next to it an also ran? Does anyone know? I certainly don't. Quite frankly, neither do the barrel makers! If one of them did he would be making every barrel a hummer, and shooters would be flocking to his shop to buy his barrels.

No doubt, the quality of the steel bar the blank is made from has a direct bearing on the manufacturing process. Barrel steel is comprised of a mixture of elements and, no matter how carefully those elements are blended, one would have to be dreaming if one thought their composition was perfect. Given that there must be a variation, throughout the bar in its composition, it follows that those variations will react differently to the heat treatment processes that the bar undergoes during the course of its manufacture.

Any variation in the composition and/or hardness of the bar will cause the cutting tools, which are used to manufacture the barrel, to react differently when they pass through it. For instance, a single point drill will shy away from a hard section, when it encounters it, and move towards a softer section. That's a good reason why our barrel blanks are not straight, straight. A reamer will cut a slightly larger hole in a soft section of steel than it will in a harder section. So will a rifling cutter, or a rifling button. Even a lead lap will cut through soft steel faster than through harder steel. So, regardless of how careful the manufacturer is, there will be variations in the bore of the individual barrel blank, and these variations will differ from blank to blank.

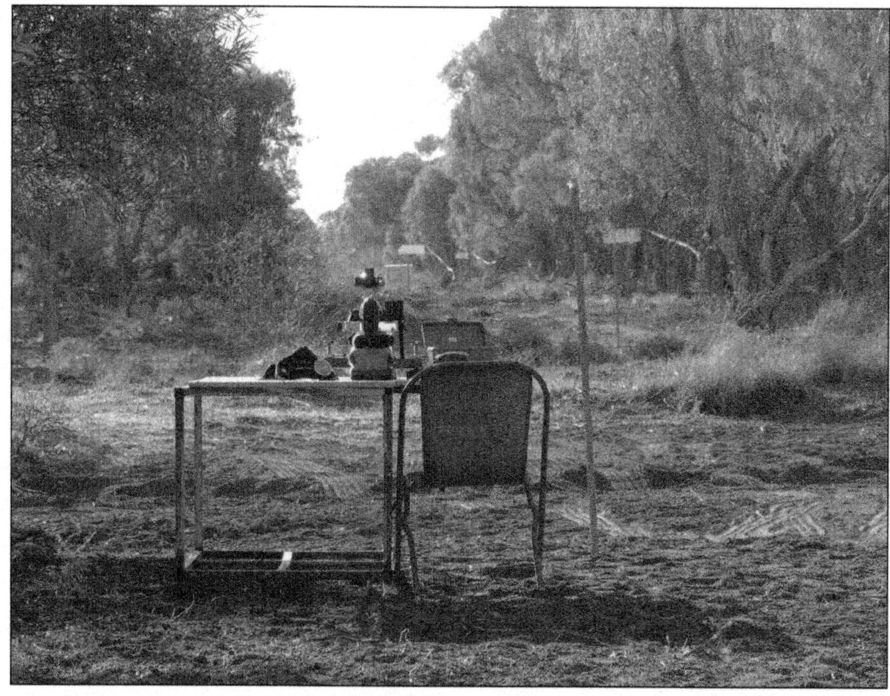

PHOTO 10-15.
The authors private range, where most of the testing in this chapter was carried out.

How do you tell a good blank from a not so good blank before it is fitted? I have absolutely no idea, other than if, after it is fitted, it shoots tiny little groups consistently, and holds into the wind better than commonsense says it should, it is a good blank, and you should treasure it. Save it for the big matches, for that is where it will do the most good. It is wasted in club shoots — use your 3rd best barrel for them.

I can, however, relate some information about my first 7 Saum barrel that may be of interest. When I fitted that barrel I was really stretched for time. After a long wait, and despite receiving preferential treatment, for which I am thankful, the reamer arrived only a few weeks before we were due to leave for 2012s away competitions. I had no 7mm barrel off-cuts with which to make my 3 testing tools, so I drilled out a piece of 6mm barrel, and reamed it to 7mm (.2756") for the job, which meant the bore was smooth with no rifling, and that led me into a trap. After I fitted and throated the barrel I inspected the throat with my bore scope, and was somewhat surprised to see that the throating reamer had not touched the grooves of the rifling at all. In fact, the rifling lands could be easily seen right back at the very front of the chamber.

I remember thinking to myself that maybe the throating reamer was a tad undersize. That was a stupid thought. Hugh Henriksen doesn't make out of spec tools — period. But, being the dumb shit I am, that's what I thought. Honestly, there 'aint no cure for stupid! If I had a piece of 7mm barrel, with which to make my 3 tools, alarm bells may have rang, as I would have seen that the reamer did, in fact, cut its correct .2845" diameter. However, that didn't happen. I could see the rifling lands prominently right at the front of the chamber, and that should have been a red flag — apparently it wasn't a big enough one. Regardless, my options were very limited. Stop, and investigate it fully, and forget about 2012s away shoots, or suck it and see how it goes. At my time of life you really can't afford to put something off for a year. You may not be around next year, so suck it and see was the only option.

Even though it did good work for me early in 2012, the barrel was mediocre to say the least. By the time we returned home in June it had just over 600 shots on it, and from then on I could not get it to shoot satisfactorily—certainly not good enough for F Open competition where the accuracy requirement, if you want to be competitive, is an honest .3MOA maximum. I threw another 500 shots at it trying everything I know, but in the end it was obvious it was never going to work, so I retired it at 1100 shots. It was pretty dumb of me to persevere with it for so long—I spent enough money in useless testing to pay for a new blank!

Why was it not a good barrel? The manufacturer's tolerance is –0 +.0005". That blank was certainly out of spec. I pushed a .2845" diameter throating reamer into it, and could still easily see rifling lands at the front of the chamber, which indicates to me that the groove size was well over the maximum allowable diameter of .2845". It was probably closer to .2850" than it was to .2845". To my mind, being oversize like that is a good reason for it not to work. The projectiles I use measure .2843" diameter at the expansion ring, and .2837" diameter just in front of it.

I would not expect those projectiles to be happy little campers in a barrel like I had, and the barrels performance bears that out. Probably, if it were possible to obtain projectiles measuring .2850" diameter at the expansion ring, the barrel would have worked, but that wasn't going to happen.

So, there's one reason a barrel will be mediocre. What have I learned from this? Well—I won't fit another of those barrels before I run my throating reamer into the back of that 1" piece I cut from the muzzle when I prepare the blank, which will tell me whether or not the barrel is oversize, and whether I should proceed with it. Additionally, I now keep a back up blank on hand, so I won't be caught short with a bad blank again. As I said, at my time of life a year lost may be lost forever.

Finally, if the rifle is for long range work, we can move back, and test accuracy there with some longer strings. Just because the rifle shoots well at 200 yards doesn't mean it will shoot well at 500 yards, or at 1000 yards. If I am having vertical problems at long range I find I can usually cure them with a variation in neck tension, either up or down.

From here on in, it's simply a case of monitoring the rifle during matches, and looking for aberrations that may indicate a loss of accuracy. Essentially, I monitor leade lengthening, with my measuring tool, and chase any increase by adding shims to my seating die. I look for vertical shots I can't explain, and also for shots that go against the wind during matches. This can be perplexing at long range, because often the flags say one thing, but the wind may well be doing something else.

Overall, my aim in this exercise is to find a good tune, while firing as few shots as possible. Quite apart from the fact that our ammunition is expensive, our barrels have a finite life, and that is best spent in competition, rather than frittered away in tuning, or unnecessary testing.

In the next chapter I will be discussing barrel tuners. *Regardless of whether you will be using a barrel tuner, or not, you should tune your barrel to its best average accuracy.* Only by doing that will you have a rifle that is a reliable and consistent performer.

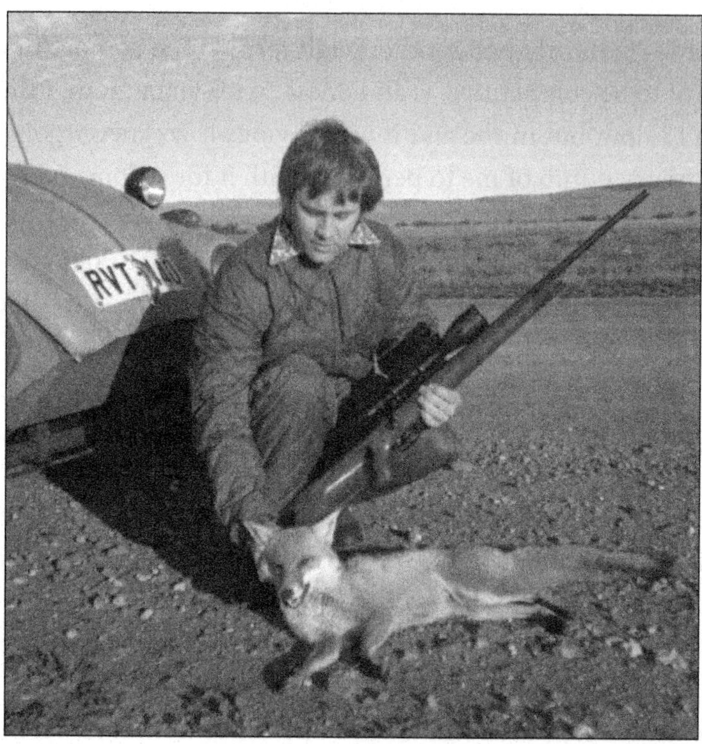

Photos 10-16 and 10-17.

Some time in the early 1970s I sent the editor of Sporting Shooter Magazine a negative strip containing the photograph on PAGE 77, thinking that would make a good cover shot for the magazine. I still think that, but obviously I was wrong, because they picked a lousy photo of me, that was on the same strip, and had the shadow of the rifles barrel across my face. If they had asked, I could have supplied the next negative strip with a better photo. That's it in Photo 10-16.

Photo 10-17 is included to show the right hand side of my .338/06.

AN M'98 MAUSER IN .257 ACKLEY IMPROVED ROBERTS

BUILT IN THE LATE 1980S

PHOTO C5-13.

Photographs are shown in the white in order that fine detail may be more easily observed.

PHOTO C5-14.

The stick was another nice piece of Roger Vardy's Australian English Walnut.

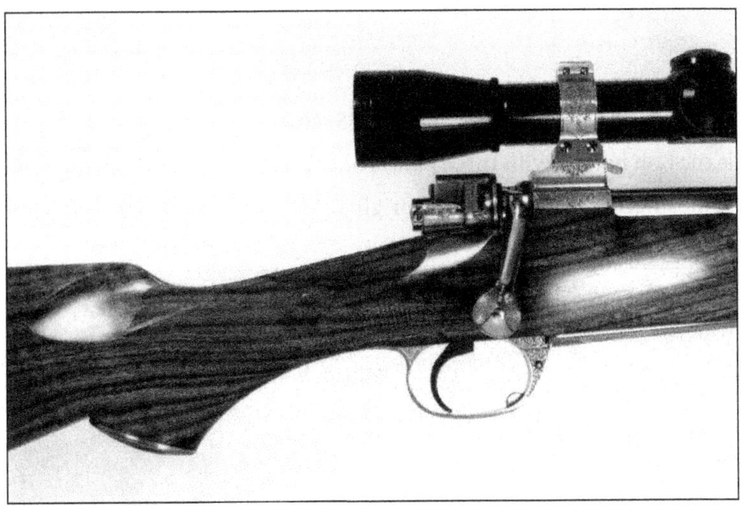

PHOTO C5-15.

This particular rifle had the 4" grip length I have on my personal hunting rifle. I made Mausers in three grip lengths, 3½", 3¾", and 4", to suite the size of the hands of my customers. The stock design was refined with every rifle I built until I believed I had found the ideal cast off at heel and toe, ideal drop at the heel, and ideal pitch angle so that in the end they pointed like an extension of your arm.

PHOTO C5-16.
A Classic bolt handle with three panels of checkering. The side swing safety is a two position design built on the original Mauser bolt shroud. Very classic.

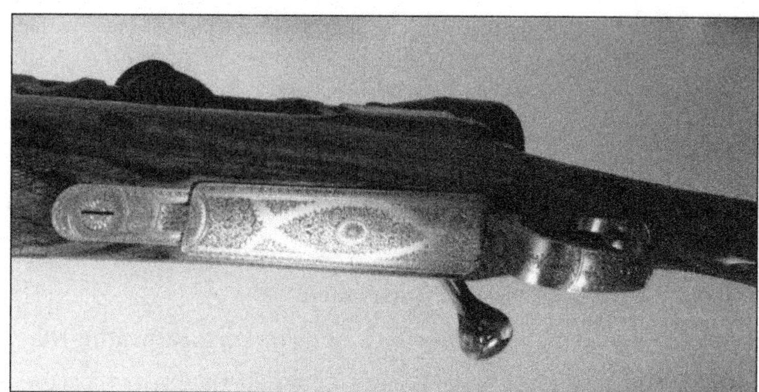

PHOTO C5-17.
Floor plate detail. Note custom made flush fitted front screw.

PHOTO C5-18.
Stock treatment around the bolt stop at the rear bridge of the action.

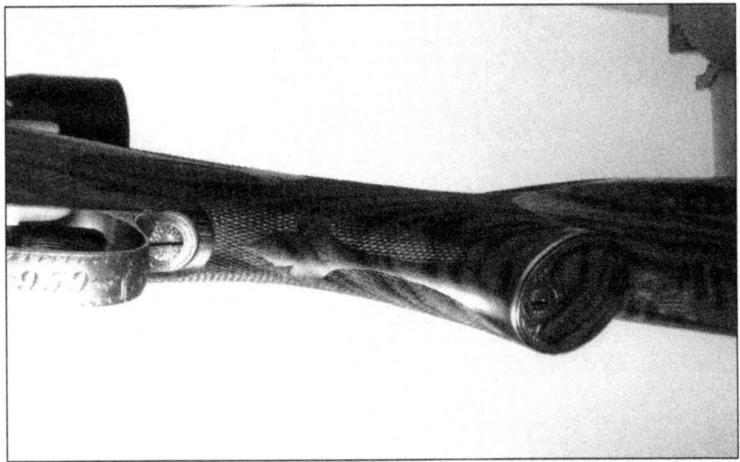

PHOTO C5-19.
Note the rear screw is shaped to fit the contour of the trigger guard. The checkering pattern wraps completely around the grip with no break.

PHOTO C5-20.
Detail of checkering underneath the forend.

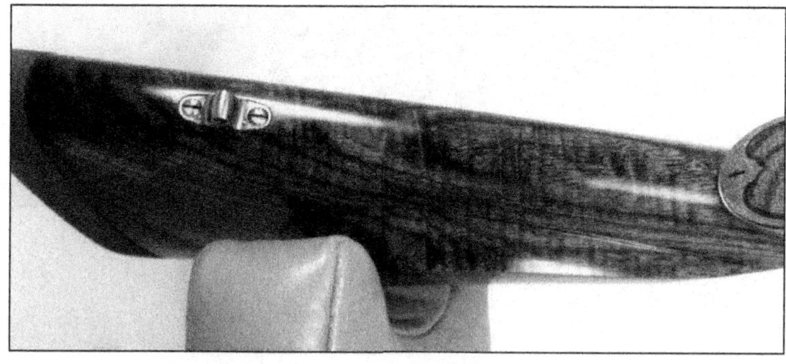

PHOTO C5-21.
Rear swivel base of 2 screw oval design.

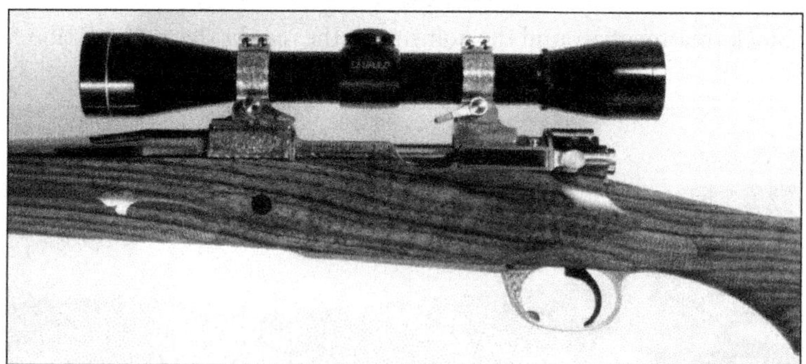

PHOTO C5-22.
Left hand side action profile. The cross-bolt hole is filled with an Ebony plug. Trigger is a Canjar M-3, modified and tuned for a 1¼ pound pull.

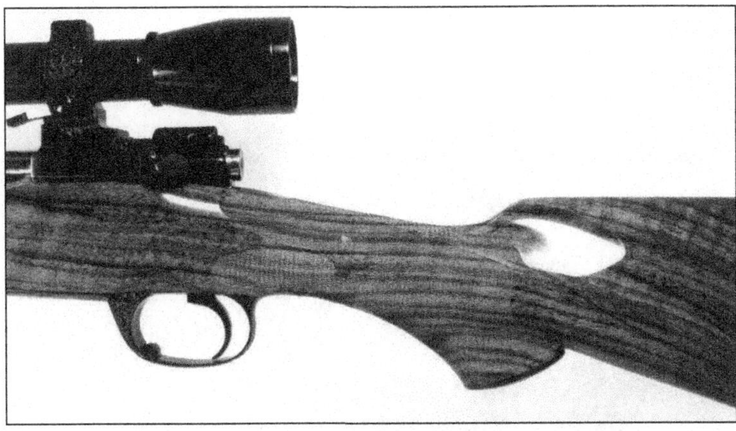

PHOTO C5-23.

The scope rings were quick detachable units made by Dave Talley in the USA.

PHOTO C5-24

These scope bases were custom made for each individual rifle and the rifle was fired on target to obtain precise alignment with the scope adjustments centred.

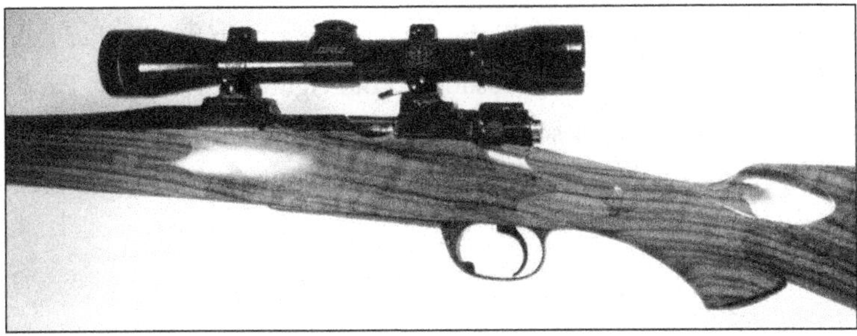

PHOTO C5-25.

These Fler-de-Lis checkering patterns took over 60 hours to complete.

Photo C5-26.

I am on the 700 yard mound at our local rifle range, trying to figure out what the Sam Hill's going on down range. Even with a spotting scope I don't have much of a clue! Here, I am testing a few loads with a different powder. My wind flags are out and placed so that I can see them through the spotting scope, which has a wide angle 20X eyepiece. A clipboard and pen are on your left. I jot down windage notes for each shot on it. On your right is my ammo box with blood sample vials I have my powder loads in. I have two shots to go before I must travel down to the target and see the result of this phase of the test. I will then load some ammo for another test on the back of my truck, which is just out of shot on your right. The rifle is my Panda 7MM REMINGTON SAUM. The telescopic sight is a March 10-60X in high Kelbly rings. The rest is a Farley, and the spotting scope a Kowa TSN-820M on a home made stand.

CHAPTER ELEVEN

BARREL TUNERS

A barrel tuner is an adjustable weight that is fitted onto the end of a barrel, in order to modify its harmonics. *It is a tool we can use to bring a slightly out of tune barrel back into tune.* It is *not* a magic bullet.

I am no expert on tuners, as my experience is limited to one design that I use on a regular basis. However, I do have some information to pass on that may prove beneficial, or at the very least make you think about what you are doing.

Tuners vary in design, depending on who is producing them, and there are many claims made about the benefits of this one or that one, some of which may or may not be true. One thing I am convinced of, though, is that they do work, but not necessarily in the way many people may think.

We discussed the tuning tools available to us in the chapter on tuning, and the desirability to tune the barrel for its best average accuracy over a wide load window, rather than for its most accurate single load. *This is especially important in matches where the shooter has only limited sighting shots;* long range competition (Big Bore / F class) being an example.

No matter how well you tune a rifle, on any given day, there is no doubt in my mind that, on any other day, it may well not be at its perfect tune. In fact, there is a very good chance that the barrel will not be at its perfect tune later on, that very day, after you finished tuning it. Therefore, it is possible to refine its tune on that different day, and restore it to what it was when you tuned it originally. The reason for this wandering tune is generally agreed to be atmospherics, and their changeability, from, not only day to day, but even hour to hour.

I said the tuner is not a magic bullet, though it is a very useful tool when understood and used properly. The reason it is not a 'magic bullet' is because it is very unlikely that you will be able to fit a tuner to a rifle, that is shooting badly, and magically turn it into a tack driver by only adjusting the tuner. It is not that simple. *A tuners function is to maintain tune, rather than create it.* Before it can be truly effective, the barrel needs to be tuned to its best average accuracy, as discussed in Chapter Ten — Barrel Tuning.

The tuners advantage is, that being an adjustable mechanical device, it can be set in a position, on the barrel, that will modify the barrels harmonics, *either speeding them up, or slowing them down.* By doing that it can bring back into tune a combination of ammunition and barrel, that has lost its tune, due to a change in atmospherics. When we tune a barrel by varying powder load, and bullet seating depth, we are adjusting the load in our ammunition to be in synch with the harmonics of our barrel.

Essentially, we are timing our projectiles to arrive at the muzzle of the barrel, every shot at, or as close as possible to, the point where the barrel is at the zenith of its oscillations, either up or down. We can change the time our projectiles arrive at the muzzle by varying powder load or bullet seating depth, thereby achieving perfect tune or taking the rifle out of perfect tune, though once perfect tune has been found we would hardly want to do that. When we adjust a tuner, we are altering, and timing the barrels harmonics to the *in barrel time of our ammunition.* In other words, *we are working backwards.* With our *original* tune we tuned our *ammunitions in barrel time to the harmonics of the barrel.* This is an important thing to understand. The tuner allows us to maintain a perfect tune that has been degraded by the effects of atmospherics, on the in barrel time of our ammunition, and allows us to adjust that tune quickly and easily.

If you will have a look at Photo 11-1, you will see the effect a tuner has on the factors we have been talking about, mainly in barrel time versus barrel harmonics. As an aside, this sequence of groups was shot when I took the sequence of photographs demonstrating my shooting method, seen starting on page 408. I started this test with my tuner screwed right in at 12:00, and screwed it out in increments as the test progressed.

In sequence #1 the shots printed with .144" of vertical, which was coincidentally the group size as well. This rifle has done better than that in the past, so I know, from experience, that the tune is close, but not perfect, or at least as good as it can be. In sequence #2, I moved the tuner out towards the muzzle, ¼ of a turn, to the 3:00 position. The group was a little larger at .188", and the vertical fractionally less, at .137" — close, but not as good as the rifle can be. In sequence #3, I, again, screwed the tuner out ¼ of a turn, to the 6:00 position. *Here I have taken a barrel, that was nearly in tune (in sequence #1), completely out of tune.* The group, at .326", with the same .326" of vertical is as bad as this rifle shoots. In sequence #4, I, again, wound the tuner out ¼ of a turn to the 9:00 position, and you can see the tune has improved, marginally, with both group size, and vertical reducing. In sequence #5, I, again, wound the tuner out ¼ of a turn, back to the 12:00 position, but this time a full turn out from its original position. This brought the barrel into perfect tune, or at least as perfect as I am ever going to shoot it, with only .051" of vertical, and the same group size. Sequence #6 was fired without the tuner fitted, and represents the basic tune of the barrel, on that day, in the atmospheric conditions that applied when the groups were fired. As you can see the group at .279", with .279" of vertical, was improved considerably with the tuner fitted.

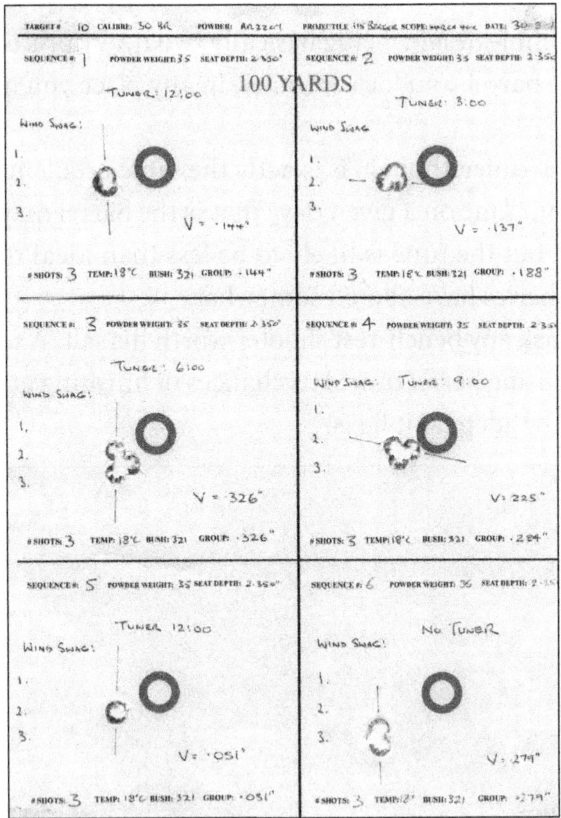

PHOTO 11-1.

This photo demonstrates the effect a barrel tuner has, on a barrel, in regard to barrel oscillations versus the in barrel time of projectiles.

I have repeated this test many times, with several different barrels, always with the same result. You could say I'm a believer!

In target oriented rifle matches with unlimited sighters, tuners negate a huge advantage many of the top competitors have — an advantage that has been gained by much experimenting and experience. Before the advent of barrel tuners, maintaining barrel tune, during a match, was a process of experience based guesswork around the competitor's perception of what the atmospheric conditions, and temperature, were likely to be when the competitor would be next on the firing line, and how he perceived those conditions would affect the tune of the barrel. If the competitor divined — and that's about what it is! — that there would be a tune affecting atmospheric change, before he was up for his next group, he would adjust his powder load slightly to compensate for the change, that adjustment being based on prior experience, and a lot of it.

Once the competitor is committed, to a course of action, he is stuck with it, and has to suffer the consequences, if he has made an incorrect choice. Those consequences are, of course, to shoot a monster.

With the advent of barrel tuners, provided the barrel has been tuned to its best average accuracy previously, the competitor can literally dial his barrel into its best tune, in a couple of minutes or less, and know that when he runs his group, or score, the barrel will be shooting as accurately as it is possible to be. There is no need to be varying the load, or second guessing the conditions. The tuner will modify the barrels oscillations to be in time with the in barrel time of your existing load, and your barrel will be at best tune. It doesn't get much better than that!

The tuner I have used extensively, and still use as I write this, is one designed and made by Gene Beggs in the U.S.A. It can be seen, along with the barrel modification required to fit it, in Photos 11-2, and 11-3. It is a deceptively simple design, being basically two heavy precision machined stainless steel washers that thread onto the barrel, and lock together, in any place you might choose. I have found it to be a very effective device.

The problem with using a Tuner, though, is exactly the same problem we encounter when we tune the barrel for best single group tune on a given day. That is the barrel may be in perfect tune when we have completed the process, but the tune is likely to be less than ideal the next day, or even later on that same day when atmospherics have altered somewhat.

If you don't believe this, ask any bench-rest shooter worth his salt. A top grade bench-rest shooters existence revolves around chasing barrel tune. His chances of finishing at the pointy end in any match are directly dependent on how adept at it he is.

PHOTO 11-2.

This is my Beggs Barrel Tuner fitted to my .22PPC practice rifle.

In a fantasy world we would be able to correlate atmospheric conditions to tuner setting and have the barrel/ammunition combo in perfect tune. Something like X% density altitude + X% humidity + X degrees temperature equals a tuner setting of 15, and the rifle will be in perfect tune. Alas, we do not live in a fantasy world (most of us anyway), so we need to deal with the one we have.

I have tried to do just that over several thousand shots, and not been able to come up with any formula that works, even some of the time. I did however learn a great deal about my tuner, and arrived at some pertinent conclusions, as follows.

1. There is no doubt in my mind, at all, that tuners work. Every time I have tested one of my rifles with a tuner fitted, and the rifle exhibited a slightly out of tune condition, I have been able to bring it into tune very quickly by adjusting the tuner.

2. The *only* way to tune a rifle with a tuner is to fire it for group, and adjust the tuner, until you obtain the tune you need.

3. There is *no way* (I know of) you can predict where the tuner needs to be positioned in order to bring the rifle into tune.

PHOTO 11-3.
The Beggs tuner disassembled. It is very simple, but works very effectively.

Given the above conclusions, I believe that having a tuner fitted to a rifle, that will be used in a match without unlimited sighters, *is a total waste of time.* That includes any form of long range shooting. The only exception would be if you had access to a 100 or 200 yard sight in range close to the main range, and could fire a few groups to find tune before the match, but that's a very unlikely scenario. Otherwise a tuner on your rifle is merely adding excess weight to the barrel, *and is just as likely to be hindering tune as it is to be enhancing it.*

So how can we use one? This is how I do it.

Photo 11-4 is a very good example of my methodology. This is the first target I fired in a bench-rest for score match in 2012 at our local club. We don't use wind flags (Western Queenslanders don't need 'em!), and the wind was very strong on the day, coming from 6.30 to 7.30, strong enough to shake you on the bench.

The rifle is a .30BR shooting the Berger 115 grain match projectile at 3000FPS. The action on this rifle is the Shilen DGA we accurised in Chapter One.

I start by firing two fouling shots into the backing board of the target close to the sighter target aiming at an existing bullet hole to see how my zero is, and foul the barrel.

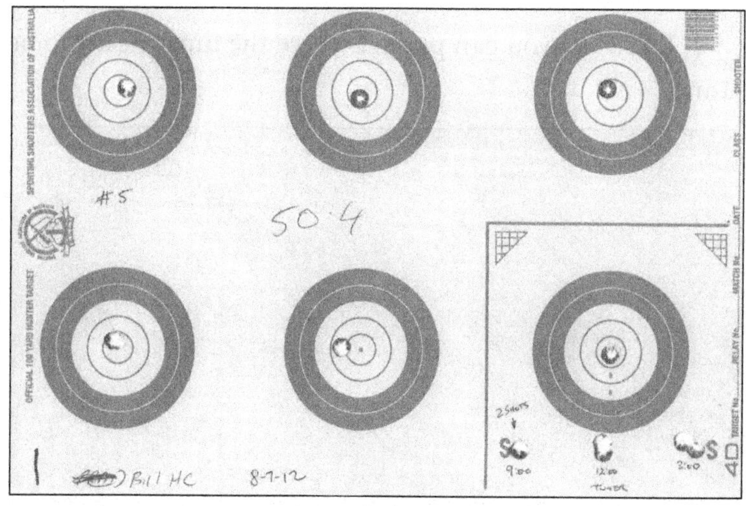

PHOTO 11-4.

Setting the tuner at the start of a 100YD score match.

In this instance my first two shots on the sighter target were made aiming at the bottom of the outside target ring with my tuner set at 12:00. You can see the rifle is exhibiting about ½ a bullet hole of vertical with those two shots. I think I can do better, so I adjust my tuner to the 3:00 position and fire another 2 shots aiming at the 'S' on the right hand side of the sighter target. I was caught by a bit of wind but the print still showed a bit of vertical, though a little bit less than the 12:00 setting. I think I can do better. Next I set the tuner at the 9:00 position and fire two more shots this time aiming about ½" to the right of the left hand 'S' on the sighter target. I don't want to pop a shot over the line or it will count for score, and that's a disaster. This time I get what I'm after. The rifle looks like it's in perfect tune, so I go with this setting.

If I have any doubts during the match it is a simple matter to check my tune on the next sighter target, with a couple of shots, and adjust the tuner if necessary to bring the rifle back into perfect tune. There is no penalty involved in doing this, as it is done in conjunction with sighter shots that are fired to test the effect of the wind. You have to fire these shots anyway. I crank my 2 shots off in 5 seconds — many top competitors can get them away in 3 seconds or less. You just need to fire an extra shot to gauge the vertical dispersion between those shots, and prove the tune of your barrel. For certain, this is a much better scenario than having made a load adjustment before the match, then firing a couple of shots on the sighter, only to have them print with a tenth or more of vertical. Hoo-boy — big group coming up!

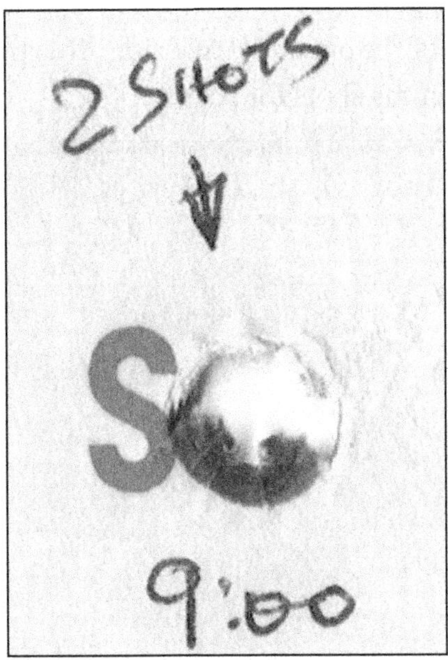

PHOTO 11-5.

A close up of the two shots with the tuner set at 9:00

Photo 11-6 is the first target from another 100 yard bench-rest for score match. I had been using the tuner on my .22PPC practice rifle, and when I refitted it to the .30BR I had it one turn too far in. Some people really have dumb kids! This time I fired my first two sighters, on the sighter target, aiming at the top of the outside target ring, with my tuner set in the 12:00 position.

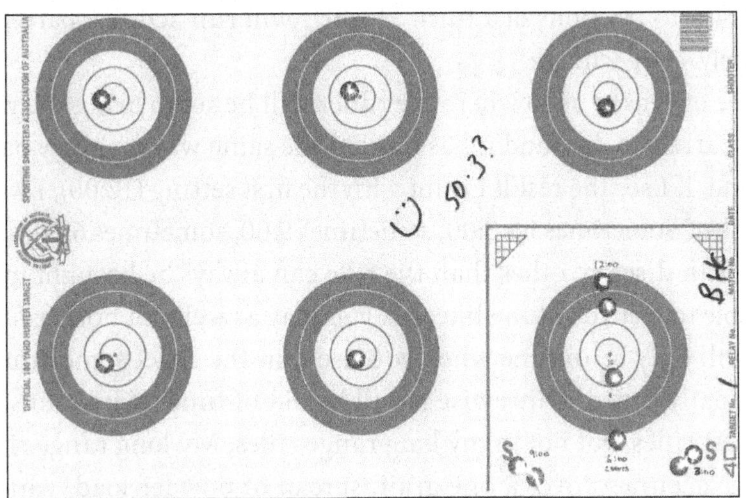

PHOTO 11-6.

Target #1 from another 100YD match. This time I didn't find tune until the 6:00 position, but I found tune none the less.

It is convenient on bench-rest targets to print your test shots at whatever o'clock position, on the target, that the tuner is set at. It helps to remember what you have done.

The shots printed with considerable vertical, so I screwed the tuner out ¼ of a turn to the 3:00 position, and fired 2 shots, aiming at the right hand S. Vertical was reduced, but I knew the rifle could do better, so I screwed the tuner out ½ of a turn, to the 9:00 position, and fired 2 shots aiming ½" to the right of the left hand S. If anything, I had a little more vertical. I shouldn't have tried to second guess the setting. I decided I should go back to the 6:00 position, so screwed the tuner back in, and fired 2 shots aiming at the bottom of the outside target ring. This time I found what I was looking for. The rifle was in best tune, and I ran my shots for score.

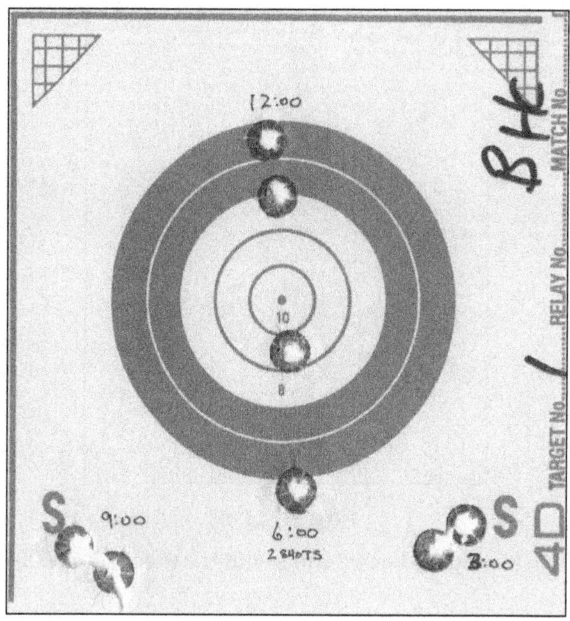

PHOTO 11-7.

A close up of the sighter target from PHOTO 11-6.

I have always been able to find best tune with this device at the 12:00, 3:00, 6:00, or 9:00 positions, without having to resort to fractions of a turn. Maybe I will run across a barrel in the future where that rule does not apply — we will see.

There is no rhyme or reason as to where the tuner will be set to bring the rifle into tune. I have had it on 4 different barrels to date and it has reacted the same way on every barrel. I always follow the same sequence and, if I see the result I want with the first setting (12:00), I will go with it without bothering to test further. Sometimes it's 3:00, sometimes 9:00, sometimes 6:00, and sometimes 12:00. There is no pattern I can discern, other than the rifle can always be brought into best tune with it.

Unless you are able to test your tune like this you may as well not bother fitting a tuner to your barrel. Your barrel will only be in tune when you use it in the exact same atmospheric conditions in which it was originally tuned. Otherwise it will be out of tune, at least to some degree. I fit the tuner to my bench-rest rifles, but not to my long range rifles. My long range rifle is tuned with the load, for best average accuracy, over a one grain spread of powder load, which is the best way, I think, to do it.

Having said that, though, lately I have been thinking my tuner may well be a worthwhile addition to my long range rifle, not during competitions, but rather as a tuning aid, or rather a tune confirmor. The tuner makes it so quick and easy to find the barrels best tune, I am thinking it would be an asset to test whether my original tune is still good enough to take away, or if I need alter my load before I leave. Have I tuned my barrel to its full potential? If I have threaded my barrel, I can screw my tuner onto it, and test the existing tune. If I can find a better tune by adjusting the tuner, obviously my original tune is not optimal, and I have more work to do. It is certainly food for thought, and something I intend to pursue.

If you have a tuner fitted, or are contemplating obtaining one, my advice is to learn its characteristics and adopt a procedure, such as I have described above. Start with the tuner screwed all the way in and backed out so its '0' mark is at the 12:00 position. Fire a 2 shot group and note the groups characteristics. If you put 2 shots in one hole, that's fine; don't stop there though. Rotate your tuner to the 9:00 position and fire another 2 shots. Find the position on the tuner where the rifle goes out of tune, and the position where it comes back into tune, and record it for future reference. If you play around a bit you will gain the experience needed to bring your rifle into perfect tune very quickly using the tuner, and keep it there throughout the day.

Many tuners have fine adjustment graduations etched on them, so don't go falling into the trap of making small incremental adjustments. Start with a ¼ turn at a time. My tuner is threaded at 28TPI, and if the thread on your tuner is finer than that you should make a coarser adjustment, more like a third of a turn. Of course, if your thread is coarser, make a finer adjustment. Just don't go making 1/25TH of a turn adjustments because your tuner is etched in 1/25TH increments.

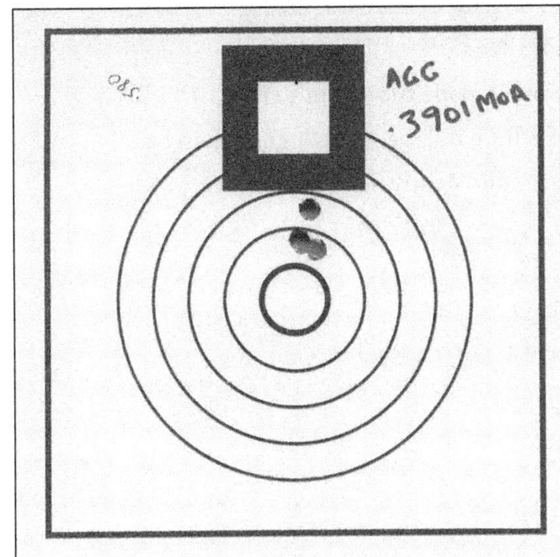

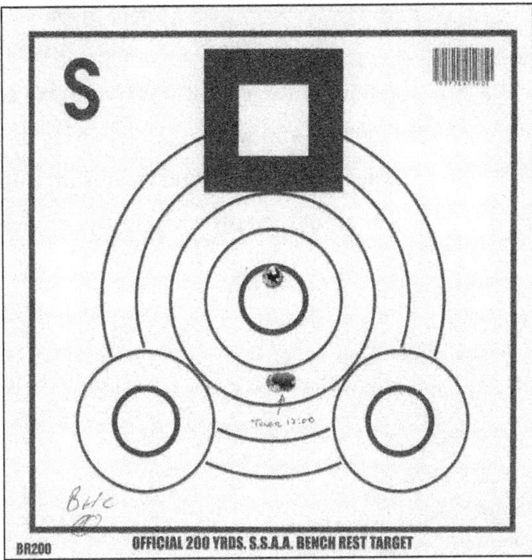

PHOTOS 11-8 AND 11-9.

This is the first target from a local Bench-Rest for group match at 200 yards. As usual, no wind flags were out, and the wind was not kind. My tuner setting at 12:00 looked good so I went with it, not bothering to test further. I would have shot a good group if I didn't roll back with the recoil on shot #3, a bad habit of mine. If tune looks good I don't bother looking further. There isn't much point in doing so. The rifle was my .30BR.

I have a friend who has a Shadetree Tuner fitted to the barrel of his .308 F Class Standard rifle, which he also uses in our local Bench-Rest Matches. The Shadetree Tuner is similar to the Beggs Tuner, with the exception that it positions the two heavy washers in front of the muzzle of the rifle, rather than behind it, like the Beggs does. From what I have seen of it, it reacts pretty much the same as my tuner. He has recently adopted my methodology (I should have kept quiet!), and his tuner, like mine, brings his rifle into perfect tune. Now, his sighter targets look just like the one you can see in Photo 11-4. Unfortunately, so do his record targets.

Of course, you would be getting a far more accurate indication of tune by firing 3 shot groups, or even 5 shot groups, but you would only be flogging out a good barrel to no purpose. If a good accurate barrel will not put 2 shots into the same hole, it's on the cards you won't be getting any extra information by banging down a third. Like in initial tuning, we want to limit the number of useless shots we put through the barrel, and save it for the real deal.

PHOTO 11-10.

The mid winter conditions that prevailed when I made the test in PHOTO 11-1. It is 8:00AM, and without cloud cover there is a little mirage, but not enough to be a problem — yet! The wind is coming from 3:00 consistently, so I only need to watch the angle of the tails when I run my groups.

A DROPPED MAGAZINE 7X57 MAUSER

BUILT ON AN M'98 MAUSER ACTION IN THE LATE 1980S

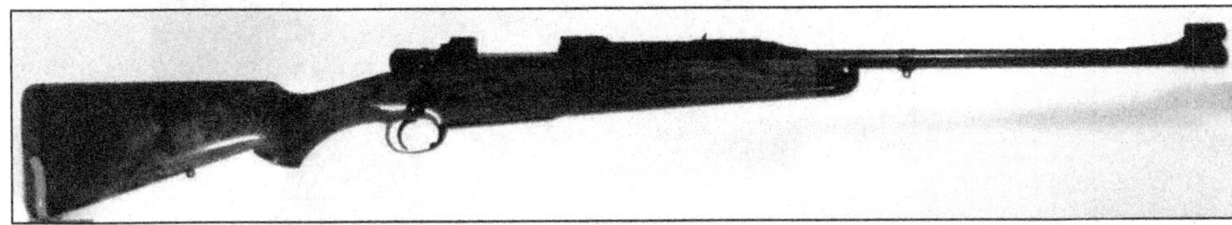

PHOTO C5-26.

This rifle is representative of the shape I was making at the end of my career.

PHOTO C5-27.

The dropped magazine is unusual on a small calibre like the 7 X 57 Mauser, however this rifle was built to be a mate for the Mauser .375 H&H on page 240.

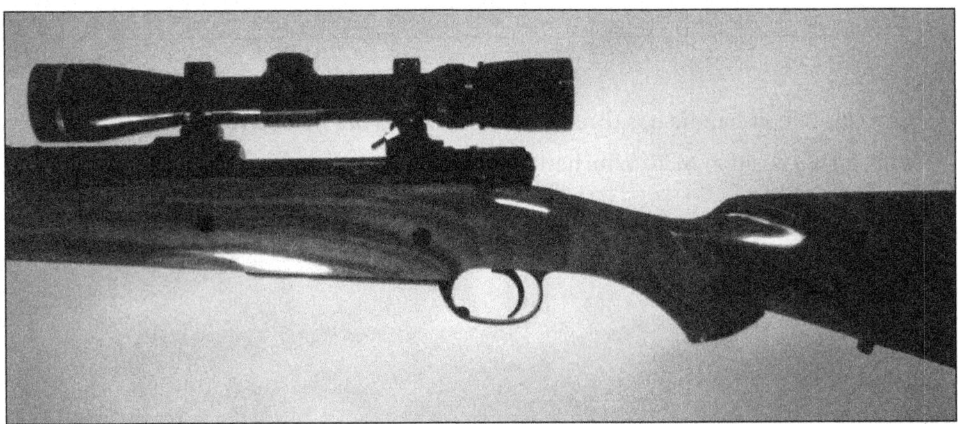

PHOTO C5-28.

Front and rear cross-bolts were capped with Ebony. The rifle was equipped for a telescopic sight with side lever quick detachable mounts, as well as open sights with a quarter rib, express rear sight, and barrel banded foresight.

PHOTO C5-29.

The classic bolt handle has three panels of checkering in a teardrop pattern. The safety is a 3 position M'70 Winchester design.

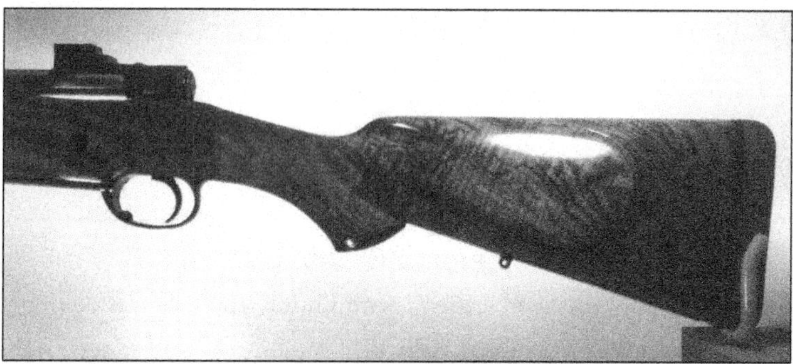

PHOTO C5-30.

LHS Butt and grip profile sans scope. The stick was a nice piece of Australian English Walnut from Roger Vardy in Victoria. When I moved to Tumbarumba, N.S.W. in 1982 I used Roger's wood nearly exclusively, and liked it.

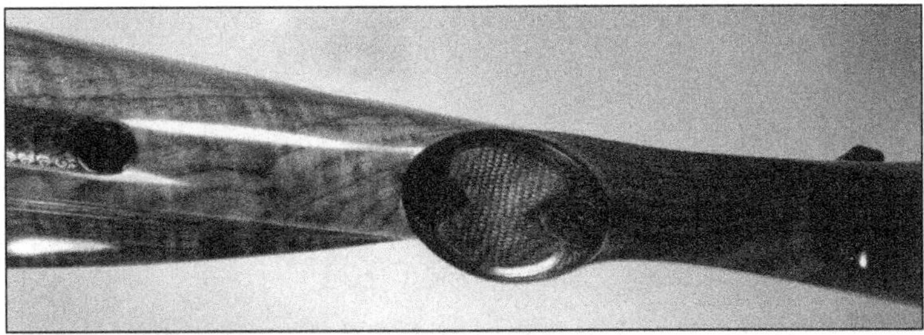

PHOTO C5-31.

The grip cap is a scalloped skeleton design with a panel of checkering. These grip caps were very popular.

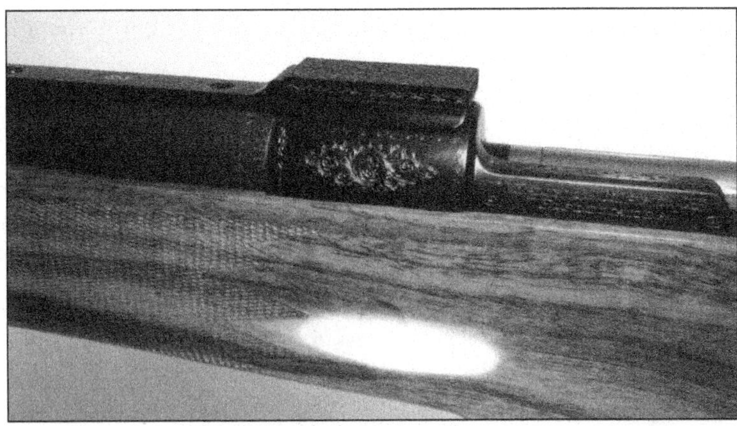

PHOTO C5-32.

I made caps that covered the telescopic sight base dovetails front and rear when the telescopic sight was removed for open sight use. Here the cap is installed on the front base dovetail.

PHOTO C5-33.

Here the cap is removed from the base. You can see the detent that retains it. These caps were stored in the butt trap when the telescopic sight was installed.

PHOTO C5-34.

These butt traps were also popular. I made the swivel stud from ½" round steel.

PHOTO C5-35.

These express rear sights were regulated by shooting on target with factory ammunition, and machined to make zero on my home range. The barrel was blued stainless steel.

PHOTO C5-36.

This ¼ rib design was also one of my trademarks.

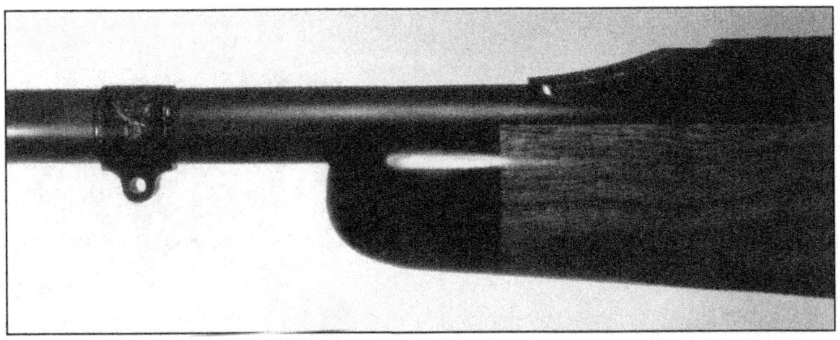

PHOTO C5-37.
The forend tip is African Ebony.

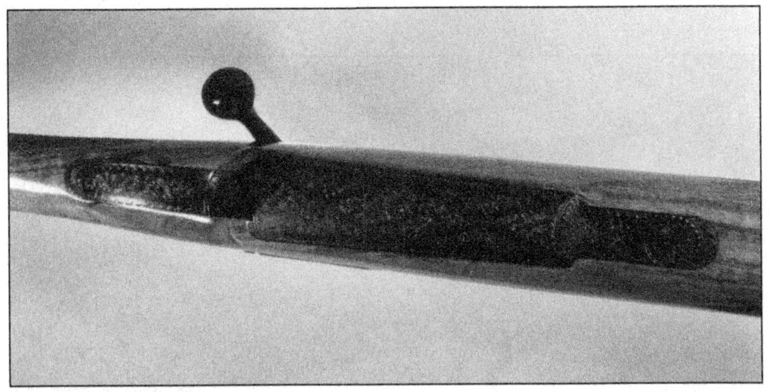

PHOTO C5-38.
Trigger guard assembly masterfully engraved by Phil Vinnicombe.

PHOTO C5-39.
The dropped magnum magazine assembly was a Dakota.

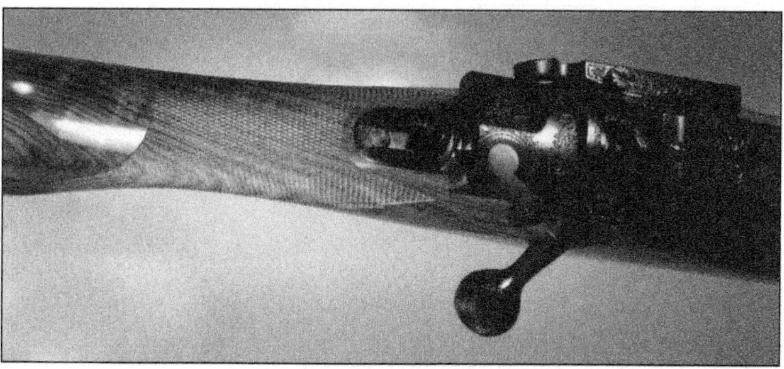

PHOTO C5-40.
The checkering pattern ran over the grip. Also note the blending of the rear tang.

PHOTO C5-41.
Checkering was a classic point pattern. Note the treatment around the bolt stop.

PHOTO C5-42.
Rear bridge with scope base cap installed.

CHAPTER TWELVE

CLEANING, RELOADING, AND OTHER STUFF

CLEANING: If you were to question ten people about their cleaning methods you would probably get ten different answers ranging from, 'I never clean my gun — ever', 'Just squirt RP7/CRC/Innox down the barrel', and many others. Maybe you will get a sensible answer from at least one person. It's surprising how many people, I run into, who firmly believe that the accuracy of their rifle suffers when they clean it. Their philosophy is simple; 'Don't clean it or you'll stuff up its accuracy', when, in reality, the accuracy has been improved — it's the zero that has been stuffed up!

When fired, centrefire rifles generate a considerable amount of gas which is employed to drive a gilding metal jacketed lead projectile, through the bore, under considerable pressure. Both the gas generated by the burning powder, and the projectile, leave behind a residue in the bore, which we call fouling. The residue the projectile leaves behind we call copper fouling, and the residue the gas leaves behind we call powder fouling.

Both of these residues are accumulative. That is, every time the rifle is fired both types of fouling, from that shot, are deposited on top of the fouling deposited from the previous shot. The more shots that are fired the more layers of fouling are deposited. Fouling can't be shot out. The projectile is moving too fast to push anything ahead of it. It simply rides over anything it encounters in the bore. As a result, unless something is done to remove the fouling it will continue to build, and will at some stage affect accuracy detrimentally.

To my mind, it is especially bad to fire a projectile through the barrel after the fouling has been allowed to harden overnight, without cleaning. If you think it doesn't matter, try pushing a dry patch through the bore first. You will see that it can't be done. If you insist on doing this you are not doing the bore of your barrel any favours.

Also powder fouling that has been allowed to remain in the bore attracts moisture, which allows any copper fouling present to create an electrolytic action between it and the steel of the bore, even in stainless steel barrels.

Be aware, that the stainless steel in your barrel is not like the stainless steel in your kitchen sink. Your kitchen sink is made from 300 series stainless steel, and you barrel is made from 400 series stainless steel, and they are very different. 300 series stainless steel is very corrosion resistant, but 400 series stainless steel is actually a high chromium steel, not a true stainless steel, even though we call it that. It will not form the red rust we see on neglected chrome molybdenum barrels, but it will corrode with much the same result, though less visible. This electrolytic action, if left unattended, will pit the bore under the copper fouling, leaving it rough and prone to pick up copper fouling even more quickly.

In my experience copper fouling can extend for the full length of the barrel, and powder fouling extends for around 12" from the end of the chamber. Possibly it could extend further if enough shots were fired, but I have never fired that many shots before doing something about it.

Accuracy deterioration from copper fouling is probably caused by stripping; that is damage to the projectile jacket on its way through the bore. A less than smooth bore will strip some of the copper jacket from the projectile, and the copper thus deposited will continue to do the same. The more build up there is, the more will be the stripping action, eventually affecting accuracy. With powder fouling, my theory is that the buildup to some 6" in front of the chamber causes a constriction that sizes the projectile down as it passes through. Projectiles are made with, what is called, the size up method because the lead core is inert, but the copper jacket is not. In each step of the projectiles manufacture it is increased in diameter slightly so that the copper jacket can maintain its spring against, and grip to, the lead core. If the projectile passes through a constriction, on its way through the bore, the reverse will happen. The projectile will be sized down to a slightly smaller diameter, passing through the constriction, and when it emerges, from the constriction, the copper jacket will spring back to fill the larger diameter of bore past the constriction, but the lead core, being inert, will not. The result will be a separation between the jacket and the core, which will be very detrimental to accuracy. In severe cases the projectile can skip over the rifling, losing its rotational velocity, and be unstable when it leaves the barrel, printing sideways through the target. We call that key holing.

Given the above it would seem sensible to keep both types of fouling to at least a reasonable level. I keep a close eye on the bores of my barrels, and have looked at many belonging to others. I have seen barrels that looked like a coal mine, with veins of gold running through the black.

Pity they weren't real veins of gold! They literally shot around corners, but when the fouling was removed they shot acceptably, and continued to do so, as long as the fouling was not allowed to build up again. That kinda gives lie to the 'never clean it' brigade.

The barrel itself will determine which fouling you will have to deal with. Barrels vary greatly in their internal finish, which has a direct bearing on how much they will attract fouling. Also, the type of powder you use will have a bearing on how much powder fouling you will have to contend with.

Modern match grade barrels usually have bores that have been lapped to a smooth finish, smooth enough not to attract copper fouling, or if they do, attract not very much of it. The less smooth the bore of the barrel is the more likely it is to strip copper from the projectile as it is forced through the barrel under high pressure, and at high speed. This copper is ironed into the pores of the metal in the bore, and as I said it is accumulative — the more shots that are fired the more copper is deposited in the bore.

There is a bewildering array of tools available on the market to tackle barrel fouling, and only personal experience will enable you to separate the sheep from the goats. In the old days, back when JC was playing full back for Jerusalem, we used pull throughs to clean our barrels, which by and large are pretty useless. I guess they are better than nothing, but not by much.

You should get yourself a good cleaning rod, in the caliber of your choice, with ball bearings at both ends of the handle. I used Parker Hale rods for many years, and they are excellent. I am currently using Montana Extreme rods as well, which are also excellent. You want the cleaning brush to follow the grooves of the rifling, both on the forward and backward stroke, and if the rod you are using is a non ball bearing type, that will not happen — the brush will skip over the rifling. The plastic coating on my old Parker Hale rods was a soft type, so I stripped it off many years ago, and polished the rods bright. I haven't bothered to do that with the Montana rods. Really, it doesn't probably matter either way.

When you purchase jags for your rod get the ones that have a spear point at the end. They are much easier to use than either the wrap around type or the loop. You can buy patches ready cut, or make your own from flannelette material you can buy from the likes of Spotlight.

You will also need some brushes, in the caliber of you choice, to fit your cleaning rod. Parker Hale rods have a male thread on the end whereas American rods, the Montana Extreme included, have a female thread on the end. Brushes are available in nylon and phosphor bronze to suit whatever caliber you may be using. Years ago they were available in brass, but I haven't been able to source those for a long time now. Personally, I don't like phosphor bronze brushes, and I'll touch on that shortly. Adapters are available to allow you to use the American male threaded brushes and jags on Parker Hale rods.

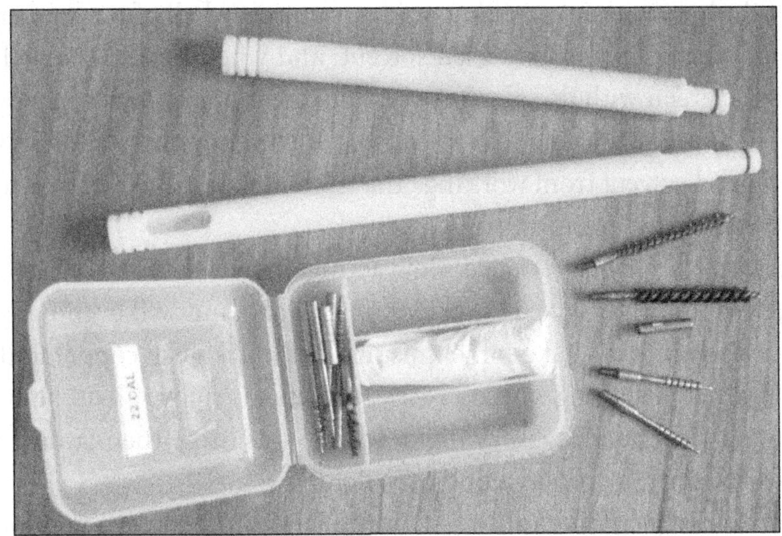

PHOTO 12-1.

Two Sinclair cleaning rod guides. The top one is for my Shilen .30BR, and the bottom one for my Remington .25/06 Ackley Improved. Below them is my .22 calibre MTM brush and jag box. The nylon bristle brush, that I am currently using, is in the middle compartment, wrapped in a tissue. To the right of the box, starting from the top, are a phosphor bronze brush (which I don't use), a nylon bristle brush, and a Dewey brush adapter that allows me to use American brushes on a Parker Hale cleaning rod. Finally, a couple of spear point jags.

There are two ways to combat copper fouling, mechanically, and chemically. There are many solvents available on the market that will deal with copper fouling, chemically dissolving it from the surface of the bore. Basically solvents can be divided into two categories, either oil or water based. Some modern solvents are a combination of both. Water based solvents can be identified by a strong ammonia odour, and are really quick action copper removers, compared to the oil based solvents, which have an oil/petrol odour. The combination solvents still smell a bit of ammonia, though not as strong as the copper removers.

Most solvents claim rust/corrosion preventative properties which I take with a grain of salt. True they will inhibit rust to a degree, but only in the short term — days, not weeks. They are simply not designed to penetrate the pores of the steel, and stay in place. Gravity will draw them towards the centre of the earth leaving the steel dry, clean and unprotected. Do not rely on them — use a dedicated rust/corrosion preventative, such as CLP Break Free, as soon as you determine your bore is free of fouling. After you have pushed the CLP soaked patch through the bore, wipe it over the outside of the rifles metalwork to protect it too.

The water based solvents speak for themselves. They offer no rust/ corrosion protection. The best way to apply them is with a nylon bristle brush to froth them up in the bore, and enhance their action. They are quick acting, and should be left in the bore for only 10 to 15 minutes before being removed and refreshed.

You will know they are working by the blue residue on your patches. One thing I have noticed with the water based solvents, I have used, is if there is a lot of copper fouling to remove, they will cease to function before all of the copper is gone. I surmise this is because they eventually form a coating on the surface of the copper that resists their action. Many times I have used them, and when the patches came out of the bore without any blue residue, considered all of the copper to be gone. I have then soaked the bore overnight with oil based solvent, and when it was removed the following day found the patches quite green with dissolved copper. Further applications of the water based solvent removed more copper. It seemed to me that the oil based solvent removed (dissolved) the 'skin' that prevented the water based solvent from working. The lesson I took from this was to use both solvents in conjunction with each other. Don't rely on just one.

Oil based solvents are, in my experience, slow acting. They should be left in the bore overnight at least. Unlike water based solvents, they will continue to act, and will eventually remove all of the copper from the bore, though it will take some time if the barrel is a bad copper fouler. I've had barrels that took a couple of weeks of soaking with oil based solvents to remove all of the copper, even though they were soaked in the same solvent, every night, while I was using them away on a trip. Using the two solvents together speeds the process along considerably.

Modern combination solvents are quite fast acting, and can be left in the bore overnight. They claim rust/corrosion prevention, but don't trust them for even medium term protection. They will dissolve all of the copper from a barrel very quickly. I am using a combination solvent at the moment that will dissolve the copper completely from the barrel, in two applications, that would take a week with my old oil based solvents.

Mechanically, you can't brush copper out of the bore with the likes of a phosphor bronze brush. The copper is ironed into the pores of the metal, and all a brush will do is scratch the surface. All that will do is, possibly, let the solvent get a better go at it. Mechanical removal can only be achieved with an abrasive paste such as JB Non Imbedding Bore Cleaning Compound. Really, you should not have to resort to such extreme measures, to remove copper fouling, if you are using a modern combination solvent.

Powder fouling is dependant on the brand and burning rate of the powder you are using. It can be light, and hardly a problem, or it can be severe, and quite a problem, that requires constant attention.

Take my .338/06 as an example. I have only ever used Dupont IMR4895 powder in it. The barrel has always picked up a deal of copper fouling, which took at least a week to remove entirely with my usual solvents. After a recent hunting trip I cleaned it in my normal way with a combination solvent, and the copper was removed in only one application. I then decided to have a look at the bore with my bore scope, something I have never done before, and was somewhat surprised to find the bore was bright and shiny. No powder fouling present at all.

I have only ever used Dupont IMR4320 powder in Lyn's 7x57 Mauser, so had a look at it at the same time. This barrel, too, always picked up a deal of copper fouling, and when I checked it with the bore scope I found only a thin film of carbon fouling in it — not enough to be worried about.

Since I have been using Mulwex ADI powders I have found I have had to be very aware of powder fouling buildup. The slower the burning rate of the powder, the more it fouls, and the more attention must be paid to it. I use AR2207 in my .30BR and it doesn't foul nearly as much as the slower burning rate AR powders I have used; AR2208, AR2209, AR2213sc, AR2217. The worst fouling one I have used is, AR2225.

The very first shot you fire through your barrel will leave carbon residue in the bore from the burning of the powder. When you fire the next shot the projectile will ride right over the residue from the last shot, and iron it into the pores of the metal under great pressure — the projectile is hitting that residue at great speed. As a result, the barrel ends up being fouled with both free carbon, and carbon that has been impacted into the bore under great pressure.

Free, or surface carbon, is easily removed with an oil, or combination, based solvent, but impacted carbon is not so easily removed. Impacted carbon fouling left behind, after cleaning the bore, continues to be built upon by subsequent firings, to the point where it will constrict the bore if it is not attended to. When it builds up sufficiently it takes on a shiny glazed, glass like appearance, and I have found nothing that will dissolve it, or any brush that will scratch it away. I have been told by people who know more about these things than me, that there is nothing that can dissolve it. It is not like the carbon buildup in the cylinder head of an engine, which is soft by comparison. This carbon has been conditioned under great pressure and is hard like glass.

The only way I have been able to remove this imbedded powder fouling is with JB Non Imbedding Bore Cleaning Compound. I was importing JB from Jim Brobst in the late 1960s, so I have been using it a long time. When you have JB in glass containers you know you are long in the tooth! There are other similar products on the market, but I can't comment as I have not used them. JB has done all I needed doing, so there has been no need to look any further. This is how I use it.

1. Use a cleaning rod guide.

2. Run a patch through the bore, wet with solvent, such as Shooters Choice, Montana Extreme or Hoppes #9. Whatever oil based solvent you have will be fine.

3. Screw a nylon bristle brush on the rod, and dampen it with the solvent you wet the bore with.

4. With a screwdriver, fill the bristles of the brush with brown (not red) JB.

5. Push the brush into the barrel only as far as the end of the chamber. When you feel it touching the end of the chamber stop.

6. Holding a bit of pressure against the end of the chamber, rotate the rod a minimum of 50 turns. What we are doing here is removing the carbon deposit that builds up between the end of the cartridge case, and the end of the chamber. If you do not do this the accumulated carbon deposit will build up, and eventually squeeze the end of the neck of the case against the projectile, especially in chambers that have minimal neck clearance. If not attended to the result will be odd fliers in a group, or odd misses on small game that you can't account for.

7. Now push the brush into the bore for about 12", letting it rotate as it goes in. Hold the rod, so that it can't rotate, and drag the brush back out of the barrel until it just clears the chamber. Push it back in letting it rotate, hold the rod and drag it back out without it rotating. Do this fifty times. That's right, fifty times. For maybe 10 to 15 of the 50 strokes I will push the brush right to the muzzle so it cleans a bit there. From my observations the barrel doesn't powder foul much past the first 12".

8. Push a few patches through the bore to remove most of the now black JB, at the same time cleaning the chamber on the way through. JB is messy, so you will have a job to clean it from the rod and inside the guide. Store the JB brush in its own container. You will be using it often, so you might as well have a dedicated brush. Photo 12-2 shows my storage solution.

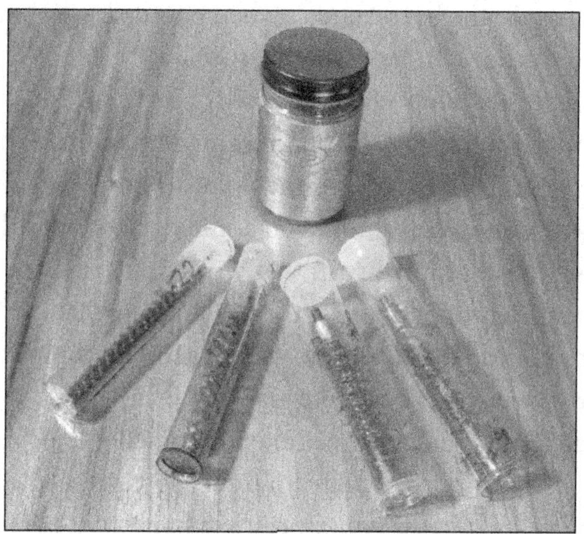

PHOTO 12-2.

The new glass bottle of JB Non Imbedding Bore Cleaning Compound shows my age. I store my brushes in these plastic containers. I don't bother washing them to clean them, but just add fresh JB to them next time they are used. If you want to wash them between uses, go knock yourself out!

9. Anoint a nylon bristle brush with your oil based nitro solvent, and push it right through the bore a few times, letting the rod turn on both the forward and back stroke. On the back stroke take note of how the rod feels. It should feel silky smooth all the way on the back stroke. If you feel it drag at all in the last 12", you have not removed all of the powder fouling, and need to give it another 50 strokes with a refreshed JB brush.

10. When your nylon bristle brush can be withdrawn through the bore, without dragging, you are finished with JB, and can be satisfied that the bore is free of carbon deposits. Dry it, oil it, and we are done.

In my experience it is a waste of time to JB a bore with anything less than 50 strokes. That seems to be the minimum figure that will work effectively. I have tried fewer strokes, and all that did was make more messy work for me. For me, 50 strokes is the minimum. I have also tried other methods of application, (Hell, I've been using this stuff for over 40 years.) but the nylon bristle brush is the most effective I have found. It works the best because the JB is trapped between the bristles of the brush, and as it is stroked through the bore it is moved around, presenting fresh JB to the bore at every stroke, unlike a charged cloth patch, for instance, that leaves most of its JB in the chamber as it passes into the bore.

I use only Brown JB, as I found the pink JB has little effect in removing powder fouling. How often should we use it? Your barrel will give you that information as you go along. It's a messy job, and I find myself avoiding it as much as possible, but you will probably have to bite the bullet every 100 shots or so. You will feel the nylon bristle brush dragging when it is withdrawn through the bore, and that will be your trigger. The more shots your barrel has through it, the faster it will powder foul, and begin to pick up copper as well. As I said, the copper is not a problem for me, as modern solvents handle it without any problems. Powder fouling they don't do so good a job on. I really hate treating my bore with JB, but unfortunately it is one of those evils we just have to put up with if we are to maintain an efficient shooting system.

It is probably not necessary to use a cleaning rod guide, when cleaning your rifle, provided you keep the rod reasonably centered in the bore. This is important as, when passing through the bore, the surface of the rod will pick up free powder fouling, and primer residue, which are both, quite abrasive. I saw a .17 Remington once that had a half moon hole worn right along the neck of the chamber by a cleaning rod. It may not be necessary to use a cleaning rod guide, but it is desirable.

The bore guides I use, and favor, are a nylon affair made by Sinclair International. See Photo 12-1 (Page 403). They are not very expensive and feature an 'o' ring that seals the chamber, which prevents solvent from leaking back into the action, and stock, which I view as a very good thing. When using abrasive pastes, such as JB Non Imbedding Bore Cleaner, a rod guide is really mandatory. You should still endeavor to move your rod in the centre of the guide — in other words don't think, because you have a rod guide, you can neglect centering the rod.

Barrels vary considerably in the way they will foul, and it's up to you to observe what is happening when you clean, and work out exactly what your particular barrel needs. Basically what I do is have a standard cleaning system, and modify it for a particular barrel if I find it is not working well enough.

This is what I do:–

1. I always use one of my Sinclair rod guides, which basically live in my rifles when I am not using them. If the bolt isn't in the rifle, then the rod guide is.

2. If possible it's best to clean the barrel while it is still warm, but not hot. If the barrel is hot, I let it cool to warm before I start to clean it. I feel a hot barrel will evaporate the solvent away from the bore too quickly. Of course, you can't always get to clean the barrel while it is still warm, and that's ok.

3. I am currently using a product called Patch-out with Accelerator, which is a fast acting combination solvent. I spear an appropriate sized patch through the middle, and wet it with Patch-out, then add some Accelerator to it, and push it through the bore. I don't let it go out of the muzzle until I've worked it back and forth a few times to get the bore good and wet. When the patch comes out of the muzzle it will be jet black with removed free powder fouling. I leave the rod in the bore, for a half hour or so, figuring the rod, clogging up the bore, will hold the solvent where it needs to be for a bit longer than would be the case if I removed it. Leaving the bore wet with solvent, for a half hour or so, gives the solvent a chance to soften up any powder fouling, that can be softened up, and gives it a head start on any copper fouling that may be present, if any is.

4. When I get back to it, I push a clean patch through the bore, and note its appearance when it emerges from the muzzle. Usually there is not much to see, as it's as black as, with powder fouling.

5. I repeat step 3, exactly as before, to remove any remaining dissolved free powder fouling.

6. A half hour or so later, when I push a clean patch through the bore there will be less black powder fouling present — those two steps have pretty well removed all of the free powder fouling in the bore.

7. I remove the spear point jag and replace it with a nylon brush, of the appropriate caliber, which I anoint with some Patch-out, and follow up with some Accelerator. I pass the brush right through the bore and back about 10 times, thoroughly wetting the bore, then remove the rod and brush. I wrap the brush in a tissue, and store it in an MTM brush container. I have these containers for every caliber I am using. I place the rifle in my man cave, lying on its side, with the rod guide in the chamber, and every time I pass by I go in and turn it over, figuring the solvent will find its way to the other side of the barrel, and do some extra dissolving work on the way. I leave it overnight.

I don't use phosphor bronze brushes in my barrels for a few reasons. First up they cause a false positive to the solvent, so you will not know if you have any copper in the barrel, because any green/ blue colour you will get is mostly coming from the brush itself. Second, the phosphor bronze brush will go a good way towards killing the action of your solvent, before it gets into the barrel. Thirdly, I have cleaned many barrels with nylon bristle brushes, and after they have been as clean as I can get them, I have done another clean with a phosphor bronze brush, *which has removed absolutely nothing.* It does not even scratch the glazed carbon fouling in the barrel, let alone remove any of it.

Nearly everyone I know uses phosphor bronze brushes, but frankly, if they are not going to do any extra work for me, I don't see the point. It's simply a matter of observing what is happening, and making up your own mind with regard to what you see. If you get no benefit from using a product, that is detrimental to the other product you use it with, why continue using it? They may have been useful in the old days, when all we had was slow acting solvents, and their ability to scratch copper fouling, allowing the solvent to get a better bite at it, speeded things up a bit. But with modern solvents that is not needed, and if they won't touch glazed on powder fouling I don't see that I need to put them in my barrel. You can make up your own mind on that.

8. The next morning I push a couple of clean patches through the barrel, and examine them to see if there has been any copper fouling in the bore. As we removed the free powder fouling, with our first two cleanings, we can easily see if there has been any copper fouling in the barrel by either a green or blue colour on the patches.

9. If I see colour on the patches I repeat step 7, and 8 until the patches come out of the bore with only solvent on them — no colour. While I am stroking the nylon brush through the bore, during step 7, I am taking particular note of how it feels on the return stroke, to gauge how much powder fouling the barrel is accumulating, as I discussed earlier.

10. When I am satisfied the barrel is copper free, I remove the bore guide, and dry the solvent from the chamber when I push another couple of patches through, then replace the rod guide. Finally I push a patch wet with CLP Break Free through the bore to protect it from rust/ corrosion. Then the

rifle is put away until I next want to use it. To my mind, CLP Break Free is the best rust/corrosion protection you can get, without having to resort to protections that leave a gummy film on the part, which becomes a nuisance. I have every confidence in it, and it has never let me down.

11. Before I fire the rifle again I push a dry patch through the bore, taking care to revolve it around in the chamber, on its way through, to remove the CLP Break Free from both areas. Actually, a very thin film (microscopic, really) will be left behind, which will provide a bit of lubrication for the first bullet as it speeds down the barrel. When I am in the field, I still apply CLP to the bore, and push it out prior to firing the first shot after cleaning. Solvents leave the bore chemically clean, and I think it wise to assist the first shot through the bore with a microscopic layer of lubricant.

If you do not know for a fact that you have a solvent that actually works, you should test it by placing a couple of drops on a projectile and see how it reacts. Any solvent will remove free powder fouling, but not all solvents are good copper removers. I have had solvents that did nearly nothing to remove copper. You will soon see if the solvent is working by the green/blue colour it will turn as it dissolves the projectiles jacket.

I mention this because many modern match grade barrels don't copper foul very much — some not at all, and if you have a solvent that isn't good, you could be suckered into thinking you have one of these barrels when, in fact, you don't.

As I said, different barrels react differently, so you will have to observe what is happening in your individual case, and adopt a procedure that works for you.

My .30BR copper fouls only a tiny bit — just a faint blue colour after step 7, and nothing thereafter. Also there is very little glazed on powder fouling from the fast burning AR2207 powder that I use in it.

Both my .338/06, and Lyn's 7x57 Mauser, copper foul heavily requiring two or three sessions with step 7 to remove it. The .338 does not powder foul at all, and the 7mms powder fouling is minimal — about like the .30BR.

My 22PPC doesn't copper foul at all, however the AR2208 powder I use in it does cause enough powder fouling to be a concern.

My .25/06 Ackley Improved copper fouls heavily, despite its Remington Custom Shop stainless steel barrel. It takes 3 or 4 step 7 sessions to remove the copper, with the patches coming out of the bore bright blue. It also powder fouls quite a deal thanks to the slow AR2213sc I use in it.

My 7MM SAUM has never copper fouled at all, but powder fouled heavily, due to the very slow AR2225 powder I use.

As you can see, barrels vary a great deal, and there is no hard and fast rule how they will foul. You just have to find out what needs to be done when you clean them, and act accordingly.

WORKING UP LOADS: Working up to a maximum load in your rifle is not a task that should be undertaken lightly. It is important to be methodical and very observant during the procedure, as you are dealing with extremely high pressures that have the potential to destroy your rifle, telescopic sight and all.

I do this job while I am chronographing my loads, as it is expedient to know what velocity the different powder charges I am using produce. We have to find a load to start with, and the best way to do that is with a reloading manual. They generally have suggested loads and maximum loads listed, but you need to be aware that those loads are valid only for the rifle they were tested in — not your rifle.

It is a big mistake to assume, when you change barrels on your rifle, that the new barrel is the same as the old barrel, and you can go ahead and use the loads from your old barrel. If you were using a maximum working load in the old barrel, that load could well be much too hot for the new barrel, and cause the rifle to blow up. You must treat every barrel/rifle as an individual, and load it accordingly — always staying on the safe side. Your eyes, and that empty space between your ears, are precious — you don't want to lose either.

If you can, compare the suggested loads from a couple of reloading manuals, and make an informed decision on which load you will begin with. If your mate says, "Just use xx grains of xxxx," disregard him. If your rifle blows up with his load he will say, "Fancy that," and you'll be left with the mess, expense, and injuries. Use a reasonable, safe, suggested load from a reloading manual to start from. If you are using an improved case, you will be safe to start with the suggested load for its parent case.

The only way to know that a suggested load is safe in your rifle is to fire it, and I have to confess that firing that first shot from a new barrel, or rifle, always gives me the heebie jeebees — it's always a relief to know the load was safe. Once we have our starting load, it's simply a matter of increasing the load, in steps, until we reach the maximum load the rifle will accept, short of destroying itself. We have to know when to stop!

We know when to stop by observing various signs, or flags, that are available to us. There are a few things we can monitor, but the problem is they may all be present, or only one or two may be present, or maybe just one. Therefore it is a good idea to be aware of all of them, but not to rely on any one of them. *Don't concentrate on one sign only — keep your eye on them all.* I'll list all of the signs you should be looking for, when you are working up to a maximum load, and discuss each in turn.

If at all possible, I think it's a good idea to work up to a maximum load when the weather is hot. If it is not possible to do this, be aware that temperature has a direct bearing on pressure. Simply put, the higher the temperature the more pressure will be developed in your load. In practical terms, the load you work up in the winter may well be much too hot to use in the summer.

A rifles maximum working load should be at least 1½ to 2 grains less than its maximum load. Never use a maximum load as your working load, as variations in pressure, from load to load, could easily tip the pressure over the critical level, and cause a blow up. If you have worked out a maximum working load in cold weather, you should reduce it by as much as up to a grain if you want to use it in summer, and then monitor it carefully as summer comes around.

Ok, here we go:

Case head expansion: There are two problems with this flag. The mechanics of it require you to measure the diameter of the case with a .0001" micrometer, at the solid head, just behind the expansion ring on the case. The expansion ring is that bright shiny mark you will see, on fired cases, that denotes the place where the case thins sufficiently to be expanded, by the pressure generated within, when the cartridge is fired. The solid head of the case is thick, and strong enough to resist expanding, when the cartridge is fired, with a normal maximum working load. However, given enough pressure, the solid head will deform (expand), and when it does, that load is considered to be excessive.

The first problem is access to that part of the solid head that needs to be measured. On most cases there is a slight bulge in front of it, and the diameter of the rim of the case is slightly larger than the solid head itself. There isn't enough room to get a normal 1", .0001" micrometer onto the section that has to be measured. If you are using a rebated rim cartridge, such as a .284 Winchester, you will have access to the point that must be measured. In such an instance check that the case is in fact round at that point — they seldom are, so, if not, mark the case so you are always measuring across the same diameter. You could obtain a specialty micrometer, with spade shaped anvils, with which to take the measurement, or file small flats on the rim of the case to give you access to the area that needs to be measured.

The second problem is this method gives you no warning as pressure builds. The amount of expansion we are looking for is only .0001". The method requires you to reload one case multiple times. Select a case and mark where you will be measuring it, so that you are always measuring across the same diameter. Measure the diameter with a .0001" micrometer, and jot the measurement down. The case head will expand slightly, for a few shots, with a normal suggested load until it settles down to a constant measurement. Fire those shots, reloading the same case each time, and measuring the case head each shot, until you observe that the measurement remains the same for a few shots. See Photo 12-3.

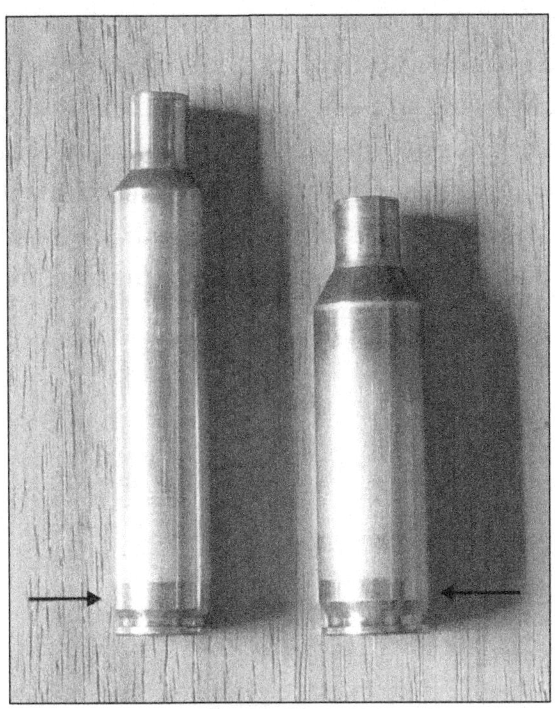

PHOTO 12-3.

The area that should be measured can easily be seen on these two well worn cases. The arrows are pointing right at them. The .25/06 Ackley Improved case on the left is slightly bulged, due to a loose factory chamber, at the visible demarcation line around 1/10" above the top of the extraction groove. This is the point where the solid head resists expanding with normal safe powder loads, even though it is not supported in the chamber. The middle of that 1/10" section is where you should be measuring case head expansion. The 7MM RSAUM case on the right has no expansion bulge at all, yet the demarcation line is still visible.

When this happens, begin increasing the load, measuring the case head between each shot. Finally, you will detect an increase in the diameter of the case head, maybe of only .0001". When that happens fire that same load again, and see if the case head continues to expand, even by only .0001". If it does expand, you have reached your maximum load for that rifle/combination, and should stop. If the measurement stays the same, fire another shot with the same load and measure again. If it is still the same move up to the next load increment, and continue until you detect an increase in the diameter of the case head, and reconfirm with the same load. When the case head increases in diameter for two consecutive shots you have reached the absolute maximum load for that rifle/combination. *Do not exceed it.* While you are doing this, remember to be looking for the other flags that I will be discussing next.

Really, if you want to use it, consider it as the final confirmation that you have indeed reached the maximum load the rifle will accept. Personally, I don't bother measuring case head expansion — you may be of a different opinion, and that's ok.

Primer Protrusion: This is one of my favorites, as it will give you an early indication that pressure is building. To enable you to read it requires that there be a firing pin tip diameter of around .075", and a clearance in the hole, the tip passes through, of around .002". Measurements like those will allow the pressure generated, in the case, to extrude the material in the primer cup into the gap between the firing pin and its hole, forming the protrusion we can easily see on the primer cup. At the same time the inertia of the firing pin is also overcome, to an extent, and it is pushed part of the way back into its hole.

Study Photo 12-4a carefully, as it is an example of very poor reloading practice. I borrowed it from a mate who 'rescued' it when he saw a guy literally hammering it out of his action. You can see a good example of primer protrusion here, obviously too much to be comfortable with, as this case has been running at too much pressure. Some primer extrusion in your loads is ok, depending on the factors we have already discussed, but this case is probably exhibiting around 50% too much. Look closely

PHOTO 12-4A.
A trifector of reloading errors.

PHOTO 12-4B.
Authors .30BR primer protrusion.

and you will see a smear from the 'N' to the 'A' in Norma. That is the result of several firings with case head extrusion into the ejector hole of the Remington Clone action. Finally, the slight crease you can see just in front of the extractor groove is the sign of an imminent case head separation, caused by incorrect full length sizing, as we discussed in Chapter 6. In Photo 12-4b you can see the primer protrusion I am comfortable with in my .30[BR]. The primers are Remington 7½ small rifle bench-rest, and these cases were fired on a very hot day. The firing pin diameter on this Shilen action is .0715", and the hole diameter is .0740", about the right dimensions needed to read primer protrusion reliably.

In some calibers — the PPCs are an example — chamber pressure is held at a high level for an extended period, and this completely overcomes the firing pins inertia, and swages the primer cup right back into the firing pin hole. When the piece of cup separates, gas under high pressure is released into the firing pin cavity, which pushes the firing pin right back, bottoming its spring, and blowing that little piece into the bolt body. I have often thought that, when this happens, the firing pin tail must come within a hair of hitting my cheek.

We call that primer disking, named after the little round disk of primer cup that is blown back into the bolt body. It is not a desirable thing to have happen, as you usually get a face full of gas with it, and that little disc will jam the firing pin and cause misfires at some later date, if you do not disassemble the bolt and remove it, usually by washing it out with solvent. Make sure you find it, as it's a sneaky little booger, and will do its best to stay hiding in the firing pin cavity, lurking, to cause you grief down the track. Have a look at Photo 12-5.

PHOTO 12-5.
An example of primer disking. You can see that the firing pin hole sized disk has been punched right out of the primer, and will be residing somewhere inside the bolt body.

Primer protrusion as a pressure guide is all well and good, however, if your bolt has a close tolerance between the firing pin and its hole, or if the hole has been bushed, as I described in Chapter 1, Page 14, then it is highly unlikely you will see any primer protrusion at all, even at your maximum load. In other words, look for it, but don't assume that the load is safe because you have not seen it yet.

On the other hand, if you are working up a load and are experiencing, like mega primer protrusion, and common sense indicates that you are not even close to the maximum load, then you should consider changing to a primer with a harder cup; perhaps a magnum primer. Either that, or consider having your firing pin hole bushed, and perhaps the firing pin diameter reduced.

Primer cup appearance: When the primer is seated in its cavity, in the case, it has, more or less, rounded edges. As the pressure in the case builds, the edges of the primer will begin to flatten out, and become less rounded. You can easily compare fired primers with primers you have yet to fire, and this will give you an indication that pressure is building, but not of how much pressure there is, or if it is approaching the point where you should stop. It is another indicator we should be looking at, along with all of the others. See Photo 12-7, page 415.

Case head extrusion: This is a sure fire indication that you have reached, actually slightly exceeded, maximum pressure. No doubt you are aware that pressure acts equally in all directions. The same pressure that expands the solid head is also pressing against the base of the case, and when enough pressure is built it will stretch the back of the case, and push the base of the case against the bolt face under great pressure. What happens is the brass flows, or extrudes, slightly, into the ejector hole, or slot in the bolt. When the bolt is rotated, to open it, the sharp edge in the ejector hole/slot shaves the portion of brass, that flowed back into the hole, leaving behind a shiny mark.

Have a close look at Photo 12-6, and you will see what I mean. These are three cases fired in my .25/06 Ackley Improved with the maximum loads, I worked up to, with 3 projectile weights. You will see the round marks from the round ejector hole on the Remington bolt. On the left hand case you can see the mark is just next to the 'N' in Win. On the middle case you can see a ridge above the 'R' in Winchester, where the brass has extruded back into the hole. On the right hand case there is a rub mark above the '2' in 270. Have a look at the .338/06 case in Photo 12-7. This case was fired in an M'98 action which has an ejector hole in the shape of a slot. You can easily see the shiny mark on the right hand side just below the second 'W' in WW Super.

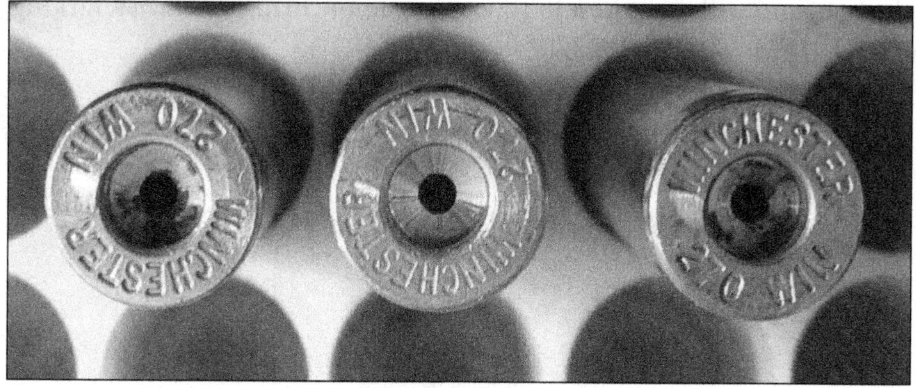

PHOTO 12-6.

Three fired cases with case head extrusion indicating maximum pressure has been reached, if not slightly exceeded.

PHOTO 12-7.

This is an interesting Photo that should be looked at closely. It was fired in my FN military actioned sporting rifle, with a firing pin tip diameter of .0765", and a firing pin hole diameter of .0795". The primers I use are Federal 215s, a 'magnum' primer. Despite the 'loose' fit between the firing pin tip and its hole, and the evidence of a very prominent ejector mark, indicating maximum pressure has certainly been exceeded, there is only a tiny amount of protrusion of the primer. Also, the primer cup is very flattened. This is a classic example of why you should be looking for every sign of excess pressure, not just concentrating on one.

Look carefully for these marks as you work up your loads, and at the first sign of them *STOP*. You have reached, and probably slightly exceeded, your maximum load.

Bolt lift: Bolt lift will give you a very good indication of when you have reached your maximum load. It's a human condition, that when we are used to the feel of something, we notice immediately if that feeling changes, even a tiny bit. While you are working up your load you will automatically note how the bolt feels when you extract cases.

When you go through the extraction cycle, initial bolt lift is straight up, until you contact the extraction cam which is usually at the root of the bolt handle. I discussed this in Chapter 9, Jam and Touch. Have a look at Photos 9-9 and 9-10. When the root of the bolt handle contacts the extraction cam, actual removal of the fired case, from the chamber, begins. The tighter the case is in the chamber the harder will be that movement, of the bolt lift, though with the power a good bolt action exerts, in the extraction cycle, you may not notice much, if any, difference in the effort required, until the maximum load has been reached.

When you have reached the maximum load you will notice a distinct extra effort required to move the bolt through the extraction cam. The case usually breaks free from the chamber about half way through the cycle, with the result that, because you are applying a deal of effort, the last half of the movement takes place in a rush, and when the root of the bolt handle hits its stop you will hear a distinct 'click'.

The pressure of your maximum load will jam the case in the chamber making it harder to extract, and when you feel the extraction tighten and hear the 'click', *STOP*— that is the maximum load for your rifle. When you extract the case examine the base for an ejector mark, as described above, and keep that case aside. When you reload that case take particular note of how the new primer seats in it. You may have enlarged the primer pocket diameter with that hot load, and the primer may be too easy to seat, or just fall out when you've seated it. If that is the case, that case has been destroyed — throw it away.

While I'm on this, whenever you load ammunition, you should take note of how easily the primer seats in all of your cases. Cases are consumables, and they wear out, usually with split necks or loose primer pockets. If I think a primer seats too loose, I take a hand de-capping rod, and see if I can push it back out with hand pressure only. If the primer moves

I de-cap it in my arbor press and discard the case. If I can't move it with hand pressure I figure it's ok to use again.

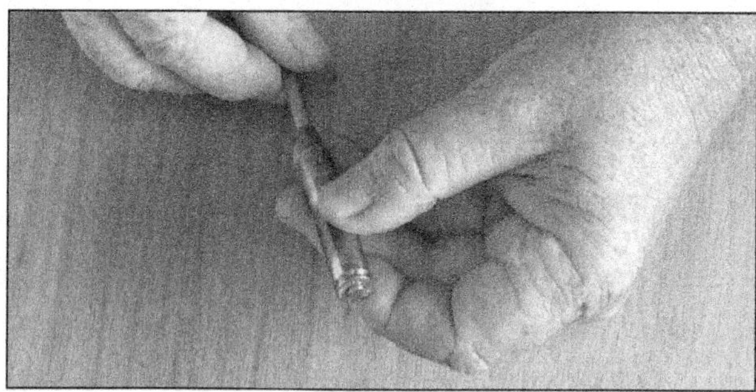

PHOTO 12-7.

Here I have noticed that a primer seated too easily in this .25/06 Ackley Improved case, so I am testing its integrity by attempting to push the primer out by hand, using a hand de-capping rod. Not much pressure is needed, if the primer pocket is, in fact, loose. As you can see, I have managed to push it half way out of the pocket, proving that the case is not suitable for reloading. De-cap it, and throw it away.

If you fire a cartridge, with a loose primer pocket, gas will leak around the gap, and cut a primer sized ring/cavity in your bolt face, which is something we don't want to happen. I have never experienced any of this when I've used cases whose primers seated easier than usual, but that I couldn't move when I attempted to push them out by hand.

Ok, we know what signs to look for. How should we go about it? Once you have established that your starting load is safe by firing it, and breathed a sigh of relief that the rifle didn't explode, you can go about increasing the load, in increments, until you reach the maximum load for that rifle. What increments should you use?

My rule of thumb is to increase the load about 1% at a time. Taking my .25/06 Ackley Improved as an example, with the 90 grain projectile, I started at 58 grains of powder and worked up to 63 grains in ½ grain increments. 1% of 58 grains is .58 grains, and 1% of 63 grains is .63 grains, so by going up in .5 grain increments I am staying on the safe side, and as the load increases the percentage of my increase decreases. At 63 grains I detected a slight 'click' when I opened the bolt, so that is where I stopped. There were no other pressure signs evident while I was working up the load.

When working out the increments by which you will increase the powder charge, when working up to maximum, use your common sense and stay on the safe side. A 2% increase in charge in my .25/06 Ackley Improved would be much too severe an increase for my liking. When the powder load begins to approach maximum the pressure begins to rise non-linearly — in other words you have an exponentially higher percentage of pressure increase with each incremental increase in powder charge.

Therefore we want our incremental increases to not be so much that the pressure becomes a severe overload with the following increment. We want to be able to note the point before that happens, and in my experience 1% increments allow that point to be observed before anything drastic happens.

Once I have found my maximum load I then examine my targets, and see what accuracy I have obtained to work out what my maximum working load is going to be. I look for the most accurate load at least 2% under my maximum load for that rifle. With my .25/06 Ackley Improved, my maximum load was at 63 grains of powder and that load caused a slight extraction click, but did not damage the case — that is no ejector mark, or loose primer pocket. My working load for that rifle is 62 grains of powder which is a 1.6% decrease. I would prefer a 2% decrease from maximum, but the rifle shoots very well with the 62 grain load, so I will be careful to monitor my cases, when I am reloading, and watch for pressure signs as the weather warms up.

If your load is safe enough, you should get at least 8-10 reloads from every case before the primer pockets begin to loosen. Monitor them as you seat the primers, and if you find that they are loosening in only 3 or 4 reloads, your load is too hot for a working load. With such a load, if you come across a weak case in amongst the batch you are using, it may not be able to withstand the pressure being generated, and burst, with severe consequences.

The final word — be careful, be vigilant and stay on the safe side.

RUNNING A BARREL IN: I am not a fan of lengthy run in procedures that take, like a couple of weeks to work through. I strongly believe that your barrel will tell you what it requires, and that information, coupled with a bit of common sense, will get you through. One thing I have been doing lately, is giving the bore 50 strokes with JB, after a barrel is fitted. That shines it up considerably before the first projectile goes through. It may help the barrel to resist picking up initial fouling, but really it's hard to know, because there is no way to test the same barrel both ways, so we are only surmising that it helps. Never-the-less I continue to do it on all of my new barrels.

I simply use a fast acting copper solvent and clean after the first shot on a new barrel. If I get no copper colour, and for my last 4 barrels I haven't, I go to two shots, then 5 shots and that's it for me. As I said, your barrel will tell you what it needs throughout its life. You just have to take notice of it.

The solvent I have been using for the past 12 months or so is Patch-out with Accelerator, and it seems to be quite effective in removing free powder fouling and copper fouling very quickly. I know shooters that use other solvents that seem to be equally effective. Again, observation will tell you whether you need to make a change. I have a shelf in my man cave I store my target rifles on. It allows me to lie them flat on their sides, as they seem to spend most of their lives with solvent in the barrel, and with an 'o' ringed bore guide in the chamber. This is because I am generally using them on a weekly basis for club shoots or practice, so they rarely get to the stage where I store them with CLP Break Free in the bore. Photo 12-9 shows my somewhat cluttered setup.

Photo 12-9.

The Author trickling powder in his very cluttered man cave. The powder scale is at eye height, and there is a magnifying glass in front of the scale graduations, to better see them. The rifles, that are in current use, are lying on their side, to better utilise the solvent in the barrels. The carboys are used for ..... storage!

What I do is wet the bore with solvent, and every time I go past my man cave I drop in and turn the rifle over, figuring that the solvent that has collected at the bottom of the bore, will now migrate to the other side, and do some more work for me on the way. Maybe it does, maybe it doesn't, but being the cheap b@$t@#d I am, it makes me feel better, so it must be good! I try to replace the solvent every 24 hours, but that often stretches to 2-3 days. I'd forget my head if it wasn't screwed on!

RELOADING: In this day and age you would think there would be enough information around that everyone would have a handle on the does and don'ts of reloading, but that doesn't seem to be the case. Only a short while ago, I ran into a guy who set his full length die height with the firing pin assembly, and ejector, in the bolt, and wondered why primers were sticking out of his fired cases. To make matters worse, when I examined his ready to go loaded ammunition, most of the primers were sticking out about 1/3RD of their depth. He couldn't seat them deeper because of the accumulation of residue in the primer pockets.

If the fired primers in your reloads stick out of the case like those in Photo 12-10, you are severely over sizing them. If they stick out like this after you have seated them, clean the accumulated carbon from the bottom of the primer pocket. Your primers should seat flush, or slightly below flush, with the back of the case, and should not protrude, from the back of the case, when they are fired.

PHOTO 12-10.

Three over full length sized .223 Remington cases

Honestly, you just can't do that, and expect the system to work properly. I have already discussed the proper setting up of a full length die in Chapter Six. Don't take shortcuts! It just won't work if you do. As for primer pocket residue, it *is* a problem now. In the old days it was easily removed with a screwdriver, but in the last few years they must have changed the mix, or something, because suddenly that residue became hard to remove, even with a sharp pointed scribe. The best way I have found to remove it is with one of the tungsten carbide primer pocket reamers available from various sources. They remove the residue instantly, and keep the primer pocket at the correct depth simultaneously. If you don't use one, you may well end up in the same circumstance as the bloke above. I couldn't keep up with it myself with a screwdriver or scribe. Photo 12-11 shows the tool.

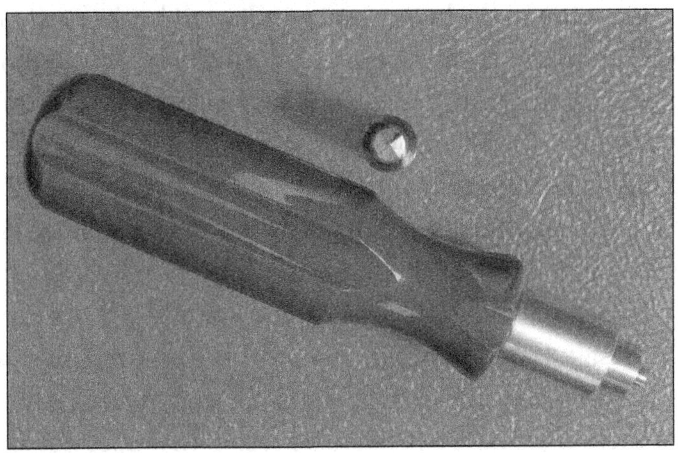

PHOTO 12-11.

These tungsten carbide primer pocket sizing reamers are available from various sources. They remove stubborn primer pocket residue in short order.

While I'm on the subject of setting up dies, it's surprising how often I have run into guys whose reloaded ammunition doesn't fit their rifle, and they can't understand why. When they ask me about it I say, "You've bumped the shoulder with your seating die," which they strenuously deny, but always turns out to be the case. It's easy to do, and with the reloading press being at the top of its stroke, utilising the maximum power it has, you will not notice it when the shoulder bumps the top of the bullet seating die, and causes a bulge just behind the shoulder. If it happens to you, it's a real mongrel, because the ammunition will have to be unloaded, so the cases can be full length re-sized, to remove the offending bulge. Make sure your seating die is around half a turn back from your case with the press ram fully up.

One thing that always catches me out is case length. I tend to use the same batch of shells over and over, when practicing, and it doesn't take long for the cases to exceed their trim length. Fortunately I seem to notice the unexplained vertical shots, caused by that condition, and then trim the cases before I blow the gun up. Its just one of those things that seems to sneak up on you, and so it bears attention.

Some time ago I bought a quality electronic scale, thinking that it might speed up my powder weighing process somewhat, but that didn't pan out. I found the electronic scale wandered off its zero too often for me to be comfortable using it, so I went back to my old RCBS powder scale, that I have been using for some 30 years. What I did find, by cross-checking with the very accurate electronic scale, was that my old RCBS scale was very accurate and consistent, if used properly. It will register a single granule of AR2208 powder, and every load will be the same weight, provided the powder is always trickled in up to the zero on the scale. In other words, if the powder is trickled in over the zero mark, do not remove granules to bring it back to the zero. You must remove at least a grain, and then trickle back up to zero. I would think the same would hold true for all powder scales. I have a magnifying glass mounted in front of the graduations, on my scale, to better see the pointer come up to zero. Unless you are going to trim individual granules to size and weight, (nobody does that, do they?) you don't need any more accuracy than that old scale provides. Just learn how to use it properly. Photo 12-9 (page 418) shows the setup.

Shooting Groups: There are several different ways to handle a rifle when tuning the barrel, and later when shooting groups, either to confirm your tune, in practice, or in a match. While it's ok to make the recommendation to shoot it off sand bags, it's a little more complicated than that. The more solid and sophisticated your setup is, the better your results will be. Its pretty hard, if not impossible, to shoot consistent sub ¼" groups over the bonnet of a vehicle. It's worth joining a bench-rest club, even if you don't shoot bench-rest, because they will have the perfect setup with which to tune your rifle. Many F Class clubs also have benches for testing on.

The club I am a member of is primarily an F Class club, and we shoot a bit of informal bench-rest as well. As a result our benches are light weight portable devices, so that we can move them off the F Class range easily. When using them you have to be very aware of their flexibility. They are not even remotely stable. Whatever you use, aim for the maximum stability you can get.

Sporting rifles, of the design I used to build, do not work very well on sand bags, due to the cast off in the butt of the stock. Of course, checkering, on the for-end, doesn't help much in the front sand bag, either. Too, many of these rifles have considerable recoil, that does not lend them to be fired any way but held firmly. My practice with such rifles is to hold the for-end in my hand, with the back of my hand resting comfortably, on a large sand bag filled with aquarium sand. The butt is held firmly into my shoulder, and I have a small sand bag, under the toe of the stock, to assist me in holding it steady. When the rifle recoils, the toe of the stock recoils away from the sand bag, so there is no sliding/tracking on it involved.

You can make a steady aim like this, though you do need to concentrate and breathe properly. It's hardly a method I'd recommend to shoot dots with. However, with those rifles I'm not looking to do that. They are not designed with that in mind, and literally hammer you on a bench. As soon as I find a load that will shoot a few three shot groups, between ¾" and 1", I pull up and go hunting with it. That degree of accuracy will stick a shot, close to where I am aiming, on any critter I want to take, and at any distance at which I want to have a crack at it.

To get the best out of a varmint rifle you really need a good bench-rest setup. There are three basic ways to fire such a rifle off sand bags. Holding it — with free recoil — or pinning it. You have to find out, by practice, to see which method suites you best.

With holding the rifle, you pretty much hold it as you would in the field, with the exception that your left hand (for righties) will not be holding the for-end, but will be manipulating the rear sand bag, or joystick on the front rest if you have one. You will be holding the rifle into your shoulder, and essentially guiding it under recoil. You need to be very practiced with this method to shoot very small groups consistently, as any slight variation in holding tension, or recoil control, will cause the shot to print away from the group. It is the hardest method to master, though some people can do very well with it.

If you are bench testing a heavy kicking varmint rifle, with a straight stock that will track in the sand bags reasonably, you may have to hold onto it very tightly to get it to shoot. If the rifle is not printing the groups you think it should, don't be afraid to alter your shooting position/style, and see if that makes a difference.

My current .25/06 Ackley Improved is such a rifle. It has a standard Remington BDL stock on it, with a lot of drop at the heel, and the round tipped forend precludes pinning it against the rest, though with the drop in the stock I doubt that would be a successful method to employ anyway. If I try to fire it normal bench-rest style it leaps out of the front bag, torquing violently in the process.

I got it to shoot very well by holding it firmly onto the sand bags, and firmly into my shoulder. I have to be very careful with my breathing and hold, and remember the sight picture as the trigger breaks, so I know if I have fired a good shot or not. It is not a very pleasant rifle to shoot off the bench. Photo 12-12 shows me velocity testing it at our local range.

Before I adopted this shooting style I had literally no control over the way the rifle recoiled, and my testing was plagued with flyers. The rifle literally did its own thing, and not the same thing very often. I knew I was doing something wrong when I kept getting 2 shots cutting, and then one well away. Changing my shooting style fixed that.

PHOTO 12-12.

I am sighting in preparation to taking a shot. The joystick on the rest is right down, and it has been useful to adjust windage whilst I was setting up for the shot. I am holding the rifle firmly onto the sandbags, and firmly into my shoulder. This rifle will not shoot well with usual bench-rest techniques.

PHOTO 12-13.

If you compare this Photo with Photo 12-12, note the position of the forend in the front rest. It has risen appreciably out of the sandbag with recoil. Even though this is not a pleasant rifle to shoot off sandbags, note that my body and head have not moved under recoil — I am staying as still as a statue, despite the rifle moving a considerable distance into my shoulder, and rearing up as well. This is important bench-rest technique, as is knowing exactly where the reticule was resting when the trigger broke — often called 'calling the shot'. This recoil is from the 75 grain projectile. The 85 and 90 grain projectiles kick harder.

On the surface, free recoil would appear to be the best method to get the best accuracy from a rifle, but that isn't necessarily the case. Essentially, with free recoil, the rifle sits in the sand bags with no part of you touching it, except the tip of your trigger finger on the trigger. Your shoulder is around ½" behind the butt, and you apply gentle pressure to the trigger, straight back, so when the rifle fires it recoils freely, to the rear, until the butt contacts your shoulder. In order for it to work you need a stock that tracks very straight, and a solid bench setup, that won't vibrate or move. Some people will squeeze the trigger with their thumb behind the trigger guard, and others may rest their thumb lightly on the right top side of the grip. Essentially, though, they are trying to interfere with the rifles free recoil as little as possible — preferably not at all.

Pinning the rifle is much like free recoil, with the exception that you hold the for-end very firmly, against the for-end stop on the front rest, with a considerable amount of pressure, with your shoulder pressing against the butt. The only parts of your body that contact the rifle are your shoulder, and the tip of your trigger finger.

Of the three methods, I very much favor pinning the rifle. I have had rifles that would not shoot well enough with free recoil, but I have never had one that would not shoot, to its potential, when pinned. Pinning also works best if your bench is not as stable as it should be, by holding the setup under tension. If you use that method you must first ensure the rifle is tracking properly in the sandbags. If it isn't, adjust the angle of your rear bag until it is. That is, when the rifle slides back and forth in the bags, the reticule moves straight up and down the target, with no deviation off to the side.

Now assume your natural shooting position, and apply pressure to the butt with your shoulder. When you do this you are driving the rifle forward, and pinning it against the stop at the front of the rest. As you drive your shoulder forward, against the butt, observe what happens to the reticule, of the telescopic sight, on the target. If it moves it should only be vertically — down, to come to rest just under the mothball on the target. If it moves at all horizontally, you are not positioned correctly behind the rifle. Relax, reposition yourself, according to the direction the reticule moved, and then drive forward again. Keep adjusting your position until you can drive your shoulder into the butt, and the reticule moves, only a small amount, straight down from your aiming point. That is the last thing you do before firing your group, or tuning shot. Having achieved that position, your body should become like a statue, and the only parts of it that move, while you fire your group, are your arms and hands, as they manipulate the bolt, load ammunition, and squeeze the trigger. Every other part of your body should be frozen in position, including your head.

How much pressure should you apply, to the butt, when pinning the rifle? I apply a lot—probably around 20 pounds. I do this because I feel the amount of pressure you apply is, probably, not as important as is applying it consistently. I feel that I can more consistently apply hard pressure, than I can soft. You will have to work that out for yourself.

Photo 12–14 is a scan of a target I shot, at 200 yards, with my 6x47 Lapua F Class rifle, shooting a 107GRN Sierra Match projectile at just over 3000FPS, testing the effect of varying shoulder pressure. You can see that a change in shoulder pressure does not change the impact point of the projectile significantly, though it does change it.

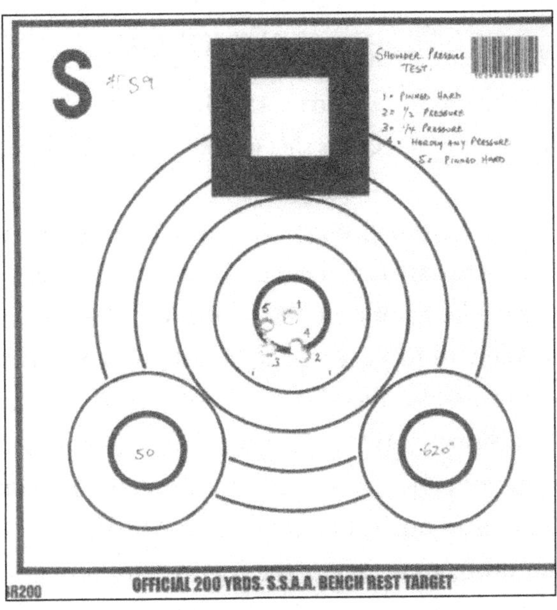

PHOTO 12-14.

A 200 yard target showing the effect of varying shoulder pressure on impact point.

Photo 12–15 is a scan of a target I shot, straight after the test in Photo 12–14, utilizing a heavy pin for every shot. The group is a tad smaller, but much the same as the group where shoulder pressure was varied significantly for three of the five shots. Non-the-less, you should strive to maintain the same shoulder pressure for every shot, and most important is to *hold your ground* when the shot breaks. I have a bad habit, in the heat of combat, to roll right back with the recoil of the rifle on occasion, and when I do that, that shot will certainly print high and out of the group. I guess that comes from firing many heavy kicking rifles in the field, and is simply a way of soaking up some shoulder wrecking recoil. Unfortunately, the bad habit has carried over to my bench shooting, even though soaking up recoil is not needed. When you break the shot you must be a statue, until the recoil has abated, and only then do you begin the reloading sequence.

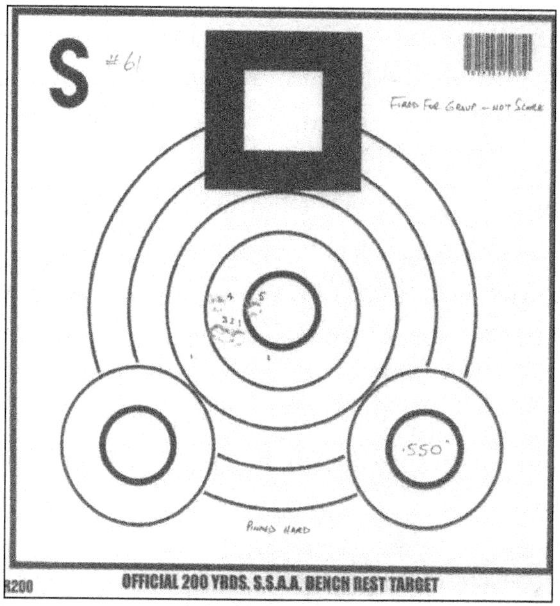

PHOTO 12-15.

This 200 yard target was shot with the rifle pinned hard.

There are two ways you can fire your groups when practicing, or in a match. In bench-rest terminology the advocates, of each, are called pickers and runners. Pickers are very good at reading the wind, and have considerable knowledge of how the condition, they are seeing in the wind flags, will affect the position their projectile will impact on the target. They try to shoot every shot in the same condition, but that is not always possible, due to the limited time they have to fire a group, so they may end up shooting in another condition, if time is running out. Of course, they have the sighter target with which to get some information, about the new condition, before continuing with their group.

Runners shoot their group in the shortest possible time. The theory behind the practice is that the shorter the time you spend shooting your group, the less variation in conditions you will be exposed to. What they do is observe the conditions, prior to shooting their group, and try and find a sign that will tell them that the following condition may hold for a short while.

A sign might be when the tails of the flags drop to 7 o'clock, and the sails swing to 6 o'clock, get ready because it's very likely the sails will swing to 9 o'clock, the tails pick up to 8 o'clock, and that condition will hold for maybe 20–30 seconds. As soon as they see the condition stabilize, they run their group very quickly— some guys can get 5 accurate shots away in 15 seconds or less. The guys with the really quick minds (really, really quick actually) watch the flags, while they are running their group, and if they see a slight drop off, or pick up, adjust their aim to compensate for it, and keep going. Their equipment is specifically designed to shoot fast, with dual port actions fitted with ejectors, and their cartridge block placed right next to the loading port. They also practice a lot to reach, and maintain, the level of expertise they need.

It is possible to be a bit of a runner in long range competition too, depending on how fast your target service is, and some competitors do use the method. I am on record, in open competition, as shooting my 12 shots away in less than 2 minutes, to score 60.5 at 800 yards. To do that you need fantastic target service (my guy deserved a medal) and the right conditions. It's not a method I'd recommend, though, as you can get caught out very badly when (not if!) the conditions change. Running, in long range competition, is called 'chasing the spotter'. To use that method, you fire your shot, and reload while the target is being serviced. As the target is returning you will see where your shot impacted by the position of the spotter. You simply adjust your aim to allow for any error, and fire again, very quickly, the instant the target stops at the top.

I'm a runner, (though not a very fast one) simply because I suck at reading wind flags. I shoot a non ejector, right port only action, with a right hand bolt, left handed, but still manage to get 5 shots away, usually in less than 25 seconds. To do that I modified the bolt of my rifle by fitting a 3/16" Whitworth cap screw to the bolt shroud. You can see the modification made to the bolt of my Shilen DGA in Photo 12–16, and my Panda in Photo 12–17.

This screw allows me to use two hands, at the same time, while running my group, and proved to be so handy that I fitted it onto my F Class rifle as well. I'm not looking for speed with the F Class rifle, but still manipulate the bolt with the screw, which keeps my motor responses working consistently, and it is really handy for cocking and un-cocking the bolt. When I've finished shooting I automatically un-cock the bolt with it, and take the tension off the firing pin spring. It's become second nature for me.

PHOTO 12-16.
The modification made to my Shilen DGA bolt.

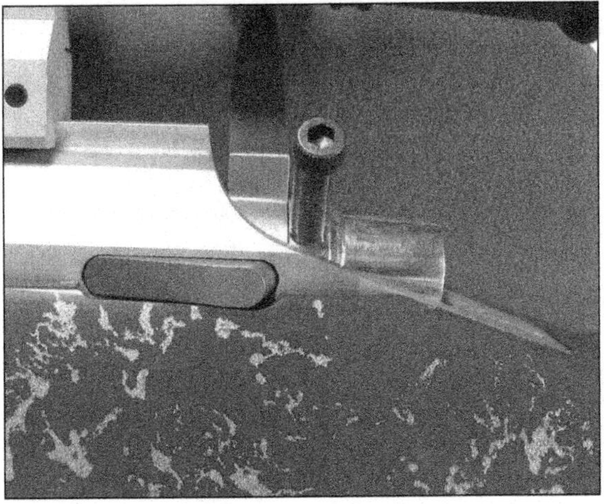

PHOTO 12-17.
The modification made to my Panda bolt.

Photos 12–18 through 12–34 are a series of photographs showing my method while running a group. The sequence shows both left and right sides of the rifle at the same time, or very close to it. I captured these photos from video I took while I shot the groups in Photo 11–1 (Page 387). The right hand photos are of me shooting the sequence #4 group, and the left hand photos are of me shooting the sequence #5 group.

PHOTO 12-18 LEFT AND RIGHT.

I am about to fire the first shot. The only things touching the rifle are my shoulder and trigger finger. My whiskers are barely brushing the comb.

PHOTO 12-19 LEFT AND RIGHT.

The shot has been fired, and the rifle is in full recoil.

PHOTO 12-20 LEFT AND RIGHT.

Recoil has abated, and I have moved the rifle forward, with my shoulder, and pinned it hard against the rest stop. It will remain pinned hard during the reloading sequence, and firing the next shot.

PHOTO 12-21 LEFT AND RIGHT.

My left hand is reaching for the stud on the back of the bolt, at the same time my right hand is reaching for the bolt handle.

PHOTO 12-22 LEFT AND RIGHT.

My left hand has reached the stud, and my left thumb is on top of the grip adding stability. My right thumb is under the bolt handle, and my fingers are on the ledge at the ejection port, to resist the torquing motion, when I rotate the bolt.

PHOTO 12-23 LEFT AND RIGHT.

The bolt has been rotated, and my left hand has withdrawn it about 1/3RD of the way to the rear. My right hand is reaching for a cartridge from the bullet block.

PHOTO 12-24 LEFT AND RIGHT.

My left hand is holding the bolt fully to the rear. My right hand has hold of a cartridge.

PHOTO 12-25 LEFT AND RIGHT.

My left hand still holds the bolt to the rear. My right hand has removed a cartridge from the loading block.

Photo 12-26 Left and Right.

My left hand still holds the bolt to the rear. My right hand is inserting a cartridge into the chamber.

Photo 12-27 Left and Right.

(Puff, Puff!) My left hand still holds the bolt to the rear. My right hand is grabbing the fired case from the bolt. You can see the cartridge sitting on the front of the loading ramp.

Photo 12-28 Left and Right.

Finally, my left hand starts to move the bolt forward, as my right hand brings the fired case out of the action.

Photo 12-29 Left and Right.

My left hand has nearly shut the bolt. My right hand has dropped the case, and is moving back towards the bolt handle.

PHOTO 12-30 LEFT AND RIGHT.
My left hand has shut the bolt. My right hand is steadying the rifle against the torque that will be applied when I rotate the bolt.

PHOTO 12-31 LEFT AND RIGHT.
My left hand is starting to move towards the trigger. My right hand has closed the bolt.

PHOTO 12-32 LEFT AND RIGHT.
My left hand has moved close to the trigger. My right hand is almost to the joystick knob.

PHOTO 12-33 LEFT AND RIGHT.
My left hand is feeling for the trigger. My right hand is on the joystick handle, and I am adjusting my aim.

Photo 12-34 LEFT AND RIGHT.
The second shot is fired. Total elapsed time — less than 5 seconds.

When you are testing any rifle, with a bit of recoil, for group you will probably find that it will shoot better pinned, than if shot free recoil. Obviously, you can't shoot the rifle pinned over the bonnet of a vehicle. You will need a good heavy front bench-rest. My .30BR throws shots when fired free recoil. My 7 Saum torques violently out of the front sand bag when fired free recoil, which tends to destroy the packing of my front sand bag, as well as flog my shoulder. It is much better behaved when I fire it pinned. By all means try every method, and pick the one that suites you best. Another plus, with pinning, is it takes some of the recoil load from your telescopic sight.

CASE PREPARATION: As far as I'm concerned, case preparation is about as much fun as a three fingered prostrate exam. It's really tedious, and for my arthritic thumbs painful to boot. However far you want to take it is up to you, though you can be pretty well assured that whatever steps you are *not* taking, everyone else is!

An accurate centre-fire rifle is certainly a result of the sum of its parts, each part contributing to the end result. Case preparation is a sub section of one of those parts, the cartridge, whose effect is hard to quantify, though is surely part of the overall equation, and a contribution to the end result. 'Contribution' is the key word here. Case preparation will not turn your badly shooting rifle into a tack driver. It will only contribute towards averaging the level of accuracy you achieve. By that I mean it reduces flyers, or stray shots, which is exactly why we suffer through it.

Every step you take in the accuracy equation is beneficial. However, you have to rationalize each step on a return of benefit basis.

I don't bother with any case preparation on my normal hunting rifles, apart from case length trimming, and correct full length sizing. If I were to be using a long range hunting rifle — something I may want to take medium game with out to around 400 yards, I would spend some time on my cases. Likewise, with a varmint rifle, and certainly with a target rifle.

The case preparation steps I undertake are as follows:–

1. Primer pocket depth equalizing. This is carried out with a tungsten carbide cutter like the one seen in Photo 12-11 (Page 419). I secure the cutter in the chuck of a battery drill held in the soft jaws of my vice, just like you see in Photo 12-35. It's simply a matter of holding the case squarely against the cutter until the cutting action stops. You will need to clear the chips out of the hole a couple of times for each case.

PHOTO 12-35.

Equalizing primer pocket depth, and squaring the bottom of the recess.

2. Lubricate the inside of the necks of the case with Imperial die sizing wax. I apply it with a cotton bud. It's a boooorrring job! Photo 12-36 refers.

PHOTO 12-36

Lubricating the inside of the case necks with Imperial Sizing Die Wax. I have a long way to go — ho-hum!

3. Pre-turn the case necks. You will achieve more consistent neck thickness and uniformity if you pre-turn the case necks, leaving only about .001" for the final cut. You can purchase case neck turning tools for this job, and some people have two tools, one to pre-turn, and one to final turn. If you have a lathe you can pre-turn your cases with it, and that is what I do. You can do the whole job with a lathe if you wish, however you must be aware that when you turn the case necks, friction from the cutting tool will heat them up. That heat will be transferred to the turning mandrill, which will heat it up, and make it expand in diameter. This will vary the thickness of your case necks. Not very helpful! We want to keep them all exactly the same. If you are going to turn necks like this you should only turn maybe ten every half hour to maintain neck thickness consistency, which is why I prefer to pre-turn only with the lathe. Otherwise, it takes too long to do. If turning with a lathe only, I would still do the job in two steps — a roughing step, and a finishing step. You would need to make one mandrill for the roughing cut, and then cut it off and make another slightly larger one for the finishing cut.

Photo 12-37 shows my tools, and Photos 12-38 through 12-46 show the method. The mandrel is turned from ½" drill rod, and the leade in taper is 5 degrees. Lubricating the cases with sizing die wax (in step 2) prevents them from galling the mandrel. You quickly adopt a routine doing this job, and it goes reasonably fast. I'm not as nimble as I once was, but can still manage 100 cases in 50 minutes. The forward cut along the case neck is a fast one, and done by hand. The surface of the case neck will look like you've cut a 28TPI thread by the time you reach the rear stop. When you get there engage the slow longitudinal feed, and it will make a fine correctly sized finish as it cuts to the end of the case automatically. Looking at Photo 12-38 you will note that I have removed the handle on my cross-slide adjustment lest I inadvertently bump it and upset my setting. The cross-slide itself is locked in position once I have determined the cut is correct. As I said, you get pretty good at having everything in the right position at the right time, and the job goes reasonably quickly.

PHOTO 12-37.

The tools needed to turn case necks on a lathe. The piece on the top right accepts the case pusher just in front of it, as well as a standard shell holder. The tip of the turning tool at the bottom is ground, and stoned, to a .015" radius. The mandrel must be turned in the lathe, and cannot be used again by simply trueing it in a 4 jaw chuck, as that will not be accurate enough to hold the extremely close tolerances needed for this job. When you start another batch of cases you must make a new mandrel.

PHOTO 12-38.

The lathe setup for case neck turning. There are stops, both at the front and at the rear of the carriage. Note, also, that I have removed the handle from the cross-slide in case I inadvertently bump it and upset my setting. When the correct diameter is found the cross-slide is locked into position.

PHOTO 12-39.

The lathe, set up, and ready to begin.

PHOTO 12-40.

The case is being driven onto the mandrel with the tail-stock feed.

PHOTO 12-41.

The case being turned back to the shoulder. The feed is by hand.

PHOTO 12-42.

Here, you can see how quickly the cut to the shoulder is made. This is not a sizing cut, but merely to get the tool back to the shoulder.

Photo 12-43.

The return cut, towards the end of the neck, is made with a slow automatic feed, to both size the diameter of the neck, and produce a fine finish. While the return cut is taking place, the case installer is removed, and the tail-stock feed is wound forward to bring the shell holder retainer into its correct position for case extraction.

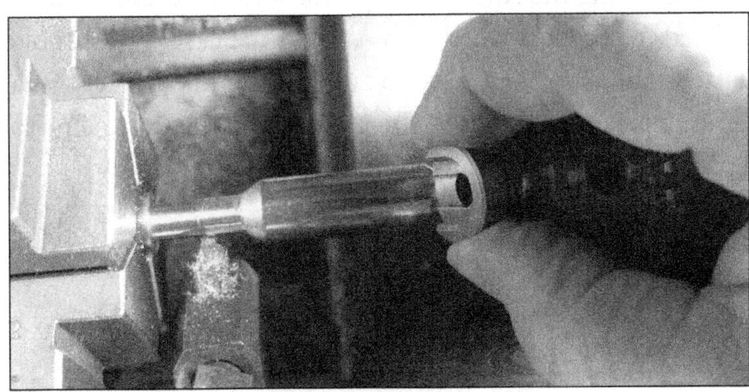

Photo 12-44.

The lathe is turned off just as the tool reaches the end of the neck. The shell holder, needed to extract the case, is dropped into position.

Photo 12-45.

The case is being extracted, from the mandrel, by winding the tail-stock feed back.

PHOTO 12-46.

The shell holder is removed, the case pusher is installed in the shell holder retainer, and we are ready to go again.

4. Chamfer the flash holes. The tools I use can be seen in Photo 12-47. This job is carried out to remove any burrs at the end of the flash hole inside the case, and equalize the length of the flash hole. I do this by hand, simply inserting the cutter through the flash hole, and slide the sleeve into the case neck, which has been sized to accept it when I pre-turned the cases. Then, hold the case against the base, and rotate the cutter handle until it ceases to cut. The depth of the cut is taken from the base of the case, which is the same place the depth of the primer pocket was taken from, so my flash holes will all be the same length. Photo 12-48 shows me doing the job.

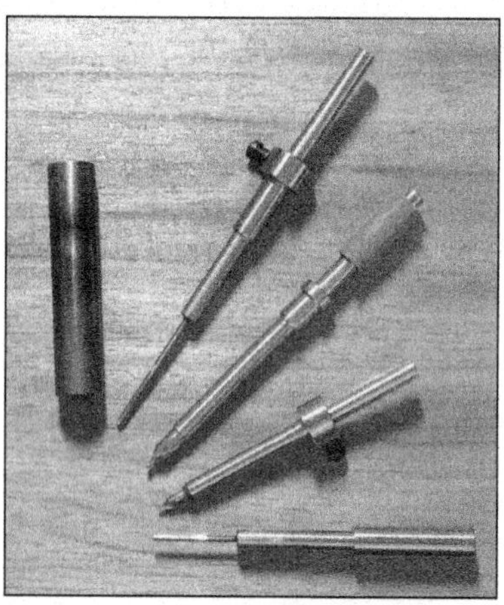

PHOTO 12-47.

Flash hole reaming and chamfering tools. The base piece on the left determines the depth of the chamfer, and is hardened on the end so the drill will not penetrate it. The chamfering tools are made from half a centre drill, and drill rod. The reamers are commercial tungsten carbide, glued into drill rod holders, though I have not bothered reaming flash holes lately.

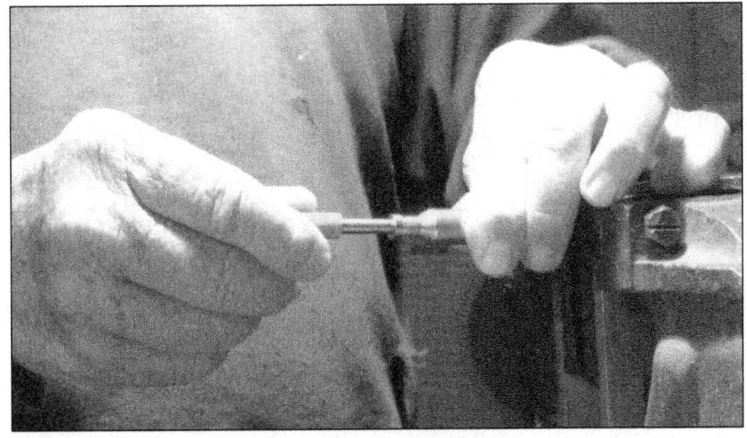

PHOTO 12-48.

I chamfer the flash holes by hand. The case is held against the base of the depth piece, and the chamfering tool wound in carefully until the cut stops.

5. Expand the case necks for final turning. There is still enough die wax in the necks to lubricate them as they are expanded. See Photo 12-49.

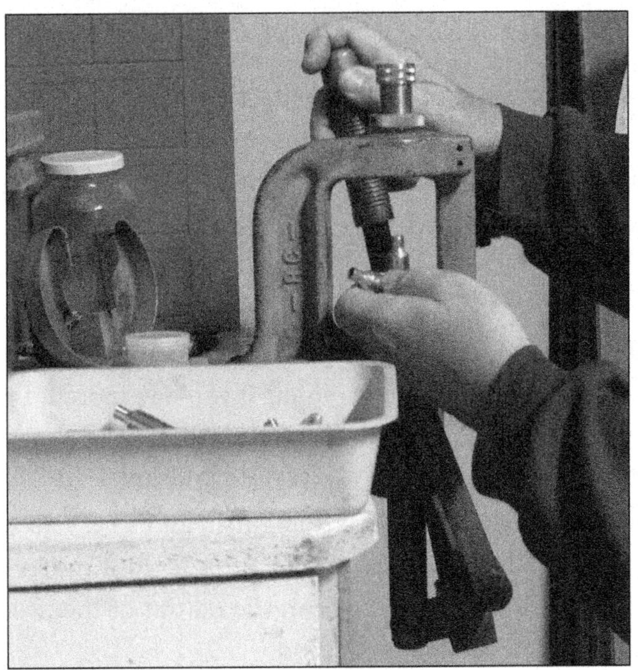

PHOTO 12-49.

Expanding the case necks, to the correct diameter, for final neck turning with a neck turning tool. Taking an expanded case out, and putting a new case in at the same time speeds the job along.

6. Final turn the case necks to correct size. I do this with a commercial neck turning tool in my milling machine. If you buy yourself a neck turning tool, be sure to order it with a tungsten carbide turning mandrel. If you neglect to do this, and opt instead for a steel turning mandrel, you will have difficultly maintaining consistent neck thickness due to variation, in the diameter of the mandrel, as it heats during turning, and cools between cases. The mandrel gets quite hot in this operation. A

tungsten carbide mandrel negates this problem, allowing cases to be turned very uniformly. Also, purchase a deluxe model, with a dial adjustable mandrel, that will enable you to adjust the thickness of your cut easily and precisely. This feature makes arriving at the exact neck thickness you want so much easier, and is well worth the extra expense.

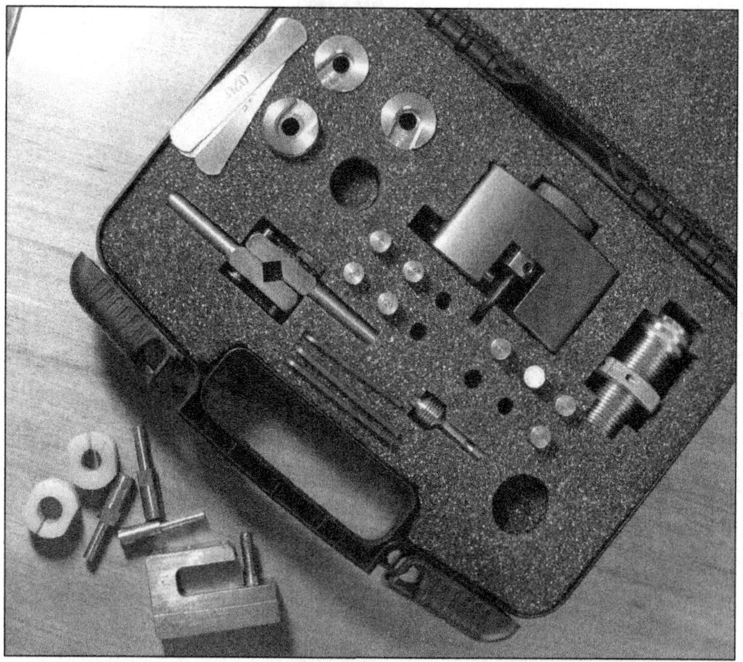

PHOTO 12-50.

My current case neck turning tools. At the bottom left is the tool I began turning case necks with in the 1970s, made by Ferris Pindell of PPC fame. Neck turning tools have come a long way since then. The Pindell tool should probably be in a museum!

The milling cut is much the same as the lathe cut, except I am now using a tungsten carbide mandrel with a coefficient of expansion that is so negligible it can be ignored. I place a drop of 50/50 STP and Mobil 1 on the mandrel, to lubricate it, prior to each cut. The advancing cut is done by hand, quite quickly, as with the lathe, and at the end of the cut I engage the automatic feed, and the mill does the retracting cut for me, with a slow feed, making a fine finish, and a very accurate cut.

The mill is slower than the lathe — it takes me 1 hour and 20 minutes to turn 100 cases. While the case is retracting, I take the opportunity to clean the oil out of the neck of the case I previously turned. Photos 12-51 through 12-55 show the method.

PHOTO 12-51.

The setup for turning case necks in the mill. A drop of 50/50 STP and Mobil 1 has been placed on the mandrel. The mandrel has been centered under the quill with a center finder.

PHOTO 12-52.

Installing the case in the shell holder. The shell holder locks the case in place for both height and center over the mandrel.

PHOTO 12-53.

The cut to the shoulder, like on the lathe, is made quite quickly by hand with the quill feed handle. The depth of the cut is determined by the quill travel stop, not by running into the end of the mandrel.

PHOTO 12-54.

The return cut is made with the quill automatic feed set on slow.

PHOTO 12-55.

While the return cut is being made, I clean the oil from the inside of the case necks.

7. Batch weigh the cases. This step probably falls into one of those wishful thinking areas — we kinda hope we are doing something positive, but probably we are not making any difference at all. At least it's highly unlikely we will be making a negative influence. The case is nothing more than a pressure vessel, and what we are trying to achieve is to equalize the volume of all of our pressure vessels (cases) in the hope that when we burn an equal weight of powder in each, they will all generate an equal amount of pressure to drive the projectile out of the barrel. Whether x grains of

powder always burned in Y volume of pressure vessel *always* produces Z psi of pressure is a moot point — probably not.

The external dimensions of our cases should be as near as 'damn it' is to swearing the same, and as we have improved those dimensions a tad with our case preparation, its reasonable to assume that case weight will reflect a variation in case internal volume. That's what we are about in sorting cases by weight. We are hoping to reduce the internal volume of our cases, into batches, with as little variation as possible. Hopefully that will equalize the pressure within each case, when it is fired, or at least reduce the variation in pressure between cases.

If you have a digital scale the job goes pretty quickly, and you only have to do it once, so I figure why not. I can't see that it can do any harm. You could be super anal and measure the internal volume of every case, but it's a matter of diminishing returns. Kinda like painting a house with an artists brush instead of a 6" painters brush. What have you gained? A hell of a lot of effort, and the house has still only been painted. I have no problems expending a reasonable amount of effort on jobs like this, but don't go overboard. You'll get far more return, with your expenditure in time, by learning to shoot.

Some brands of cases are of higher quality than others, and some calibers in the same brand are better than others. The Remington 7mm Saum cases you see me preparing in the photos are, quite frankly, bloody awful — they should be ashamed. The preparing of the flash holes and primer pocket are mandatory in this case, not an option, they are so bad. You will see I am preparing a wedge of cases, 450 in all. These cases will do me for probably 3 barrels, and I am preparing so many in order to make my batches somewhat larger, so I don't have so many batches with a small number of cases in them. The weight of these cases varies over 7 grains, and I will batch them in .5 grain lots. In this instance I am looking for batches of at least 24 cases, which is the number of shots fired in ½ a days match. A batch of 48 cases would be much better, as that represents a full days match — 4 ranges x 12 shots/range. Sometimes there are 15 shot matches, or even 20 shot matches, so I will try to rationalize my batches to allow for this.

Photo 12-56.

The cases have been batched into ½ grain lots. The quality of these cases sucks — they vary by over 7 grains overall. For my current barrel I used the three blocks on the right, and made 2 batches from the cases on the extreme right. I only have enough cases for each barrel for a bit over one days match shooting, and reload them at the end of each day for the following day. Before I leave for an away match I pre-weigh all of my powder into the vials you saw in Chapter 10 (Photo 10-1, Page 360) to make the job go a bit quicker. When I need them, the cases in the far left block will be batched again into 2 groups, which will drop their spread to ¼ grain (maybe!), and I will re batch the out of spec cases on the far left.

Once batched, I keep the cases together in cartridges boxes marked A, B etc, and try to shoot each batch the same number of times, though that's pretty hard to do consistently. I am trying, though—very trying!

8. Anneal the case necks. You can buy an expensive machine to do this job or you can do it, with less precision with an oxy torch, or a MAP gas torch. I have a mate with a machine, and he says it works ok. I used oxy when I had the bottles, but when they got too expensive to keep I switched over to a MAP gas torch. If you use oxy the flame is very hot, even when turned right down, and you have to be careful not to overheat the necks, or even melt them. Also, with oxy, use a quiet carburizing flame, not a neutral, or an oxidizing flame. Have a bit of an acetylene feather at the end of the tip. Map gas is much more forgiving, even flat out.

Many years ago I made the shell holders, you can see in Photo 12-57, that fit in a battery drill, and allow me to rotate the cases while they are being held in the flame of the torch, oxy or MAP. The holders keep the flame, and heat, away from the head of the case—the last thing you want to do is draw the hardness at the case head. That's a recipe guaranteed to blow your head off.

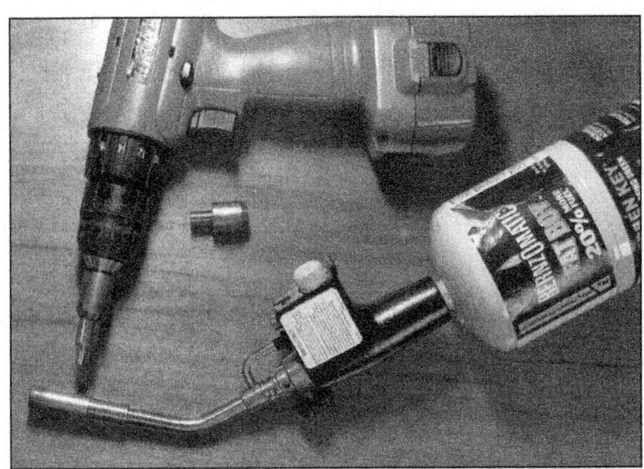

PHOTO 12-57.

Tools for annealing case necks. The case holders are made from old stainless barrel steel.

PHOTO 12-58.

Annealing a case neck. As soon as the case neck reaches a dull red colour I flip the drill over and the case drops into the water in the bucket. I am doing the job in the dark — the photo was taken with a flash.

I'm not real technical with this job. I do it in a dark room, the better to see the colour of the case necks when I bring them up to temperature. The Map gas torch is set up so that its flame plays above the surface of a bucket of water. I place a case in the holder, start the drill running in slow speed, and bring the neck of the case into the flame at an angle until it just glows barely dull red, and then drop the case into the bucket of water. The case is held in the flame for a count of 5. When I have finished the batch of cases, I shake the water out of them, blow them out with compressed air, and put them out in the sun for an hour or so to dry right off.

To gauge the anneal of my cases I simply try a projectile in a few fired case necks. I think that, when fired, the case neck should relax enough to allow a projectile to pass easily through. If it won't it's a sign that the neck has work hardened, is springing back too much, and needs to be annealed again. When the cases have dried I apply a thin coat of Imperial die wax to protect them from corrosion, The annealing burns all of the oil/wax from the surface of the case leaving it unprotected. The wax literally soaks into the brass by the time I get to use the cases.

PHOTO 12-59.
Annealed cases on the left, and un-annealed cases on the right.

9. Chamfer the inside and outside of the case neck. I use an ordinary Wilson chamfering tool for the outside of the neck, and a long tapered cutter in a battery drill, set on low, for the inside. I give the inside of the neck a good chamfer to facilitate even seating of boat tail projectiles.

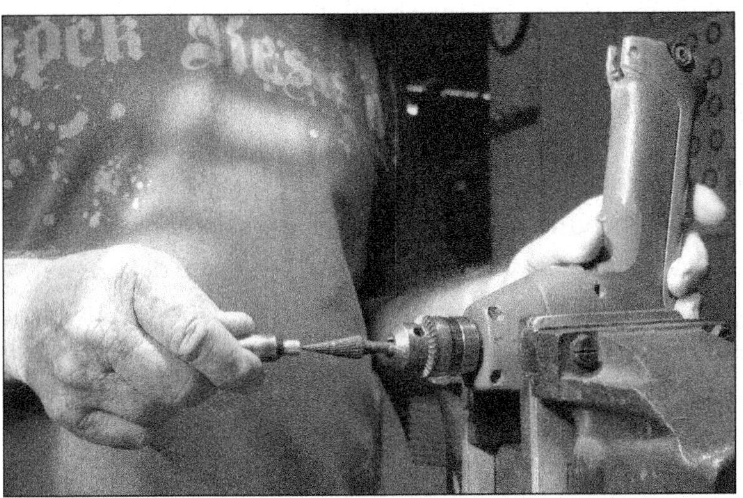

PHOTO 12-60.
About to chamfer the inside of a case neck. Thank goodness I'm close to the end of this job!

All in all case prep is one job I am glad to see the end of. Its one of those processes whose benefits you have to take on faith, as those benefits are not seen in an immediate improvement in accuracy. *You are just as likely to shoot a smaller group with unprepared cases than you are with prepared cases.* Sounds stupid, but the variables in the system are such, that can, and does happen. However, were it possible to wear out the same barrel twice, once with prepared cases, and once with unprepared cases, and measure all of the groups fired, I would bet my left nut that the prepared cases would win the competition hands down. And that's what it's all about — reducing the variables to lessen the stray shots, and achieve a better performance average.

That's it for me, and frankly it's more than I want to do, but I figure I'd better at least wave the flag, and do the basics. There are lots of nifty tools around that will measure other things, and further refine your batches. In my case I'd probably end up with batches of 3 cases, and that wouldn't work. As I said a while back, you have to balance effort versus gain, and strike a happy medium. That having been said, though, a lot of the perceived gain from this sort of thing is in the mind, so if you think it's better it probably is (for you).

Neck Weld: Something that is not generally known but bears keeping an eye on, is your projectiles will weld themselves to your case necks over time, and cause a sharp rise in pressure when the cartridges are fired. Anyone who has stored loaded ammunition for a time needs to be aware of this, especially if the load you are using is close to the maximum usable load in that barrel. The extra pressure generated in a cartridge, with a welded projectile, could easily cause a case head failure with disastrous results.

Hunters and varmint shooters, especially, need to be aware of this problem, and I am one who has been caught out with it. We tend to load a wedge of cartridges for a trip, and when game is scarce we bring a lot of them home to be used next time, and that can be a year away. Target shooters, too, should be aware, as it can affect them as well.

It doesn't take long for the welding process to begin — I have noticed its effect in ammunition that has been loaded for only a week or so — so much so that when I preload ammunition, for an away competition, I seat the projectile plus .050" by inserting a washer in my seating die, and then re-seat them, on the morning of the match, to the correct overall length. You know something's going on when you hear quite a few of them go '*crack*', as they break the weld, when you re-seat them. That's what I do with any old hunting ammunition I am going to take with me on an expedition. You just need to seat them deeper enough to hear them crack loose — .010" is plenty. The extra bullet jump won't cause you to miss a critter out to a couple of hundred yards.

Why does it happen? — I don't know. Probably a case of two dissimilar metals, held together under pressure, with a thin carbon deposit in between, setting up an electrolytic action, or something like that. Whatever it is it's a fact, and we have to be aware of it so we can deal with it, and avoid an accident.

the intentions of mice and men: It was not my intention to write this book for target shooters, but rather for hunters and varmint shooters. *I am not a target shooter.* I'm a hunter who has done a bit of target shooting, but more than anything I have been a student of centre-fire rifle accuracy all of my adult life. I have referred to target shooting, and what they do, a bit in this book, because target shooting is the test bed for new ideas and procedures. You simply don't know how good you or your equipment is, until you test it against others in open competition. Only that separates the sheep from the goats.

While the last thing I would consider, would be to take my target rifle hunting — that'd be like trying to hump a Porcupine— the principals, and procedures, that have produced its accuracy apply as equally to hunting, and varmint rifles, as they do to it. The target rifles design sucks as a hunting, or even varmint platform, but the procedures used in its manufacture, and ammunition preparation, apply equally to all platforms.

working out zero: Many years ago I was very anal about trajectory and zero — I still am. Back then I used to trajectory test my rifles by shooting them, in 50 yard increments out to 500 yards, then plot the trajectory on a graph, and work out from that where I wanted my zero distance to be. I was pretty good at hitting distant things in the field, and that came about in good part from the trajectory testing I did.

These days modern computer programs make those deliberations more accurate, but you still have to do the leg work for their calculations to apply in the real world. I use a free program, which was available from Berger Bullets (Berger Ballistics 11), which I have found to be very accurate. Unfortunately it is no longer available, and is only compatible up to Windows XP service pack 2. Other programs may work as well.

You still have to find out what the trajectory of your working load will be in the real world by shooting it. What I do is get a very good zero for my rifle at 200 yards. Then without touching the sight, I shoot it on target at 100 yards, 300 yards, and 400 yards, and write down the drop figures I obtain. I do the shooting from out of the window of Lyn's Suzuki Sierra — it's quicker than setting up a bench at those ranges.

PHOTO 12-61.

Trajectory testing out to 400 yards is easier out of the window of Lyn's Zippy than setting up portable benches at the different ranges.

PHOTO 12-62.

Comparing this Photo to Photo 12-61, you can see by the way the barrel has reared up, under recoil, this .25/06 Ackley Improved really leans on you, even shooting the light 75^{GN} projectile, which its working load gets out at 3830 FPS.

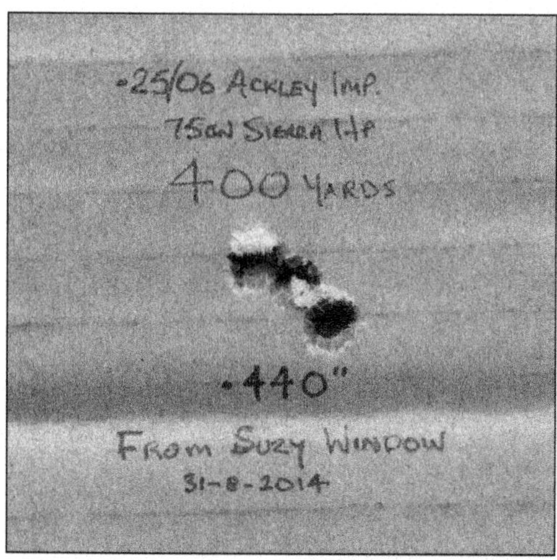

PHOTO 12-63.

I might as well show off! I shot this target from the window of Lyn's Suzuki while testing the 75^{GN} Sierra HP projectile in my 25/06 Ackley Improved at 400 yards. If you think I can repeat it, you're off your rocker!

Then I go and fire up the computer, input the environmental data etc, and see how the trajectory data matches the data I obtained in the real world. It rarely does, so I adjust the parameters available to me, mostly the ballistic coefficient parameter, until the computer data closely matches the real world data I obtained. Having achieved that, or as close as I can get to it, I can then ask the program to plot the trajectory for me, in ten yard increments, out to whatever distance I want. I usually pick a maximum distance of 500 yards.

With that information I can adjust my zero distance in the program, and see what effect that makes on my overall trajectory. For my varmint rifle I prefer it not to shoot more than 1.8" above the line of sight, so I adjust my zero range to make that happen. Once I have that information I can see how high I must make my zero at 200 yards, which is the distance I always zero my varmint rifles at, to give me the optimum trajectory I'm after. Double check a couple of distances in the real world, and I'm good to go. Simple!

LOADING LARGE BATCHES OF AMMUNITION: I don't do that anymore. It's really hard to know how many shots you will need for a trip. Australia is a land of extremes, and sometimes when you arrive at your favorite shooting haunt there is game in the hundreds, and other times there is nearly nothing. In the past I always budgeted for the best case scenario, and when I encountered the worst case scenario, ended up taking a lot of ammunition home with me.

These days I only take about 30 loaded rounds with me — enough to last for the first day. I also take my small press, bullet seating dies, sized and primed cases, projectiles, and powder pre-weighed in the vials you can see in Photo 10-1 on page 360 . If there is plenty of game around it's no problem to quickly load the ammunition I need, as all I have to do is pour the powder into the cases, from the vials, and seat a bullet on them. My ammo is always fresh, and if there isn't much game around I can take my unused cases back home, and have them available, if I want to do any further testing with that rifle. I'm always tinkering around, and this is a much better system for me than having to unload old ammunition.

SIGHTING IN: Being an avid crow shooter taught me early on the importance of sighting in your rifle correctly. It is important to understand that the way you hold a rifle, and thereby influence its recoil, has a direct effect on the rifles zero.

Recoil, and the way we control it, or maybe better, whether we control it or not, has a direct effect on whether or not our shot will impact in the place we intend it to. In this regard light recoiling rifles, such as the .17 calibers, are easier to shoot accurately than heavy recoiling rifles, such as anything over 6MM calibre.

In my experience the hot shot 17s, such as the .17/222 Improved Magnum, and the hot shot .22s shooting a 60[GN] HP projectile, at around 4000FPS, were far more consistent long range crow killers than my .25/06 Ackley Improved, spitting the 87[GN] bullet out at 3650FPS. On paper, at 400 yards, the .25/06 Improved is the superior cartridge, but in the real world, you have to be able to shoot it.

What all of this boils down to is this. The only time you should sight your rifle in, on a bench, with sand bags, is if that is the way you are going to use it. *That is the only way your zero will be valid.* If you use the rifle any other way your zero will be off. Ok, you will still hit a pig in the guts at 50 yards, but if you want to hit a crow at 250 yards, in any other shooting position, that just 'aint gunna happen.

If you want to hit that crow and his mates consistently, you have to sight your rifle in using the shooting position you will be using, in the field, crow shooting. If you are going to shoot over the roof of a ute, then that's how you should sight your rifle in. I did most of my crow shooting out of the window of a vehicle, and that's how I sighted my crow rifles in. On Page 78 is a photo of Tony Greenfield sighting in my .14/221 Walker. That's how he will be using it, for that nights fox shooting, so he is sighting it in the same way.

This is a rule you must follow if you are to be successful at hitting things, where you want to, in the field.

Unless you are very confident in your ability, and in your rifles accuracy, you should fire a 3 shot group, and make your sight correction according to the centre of that groups impact. The size of the group is not important. Sighting in to the average of the shots is. If you sight in with a single shot you will end up chasing your own tail. A three shot group is a concrete base from which to make a positive adjustment. A single shot is not.

I sight my rifles in at 200 yards. Experience taught me early on that a rifle that was sighted in at 100 yards usually had a windage or elevation error, at the longer ranges, that could not be detected at the close range.

I obtained a superior zero at the longer range.

The scope adjustments are just bolts that bear against the erector tube, inside the scope, which is held against the adjusters, usually with a leaf spring. The tolerances in these instruments are miniscule, and when you wind the adjuster out sometimes the spring does not have enough power to force the erector tube properly against it. What happens is you make an adjustment and the zero doesn't alter, so you make another (or two), and then when you fire the rifle the recoil finally jars the erector loose, and you have over adjusted. The fix is, when you wind the adjuster out, wind it at least 5 clicks past the adjustment you want, and then tap around the adjusting turret a few times with the handle of a screw driver. Then wind the adjuster back in the 5 clicks to make the adjustment you originally wanted. You will find that when you do it like this your adjustments will be more precise, and less frustrating.

This job needs to be done in the early morning, or in the late evening, when the wind is at its most benevolent — preferably non existent. In long range target shooting we call this a 'no wind zero', and it is very important if you expect to make accurate predictions of where to hold off when the wind blows. When you have an accurate no wind zero, zero the scale on your windage adjustments. For elevation, work out the trajectory of your rifle and base your 200 yard zero on that. When I was doing my crow and fox shooting, I worked that out in the real world by testing the trajectory of my rifles out to 500 yards, and plotting their trajectory on graph paper. I was very anal about zero, and trajectory, in those days, and that is a good reason why I was so successful at hitting long range targets. If I may be allowed a little bit of self indulgence, I was very good at it, and this was brought about, mainly, by a good deal of intelligent preparation.

When you are shooting at game, regardless, whether or not it is vermin, you owe it to them to dispatch them cleanly and quickly. Unless you go into the field with a properly sighted in rifle, have learned its trajectory, and can operate it to the best of your ability, you are not holding up your end of the contract. If I have learned anything in my time, taking many thousands of head of game, it is this. When you break the trigger, the result is never certain. Many things can happen between the instant you break the trigger, and the instant the projectile arrives at the animal, or bird, whose life you are about to extinguish. Be sure that you have done everything in your power to make that shot count. Nothing less is acceptable.

PHOTO 12-64.

The author just leaving the ground on a Brumby cull in western Queensland. Hanging with my body three quarters of the way out of this chopper was a real buzz. Real 'Apocalypse Now'. I remember thinking, "Bloody hell, I hope I did this seat belt up properly!"

PHOTO 12-65.

Our camp in the Thomson channel country, 2002. This was our first trip with a small off road caravan, having just graduated from a trailer and tent. Such luxury in the bush. On our previous trip, in northern NSW, we were rained in on black soil for a week, and decided we needed a little more comfort in our old age!

AFTERWORD

Producing this book has been a long hard road. Getting my thoughts on paper was the easy part. How my poor wife translated my Arabic like scribble into type is quite beyond me, and then the editing, proof reading, etc — wow — what a nightmare!

Now that it is completed, I am over 70 years old and still an active shooter. In 2006 I developed an epiretinal membrane on my right eye that started to affect the amount of detail I could resolve with that eye, though, at the time, I was unaware of what was happening. By the end of 2007 that eye was causing me considerable problems, to the extent that I had to change over to shooting left handed, in order to see the target. That was a trial.

My health became a problem for hunting around this time, so I took up F Class shooting around the end of 2008, and made a 6X47 Lapua on a Panda F Class action I had obtained. I had, and have, no interest in either .223 Remington or 308 Winchester cartridges, so opted for F Open Class, where you could use pretty well whatever calibre your little heart desired. In 2009 I attended my first Open Class shoot at the Raglan Shooting Complex, 55KM south of Rockhampton, on the central coast of Queensland. I placed 1ST in the lead up, to the Central Queensland Championships, in which I came in $5^{TH,}$ and 2ND in the Palma match held on the following day.

Health problems precluded any traveling for three years. By 2011 my eyes were a considerable problem, so I spent $15,000 on them without much, if any, improvement. The image from my right eye is still badly distorted, and I still can't resolve much detail, especially in my right eye from which colour is very wishy washy. My left eye has a large permanent floater right in the middle of my vision. I guess, at least, I can still see a bit.

F Class shooting is a great source of frustration for me, as I am unable to resolve the subtle variations in mirage speed, or flag angle, that are so important to making a successful shot. Still, it does give me something to bitch about, and I do a lot of that!

In 2012 we returned to Raglan again, where I took 3RD place in the lead up (1 point from 1ST), won the Central Queensland Championships, won the Palma, and won the Queensland Long Range Championships, top scoring by 22 points. From Raglan we moved on to Mackay for the North

Queensland Queens Prize shoot. There I took 12TH out of 32 competitors in the lead up, 6TH out of 37 competitors, only 3 points from $1^{ST,}$ in the Queens, and 7TH out of 37 in the grand aggregate, 7 points from $1^{ST.}$ I guess there is still some life left in the old dog yet!

While there is rarely a week goes by that I haven't been shooting on our local rifle range, I haven't been hunting for some 5 years. I will take steps to do something about that next year. In the meantime I plan to continue shooting as long as I can.

I feel really lucky to have lived in a time when there was so much to be discovered about accuracy, and a fine rifle was appreciated for its form and function. I cringe when I see the ugly, so called, 'Tactical' junk that is so much in vogue these days. Throw me and my Mauser sporting rifle, and Joe Bloggs with his Tac x super gun into a mob of pigs, and I'm pretty confident I know who would score the most. Quite frankly, I'd be worried to go up against a hamster, armed with the stuff that's on offer these days, let alone risk going after something that has the potential to harm me.

Anyway, I hope you have gleaned some useful information from my ramblings. As for me, if I have contributed to only one person not making an unsafe trigger I will feel that my efforts were worth while.

Gongs won in early 2012 at Raglan and Mackay.

APPENDIX I

In the following pages are drawings depicting the pre-turn dimensions I used for many of the actions I fitted barrels to over the years.

They are placed here as an addition to Chapter 3, Fit The Barrel, so that you can get an idea of what you are liable to encounter when fitting barrels to these various actions. Again, I would warn you — *do not take any of these measurements verbatim.* You should always base your measurements on what you have in front of you, doing this job, and never on what is printed in a book. If I have learned anything writing this book, it is this: *the possibility that there will be errors, in a book, is highly likely.*

Threading a stainless steel barrel blank. The setup method used here was Method 2 (Chapter 2 Page 57). This photo is circa 1970.

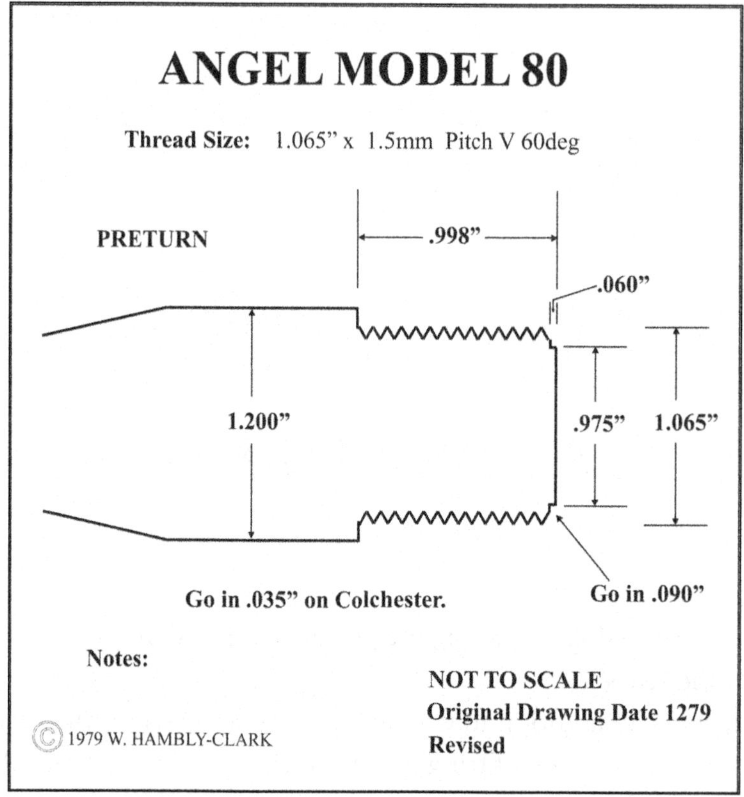
ANGEL MODEL 80
Thread Size: 1.065" x 1.5mm Pitch V 60deg
PRETURN
.998"
.060"
1.200"
.975"
1.065"
Go in .035" on Colchester.
Go in .090"
Notes:
NOT TO SCALE
Original Drawing Date 1279
Revised
© 1979 W. HAMBLY-CLARK

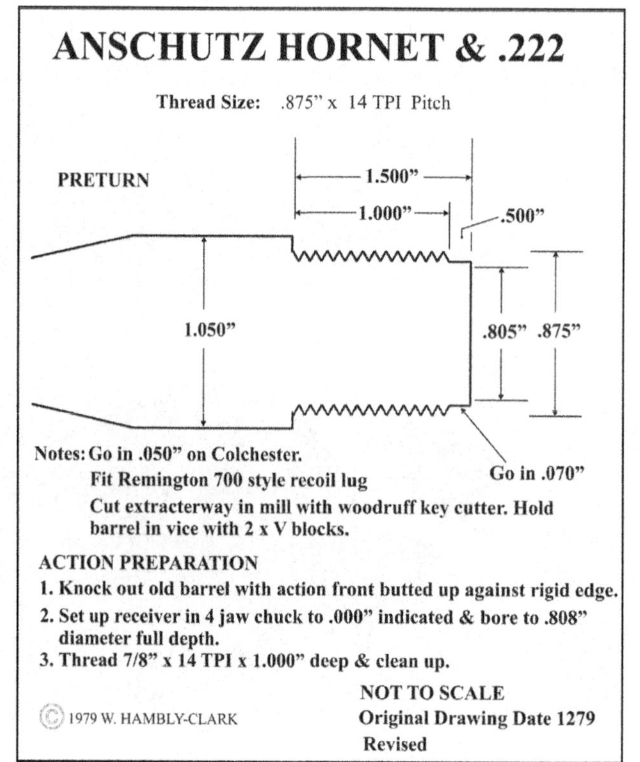
ANSCHUTZ HORNET & .222
Thread Size: .875" x 14 TPI Pitch
PRETURN
1.500"
1.000"
.500"
1.050"
.805"
.875"
Notes: Go in .050" on Colchester.
Fit Remington 700 style recoil lug
Go in .070"
Cut extracterway in mill with woodruff key cutter. Hold barrel in vice with 2 x V blocks.
ACTION PREPARATION
1. Knock out old barrel with action front butted up against rigid edge.
2. Set up receiver in 4 jaw chuck to .000" indicated & bore to .808" diameter full depth.
3. Thread 7/8" x 14 TPI x 1.000" deep & clean up.
NOT TO SCALE
Original Drawing Date 1279
Revised
© 1979 W. HAMBLY-CLARK

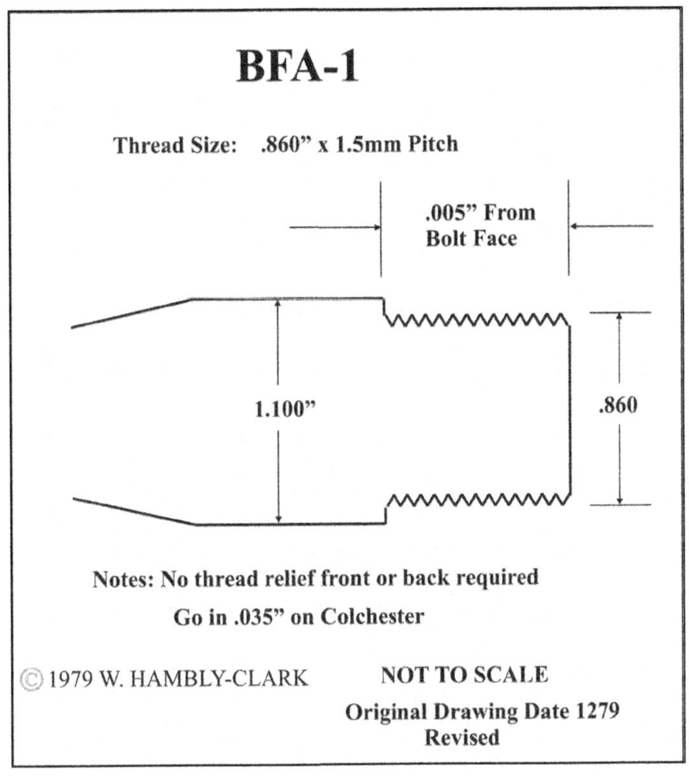
BFA-1
Thread Size: .860" x 1.5mm Pitch
.005" From Bolt Face
1.100"
.860
Notes: No thread relief front or back required
Go in .035" on Colchester
© 1979 W. HAMBLY-CLARK
NOT TO SCALE
Original Drawing Date 1279
Revised

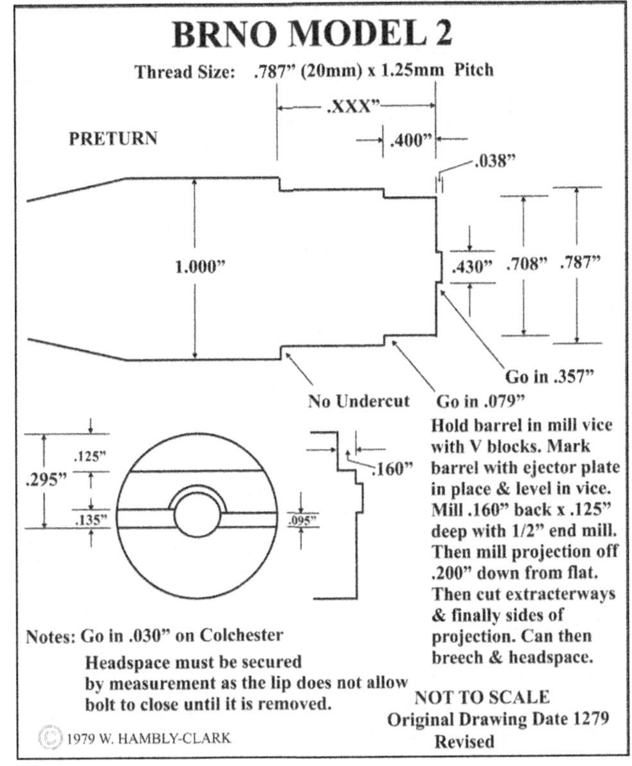
BRNO MODEL 2
Thread Size: .787" (20mm) x 1.25mm Pitch
.XXX"
PRETURN
.400"
.038"
1.000"
.430"
.708"
.787"
Go in .357"
No Undercut
Go in .079"
Hold barrel in mill vice with V blocks. Mark barrel with ejector plate in place & level in vice. Mill .160" back x .125" deep with 1/2" end mill. Then mill projection off .200" down from flat. Then cut extracterways & finally sides of projection. Can then breech & headspace.
.125"
.295"
.135"
.095"
.160"
Notes: Go in .030" on Colchester
Headspace must be secured by measurement as the lip does not allow bolt to close until it is removed.
NOT TO SCALE
Original Drawing Date 1279
Revised
© 1979 W. HAMBLY-CLARK

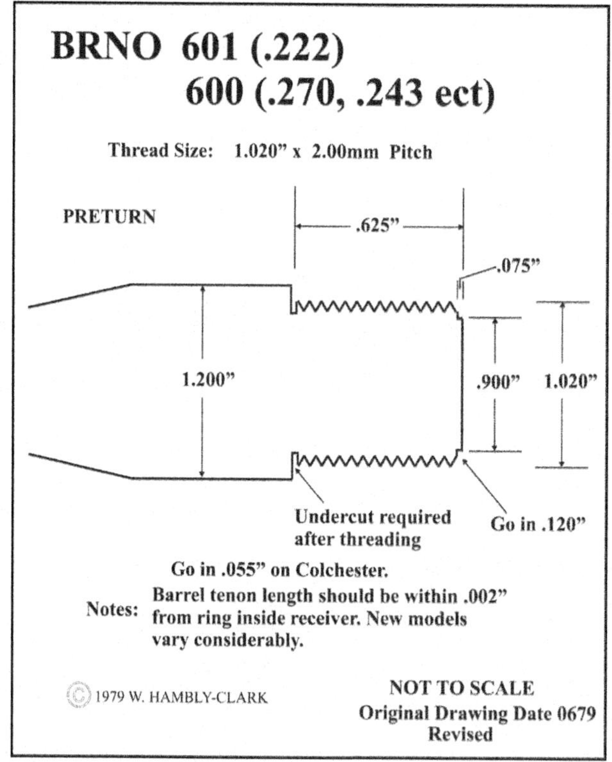
BRNO 601 (.222)
600 (.270, .243 ect)
Thread Size: 1.020" x 2.00mm Pitch
PRETURN
.625"
.075"
1.200"
.900"
1.020"
Undercut required after threading
Go in .120"
Go in .055" on Colchester.
Notes: Barrel tenon length should be within .002" from ring inside receiver. New models vary considerably.
© 1979 W. HAMBLY-CLARK
NOT TO SCALE
Original Drawing Date 0679
Revised

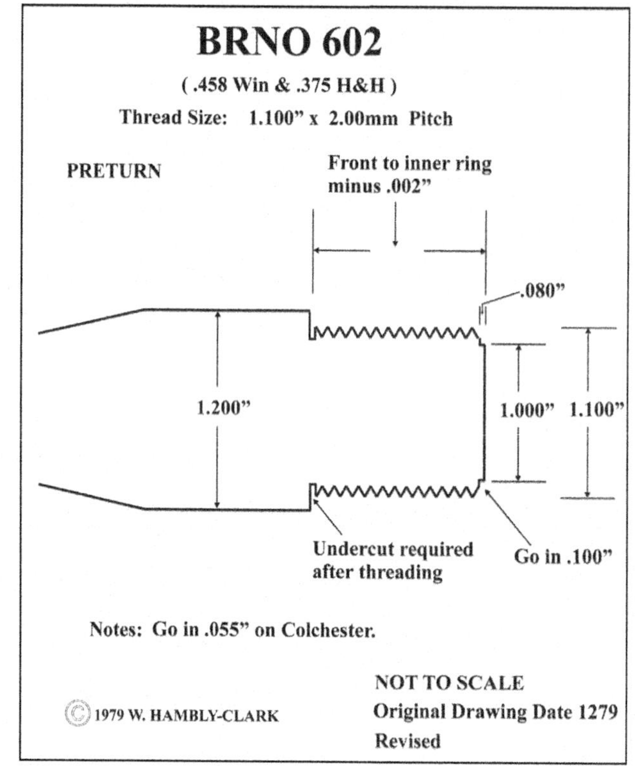
BRNO 602
(.458 Win & .375 H&H)
Thread Size: 1.100" x 2.00mm Pitch
PRETURN
Front to inner ring minus .002"
.080"
1.200"
1.000"
1.100"
Undercut required after threading
Go in .100"
Notes: Go in .055" on Colchester.
© 1979 W. HAMBLY-CLARK
NOT TO SCALE
Original Drawing Date 1279
Revised

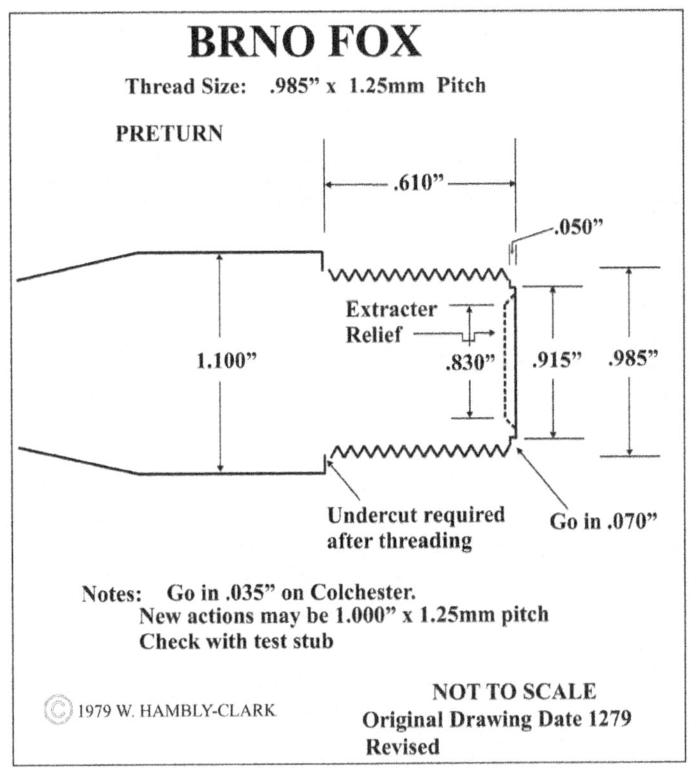
BRNO FOX
Thread Size: .985" x 1.25mm Pitch
PRETURN
.610"
.050"
Extracter
Relief
1.100"
.830"
.915"
.985"
Undercut required
after threading
Go in .070"
Notes: Go in .035" on Colchester.
New actions may be 1.000" x 1.25mm pitch
Check with test stub
© 1979 W. HAMBLY-CLARK
NOT TO SCALE
Original Drawing Date 1279
Revised

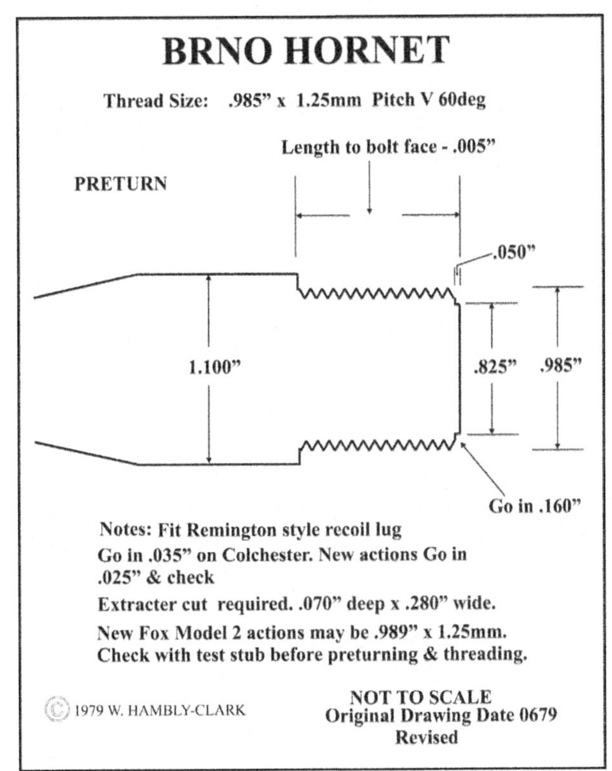
BRNO HORNET
Thread Size: .985" x 1.25mm Pitch V 60deg
Length to bolt face - .005"
PRETURN
.050"
1.100"
.825"
.985"
Go in .160"
Notes: Fit Remington style recoil lug
Go in .035" on Colchester. New actions Go in
.025" & check
Extracter cut required. .070" deep x .280" wide.
New Fox Model 2 actions may be .989" x 1.25mm.
Check with test stub before preturning & threading.
© 1979 W. HAMBLY-CLARK
NOT TO SCALE
Original Drawing Date 0679
Revised

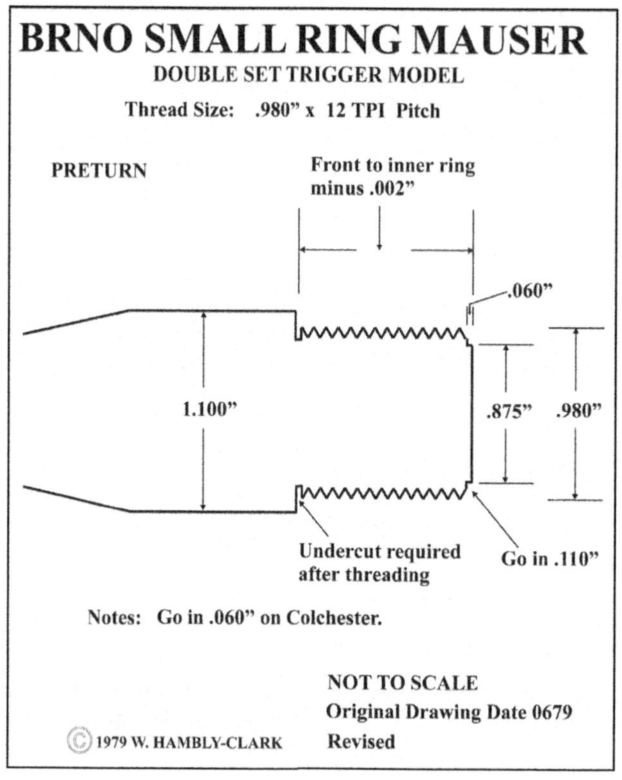
BRNO SMALL RING MAUSER
DOUBLE SET TRIGGER MODEL
Thread Size: .980" x 12 TPI Pitch
PRETURN
Front to inner ring minus .002"
.060"
1.100"
.875"
.980"
Undercut required after threading
Go in .110"
Notes: Go in .060" on Colchester.
NOT TO SCALE
Original Drawing Date 0679
© 1979 W. HAMBLY-CLARK
Revised

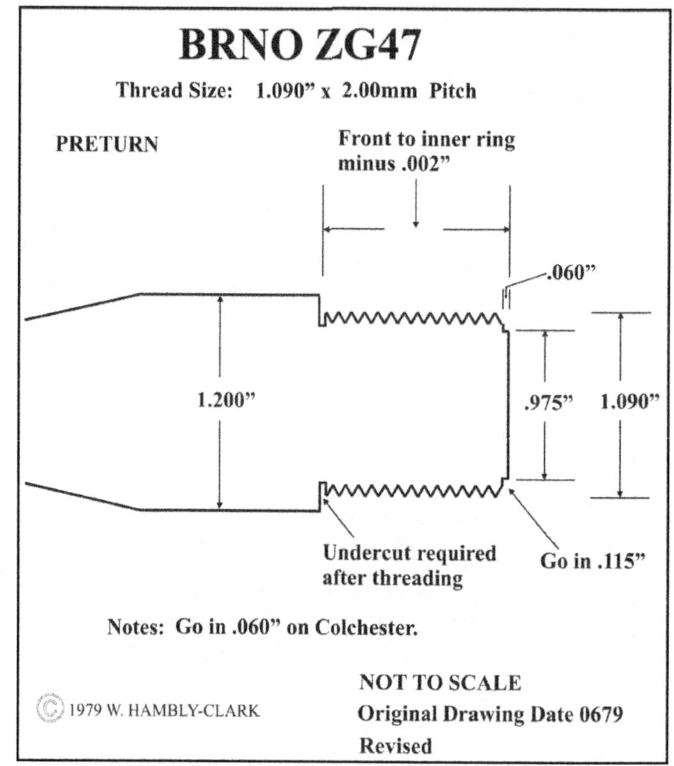
BRNO ZG47
Thread Size: 1.090" x 2.00mm Pitch
PRETURN
Front to inner ring minus .002"
.060"
1.200"
.975"
1.090"
Undercut required after threading
Go in .115"
Notes: Go in .060" on Colchester.
NOT TO SCALE
© 1979 W. HAMBLY-CLARK
Original Drawing Date 0679
Revised

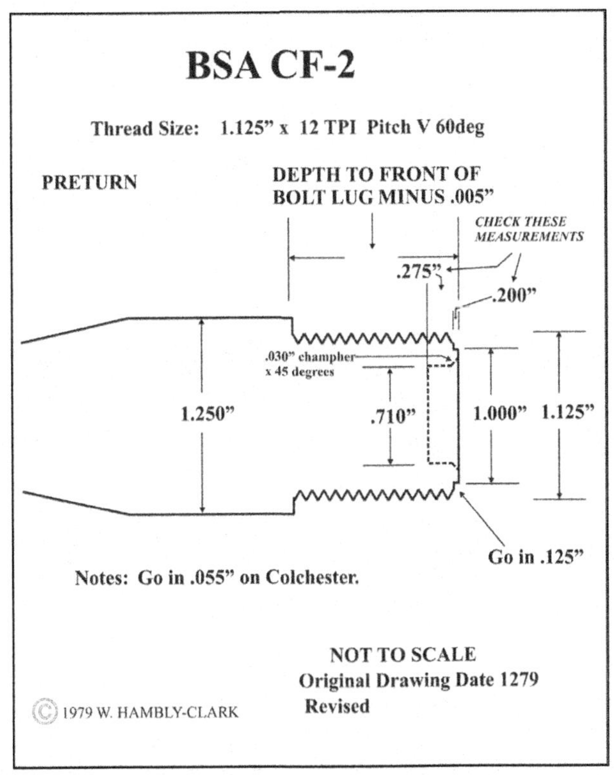
BSA CF-2
Thread Size: 1.125" x 12 TPI Pitch V 60deg
PRETURN
DEPTH TO FRONT OF
BOLT LUG MINUS .005"
CHECK THESE
MEASUREMENTS
.275"
.200"
.030" champher
x 45 degrees
1.250"
.710"
1.000"
1.125"
Go in .125"
Notes: Go in .055" on Colchester.
NOT TO SCALE
Original Drawing Date 1279
Revised
© 1979 W. HAMBLY-CLARK

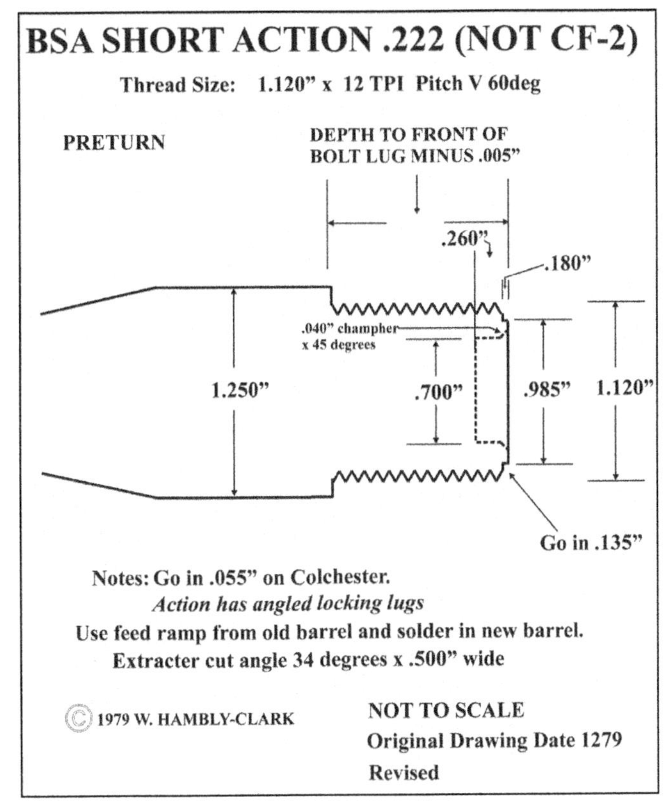
BSA SHORT ACTION .222 (NOT CF-2)
Thread Size: 1.120" x 12 TPI Pitch V 60deg
PRETURN
DEPTH TO FRONT OF
BOLT LUG MINUS .005"
.260"
.180"
.040" champher
x 45 degrees
1.250"
.700"
.985"
1.120"
Go in .135"
Notes: Go in .055" on Colchester.
Action has angled locking lugs
Use feed ramp from old barrel and solder in new barrel.
Extracter cut angle 34 degrees x .500" wide
© 1979 W. HAMBLY-CLARK
NOT TO SCALE
Original Drawing Date 1279
Revised

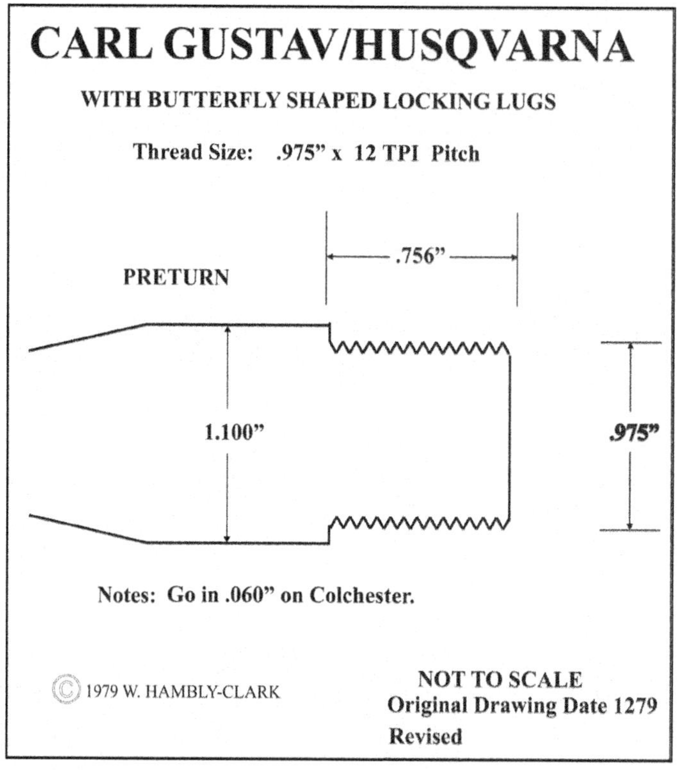
CARL GUSTAV/HUSQVARNA
WITH BUTTERFLY SHAPED LOCKING LUGS
Thread Size: .975" x 12 TPI Pitch
.756"
PRETURN
1.100"
.975"
Notes: Go in .060" on Colchester.
© 1979 W. HAMBLY-CLARK
NOT TO SCALE
Original Drawing Date 1279
Revised

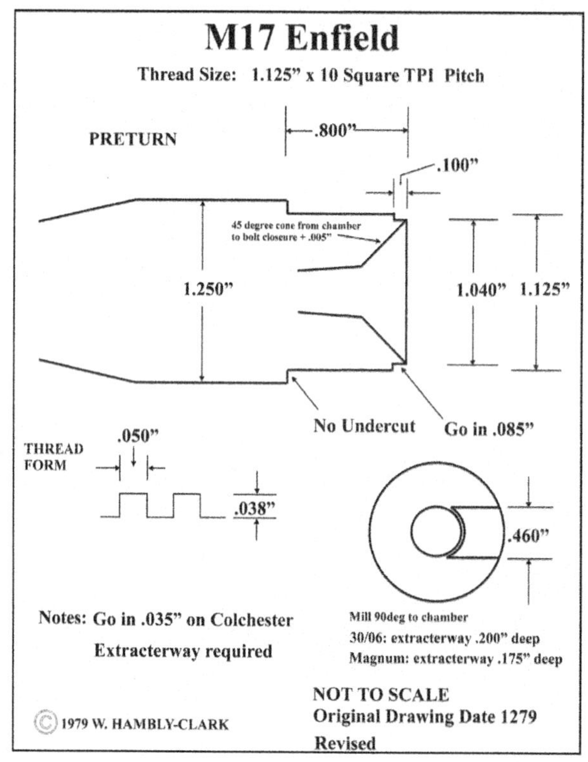
M17 Enfield
Thread Size: 1.125" x 10 Square TPI Pitch
PRETURN
.800"
.100"
45 degree cone from chamber to bolt closeure + .005"
1.250"
1.040"
1.125"
No Undercut
Go in .085"
THREAD FORM
.050"
.038"
.460"
Notes: Go in .035" on Colchester
Extracterway required
Mill 90deg to chamber
30/06: extracterway .200" deep
Magnum: extracterway .175" deep
NOT TO SCALE
Original Drawing Date 1279
Revised
© 1979 W. HAMBLY-CLARK

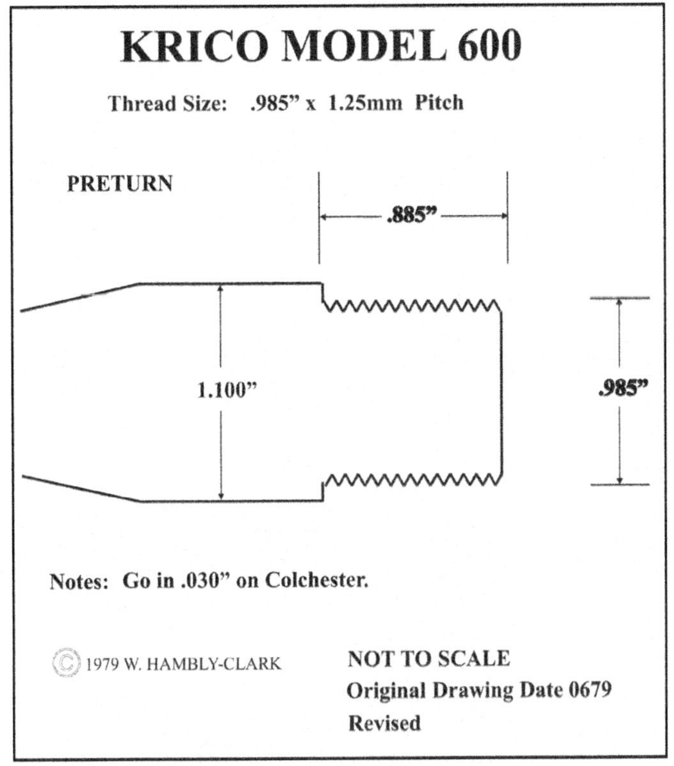
KRICO MODEL 600
Thread Size: .985" x 1.25mm Pitch
PRETURN
.885"
1.100"
.985"
Notes: Go in .030" on Colchester.
© 1979 W. HAMBLY-CLARK
NOT TO SCALE
Original Drawing Date 0679
Revised

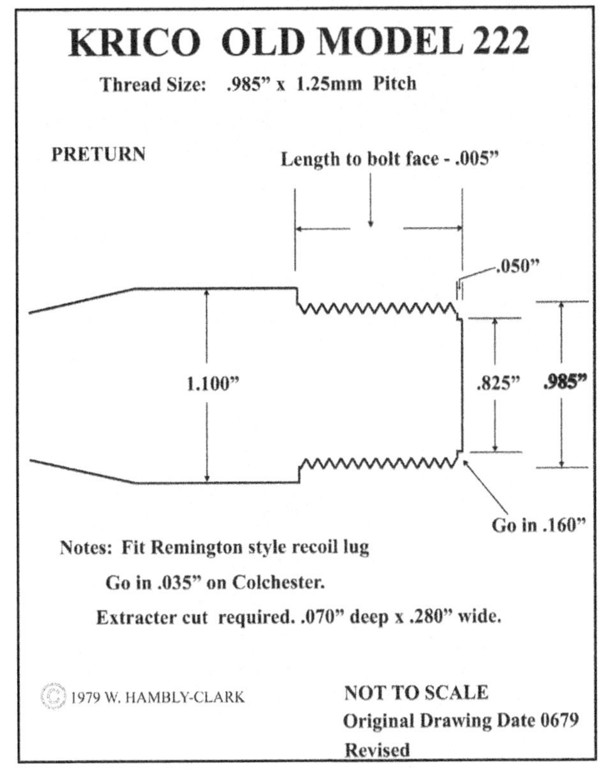
KRICO OLD MODEL 222
Thread Size: .985" x 1.25mm Pitch
PRETURN
Length to bolt face - .005"
.050"
1.100"
.825"
.985"
Go in .160"
Notes: Fit Remington style recoil lug
Go in .035" on Colchester.
Extracter cut required. .070" deep x .280" wide.
© 1979 W. HAMBLY-CLARK
NOT TO SCALE
Original Drawing Date 0679
Revised

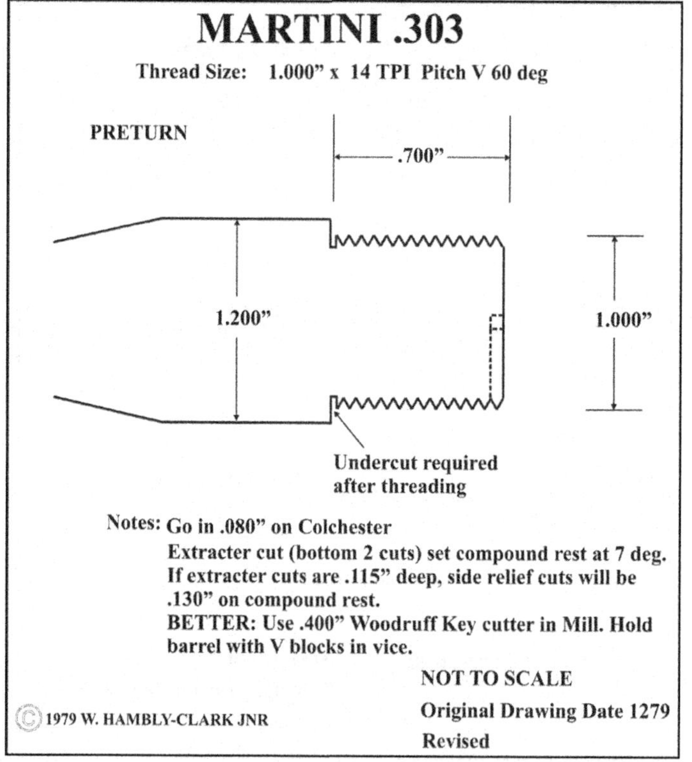
MARTINI .303
Thread Size: 1.000" x 14 TPI Pitch V 60 deg
PRETURN
.700"
1.200"
1.000"
Undercut required
after threading
Notes: Go in .080" on Colchester
Extracter cut (bottom 2 cuts) set compound rest at 7 deg.
If extracter cuts are .115" deep, side relief cuts will be
.130" on compound rest.
BETTER: Use .400" Woodruff Key cutter in Mill. Hold
barrel with V blocks in vice.
NOT TO SCALE
© 1979 W. HAMBLY-CLARK JNR
Original Drawing Date 1279
Revised

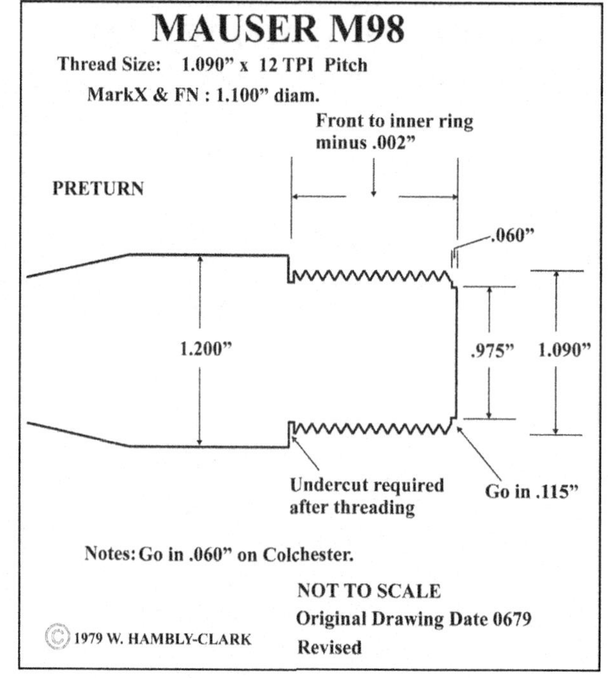
MAUSER M98
Thread Size: 1.090" x 12 TPI Pitch
MarkX & FN : 1.100" diam.
Front to inner ring
minus .002"
PRETURN
.060"
1.200"
.975"
1.090"
Undercut required
after threading
Go in .115"
Notes: Go in .060" on Colchester.
NOT TO SCALE
Original Drawing Date 0679
© 1979 W. HAMBLY-CLARK
Revised

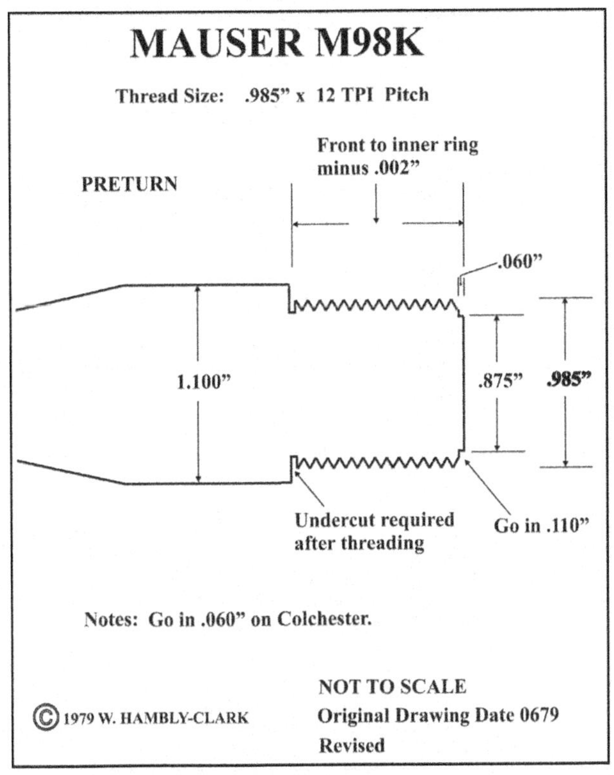
MAUSER M98K
Thread Size: .985" x 12 TPI Pitch
Front to inner ring
minus .002"
PRETURN
.060"
1.100"
.875"
.985"
Undercut required
after threading
Go in .110"
Notes: Go in .060" on Colchester.
NOT TO SCALE
© 1979 W. HAMBLY-CLARK
Original Drawing Date 0679
Revised

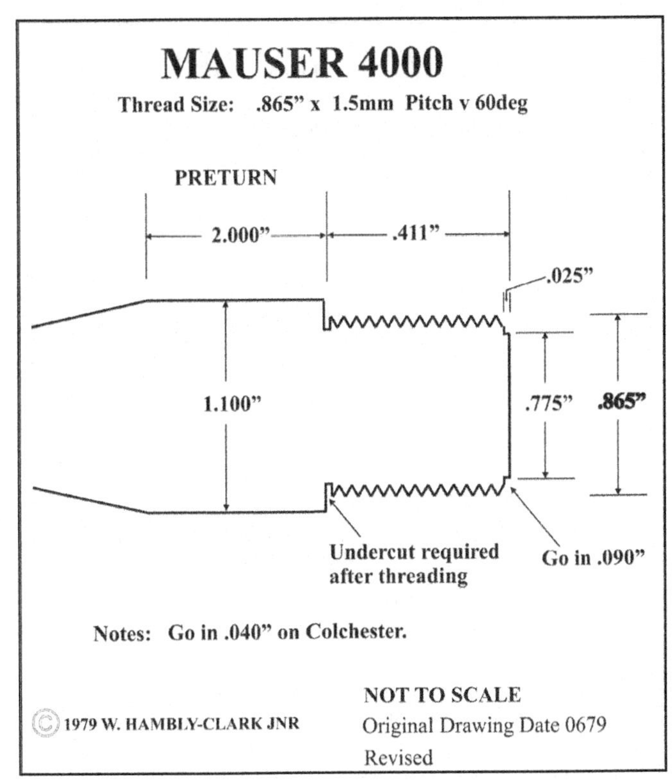
MAUSER 4000
Thread Size: .865" x 1.5mm Pitch v 60deg
PRETURN
2.000"
.411"
.025"
1.100"
.775"
.865"
Undercut required
after threading
Go in .090"
Notes: Go in .040" on Colchester.
NOT TO SCALE
© 1979 W. HAMBLY-CLARK JNR
Original Drawing Date 0679
Revised

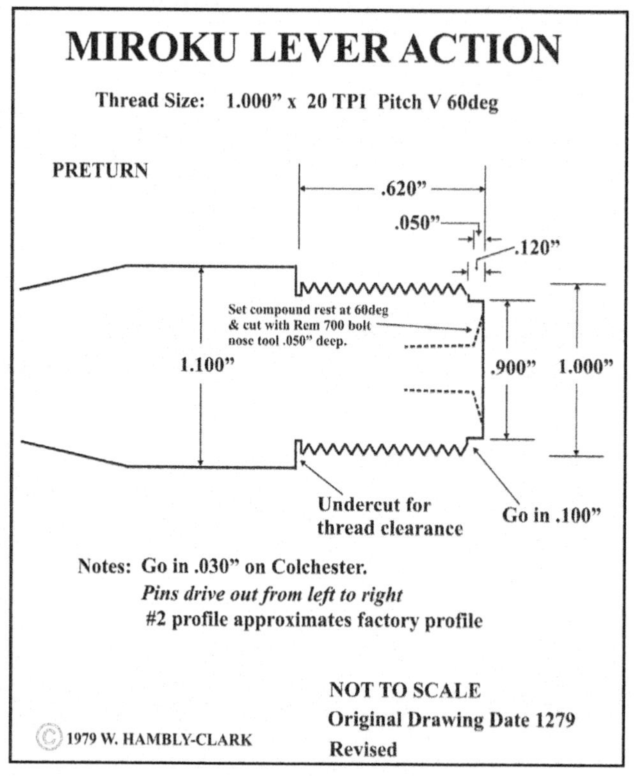
MIROKU LEVER ACTION
Thread Size: 1.000" x 20 TPI Pitch V 60deg
PRETURN
.620"
.050"
.120"
Set compound rest at 60deg
& cut with Rem 700 bolt
nose tool .050" deep.
1.100"
.900"
1.000"
Undercut for
thread clearance
Go in .100"
Notes: Go in .030" on Colchester.
Pins drive out from left to right
#2 profile approximates factory profile
NOT TO SCALE
Original Drawing Date 1279
Revised
© 1979 W. HAMBLY-CLARK

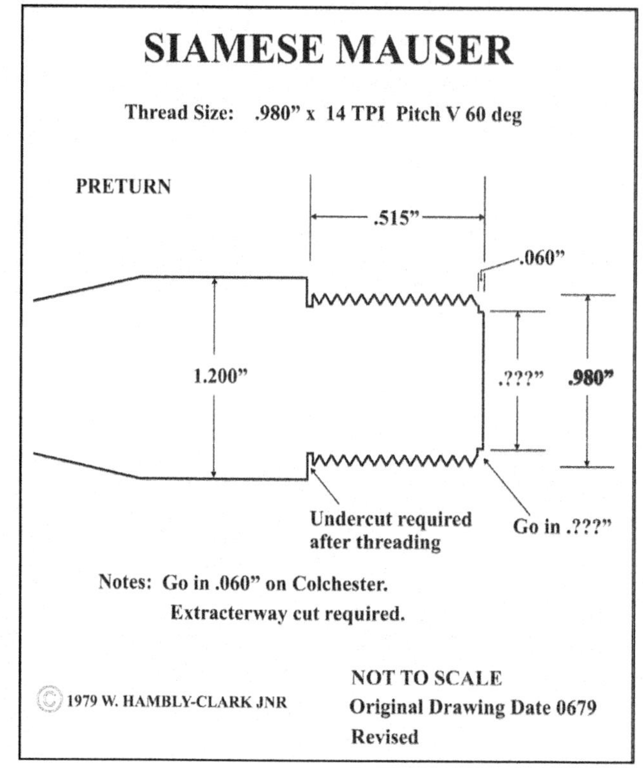
SIAMESE MAUSER
Thread Size: .980" x 14 TPI Pitch V 60 deg
PRETURN
.515"
.060"
1.200"
.???"
.980"
Undercut required
after threading
Go in .???"
Notes: Go in .060" on Colchester.
Extracterway cut required.
NOT TO SCALE
Original Drawing Date 0679
Revised
© 1979 W. HAMBLY-CLARK JNR

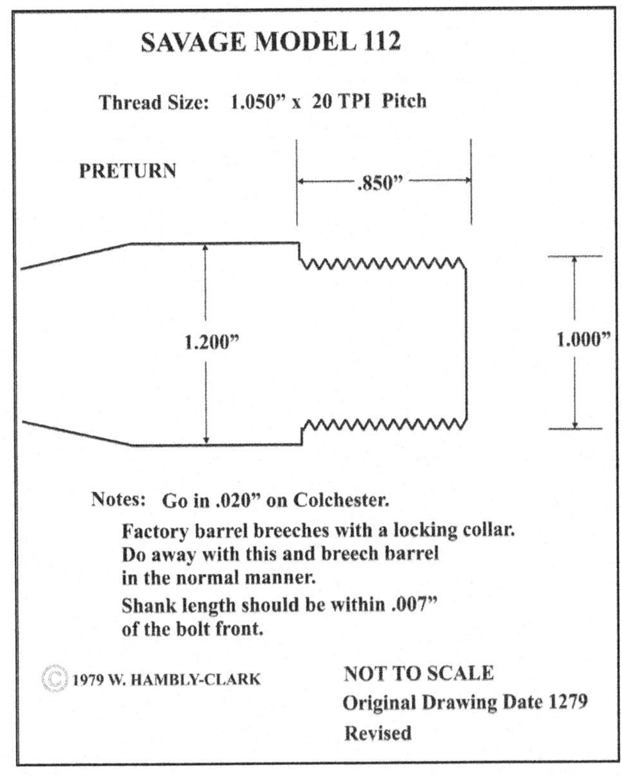
SAVAGE MODEL 112
Thread Size: 1.050" x 20 TPI Pitch
PRETURN
.850"
1.200"
1.000"
Notes: Go in .020" on Colchester.
Factory barrel breeches with a locking collar.
Do away with this and breech barrel
in the normal manner.
Shank length should be within .007"
of the bolt front.
© 1979 W. HAMBLY-CLARK
NOT TO SCALE
Original Drawing Date 1279
Revised

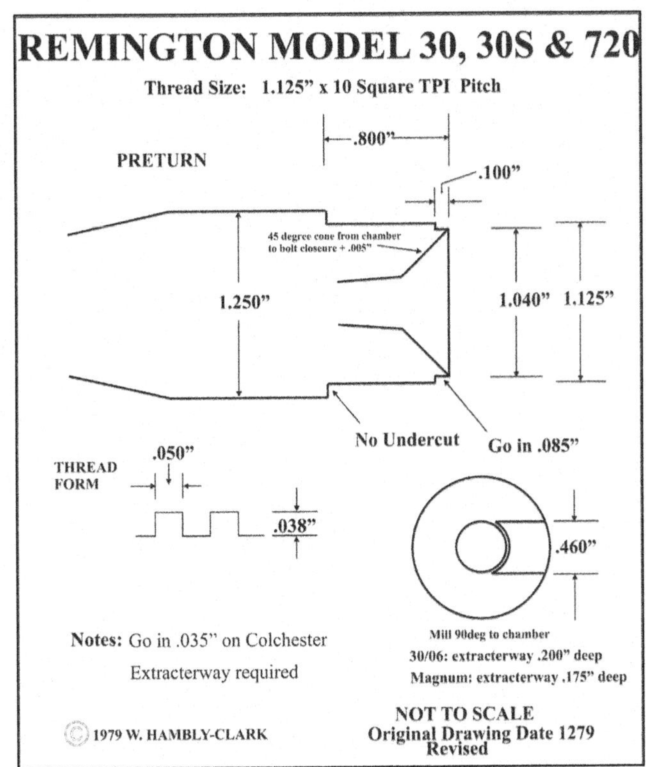
REMINGTON MODEL 30, 30S & 720
Thread Size: 1.125" x 10 Square TPI Pitch
PRETURN
.800"
.100"
45 degree cone from chamber
to bolt closure + .005"
1.250"
1.040"
1.125"
No Undercut
Go in .085"
THREAD
FORM
.050"
.038"
.460"
Notes: Go in .035" on Colchester
Extracterway required
Mill 90deg to chamber
30/06: extracterway .200" deep
Magnum: extracterway .175" deep
© 1979 W. HAMBLY-CLARK
NOT TO SCALE
Original Drawing Date 1279
Revised

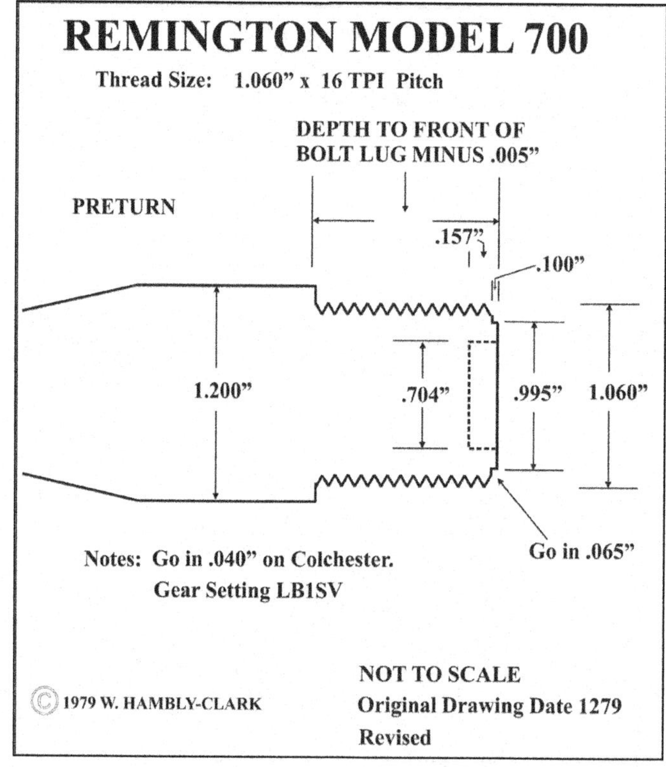
REMINGTON MODEL 700
Thread Size: 1.060" x 16 TPI Pitch
DEPTH TO FRONT OF
BOLT LUG MINUS .005"
PRETURN
.157"
.100"
1.200"
.704"
.995"
1.060"
Go in .065"
Notes: Go in .040" on Colchester.
Gear Setting LB1SV
NOT TO SCALE
© 1979 W. HAMBLY-CLARK
Original Drawing Date 1279
Revised

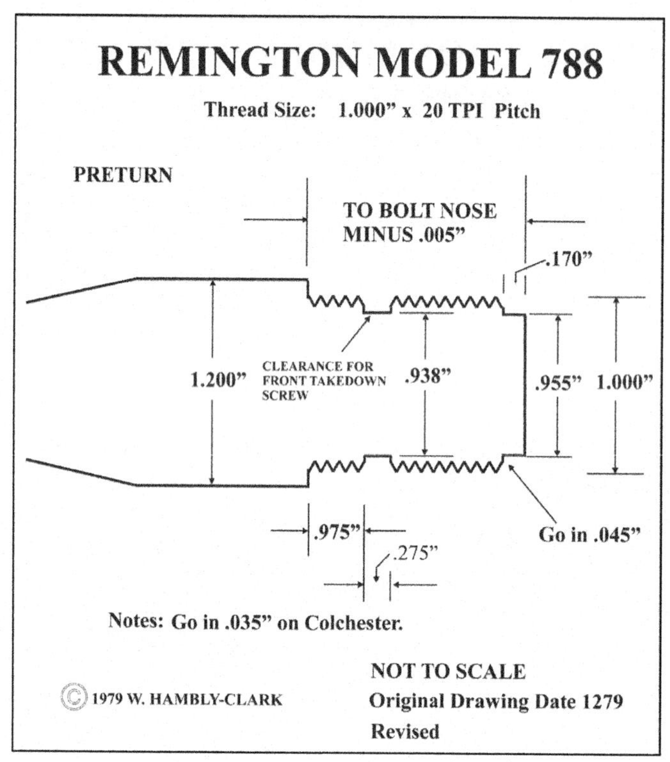
REMINGTON MODEL 788
Thread Size: 1.000" x 20 TPI Pitch
PRETURN
TO BOLT NOSE
MINUS .005"
.170"
1.200"
CLEARANCE FOR
FRONT TAKEDOWN
SCREW
.938"
.955"
1.000"
.975"
.275"
Go in .045"
Notes: Go in .035" on Colchester.
NOT TO SCALE
© 1979 W. HAMBLY-CLARK
Original Drawing Date 1279
Revised

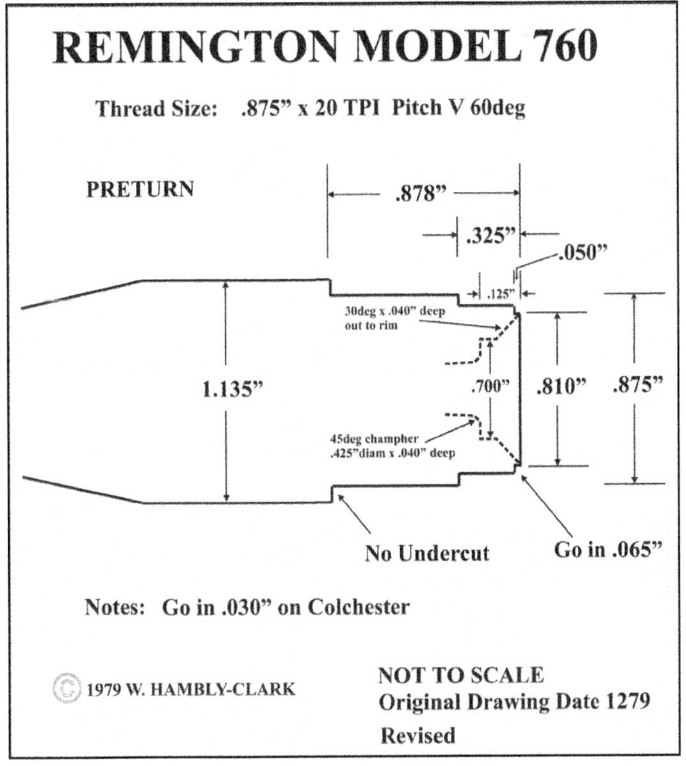
REMINGTON MODEL 760
Thread Size: .875" x 20 TPI Pitch V 60deg
PRETURN
.878"
.325"
.050"
.125"
30deg x .040" deep out to rim
1.135"
.700"
.810"
.875"
45deg champher .425"diam x .040" deep
No Undercut
Go in .065"
Notes: Go in .030" on Colchester
© 1979 W. HAMBLY-CLARK
NOT TO SCALE
Original Drawing Date 1279
Revised

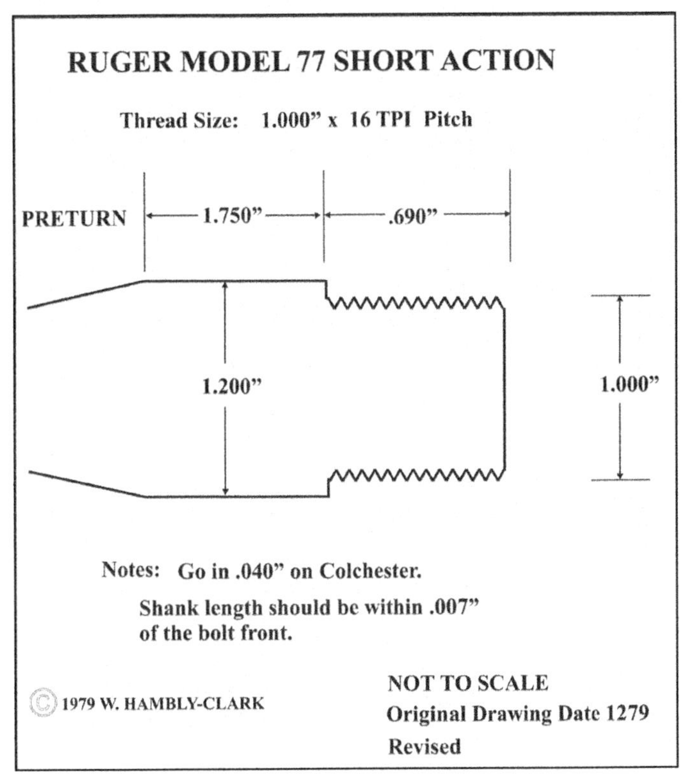
RUGER MODEL 77 SHORT ACTION
Thread Size: 1.000" x 16 TPI Pitch
PRETURN
1.750"
.690"
1.200"
1.000"
Notes: Go in .040" on Colchester.
Shank length should be within .007" of the bolt front.
© 1979 W. HAMBLY-CLARK
NOT TO SCALE
Original Drawing Date 1279
Revised

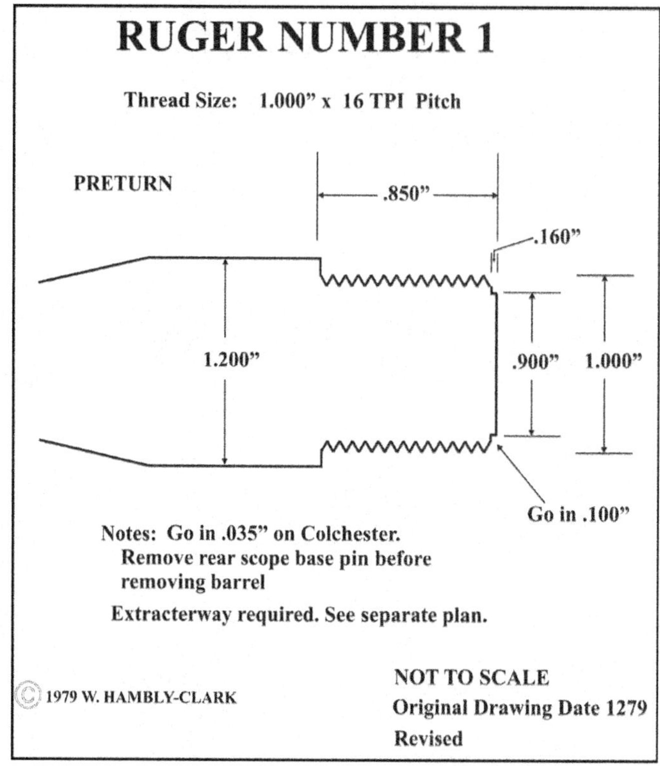
RUGER NUMBER 1
Thread Size: 1.000" x 16 TPI Pitch
PRETURN
.850"
.160"
1.200"
.900"
1.000"
Go in .100"
Notes: Go in .035" on Colchester.
Remove rear scope base pin before removing barrel
Extracterway required. See separate plan.
© 1979 W. HAMBLY-CLARK
NOT TO SCALE
Original Drawing Date 1279
Revised

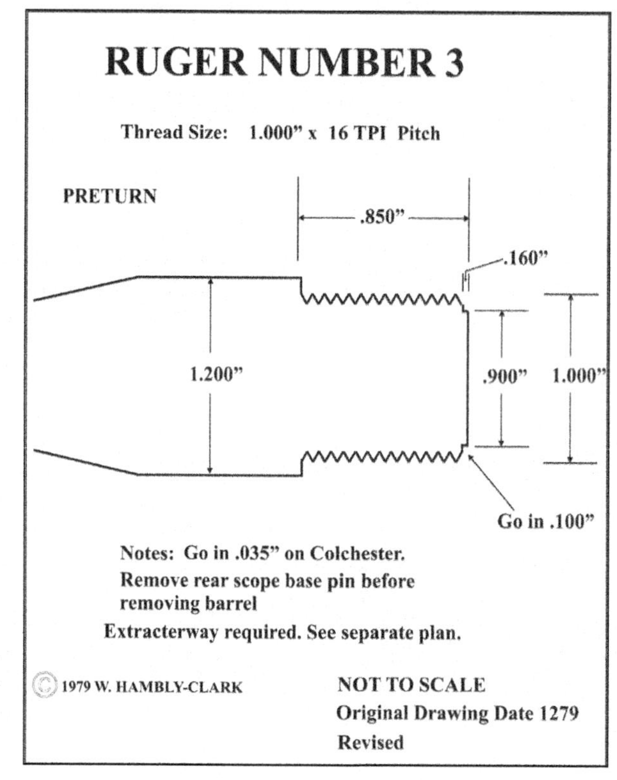
RUGER NUMBER 3
Thread Size: 1.000" x 16 TPI Pitch
PRETURN
.850"
.160"
1.200"
.900"
1.000"
Go in .100"
Notes: Go in .035" on Colchester.
Remove rear scope base pin before removing barrel
Extracterway required. See separate plan.
© 1979 W. HAMBLY-CLARK
NOT TO SCALE
Original Drawing Date 1279
Revised

RUGER No1 & No3 EXTRACTERWAY

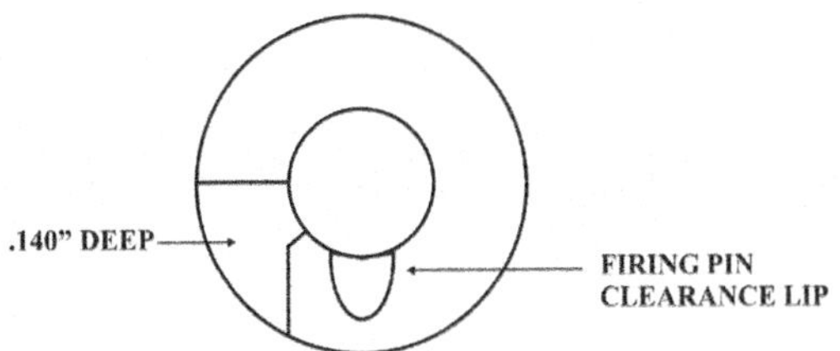

EXTRACTERWAY:

1. SCRIBE LINE STRAIGHT UP FROM LEDGE ON LEFT HAND SIDE OF RECEIVER.
2. THERE IS ANOTHER SMALL HORIZONTAL LEDGE HALF WAY UP ON THE LEFT HAND SIDE. SCRIBE A HORIZONTAL LINE FROM THEI LEDGE.
3. FIT TEMPLATE AND SCRIBE IN THIRD LINE.
4. MILL EXTRACTERWAY .130" DEEP WITH 3/16" END MILL IN LATHE.

FIRING PIN CLEARANCE LIP (MOD 1/88)

1. DO THIS IN LATHE AFTER EXTRACTERWAY CUT.
2. USE ORDINARY FACING TOOL
3. SET COMPOUND REST AT 10 DEGREES ON THREADING SET MARK.
4. FACE CONE .050" DEEP, WHICH WILL LEAVE A FLAT ON THE OUTSIDE .070" WIDE.
5. POLISH

SAKO L57

Thread Size: .984" x 1.5mm Pitch

PRETURN

.800"

.120"

1.100"

.860" **.984"**

Undercut required after threading

Go in .125"

Notes: Go in .035" on Colchester

Extracter relief required. See separate drawing.

NOT TO SCALE

Original Drawing Date 1279

Revised

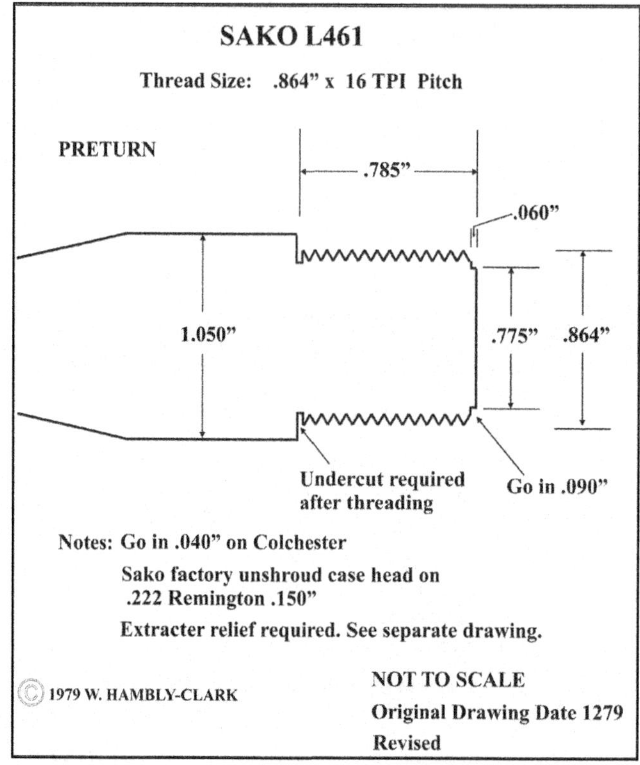
SAKO L461
Thread Size: .864" x 16 TPI Pitch
PRETURN
.785"
.060"
1.050"
.775"
.864"
Undercut required after threading
Go in .090"
Notes: Go in .040" on Colchester
Sako factory unshroud case head on .222 Remington .150"
Extracter relief required. See separate drawing.
© 1979 W. HAMBLY-CLARK
NOT TO SCALE
Original Drawing Date 1279
Revised

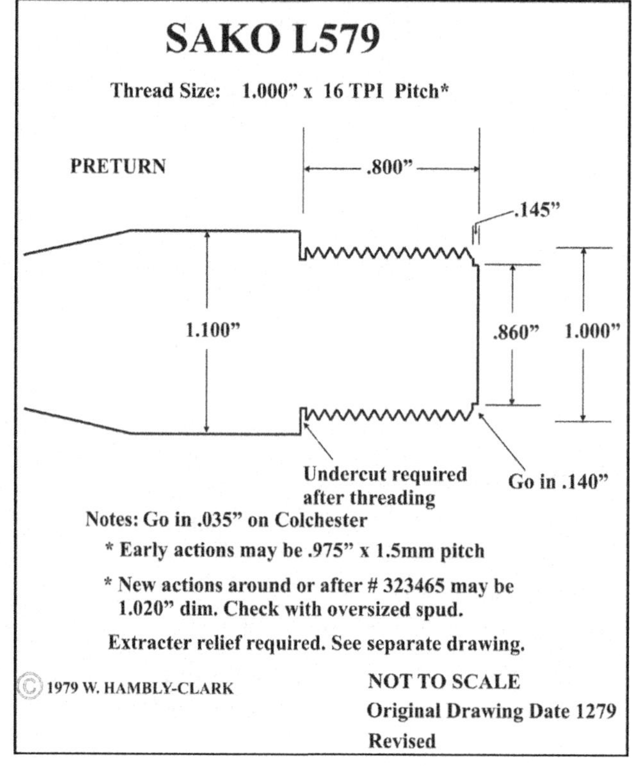
SAKO L579
Thread Size: 1.000" x 16 TPI Pitch*
PRETURN
.800"
.145"
1.100"
.860"
1.000"
Undercut required after threading
Go in .140"
Notes: Go in .035" on Colchester
* Early actions may be .975" x 1.5mm pitch
* New actions around or after # 323465 may be 1.020" dim. Check with oversized spud.
Extracter relief required. See separate drawing.
© 1979 W. HAMBLY-CLARK
NOT TO SCALE
Original Drawing Date 1279
Revised

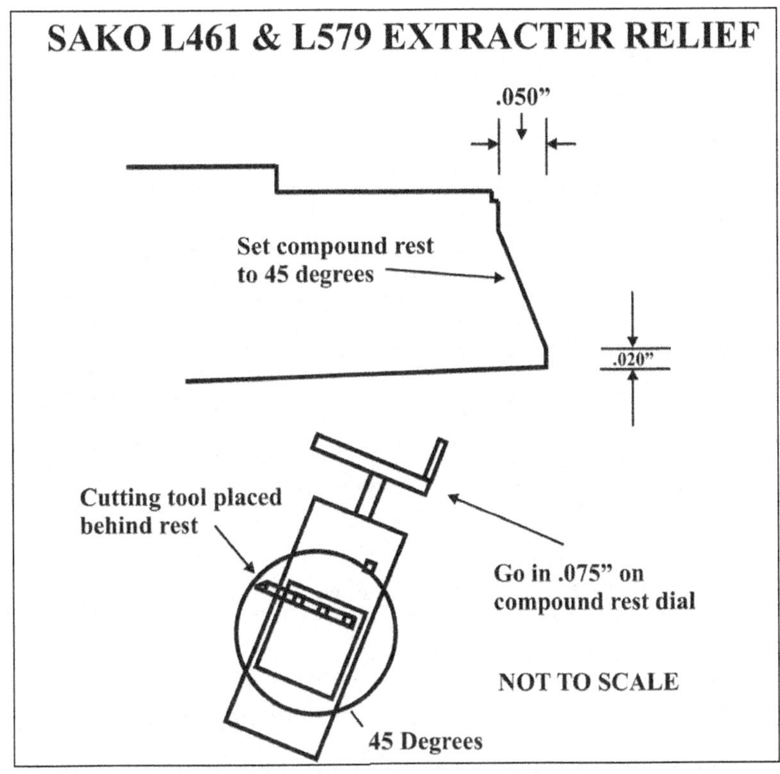
SAKO L461 & L579 EXTRACTER RELIEF
.050"
Set compound rest
to 45 degrees
.020"
Cutting tool placed
behind rest
Go in .075" on
compound rest dial
NOT TO SCALE
45 Degrees

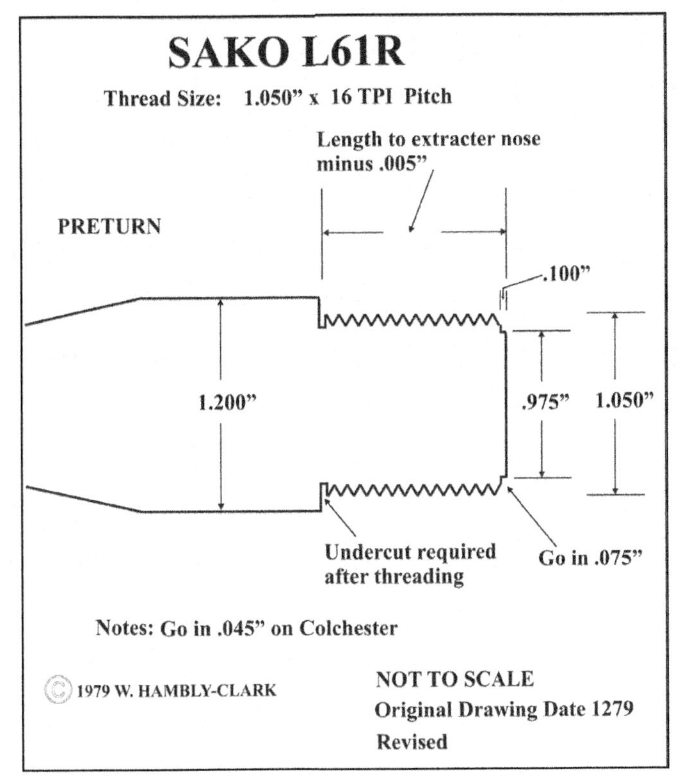
SAKO L61R
Thread Size: 1.050" x 16 TPI Pitch
Length to extracter nose
minus .005"
PRETURN
.100"
1.200"
.975"
1.050"
Undercut required
after threading
Go in .075"
Notes: Go in .045" on Colchester
© 1979 W. HAMBLY-CLARK
NOT TO SCALE
Original Drawing Date 1279
Revised

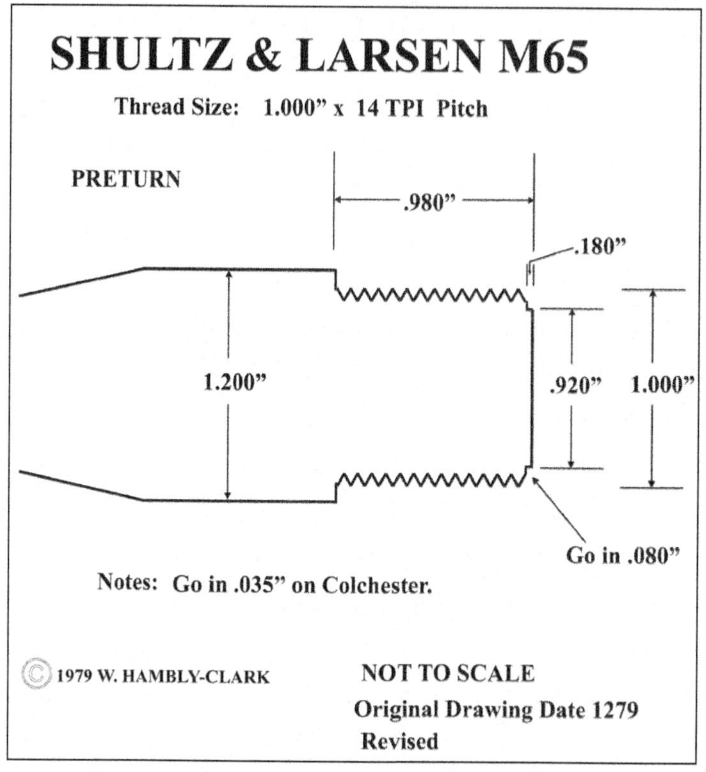
SHULTZ & LARSEN M65
Thread Size: 1.000" x 14 TPI Pitch
PRETURN
.980"
.180"
1.200"
.920"
1.000"
Go in .080"
Notes: Go in .035" on Colchester.
© 1979 W. HAMBLY-CLARK
NOT TO SCALE
Original Drawing Date 1279
Revised

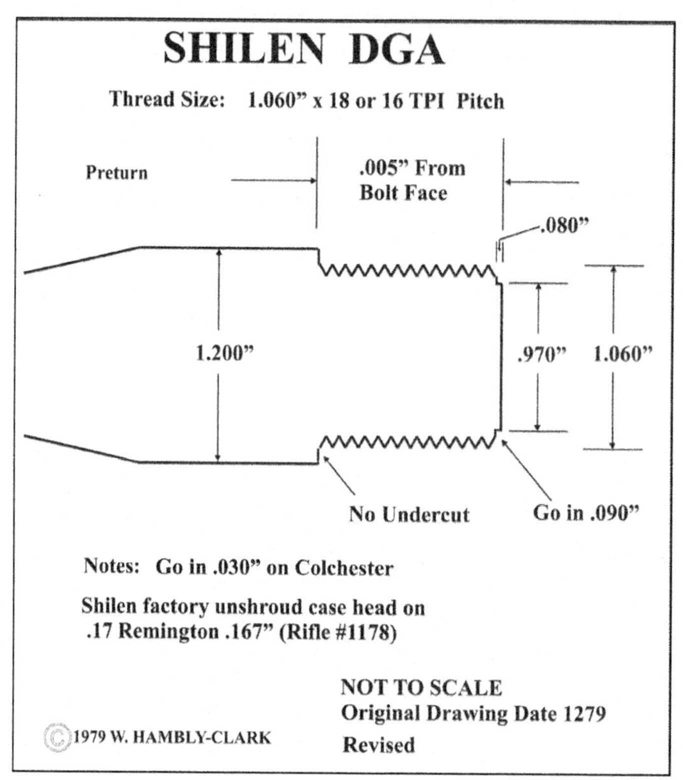
SHILEN DGA
Thread Size: 1.060" x 18 or 16 TPI Pitch
Preturn
.005" From
Bolt Face
.080"
1.200"
.970"
1.060"
No Undercut
Go in .090"
Notes: Go in .030" on Colchester
Shilen factory unshroud case head on
.17 Remington .167" (Rifle #1178)
NOT TO SCALE
Original Drawing Date 1279
© 1979 W. HAMBLY-CLARK
Revised

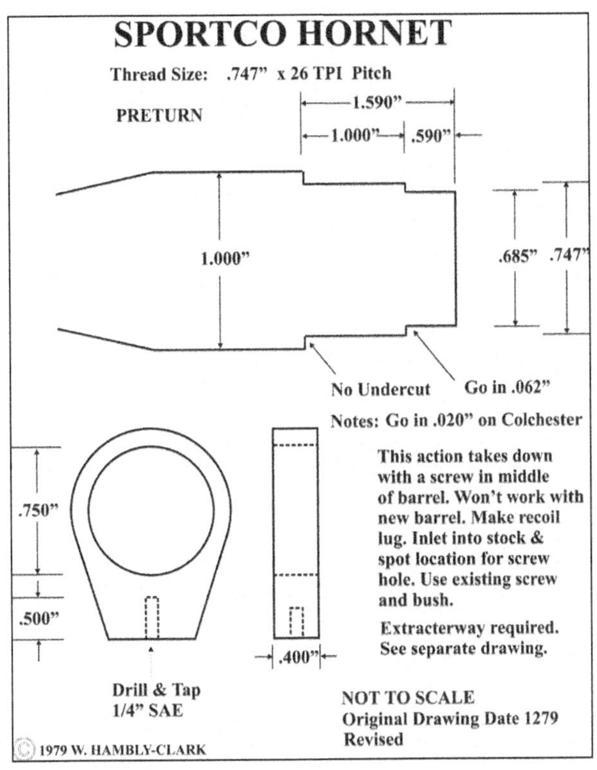
SPORTCO HORNET
Thread Size: .747" x 26 TPI Pitch
PRETURN
1.590"
1.000"
.590"
1.000"
.685"
.747"
No Undercut
Go in .062"
Notes: Go in .020" on Colchester
.750"
.500"
.400"
This action takes down with a screw in middle of barrel. Won't work with new barrel. Make recoil lug. Inlet into stock & spot location for screw hole. Use existing screw and bush.
Extracterway required. See separate drawing.
Drill & Tap 1/4" SAE
NOT TO SCALE
Original Drawing Date 1279
Revised
© 1979 W. HAMBLY-CLARK

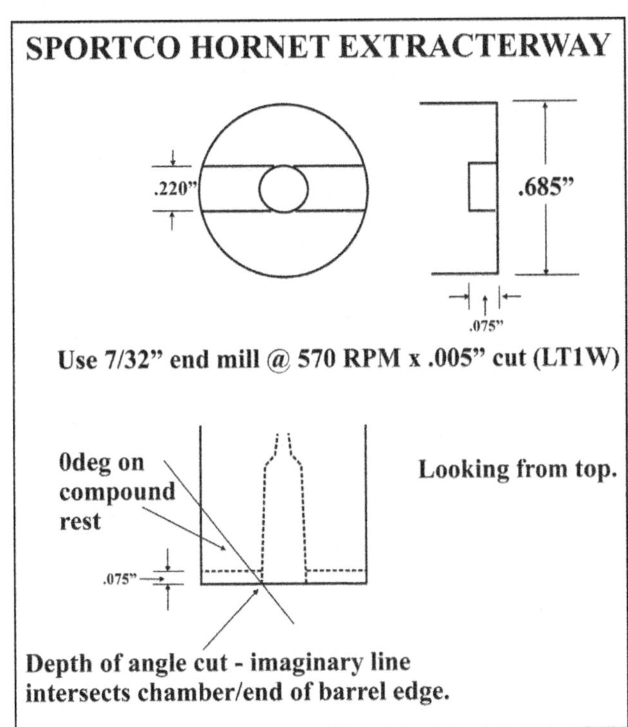
SPORTCO HORNET EXTRACTERWAY
.220"
.685"
.075"
Use 7/32" end mill @ 570 RPM x .005" cut (LT1W)
0deg on compound rest
Looking from top.
.075"
Depth of angle cut - imaginary line intersects chamber/end of barrel edge.

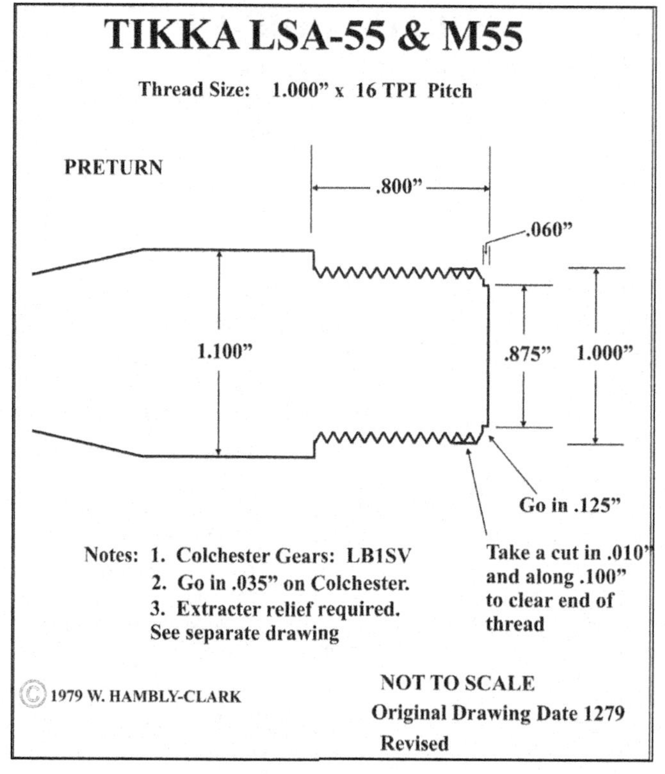
TIKKA LSA-55 & M55
Thread Size: 1.000" x 16 TPI Pitch
PRETURN
.800"
.060"
1.100"
.875"
1.000"
Go in .125"
Notes: 1. Colchester Gears: LB1SV
2. Go in .035" on Colchester.
3. Extracter relief required.
See separate drawing
Take a cut in .010"
and along .100"
to clear end of
thread
© 1979 W. HAMBLY-CLARK
NOT TO SCALE
Original Drawing Date 1279
Revised

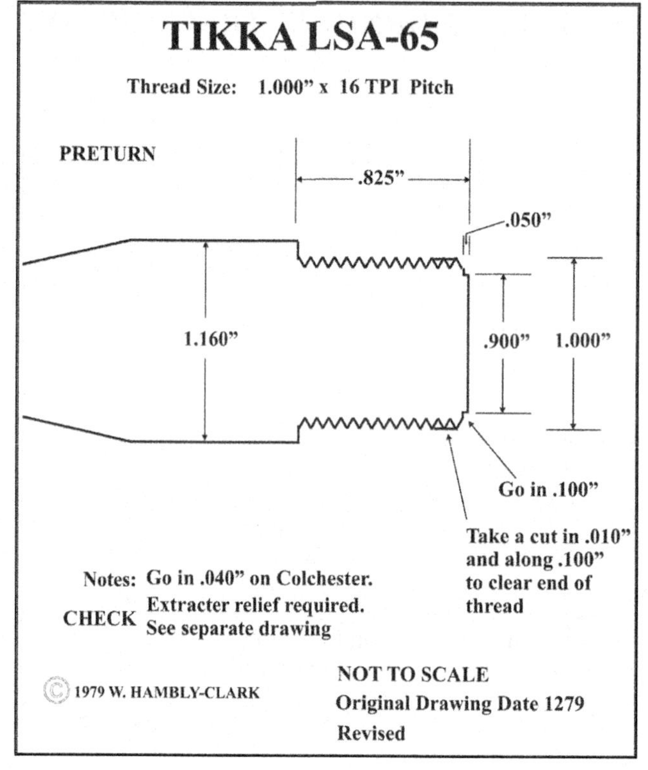
TIKKA LSA-65
Thread Size: 1.000" x 16 TPI Pitch
PRETURN
.825"
.050"
1.160"
.900"
1.000"
Go in .100"
Take a cut in .010"
and along .100"
to clear end of
thread
Notes: Go in .040" on Colchester.
CHECK Extracter relief required.
See separate drawing
© 1979 W. HAMBLY-CLARK
NOT TO SCALE
Original Drawing Date 1279
Revised

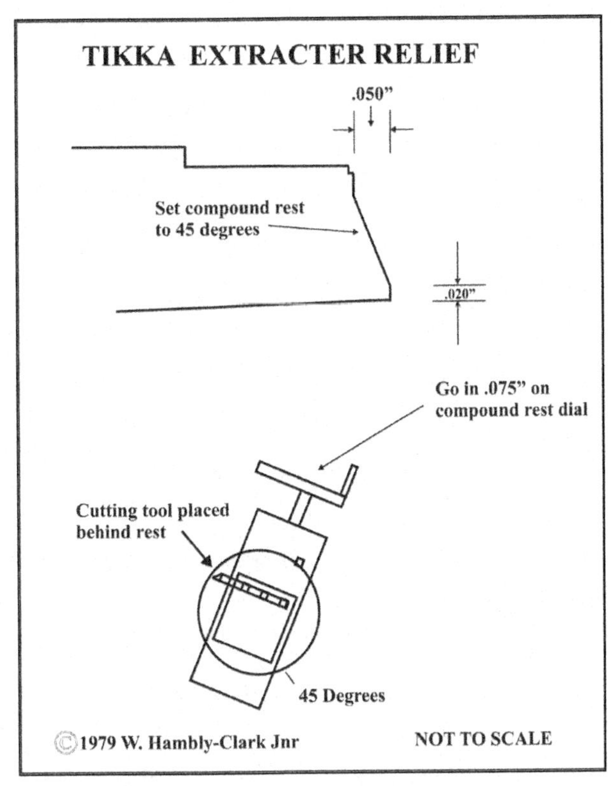
TIKKA EXTRACTER RELIEF
.050"
Set compound rest
to 45 degrees
.020"
Go in .075" on
compound rest dial
Cutting tool placed
behind rest
45 Degrees
©1979 W. Hambly-Clark Jnr
NOT TO SCALE

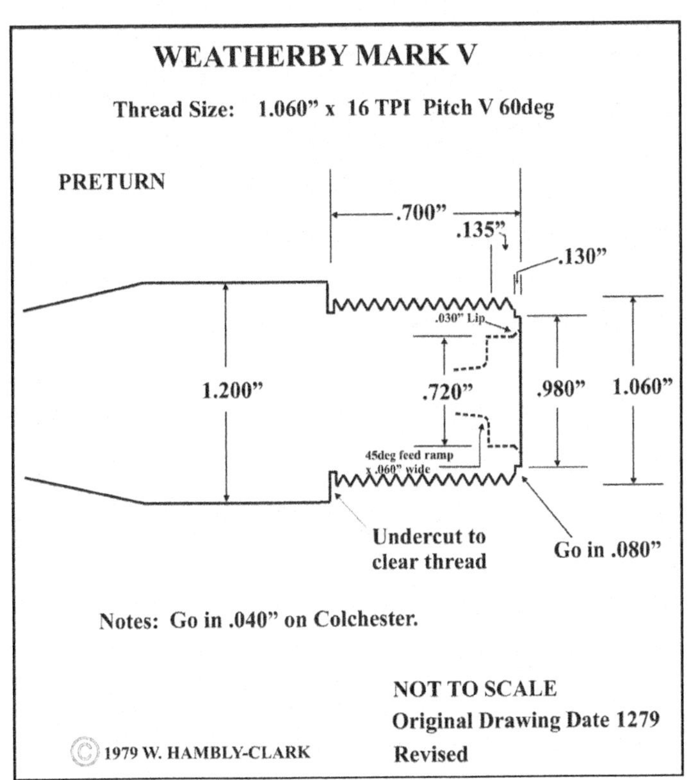
WEATHERBY MARK V
Thread Size: 1.060" x 16 TPI Pitch V 60deg
PRETURN
.700"
.135"
.130"
.030" Lip
1.200"
.720"
.980"
1.060"
45deg feed ramp
x .060" wide
Undercut to
clear thread
Go in .080"
Notes: Go in .040" on Colchester.
NOT TO SCALE
Original Drawing Date 1279
Revised
© 1979 W. HAMBLY-CLARK

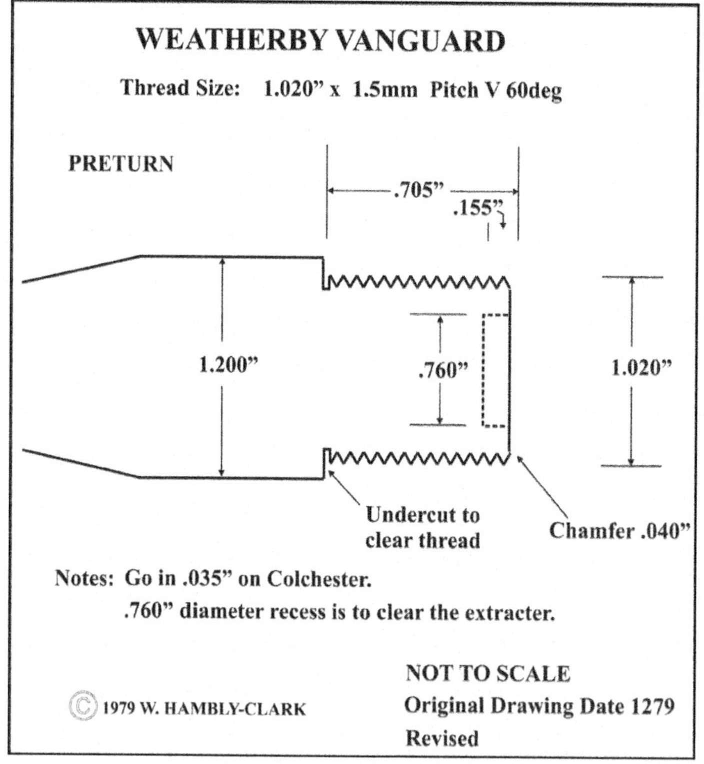
WEATHERBY VANGUARD
Thread Size: 1.020" x 1.5mm Pitch V 60deg
PRETURN
.705"
.155"
1.200"
.760"
1.020"
Undercut to clear thread
Chamfer .040"
Notes: Go in .035" on Colchester.
.760" diameter recess is to clear the extracter.
NOT TO SCALE
© 1979 W. HAMBLY-CLARK
Original Drawing Date 1279
Revised

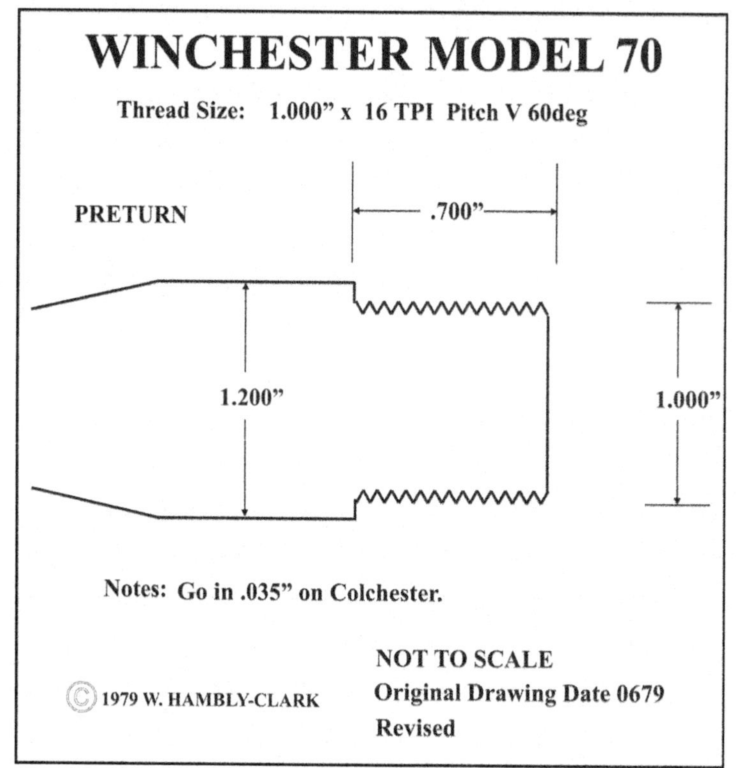
WINCHESTER MODEL 70
Thread Size: 1.000" x 16 TPI Pitch V 60deg
PRETURN
.700"
1.200"
1.000"
Notes: Go in .035" on Colchester.
NOT TO SCALE
© 1979 W. HAMBLY-CLARK
Original Drawing Date 0679
Revised

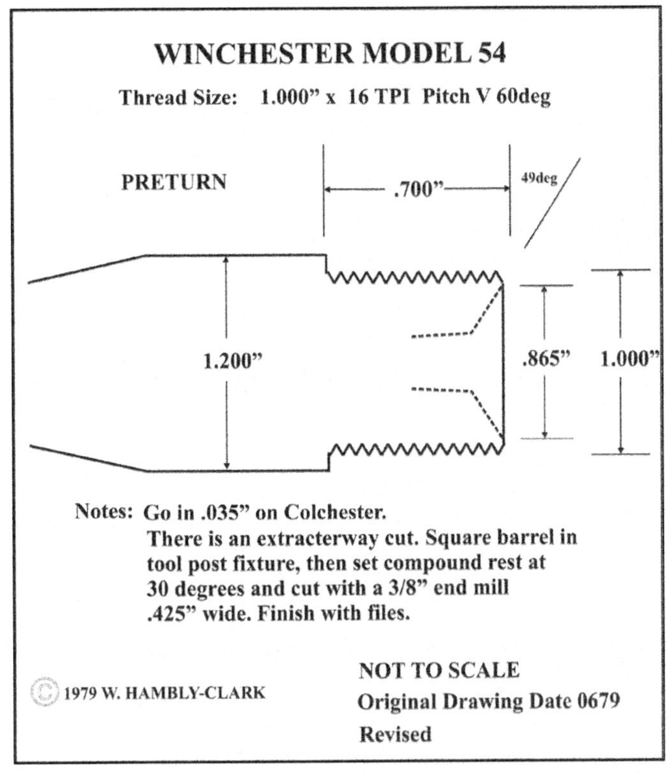
WINCHESTER MODEL 54
Thread Size: 1.000" x 16 TPI Pitch V 60deg
PRETURN
.700"
49deg
1.200"
.865"
1.000"
Notes: Go in .035" on Colchester.
There is an extracterway cut. Square barrel in tool post fixture, then set compound rest at 30 degrees and cut with a 3/8" end mill .425" wide. Finish with files.
© 1979 W. HAMBLY-CLARK
NOT TO SCALE
Original Drawing Date 0679
Revised

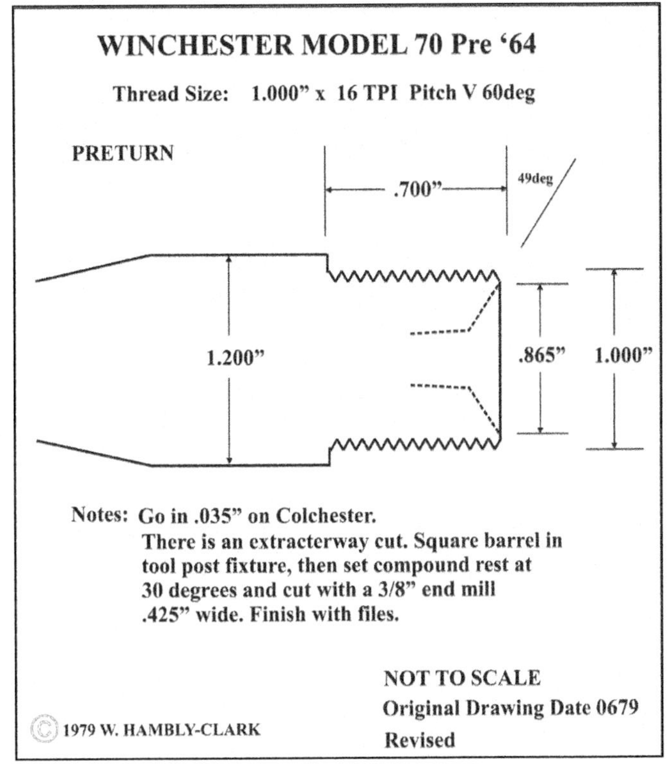
WINCHESTER MODEL 70 Pre '64
Thread Size: 1.000" x 16 TPI Pitch V 60deg
PRETURN
.700"
49deg
1.200"
.865"
1.000"
Notes: Go in .035" on Colchester.
There is an extracterway cut. Square barrel in tool post fixture, then set compound rest at 30 degrees and cut with a 3/8" end mill .425" wide. Finish with files.
© 1979 W. HAMBLY-CLARK
NOT TO SCALE
Original Drawing Date 0679
Revised

APPENDIX 2

You may be wondering what I meant in my last sentence about Tony (Greenie) Greenfield when I wrote, "Bomb me a hole," so I thought I should explain.

Tony was a quintessential bushie and a bit of a wag. His financial overloads had him on a strict budget, so he used to save up his fuel money until I came up to go fox shooting. I said it before and I'll say it again, "He was a good mate."

It was early January, and as hot as hell on a hot hell day. We had been mustering sheep on our Yamaha RT3 bikes since dawn, and had just got them into the yard in time to be back at the homestead for lunch. As he shut the yard gate Greenie reckoned it'd be a good idea to go for a dip in the well on the way home to cool off.

The well was probably about 2KM from the homestead. It was a raised turkey nest with a concrete top about 1 meter wide. I guess it was about 10 meters square or thereabouts. It was fed by a wind mill close by, and was usually mostly full.

Greenie mounted his bike and was off in a cloud of dust. You probably don't know, but those old RT3 Yamahas used to kick back, like a really pissed off mule, when you kick started them. I got a good smack in the foot, but wasn't all that far behind. Greenie was faster than me, and by the time I reached the well he had all of his gear off. As I slid to a halt he started to sprint up the slope of the well yelling, "I'll bomb you a hole."

I sort of thought, "Huh!" I ripped all my duds off as I saw Greenie sprint to the top of the well and launch himself into the air. I followed suite right behind him.

I hit the top of the well running flat out and launched myself into the air, and then looked down at the water. I think the words that went through my mind were, "Oh S@#T!" The wells water level was probably down about two feet. Floating in the water were four dead kangaroos and three dead foxes, all badly decomposed. The surface of the water was covered with a 3"– 4" layer of sickly green frothed up slime, except for the hole my mate had so thoughtfully bombed for me. Inside the hole, the water was green, and not a nice shade of green either.

I had no where to go but down!

I really think I will take those words to my grave. "*I'll bomb you a hole!*"

The tank at a cleaner time. Tony Greenfield is floating on the tube with my son sometime around 1973. When the above incident occurred, the water level in the tank was down around two feet, and had been for some time. Foxes and kangaroos would come in for a drink, and were forced to lean a long way into the tank to reach the water. If they overbalanced and fell in, there was no way out, and they eventually drowned. Life in the bush can be very unkind.

APPENDIX 3

PARTING SHOT

'Centrefire Rifle Accuracy' has been a work in progress for me. Since the first edition I have often come in contact with other shooters, and seeing what they are doing (incorrectly), realized I needed more information in the book. I swear; this 3rd edition is the last time I update it — surely there is enough in there by now.

In the last quarter of 2014 I was finally able to go hunting again, after a five year break caused by bad health, as a result of my knee replacement surgery, amongst other things. My knee won't bend far enough to allow me to ride my motorcycle any more, and in the event I was to fall off it (which I have a bad habit of doing — often) the resulting injury to the knee could be a disaster. So, I have had to settle for the next best thing, a little Suzuki Sierra Jimny.

The first day out with Zippy, I was poking along a track when a medium sized boar came up out of a wash about 140 yards away. He spotted me instantly, and was off like a rocket running directly across my front. I piled out of Zippy with my .338, and without thinking, cranked the shot off as the reticule just passed his nose, and was rewarded with a loud 'thwack' as the projectile struck home. I said out loud, "Wow, it's a long time since I've done that." Honestly, I think that shot, after so long a break, was more a credit to my rifle design than it is to me.

All through our area, and probably every where else, doggers have made pigs extremely shy of vehicles. Any pig you see from a vehicle, now, is always running flat out. They well know what it's all about. It seems every kid in our area has a Toyota 4wd with a cage on the back, and 3 or more big dogs in it. Personally, I can't work out what they see in it. I guess they get off on watching the violence and blood. The dogs, after all, are doing all of the work. I can't even figure out how they afford it. When I was their age my vehicle was a clapped out 20 year old Volkswagon Beetle. I'd have given my left nut for a 4wd, but that was so far out of reach it might as well have been on another planet. They don't get all that many pigs either, but they do chase them all out of the area they are in. Any tusks they get should be hanging in the dog kennel, not on their wall. If you think I have a very low opinion of doggers, you'd be dead right. It's not, even remotely, my idea of 'fair chase'.

My hunting is much more sedate now. I can't walk long distances, and have to be very careful how I move across uneven ground, as I don't fall very well any more. No more running mobs of pigs down, on foot, like I used to. Never-the-less, I still get a rush of adrenaline when I'm sneaking up a channel with the wind in my face, and the chance of a contact, even after all this time. Must be in my blood or something.

Zippy and me on my first trip away hunting, after a five year break, and the little boar that fell victim to the good design of my .338. The bend you can see in my right knee is close to the maximum it can make. As you can see, it's very dry. We are really hanging out for some decent rain in this country.

I've fitted a dual battery system, radio, and HID spotlight through the roof, and a set of mud tyres. I'm working on some more modifications as well. I don't expect to be spending much time home next year, or many after that, if we get some half way decent seasons.

Some people have wondered why I gave up Gunsmithing, and took up a real job. I honestly believed that one day I would clutch my chest and fall, dead, over the job I was working on, but that isn't going to eventuate, or at least it won't be on a paying job.

Aspiring Gunsmiths should take a lesson from my experience. At the height of my skill, and with many things I still wanted to do and try, work simply stopped. It just stopped dead. I was working on a custom rifle one day, and suddenly realized I had about a months work left, and that was it. It was a bit of a shock, and I didn't know what to do. We had no back up money. Gunsmithing only allowed us a frugal lifestyle. It didn't pay enough to allow us to accumulate money in the bank. Financially, things were getting a bit desperate.

I was talking about the problem to a guy I knew, and he suggested I should apply for a position with Corrective Services, which I did, and was accepted.

Gun work never picked up — I never received another enquiry. It was as if I had ceased to exist as a Gunsmith. Had it picked up I would have dumped the job and carried on, but as time went on that became less of an option.

What do I take from this? With hind sight I think it was caused by a lack of advertising. In the early days I wrote articles in some of the gun magazines, and that brought me to the attention of potential customers. Many people still mention those old pieces to me, even today. The simple fact was we could not afford to pay for advertising, and when I stopped writing for the magazines people just forgot me. From my end, I just didn't think I had anything to say — I'm not one to just waffle on ad infinitum about nothing, though you wouldn't know it given this book.

I thought my work would be advertisement enough, but it wasn't. If you are aspiring to be a Gunsmith, don't make the same mistake I did. Factor in an advertising budget to the cost of your work. Blow your own trumpet. The internet, and digital photography, make that so easy to do these days. What ever you do, don't ignore advertising, or no matter how good you are you will go the way of the Dodo, just like I did.

CPSIA information can be obtained
at www.ICGtesting.com
Printed in the USA
BVOW07s0848221017
498337BV00010B/238/P